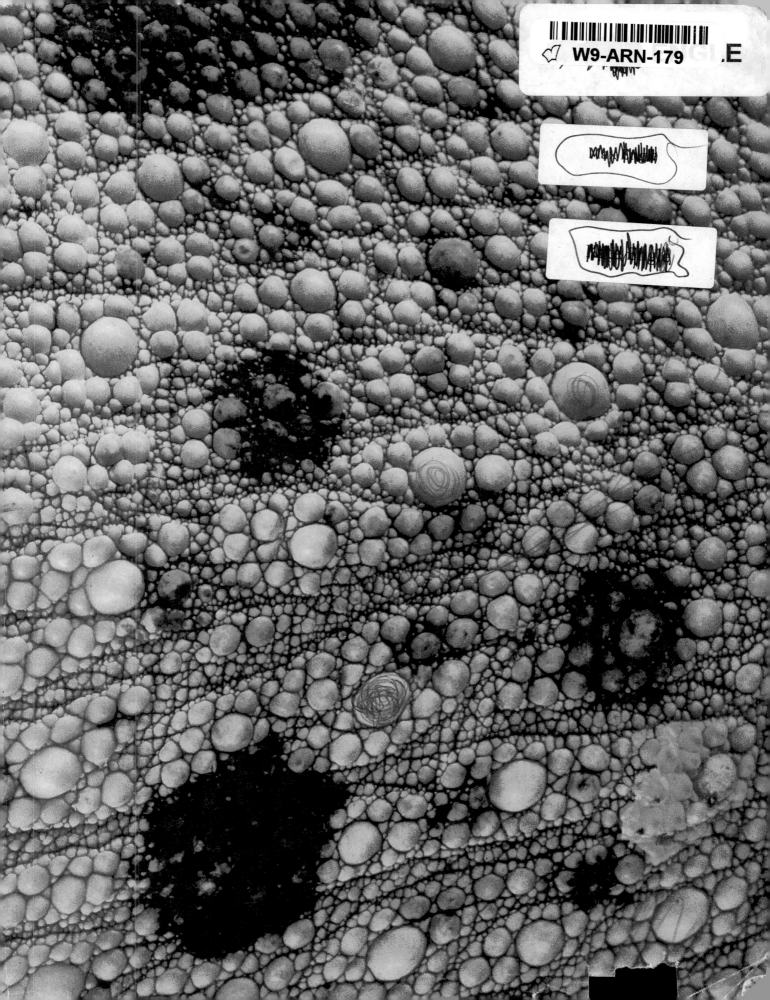

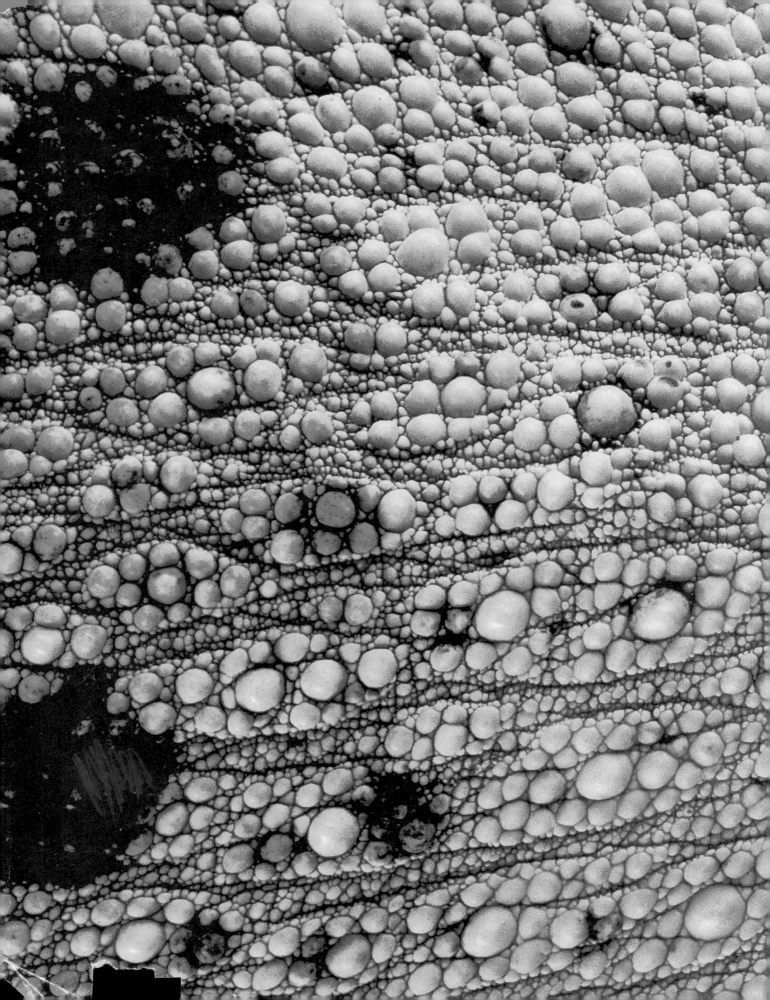

HARCOURT
Science

Harcourt School Publishers

Orlando • Boston • Dallas • Chicago • San Diego

www.harcourtschool.com

The **panther chameleon** (*Chamaeleo pardalis*) is native to the eastern and northern coasts of Madagascar and some surrounding islands. The panther chameleon lives in hot, humid rain forests and it eats insects. It can grow to be as long as 30 cm (about 1 ft). It feeds by capturing insects with a sticky tongue that can be as long as its entire body. The tongue can extend out and capture an insect in less than 1/16th of a second. The inside covers of this book show a closeup of the skin of the panther chameleon.

Printed in the United States of America

ISBN 0-15-322922-5

4 5 6 7 8 9 10 032 10 09 08 07 06 05 04 03 02

Authors

Marjorie Slavick Frank
Former Adjunct Faculty Member
Hunter, Brooklyn, and
    Manhattan Colleges
New York, New York

Robert M. Jones
Professor of Education
University of Houston–
    Clear Lake
Houston, Texas

Gerald H. Krockover
*Professor of Earth and Atmospheric
    Science Education*
School Mathematics and
    Science Center
Purdue University
West Lafayette, Indiana

Mozell P. Lang
Science Education Consultant
Michigan Department
    of Education
Lansing, Michigan

Joyce C. McLeod
Visiting Professor
Rollins College
Winter Park, Florida

Carol J. Valenta
*Vice President—Education, Exhibits,
    and Programs*
St. Louis Science Center
St. Louis, Missouri

Barry A. Van Deman
*Program Director, Informal Science
    Education*
Arlington, Virginia

UNIT A

LIFE SCIENCE

Living Systems

UNIT B

LIFE SCIENCE

Systems and Interactions in Nature

UNIT C

EARTH SCIENCE
Processes That Change the Earth

UNIT D · EARTH SCIENCE
The Solar System and Beyond

Hi!
Person
who ever
has
this
book!

UNIT E

PHYSICAL SCIENCE

Building Blocks of Matter

UNIT F

PHYSICAL SCIENCE
Energy and Motion

Planning an Investigation

How do scientists answer a question or solve a problem they have identified? They use organized ways called **scientific methods** to plan and conduct a study. They use science process skills to help them gather, organize, analyze, and present their information.

Justin is using this scientific method for experimenting to find an answer to his question. You can use these steps, too.

STEP 1 Observe and ask questions.

- Use your senses to make observations.
- Record **one** question that you would like to answer.
- Write down what you already know about the topic of your question.
- Decide what other information you need.
- Do research to find more information about your topic.

What design of paper airplane will fly the greatest distance? I need to find out more about airplane wings.

STEP 2 Form a hypothesis.

- Write a possible answer to your question. A possible answer to a question that can be tested is a **hypothesis**.
- Write your hypothesis in a complete sentence.

My hypothesis is: This airplane, with the narrow wings, will fly farthest.

STEP 3 Plan an experiment.

- Decide how to conduct a fair test of your hypothesis by controlling variables. **Variables** are factors that can affect the outcome of the investigation.
- Write down the steps you will follow to do your test.
- List the equipment you will need.
- Decide how you will gather and record your data.

I'll launch each airplane three times. Each airplane will be launched from the same spot, and I'll use the same amount of force each time.

STEP 4 Conduct the experiment.

- Follow the steps you wrote.
- Observe and measure carefully.
- Record everything that happens.
- Organize your data so you can study it carefully.

I'll record each distance. Then I'll find the average distance each airplane traveled.

STEP 5 Draw conclusions and communicate results.

- Analyze the data you gathered.

- Make charts, tables, or graphs to show your data.

- Write a conclusion. Describe the evidence you used to determine whether your test supported your hypothesis.

- Decide whether your hypothesis was correct.

My hypothesis was correct. The airplane with the narrow wings flew farthest.

INVESTIGATE FURTHER

What if your hypothesis was correct . . .

You may want to pose another question about your topic that you can test.

What if your hypothesis was incorrect . . .

You may want to form another hypothesis and do a test on a different variable.

I'll test this new hypothesis: The airplane with the narrow wings will also fly for the longest time.

Do you think Justin's new hypothesis will be correct? Plan and conduct a test to find out!

Using Science Process Skills

When scientists try to find an answer to a question or do an experiment, they use thinking tools called **process skills**. You use many of the process skills whenever you speak, listen, read, write, or think. Think about how these students use process skills to help them answer questions, do experiments, and investigate the world around them.

What Greg plans to investigate

Greg is finding leaves in the park. He wants to make collections of leaves that are alike in some way. He looks for leaves of different sizes and shapes.

Process Skills

Observe—use the senses to learn about objects and events

Compare—identify characteristics about things or events to find out how they are alike and different

Measure—compare an attribute of an object, such as its mass, length, or volume, to a standard unit, such as a gram, centimeter, or liter

Classify—group or organize objects or events in categories based on specific characteristics

How Greg uses process skills

He **observes** the leaves and **compares** their sizes, shapes, and colors. He **measures** each leaf with a ruler. Then he **classifies** the leaves, first into groups based on their sizes and then into groups based on their shapes.

What Pilar plans to investigate

It's been raining for part of the week. Pilar wants to know if it will rain during the coming weekend.

How Pilar uses process skills

She **gathers and records data** to make a prediction about the weather. She observes the weather each day of the week and records it. On a chart, she **displays data** she has gathered. On Friday, she **predicts**, based on her observations, that it will rain during the weekend.

Process Skills

Gather, Record, Display, or Interpret Data

- gather data by making observations and use them to make inferences or predictions
- record data by writing down observations
- display data by making tables, charts, or graphs

Predict—form an idea of an expected outcome, based on observations or experience

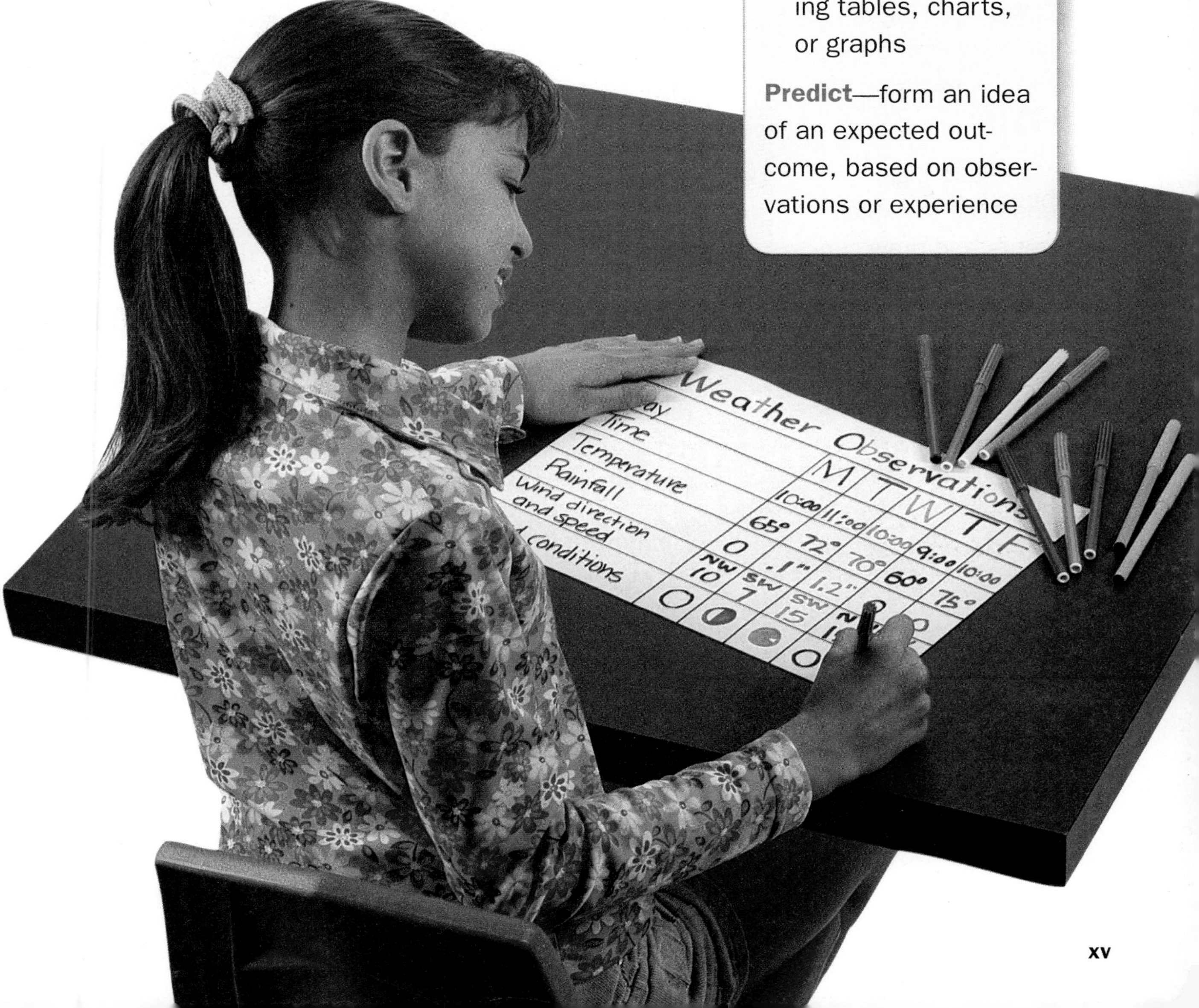

Hypothesize—make a statement about an expected outcome, based on observation, knowledge, and experience

Plan and Conduct a Simple Investigation—identify and perform the steps necessary to find the answer to a question, using appropriate tools and recording and analyzing the data collected

Infer—use logical reasoning to explain events and draw conclusions based on observations

What Tran plans to investigate

Tran is interested in knowing how the size of a magnet is related to its strength.

How Tran uses process skills

He **hypothesizes** that larger magnets are stronger than smaller magnets. He **plans and conducts a simple investigation** to see if his hypothesis is correct. He gathers magnets of different sizes and objects of different weights that the magnets will attract. Tran tests each item with each magnet and records his findings. His hypothesis seems to be correct until he tests the last object, a toy truck. When the large bar magnet cannot pick up the truck, but the smaller horseshoe magnet can, he **infers** that the largest magnets are not always the strongest.

What Emily plans to investigate

Emily sees an ad about food wrap. The people in the ad claim that Tight-Right food wrap seals containers better than other food wraps. Emily plans a simple experiment to find out if this claim is true.

How Emily uses process skills

She **identifies and controls variables** in the experiment by choosing three bowls that are exactly the same. She labels the bowls A, B, and C, places them on a tray, and adds exactly 350 mL of water to each bowl. She cuts a 25-cm-long piece of Tight-Right food wrap and covers bowl A. She cuts 25-cm-long pieces of two other brands of food wrap and covers bowls B and C. She seals the food wrap on all three bowls as tightly as she can. Emily **experiments** with the seals by shaking the tray on which the bowls are placed. Water sloshes up the sides of the bowls and leaks out onto the tray from bowls B and C, but not from bowl A. From her observations she infers that the claim for Tight-Right food wrap is true.

Process Skills

Identify and Control Variables—identify and control factors that affect the outcome of an experiment

Experiment—design ways to collect data to test hypotheses under controlled conditions

Reading to Learn

Scientists use reading, writing, and numbers in their work. They **read** to find out everything they can about a topic they are investigating. So it is important that scientists know the meanings of science vocabulary and that they understand what they read. Use the following strategies to help you become a good science reader!

Before Reading

- Read the **Find Out** statements to help you know what to look for as you read.
- Think: I need to find out how living things get the energy they need.

- Look at the **Vocabulary** terms.
- Be sure you can pronounce each term.
- Look up each term in the Glossary.
- Say the definition to yourself. Use the term in a sentence to show its meaning.

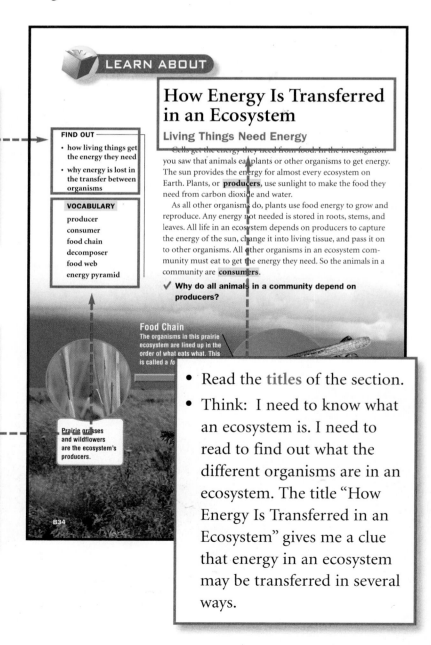

LEARN ABOUT

How Energy Is Transferred in an Ecosystem

Living Things Need Energy

Cells get the energy they need from food. In the investigation you saw that animals eat plants or other organisms to get energy. The sun provides the energy for almost every ecosystem on Earth. Plants, or **producers**, use sunlight to make the food they need from carbon dioxide and water.

As all other organisms do, plants use food energy to grow and reproduce. Any energy not needed is stored in roots, stems, and leaves. All life in an ecosystem depends on producers to capture the energy of the sun, change it into living tissue, and pass it on to other organisms. All other organisms in an ecosystem community must eat to get the energy they need. So the animals in a community are **consumers**.

✓ Why do all animals in a community depend on producers?

FIND OUT
- how living things get the energy they need
- why energy is lost in the transfer between organisms

VOCABULARY
producer
consumer
food chain
decomposer
food web
energy pyramid

Food Chain
The organisms in this prairie ecosystem are lined up in the order of what eats what. This is called a fo

Prairie grasses and wildflowers are the ecosystem's producers.

B34

- Read the **titles** of the section.
- Think: I need to know what an ecosystem is. I need to read to find out what the different organisms are in an ecosystem. The title "How Energy Is Transferred in an Ecosystem" gives me a clue that energy in an ecosystem may be transferred in several ways.

During Reading

Find the **main idea** in the first paragraph.

- In food chains, there are more producers than consumers.

Find the **details** in the next paragraph that support the main idea.

- Only 10 percent of the energy at any level is passed on to the next level.

- High-level consumers, such as wolves, have relatively small populations. There isn't enough energy for large populations of wolves.

- All other organisms in an ecosystem must eat to get the energy they need.

Energy Pyramids

In the food chains of most ecosystems, there are many more producers than there are consumers. Producers use about 90 percent of the food energy they make during photosynthesis for their life processes. Only 10 percent of the energy is stored in plant tissue. When a consumer eats the plant tissue, it uses about 90 percent of the plant's stored food energy to stay alive. It stores the other 10 percent in its body tissue. This huge loss of stored food energy occurs at each level in a food chain. An **energy pyramid** shows the amount of energy available to pass from one level of a food chain to the next.

Remember, only 10 percent of the energy at any level of a food chain is passed on to the next higher level. Since less energy is available to organisms higher up the food chain, there are usually fewer organisms at these levels. High-level consumers, such as wolves, have relatively small populations. There is not enough energy available to support a large population of wolves.

The size of each level of an energy pyramid is related to the sizes of the populations at that level. The producer population is usually the largest, since it provides energy for all consumer levels in the pyramid.

✓ **How much of the food energy that is taken in by an organism is used for its own life processes?**

Energy Pyramid

◄ **Third-level consumers** Hawks are at the top of this energy pyramid. They eat snakes. There are few hawks because most of the energy has been used at lower levels of the pyramid.

hawk

◄ **Second-level consumers** There are far fewer snakes than grasshoppers. This is because grasshoppers use 90 percent of the food energy they get for their own life processes.

snakes

◄ **First-level consumers** Since plants use 90 percent of the food energy they produce, there are fewer grasshoppers than there are grasses and other plants.

grasshoppers

◄ **Producers** Producers, such as grasses and other plants, form the base of an energy pyramid.

grass

Check your understanding of what you have read.

- Answer the question at the end of the section.

- If you're not sure of the answer, reread the section and look for the answer to the question.

After Reading

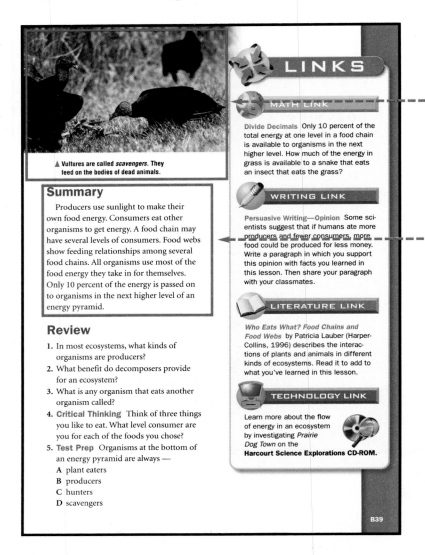

▲ Vultures are called *scavengers*. They feed on the bodies of dead animals.

Summary

Producers use sunlight to make their own food energy. Consumers eat other organisms to get energy. A food chain may have several levels of consumers. Food webs show feeding relationships among several food chains. All organisms use most of the food energy they take in for themselves. Only 10 percent of the energy is passed on to organisms in the next higher level of an energy pyramid.

Review

1. In most ecosystems, what kinds of organisms are producers?
2. What benefit do decomposers provide for an ecosystem?
3. What is any organism that eats another organism called?
4. **Critical Thinking** Think of three things you like to eat. What level consumer are you for each of the foods you chose?
5. **Test Prep** Organisms at the bottom of an energy pyramid are always —
   A plant eaters
   B producers
   C hunters
   D scavengers

LINKS

MATH LINK

Divide Decimals Only 10 percent of the total energy at one level in a food chain is available to organisms in the next higher level. How much of the energy in grass is available to a snake that eats an insect that eats the grass?

WRITING LINK

Persuasive Writing—Opinion Some scientists suggest that if humans ate more producers and fewer consumers, more food could be produced for less money. Write a paragraph in which you support this opinion with facts you learned in this lesson. Then share your paragraph with your classmates.

LITERATURE LINK

Who Eats What? Food Chains and Food Webs by Patricia Lauber (Harper-Collins, 1996) describes the interactions of plants and animals in different kinds of ecosystems. Read it to add to what you've learned in this lesson.

TECHNOLOGY LINK

Learn more about the flow of energy in an ecosystem by investigating *Prairie Dog Town* on the **Harcourt Science Explorations CD-ROM.**

B39

Study the photographs.

- Read the caption with each photograph.
- Think: What kinds of organisms are shown in the photographs? What do they eat?

Summarize what you have read.

- Think about what you've already learned about energy transfer in an ecosystem.
- Ask yourself: Why does an ecosystem depend on its producers? What kinds of foods do the consumers eat?

For more reading strategies and tips, see pages R38–R49.

Reading about science helps you understand your conclusions from your investigations.

Writing to Communicate

Writing about what you are learning helps you connect the new ideas to what you already know. Scientists **write** about what they learn in their research and investigations to help others understand the work they have done. As you work like a scientist, you will use the following kinds of writing to describe what you are doing and learning.

In **informative writing**, you may

- describe your observations, inferences, and conclusions.
- tell how to do an experiment.

In **narrative writing**, you may

- describe something, give examples, or tell a story.

In **expressive writing**, you may

- write letters, poems, or songs.

In **persuasive writing**, you may

- write letters about important issues in science.
- write essays expressing your opinions about science issues.

Writing about what you have learned about science helps others understand your thinking.

Using Numbers

Scientists **use numbers** when they collect, display, and interpret their data. Understanding numbers and using them correctly to show the results of investigations are important skills that a scientist must have. As you work like a scientist, you will use numbers in the following ways:

Measuring

Scientists make accurate measurements as they gather data. They use measuring instruments such as thermometers, clocks and timers, rulers, a spring scale, and a balance, and they use beakers and other containers to measure liquids.

For more information about using measuring tools, see pages R2–R6.

Interpreting Data

Scientists collect, organize, display, and interpret data as they do investigations. Scientists choose a way to display data that helps others understand what they have learned. Tables, charts, and graphs are good ways to display data so that it can be interpreted by others.

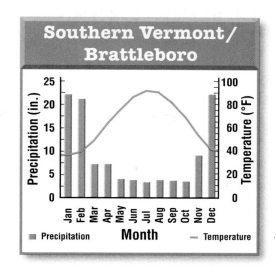

Using Number Sense

Scientists must understand what the numbers they use represent. They compare and order numbers, compute with numbers, read and understand the numbers shown on graphs, and read the scales on thermometers, measuring cups, beakers, and other tools.

Good scientists apply their math skills to help them display and interpret the data they collect.

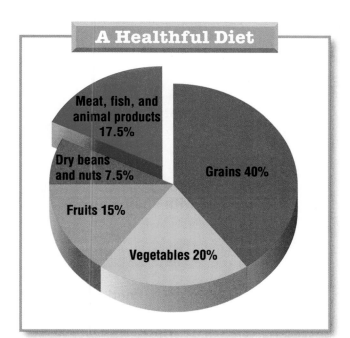

In *Harcourt Science* you will have many opportunities to work like a scientist. An exciting year of discovery lies ahead!

Safety in Science

Doing investigations in science can be fun, but you need to be sure you do them safely. Here are some rules to follow.

1 **Think ahead.** Study the steps of the investigation so you know what to expect. If you have any questions, ask your teacher. Be sure you understand any safety symbols that are shown.

2 **Be neat.** Keep your work area clean. If you have long hair, pull it back so it doesn't get in the way. Roll or push up long sleeves to keep them away from your experiment.

3 **Oops!** If you should spill or break something, or get cut, tell your teacher right away.

4 **Watch your eyes.** Wear safety goggles anytime you are directed to do so. If you get anything in your eyes, tell your teacher right away.

5 **Yuck!** Never eat or drink anything during a science activity.

6 **Don't get shocked.** Be especially careful if an electric appliance is used. Be sure that electric cords are in a safe place where you can't trip over them. Don't ever pull a plug out of an outlet by pulling on the cord.

7 **Keep it clean.** Always clean up when you have finished. Put everything away and wipe your work area. Wash your hands.

In some activities you will see these symbols. They are signs for what you need to be safe.

Be especially careful.

Wear safety goggles.

Be careful with sharp objects.

Don't get burned.

Protect your clothes.

Protect your hands with mitts.

Be careful with electricity.

Living Systems

Living Systems

UNIT EXPERIMENT

Plants and Light

Living organisms respond to certain factors in their environments. One environmental factor that plants respond to is light. While you study this unit, you can conduct a long-term experiment related to this response. Here are some questions to think about. How do plants respond to light? For example, will plants grow toward a light source? Plan and conduct an experiment to find answers to these or other questions you have about plants and light. See pages x–xvii for help in designing your experiment.

From Single Cells to Body Systems

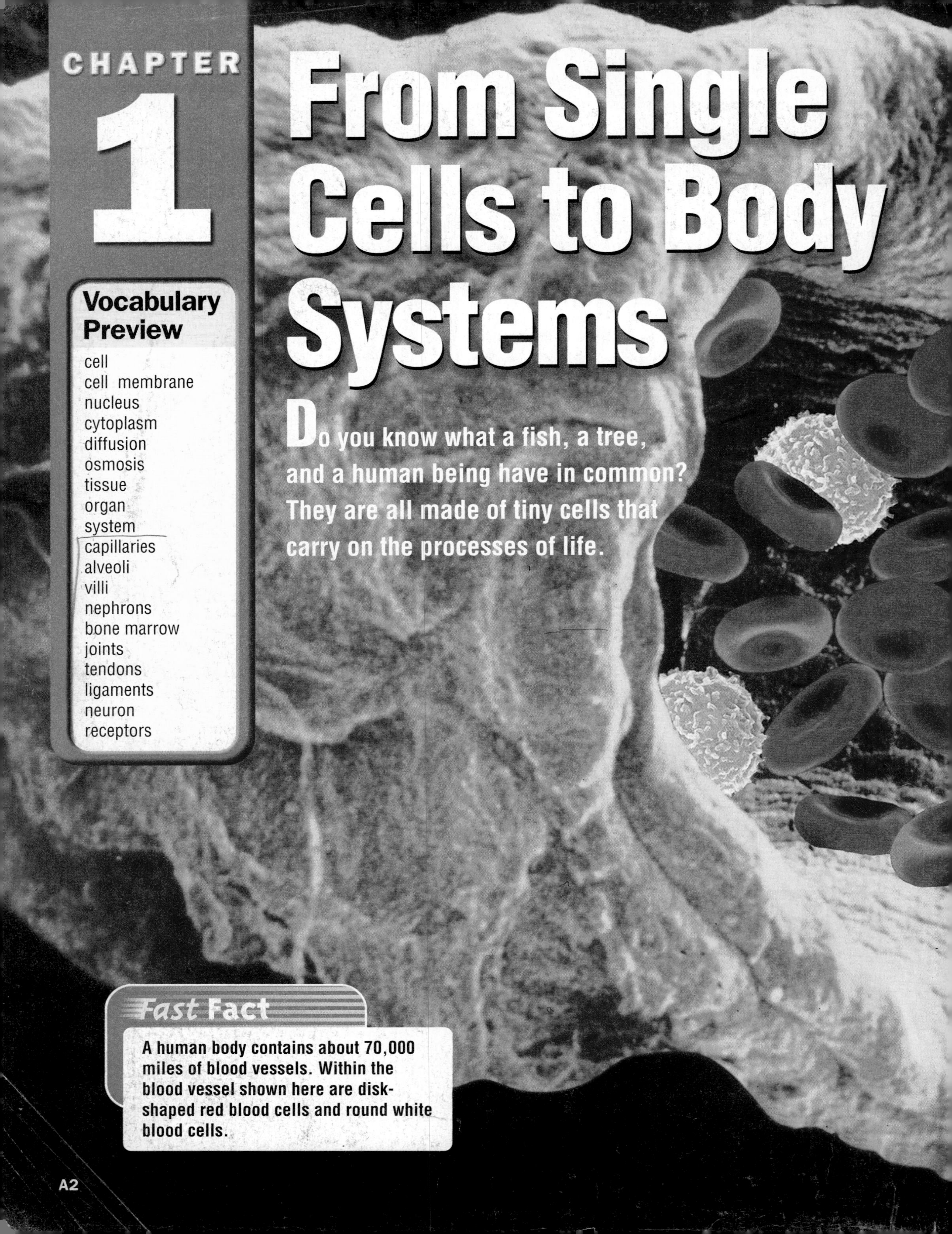

Vocabulary Preview

cell
cell membrane
nucleus
cytoplasm
diffusion
osmosis
tissue
organ
system
capillaries
alveoli
villi
nephrons
bone marrow
joints
tendons
ligaments
neuron
receptors

Do you know what a fish, a tree, and a human being have in common? They are all made of tiny cells that carry on the processes of life.

Fast Fact

A human body contains about 70,000 miles of blood vessels. Within the blood vessel shown here are disk-shaped red blood cells and round white blood cells.

A scanning electron microscope (SEM) can magnify objects as much as 900,000 times. This electron micrograph shows human face cells magnified 100,000 times.

A single square inch of human skin has more than 19 million cells.

1

What Are Cells, and What Do They Do?

In this lesson, you can . . .

INVESTIGATE what cells look like.

LEARN ABOUT cells.

LINK to math, writing, health, and technology.

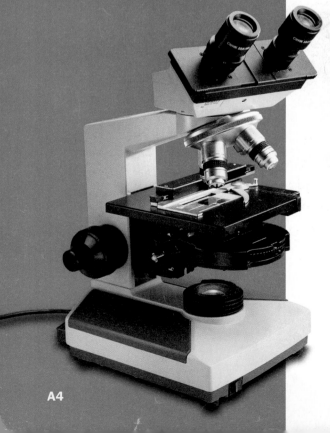

INVESTIGATE

Observing Cells

Activity Purpose If you're looking at a landscape from far away, you might use a telescope to make the details clearer. Suppose you focus the telescope on a distant farm. You can see crates of freshly harvested onions. Now suppose you use a microscope to magnify the scene more and more. What details about an onion might you **observe**? In this investigation you'll observe a thin layer of an onion skin. Then you will observe and **compare** other plant cells and animal cells.

Materials

- Microslide Viewer
- Microslide of cell structure
- colored pencils

Alternate Materials

- slice of onion
- microscope slide
- coverslip
- dropper
- red food coloring
- microscope
- colored pencils

Activity Procedure

1 Insert the Cell Structure Microslide in the slot on the Microslide Viewer. Turn the focus knob until you can see the cells clearly. (Picture A)

2 **Observe** the onion skin cells and the human cheek cells. **Record** your observations by using the colored pencils to make drawings.

◀ This microscope allows a person to study a thin slice of material under high magnification.

3 Now **observe** the green leaf cells and the nerve cells. Again, **record** your observations by making drawings. (Picture B)

4 Now **compare** your drawings. Make a Venn diagram with two large, overlapping circles. Label the circles *Plant Cells* and *Animal Cells*. Label the area where the circles overlap *Both Cells*. Draw the cell parts that you **observed** in the proper circles. Leave enough room to label the parts as you read about them in this lesson.

Picture A

Draw Conclusions

1. **Compare** the outer layers of plant and animal cells.

2. In the centers of most cells are structures that determine how cells function. How many of these structures are there in each of the cells you **observed**?

3. **Scientists at Work** Scientists often **infer** characteristics of a group of objects by **observing** just a few of the objects. From your observations, what do you infer about the number of determining structures in a cell?

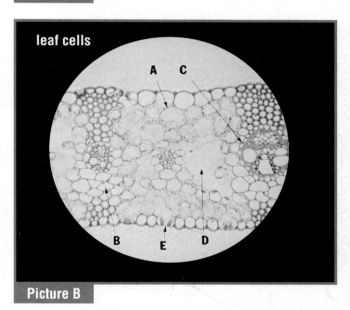
leaf cells
Picture B

Investigate Further Now that you have **observed** photomicrographs of cells, what questions do you have about living cells? Use the materials in the *Alternate Materials* list to **plan and conduct a simple experiment** based on this hypothesis: All cells have certain parts in common. See page R3 for tips on using a microscope.

Process Skill Tip

You can **infer** based on what you **observe**, or based on other information you have about a subject.

A5

Cells

FIND OUT

- **what cells are**
- **how cells are organized**
- **what cells do**

VOCABULARY

cell
cell membrane
nucleus
cytoplasm
diffusion
osmosis
tissue
organ
system

The Discovery of Cells

The Microslide and viewer you used in the investigation enabled you to observe parts of plants and animals under magnification. Without magnification, you couldn't have seen the structures you did. A microscope magnifies objects in a similar way. In fact, the photomicrographs you observed were taken through a microscope. The first microscopes were invented in the early 1600s. One scientist who built and used an early microscope was Robert Hooke.

In 1665 Hooke observed a thin slice of cork through a microscope. The tiny walled spaces he saw in the cork reminded him of tiny rooms. So he called them cells. Over the next 200 years, scientists learned more and more about cells. They learned that the **cell** is the basic unit of structure and function of all living things. The time line below shows some important early discoveries about cells.

✔ **Why were cells not observed before the 1600s?**

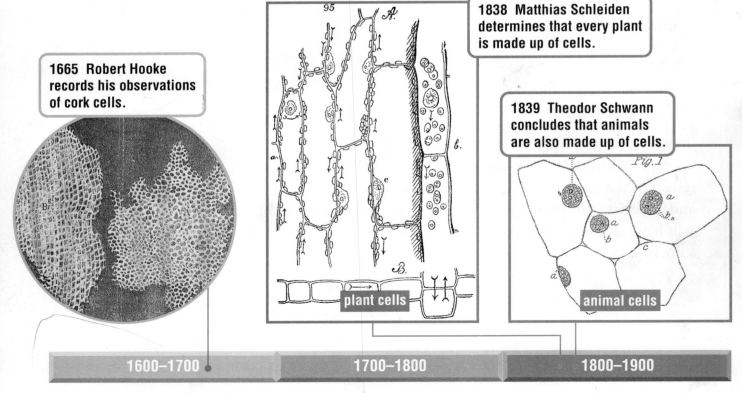

1665 Robert Hooke records his observations of cork cells.

1838 Matthias Schleiden determines that every plant is made up of cells.

1839 Theodor Schwann concludes that animals are also made up of cells.

plant cells

animal cells

1600–1700   1700–1800   1800–1900

Kinds of Cells

Scientists have classified about a million kinds of plants and animals. But as different as those plants and animals seem to be, all of them are made of cells.

The simplest organisms, such as bacteria, are each a single cell. Most plants and animals, however, are made up of many cells. Humans, for example, are made up of trillions of cells. An organism with many cells usually has many different kinds of cells. Each kind of cell has a particular function.

The size and shape of a cell depend on its function. Red blood cells, for example, are small and disc-shaped. They can easily fit through the smallest blood vessels. Muscle cells are long and thin. When they contract, or shorten, they produce movement. Nerve cells, which carry signals from the brain to the muscles, are very long.

Plants also have different kinds of cells. Some plant cells take in water from the soil. Others protect the plant. And still others make food.

Cells work together to perform basic life processes that keep an organism alive. These processes include releasing energy from food, getting rid of body wastes, and making new cells for growth and repair. In addition to performing a particular function for the organism, each individual cell can perform all the basic life processes for itself.

✔ **Why might bone cells be different from muscle cells?**

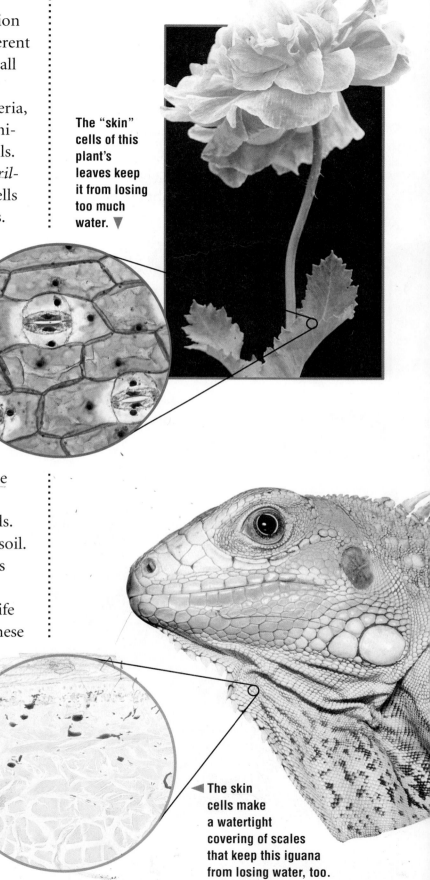

The "skin" cells of this plant's leaves keep it from losing too much water. ▼

◄ The skin cells make a watertight covering of scales that keep this iguana from losing water, too.

Plant and Animal Cells

Although cells are the basic unit of all living organisms, cells contain even smaller structures called *organelles* (awr•guh•NELZ). Each organelle has a particular function in the life processes of a cell.

All cells—except those of bacteria—have similar organelles. For example, every cell is enclosed by a thin covering called the **cell membrane**. The cell membrane holds the parts of the cell together. It also separates the cell from its surroundings.

Most cells have a nucleus (NOO•klee•uhs). The **nucleus,** which is enclosed in its own membrane, determines the cell's activities. One function of the nucleus is to control cell reproduction. Cells can grow only to a certain size. So the number of cells has to increase in order for plants and animals to grow.

Inside the nucleus are threadlike structures called *chromosomes* (KROH•muh•sohmz).

THE INSIDE STORY

Comparing Plant and Animal Cells

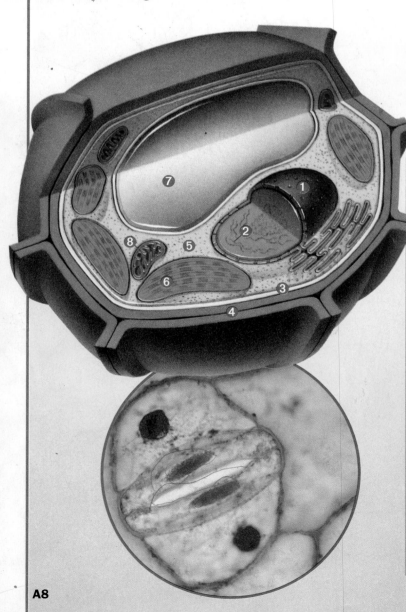

Plant cells have different shapes and sizes, but they all have the same parts. The diagram shows what you might observe if you could look inside a leaf cell. The organelles you see are working parts of a complete cell. Each organelle has its own specific function.

Plant Cell Structures

Nucleus— ❶	the organelle that determines all of a plant cell's activities and the production of new cells
Chromosomes— ❷	threadlike structures that contain information about the characteristics of the plant
Cell membrane— ❸	a covering that holds the plant cell together and separates it from its surroundings
Cell wall— ④	a rigid layer that supports and protects the plant cell
Cytoplasm— ❺	a jellylike substance that contains many chemicals to keep the cell functioning
Chloroplasts— ⑥	organelles that make food for the plant cell
Vacuole— ❼	an organelle that stores food, water, or wastes
Mitochondria— ❽	organelles that release energy from food

These contain information about the characteristics of the organism. When a cell reproduces, identical chromosomes go into each new cell.

Between the cell membrane and the nucleus is the cytoplasm (SYT•oh•plaz•uhm). **Cytoplasm** is a jellylike substance containing many chemicals to keep the cell functioning.

There are several kinds of organelles in the cytoplasm. Each is enclosed in a membrane. *Mitochondria* (myt•oh•KAHN•dree•uh) release energy from food. *Vacuoles* (VAK•yoo•ohlz) are storage organelles. They store food, water, or waste materials.

Two organelles make plant cells different from animal cells. In addition to a cell membrane, a plant cell is surrounded by a rigid *cell wall*, which gives it strength. Plant cells also have *chloroplasts*, which make food.

✔ **How do plant cells and animal cells differ?**

The functions that allow an animal to live and grow are also carried out in its cells. Although the iguana's skin cells are a different shape and size from its blood cells, each cell typically contains the same parts. As you look at the diagram of an animal cell, notice how it differs from the plant cell.

Animal Cell Structures

Nucleus— ❶ the organelle that determines all of an animal cell's activities and the production of new cells

Chromosomes— ❷ threadlike structures that contain information about the characteristics of the animal

Cell membrane— ❸ a covering that holds the animal cell together and separates it from its surroundings

Cytoplasm— ❹ a jellylike substance that contains many chemicals to keep the cell functioning

Vacuoles— ❺ organelles that store food, wastes, or water

Mitochondria— ❻ organelles that release energy from food

Materials Move into and out of Cells

Most of the activities of a cell require energy. That energy is supplied by the mitochondria. Mitochondria use food, oxygen, and water to produce energy. This process produces carbon dioxide. How do cells get needed materials like food, water, and oxygen? And how do they get rid of wastes, like carbon dioxide?

Many materials move into and out of cells by diffusion. In the process of **diffusion**, particles of a substance move from an area where there are a lot of particles of the substance to an area where there are fewer particles of the substance.

For example, red blood cells carry oxygen from the lungs to all parts of the body. There is a lot of oxygen in red blood cells and very little in other body cells. So oxygen diffuses out of red blood cells and into body cells. At the same time, there is a lot of carbon dioxide in body cells and very little in the blood. So carbon dioxide diffuses out of body cells and into the blood.

Diffusion of materials into and out of cells takes place through the cell membrane. You might think of a cell membrane as a filter. It allows some particles to pass through, but it keeps other particles out. Water and materials dissolved in water—such as sugar—diffuse easily through cell membranes. Diffusion doesn't require energy from the cell.

The movement of water and dissolved materials through cell membranes is so important to living organisms that it is given a special name— **osmosis**. Cells get most of their water by osmosis.

When a plant gets too little water, water leaves the cells because the concentration of water is higher inside the cells than outside.

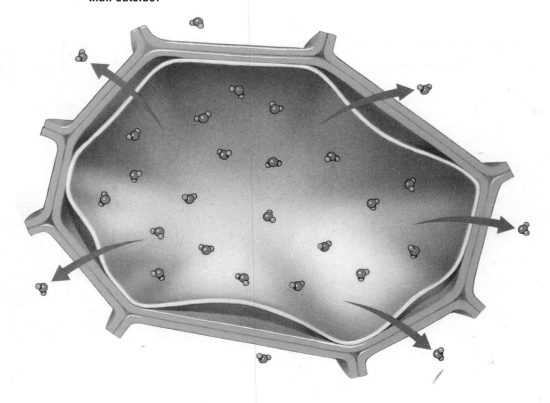

▲ If the soil is dry, water moves from the plant's cells into the soil. The cells shrink, and the plant wilts.

▲ If the soil is moist, water moves back into the plant's cells. The cells expand, and the plant recovers.

By drinking, animals replace the water their cells lose. ▼

Osmosis keeps plants from wilting. Since there is usually more water in the soil than in the roots of plants, water flows into plant cells. Water flowing into plant cells fills the vacuoles, which pushes the cytoplasm tightly against the cell walls. This causes plant stems and leaves to stand straight.

If the soil is very dry, there is more water in the plant than in the soil. Water leaves the plant by osmosis. The loss of water from the plant's vacuoles causes cytoplasm to shrink away from cell walls. The plant wilts and may die if it loses too much water.

✔ **What is osmosis?**

Tissues, Organs, and Systems

In an organism made up of many cells, similar cells work together. Cells that work together to perform a specific function form a **tissue**. There are four kinds of tissues in humans.

Most of the mass of an animal is *muscle tissue*. Muscle tissue is made up of cells that contract when they receive signals from the brain. The contraction and relaxation of muscle tissue move the skeleton. The signals that cause muscle tissue to contract travel through another kind of tissue—*nervous tissue*. The brain and spinal cord, as well as the places where sight, hearing, taste, smell, and touch begin, are all nervous tissue.

Connective tissue is the third kind of tissue. It includes the tissue in bones, cartilage, and tendons. Blood is also a connective tissue.

The final kind of tissue is *epithelial* (ep•ih•THEE•lee•uhl) *tissue*. Epithelial tissue includes the body covering of an animal. It also lines most internal organs.

Just as cells that work together form a tissue, tissues that work together form an **organ**. Each organ in an animal's body is made of several kinds of tissues. Skin, for example, is an organ. It is made of many layers of epithelial tissue, as well as muscle tissue, nervous tissue, and a cushioning layer of connective tissue.

Each organ in an animal's body performs a major function that keeps the animal alive. The heart, for example, is an organ that pumps blood throughout the animal's body.

Organs that work together to perform a function form a **system**. A human has ten

In this diagram, you can see the four levels of organization in the digestive system. ▼

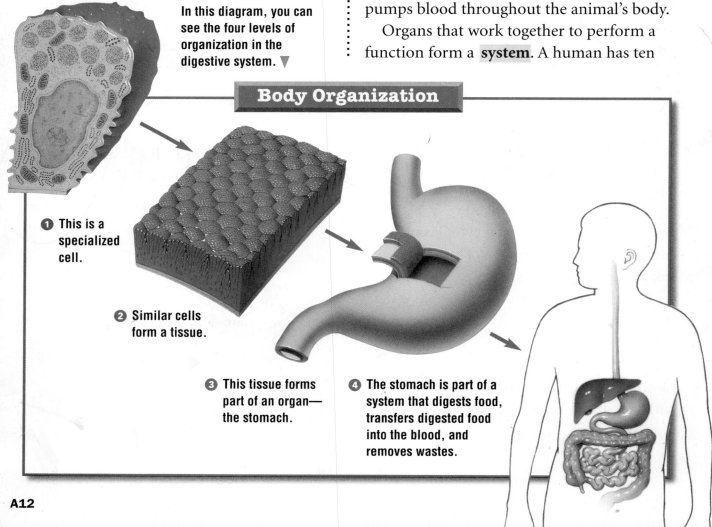

Body Organization

❶ This is a specialized cell.

❷ Similar cells form a tissue.

❸ This tissue forms part of an organ— the stomach.

❹ The stomach is part of a system that digests food, transfers digested food into the blood, and removes wastes.

major body systems. You will learn about some of those systems in the next two lessons.

Plant cells also form tissues, such as the bark of a tree. And plant tissues work together, forming organs, such as roots and leaves. You will learn more about plants in Chapters 2 and 4.

✔ **What kind of tissue gives an organism the ability to move?**

Summary

All living things are made up of one or more cells. Each cell is able to perform the functions that support life. Plant cells differ from animal cells in that they have cell walls and chloroplasts. Cells obtain the materials they need through the cell membrane. Cells with similar functions form tissues. Tissues that function together make up an organ. Organs working together form a body system.

Review

1. What is the function of a cell's nucleus?
2. How do vacuoles in plant cells help keep the plant upright?
3. What is the difference between diffusion and osmosis?
4. **Critical Thinking** If you stand at one end of a room and spray perfume into the air, a person at the other end of the room will soon smell the perfume. Explain.
5. **Test Prep** One example of a tissue is —
   A heart   **C** muscle
   B nucleus   **D** mitochondria

LINKS

MATH LINK

Solve Problems Suppose a single cell divides into two cells every 15 min. If each of those also divides into two, and so on, how long will it take for a single cell to produce 500 cells?

WRITING LINK

Informative Writing—Compare and Contrast Write two or three paragraphs for your teacher comparing plant cells and animal cells.

HEALTH LINK

Interview a Doctor Find out how studying cells helps doctors understand the human body. Brainstorm with a family member to come up with questions you can ask your doctor the next time you have an appointment.

GO ONLINE TECHNOLOGY LINK

Learn more about cells and body systems by using the activities and information provided on the Harcourt Learning Site.
www.harcourtschool.com

WELCOME TO
THE
LEARNING
SITE

LESSON 2

How Do Body Systems Transport Materials?

In this lesson, you can . . .

 INVESTIGATE cells and tissues.

 LEARN ABOUT four human body systems.

 LINK to math, writing, social studies, and technology.

The materials your body uses to produce energy must be replaced.

INVESTIGATE

Cells and Tissues

Activity Purpose Your body is made up of cells that are organized into tissues, organs, and systems. Cells are highly specialized for the functions they perform for the body. Even cells that make up similar tissues can differ in many ways. In this investigation you will **observe** and **compare** under magnification several kinds of cells and tissues.

Materials

- Microslide Viewer
- Microslide of animal tissues
- colored pencils

Alternate Materials

- prepared slides of epithelial, connective, and nervous tissues
- microscope

Activity Procedure

1 Insert the Animal Tissues Microslide in the slot of the Microslide Viewer. Turn the focus knob until you can see the cells and tissues clearly. (Picture A)

2 **Observe** the voluntary muscle cells. **Record** your observations by using the colored pencils to make a drawing. Label your drawing with the name of the tissue. Then describe the tissue. You may use the Microslide text folder to help you write your description. (Picture B)

Picture A

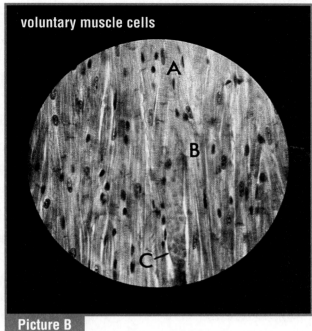

voluntary muscle cells

A
B
C

Picture B

3 Repeat Step 2 for the smooth muscle cells and the heart muscle.

4 **Compare** the three kinds of muscle tissue.

Draw Conclusions

1. How are the three kinds of muscle tissue alike? How are they different?

2. The dark-stained organelles you **observed** in the muscle tissues are mitochondria. Which kind of muscle tissue has the most mitochondria?

3. **Scientists at Work** When scientists **compare** objects, they often **infer** reasons for any differences. What do you infer about why one kind of muscle tissue has more mitochondria than the others?

Investigate Further Now that you have **observed** several kinds of tissues, develop a testable question about differences among tissues. Use the materials in the **Alternate Materials** list to study other kinds of tissues. Observe the tissues under the microscope, and draw and label any differences you see. **Form a hypothesis** about how these tissues are different from the muscle tissues you observed. See page R3 for tips on using a microscope.

Process Skill Tip

Making drawings of objects allows you to **compare** them and **infer** reasons for differences between them.

A15

Human Body Systems

From Cells to Systems

The tissues you observed in the investigation combine in various ways to form body organs. Certain organs work together to form body systems. Each body system has a specific task that helps keep you alive. But your body systems also work together. On its own, a single body system cannot keep you alive.

The digestive system, for example, breaks down food into nutrients the body needs for energy. But without the circulatory system, the nutrients couldn't travel to the parts of the body that need them. The circulatory system also delivers the oxygen needed to release energy from food. However, without the respiratory system, oxygen couldn't get into the circulatory system. And all body processes produce wastes that must be removed. The excretory and respiratory systems share this function, with transportation provided by the circulatory system.

As you can see, working together is important for living organisms. Cells work together to form tissues. Tissues work together to form organs. Organs work together to form systems. And systems work together to keep you alive.

✓ **How do body systems depend on each other?**

These red blood cells are part of a tissue—blood. ▼

Blood vessels are one kind of organ in the circulatory system. ▶

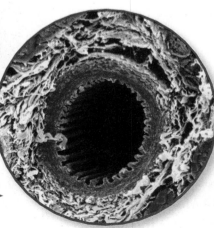

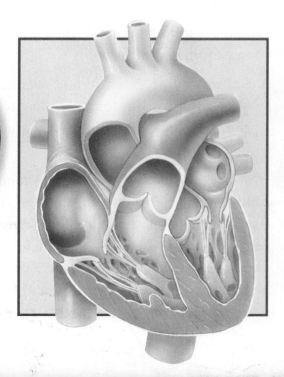

The heart is another organ of the circulatory system. It is made of muscle tissue. ▶

The Circulatory System

The circulatory system transports oxygen, nutrients, and wastes through the body in the blood. The liquid part of blood, called *plasma*, is mostly water. Plasma also contains dissolved nutrients and waste products such as carbon dioxide. The solid part of blood includes red blood cells and white blood cells. Red blood cells absorb oxygen from air in the lungs and transport it to every cell in the body. White blood cells help the body fight infection. They attack and destroy viruses and bacteria that enter the body.

Blood also contains *platelets*—tiny pieces of blood cells inside membranes. Platelets cause blood to clot when a blood vessel is cut. They also help repair damage to blood vessels.

The heart, an organ made of muscle tissue, pumps blood through blood vessels. The heart has four chambers, or parts. Oxygen-rich blood from the lungs enters one chamber. It moves to the next chamber, from which it is pumped to the body. Oxygen-poor blood from the body enters the third chamber. It moves to the fourth chamber, from which it is pumped to the lungs.

Blood leaves the heart through blood vessels called *arteries.* Arteries lead to capillaries. **Capillaries** are blood vessels so small that blood cells have to move through them in single file. There are capillaries throughout the body, so nutrients and oxygen can reach every cell. Waste products from cells

are picked up by plasma in the capillaries. Capillaries lead to larger vessels, called *veins,* which return blood to the heart.

✔ **Why are platelets important?**

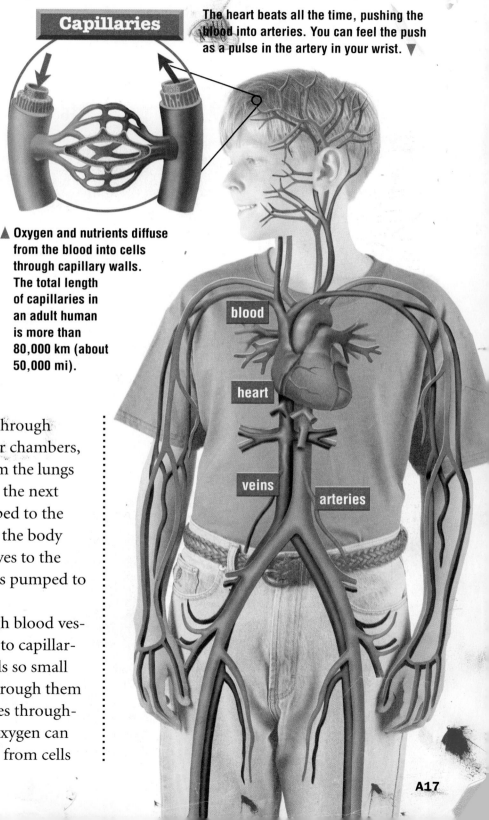

Capillaries

▲ Oxygen and nutrients diffuse from the blood into cells through capillary walls. The total length of capillaries in an adult human is more than 80,000 km (about 50,000 mi).

The heart beats all the time, pushing the blood into arteries. You can feel the push as a pulse in the artery in your wrist. ▼

blood

heart

veins

arteries

The Respiratory System

Your body uses a lot of energy. So your cells need a lot of food and oxygen. You get the oxygen your cells need by breathing. When you inhale, several liters of air are pulled into your body. The air is filtered by tiny hairs in your nose and warmed by capillaries that line the nasal passages. Warm, clean air then travels down your *trachea*, or windpipe.

The lungs are the major organs of the respiratory system. ▼

trachea

bronchi

In your chest, the trachea branches into two tubes called *bronchi* (BRAHNG•kee). Each tube leads into a lung. In the lungs, the bronchi divide into smaller and smaller tubes. At the end of the smallest tubes are tiny air sacs called **alveoli** (al•VEE•oh•lee). The walls of the alveoli are only one cell thick and are surrounded by capillaries.

The capillaries surrounding the alveoli get blood from the *pulmonary arteries* coming from the heart. This blood contains a lot of carbon dioxide. Carbon dioxide is a waste produced by the process that releases energy in cells. Carbon dioxide diffuses through the thin walls of the alveoli and into air that will be exhaled. At the same time, oxygen from inhaled air diffuses through the alveoli and into red blood cells in the capillaries. The oxygen-rich blood then flows from the capillaries into the *pulmonary veins* and back to the heart. From the heart, oxygen-rich blood is pumped to other parts of the body.

✔ **What happens in the alveoli?**

▲ The gas exchange of oxygen and carbon dioxide takes place in the alveoli.

The lungs are on a separate circuit of the circulatory system. The heart pumps oxygen-poor blood through the pulmonary arteries to the lungs. The oxygen-rich blood travels through the pulmonary veins back to the heart. ▼

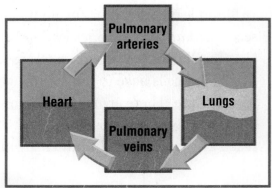

The Digestive System

Your digestive system provides the nutrients your cells need to produce energy. To provide nutrients, the digestive system performs two functions. The first is to break food into nutrients. The second is to get the nutrients into the blood. Then the circulatory system transports them to your cells.

Digestion begins as you chew food, breaking it into smaller pieces so that you can swallow it. Glands in your mouth produce saliva. Saliva moistens food and begins to break down starchy foods, such as pasta, into sugars. (If you chew an unsalted cracker for a while, it will begin to taste sweet.)

When you swallow, food passes through the *esophagus* (ih•SAHF•uh•guhs), a long tube that leads to the stomach. Gastric juice, produced by the stomach, contains acid and chemicals that break down proteins.

After several hours in the stomach, partly digested food moves into the small intestine. Digestion of food into nutrients is completed by chemicals produced in the small intestine. Nutrients diffuse through the **villi**, projections sticking out of the walls of the small intestine, into the blood. From the small intestine, undigested food passes into the large intestine. There, water and minerals pass into the blood, and wastes are removed from the body.

Two other organs have a role in digestion. The *liver* produces bile, which is stored in the *gallbladder* until it's needed. Bile breaks down fats into smaller particles that can be more easily digested. The *pancreas* produces a fluid that neutralizes stomach acid and chemicals that help finish digestion.

✔ **In what organ of the digestive system do nutrients enter the blood?**

As food passes through the digestive system, chemicals break it down into nutrients the body cells need. ▼

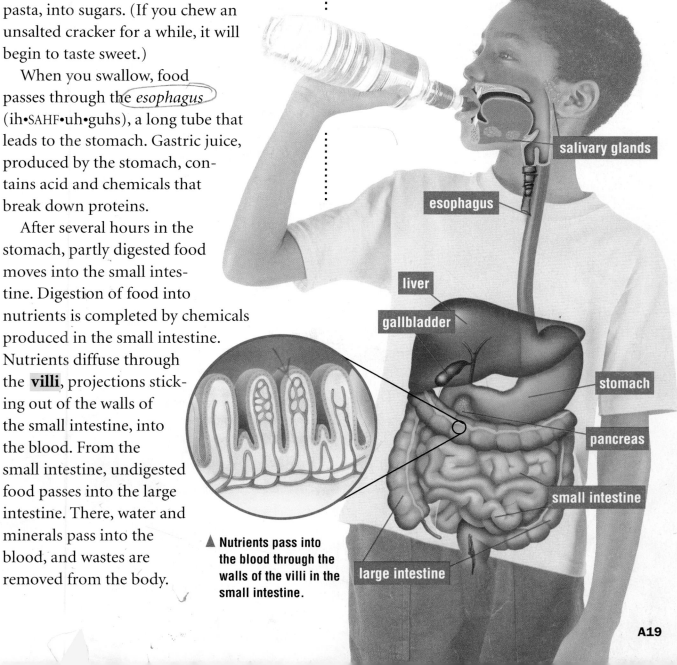

salivary glands

esophagus

liver

gallbladder

stomach

pancreas

small intestine

large intestine

▲ Nutrients pass into the blood through the walls of the villi in the small intestine.

The Excretory System

The circulatory system supplies food and oxygen to the body's cells. It carries away waste products from the production of energy. The wastes must then be removed from the blood. This is the function of the excretory system.

Cell wastes include carbon dioxide and ammonia. As you learned, the respiratory system gets rid of carbon dioxide. Ammonia is carried by the blood to the liver, where it is changed to urea.

From the liver, urea is carried by the blood to the kidneys. These organs are located behind the liver and stomach. As blood flows through capillaries in the kidneys, urea and water enter tubes called **nephrons**.

Urine, which is urea, water, and other waste products, flows from the kidneys through tubes called *ureters*. The ureters empty into a muscular organ called the bladder. When the bladder is full, urine leaves the body through a channel called the *urethra*.

The kidneys, ureters, bladder, and urethra make up the excretory system. This system takes wastes from the blood and removes them from the body as urine. ▼

nephron

▲ **Wastes and water are removed from the capillaries that run through the kidneys. Materials that the body needs are returned to the capillaries.**

The excretory system keeps the amount of water in the body fairly constant.

Daily Water Gain and Water Loss in Adults			
Water Gain		**Water Loss**	
From cell activities	400 mL	In solid wastes	100 mL
From eating	900 mL	From skin and lungs	1000 mL
From drinking	1300 mL	As urine	1500 mL
Total	2600 mL	Total	2600 mL

Cell wastes aren't the only wastes the body needs to get rid of. When you exercise, your body gets warm. Excess heat is eliminated by sweating. Sweat is a salty liquid that evaporates from the skin. Evaporation pulls heat from capillaries just below the skin. The blood and the entire body are cooled.

✓ **How do cell wastes get to the kidneys?**

Summary

Body cells are organized into tissues, organs, and systems that work together to keep the body alive. The circulatory system transports materials throughout the body. In the respiratory system, oxygen diffuses into the blood and carbon dioxide diffuses out of the blood. The digestive system breaks down food into nutrients that can be used by cells. The excretory system removes cell wastes from the blood.

Review

1. How do the functions of red blood cells and white blood cells differ?

2. In what way do the respiratory and circulatory systems work together?

3. What does the pancreas do?

4. **Critical Thinking** Between the trachea and the esophagus is a flap of skin called the *epiglottis*. What do you think its function is?

5. **Test Prep** Inhaled oxygen diffuses through the walls of the —

   A ureters
   B bronchioles
   C pulmonary arteries
   D alveoli

LINKS

MATH LINK

Use Mental Math Count the number of times your heart beats in 15 sec. Then multiply the number by 4 to find your approximate heartbeat rate per minute. At that rate, how many times would your heart beat in one year?

WRITING LINK

Informative Writing—Report Find out more about one of the body systems. Write a brief report for your teacher. Describe in detail the organs of the system. Also explain how the system functions.

SOCIAL STUDIES LINK

Early Physicians Some of the first recorded information about physicians described Imhotep, who lived in Egypt during the Third Dynasty (about 2700–2500 B.C.). Find out about Imhotep and his contributions to ancient medicine.

TECHNOLOGY LINK

Learn more about the functioning of the heart by investigating *One Heart— Two Amazing Pumps* on the **Harcourt Science Explorations CD-ROM.**

How Do Bones, Muscles, and Nerves Work Together?

In this lesson, you can . . .

INVESTIGATE how muscles cause movement.

LEARN ABOUT the skeletal, muscular, and nervous systems.

LINK to math, writing, art, and technology.

INVESTIGATE

How Muscles Cause Movement

Activity Purpose Your respiratory, circulatory, digestive, and excretory systems function automatically, without the need for you to give them directions. Other systems in your body are under your control, at least some of the time. When you run for a bus, for example, you direct your skeleton, muscles, and nerves to work together. In this investigation you'll **observe** what your muscles do when you bend your arm.

Materials
■ tape measure

Activity Procedure

1. Place your left hand on top of your right arm, between the shoulder and elbow. Bend and straighten your right arm at the elbow. **Observe** the movement by feeling the muscles in your right arm. (Picture A)

2. The muscle on the front of the upper arm is called the *biceps.* The muscle on the back of the upper arm is called the *triceps.* **Compare** the biceps and the triceps as you bend and straighten your arm. **Infer** which muscle controls the bending movement and which controls the straightening movement.

◀ In-line skating requires the coordination of your skeletal system, muscular system, and nervous system.

Picture A

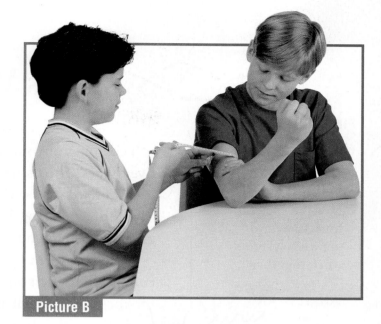

Picture B

3 Have a partner use the tape measure to **measure** the distance around your upper arm when it is straight and when it is bent. **Record** the measurements. (Picture B)

4 Repeat Steps 2 and 3, using your right hand and your left arm.

5 **Compare** the sets of measurements.

Draw Conclusions

1. What did you **infer** about the muscles controlling the bending and the straightening of your upper arm?

2. Why are two muscles needed to bend and straighten your arm? Why can't one muscle do it?

3. **Scientists at Work** Scientists often hypothesize about things they **observe**. **Hypothesize** about any differences between the measurements of your right arm and the measurements of your left arm.

Investigate Further **Plan and conduct an experiment** with different pairs of muscles. For example, try bending your leg at the knee while **observing** the muscles in your thigh. See if these measurements also support your hypothesis. **Draw conclusions** about differences in muscle sizes from the data you collected. Decide whether more data is needed to support your conclusions.

Process Skill Tip

When you **hypothesize**, you tell what you think will happen based on what you **observe**. A hypothesis can be tested by doing an experiment.

A23

Systems Working Together

Bones and Joints

FIND OUT

- what the structure and function of bones are
- how the skeletal, muscular, and nervous systems work together

VOCABULARY

bone marrow
joints
tendons
ligaments
neuron
receptors

The bones of your body are living organs made up of connective tissues. The tissues include an outer protective membrane, a layer of hard material, and a soft center containing bone marrow. **Bone marrow** is a connective tissue that produces red blood cells and white blood cells.

Bone cells form canals throughout the hard layer. The cells are connected to each other and to blood vessels. Bone cells secrete the rocklike material, made of calcium, that gives bones their strength and hardness. The protective membrane surrounding bones repairs them if they are broken.

Your body contains several kinds of bones. These include long bones in your arms and legs, flat bones in your shoulders and hips, and short bones in your fingers and toes. Other kinds of bones include the irregular bones in your wrists and ankles.

Bones meet at **joints**, where they are attached to each other and to muscles. Different kinds of joints allow different kinds of movement. Hinge joints, for example, allow back-and-forth movement, like the movement of a door hinge. Ball-and-socket joints allow circular motion, like the motion of a joystick. Some joints, such as the ones in your skull, don't allow any movement.

✔ **What kind of tissue are bones made of?**

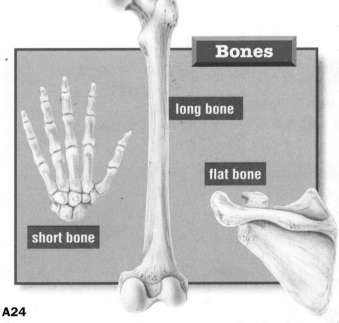

Bones

long bone

flat bone

short bone

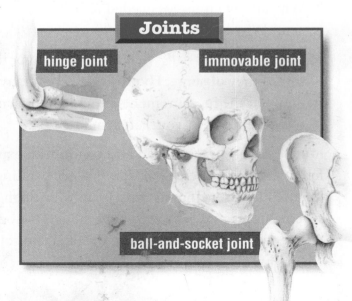

Joints

hinge joint

immovable joint

ball-and-socket joint

The Skeletal System

Bones are organized into a skeleton, which provides support for your body. Your skeleton also protects many of your internal organs. For example, your skull completely encloses your brain.

The outer layer of a bone provides a surface for the attachment of muscles. On each side of a joint, muscles are attached to bones by **tendons**, tough bands of connective tissue. Bones are attached to each other by **ligaments**, bands of connective tissue that hold the skeleton together.

An adult human skeleton has 206 bones. Each hand has 27 bones and each foot has 26 bones. The skull is made up of 23 bones. Not all of the skeleton is bone. Your outer ears and the tip of your nose are *cartilage*—another type of connective tissue. Cartilage also coats the ends of bones where they meet at a joint. This allows smooth movement between bones.

✔ **How are muscles attached to bones?**

The Muscular System

There are three kinds of muscles—voluntary muscles, smooth muscles, and cardiac muscles. *Voluntary muscles* move bones and hold your skeleton upright. These muscles are made up of groups of muscle tissues bound together by connective tissue. They are generally attached to two or more bones, either directly or through tendons. Where muscles attach to bones at a joint, they work in opposing pairs. As you observed in the investigation, one muscle contracts to bend a joint. Another contracts to straighten it.

Smooth muscles contract slowly and move substances through the organs they surround. These muscles run in bands around the walls of blood vessels and digestive organs.

Cardiac muscles make up the walls of the heart. Their function is to pump blood. Some cardiac muscles work together to set the heartbeat rate. They ensure that all the cardiac muscles beat at the same time.

✔ **Why must voluntary muscles work in pairs?**

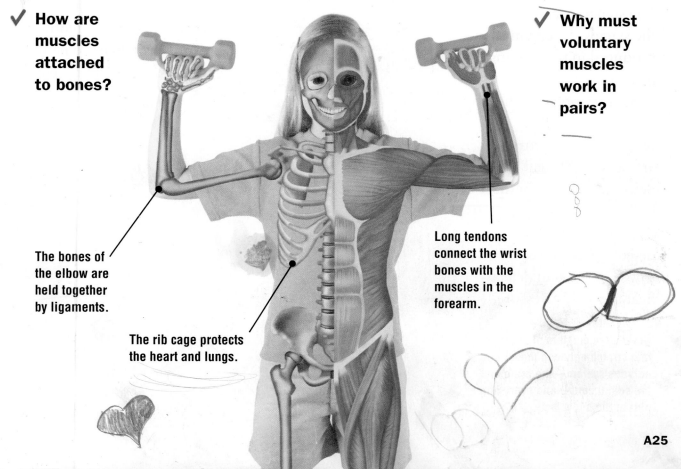

The bones of the elbow are held together by ligaments.

The rib cage protects the heart and lungs.

Long tendons connect the wrist bones with the muscles in the forearm.

The Nervous System

Your nervous system allows you to experience things and to react to your environment. It connects all the tissues and organs of your body to your brain. The nervous system consists of two parts—the central nervous system and the peripheral nervous system. The central nervous system is made up of the brain and the spinal cord. The spinal cord is a bundle of nerves, about as thick as a pencil. It runs from the base of the brain to the hips.

The peripheral nervous system consists of sensory organs, such as the eyes and ears, and body nerves. Nerves are bundles of nerve cells, or neurons. A **neuron** is a specialized cell that can receive signals and transmit them to other neurons.

Signals traveling along nerves cross the gap between neurons. This gap is called a *synapse.* The signal is carried across the synapse by chemicals produced in the sending neuron.

Sensory organs contain neurons called receptors. **Receptors** are nerve cells that detect conditions in the body's environment. Receptors in the ears detect sound waves. Those in the skin detect heat and cold, pressure,

spinal cord

Nerves are clusters of neurons that stretch between the central nervous system—the brain and the spinal cord—and every other part of the body. ▶

touch, and pain. Receptors in the eyes detect light and color. Those in the mouth and nose detect tastes and smells. Each receptor sends a signal through nerves to the central nervous system.

The central nervous system interprets signals it receives from nerves and determines what response is needed. Signals sent by the brain travel through nerves and direct all of the body's muscles. The brain also controls the body's automatic functions, such as respiration, circulation, and digestion.

Some muscle actions are automatic responses to situations. These are called *reflexes.* For example, when a pain signal from a skin receptor reaches the spinal cord, the nerve carrying the signal transmits it directly to a nerve that controls muscles, as well as to a nerve traveling to the brain. The reflex action of the muscles to avoid the source of pain happens before the signal reaches the brain. In other words, you react to pain before you even feel pain.

✔ **What takes place at a synapse?**

A synapse is the gap between neurons. ▼

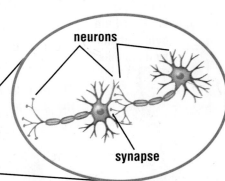

neurons

synapse

If you accidentally touch a very hot object, your hand pulls back in a reflex action. This happens before the information reaches your brain. The signal from a heat receptor makes a "shortcut," triggering a neuron in the spinal cord that makes the muscles in your arm move your hand out of danger.

Summary

Bones are living organs that make up the skeletal system. Skeletal bones move because of the action of pairs of voluntary muscles. Smooth muscles line the digestive organs and blood vessels. Cardiac muscles make up the walls of the heart. Muscles are controlled by the central nervous system. Nerves are bundles of neurons. They carry signals from sensory organs to the brain and from the brain to the muscles.

Review

1. What is produced in bone marrow?
2. What function do ligaments perform?
3. What kinds of muscles move food through the digestive system?
4. **Critical Thinking** What kind of action is a sneeze caused by pepper in the air? Explain.
5. **Test Prep** Tendons are connective tissue that —
   - **A** makes blood cells
   - **B** carries signals from receptors
   - **C** connects one bone to another
   - **D** connects a bone to a muscle

  LINKS

 MATH LINK

Collect/Organize Data Work with a partner to test your reaction time. Have your partner hold a meterstick vertically so that the lower end is just above the open fingers of your hand. When your partner lets the meterstick go—without warning—catch it between your fingers. Record the measurement where your fingers grasp the stick. Repeat the activity several times, and graph your results.

 WRITING LINK

Informative Writing—Description Fill one bowl with ice-cold water, one with hot—but not too hot—water, and one with lukewarm water. Leave one hand in the cold water and one in the hot water for about a minute. Then put both hands into the lukewarm water. Write a paragraph describing the results.

 ART LINK

Pointillism Pointillist paintings are composed of small, separate dots of color, like a photograph. The brain interprets the dots as a picture. Try making a pointillist painting of your own.

 TECHNOLOGY LINK

Learn more about the benefits of exercise by viewing *The Importance of Exercise* on the **Harcourt Science Newsroom Video** in your classroom video library.

CNN
Turner
Le@rning

POTATO VACCINES

Scientists are using biotechnology to turn common potatoes into vaccines against deadly diseases such as cholera.

Why Potato Vaccines?

Potatoes are an inexpensive, nutritious food that most children like to eat mashed, baked, or French fried. Biologists are using genetic engineering to insert a new gene into potatoes. This gene causes the plants to produce a chemical, called a B-protein, that is a harmless part of cholera toxin, or poison. When children eat a certain amount of these genetically altered potatoes, they become vaccinated against cholera.

Potatoes are a good choice for edible vaccines because most people like them.

This white blood cell is attacking *E. coli* bacteria.

What Is Cholera?

Cholera is an infectious disease that affects about 5 million people a year, particularly in poor areas of the world. It's highly contagious, so outbreaks of cholera can easily become epidemics. Cholera toxin causes pores in cells lining the intestines to remain open when they should be closed. Water diffuses from the blood into the intestines and then out of the body as diarrhea. People with cholera can lose so much water so quickly that they become very sick and may even die.

How Does the Potato Vaccine Work?

Scientists at the Loma Linda University School of Medicine in California have added the gene that produces the cholera toxin's B-protein to the genes of potato plants. The B-protein attaches to cells in the intestines and triggers the production of antibodies against cholera.

Scientists tested the potato vaccines by feeding genetically altered potatoes to mice. Then they examined tissue from the mice's intestines to see what happened when it was exposed to cholera toxin. They found that only half as much water passed through this tissue compared with tissue from mice that had not eaten the altered potatoes.

People seldom eat potatoes raw, so scientists had to make sure that cooking wouldn't destroy the vaccine. They found that after cooking, the genetically altered potatoes had about half the vaccine they started with. But this is still enough vaccine to be effective. One cooked potato a week for one month provides enough cholera toxin B-protein to protect against the disease for years.

Other uses of the potato vaccine

Toxins produced by the cholera bacteria are nearly identical to toxins produced by another dangerous intestinal bacteria called *E. coli*. So the potato vaccine that works against cholera may also work against *E. coli* toxins. Scientists are also looking for ways to improve the potato vaccine so that it will help destroy the bacteria directly, not just the toxins the bacteria produce.

THINK ABOUT IT

1. Why do you think potato vaccines would be easier to distribute and give to people than injected vaccines?

2. What would be an advantage of inserting vaccine-producing genes into foods that are eaten raw, such as bananas?

CAREERS
GENETICIST

What They Do
Geneticists study the ways genes and chromosomes combine to produce variety in plants and animals.

Education and Training
People wishing to become geneticists should earn an M.D. degree, or a Ph.D. degree in cell biology.

WEB LINK
For Science and Technology updates, visit the Harcourt Internet site.
www.harcourtschool.com

"What a sight . . . the Earth below us, the clouds that look like they're hugging it. It's even more incredible than I imagined."

Bernard A. Harris, Jr.

ASTRONAUT, PHYSICIAN

When Bernard A. Harris, Jr., opened the hatch of the space shuttle *Discovery* and stepped outside, he became the first African American ever to walk in space. It was an amazing moment for a man who, from the age of 13, had dreamed of becoming an astronaut. His dream had been born as, watching on television, he saw Neil Armstrong take that first step on the moon. Although he kept his goal a secret, Dr. Harris worked constantly toward it, studying biology and medicine.

Dr. Harris's first trip in space was aboard the space shuttle *Columbia* in 1993. He and his crewmates experimented to find out the effects of space travel on the human body. The researchers learned that for every month astronauts spend in space, they lose 22.4–44.5 newtons (5–10 lb) of their body weight. In addition, they lose 20 percent of their blood volume because their bone marrow makes less blood.

While in space, Dr. Harris used sound waves to "see" his own heart and discovered that, under the conditions of near weightlessness, it shrank and shifted in his chest. "I had to listen for it in a slightly different place," he recalls.

Today, Dr. Harris is vice-president of SPACE-HAB, Inc., a company that furnishes payloads and experimental modules for NASA's space shuttles. He is also active in the STARS program (Space Technology and Research Students). This is a program that enables students to participate in experiments that are conducted in space.

THINK ABOUT IT

1. Why did Dr. Harris have to listen for his heart in a different place?

2. What physical effects might astronauts experience if they remain in space for months?

BALLOON LUNGS

How do lungs work?

Materials

- 2 balloons
- scissors
- plastic soda bottle

Procedure

❶ Remove the cap and cut the bottom off the bottle.

❷ Put one balloon into the bottle. Secure the lip of the balloon to the top of the bottle.

❸ Cut the lip off the second balloon. Stretch the large part of the second balloon over the bottom of the bottle.

❹ With your fingers, pull down on the second balloon and then release it. Observe what happens to the first balloon.

Draw Conclusions

When you pull on the second balloon, what happens inside the bottle? What part of the respiratory system does each part of your model represent?

SKELETAL SYSTEMS

What adaptations do skeletons show?

Materials

- butcher paper
- 5 people
- meterstick
- marker

Procedure

❶ Measure out about 7 m of butcher paper.

❷ Have one person lie in the center of the paper. This person should stretch out his or her arms as shown.

❸ Have two other people lie end-to-end on each side of the first person.

❹ Use the marker to draw around the first person, including the top edge of his or her outstretched arms and thumbs.

❺ To complete the top edge, draw a sloping line the lengths of the people on both sides as shown. Draw the lower edge with four points and four scallops as shown.

Draw Conclusions

While the skeletal systems of all mammals are similar, there are differences due to various adaptations. The skeletons of bats show adaptations for flight. If humans could fly, how many times longer than their bodies would their wings need to be? What other skeletal adaptations of mammals can you think of?

Vocabulary Review

Use the terms below to complete the sentences. The page numbers in ( ) tell you where to look in the chapter if you need help.

cell (A6)
cell membrane (A8)
nucleus (A8)
cytoplasm (A9)
diffusion (A10)
osmosis (A10)
tissue (A12)
organ (A12)
system (A12)
capillaries (A17)

alveoli (A18)
villi (A19)
nephron (A20)
bone marrow (A24)
joints (A24)
tendons (A25)
ligaments (A25)
neuron (A26)
receptors (A26)

1. The _____ are projections of the inside wall of the small intestine.

2. The smallest blood vessels are the _____.

3. Similar cells work together in a _____, which is part of an _____, which is part of a _____.

4. Cells that detect conditions in the body's environment are _____.

5. The _____ determines cell activities, and the _____ regulates what enters and leaves the cell.

6. Air sacs in the lungs through which oxygen and carbon dioxide diffuse into and out of the blood are the _____.

7. The _____ is the basic unit of structure of all living things.

8. At _____, bones are connected to each other by _____, while _____ connect bones to muscles.

9. A _____ is a cell that can receive and transmit signals.

10. The structure in the kidney that filters urea and water from the blood is a _____.

11. Particles move from areas where there are a lot of them to areas where there are fewer of them by _____. Water and materials dissolved in water pass through a membrane by _____.

12. The jellylike substance between the cell membrane and the nucleus is the _____.

13. Blood cells are produced in _____.

Connect Concepts

Complete the chart by filling in terms from the Word Bank. Some terms are used more than once.

smooth muscle
oxygen
small intestine
nutrients
cardiac muscle

lungs
esophagus
alveoli
voluntary muscle

Food
travels down the **14.** to the stomach and then to the **15.**, where **16.** pass into the blood.

Air
travels down the trachea to the **17.**, where **18.** diffuses into the blood through the walls of the **19.**

16. and **18.**
are carried by the blood to muscle cells. The energy they produce in **20.** tissue is used to move bones. The energy they produce in **21.** tissue is used to move food through the digestive system. The energy they produce in **22.** tissue is used to move blood through the circulatory system.

Check Understanding

Write the letter of the best choice.

23. The tissue that makes up bones, tendons, and ligaments is —
    A connective tissue
    B epithelial tissue
    C muscle tissue
    D voluntary tissue

24. Bile, produced by the liver, breaks down —
    F muscle tissue
    G fats
    H stomach acid
    J white blood cells

25. The urea and water that make up urine are removed from the blood in the —
    A bladder
    B kidneys
    C pancreas
    D urethra

26. A plant stands up straight because of water pressure against the —
    F cell walls
    G nucleus
    H cellular membrane
    J chloroplasts

27. Neurons transmit signals across a —
    A synapse
    B nucleus
    C cell wall
    D receptor

28. The liver is an organ of the —
    F digestive system only
    G excretory and digestive systems
    H circulatory system only
    J circulatory and excretory systems

Critical Thinking

29. A nerve can carry signals both to the brain and from the brain. Why can't an individual neuron do this?

30. Platelets in the blood cause clotting. Why is this important?

31. On each side of the heart, a valve allows blood to travel from the upper chamber to the lower chamber. Why is this important?

Process Skills Review

32. If you are **observing** cells under a microscope, what will lead you to **infer** that the cells are animal cells?

33. How would you test the **hypothesis** that there is never a ball-and-socket joint between a hinged joint and the end of a limb of a skeleton?

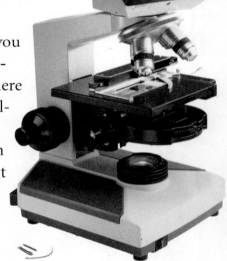

Performance Assessment

Body Systems

Use colored pencils to draw the organs and vessels of the excretory system on a human body outline. Label each part. Describe how this system works to eliminate waste from the body cells.

2

Classifying Living Things

Vocabulary Preview

classification
kingdom
moneran
protist
fungi
genus
species
vertebrates
mammals
reptiles
amphibians
fish
birds
invertebrates
vascular plants
nonvascular plants

Have you ever noticed how some living things have the same kinds of parts? A cat and a dog each have fur, four legs, and a tail. An ant and a cockroach each have six legs. Scientists look at the similarities among living things and put them into groups.

Fast Fact

A kelp may look like a plant, but it's not. The leaflike and stemlike parts of a kelp are different from those of plants. Instead, kelps belong to the protist kingdom. Other protists include microscopic amoebas and paramecia.

A duckbill platypus looks like a mixed-up animal. You might think it's a bird because it has a bill and lays eggs. But scientists say it's a mammal, like a dog or cat, because it has fur and produces milk for its young.

This Ithaca bog beetle was in an insect collection at Cornell University in Ithaca, New York, for 85 years before anyone realized it had no scientific name. Scientists think there are many more living things to be classified and named. Many haven't even been discovered yet.

Numbers of Living Things

Type of Living Thing	Number of Known Species, or Kinds
Insects	1,000,000
Fish	30,000
Orchids	20,000

How Do Scientists Classify Living Things?

In this lesson, you can . . .

 INVESTIGATE ways to group nonliving objects.

 LEARN ABOUT classification.

 LINK to math, writing, art, and technology.

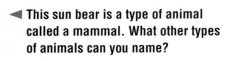

◄ This sun bear is a type of animal called a mammal. What other types of animals can you name?

Classifying Shoes

Activity Purpose You've probably looked for a certain book in a library. Imagine how hard it would be to find a book in a library full of books if they were not grouped by topic. In this activity you will practice **classifying** some familiar items.

Materials

- shoes
- newspaper or paper towels

Activity Procedure

1 Take off one shoe and put it with your class-mates' shoes. If you put the shoes on a desk or table, cover it first with newspaper or paper towels. (Picture A)

2 Find a way to **classify** the shoes. Begin by find-ing two or three large groups of shoes that are alike. Write a description of each group. (Picture B)

3 **Classify** the large groups of shoes into smaller and smaller groups. Each smaller group should be alike in some way.

Picture A

Picture B

4 Write a description of each smaller group.

5 Stop classifying when you have sorted all the shoes into groups with two or fewer members.

Draw Conclusions

1. What features did you use to **classify** the shoes?

2. **Compare** your classification system with a classmate's system. How are your systems alike? How are they different?

3. **Scientists at Work** Scientists **classify** living things to show how living things are alike. Why might it be important for scientists to agree on a set of rules for classifying living things?

Investigate Further **Classify** other groups of things such as toys, cars, or pictures of plants and animals. Write a brief explanation of your classification system.

Classification

Grouping Living Things

FIND OUT

- why scientists group living things

- the names of the five largest groups of living things

VOCABULARY

classification
kingdom
moneran
protist
fungi
genus
species

If you were asked to go to the grocery store to buy fresh peaches, how would you find them? You know how your grocery store is set up, so you would probably go to the produce department and find the fruit section. There you would look for peaches. If a store put some fruit with the cereal and some with the meat, finding peaches would be much more difficult.

Like grocery shoppers, scientists need to be able to find things easily. Just as you did with shoes in the investigation, scientists look at living things and identify their characteristics. They then group together living things that have similar features. This act of grouping things by using a set of rules is called **classification** (klas•uh•fih•KAY•shuhn).

✔ **How do scientists group living things?**

The living things shown in the forest scene and in the smaller photos belong to several different groups.

Bacterium

Paramecium

Water strider

The Five Kingdoms

Kingdom	Important Characteristics	Examples
Animals	Many-celled, feed on living or once-living things	Monkeys, birds, frogs, fish, spiders
Plants	Many-celled, make their own food	Trees, flowers, grasses, ferns, mosses
Fungi	Most many-celled, absorb food from other living things or dead things such as logs	Mushrooms, yeasts, molds
Protists	Most one-celled, make their own food or feed on living or once-living things	Algae, amoebas, diatoms
Monerans	One-celled, no cell nuclei, some make their own food, some feed on living or once-living things	Bacteria

Grouping by Similarities and Differences

Scientists classify for many reasons. Classifying living things makes it easier to find and share information about them. When scientists discover a new living thing, classification can show how the new living thing relates to others that are already classified.

All living things can be classified into one of five kingdoms. A **kingdom** (KING•duhm) is the largest group into which living things can be classified. Every member of a kingdom has some characteristics that are the same as those of other members. For example, bacteria are monerans. Every member of the **moneran** (muh•NER•uhn) kingdom has only one cell. The cell has no nucleus.

Compare the bacterium to the paramecium on page A38. Paramecia are protists. Most members of the **protist** (PROH•tist) kingdom also have only one cell. However, each cell does have a nucleus.

Fungi make up a third kingdom. **Fungi** (FUHN•jy) have nuclei, and most are many-celled. In some ways they are like plants, but they can't make their own food as plants do. You have eaten fungi if you've ever eaten mushrooms.

Plants and animals make up the other two kingdoms. Every day you see members of these two kingdoms, such as grass, flowers, cats, and dogs.

✔ **How are monerans and protists the same? How are they different?**

Forming Smaller Groups

Classification doesn't stop at the kingdom level. Scientists study the living things in each kingdom to see how they are alike and how they are different. They use characteristics to make smaller and smaller groups, and they give each smaller group a name. The most specific classification groups have only one type of living thing. The chart below shows how brown bears can be classified by using this method.

Most living things have a common name such as *brown bear*. But common names may be different in different places. It's important to have names that scientists everywhere recognize. For this reason, scientists name animals with the labels of the two smallest classification groups. The name of the second smallest group, the **genus** (JEE•nuhs), is joined with the name of the smallest group, the **species** (SPEE•sheez). For example, the scientific name for a house cat is *Felis domesticus*, and a brown bear is called *Ursus arctos*.

✓ **How do scientists form smaller groups of living things?**

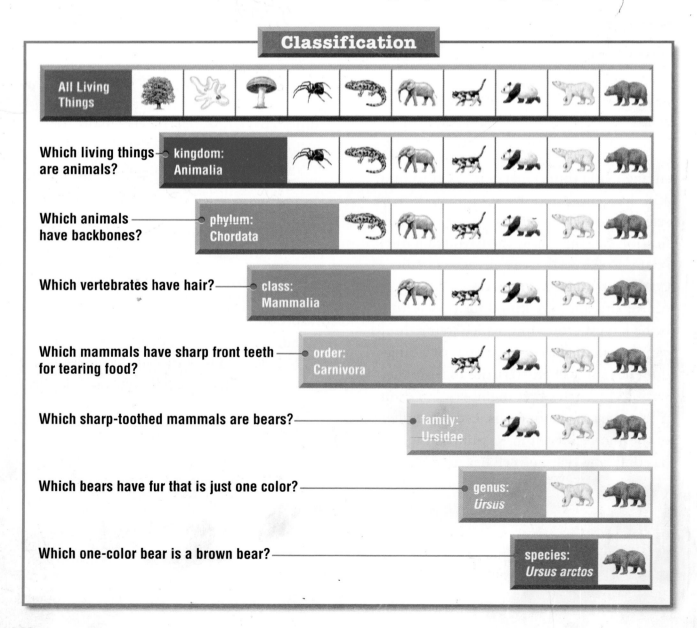

Classification

All Living Things

Which living things are animals?
kingdom: Animalia

Which animals have backbones?
phylum: Chordata

Which vertebrates have hair?
class: Mammalia

Which mammals have sharp front teeth for tearing food?
order: Carnivora

Which sharp-toothed mammals are bears?
family: Ursidae

Which bears have fur that is just one color?
genus: Ursus

Which one-color bear is a brown bear?
species: Ursus arctos

This bear cub's scientific name is *Ursus* (genus) *arctos* (species).

Summary

Scientists organize living things to make studying and discussing them easier. Scientists classify all living things into five kingdoms—monerans, protists, fungi, plants, and animals. The five kingdoms are divided into smaller groups.

Review

1. Why do scientists organize information about living things?
2. What are the five kingdoms of living things?
3. How do scientists name each type of living thing?
4. **Critical Thinking** There are probably millions of living things that scientists haven't discovered yet. If scientists were to find a living thing that didn't fit into any of the five kingdoms, what would they need to do?
5. **Test Prep** Which kingdom contains one-celled living things without nuclei?

   A plants   **C** fungi
   B monerans   **D** protists

LINKS

 MATH LINK

Display Data Suppose you have found a cave in which animals—three snakes, six bats, and a bear—are living. To report your discovery to your classmates, make a bar graph showing the types and numbers of animals in the cave.

 WRITING LINK

Informative Writing—Description Suppose you've discovered a new species of living thing. For your teacher, write two or three paragraphs to describe how you found it, what its characteristics are, and how you decided on its name.

 ART LINK

Designing Labels Think about how you could improve the organization of your books, games, or CDs. Classify them and then design picture labels for each group. Put the labels on your books, games, or CDs so that you can more easily find the ones you want.

 TECHNOLOGY LINK

Learn more about some bears by viewing *China Panda* on the **Harcourt Science Newsroom Video** in your classroom video library.

How Are Animals Classified?

In this lesson, you can . . .

 INVESTIGATE a model of a backbone.

 LEARN ABOUT vertebrate classification.

 LINK to math, writing, health, and technology.

 **INVESTIGATE**

Building a Model Backbone

Activity Purpose Animals are classified into several groups. Animals in one of these groups all have a backbone that protects the spinal cord and helps support the body. In this investigation you will **make and use a model** backbone.

Materials
- chenille stem
- wagon-wheel pasta, uncooked
- candy gelatin rings

Activity Procedure
CAUTION

1 CAUTION **Never eat anything you use in an Investigate.** Bend one end of the chenille stem. Thread six pieces of wagon-wheel pasta onto the stem. Push the pasta down to the bend in the stem. Bend the stem above the pasta to hold the pasta in place.

2 Bend and twist the stem. What do you see and hear?

3 Take all the pasta off the chenille stem except one. Thread a candy gelatin ring onto the stem, and push it down. (Picture A)

◀ Birds have a backbone. Worms, like the one the bird is eating, don't.

Picture A

Picture B

4 Add pasta and rings until the stem is almost full. Bend the stem above the pasta and rings to hold them in place. (Picture B)

5 Bend and twist the stem. What do you see and hear?

6 Draw pictures of the model backbones you made. **Compare** your models with that shown in the picture on page A57.

Draw Conclusions

1. A real backbone is made of bones called vertebrae (VER•tuh•bray) and soft discs that surround the spinal cord. What does each part of your final model stand for?

2. How is your final model like a real backbone?

3. Study your final model again. What do the soft discs do?

4. **Scientists at Work** Scientists use models to study how things work. **Make a model** to test this **hypothesis:** A piece of dry, uncooked spaghetti or some other material would work better than a chenille stem to stand for the spinal cord in a model. **Experiment** to see. Then write a report of your experiment. Be sure to include the results of any tests you conducted with other materials, and any conclusions you drew about using those materials in a model backbone.

Some objects are too big, too small, or too far away to observe directly. You can't observe your backbone directly because it is inside your body. But you can **make a model** to learn more about it.

Animal Classification

Animals with a Backbone

You are probably familiar with many members of the animal kingdom. An animal is a living thing made up of many cells that have nuclei. Animals can't make their own food. They must eat to survive. Scientists divide the animal kingdom into two large groups. One group of animals has backbones.

Animals that have a backbone are called **vertebrates** (VER•tuh•brits). Most vertebrates have sharp senses and large brains. These characteristics help them survive in their surroundings.

The large group of vertebrates is divided into several smaller groups. **Mammals** (MAM•uhlz) have hair and produce milk for their young. Cats and dogs are mammals that you may have as pets. Lizards, snakes, and turtles are reptiles. **Reptiles** (REP•tylz) have dry, scaly skin. **Amphibians** (am•FIB•ee•uhnz) have moist skin and no scales. Most of them begin life in water, but they live on land as adults. Frogs, toads, and newts are amphibians.

Sharks, eels, bass, and tuna are fish. **Fish** are vertebrates that live their entire lives in water. Most fish have hard scales covering their bodies and gills to take the oxygen they need directly from the water.

Mongoose

Frog

◄ A mongoose and a frog are both vertebrates. What characteristic do they share with a snake?

Snake skeleton

Snail

Tortoiseshell beetle

Sea sponge

Snails, sea sponges, and beetles are invertebrates. None of these animals has a backbone.

▲ Although a shark's backbone isn't made of bone, a shark is still a vertebrate.

Birds are vertebrates with feathers. A bird's feathers keep it warm and help it to fly. Owls, robins, and parrots are birds. Some birds, such as penguins, don't fly.

✓ **What characteristic do all vertebrates have in common?**

Only a small part of all the animals in the world have a backbone. ▼

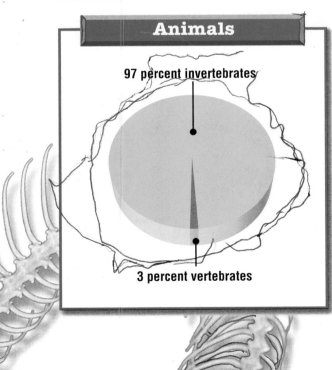

Animals

97 percent invertebrates

3 percent vertebrates

Animals Without a Backbone

Animals without a backbone are called **invertebrates** (in•VER•tuh•brits). There are many more types of invertebrates than types of vertebrates. Most invertebrates are smaller than vertebrates.

Arthropods (AR•throh•pahdz) are invertebrates with legs that have several joints. Their bodies have two or more parts, and they often have an outer covering that protects them. There are several groups of arthropods. Insects make up the largest group. Adult insects, such as beetles and bees, have six legs. Spiders aren't insects. They and other arthropods, such as mites, horseshoe crabs, and scorpions, have eight legs.

Mollusks (MAHL•uhsks) are invertebrates that may or may not have a hard outer shell. Snails, clams, and squids are mollusks.

Invertebrates also include several groups of *worms.* Worms have no shells, legs, or eyes. Earthworms, tapeworms, and flatworms belong to different groups of invertebrates.

✓ **What characteristic do all invertebrates have in common?**

Body Parts for Jumping

Frogs and grasshoppers are in different animal groups. Both animals are known for their ability to jump. Their back legs are different, but they work in much the same way.

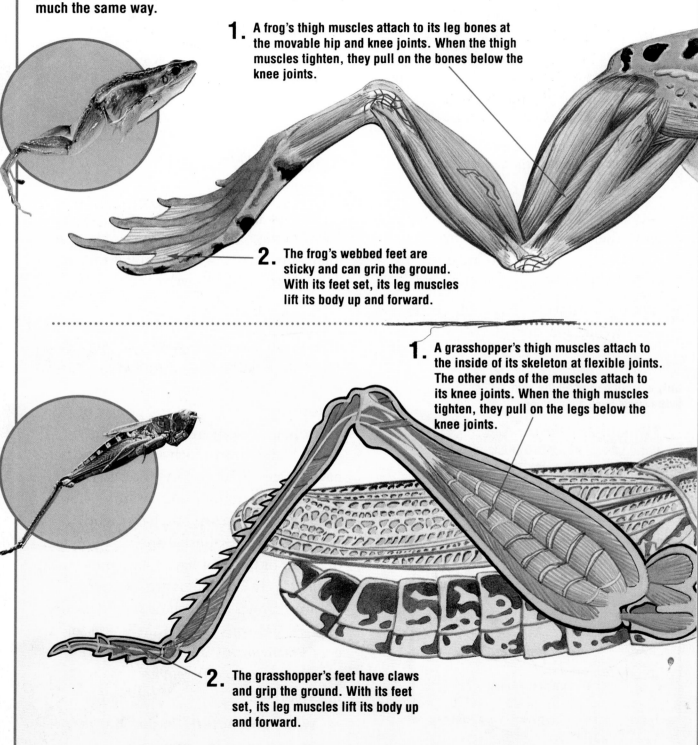

1. A frog's thigh muscles attach to its leg bones at the movable hip and knee joints. When the thigh muscles tighten, they pull on the bones below the knee joints.

2. The frog's webbed feet are sticky and can grip the ground. With its feet set, its leg muscles lift its body up and forward.

1. A grasshopper's thigh muscles attach to the inside of its skeleton at flexible joints. The other ends of the muscles attach to its knee joints. When the thigh muscles tighten, they pull on the legs below the knee joints.

2. The grasshopper's feet have claws and grip the ground. With its feet set, its leg muscles lift its body up and forward.

A Closer Look at Animals

Not all animals have a backbone, but most animals have skeletons and muscles that work together to allow the animals to move. The skeletons of vertebrates are made up of bones that support their bodies from the inside. Muscles attach to the bones at movable joints.

Most invertebrates have skeletons that form hard outer coverings. These skeletons are made of a material much like human fingernails. Muscles attach on the inside of these coverings at flexible joints.

✓ **Where do muscles attach to the skeletons of animals?**

Summary

Vertebrates, such as mammals, reptiles, amphibians, birds, and fish, have backbones. Invertebrate animals, such as arthropods, mollusks, and worms, do not have backbones.

Review

1. Which group of vertebrates begins life in water and later lives on land?
2. How is a spider different from an insect?
3. How are the skeletons of vertebrates and invertebrates different?
4. **Critical Thinking** How might having sharp senses and large brains help vertebrates survive?
5. **Test Prep** Which animals are **NOT** vertebrates?
   A reptiles
   B mammals
   C amphibians
   D arthropods

LINKS

MATH LINK

Display Data Vertebrate skeletons are made up of bones. The adult human spine has 33 bones. Find out how many bones the spines of five other vertebrates have. Make a bar graph to show what you learn.

WRITING LINK

Informative Writing—Explanation
You've learned that skeletons support animals' bodies and help them move. Skeletons also protect animals' organs. Would you prefer to have a hard outer shell or the skeleton you have now? Write a paragraph to explain your answer to a classmate.

HEALTH LINK

Prevention Calcium helps build strong bones. Eating calcium-rich foods helps prevent bone problems as you get older. Find out which foods are rich in calcium. Then make a chart to post in your kitchen at home.

TECHNOLOGY LINK

Learn more about vertebrates by investigating *Vertebrate Challenge* on the **Harcourt Science Explorations CD-ROM.**

How Are Plants Classified?

In this lesson, you can . . .

INVESTIGATE plant stems.

LEARN ABOUT plant classification.

LINK to math, writing, literature, and technology.

INVESTIGATE

Plant Stems

Activity Purpose You have learned that animals can be classified by whether they have a backbone. Plants also can be classified by their parts. One of those parts is the stem. In this investigation you will **observe** a stalk of celery to help you **infer** what stems do. Although a celery stalk is actually a celery leaf, it acts like a stem.

Materials

- fresh celery stalk with leaf blades
- plastic knife
- two containers
- water
- red food coloring
- blue food coloring
- paper towels
- hand lens

Activity Procedure

1 Use the plastic knife to trim the end off the celery stalk. Split the celery from the middle of the stalk to the bottom. Do not cut the stalk completely in half. (Picture A)

2 Make a chart like the one here.

Time	Observations

▼ These flowers and mosses are two different types of plants. They move water in different ways.

Picture A

Picture B

3 Half-fill each container with water. Add 15 drops of red food coloring to one container. Add 15 drops of blue food coloring to the other container.

4 With the containers side by side, place one part of the celery stalk in each container of colored water. You may need to prop the stalk up so the containers don't tip over. (Picture B)

5 **Observe** the celery every 15 minutes for an hour. **Record** your observations on your chart.

6 After you have completed your chart, put a paper towel on your desk. Take the celery out of the water. Cut about 2 cm off the bottom of the stalk. Use the hand lens to **observe** the pieces of stalk and the freshly cut end of the stalk.

Draw Conclusions

1. Where did the water travel? How do you know?

2. How fast did the water travel? How do you know?

3. **Scientists at Work** Scientists **infer** what happens in nature by making careful observations. Based on this investigation, what can you infer about the function of stems?

Investigate Further **Hypothesize** about how you could change a white carnation into a flower with two colors. **Plan and conduct an experiment** to test your hypothesis.

Process Skill Tip

When you **infer**, you use what you observe to explain what happened. Inferring is like using clues to solve a mystery. Observing carefully, like finding good clues, can help you infer correctly.

Plant Classification

Plants with Tubes

FIND OUT

- how the plant kingdom is divided
- members of each main group of plants

VOCABULARY

vascular plant
nonvascular plant

All plants are members of the plant kingdom. Plants have many cells, and their cells have nuclei. Unlike animals, plants do not need to eat other living things to survive. Instead, they make their own food. Scientists divide the plant kingdom into two main groups. One group of plants has tubes. The other group does not.

Vascular (VAS•kyuh•ler) **plants** have tubes. These tubes can be found in roots, stems, and leaves. Water and nutrients enter a plant through the roots. The tubes in the roots then carry this mixture to the stems. You observed some stemlike tubes in the investigation. Tubes in stems carry the water and nutrients to tubes in a plant's leaves. A different set of tubes carries the food the leaves make to the other parts of the plant. Some food tubes run from the leaves to the roots.

Ferns are a type of vascular plant. The tubes of fern stems form a network. They often split apart and rejoin. Cells that make up the tubes are stiff. This helps provide support for the fern as its stems grow.

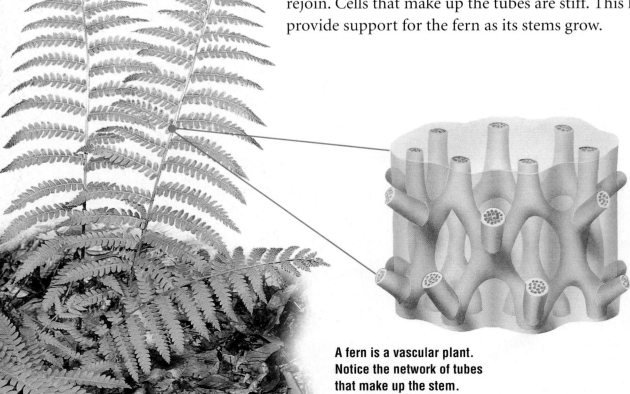

A fern is a vascular plant. Notice the network of tubes that make up the stem.

Sapwood

Growth ring

Heartwood

Bark

Trees are another type of vascular plant. The stems of trees contain cells that are woody, or very hard. Most large bushes also have woody stems. The largest woody stem of a tree is called the trunk. Look at the detailed slice of the tree trunk. The center of the trunk is made of clogged tubes called *heartwood*. Around the heartwood is a ring of *sapwood*. The sapwood tubes carry water and nutrients. Each year, a new set of tubes forms, and an old set dies, adding a growth ring to the trunk. The outside layer of the trunk is called the bark. The bark contains living tubes that carry food, and dead cells that protect the trunk.

There are many other types of vascular plants. Any plant that has flowers or cones is a vascular plant.

✔ **What is carried by the tubes of vascular plants?** water nutrients food

The giant sequoia is a conifer. Conifers (KAHN•uh•ferz) are vascular plants that produce cones. As new sapwood is added each year, a new growth ring forms in the trunk. ▶

Plants Without Tubes

Have you ever seen something that looked like a green carpet growing on stones and walkways? If so, you probably saw moss. Moss is a nonvascular plant. **Nonvascular** (nahn•VAS•kyuh•ler) **plants** don't have tubes. Water must soak into the plants and pass slowly from cell to cell. Food made in the plants must travel with the water from cell to cell. For this reason, nonvascular plants live in damp places and don't grow to be large or tall.

Mosses are often the first plants to grow on bare rock. Their rootlike structures help break down the rock into soil. When the mosses die, their dead bodies help to enrich the soil, making it more fertile. Nonvascular plants need fertile, moist soil in which to grow.

Nonvascular plants have no roots, stems, or leaves. The lobes, or rounded parts, of the liverwort may look like leaves, but they are not true leaves because they have no tubes.

✓ **How does water travel through a nonvascular plant?**

Enlarged, these liverworts look like small palm trees with leafy bases. However, liverworts have no tubes. So, they have no true stems or leaves. ▶

▲ Moss grows in shady, damp places.

▲ These plants are liverworts. Liverworts also grow in damp places.

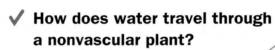

Summary

Scientists have classified plants into two main groups. Vascular plants, such as ferns and trees, have tubes. Because they have tubes to carry water, nutrients, and food, vascular plants can grow quite tall.

Nonvascular plants, such as mosses, do not have tubes. So water must move from cell to cell. These plants need to live in a moist place, and they do not grow to be very large.

Review

1. What are the two main groups of plants?

2. Where are the tubes of vascular plants found?

3. Because nonvascular plants do not have tubes, in what kind of place do they need to grow?

4. **Critical Thinking** What probably would happen to a plant if its main stem were crushed or broken?

5. **Test Prep** Which of these is an example of a nonvascular plant?

   A conifer   **C** moss

   B fern   **D** flower

LINKS

MATH LINK

Collect/Organize/Display Data The width of a growth ring depends on the amount of rainfall the tree received that year. Wide rings form in rainy years. Narrow rings form in dry years. Examine a tree stump or the end of a log. Count the growth rings, and then measure the width of each ring. Make a line graph or a bar graph to show what you see. What can you infer from your graph?

WRITING LINK

Informative Writing—Description Gather several types of plants, and examine their characteristics. Write clues describing each plant. Your clues can be about color, smell, height, size, or the plant's use, or they may tell where it was found. Read your clues to your classmates, and see if they can guess your plant.

LITERATURE LINK

Sugaring Time Would you like to learn how maple syrup is made from sap that flows through the tubes in maple trees? Read *Sugaring Time* by Kathryn Lasky.

GO ONLINE   TECHNOLOGY LINK

Learn more about plant classification by visiting the Harcourt Learning Site for related links, activities, and resources.
www.harcourtschool.com

WELCOME TO THE LEARNING SITE

Naming Living Things

Marmota monax (gopher or woodchuck)

People have classified living things for a long time. Cave people probably sorted animals into groups such as those that were good to eat and those that were likely to eat you. Classification is an important first step in the study of almost anything.

The history of classification shows how ideas in science can change through time. As scientists learn more, they change their ideas about how things work. For example, the first recorded classification system for living things that we know about was developed by Aristotle. Aristotle was a philosopher,

Gopherus polyphemus (gopher tortoise)

In different parts of the United States, both of these animals are called gophers. The scientific name of each helps you know to which animal a scientist is referring.

teacher, and scientist in ancient Greece. In about 350 B.C. he classified living things into two large groups—plants and animals. He divided animals by how they looked, how they behaved, and where they lived. He divided plants by their size and shape. He said that the three main divisions of the plant kingdom were trees, shrubs, and herbs (small plants such as grasses).

A New System

Aristotle's system didn't work for all plants and animals. However, it was used for more than 2000 years. In 1753 Carolus Linnaeus published the system that is the basis for the system we use today. Linnaeus, like Aristotle, divided living things into two kingdoms. However, for more exact sorting, he then broke the kingdoms into many smaller groups. The smallest group is the species. Today, scientists use genus and species names to identify living things.

Which Cat?

Genus and species names are important because they help scientists and other people talk about exactly the same organisms. For example, people use different names for one kind of large cat—*puma*, *panther*, and *mountain lion*. However, a scientist uses only the name *Felis concolor*. That way you know exactly which type of cat he or she is talking about.

As microscopes and other instruments for the study of living things became better, people began to realize that there were probably more than two kingdoms. Fungi were the first organisms classified as a new kingdom. After a lot of study, living things were divided into five different kingdoms. Some scientists now suggest that there may be as many as seven kingdoms.

As we learn more, our ideas about how living things are related change. As those ideas change, the way we classify the world of living things also changes. Each change in the classification system is a direct result of more study and better understanding of the relationships of living things.

THINK ABOUT IT

1. Linnaeus classified living things. Give examples of two other classification systems and what they classify.
2. How have changes in technology affected the classification of living things?

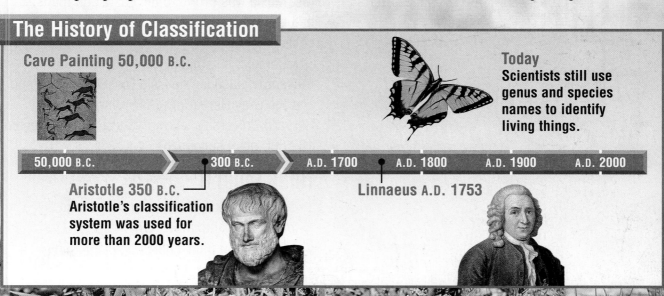

The History of Classification

Cave Painting 50,000 B.C.

Today
Scientists still use genus and species names to identify living things.

| 50,000 B.C. | 300 B.C. | A.D. 1700 | A.D. 1800 | A.D. 1900 | A.D. 2000 |

Aristotle 350 B.C.
Aristotle's classification system was used for more than 2000 years.

Linnaeus A.D. 1753

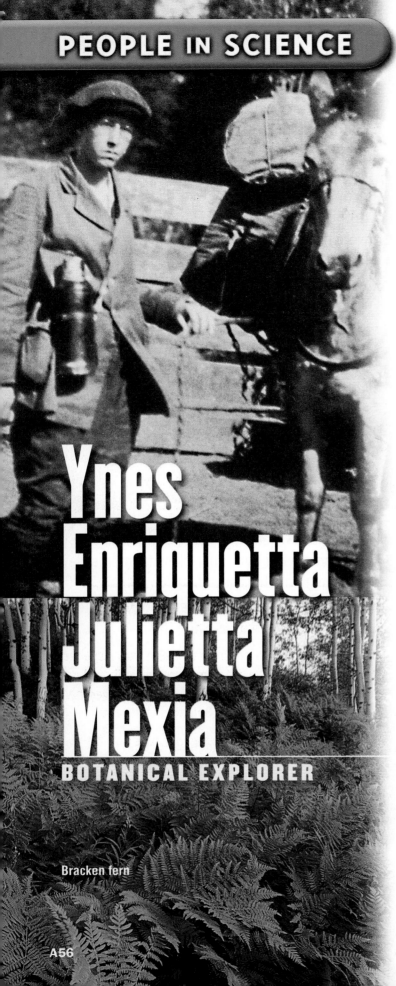

Ynes Enriquetta Julietta Mexia

BOTANICAL EXPLORER

Bracken fern

Ynes Mexia spent the last 13 years of her life, from 1925 to 1938, collecting plant specimens outside the United States. She was the daughter of an agent for the Mexican government, so she knew other languages and understood other cultures. This helped her when she traveled. She visited many places, including Mexico, Alaska, Brazil, Ecuador, Argentina, Bolivia, and Peru. During her trips she discovered almost 50 new plant species.

While living in San Francisco, Ms. Mexia traveled with the local Sierra Club. She took classes in natural science at the University of California and became interested in botany (BAHT•uhn•ee). She took a class on flowering plants, and it changed her life.

The botany class led to her first collecting trip, with botanist Roxanna S. Ferris. The trip was cut short when Ms. Mexia fell from a cliff. She broke several ribs and injured her hand. But before her fall, she had already collected 500 species of plants. One new species was named in Ms. Mexia's honor.

Nearly all Ms. Mexia's trips were to tropical countries. Because of the humid climates, it was difficult to dry and preserve plant samples. Alice Eastwood, a noted botanist, taught Ms. Mexia how to collect and preserve plants. Later, Ms. Mexia was proud to tell Eastwood that she had been able to preserve every specimen she collected!

Ms. Mexia's samples went to important museums, such as the Field Museum in Chicago and the Gray Herbarium (her•BAIR•ee•uhm) at Harvard University. During 13 years she collected 137,600 plant specimens.

THINK ABOUT IT

1. Do you think it is easier to collect and preserve plants now? Why?
2. How do you think collecting plants helps scientists understand more about plant classification?

BACKBONE CONSTRUCTION

How do backbones give vertebrates flexible support?

Materials

- construction paper
- tape
- scissors
- book

Procedure

1 Roll the paper into a tube about 5 cm across. Tape all along the edge.

2 Stand the tube on one end. Will the tube hold up a pair of scissors? A book? More than one book?

3 Squeeze the tube gently to make an oval. Make slits about 2 cm apart all down the tube. Cut the slits from each side almost to the middle.

4 Experiment to see how much weight the tube will now hold up.

Draw Conclusions

What happened each time the tube gave way? How did the cuts change the tube?

PLANTS AND WATER

Why do leaves give off water?

Materials

- pencil
- water
- marker
- scissors
- piece of thin cardboard
- leaf with a long stem
- modeling clay
- 2 clear plastic cups

Procedure

1 Carefully use the pencil to poke a hole in the center of the cardboard. Then push the leaf stem through the hole. Use the clay to close up the hole around the stem. Be careful not to pinch the stem.

2 Fill one cup about $\frac{2}{3}$ full with water. Mark the water line with the marker.

3 Snip off about 1 cm from the stem end. Place the cut stem into the water, resting the cardboard on the rim of the cup. Place the empty cup over the leaf. Set the cups in the sun.

4 After a few hours, observe both cups and the stem. Record your observations.

Draw Conclusions

What can you infer from your observations?

Vocabulary Review

Use the terms below to complete the sentences. The page numbers in ( ) tell you where to look in the chapter if you need help.

classification (A38)
kingdom (A39)
monerans (A39)
protists (A39)
fungi (A39)
genus (A40)
species (A40)
vertebrate (A44)
mammal (A44)

reptile (A44)
amphibian (A44)
fish (A44)
bird (A45)
invertebrate (A45)
vascular plants (A50)
nonvascular plants (A52)

1. The largest group into which scientists classify living things is a ____.

2. An animal that does not have a backbone is an ____.

3. Plants are either ____ or ____, depending on the presence of tubes.

4. ____ and ____ are the smallest groups into which living things are classified.

5. An animal with a backbone is a ____.

6. The two kingdoms of microscopic living things are ____ and ____.

7. ____, ____, ____ are vertebrates.

8. ____ and ____ are also vertebrates.

9. Scientists use ____ to organize living things.

10. ____ have many cells with nuclei and absorb food from other living things.

Connect Concepts

Use the terms in the Word Bank to complete the concept map.

animals
classification
fungi
genus
kingdoms
monerans
plants
protists
species

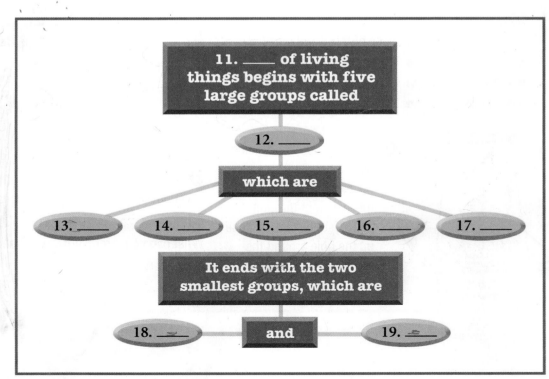

11. ____ of living things begins with five large groups called

12. ____

which are

13. ____   14. ____   15. ____   16. ____   17. ____

It ends with the two smallest groups, which are

18. ____   and   19. ____

Check Understanding

Write the letter of the best choice.

20. Which of the following is a type of moneran?
    - A algae
    - B bacteria
    - C fish
    - D mushroom

21. Which characteristic makes vertebrates different from invertebrates?
    - F Vertebrates have a backbone.
    - G Vertebrates do not have a backbone.
    - H Vertebrates are monerans.
    - J Invertebrates have a backbone.

22. In a nonvascular plant, water travels —
    - A through the roots
    - B through the sapwood
    - C from cell to cell
    - D through the flowers

23. Which part of a vascular plant has tubes for carrying food?
    - F leaves
    - G heartwood
    - H bark
    - J ferns

24. Which of the following is **NOT** a kingdom?
    - A fungi
    - B animals
    - C plants
    - D vertebrates

25. Where do muscles attach to the skeletons of invertebrates?
    - F at flexible shell joints
    - G at the backbone
    - H where bones meet
    - J at movable bone joints

26. Which of the following vertebrates have hair and give milk for their young?
    - A reptiles
    - B mammals
    - C amphibians
    - D birds

27. What makes a moneran different from a protist?
    - F A moneran has no nucleus.
    - G A moneran has a backbone.
    - H A moneran has tubes.
    - J A moneran has jointed legs.

Critical Thinking

28. Why is it important that scientists share what they learn from their research?

29. A dog has a backbone and fur. To which kingdom and to which two smaller groups does it belong?

Process Skills Review

30. Which three items would you **classify** in one group? Explain your answer.

    shoelace, stop sign, button, zipper

31. Which would make the better **model** for showing how water is carried inside a tree? Explain your answer.

    a frozen-treat stick and paper

    a cardboard tube and a rubber hose

32. Think about your observations of the feet of ducks and chickens. Which animals would you **infer** are the better swimmers? Explain your answer.

Performance Assessment

Sorting Scheme

Work with a group to make rules for classifying items in your desks or in your classroom. Sort the items into several "kingdoms." Then sort the members of each kingdom into as many smaller groups as you can.

Animal Growth and Heredity

Human children look like their parents. So do the young of many animals, such as this turtle. The young of many other organisms, however, do not look anything like their parents. Many organisms go through big changes as they grow and mature.

Fast Fact

It's sometimes hard to determine how long wild animals live, but we do know how long domesticated animals, like dogs and cats, and zoo animals live. Some can live as long as human beings.

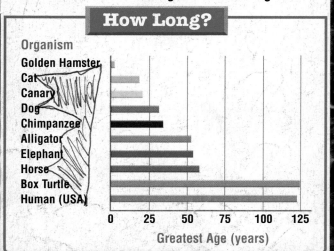

How Long?

Organism

Golden Hamster
Cat
Canary
Dog
Chimpanzee
Alligator
Elephant
Horse
Box Turtle
Human (USA)

0   25   50   75   100   125

Greatest Age (years)

Fast Fact

Fast Fact

Many animals mature quickly. Mice, for example, start having young of their own when they are only four months old. By the time they are a year old, they may already be great-grandparents.

About 3 billion of your body's cells die every minute. Thanks to a process called mitosis, about the same number of new cells are formed every minute.

Eastern box-turtle

How Do Animals Grow and Reproduce?

In this lesson, you can . . .

 INVESTIGATE cell reproduction.

 LEARN ABOUT how organisms grow.

 LINK to math, writing, language arts, and technology.

◀ **The cells that make up the tiger cub will reproduce rapidly as the cub grows into an adult.**

 **INVESTIGATE**

Cell Reproduction

Activity Purpose Cells are the basic units of all living things. Cells make up bones, muscles, skin, and blood. They make up leaves, roots, stems, and flowers. Every part of an animal or a plant is made up of cells. As these cells grow and reproduce, the organism grows and develops. In this investigation you will **observe** how plant and animal cells reproduce.

Materials

- Microslide Viewer
- Microslide of plant mitosis
- Microslide of animal mitosis

Alternate Materials

- microscope
- prepared slides of plant cells dividing
- prepared slides of animal cells dividing

Activity Procedure

1 Insert the Plant Mitosis Microslide into the slot in the Microslide Viewer. Turn the focus knob until you can see the cells clearly. (Picture A)

2 **Observe** the plant cells dividing. **Record** what you observe in each stage of cell division. The descriptions on the microslide card may help you. Then draw pictures of what you see at each stage.

3 Now insert the Animal Mitosis Microslide into the slot in the Microslide Viewer. Again turn the focus knob until you can see the cells clearly.

Picture A

Picture B

4 **Observe** the animal cells dividing. **Record** what you observe in each stage of cell division. Again you may use the descriptions on the Microslide card to help you. Then draw pictures of what you see at each stage. (Picture B)

5 Now **compare** the stages of plant cell division with the stages of animal cell division. How are the stages alike? How are they different? **Record** your observations.

Draw Conclusions

1. What part of the cell changes as cell division occurs? What changes take place?

2. How many new cells does each dividing cell produce?

3. What similarities and differences did you **observe** between the dividing plant cells and the dividing animal cells?

4. **Scientists at Work** Scientists **observe** cells and ask questions based on their observations. What questions do you have about cell division, based on what you observed?

Investigate Further Now that you have observed photomicrographs of plant and animal cells dividing, use the materials on the *Alternate Materials* list to observe other cells dividing. See page R3 for tips on using a microscope.

> **Process Skill Tip**
>
> As you **observe** each slide, make a note of every detail—even if it doesn't seem important. Details will help you track exactly how a dividing cell changes from one stage to the next.

How Organisms Grow

Growth

FIND OUT

• about growth and cell division

• about regeneration

• about mitosis and meiosis

VOCABULARY

chromosome
mitosis
asexual reproduction
sexual reproduction
meiosis

You began life as a single cell. That one cell divided into two cells. The two cells divided into four cells, the four cells into eight cells, and so on. By the time you were born, your body was already made up of billions of cells.

It may be hard to observe, but you're probably a little taller than you were a month ago. In that short time, your bone cells have divided again and again to make more bone tissue. Muscle and skin cells have also been dividing. As cells throughout your body continue dividing, your body will continue growing. By the time you are an adult, your body will have more than 100 trillion cells.

You know that body systems are made up of organs, organs are made of tissues, and tissues are made up of cells. The cells that make up each tissue have specific functions as part of an organ. So when bone cells divide, for example, they must produce cells exactly like themselves. Nearly all body cells produce exact copies of themselves. Producing identical cells enables new cells to perform the same functions as older cells. This allows organs to continue functioning properly as they grow.

✔ **Why do bone cells make exact copies of themselves?**

DAY 1

A chick begins life as an egg—a single cell.

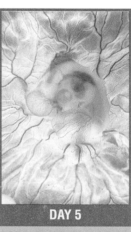

DAY 5

After 5 days the single cell has divided into many cells.

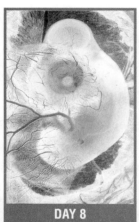

DAY 8

By Day 8, eyes begin to develop.

DAY 14

At 14 days the chick has developed tiny feathers.

DAY 21+

After 21 days the chick is fully developed.

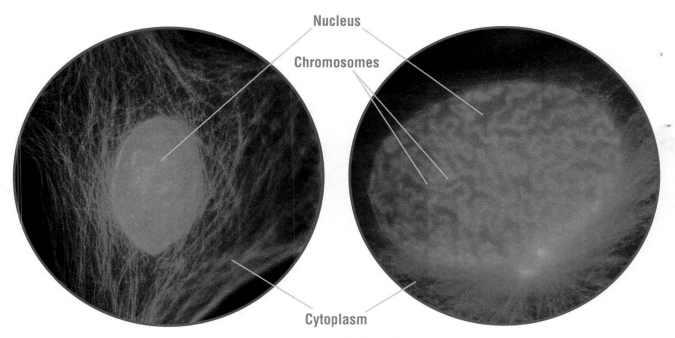

Nucleus

Chromosomes

Cytoplasm

Before a cell divides, the chromosomes shorten, thicken, and become visible.

Cell Division

Every square centimeter of your skin has about 150,000 skin cells. The top layer of skin is damaged by contact with the world around you. Its cells are always dying. Fortunately, skin cells reproduce quickly and replace the dead cells. In fact, the surface layer of your skin will be replaced twice today. Like most cells, skin cells reproduce by dividing in two. But what makes cells divide?

You know that the nucleus controls everything a cell does. So it is the nucleus that "tells" a cell when to divide. Inside the nucleus are threadlike strands. Each strand is called a **chromosome** (KROH•muh•sohm). Chromosomes are made up of a chemical called DNA, which forms a chemical code. This code determines the shape and function of a cell. It also determines when a cell will divide.

Whenever a cell divides, each new cell must get an exact copy of the parent cell's chromosomes. Having an identical set of chromosomes gives each new skin cell, for example, the same DNA code as its parent cell. This ensures that it will look and act like older skin cells.

The process of cell division is called **mitosis** (my•TOH•sihs). The nucleus of a cell prepares for mitosis by making an exact copy of its chromosomes. After the chromosomes have been copied, but before mitosis begins, a cell has enough DNA for two cells. During mitosis each chromosome separates from its copy. The two groups of chromosomes pull apart. Then the cell membrane pinches in at the middle, forming two new cells. Each new cell has the same DNA—and therefore the same shape and function—as its parent cell.

✔ **What happens in the nucleus before a cell divides?**

Mitosis

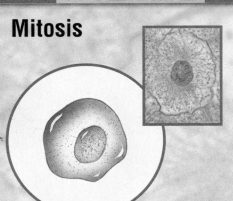

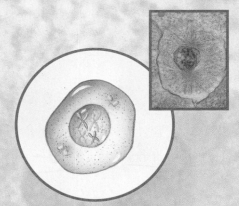

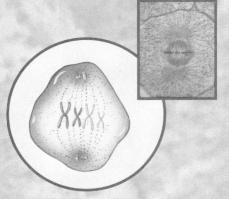

▲ Before mitosis the chromosomes (made up of DNA) make copies of themselves. Each chromosome and its copy are connected.

▲ As mitosis begins, the chromosomes grow thick and short. The nuclear membrane disappears.

▲ A network of thin tubes, called a spindle, forms. As the spindle gets longer, the chromosomes and their attached copies form a straight line in the middle of the cell.

This starfish escaped a hungry predator by dropping one of its arms. When regeneration is complete, the starfish will have a new arm. ▼

Regeneration

At one time or another, you have probably scraped your knee or cut your finger. If you cleaned the wound and kept it clean, after a few days all signs of the wound vanished. As soon as your body is wounded, it begins repairing itself.

Healing is a kind of *regeneration* (rih•jen•uh•RAY•shuhn), or tissue replacement. Skin cells divide, and regenerated skin grows over the cut. In humans, regeneration is limited mostly to healing wounds.

Plants and some animals, however, can regenerate major body parts. For example, if a large animal grabs a lizard by its tail, the tail may drop off. If this happens, the lizard's remaining tail cells begin rapid mitosis. Before long, the lizard has regenerated a new tail.

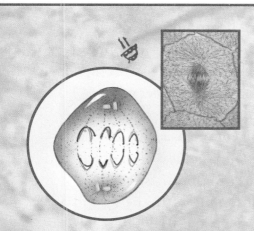

▲ The spindle shortens, and the chromosome copies separate. One chromosome from each copied pair moves to one side of the cell while the other chromosome moves to the other side.

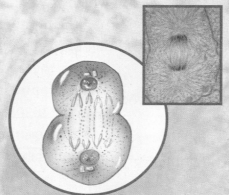

▲ As mitosis ends, the spindle falls apart. The cell membrane begins to pinch in, creating two new cells. A nuclear membrane forms around each set of chromosomes.

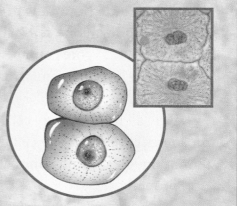

▲ After mitosis the chromosomes grow thinner and longer inside each new nucleus. Each new cell will now copy its own chromosomes.

Planaria (pluh•NEHR•ee•uh), a type of freshwater flatworm, can regenerate most of its body. If a planarian is cut in two, each piece regenerates the missing parts through mitosis. And chopping a sponge into many pieces is never deadly. The pieces simply regenerate many new, complete sponges.

✔ **How does mitosis help heal a wound?**

Asexual Reproduction

Many one-celled organisms, such as bacteria and protozoa, reproduce by simple cell division, or *fission*. This type of reproduction—without the joining of male and female cells—is called **asexual reproduction**. In fission the parent produces offspring through the process of mitosis.

Yeast—a one-celled fungus—reproduces asexually by a process called *budding*. A tiny

bud forms on the parent cell. Mitosis takes place within the parent cell, and a copy of the parent's chromosomes enters the growing bud. When the bud is fully grown, it separates from the parent cell.

Some plants also reproduce asexually. You will learn about asexual reproduction in plants in the next chapter.

✔ **How many parents are needed in asexual reproduction?**

A paramecium (par•uh•MEE•see•uhm) is a one-celled organism that lives in lakes and ponds. This paramecium is in the process of reproducing asexually. ▶

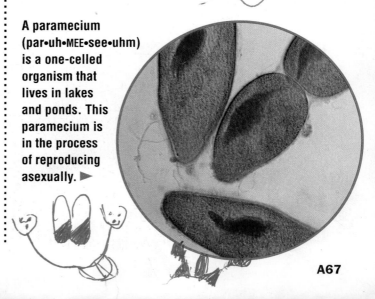

A67

Sexual Reproduction

Most organisms reproduce sexually. In **sexual reproduction**, cells from two parents unite to form one cell, called a *zygote* (ZY•goht). The zygote contains chromosomes from both the female parent and the male parent.

Nearly all human body cells have 46 chromosomes each. If a body cell has more or fewer than 46 chromosomes, it won't function properly.

If two body cells were to unite, the zygote they formed would have 92 chromosomes. Every body cell would then have 92 chromosomes, instead of 46. In the next generation, the zygote and all the body cells would each have 184 chromosomes, and so on. With each new generation, the number of chromosomes would double.

This never happens, though, because the human body produces reproductive cells, which have only 23 chromosomes each—half the number of chromosomes found in body cells. **Meiosis** (my•OH•sis) is the process that reduces the number of chromosomes in reproductive cells.

In the first stage of meiosis, the cell copies its chromosomes and divides. Both of the new cells have 46 chromosomes. This process is similar to mitosis. In the second stage of meiosis, the two cells divide again. However, this time they do not copy their chromosomes first. Each of the four new cells is a reproductive cell, or *gamete* (GAM•eet). Gametes have half the number of chromosomes that are in a body cell.

✔ **Why must gametes have half the number of chromosomes that are in a body cell?**

Meiosis

The cells at the top of the diagram are body cells. The cells in the center of the diagram are reproductive cells. Because of meiosis, the reproductive cells have half the number of chromosomes that are in body cells. The cell at the bottom of the diagram is a zygote, with the same number of chromosomes as in body cells.

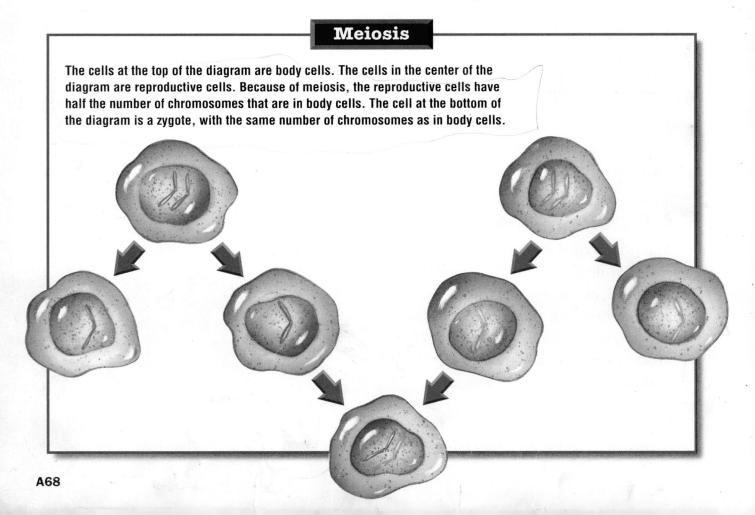

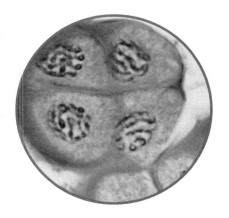

▲ **Each of these gametes has half the number of chromosomes of a body cell.**

Summary

Organisms grow when their cells divide. Body cells divide through the process of mitosis. Before mitosis, a cell makes copies of its chromosomes. After mitosis each of the new cells has an exact copy of the original cell's chromosomes. Reproductive cells have half the number of chromosomes that are in body cells. Meiosis reduces the number of chromosomes.

Review

1. What are chromosomes? Why are they important to cells?

2. How can some animals regenerate body parts?

3. Why must chromosomes be duplicated before mitosis?

4. What is asexual reproduction?

5. **Critical Thinking** Suppose an organism has 12 chromosomes in its body cells. How many chromosomes do its reproductive cells and zygotes have?

6. **Test Prep** During mitosis, what part of the cell pinches in to make two new cells?
   A the nucleus
   B the chromosomes
   C the DNA
   D the cell membrane

LINKS

MATH LINK

Use Divisibility Rules The list of organisms below shows the numbers of chromosomes in their body cells. Determine how many chromosomes each organism's reproductive cells have.

alligator, 32	housefly, 12
earthworm, 36	chimpanzee, 48
pigeon, 80	lettuce, 18

WRITING LINK

Informative Writing—Explanation Write an article for your school newspaper explaining the importance of meiosis. Briefly describe meiosis, and explain how it enables an organism to keep the same number of chromosomes in its body cells after sexual reproduction.

LANGUAGE ARTS LINK

Sequencing Mitosis Cut a sheet of paper into 10 pieces. On each piece, write something that happens during mitosis—for example, *spindle forms* or *nuclear membrane disappears*. Exchange pieces of paper with a classmate. Challenge each other to put the pieces in order.

GO TECHNOLOGY LINK
ONLINE

Learn more about cell division and reproduction by visiting this Internet site.
www.scilinks.org/harcourt

SCLINKS
THE WORLD'S A CLICK AWAY

LESSON 2

What Is a Life Cycle?

In this lesson, you can . . .

 INVESTIGATE the stages of a mealworm's life.

 LEARN ABOUT the stages of life.

 LINK to math, writing, art, and technology.

This butterfly is about to begin the adult stage of its life cycle.

 **INVESTIGATE**

The Stages of a Mealworm's Life

Activity Purpose Many animals change as they grow and develop. The way an animal behaves and looks when it is young may change by the time it is an adult. In this investigation you will **observe** how a mealworm changes as it grows.

Materials
- mealworm culture
- paper plate
- hand lens

Activity Procedure

1 Your teacher will give you a mealworm from the mealworm culture.

2 Put the mealworm on the paper plate. Using the hand lens, **observe** the mealworm closely. Draw what you see. (Picture A)

3 Label these parts on your drawing: head, segment, antenna, outer shell, claw, mouth, and leg.

4 **Observe** the mealworm's movements. Does it move straight forward or from side to side? Does it move quickly or slowly? **Record** your observations.

5 Now your teacher will give you a beetle from the mealworm culture. Repeat Steps 2–4 with the beetle.

Picture A

Picture B

6 Finally, **observe** the mealworm culture. Try to find evidence of other stages of a mealworm's life, such as eggs and pupa cases. Draw pictures of what you find.

7 **Compare** your drawings of the eggs and pupa cases with your drawings of the mealworm and the beetle. Form a **hypothesis** about the order of these life stages. Then list the ways in which a mealworm changes as it grows. (Picture B)

Draw Conclusions

1. How are the mealworm and the beetle similar?

2. How is the beetle different from the mealworm?

3. **Scientists at Work** Scientists often **observe** an organism and then **hypothesize** about their observations. What observations enabled you to form your hypothesis about the order of the life stages?

Investigate Further **Plan and conduct an experiment** to test your hypothesis about the life stages of a mealworm. Decide what equipment or technology you will need to use to test your hypothesis. Then use the equipment or technology in your experiment.

Process Skill Tip

As you **observe** stages in the life of an organism, you may find it helpful to **hypothesize** about the order in which the stages occur.

A71

The Stages of Life

FIND OUT

- what life cycles are
- how animals change as they grow
- how complete metamorphosis differs from incomplete metamorphosis

VOCABULARY

life cycle
direct development
metamorphosis

Life Cycles

Most organisms grow and mature through several distinct stages of life. These stages make up the organism's **life cycle**. All life cycles begin with a young organism struggling to survive in the world. Some organisms are born alive. Others develop in eggs and then hatch. Still others sprout from spores or seeds.

During each stage of life, a person changes physically. ▶

Depending on its type, a young organism spends anywhere from a few minutes to many years growing and developing. When an organism reaches its final form and size, it is an adult. During the adult stage, an organism is able to reproduce. Some organisms reproduce during their entire adult lives. Others stop reproducing as they get older.

Many organisms change a lot as they mature. But the young of some animals are identical to the adults, except in size. These organisms grow larger, but they keep the same body features, such as shape, all their lives. This kind of growth is called **direct development**. Spiders and earthworms have direct development. A young earthworm looks just like an adult earthworm, except smaller. What other animals can you think of that show this type of development?

These young scorpions are identical to the adult carrying them, except in size and color. ▼

✔ **What is a life cycle?**

A72

Incomplete Metamorphosis

Some animals, especially insects, have one kind of body when they are young and a very different kind of body when they are adults. The changes in the shape or characteristics of an organism's body as it grows and matures are called **metamorphosis** (met•uh•MOR•fuh•sis).

The life cycles of many insects, including beetles, butterflies, and grasshoppers, include metamorphosis. Some insects, such as cockroaches and grasshoppers, go through *incomplete metamorphosis*. These insects have only three stages of development: egg, nymph (NIMF), and adult. At each stage the insect looks different from the way it looks at another stage.

When a cockroach nymph first hatches, it doesn't have wings. After a period of growth, tiny wing buds appear on its body. As the nymph continues growing, wings develop from the wing buds. It takes about three months for a young cockroach to become an adult with fully formed wings.

During late spring and early summer, you may come across tiny, wingless hopping insects that look like grasshoppers. They are, in fact, grasshopper nymphs.

Cockroaches, grasshoppers, and other insects that go through incomplete metamorphosis must shed their outer skeletons as they grow. This process is called *molting*. Each time a grasshopper molts, a larger skeleton forms around its body. This gives the insect room to grow for a while.

✓ **Name the stages of incomplete metamorphosis.**

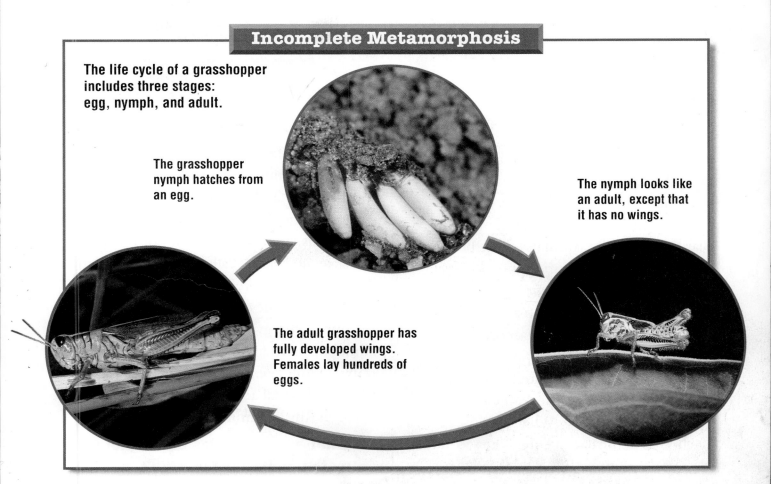

Incomplete Metamorphosis

The life cycle of a grasshopper includes three stages: egg, nymph, and adult.

The grasshopper nymph hatches from an egg.

The nymph looks like an adult, except that it has no wings.

The adult grasshopper has fully developed wings. Females lay hundreds of eggs.

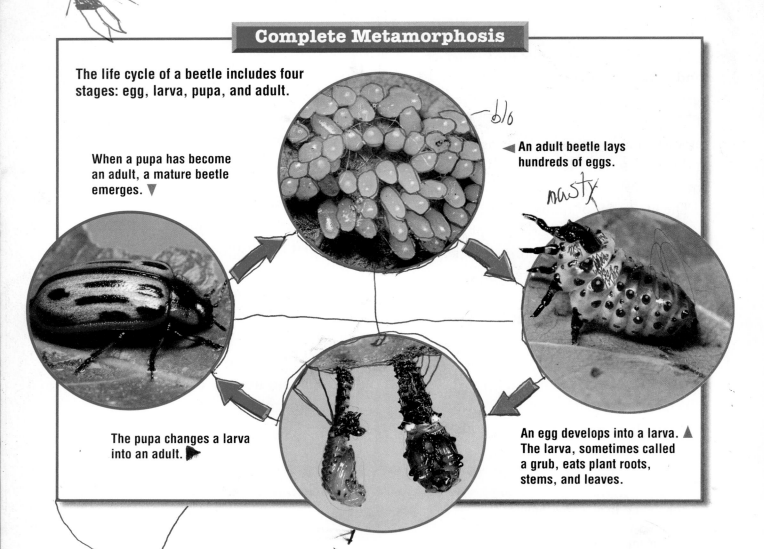

Complete Metamorphosis

The life cycle of a beetle includes four stages: egg, larva, pupa, and adult.

When a pupa has become an adult, a mature beetle emerges. ▼

◀ An adult beetle lays hundreds of eggs.

The pupa changes a larva into an adult. ▶

An egg develops into a larva. ▲ The larva, sometimes called a grub, eats plant roots, stems, and leaves.

Complete Metamorphosis

Have you ever been startled by a fuzzy, many-legged caterpillar creeping along a tree trunk? It's hard to imagine, but that same creature may one day be a moth or beautiful butterfly. Animals whose bodies change dramatically during their life cycles go through *complete metamorphosis*. A beetle is another example of an animal that goes through complete metamorphosis.

An insect's life cycle that includes complete metamorphosis has four distinct stages. During the first stage, the insect develops inside an egg. When the insect hatches from the egg, it enters the second stage of development. It is then called a *larva* (LAR•vuh). A larva lacks wings and looks very different from an adult. It spends nearly all its time eating and storing energy for the next stage of its life cycle.

During the third stage of complete metamorphosis, insects neither eat nor move. At this stage, an insect is called a *pupa* (PYOO•puh). The pupa's body breaks down many of the organs and tissues it had as a larva. Most of the pupa's energy goes into developing an adult body. When the stage is complete, the pupa no longer exists and the adult insect emerges. Like all adult insects, the female lays eggs, the beginning of a new life cycle.

✓ **What are the stages of complete metamorphosis in insects?**

▲ This palm beetle lives in the Amazon rain forest.

Summary

All organisms have life cycles. Most organisms begin as young and develop into adults. The life cycles of some organisms show direct development. These organisms change only in size as they mature. Other life cycles include incomplete metamorphosis, with three stages of development. A life cycle that includes complete metamorphosis has four stages of development.

Review

1. What is the last stage in the life cycle of a beetle?
2. In what kind of development do the young look like miniature adults?
3. Why does a grasshopper nymph molt?
4. **Critical Thinking** Why doesn't a developing pupa move around?
5. **Test Prep** During the third stage of complete metamorphosis, the larva becomes—

    A a cocoon
    B a pupa
    C an egg
    D an adult

LINKS

MATH LINK

Solve Problems Monarch butterflies and June bugs go through complete metamorphosis. A monarch caterpillar (the larva) eats milkweed leaves for about a month before becoming a pupa. A June bug larva feeds underground for about three years. How many times as long as a monarch caterpillar eats does a June bug larva eat?

WRITING LINK

Expressive Writing—Poem Choose an animal, such as a frog, and write a poem for your class about its life cycle.

ART LINK

Mobile Research the complete metamorphosis of the monarch butterfly. Then make a hanging mobile illustrating the four stages of the monarch's life cycle. Share your mobile with your class.

GO ONLINE TECHNOLOGY LINK

Learn more about complete metamorphosis of butterflies by visiting the Smithsonian Institution Internet site. **www.si.edu/harcourt/science**

✳ Smithsonian Institution®

LESSON **3**

Why Are Offspring Like Their Parents?

In this lesson, you can . . .

 INVESTIGATE inherited characteristics.

 LEARN ABOUT inherited traits.

 LINK to math, writing, social studies, and technology.

◄ This child and parent share obvious traits.

Inherited Characteristics

Activity Purpose   What color are your hair and eyes? How long are your eyelashes? Are you right-handed or left-handed? These are just a few of the characteristics you have gotten from your parents. You may have some traits in common with your classmates. In this investigation you will **observe** three inherited traits. Then you will **use numbers** to see how common those traits are among your classmates.

Materials
■ mirror

Activity Procedure

1 Make a chart like the one on the next page.

2 **Tongue Rolling** Use the mirror to **observe** what you are doing. Stick out your tongue, and try to roll its edges up toward the center. **Record** your results in the chart. (Picture A)

3 **Ear Lobes** Use the mirror to **observe** the shape of your ear lobes. Are they attached to your cheek, or do they hang free? **Record** your results in the chart.

4 **Folded Hands** Clasp your hands in front of you. **Observe** which of your thumbs falls naturally on top. **Record** your results in the chart. (Picture B)

Picture A

Picture B

5 Your teacher will now ask students to report the results of their observations. Tally the results in the chart as students report them. Total the number of students for each characteristic. Then **calculate** what fraction of the class has each characteristic.

Characteristic	Results (Circle one.)		Class Totals
Tongue rolling	Yes	No	
Ear lobes	Attached	Free	
Folded hands	Left	Right	

Draw Conclusions

1. **Infer** whether a person could learn tongue rolling. Explain.

2. What other inherited characteristics could you have **observed**?

3. **Scientists at Work** Scientists often **use numbers** to summarize the data they collect. Which trait in each pair occurred most often in your class?

Investigate Further Do your class results suggest how often these traits occur in other people? Choose one or two of these characteristics. **Hypothesize** whether the results will be the same for another group. Then ask some of your friends, neighbors, and family members to participate in this activity, and **collect data. Draw conclusions,** and share them with your class.

Inherited Traits

From Parent to Offspring

FIND OUT

• how characteristics are inherited

• what genes are

VOCABULARY

inherited trait
dominant trait
recessive trait
gene

You may have friends who look a lot like one of their parents. They might share the same smile, eyes, type of hair, or skin color. Many of the characteristics of organisms are passed to their offspring. A characteristic that is passed from parent to offspring is an **inherited trait**. In many animals, hair color or fur color is an inherited trait. So is eye color.

Sometimes an offspring has a trait that it doesn't seem to have inherited from its parents. Two brown-haired human parents might have a child with blond hair. In the picture below, observe that the mother cat is orange. All but one of her kittens are orange, too. The gray kitten must have inherited its fur color from its parents. But how could orange parents produce a gray kitten?

Some behaviors are also inherited. Most dogs, for example, can swim without having been taught. But this is not an inherited behavior among humans.

Sometimes a trait doesn't seem to have been inherited. ▼

✔ **What is an inherited trait?**

How Characteristics Are Inherited

◄ Gregor Mendel

Gregor Mendel, a monk and a scientist, spent much of his time working with plants in a monastery garden. He observed that some pea plants were tall while others were short. He also observed that some plants produced green peas and others produced yellow peas. He knew the traits were inherited, but he didn't understand how.

In 1857 Mendel began experimenting by breeding different pea plants. This is called *crossbreeding*. He kept detailed records of his results, which were published in 1865.

Mendel first bred a tall pea plant with a short pea plant. All the offspring, the first generation, were tall plants. He then bred two of these tall plants. In the second generation, three-fourths of the offspring were tall and one-fourth were short.

Mendel hypothesized that every trait is controlled by a pair of *factors*. For each trait, an offspring inherits one factor from each parent. The way the factors combine determines which trait appears in the offspring.

Mendel further hypothesized that the first-generation pea plants must have a hidden factor for shortness. Why? In the second generation, one-fourth of the offspring were short.

In peas, tallness is a strong trait, or **dominant trait**. Shortness is a weak trait, or **recessive trait**. Factors for both dominant and recessive traits may occur in an organism's chromosomes. However, recessive traits can be seen only if both parents pass the factor for it to the offspring. If only one parent pea plant, for example, passes a factor for shortness, the factor remains hidden. Then none of the offspring are short.

✓ **How did Mendel know that the tall pea plants in the first generation had a hidden factor for shortness?**

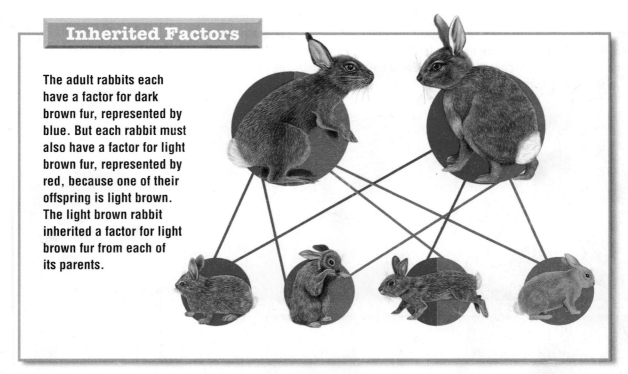

Inherited Factors

The adult rabbits each have a factor for dark brown fur, represented by blue. But each rabbit must also have a factor for light brown fur, represented by red, because one of their offspring is light brown. The light brown rabbit inherited a factor for light brown fur from each of its parents.

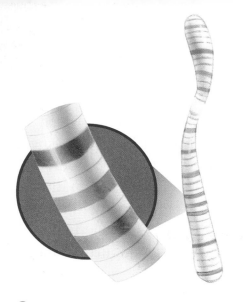

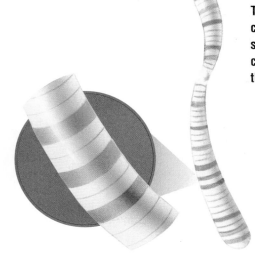

The gene for fur color occurs in the same spot on both chromosomes of the pair.

Genes

Today Mendel's factors are called genes. **Genes** contain the DNA codes for all the traits an organism inherits. Genes are on chromosomes. The genes for a particular trait always occupy the same place on a chromosome.

In wild rabbits, dark brown fur is a dominant trait. Light brown fur is a recessive trait. If a rabbit inherits even one gene for dark brown fur, it will have dark brown fur. Mendel's hidden factors were genes for recessive traits. Offspring must inherit two genes for recessive traits—one from each parent—for a recessive trait to be seen.

You can use a chart to calculate the chances that an offspring will inherit a particular combination of genes. The charts below show the chances that the offspring of two rabbits will inherit a particular fur

Dominant Traits

The chart at the left shows that all the offspring have dark brown fur. So the dark brown rabbit had two genes for dark brown fur. The chart at the right shows that half the offspring will have dark brown fur and half will have light brown fur. So the dark brown rabbit had one gene for dark brown fur and one gene for light brown fur. A trait with two identical genes is called *purebred*. The same trait with two different genes is called *hybrid*.

The dark brown rabbit may be purebred, having two genes for dark brown fur, or it may be hybrid, having one gene for dark brown fur and one gene for light brown fur. The light brown rabbit must be purebred and have two genes for light brown fur. ▼

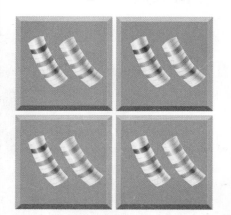

color. Dark brown fur is a dominant trait. The gene for dark brown fur is highlighted in purple. Any box with a purple-highlighted gene in it stands for an offspring with dark brown fur. Light brown fur is a recessive trait. The gene for light brown fur is highlighted in orange. Only a box with two orange-highlighted genes stands for an offspring with light brown fur.

✓ **Why must baby rabbits have two genes for light brown fur if they are to have light brown fur?**

Summary

Many traits are inherited by offspring from their parents. Gregor Mendel's experiments with peas led to the discovery of the factors of inheritance. Genes—Mendel's "factors"—are on chromosomes. Each trait is controlled by a pair of genes. Gene combinations determine if traits are seen (dominant traits) or hidden (recessive traits).

Review

1. What are characteristics called that an offspring inherits from its parents?
2. What did Mendel hypothesize about inherited traits?
3. What is a dominant trait?
4. **Critical Thinking** Will an offspring show a recessive trait if only one of its parents has the gene for that trait? Explain.
5. **Test Prep** Mendel's "factors" are now known as —
   A genes
   B chromosomes
   C DNA
   D traits

LINKS

MATH LINK

Find Probability If you toss a coin 100 times, you might expect it to land heads up 50 times and tails up 50 times. That is, the chance, or probability, of its landing heads up is the same as the probability of its landing tails up. What is the probability that two coins, flipped at the same time, will both land heads up? Make a table with four columns: *Heads/Heads, Heads/Tails, Tails/Heads, Tails/Tails.* Then get two coins from your teacher. Flip them together 100 times. Record your results in the table. What is the probability that two coins will land heads up?

WRITING LINK

Expressive Writing—Song Lyrics Write a song for a pet about one of his or her best traits, such as the color of his or her eyes or fur.

SOCIAL STUDIES LINK

Research Obtain a book about James Watson and Francis Crick, the scientists who helped discover the structure of DNA. Write a paragraph about what they did.

TECHNOLOGY LINK

Learn more about inherited traits by viewing *Better Turkeys* on the **Harcourt Science Newsroom Video.**

BIONIC DOG

As dogs grow older, they sometimes develop a painful disorder called hip dysplasia (dihs·PLAY·zhuh). Now veterinarians are able to replace one or both damaged hips with artificial parts.

Why Treat Hip Dysplasia?

Hip dysplasia is an abnormal development and growth of the hip joint, leading to arthritis. It causes pain whenever a dog stands, walks, runs, or jumps. In the early stages of the disorder, medicine can help, but when the pain becomes severe, medication is not enough. Dogs who were once very active no longer want to move. As the disorder progresses, the dog feels pain all the time, even when lying down. A dog may suffer so much that it has to be "put to sleep."

Total Hip Replacement (THR)

A total hip replacement, or THR, can save many dogs with hip dysplasia. In THR the damaged hip is replaced with a steel and plastic joint, often called an implant. Most dogs can walk immediately after surgery. After a recovery period of about two months, they can run, jump, and play as if they had a normal hip. Over 95 percent of all THR surgeries performed on dogs are successful, and the new hip lasts for the rest of the dog's life.

Large dogs are more likely than small dogs to have hip dysplasia.

How Does THR Work?

Any dog that is at least 9 months old and weighs at least 30 pounds can be considered for THR. A few hours before the surgery, the hair on the dog's leg is shaved and the skin bathed with medicine to prevent infection. During the surgery, which takes 90–120 minutes, the dog is given an anesthetic.

The artificial hip the dog receives consists of three parts. The femoral stem attaches to the femur in the dog's leg. The femoral head replaces the ball of the hip's ball-and-socket joint. A part called the acetabular cup replaces the original socket of the hip joint.

The implants are cemented to healthy bones with surgical cement. Hip implants for dogs are made from the same materials and implanted the same way as those for human hip replacements.

Instead of a THR, a dog can have a femoral head osteotomy, which is removal of the top of the femur of the diseased hip. However, this leaves the dog with less movement than a THR. For a very young dog with hip dysplasia, surgery is done to save as much of the damaged hip as possible.

THINK ABOUT IT

1. Why do you think hip dysplasia usually occurs in bigger dogs rather than smaller dogs?
2. Why do you think a young pup is not given a THR?

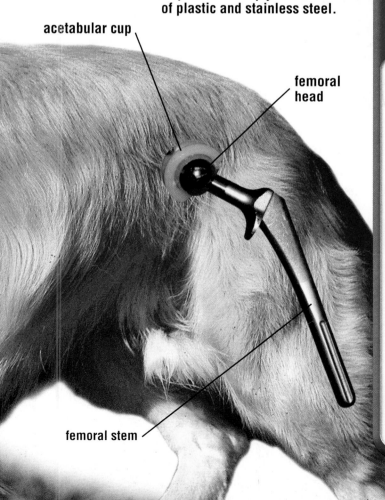

Replacement hip joints are made of plastic and stainless steel.

acetabular cup

femoral head

femoral stem

CAREERS
VETERINARY TECHNICIAN

What They Do

Veterinary technicians, or vet techs, assist veterinarians in private practice and in animal hospitals. Some vet techs assist veterinary surgeons who perform THRs. They may also work as research assistants in pharmaceutical companies.

Education and Training

A person wanting to become a vet tech should attend a two-year or four-year college accredited by the American Veterinary Medical Association and major in animal science technology.

WEB LINK
For Science and Technology updates, visit the Harcourt Internet site.
GO ONLINE www.harcourtschool.com

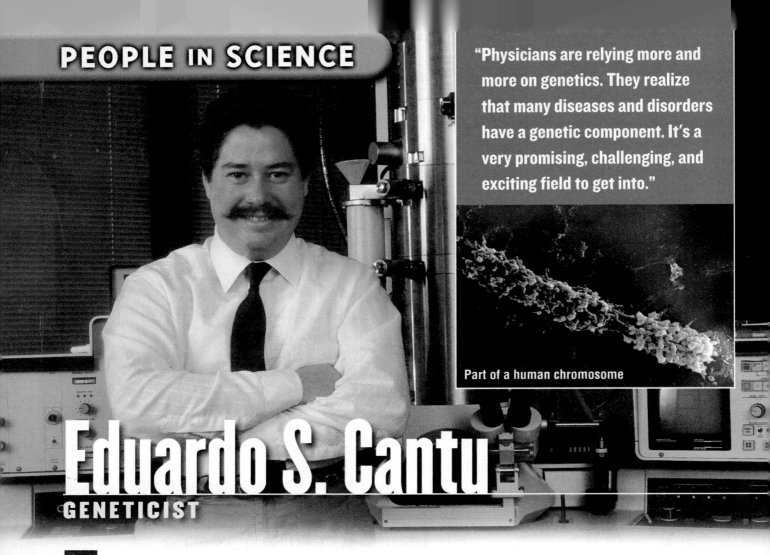

"Physicians are relying more and more on genetics. They realize that many diseases and disorders have a genetic component. It's a very promising, challenging, and exciting field to get into."

Part of a human chromosome

Eduardo S. Cantu
GENETICIST

Every human baby is born with about 30,000 different genes—and the possibility of more than 3000 genetic disorders. Most of these disorders are very rare, but geneticist Eduardo S. Cantu says that 50 to 100 of them could be considered common. Dr. Cantu, a scientist at the Medical University of South Carolina, studies ways in which genes and chromosomes affect a person's health.

As director of the Medical University's cytogenetic section, Dr. Cantu and his staff run tests that help physicians diagnose genetic disorders. Most of the tests they perform are used to diagnose genetic disorders before birth. The physician collects some of the fluid that surrounds a developing fetus, or unborn child. Then Dr. Cantu and his staff examine the fluid, which contains cells from the fetus, under a microscope. The genes in the cells provide a great deal of information about the unborn child, including whether it is likely to develop certain kinds of cancers and other diseases.

Dr. Cantu, who was born and raised in Texas, began his science education at Pan American University. His interest in genetics began when he was a graduate student. He had intended to study birds, but he found a genetics course so fascinating that he decided to change his course of study. It is a decision that Dr. Cantu is very glad he made.

THINK ABOUT IT

1. What is one kind of information that can be gained by studying the genes in the cells of a fetus?

2. Why do you think genetic research is a growing field of study?

DNA

How does DNA fit into a cell?

Materials

- sewing thread
- meterstick
- gelatin capsule

Procedure

❶ Measure 10 m of thread. The thread stands for the DNA in a cell.

❷ Open the gelatin capsule. The gelatin capsule stands for the nucleus of a cell.

❸ Put all the thread into the capsule in whatever way you can. Then close the capsule.

Draw Conclusions

How did you get all the thread into the gelatin capsule? How does so much DNA fit into the nucleus of a cell?

CHROMOSOMES

How do chromosome pairs separate?

Materials

- embroidery thread
- meterstick

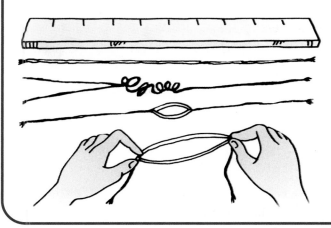

Procedure

❶ Measure 1 m of embroidery thread. The thread represents a chromosome.

❷ Starting at one end, separate the thread into two pieces.

❸ Again measure 1 m of embroidery thread.

❹ Now separate the thread into two pieces, starting in the middle.

Draw Conclusions

Was it easier to separate the thread into two pieces by starting from one end or from the middle? During mitosis, where do chromosome pairs separate?

Vocabulary Review

Use the terms below to complete the sentences. The page numbers in ( ) tell you where to look in the chapter if you need help.

chromosomes (A6)   direct
mitosis (A64)   development (A72)
asexual   metamorphosis (A73)
   reproduction (A67)   inherited trait (A78)
sexual   dominant trait (A79)
   reproduction (A68)   recessive trait (A79)
meiosis (A68)   gene (A80)
life cycle (A72)

1. The term _____ applies to an organism whose body shape, form, or characteristics change during its life cycle.

2. In humans, hair color is an example of an _____.

3. The process that reduces the number of chromosomes in certain cells is called _____.

4. An organism in the adult stage of its _____ is able to reproduce.

5. The offspring of some animals are just like the adults, except for size. This is an example of _____.

6. During _____, duplicated _____ in the cell's nucleus separate, and the cell pinches into two cells.

7. In order for a _____ to be seen, an offspring must receive a factor for the trait from each parent. In order for a _____ to be seen, an offspring needs to receive a factor from only one parent.

8. A _____ carries the DNA code for a particular trait.

9. Reproduction without the joining of cells from the female parent and the male parent is called _____. Reproduction in which cells from two parents unite to form a zygote is called _____.

Connect Concepts

Choose terms from the Word Bank that complete the concept map.

mitosis   recessive
function   nucleus

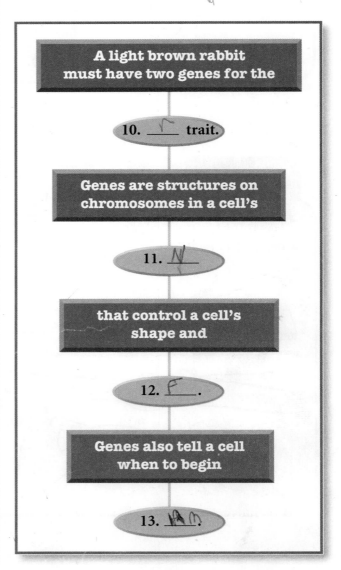

A light brown rabbit must have two genes for the

10. _____ trait.

Genes are structures on chromosomes in a cell's

11. _____

that control a cell's shape and

12. _____.

Genes also tell a cell when to begin

13. _____

Check Understanding

Write the letter of the best choice.

14. In order for a new cell to function just like its parent cell, it must receive an exact copy of its parent cell's —
    A chromosomes   C cell wall
    B gametes   D recessive traits

15. Your bones and muscles grow larger as a result of —
    F meiosis   H direct
    G metamorphosis   development
                       J mitosis

16. What does **NOT** happen during mitosis?
    A the chromosomes duplicate
    B a spindle fiber forms
    C the number of chromosomes is halved
    D the nuclear membrane disappears

17. All the traits that parents pass to their offspring are called —
    F recessive traits   H physical traits
    G dominant traits   J inherited traits

18. If an offspring receives two genes, one from each parent, for a particular recessive trait, that trait will —
    A not be seen   C be seen halfway
    B be seen   D none of the above

19. Which sequence illustrates incomplete metamorphosis?
    F egg, larva, pupa, butterfly
    G kitten, cat
    H egg, nymph, adult
    J young raccoon, adult raccoon

20. When meiosis occurs, the number of chromosomes —
    A is doubled   C stays the same
    B is halved   D is tripled

Critical Thinking

21. A dark brown rabbit mates with a light brown rabbit. Out of four offspring, how many are likely to be dark brown?

22. Mitosis is necessary for the individual, but meiosis is necessary for the species. Explain this statement.

Process Skills Review

23. Choose an item in your classroom. It may be living or nonliving. **Observe** the item using as many of your senses as possible. Make at least seven observations about the item's characteristics.

24. **Compare** the life cycle of a grasshopper with that of a butterfly. Which insect's life cycle shows complete metamorphosis?

25. Describe the expected results of a cross between a dark brown rabbit and a light brown rabbit. **Use numbers** to describe the results in the second generation.

Performance Assessment

Charting Traits

Consider two inherited traits, such as tongue rolling and free or attached ear lobes. Choose symbols to represent genes for the dominant traits and genes for the recessive traits. For each trait, make charts showing the possible offspring when one parent has the dominant traits and the other parent has the recessive traits.

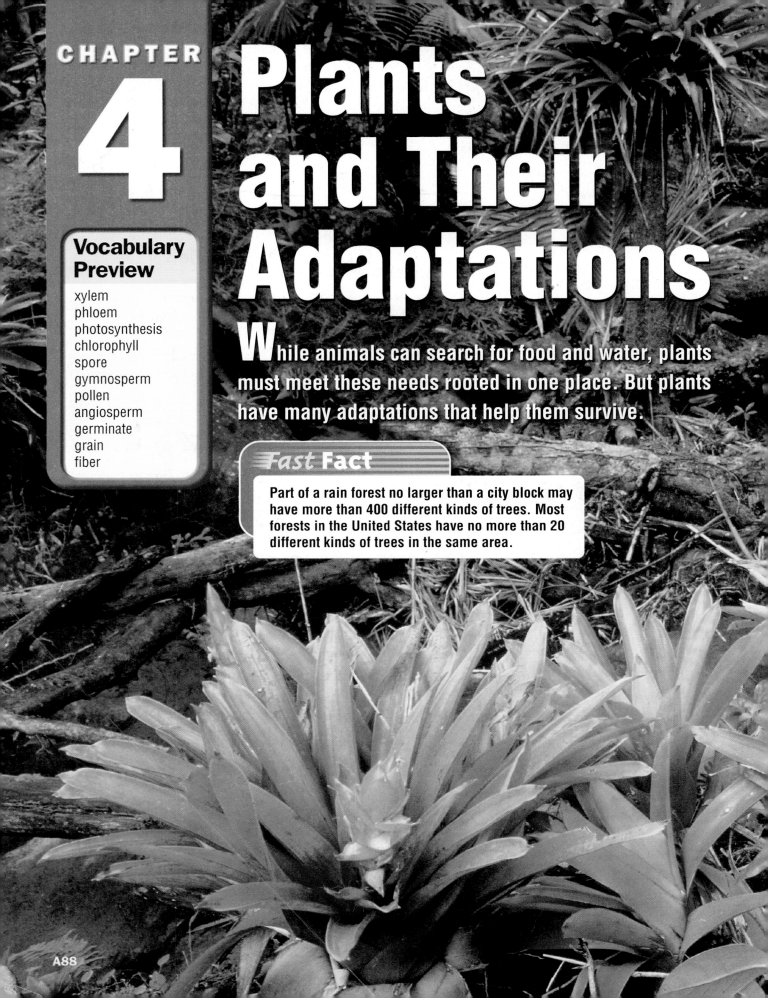

CHAPTER 4

Plants and Their Adaptations

Vocabulary Preview

xylem
phloem
photosynthesis
chlorophyll
spore
gymnosperm
pollen
angiosperm
germinate
grain
fiber

While animals can search for food and water, plants must meet these needs rooted in one place. But plants have many adaptations that help them survive.

Fast Fact

Part of a rain forest no larger than a city block may have more than 400 different kinds of trees. Most forests in the United States have no more than 20 different kinds of trees in the same area.

Have you ever heard the expression "as American as apple pie"? It may surprise you to learn that the apple is not a native American plant and that apple pie was invented in Europe.

Food Origins

Food	Probable Origin
Apple	Southeast Europe
Banana	Southeast Asia
Oats	Western Europe
Pineapple	Latin America
Potato	Peru
Rice	India
Tomato	Mexico

Buffalo grass has a thick network of roots. These roots and the soil they hold are called *sod*. The roots hold the soil so well that many settlers on the American plains used sod to build their homes.

What Are the Functions of Roots, Stems, and Leaves?

In this lesson, you can . . .

 INVESTIGATE the parts of plants.

 LEARN ABOUT plant parts and their functions.

 LINK to math, writing, social studies, and technology.

The silver sword grows only in Hawai'i.

The Parts of a Vascular Plant

Activity Purpose Towering oak trees and potted geraniums have many parts in common. Vascular plants have roots, stems, and leaves. The sizes and shapes of these parts differ, but each part has a function that helps the plant live. In this investigation you will **observe** a plant and identify its parts.

Materials

- potted plant
- hand lens
- ruler
- newspaper
- plastic knife

Activity Procedure

1 Make a drawing of the plant. List all the parts of the plant that you can name.

2 **Observe** the leaves. What colors are they? Use the ruler to measure the length and width of the leaves. Are they all the same shape and size? Are they wide or narrow? Are they long or short? Do they grow singly or in pairs? Observe them more closely with the hand lens. What more can you say about them? Identify and label the leaves in your drawing. (Picture A)

3 **Observe** the stem. Does it bend? Does it have branches? Identify and label the stem in your drawing.

4 Hold the pot upside down over the newspaper. Tap the pot gently until the plant and the soil come out. If the plant won't come out, run the plastic knife around between the soil and the inside of the pot. (Picture B)

Picture A

Picture B

5 Shake the soil from the roots until you can see them clearly. **Observe** the roots. Is there a single root, or are there many small roots? What shape are the roots? Use the ruler to **measure** the length of the roots. Are they thick or thin? Long or short? Use the hand lens to observe them more closely. What more can you say about them? Identify and label the roots in your drawing.

6 Put the soil and the plant back into the pot. Water the plant lightly to help it recover from being out of the pot.

Draw Conclusions

1. What are the parts of the plant you **observed**?

2. **Compare** the plant parts you identified with the parts of a large tree. How are they the same? How are they different?

3. **Scientists at Work** Scientists learn by making observations. What did you **observe** about each part of the plant?

Investigate Further What questions about plant parts could you answer if you had other measuring tools? **Form a hypothesis** about the functions of plant parts. Then **plan and conduct an experiment** to test your hypothesis.

Process Skill Tip

When you **observe** something, you should use as many of your senses as you can. Don't just look at the plant. Touch it to see what it feels like and how thick or strong or dry it is. Smell its leaves and roots.

A91

What Vascular Plant Parts Do

Common Parts

FIND OUT

- how vascular plants grow in different environments
- what roots, stems, and leaves do

VOCABULARY

xylem
phloem
photosynthesis
chlorophyll

There are more than half a million types of vascular plants on Earth. They range from tiny desert plants, smaller than a pencil eraser, to giant redwood trees, taller than a 25-story building. No matter how different they appear, vascular plants have three parts in common—roots, stems, and leaves.

These parts make it possible for vascular plants to live and grow almost everywhere. Vascular plants are found in dry deserts, wet jungles, and cold Arctic plains. Vascular plants are able to live in different environments because their roots, stems, and leaves are adapted to the environments in which they live.

✓ **What parts are common to vascular plants?**

◄ Some plants are able to grow in unfavorable locations.

These crocuses bloom in low temperatures that would kill many other plants. ▼

Some tall trees have roots that spread out as far as their branches. They help keep the trees from falling over.

A thick mat of fibrous roots allows grasses to take in large amounts of water from the soil. ▶

Dandelions have long taproots. If you try to pull a dandelion out of the ground, part of the root may remain. The dandelion will grow back from the part that is left in the ground. ▶

Roots

The roots of many trees spread as far or farther from the trunk as their branches do. Most plant roots act as anchors. They keep the plant from falling over or blowing away in the wind. Roots also take in water and nutrients from the soil through tiny parts called *root hairs*. Some roots also store food for the plant.

Different types of roots are adapted to different environments. Some small desert plants have roots that spread far from the plant but grow close to the surface. These roots are able to take in large amounts of the little rain that falls in the desert.

Forest trees don't need the spreading roots of desert plants because there is more water in the forest soil. These trees need deep roots to anchor them. Some tree roots, called *prop roots*, begin above the ground.

These help keep trees that grow in loose, wet soil from being blown over by the wind.

Many plants have *fibrous* (FY•bruhs) *roots*, which look a little like tree branches. The fibrous roots of some grasses form a thick and tangled mat just under the surface of the soil. Fibrous roots help prevent soil erosion by wind and water because they anchor the soil as well as the plant.

Some plants have a single, thick root that grows straight down. These roots, called *taproots,* can reach water that is deep in the ground. Some taproots store food for the plant as well.

In tropical rain forests there are plants that grow on branches high in the trees. Their roots attach themselves to the trees and take water directly from the moist air.

✔ **What do plant roots do?**

Storage Roots

Some plants store extra food and water to help them survive brief changes in their environments. Most plants cannot make food in the winter. In dry periods they may not be able to get all the water they need from the soil.

In good weather plants produce more food than they need and take in extra water. Some plants store extra food and water in their roots. Others store it in their stems.

Some plants store so much extra food in their roots that people grow them for their own food. You've probably eaten several

◀ This sugar beet root stores food for the plant in the form of sugar. Sugar beets are grown and sold for their sugar.

◀ The sugar cane plant stores sugar in its stems. Sugar cane is also grown and sold for its sugar.

kinds of storage roots. Beets, carrots, sweet potatoes, and turnips are called root vegetables. Because much of the food they store is in the form of sugar and starch, many root vegetables have a sweet taste.

✔ **What do some roots store?**

Stems

Stems do several things for plants. They hold the plant up, and they support the leaves so that they will be in sunlight. Stems also carry water and food to other parts of the plant.

Most plant stems grow upward. The leaves of long-stemmed plants can reach sunlight even in shady places. Some stems even turn during the day. This helps keep the leaves in sunlight, too.

Some plant stems grow sideways, instead of up. Wherever the stem touches the ground, it forms a root from which a new plant grows. Strawberry and spider plants are examples of this type of plant.

Many desert plants have stems that store food and water. The stem of the barrel cactus stores water for the plant. When rain is scarce, the cactus uses water from its stem.

Small plants, such as daisies and dandelions, usually have soft, green, flexible stems. The water inside the stem makes it firm enough to hold the plant up. You might have noticed that a cut flower begins to droop after a few days. Without a root, it can no longer get enough water to keep its stem firm. Most soft-stemmed plants live for just one growing season.

Large plants, such as bushes and trees, need extra support. For this reason, they usually have stiff, woody stems. Woody plants do not die at the end of one growing season but continue to grow year after year. Some woody plants, such as the redwoods of California, may live for hundreds or even thousands of years.

Recall that plant stems contain narrow tubes that carry water, nutrients, and food. The tubes that transport water and nutrients are called **xylem** (ZY•luhm). They move water and nutrients upward, from the roots to the leaves. The strings you find when you bite into a stalk of celery are xylem tubes.

The tubes that carry food are called **phloem** (FLOH•em). They move the food made in the leaves to other parts of the plant. The food that plants make and store is needed for growth by roots, stems, and leaves.

In plants with flexible stems, xylem and phloem are in bundles scattered all through the stem. In plants with woody stems, the xylem and phloem are arranged in rings. The xylem is toward the inside of the stem, while the phloem is toward the outside of the stem.

During each growing season, the stem of a woody plant gets thicker as new rings of xylem and phloem form. More xylem than phloem forms each year, so most of the thickness of a tree trunk is xylem. Older rings of xylem no longer transport water. They harden as they become filled with transported materials. This old xylem is the heartwood of a tree. People use the heartwood of many kinds of trees as lumber to build houses and to make furniture.

✓ **Name the two types of tubes that transport materials in plant stems.**

Each year, trees produce a new layer of xylem, forming a *growth ring.* Counting the growth rings of a cut tree can tell you how many years old the tree was.

xylem

phloem

The trunk and branches of a tree are the plant's woody stems. The wood of a tree is old xylem. The bark is old phloem that is pushed outward as the trunk and branches grow thicker. ▶

Leaves

Leaves have many shapes and sizes. Some are smaller than a postage stamp, while others are large enough to cover a school bus. But whether they are big or small, most leaves are thin and flat. This helps them make food.

Leaves are the "food factories" of plants. They use water and nutrients from the soil, carbon dioxide from the air, and energy from sunlight to make food. The food-making process called **photosynthesis** also produces oxygen, which the plants release into the air.

A *pigment*, or coloring matter, called **chlorophyll** (KLAWR•uh•fil) helps plants use light energy to produce sugars. Chlorophyll gives leaves their green color. In the fall, as the days get shorter, most leaves stop making chlorophyll. Then other pigments already in the leaves can be seen. So it's not frost but simply a lack of chlorophyll that makes the beautiful fall colors seen throughout most of the country.

A leaf is not as simple as it may appear. Inside are layers of cells containing microscopic *chloroplasts* (KLAWR•uh•plasts), which are full of chlorophyll. The food-making process takes place inside the chloroplasts. There are also veins, or bundles of xylem and phloem, running through a leaf. Veins bring water and nutrients to the chloroplasts and take sugars from them.

Carbon dioxide enters a leaf, and oxygen and water leave it, through tiny holes called *stomata* (stoh•MAH•tuh). Stomata open wide when the plant has plenty of water. They close to conserve water when necessary. A waxy outer layer on the top of most leaves also helps conserve water.

The leaves or stems of some plants are adapted as *tendrils*. Tendrils wrap themselves around poles or attach themselves to rough surfaces to help the leaves reach the sunlight they need to make food.

Some leaves "catch" food. The Venus' flytrap grows in places where the soil may not have all the nutrients the plant needs to make food. The plant's traplike leaves are adapted to snap shut when an insect lands on them. The leaves release chemicals that digest the insect and take from it the nutrients the plant needs.

Some leaves also store food. The fleshy layers of an onion bulb—the part we eat—are really leaves.

✔ **What is the main thing leaves do?**

The spines (leaves) of a cactus are an adaptation that protects the plant's food and water from desert animals. ▼

Summary

Each part of a vascular plant has a different function. Roots anchor a plant and take in nutrients and water from the soil. A stem supports a plant and moves materials between the plant's parts. Leaves make the plant's food. All of these parts may be adapted to the environment and the needs of the plant.

Review

1. Why are the parts of some plants very different from those of other plants?

2. How are taproots and fibrous roots different?

3. Why do plants store food?

4. **Critical Thinking** What would happen to a green plant if you left it in a dark room for a long time?

5. **Test Prep** Some leaves change color in the fall. This is because —

   A they need to be replaced
   B they stop making chlorophyll
   C there is too much sunlight
   D the trees are dying

MATH LINK

Use Variables A ratio is a comparison that uses numbers. If a leaf is 6 cm long and 2 cm wide, the ratio of its length to its width is 3 to 1. Use a ruler to measure the length and width of a number of different leaves. Round each measurement to the nearest centimeter and record your measurements. What observations can you make about the ratio of length to width?

WRITING LINK

Informative Writing—Description Suppose there were a world without trees. Write a story describing what such a world would be like. How would the world be different? What products would be missing from people's lives? Share your story with your classmates.

SOCIAL STUDIES LINK

Map Choose a type of plant and find out where in the United States it grows. Use a computer to make a map and identify the places where the plant grows. Then use the computer to make a chart showing the plant type, location, and climate.

GO ONLINE TECHNOLOGY LINK

Learn more about plants by visiting the Harcourt Learning Site.

WELCOME TO **THE LEARNING SITE**

www.harcourtschool.com

How Do Plants Reproduce?

In this lesson, you can . . .

 INVESTIGATE nonvascular plants.

 LEARN ABOUT plant reproduction.

 LINK to math, writing, language arts, and technology.

INVESTIGATE

Nonvascular Plants

Activity Purpose Scientists classify plants by the way they transport water. You read in Lesson 1 that the stems of many plants have xylem that carries water from the roots to other parts of the plant. Now you will **observe** plants that have similar-looking parts. You will **infer** what these parts do by **comparing** them to the plant parts you observed in Lesson 1.

Materials
- moss
- liverwort
- hand lens

Activity Procedure

1 **Observe** the moss and the liverwort. **Record** what you see.

2 Now **observe** the plants with a hand lens. Can you see different parts? Do any of the parts you see look like the parts of the potted plant you observed in Lesson 1? (Picture A)

3 **Observe** the plants by touching them with your fingers. Are they soft or firm? Are they dry or moist? What else can you tell by feeling them? Describe what they feel like.

◄ Moss often grows in moist, shady forests. Many tiny plants grow close together to form a mat on tree trunks, rocks, or damp soil.

Picture A

Picture B

4 Touch the plants with a pencil or other object while you **observe** them through the hand lens. Do the parts bend, or are they stiff? Do you see anything new if you push a part of the plant to one side? Describe what you see.

5 **Observe** the plants by smelling them. Do they have any kind of odor? Try to identify the odors. Describe what you smell. (Picture B)

6 Make drawings of the moss and liverwort, identify the parts you observed, and **infer** what each part does.

Draw Conclusions

1. What plant parts did you **observe** on the moss? What parts did you observe on the liverwort?

2. What do you **infer** each part of the plant does?

3. **Scientists at Work** Scientists use observations to **compare** things. Use the observations you made in this investigation to compare the moss and liverwort with a vascular plant.

Investigate Further **Observe** a fern. Based on your observations, would you **classify** a fern as a nonvascular plant, like the moss and the liverwort, or as a vascular plant, like the potted plant in Lesson 1?

Process Skill Tip

By knowing what observations help you **compare** things, you will be able to make better observations.

Different Methods of Reproduction

Nonvascular Plants

FIND OUT

• how nonvascular and vascular plants reproduce

VOCABULARY

spore
gymnosperm
pollen
angiosperm
germinate

The spore capsules of moss plants contain hundreds of tiny spores. Each spore can grow into a new plant. ▼

Recall from page A52 that mosses and liverworts are simple plants that usually grow in damp places. They need to stay moist because they do not have xylem tubes to transport water. They also lack phloem tubes.

Remember, plants that don't have xylem and phloem are nonvascular plants. Nonvascular plants can move water, nutrients, and food only from one cell to the next. This is the reason why nonvascular plants are so small. Vascular plants, which have xylem and phloem, can grow much larger.

As you observed in the investigation, nonvascular plants have parts that look similar to those of vascular plants. Their leaflike parts, for example, have chloroplasts and use sunlight to manufacture food. Their thin, rootlike structures anchor the plants in the ground and take in some water and nutrients. Their stemlike parts hold the leaflike parts up to the sunlight. However, these similar-looking parts are not true leaves, roots, or stems,

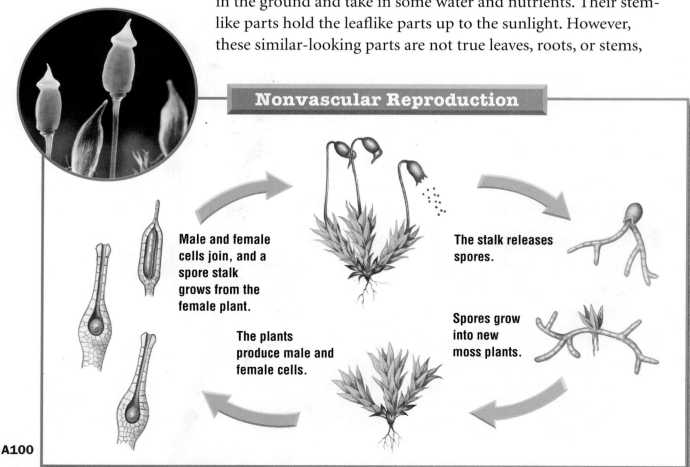

Nonvascular Reproduction

Male and female cells join, and a spore stalk grows from the female plant.

The stalk releases spores.

Spores grow into new moss plants.

The plants produce male and female cells.

because they do not have xylem and phloem.

Nonvascular plants do not have flowers, so they don't reproduce with seeds. Instead, they reproduce with spores (SPOHRZ). A **spore** is a single reproductive cell that grows into a new plant. During their life cycle, mosses produce male and female reproductive cells on separate plants. A male cell and a female cell unite and produce a stalk that grows out of the female plant. The stalk releases the spores that will grow into new moss plants.

✔ **What are the two major groups of plants, and how are they different?**

Simple Vascular Plants

Simple vascular plants include ferns and horsetails. Many people think of ferns as plants with lacy leaves. In fact, there are

more than 11,000 kinds of ferns, with many different kinds of leaves.

About 325 million years ago, vast forests of tall tree ferns covered much of the Earth. Today most ferns are found in the tropics, though some grow in cool forests. A few kinds even grow in the Arctic.

Horsetails are much less common than ferns. There are only about 20 kinds of horsetails. Most are small, and all contain silica, a gritty material like sand. Years ago, people used dried horsetails to scrub pots and pans.

Like mosses and liverworts, simple vascular plants reproduce with spores. Also like nonvascular plants, ferns and horsetails have two different stages in their life cycles.

As is the case with mosses, ferns produce male and female reproductive cells. However, in ferns the united cell, or *zygote*, divides and grows into a separate spore-producing plant.

✔ **How do simple vascular plants reproduce?**

◀ The underside of a fern leaf contains spore cases.

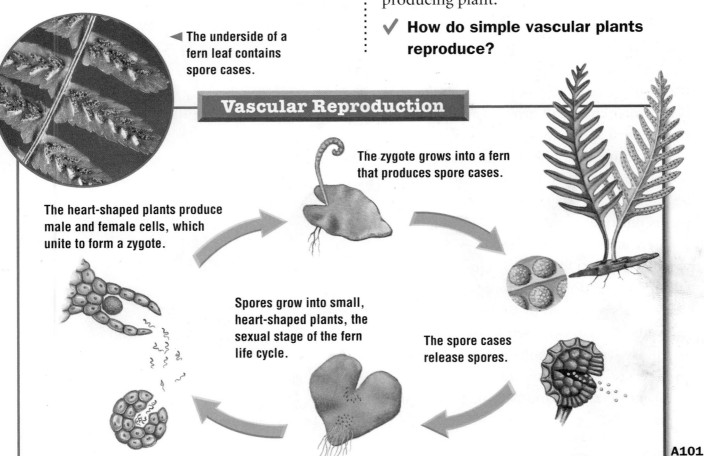

Vascular Reproduction

The heart-shaped plants produce male and female cells, which unite to form a zygote.

The zygote grows into a fern that produces spore cases.

Spores grow into small, heart-shaped plants, the sexual stage of the fern life cycle.

The spore cases release spores.

▲ The cones of
spruce trees hang
down. The cones
of pines grow up.

Conifers, such as this Norway
spruce, are common in cold
northern climates. ▶

Cone-Bearing Vascular Plants

Spore-producing plants make large numbers of spores. This adaptation makes sure that at least some of the spores will grow into new plants. Seed-producing plants make relatively fewer seeds, but a seed has a better chance of growing into a new plant than a spore does. This is because a seed contains a supply of food. This stored food helps the new plant grow until it can begin making its own food. Most vascular plants reproduce with seeds.

There are two kinds of seed-producing vascular plants. One type produces seeds with no protection. The other type produces seeds protected by some kind of fruit.

Plants with unprotected seeds are called **gymnosperms** (JIM•noh•spermz). The most common gymnosperms are the *conifers* (KAHN•uh•ferz), or cone-bearing plants, such as pine trees.

Most conifers produce both male and female cones on the same tree. Male cones produce **pollen**, structures that contain the male reproductive cells.

Female cones vary in size from 2 cm (about $\frac{3}{4}$ in.) to more than 75 cm (about 2 ft). Their shapes vary, too, but most have a kind of stem from which thin, woody plates grow. These plates are called *scales.*

Wind carries pollen from male cones to female cones. There the male and female reproductive cells unite. The resulting zygotes divide and grow into seeds. During dry weather the scales open and the seeds are released.

✔ **What is a gymnosperm?**

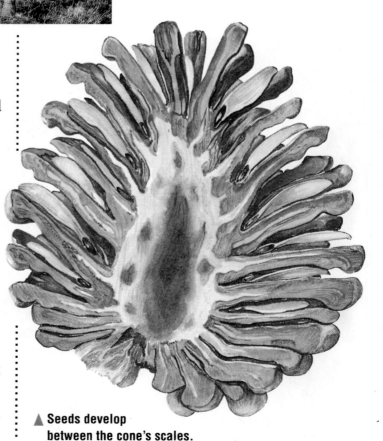

▲ Seeds develop
between the cone's scales.

Flowering Vascular Plants

Most of the plants you are familiar with are flowering plants, or **angiosperms** (AN•jee•oh•spermz). There are more than 235,000 kinds of angiosperms on Earth. These include grasses, herbs, shrubs, and many trees. Flowering plants are important sources of wood, fiber, and medicine. Nearly all the food that people eat comes directly or indirectly from flowering plants.

Flowers are an adaptation that is important to the success of angiosperms. They help make sure that pollen gets from the male part of a flower to the female part. Unlike gymnosperms, which are pollinated only by the wind, angiosperms are also pollinated by insects and other small animals. The colors, shapes, and odors of flowers attract these

▲ An apple begins as a flower.

◀ There are more than 235,000 kinds of flowering plants. Flowers are important to the success of angiosperms.

▲ The seeds of the apple tree are protected by the fruit. As the fruit rots, it provides extra food for the growth of a new apple tree.

animals, which carry pollen from one flower to another as they move about.

Angiosperm seeds are also an adaptation for success. Unlike the gymnosperms, which produce unprotected seeds, angiosperms produce fruits that protect their seeds. These fruits include apples, oranges, tomatoes, peanuts, and acorns.

A fruit protects the seed or seeds inside it in several ways. It usually keeps birds and other animals from getting at them, even if they eat the outer part of the fruit. A fruit also serves as a covering that protects the seeds from cold weather. In addition, a rotting fruit provides extra food for a new plant when it begins to grow.

✔ **What is an angiosperm?**

Seed Dispersal

Once the eggs of a plant have been fertilized and fruits have formed, the plant is ready to release the seeds. If the fruits fall next to the parent plant, the seeds do not have a good chance of growing. But plants are adapted in many ways to disperse, or scatter, fruits and seeds to places far away from the parent plant.

Maple trees, for example, produce wing-shaped fruits that spin as they fall. Spinning slows down their fall and makes it possible for wind to carry the fruit and its attached seed away from the parent tree.

In the Amazon rain forest, the fruits of some trees are dispersed by dropping into the Amazon River. The fruits are carried down the river, where they may wash up on a distant shore. There the seeds may sprout.

Many plants depend on animals to scatter their seeds. Oak trees, for example, produce fruits called acorns. Squirrels eat some acorns when they fall, and bury others to eat during the winter. The seeds inside buried acorns may sprout and grow into new oak trees.

Some seeds are covered by a fruit called a bur. The outside of a bur is usually rough, and it sticks to the fur of any passing animal. When it finally falls off, it may land on the ground and the seed inside may sprout.

✔ **Name two ways in which plants disperse seeds.**

The rough outside of a bur sticks to the fur of a passing animal or to a human's clothes.

Each dandelion seed is attached to a bit of fluff that can be blown by a light wind.

The seeds of this berry will be left in some other place with the bird's droppings.

When an animal eats a fruit, the seed may fall to the ground and sprout.

Seed Germination

A seed survives inside its protective seed coat until conditions are right for it to grow. These conditions usually include fertile soil, warm temperatures, and enough rainfall or moisture. Most seeds can survive for several years, and some seeds have survived for hundreds of years. When conditions are right, a seed will sprout, or **germinate** (JER•mih•nate).

First, the seed takes in water. This makes the seed larger. As the seed swells, the seed coat splits. The *embryo*, or tiny plant within the seed, then begins to grow and develop the parts it needs to live on its own. The first part to develop is the root, which begins to grow down, toward the center of the Earth.

Next, the stem emerges from the seed and begins to grow up, toward the light. The seed leaves are attached to the stem. At this stage, the growing plant, now called a *seedling*, uses food stored in the seed leaves to grow. Later the first true leaves, which have also emerged from the seed, will begin to make food.

As it grows, the seedling produces longer and thicker roots. The stem gets taller and stronger. When the seedling is growing well and its leaves are making all the food the plant needs, the seed leaves drop off. The young, rapidly growing plant can now live on its own.

✔ **What is the first part to emerge from a germinating seed?**

▲ This seed has landed on rain-soaked, fertile soil. It will take in moisture, swell, and germinate.

▲ The first part to emerge from the seed is the root.

▲ As the root gets longer and thicker, a stem begins to emerge.

▲ The seedling now has a well-developed root system, and its first true leaves are producing food.

Comparing Life Cycles

Both animals and plants go through stages in their lives. A flowering plant sprouts from a seed, grows and matures, flowers, and produces seeds of its own. An animal is born, grows into an adult, and reproduces its own kind. Each organism completes a cycle of life.

Some young animals look very much like their parents. Puppies and kittens are very small when they are born, but you can easily see what they will grow up to become.

Other young animals look very different from their parents. Who would guess that a caterpillar becomes a beautiful butterfly or that a fishlike tadpole becomes a frog?

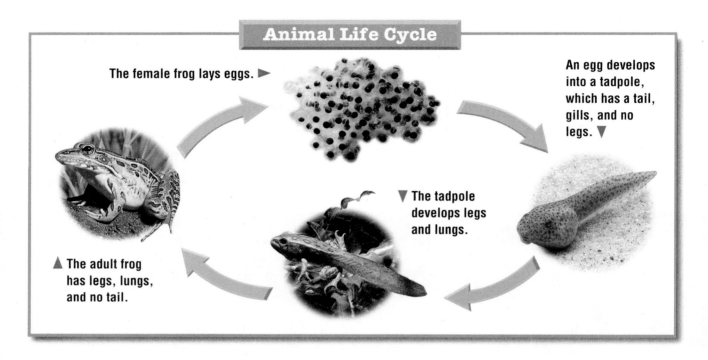

Animal Life Cycle

The female frog lays eggs. ▶

An egg develops into a tadpole, which has a tail, gills, and no legs. ▼

▼ The tadpole develops legs and lungs.

▲ The adult frog has legs, lungs, and no tail.

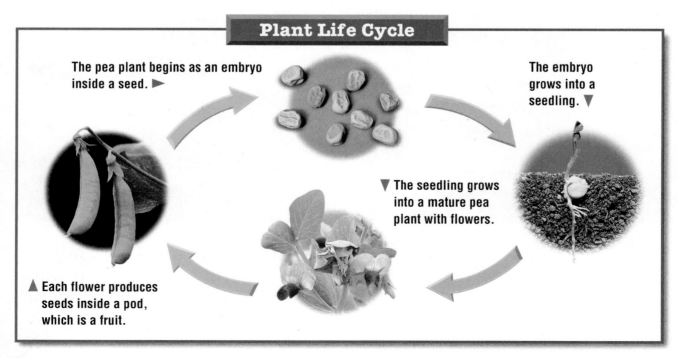

Plant Life Cycle

The pea plant begins as an embryo inside a seed. ▶

The embryo grows into a seedling. ▼

▼ The seedling grows into a mature pea plant with flowers.

▲ Each flower produces seeds inside a pod, which is a fruit.

In its earliest stages, a flowering plant is also very different from its parent plants. It starts as an embryo inside a seed. When the seed sprouts, the embryo grows into a seedling that does not look much like the mature plant. As the plant grows and matures, it looks more and more like the plants it came from.

✔ **How does the life cycle of a flowering plant compare to that of an animal?**

Summary

Vascular plants have xylem and phloem. Nonvascular plants do not have these tubes. Nonvascular plants and simple vascular plants reproduce with spores. Gymnosperms and angiosperms are seed-producing vascular plants. Like animals, plants go through several stages in their life cycles.

Review

1. Why are nonvascular plants so small?
2. How do ferns reproduce?
3. How do conifers produce seeds?
4. **Critical Thinking** Why do you think night-blooming plants have less colorful flowers than day-blooming plants?
5. **Test Prep** The fruit produced by an angiosperm —
   A makes the seeds taste better
   B protects the seeds inside
   C attracts birds and insects
   D is more attractive than the cone of a gymnosperm

LINKS

MATH LINK

Display Data Take a look at the plants around you—at home, at school, in parks. Are most of them vascular or nonvascular? Are they gymnosperms or angiosperms? Use a computer graphing program to make a circle graph that compares the percentages of the types of plants you find.

WRITING LINK

Informative Writing—Explanation Write a paragraph explaining how you use plants each day. How many times do you use them? For what purposes? Would it be hard to get through a day without plants? Share your paragraph with your classmates.

LANGUAGE ARTS LINK

Prefixes In the word *nonvascular*, the prefix *non-* means "not." What do you think the words *nonsense*, *nonbreakable,* and *nonfat* mean? What other *non-* words can you think of? Make a list of words that begin with *non-* and write down what each one means.

GO ONLINE TECHNOLOGY LINK

Learn more about flowering plants by visiting the Smithsonian Institution Internet site.
www.si.edu/harcourt/science

 Smithsonian Institution®

How Do People Use Plants?

In this lesson, you can . . .

 INVESTIGATE how heat and moisture can change popcorn.

 LEARN ABOUT the many uses of plants.

 LINK to math, writing, music, and technology.

How many uses of plants or plant products do you see here? ▽

Popcorn

Activity Purpose People eat many kinds of seeds as food, but popcorn is probably the most interesting, and the most fun. Popped popcorn is the exploded seeds of a type of corn plant. Popcorn seeds contain water, although you can't see it or feel it. Heating the seeds turns the water quickly to steam. As the steam expands, the popcorn seeds pop. In this investigation you will **predict** and **measure** how popping the seeds affects their volume and mass.

Materials
- large plastic measuring cup
- unpopped popcorn
- balance

Activity Procedure

1 Cover the bottom of the measuring cup with unpopped popcorn seeds.

2 **Estimate** the volume of the unpopped seeds. Put the cup on the balance, and **measure** the mass of the unpopped seeds. (Picture A)

3 **Predict** what will happen to the mass and the volume when the seeds are popped.

Picture A

Picture B

4. Your teacher will help you pop the popcorn. Return the popped seeds to the measuring cup.

5. **Measure** the volume and mass of the cup of popped popcorn. Were your **predictions** correct? (Picture B)

Draw Conclusions

1. How did the volume of the popcorn change?

2. How did the mass change? Explain.

3. **Scientists at Work** One reason why scientists **experiment** is to test predictions. If an experiment doesn't turn out the way they predicted, it may mean that their predictions were wrong. Or it may mean that they did not consider everything that could affect the experiment. Did you predict the volume and mass of the popped popcorn correctly? Explain.

Investigate Further What other questions do you have about popcorn? **Plan and conduct an experiment** to answer your questions.

The Uses of Plants

Plants as Food

FIND OUT

• how people use plants as food

• how people use plants as medicine

VOCABULARY

grain
fiber

People use plants more for food than for any other purpose. For example, breakfast cereal is made of **grain**, or the seeds of certain grasses. If you have a sandwich for lunch, you are eating grain again. The bread in the sandwich was made by grinding the seeds of wheat into flour. Does your sandwich have lettuce and tomato on it? Then you're also eating a plant leaf and a fruit. And if the sandwich is seasoned with mustard, you're eating something made from seeds.

People eat many different parts of many different plants. Beans, lentils, corn, and rice, for example, are seeds. Beets, radishes, turnips, and carrots are roots. Bamboo shoots and asparagus are stems. Spinach, lettuce, kale, and cabbage are leaves. Cherries, pears, oranges, and olives are fruits. Artichokes, cauliflower, and broccoli are flowers. And if you like cinnamon in your apple pie, you are eating the bark, the outer part of the stem, of a tree.

✔ **Name the plant parts that people eat.**

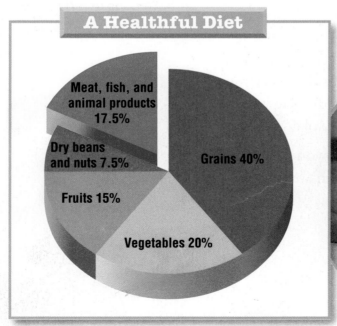

A Healthful Diet

Meat, fish, and animal products 17.5%

Dry beans and nuts 7.5%

Grains 40%

Fruits 15%

Vegetables 20%

In a healthful diet, most of the foods come from plants.

A110

The Food Guide Pyramid

Grains form the largest part of this pyramid because they are the foundation of a healthful diet. The next level is shared by vegetables and fruits. Drinking fruit juice is more healthful than drinking soda, but you should also eat the fruits themselves.

Meats and dairy products are in a small part of the pyramid because they contain fats. Too much fat can harm your health. Fish and poultry have less fat than other meats. Milk, cheese, and yogurt are good for you, but they also are high in fat. Foods that are very high in fat, oil, or sugar are not healthful.

FATS, OILS, SWEETS
Foods in this group are generally not healthful, so don't eat a lot of them.

MEAT, POULTRY, FISH, DRY BEANS, EGGS, NUTS GROUP
Eat 2–3 servings of foods from this group daily. A serving is one egg or about 3 oz of meat.

MILK, YOGURT, CHEESE GROUP
These foods contain fats, so limit yourself to 2–3 servings a day. A cup of milk is one serving.

VEGETABLE GROUP
Eat 3–5 servings of vegetables a day. A half cup of chopped vegetables is one serving.

FRUIT GROUP
Eat 2–4 servings a day. A banana is one serving.

BREAD, CEREAL, RICE, PASTA GROUP
Eat 6–11 servings a day. A slice of bread, for example, is one serving.

The leaves of the aloe plant store food. That food, a jellylike substance, is used in soaps, shampoos, makeup, skin creams, and sunscreens.

This fluffy cotton boll is made of tiny white fibers. The fibers are woven into cotton cloth, which is made into clothing. ▼

Plants as Medicines

Plants contain many substances that can be used to treat illnesses. Native Americans used the leaves and roots of hundreds of plants as medicines. They used them to reduce fevers, relieve pain, calm upset stomachs, and treat other problems.

About 40 percent of the medicines we use today are made from plants. For example, an important heart medicine called digitalis is made from the leaves of the foxglove plant. Foxglove grows in many parts of the United States. Quinine is made from the bark of a tree that grows in the Andes Mountains of South America. Quinine is used to treat malaria.

One of the best-known and most widely used pain medicines is also one of the oldest. Aspirin is a medicine invented in the 1800s. But thousands of years earlier, people took an almost identical medicine by chewing the bark of the willow tree.

✔ **What did some people do for pain before aspirin was invented?**

Other Uses for Plants

Clothing is another important product people get from plants. Blue jeans, for example, are made of fibers from the cotton plant. A **fiber** is any material that can be separated into thread. The dye that gives blue jeans their color was once made from the indigo plant.

Many kinds of trees provide wood for different purposes. Homes are often made of wood, and a lot of the furniture in most homes is wood. Musical instruments, such as guitars, violins, and pianos, are made with wood. And pulp, which is made from wood, is used to make paper.

Soaps and shampoos contain plant substances that can help make skin smooth and hair shiny. Many perfumes are made from flower petals. It takes about 100 kg (220 lb) of rose petals to make 30 mL (about 1 oz) of fragrance. This is one of the reasons why perfumes are expensive.

✔ **Name two products made from trees.**

This cancer medicine was once made from the bark of the Pacific Yew. ▼

Summary

People eat the leaves, stems, roots, seeds, fruits, and flowers of various plants. When they are sick, people often use medicines made from plants. In fact, many things people use every day come from plants.

Review

1. Name three foods that are seeds or are made from seeds.
2. From which food group should you eat the most servings each day?
3. What percentage of the medicines people use comes from plants?
4. **Critical Thinking** Nutritionists say people shouldn't eat many French fries. In which food groups do French fries belong? What part of this food may not be healthful?
5. **Test Prep** Aloe is a plant that is used to make —
   - **A** dye
   - **B** skin cream
   - **C** aspirin
   - **D** fiber

LINKS

MATH LINK

Collect Data Most people should eat no more than 30 g of fat each day. Food labels list the fat in each serving. Add up the fat in the food you eat in one week. How close to 30 g per day is the amount of fat in your diet?

WRITING LINK

Persuasive Writing—Business Letter Some people think it's healthful to eat only plants. Others think it's important to eat both meat and plants. Write a letter to a health organization requesting information about the reasons for and against both of these diets.

MUSIC LINK

Wooden Instruments Today, some musical instruments are still made of wood. Report to the class on one of them. Explain why it is made of wood instead of some other material. Include a picture of the instrument, and play part of a recording of the instrument.

TECHNOLOGY LINK

Learn more about using plants for food by viewing *Genetic Tomatoes* on the **Harcourt Science Newsroom Video** in your classroom video library.

CNN Turner Le@rning

Corn Cards and Super Slurpers

Chemists and agricultural scientists are working together to find new ways to use plants. Their goal is to make useful products that won't cause pollution.

Why Use Plants to Make Plastic?

Products made from plastics make life simpler, but plastics can cause problems, too. Most plastics are made from petroleum, and when you throw them away, they aren't really gone. Petroleum-based plastics don't decompose (break down) in the environment. Each year people throw away almost 20 million tons of plastics. That's a lot of trash. Now scientists who work with plants have discovered how to use corn to produce plastics that do decompose. In a landfill or a

Corn is one of America's most commonly grown crops.

backyard compost pile, these plastics break down into hydrogen, oxygen, and small bits of organic matter called humus. Humus helps enrich the soil.

Diapers? Not As Corny As It Sounds

What are corn-based plastics good for? Plenty! Companies use these environmentally friendly materials to make products ranging from disposable diapers to prepaid telephone calling cards.

Packaging "peanuts" made from cornstarch protect fragile products. After they have been exposed to moisture and sunlight for a few months, they fall apart.

Chemists at a U.S. Department of Agriculture laboratory discovered a way to use cornstarch to make a material they called hydrosorb. Its nickname is "Super Slurper." Why? Because it can soak up more than 300 times its own weight in water. Diapers containing hydrosorb help keep babies dry. Super Slurper filters remove water from fuels such as gasoline and heating oil. When mixed with soil, hydrosorb holds moisture near the roots of plants, helping them grow with less irrigation.

PLA Plastics

Other scientists have found ways to recombine the hydrogen, oxygen, and carbon in corn to make a material called polylactic acid resin, or PLA. Plastics made from PLA can be

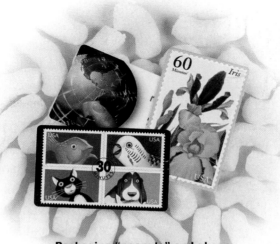

Packaging "peanuts" and phone cards can be made from corn.

used just like petroleum-based plastics to make toys, TV sets, and other products.

Nebraska farmers grow nearly 30 million tons of corn each year. Scientists at the University of Nebraska say that they haven't found anything made with petroleum-based plastic that can't also be made from plastic that comes from corn.

THINK ABOUT IT

1. What other products could Super Slurpers be used for?
2. What are some advantages and disadvantages of corn-based plastics?

CAREERS
AGRONOMIST

What They Do Agronomists study soils and plants to develop better ways to grow crops and to keep agricultural land productive.

Education and Training People wishing to become agronomists study plant biology and soil chemistry in college and graduate school.

WEB LINK
For Science and Technology updates, visit the Harcourt Internet site.
www.harcourtschool.com

"Our food, many of the things we wear, and even some parts of our homes come from plants. People also get enjoyment from looking at plants."

Shirley Mah Kooyman
BOTANIST

Because we depend on plants for so many things, the health of plants is important to our survival. Shirley Mah Kooyman feels that plants are sometimes taken for granted—that people forget they are living things. Ms. Kooyman is a botanist, or plant scientist, in Chanhassen, Minnesota. An important part of her work is discovering what makes plants grow. The knowledge that she gains is used by other scientists, who work to find ways to grow healthier plants that produce larger crops.

In her work, Ms. Kooyman seeks to better understand some of the growth processes of plants. She knows that in addition to light energy, water, proper temperature, and rich soil, plants need certain hormones. Hormones are chemical "messengers" that "tell" plants to grow. Plant hormones are produced in stems and roots. From there they travel to other parts of the plant.

Today scientists are able to make artificial plant hormones. Artificial hormones placed on a root tip make the root grow, just as natural hormones do. The advantage of artificial hormones is that they can be produced in greater amounts than natural hormones. Farmers can use artificial hormones to speed up plant growth and produce larger crops. This will make plant products more affordable. In addition to working with plant hormones in a laboratory and in the field, Ms. Kooyman teaches people about plants and the joys of gardening.

THINK ABOUT IT

1. Why is it important to understand what makes plants grow?
2. How might artificial hormones be used to produce a large crop of tomatoes?

WATER IN PLANTS

How does water move through plants?

Materials

- 5 toothpicks
- dropper
- water

Procedure

❶ Break the toothpicks in half, but don't separate the parts. The two halves should remain connected.

❷ Arrange the toothpicks like the spokes in a wagon wheel.

❸ Put several drops of water in the center of the "wheel."

❹ Observe any changes to the toothpicks.

Draw Conclusions

What happened to the water you put on the toothpicks? What happened to the toothpicks? Relate this to the way water moves through plants.

LEAF CASTS

How can you observe stomata?

Materials

- potted plant
- clear fingernail polish
- microscope slide
- microscope

Procedure

❶ Paint a 2-cm square of fingernail polish on the underside of one leaf. Let the polish dry.

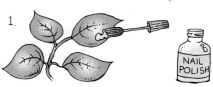
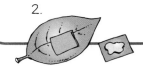

❷ Add another layer of polish and let it dry. Repeat until you have 6 layers of polish.

❸ Once the last layer of polish is dry, peel it off the leaf.

❹ Put the polish, which contains a cast of the leaf epidermis, on a microscope slide.

❺ Observe the slide by using the microscope.

Draw Conclusions

You should observe two types of cells. Compare the cells. Explain any differences between them. How do the guard cells form the stomata?

Vocabulary Review

Use the terms below to complete the paragraph. The page numbers in ( ) tell you where to look in the chapter if you need help.

xylem (A95)   **gymnosperms** (A102)

phloem (A95)   **pollen** (A102)

photosynthesis (A96)   **angiosperms** (A103)

chlorophyll (A96)   **germinate** (A105)

spores (A101)

A plant that contains tubes for the transport of water and food is called a vascular plant. The tubes that transport food are **1.** tubes; those that transport water are **2.** tubes. Plants that do not have these tubes are nonvascular plants. Whether or not they have transport tubes, all plants have a green pigment called **3.** , which enables them to make their own food. As plants make food, they use carbon dioxide and release oxygen. This process is called **4.** .

Plants have various means by which they reproduce. Plants will produce either seeds or **5.** , which will grow into a new plant when conditions are favorable. Conifers, or **6.** , produce unprotected seeds in cones. The flowers of **7.** produce protected seeds. In a flower, **8.** contains the male reproductive cells. When conditions are right, a seed will sprout, or **9.** .

Connect Concepts

Write terms from the Word Bank to complete the chart.

angiosperms   seeds

gymnosperms   spores

nonvascular plants   vascular plants

The Two Main Groups of Plants Are
10. _____, which have no xylem or phloem.
11. _____, which have xylem and phloem tubes.

The Two Groups of Vascular Plants Are
12. plants that use _____ to reproduce.
13. plants that use _____ to reproduce.

The Two Groups of Seed-Producing Plants Are
14. _____, which include conifers, such as pines.
15. _____, which include flowering apple trees.

Check Understanding

Write the letter of the best choice.

16. Most leaves are thin and flat because —
    A they look better that way
    B this helps them make food
    C they protect the plant from insects and birds
    D they absorb water from the air

17. Nonvascular plants are limited in size because —
    F they must pass water and nutrients from one cell to the next
    G they do not make their own food
    H birds and other animals like to eat them
    J they live in shady places

18. Large, colorful flowers are useful for a plant because —

    A they look pretty

    B they make food for plants

    C they attract insects and birds that spread pollen

    D they collect moisture

19. For a more healthful diet, eat more of foods that are —

    F near the top of the Food Guide Pyramid

    G mostly from the milk group

    H high in sugar

    J near the bottom of the Food Guide Pyramid

Critical Thinking

20. Could a plant live if all its leaves were cut off? Explain your answer.

21. In what way are fruits better than cones for carrying seeds?

22. How does successful seed dispersal help to ensure that a plant species will survive?

Process Skills Review

23. What can you **observe** about a plant to help you identify the kind of plant it is?

24. **Infer** which products in your classroom are made from plants or plant parts.

25. **Predict** what would happen if trees did not have fruits or cones.

Performance Assessment

Design a Plant

Choose one condition from each set. Design a plant with roots, stems, and leaves that could live in a place with the conditions you choose.

a lot of rain
some rain
almost no rain

hot temperatures
moderate temperatures
cold temperatures

a lot of light
some light
almost no light

UNIT A EXPEDITIONS

There are many places where you can observe living systems. By visiting the places below, you can learn about some of the differences among living things. You'll also have fun while you learn.

Huntsville-Madison County Botanical Garden

WHAT An ornamental garden displaying a wide assortment of plant species

WHERE Huntsville, Alabama

WHAT CAN YOU DO THERE? Take the Garden Tour, explore the trails, and study the adaptations of the many plants.

Butterfly Pavilion & Insect Center

WHAT An insect zoo that is home to more than a thousand spectacular butterflies

WHERE Westminster, Colorado

WHAT CAN YOU DO THERE? Observe subtropical plants and see different kinds of butterflies from around the world.

GO ONLINE Plan Your Own Expeditions

If you can't visit the Huntsville-Madison County Botanical Garden or the Butterfly Pavilion & Insect Center, visit a garden or zoo near you. Or log on to The Learning Site at **www.harcourtschool.com** to visit these science sites and other places where you can observe living systems.

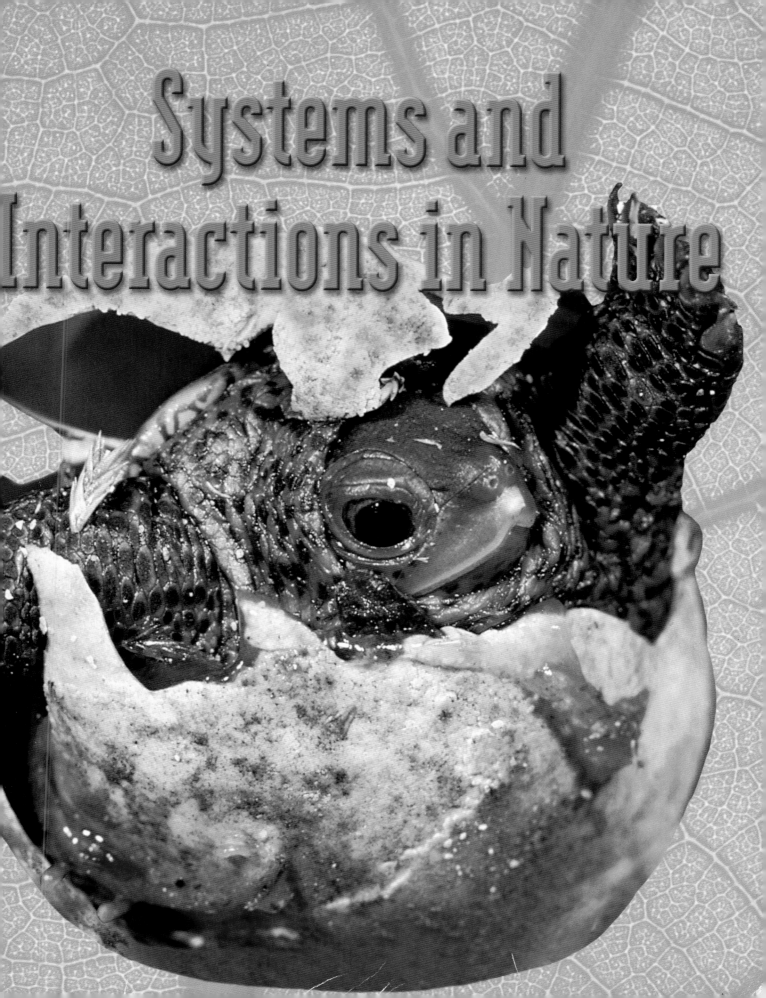

Systems and Interactions in Nature

UNIT B · LIFE SCIENCE

Systems and Interactions in Nature

UNIT EXPERIMENT

Cleaning Up Pollution

Living organisms interact with each other and with the physical environment. Human activity can sometimes pollute the physical environment. While you study this unit, you can conduct a long-term experiment related to pollution. Here are some questions to think about. How can visible pollution be removed from water? For example, can certain materials be used to filter polluted water? Plan and conduct an experiment to find answers to these or other questions you have about cleaning up pollution. See pages x–xvii for help in designing your experiment.

1 Cycles in Nature

Vocabulary Preview

nitrogen cycle
carbon-oxygen
 cycle
respiration
water cycle
evaporation
condensation
precipitation
transpiration

The water you washed with this morning has been around for millions of years. It has been rain, snow, sleet, and hail. It has flowed over thousands of waterfalls and been frozen in hundreds of glaciers. Dinosaurs might have drunk it. But it has always returned to the ground, the ocean, and the air again and again.

Fast Fact

About 70 percent of Earth's surface is covered by salt water. Most of it is in Earth's four oceans.

Earth's Oceans		
Ocean	Surface Area (millions of km²)	Volume (millions of km³)
Pacific	166.0	723.7
Atlantic	82.0	321.9
Indian	73.6	292.1
Arctic	12.2	13.5

If all of Earth's glaciers and ice caps were to melt, the oceans would rise about 60 meters (200 feet), covering thousands of large coastal cities, such as Venice, Italy.

Fast Fact

Waterfalls move. Niagara Falls is moving toward Lake Erie as it slowly wears away the rock at its top. It will reach the lake in about 23,000 years.

How Does Nature Reuse Materials?

In this lesson, you can . . .

 INVESTIGATE how plants use carbon dioxide.

 LEARN ABOUT how materials are reused in nature.

 LINK to math, writing, social studies, and technology.

▼ Every cell in this bison's body uses oxygen and produces carbon dioxide.

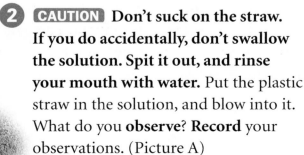

B4

 **INVESTIGATE**

How Plants Use Carbon Dioxide

Activity Purpose Remember that every time you inhale, or take a breath, your lungs take in oxygen. That oxygen then goes to your blood cells, which carry it to every other cell in your body. Body cells use oxygen for their life functions, or activities. Cell functions produce carbon dioxide, which the blood carries back to the lungs. When you exhale, or breathe out, carbon dioxide leaves your body. In this investigation you will **observe** how plants use carbon dioxide.

Materials

- safety goggles
- 2 beakers, 250 mL
- water
- dropper
- bromothymol blue (BTB), an indicator
- plastic straw
- elodea
- 2 test tubes with caps
- funnel
- clock

Activity Procedure

1 **CAUTION** **Put on safety goggles, and leave them on until you complete Step 4.** Fill one beaker about two-thirds full of water. Use the dropper to add BTB to the water until you have a blue solution. BTB is an indicator. It changes color when carbon dioxide is present.

2 **CAUTION** **Don't suck on the straw. If you do accidentally, don't swallow the solution. Spit it out, and rinse your mouth with water.** Put the plastic straw in the solution, and blow into it. What do you **observe**? **Record** your observations. (Picture A)

3 Put the elodea into one test tube, and use the funnel to fill the tube with BTB solution from the beaker. Fill the other test tube with the BTB solution only.

4 Seal the test tubes with the caps. Carefully turn the test tubes upside down, and place them in the empty beaker. (Picture B)

5 Put the beaker containing the two test tubes in a sunny window for 1 hour. **Predict** what changes will occur in the test tubes. After 1 hour, **observe** both test tubes, and **record** your observations.

Picture A

Draw Conclusions

1. What changes did you **observe** in the BTB solution when you blew into it through the straw? Explain.

2. What changes did you **observe** in the test tube of BTB solution after the elodea had been in it for 1 hour?

3. **Compare** the color of the BTB solution in the test tube that had the elodea with the color of the BTB in the test tube that did not have the elodea. Describe any differences.

4. **Scientists at Work** Scientists **observe** changes that happen during experiments. Then they **infer** what caused the changes. What can you infer about any changes that took place in the test tubes?

Investigate Further What is the importance of sunlight in this investigation? **Hypothesize** about the importance of sunlight. Then **plan and conduct a simple experiment** to test your hypothesis.

Picture B

Process Skill Tip

When you **infer** the cause of something, you try to explain why it happened. Your inference is based on what you **observe**.

How Natural Materials Are Reused

Natural Cycles

Many materials on Earth are used and then reused by living organisms. Earth also stores some materials for later use. The air, for example, stores large amounts of oxygen, nitrogen, and carbon in the form of carbon dioxide. Materials such as iron, copper, magnesium, and calcium are stored in rocks.

Running water slowly wears away rocks, releasing stored materials. The materials dissolve in rivers and lakes or become part of the soil. When an animal drinks water, it gets some of the materials it needs. Animals also get materials they need by breathing and by eating. Animals release materials into the environment in their wastes.

Plants get the materials they need from the soil and from the air. Plants release some materials into the environment during photosynthesis. When plants and animals die, their bodies decay. This releases more materials into the environment. The cycles continue as new plants and animals use these materials.

✔ **Where do animals and plants get the materials they need?**

FIND OUT

- how materials are reused in nature
- about the nitrogen and carbon–oxygen cycles
- how people can upset nature's recycling

VOCABULARY

nitrogen cycle

carbon–oxygen cycle

respiration

Animals get the materials they need by eating and by drinking water. ▼

Lightning "fixes" a small amount of nitrogen.

Plants use nitrogen in the soil to make proteins.

Animals get nitrogen by eating plants and other animals.

Most nitrogen gas is fixed by bacteria in the soil or in nodules on some plant roots.

Animal wastes and decaying plants and animals return nitrates and ammonia to the soil.

The Nitrogen Cycle

All living organisms need nitrogen (NY•truh•juhn). Plants make proteins from nitrogen in the soil. Animals get the nitrogen they need to make proteins when they eat plants or other animals that eat plants.

Earth's atmosphere is about 78 percent nitrogen. But most organisms can't use nitrogen in this form. In the **nitrogen cycle**, nitrogen gas is *fixed*, or changed, into forms of nitrogen that plants can use. These forms are nitrates and ammonia (uh•MOHN•yuh).

Bacteria in the soil and in nodules (NAHJ•ools), or small lumps, on the roots of certain plants fix most of the nitrogen gas.

A small amount of nitrogen gas is also fixed by lightning. Most fixed nitrogen remains fixed—only a small amount changes back into nitrogen gas.

Nitrates and ammonia are returned to the soil in two ways. First, they are returned through animal wastes. Solid waste from animals contains nitrates. The liquid waste, or urine, that animals produce contains ammonia. Second, when animals and plants die, bacteria release nitrates and ammonia from decaying protein.

✓ **What are two forms of fixed nitrogen?**

Farmers spread animal wastes on their fields to return nitrates to the soil.

The Carbon–Oxygen Cycle

In the carbon–oxygen cycle, carbon and oxygen move among plants, animals, and the environment. All life on Earth is involved in this cycle because carbon and oxygen make up much of the bodies of all living organisms.

The cycling of carbon and oxygen through the environment depends on two processes—photosynthesis and respiration. During photosynthesis, plants and some other organisms take in carbon dioxide from the air or the water in which they live. Using energy from the sun, the carbon is turned into food, and oxygen is released into the environment. This carbon is stored by plants, or passed along to animals that eat plants.

Respiration is the process that releases energy from food. During respiration, oxygen is taken from the air or water, and carbon dioxide is released into the environment.

FUELS Over millions of years, the carbon in some decaying ocean organisms turned into petroleum.

PHOTOSYNTHESIS Microscopic plantlike organisms make their own food by photosynthesis. These organisms take in carbon dioxide and release oxygen. Oceans contain so many of these organisms that almost 90 percent of the oxygen in the atmosphere comes from photosynthesis in the oceans.

RESPIRATION All ocean organisms use oxygen and release carbon dioxide during respiration, the process that turns food into energy.

RESPIRATION All land organisms use oxygen and release carbon dioxide during respiration.

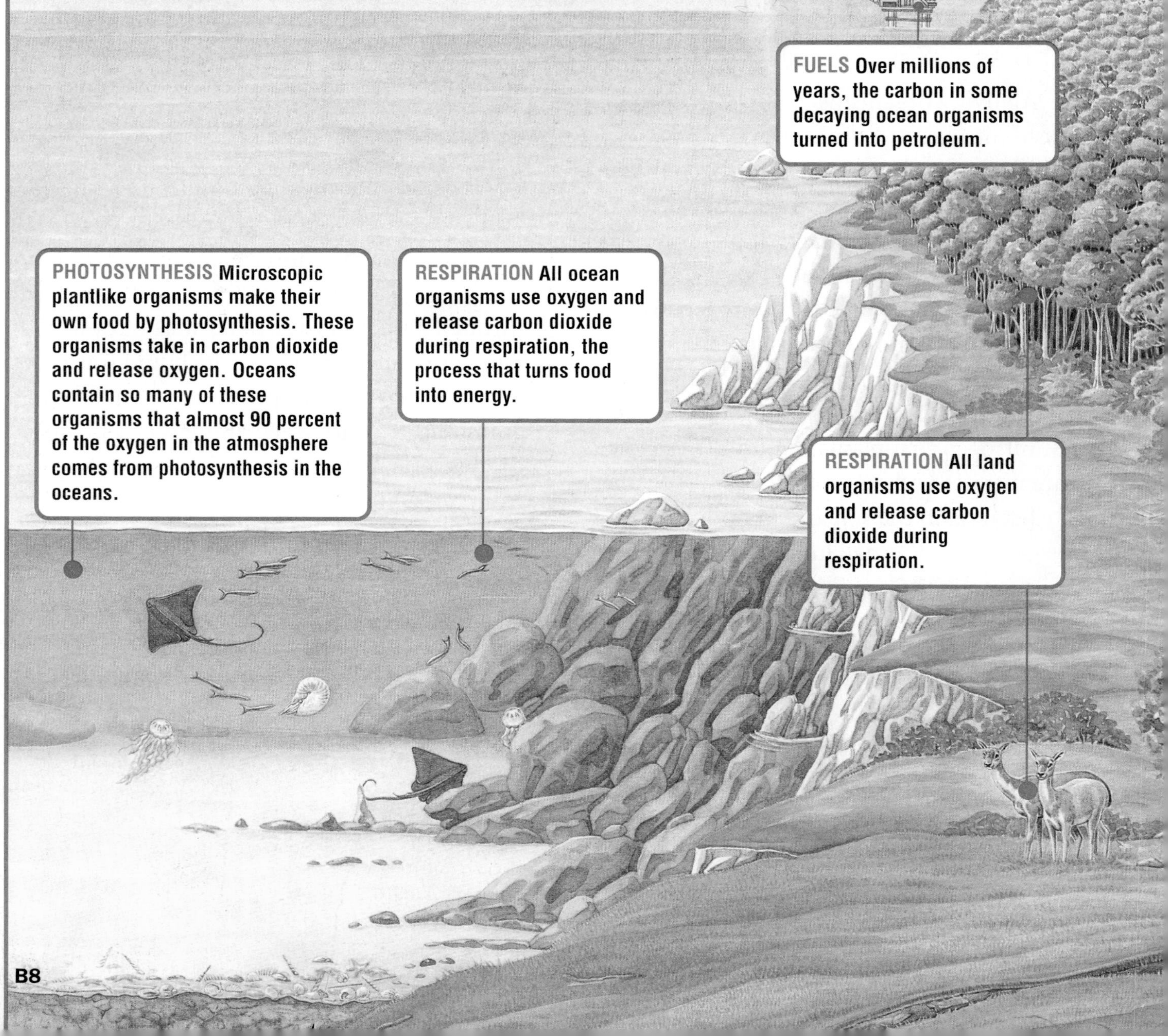

SOLAR ENERGY Sunlight provides the energy for photosynthesis in plants.

COMBUSTION Oxygen is used in the burning, or *combustion,* of fuels, such as coal. Carbon dioxide is a byproduct of combustion.

FUELS Dense forests once covered large parts of Earth. As these forests died, carbon in the plants became coal.

DECAY Some carbon is stored for a while in the bodies of dead organisms. Bacteria and fungi break down the tissues of dead animals and plants and use some of the carbon as food. The rest is released into the atmosphere as carbon dioxide.

PHOTOSYNTHESIS Plants use sunlight, water, and carbon dioxide in photosynthesis. Plants release oxygen into the atmosphere as a byproduct of photosynthesis.

B9

Changing the Balance

For hundreds of millions of years, the carbon–oxygen cycle stayed in balance, mostly by the processes of photosynthesis and respiration. However, since the beginning of the Industrial Revolution, about 200 years ago, human activity has started to change the balance.

During the Industrial Revolution, humans began to use machines fueled by wood and coal. Factories needed huge amounts of these fuels. Large areas of forests were cut for timber, and deep mines were dug to remove coal from inside the Earth. The burning of wood and coal put tons of carbon dioxide into the air each year.

Slowly, new methods made it possible to replace wood and some coal with fuels such as natural gas and petroleum. Factories, most energy stations, heating systems, and cars, trucks, and airplanes all use fuels. Burning these fuels adds even more carbon dioxide to the air.

Adding carbon dioxide to the air is a problem, because excess carbon dioxide is poisonous to animals. Although many people no longer use wood for fuel, large numbers of trees are still cut down for forest products, such as paper and lumber. Sometimes new trees are planted to replace the ones that are cut. But the total size of Earth's forests is smaller each year.

Forests are also cut to make room for other human needs, such as new farms and homes and growing cities. With forests becoming smaller, there are fewer trees to

Forests use large amounts of carbon dioxide. Smaller forests mean fewer trees to use the excess carbon dioxide in the air.

use the added carbon dioxide in the air. As a result, carbon dioxide continues to build up in the air.

✓ **How do trees and other plants help keep the carbon–oxygen cycle balanced?**

Summary

Most of the materials that organisms need are cycled through nature. Bacteria and lightning fix nitrogen gas into forms that plants can use to make proteins. Animal wastes and decaying organisms return nitrates and ammonia to the soil. Plants and animals cycle oxygen and carbon through the processes of photosynthesis and respiration. But human activities, such as burning fuels and cutting down forests, upset the balance of the carbon–oxygen cycle.

Review

1. Name two places where carbon is stored.
2. Where do bacteria fix nitrogen gas?
3. How do photosynthesis and respiration affect the carbon–oxygen cycle?
4. **Critical Thinking** How might building a shopping mall on land where there is now a park affect the amount of carbon dioxide in the air?
5. **Test Prep** Which human activity does **NOT** increase the amount of carbon dioxide in the air?

   A cutting down trees

   B heating buildings with coal

   C driving cars

   D planting corn

LINKS

MATH LINK

Solve Problems Each year human activity adds more than 7 billion tons of carbon dioxide to the air. This amount increases by 5 percent each year. If people added 7 billion tons of carbon dioxide to the air in the year 2000, how much did they add in 2001? In 2002?

WRITING LINK

Narrative Writing—Story Write a story for your family from the point of view of a material such as tin, copper, or iron. Begin your story inside a rock. Then describe what happens as you begin to dissolve in water and enter a natural cycle.

SOCIAL STUDIES LINK

Transportation Before the early 1900s, people didn't use cars to travel. Find out how people got around without cars. Write a report or make a poster showing methods of transportation people used before cars were invented.

TECHNOLOGY LINK

Learn more about cycles in nature by visiting this Internet site.
www.scilinks.org/harcourt

SC*LINKS*
THE WORLD'S A CLICK AWAY

Why Is the Water Cycle Important?

In this lesson, you can . . .

INVESTIGATE how water moves through air.

LEARN ABOUT the water cycle.

LINK to math, writing, literature, and technology.

INVESTIGATE

Water, Water Everywhere

Activity Purpose   Every day, you have some contact with water. You drink it, you bathe in it, and maybe you watch it fall from the sky. But have you ever wondered where water comes from, where it goes, or why we never run out of it? In this activity you will **observe** how water is recycled.

Materials

- graduate
- water
- small plastic cup
- zip-top plastic bag

Activity Procedure

1. Using the graduate, **measure** and pour 100 mL of water into the cup. (Picture A)

2. Open the plastic bag, and carefully put the cup inside. Then seal the bag. Be careful not to spill any water from the cup.

3. Place the sealed bag near a sunny window. **Predict** what will happen to the water in the cup. (Picture B)

◄ The warmth of the sun will change the snow into liquid water.

Picture A

Picture B

④ Leave the bag near a window for 3 to 4 days. **Observe** the cup and the bag each day. **Record** what you see.

⑤ Remove the cup from the bag. **Measure** the amount of water in the cup by pouring it back into the graduate. **Calculate** any difference in the amount of water you poured into the cup and the amount of water you removed from the cup.

Draw Conclusions

1. What did you **observe** during the time the cup was inside the bag?

2. Where do you infer the water in the bag came from? Explain.

3. **Scientists at Work** Scientists often **infer** the cause of something they **observe**. What can you infer about the amount of water in the bag?

Investigate Further How could you test the following **hypothesis?** The amount of water in the bag is the same as the amount of water missing from the cup. Decide what equipment you would need to use. Then **plan and conduct a simple experiment** that would test the hypothesis.

Process Skill Tip

If you carefully **observe** the results of an experiment, you can often **infer** what caused those results.

Why the Water Cycle Is Important

The Water Cycle

As seen from space, Earth looks like a big blue marble. Seas, oceans, lakes, and rivers cover about 75 percent of Earth's surface. Earth's water moves through the environment in what is called the **water cycle**. In the investigation, you inferred that liquid water in the cup became water vapor in the air. The water vapor then became liquid water in the plastic bag.

The heat of the sun changes water on Earth's surface into water vapor. This process is called **evaporation** (ee•vap•uh•RAY•shuhn). The temperature of the air high above the Earth is cold. There water vapor changes back into liquid water through a process called **condensation** (kahn•duhn•SAY•shuhn). Tiny droplets of water appear, forming

FIND OUT

- how water moves through the environment on Earth
- how human activity can affect the water cycle

VOCABULARY

water cycle
evaporation
condensation
precipitation
transpiration

If all of Earth's water could be held in a 1-liter bottle, the contents would be divided up like this:

Salt water: 972 mL

Fresh water: 28 mL

a cloud. After a lot of water vapor condenses, the water may fall back to the Earth as rain. If the air temperature is very cold, the water droplets may freeze and fall as snow or hail. Any form of water that falls from clouds is called **precipitation** (pree•sip•uh•TAY•shuhn).

All living organisms need water to survive. In fact, living organisms are made up of mostly water. About 70 percent of the human body is water. Living organisms get the water they need in different ways. Plants use their roots to take in water that seeps into the soil. Most animals get the water

they need by drinking from lakes or streams. Some animals get all the water they need from the food they eat.

Plants and animals also put water back into the environment. Plants give off water through their stomata. This process is called **transpiration** (tran•spuh•RAY•shuhn). Animals give off water vapor from their lungs when they exhale. And most of the urine animals produce is water.

✔ **What are the main processes in the water cycle?**

All the water on Earth keeps recycling. The heat of the sun evaporates water from the ocean's surface. High in the air, water condenses into tiny droplets to form clouds. Winds sweep clouds over the land. When clouds rise over a mountain, water falls as precipitation. Some rainwater runs off the land and returns to the ocean or to lakes. Some rainwater seeps into the Earth and becomes groundwater.

The 28 mL of fresh water is divided up like this:

Ice caps: 22 mL
Glaciers: 1.5 mL

Groundwater: 4 mL

Lakes and rivers: 2 drops

Water in soil and air: 1 drop

Average Daily Water Use

Laundry	60 gal
Bath	36 gal
Dishwashing	12 gal
Lawn watering	10 gal/min
Cooking	8 gal
Toilet per flush	5–6 gal
Shower	5 gal/min
Leaky faucet	5 gal/hr
Leaky toilet	3 gal/hr
Drinking water	0.26 gal

Humans and the Water Cycle

The amount of water on Earth today is nearly the same as it was billions of years ago. Yet every year the need for water grows. In addition to drinking, bathing, cooking, and waste removal, people use water to grow crops, feed livestock, and make materials, such as plastic, aluminum, and paper.

Less than 1 percent of the Earth's fresh water can be used because most of it is frozen in ice caps and glaciers. Yet the limited sources of fresh water are sometimes affected by human activity. Rainwater running off the land washes harmful chemicals such as oil

Although trash is more visible, this stream also carries harmful chemicals, such as pesticides, motor oil, and gasoline. ▶

and road salt into lakes and rivers. Expensive forms of water treatment must be used to make lakes and rivers safe for human use.

Rainwater seeping into the soil carries harmful chemicals such as fertilizers and pesticides into groundwater supplies. It stays there for thousands of years. Groundwater supplies provide many people with water for use in their homes. Farmers also use underground supplies to water their crops.

There are ways to conserve water and to improve water quality. For example, in

Some desert landscaping uses native plants instead of grass and trees. ▼

many states, factories must remove harmful chemicals from their waste water. In some places, used motor oil is recycled into new products. And people everywhere can conserve water by using washing machines and toilets that don't need much water. People in arid places can also landscape with native plants instead of grasses and trees that need a lot of water.

✔ **How do harmful chemicals on the land get into groundwater?**

Summary

In the water cycle, water on Earth's surface evaporates into the atmosphere. There it condenses into cloud droplets and then falls back to Earth as precipitation. Plants and animals return water to the environment through transpiration and respiration. Fresh water is a limited resource that people need to conserve and keep clean.

Review

1. What is the process by which liquid water becomes water vapor?
2. What is the process by which water vapor becomes cloud droplets?
3. Where is most of Earth's fresh water?
4. **Critical Thinking** What do you think causes dew to form on plant leaves during a cool night?
5. **Test Prep** About how much of all the fresh water on Earth can be used by people and other land organisms?
   A less than 1 percent
   B more than 10 percent
   C more than 97 percent
   D 100 percent

LINKS

MATH LINK

Compare Numbers An average person uses about 60 gallons of water a day. Calculate how much water a person uses in a month (30 days) and in a year (365 days). How much would a family of four people use in a year?

WRITING LINK

Informative Writing—Business Letter The United States government has passed laws to improve the quality of the nation's water. Find out about the Clean Drinking Water Act or other laws that protect surface water and groundwater. Draft a letter to the Environmental Protection Agency or to your representative to Congress, asking for information about these laws.

LITERATURE LINK

A Drop of Water by Walter Wick (Scholastic, 1998). Check out this book or *Squishy, Misty, Damp and Muddy: The In-Between World of Wetlands* by Molly Cone (Sierra, 1997). Learn about the importance of water and wetlands.

TECHNOLOGY LINK

Learn more about the water cycle and water treatment by viewing *Natural Water Treatment* on the **Harcourt Science Newsroom Video.**

WETLANDS WITH A PURPOSE

Wetlands are among the most productive ecosystems on Earth. Many kinds of organisms—fish, birds, reptiles, amphibians, insects, and mammals—find food and shelter in wetlands.

What Wetlands Do

In addition to providing habitats for wildlife, wetlands improve water quality. Aquatic plants and microorganisms that live on the plants filter waste materials and pollutants from the water.

Scientists are combining technology with ecology to build artificial wetlands to treat wastewater. An artificial wetland is a wetland with a purpose. Over 500 communities in the United States have already built artificial wetlands to treat sewage effluent (wastewater) and storm runoff.

Technology Imitates Nature

Artificial wetlands are designed to do what natural wetland ecosystems do. The processes are carried out by water, plants, animals, microorganisms, sun, soil, and air working together. What happens is that microorganisms, such as the bacteria and fungi in the soil and on the plants, change organic wastes into nutrients that plants can use. The plants take in materials such as nitrogen and phosphorus from the wastewater.

The Show Low wetland in northeastern Arizona was one of the first artificial wetlands in the country. In 1979 the U.S. Forest Service, the Arizona Fish and Game Commission, and Show Low city officials teamed up to build the wetland. Wastewater was pumped into a natural low area, making Pintail Lake. Then 14 small islands were built

Great blue heron chicks

An artificial wetland

in the lake to attract water birds. The islands and the shoreline were seeded with wetland plants, such as cattails, water grass, duckweed, and bulrushes. In the following years, several more marshes and lakes were made. Now the wetlands complex covers about 81 hectares (200 acres) and receives 5.37 million liters (about 1.42 million gallons) of wastewater daily. Instead of being released into a nearby river, the water stays in the treatment area until it evaporates.

Why Build Wetlands?

Artificial wetlands are very efficient at removing pollutants from municipal, agricultural, and industrial wastewater at little or no cost. It takes less energy, fewer supplies, and far fewer people to run an artificial wetland than it does to run a conventional water treatment plant.

Artificial wetlands are an example of human technology working with natural processes. In addition to treating wastewater, artificial wetlands provide habitats for wildlife and an environment in which people can enjoy and explore nature.

THINK ABOUT IT

1. For what purposes are wetlands built?
2. How do artificial wetlands combine technology with natural processes?

CAREERS
HEAVY-MACHINE OPERATOR

What They Do Heavy-machine operators drive earth-moving and construction machines, such as road scrapers, cranes, forklifts, bulldozers, and front-end loaders.

Education and Training People wishing to become heavy-machine operators may attend special trade schools to learn the basics of how to drive and operate the machinery. They also need on-the-job training and experience.

WEB LINK
For Science and Technology updates, visit the Harcourt Internet site.
www.harcourtschool.com

Marjory Stoneman Douglas

CONSERVATIONIST

"There are no other Everglades in the world. It is a river of grass."

While others saw in the Everglades nothing but a marshy wasteland, Marjory Stoneman Douglas saw "the simplicity, the diversity, the related harmony of the forms of life they enclose." Ms. Douglas began observing the Everglades as a reporter for the Miami Herald in 1919. At that time most people believed that the Everglades were a problem to be overcome in the path of development. Ms. Douglas, however, discovered a thriving ecosystem in the Everglades, a vast, shallow "river of grass" that flows south from Florida's Lake Okeechobee to the Gulf of Mexico.

Ms. Douglas became a leader among those working to save the Everglades. She wanted the government to establish an Everglades National Park. That dream was realized in 1947, the same year Ms. Douglas's book *The Everglades: River of Grass* was published. In 1970 Ms. Douglas founded an organization called Friends of the Everglades, which includes research scientists, engineers, and other citizens. This group was able to prevent the construction of an airport in the Everglades.

Following Ms. Douglas's death in 1998 at the age of 108, John Flicker, president of the National Audubon Society, said, "Marjory Stoneman Douglas showed us that the pen is truly mightier than the sword, and the bulldozer, and the excavator. She introduced the nation and the world to the wonder of an environment overlooked and misunderstood, [and she] stood against formidable forces intent upon destroying this irreplaceable national treasure. She showed us that one person can change the world."

THINK ABOUT IT

1. Why do you think people considered the Everglades a problem to be overcome?
2. Why was action to save the Everglades necessary?

THE CARBON CYCLE

Where can you find carbon?

Materials

- candle
- match
- aluminum pie pan
- white paper
- charcoal
- pencil
- hand lens

Procedure

1 Your teacher or another adult will light the candle and hold it under the aluminum pie pan for a few seconds.

2 Observe the black soot that forms on the pan.

3 After the pan cools, use your finger to scrape off some of the soot. Wipe your finger on the white paper.

4 Now rub the charcoal on the paper. Then make several marks on the paper with the pencil.

5 Using the hand lens, compare the materials on the paper.

Draw Conclusions

What material is in the soot, the charcoal, and the pencil? How did this material become part of each? Where else can you find this material?

THE WATER CYCLE

What are the parts of the water cycle?

Materials

- safety goggles
- 500-mL beaker
- water
- hot plate
- hot pad
- tongs
- glass plate

Procedure

1 **CAUTION** **Put on the safety goggles.** Put about 400 mL of water in the beaker.

2 Heat the beaker on the hot plate until the water starts to boil.

3 Using the hot pad and the tongs, hold the glass plate above the beaker to catch the steam.

4 Observe the water drops that form on the glass plate and fall back into the beaker.

Draw Conclusions

Where in the model were evaporation, condensation, and precipitation taking place? Heat from the hot plate caused the water to boil. What heat source causes evaporation in nature?

Vocabulary Review

Use the terms below to complete the sentences. The page numbers in ( ) tell you where to look in the chapter if you need help.

nitrogen cycle (B7)

carbon–oxygen cycle (B8)

respiration (B8)

water cycle (B14)

evaporation (B14)

condensation (B14)

precipitation (B15)

transpiration (B15)

1. Plants give off water from their stomata in a process called _____.

2. Ammonia is a usable form of an atmospheric gas that bacteria in the soil fix as part of the _____.

3. _____ such as rain, snow, and sleet is part of the _____.

4. As part of the _____, plants use carbon dioxide and give off oxygen into the atmosphere. Photosynthesis and _____ are important processes in this cycle.

5. Cold temperatures high in the atmosphere cause the _____ of water vapor.

6. After the _____ of liquid water on Earth's surface, water vapor rises into the atmosphere.

Connect Concepts

Fill in the concept map using terms from the Word Bank.

condense   **evaporate**

precipitation   **water vapor**

clouds

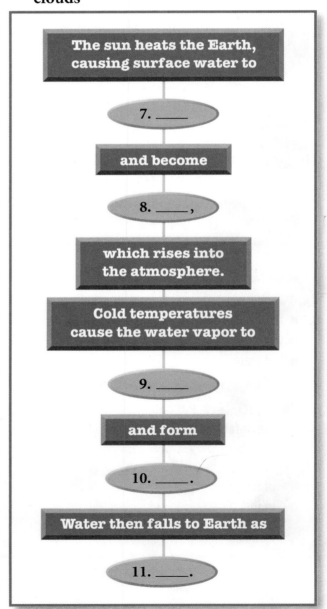

The sun heats the Earth, causing surface water to

7. _____

and become

8. _____,

which rises into the atmosphere.

Cold temperatures cause the water vapor to

9. _____

and form

10. _____.

Water then falls to Earth as

11. _____.

Check Understanding

Write the letter of the best choice.

12. The environment stores many materials. The atmosphere stores a lot of —
    A nitrogen gas   C water vapor
    B oxygen   D carbon dioxide

13. When nitrogen is fixed, it is —
    F dissolved in water
    G removed from lightning
    H changed into a usable form
    J made into a protein

14. Most of the oxygen in the air comes from photosynthesis in —
    A rain forests   C the soil
    B the oceans   D lakes and rivers

15. Fuels contain mostly —
    F fixed nitrogen   H bacteria
    G carbon   J gases

16. What human activity does **NOT** cause an increase in the amount of carbon dioxide in the atmosphere?
    A cutting down trees
    B burning fuels
    C planting trees
    D none of the above

17. Where is most of the fresh water on Earth?
    F lakes   H rivers
    G glaciers   J oceans

18. Plants give off water during —
    A transpiration   C condensation
    B respiration   D evaporation

19. Most nitrogen is fixed by —
    F lightning   H bacteria
    G rocks   J water

Critical Thinking

20. If a region's forests are cut down, do you think the amount of rainfall in that region will increase or decrease? Explain your answer.

21. Explain how buying a car that gets good gas mileage might reduce the amount of carbon dioxide that is added to the atmosphere.

22. How might solar-powered buildings and cars reduce the amount of carbon dioxide that is added to the atmosphere?

Process Skills Review

23. You know that materials such as water, nitrogen, carbon dioxide, and oxygen cycle through the environment. Based on what you know, what can you **predict** about supplies of fuels in the future? Are fuels cycled like water and nitrogen, and therefore unlimited in supply, or is their supply limited?

24. How can you **infer** that some rainwater evaporates after a storm?

Performance Assessment

Water Cycle Art

Make a mural or poster that traces a drop of water through the water cycle. Include how long the drop of water stays in each stage of the cycle. For example, it might stay 10 years in a lake, 12 days in a cloud, and so on. Label each part of the cycle.

2 Living Things Interact

Vocabulary Preview

individual
population
community
ecosystem
habitat
niche
producer
consumer
food chain
decomposer
food web
energy pyramid
competition
symbiosis
instinct
learned behavior
exotic
extinct
endangered
threatened

When poet John Donne wrote "No man is an island," he was talking about how people need and depend on other people. In fact, almost every living thing on Earth needs and depends on other living things. We are all part of the biosphere, Earth's life zone.

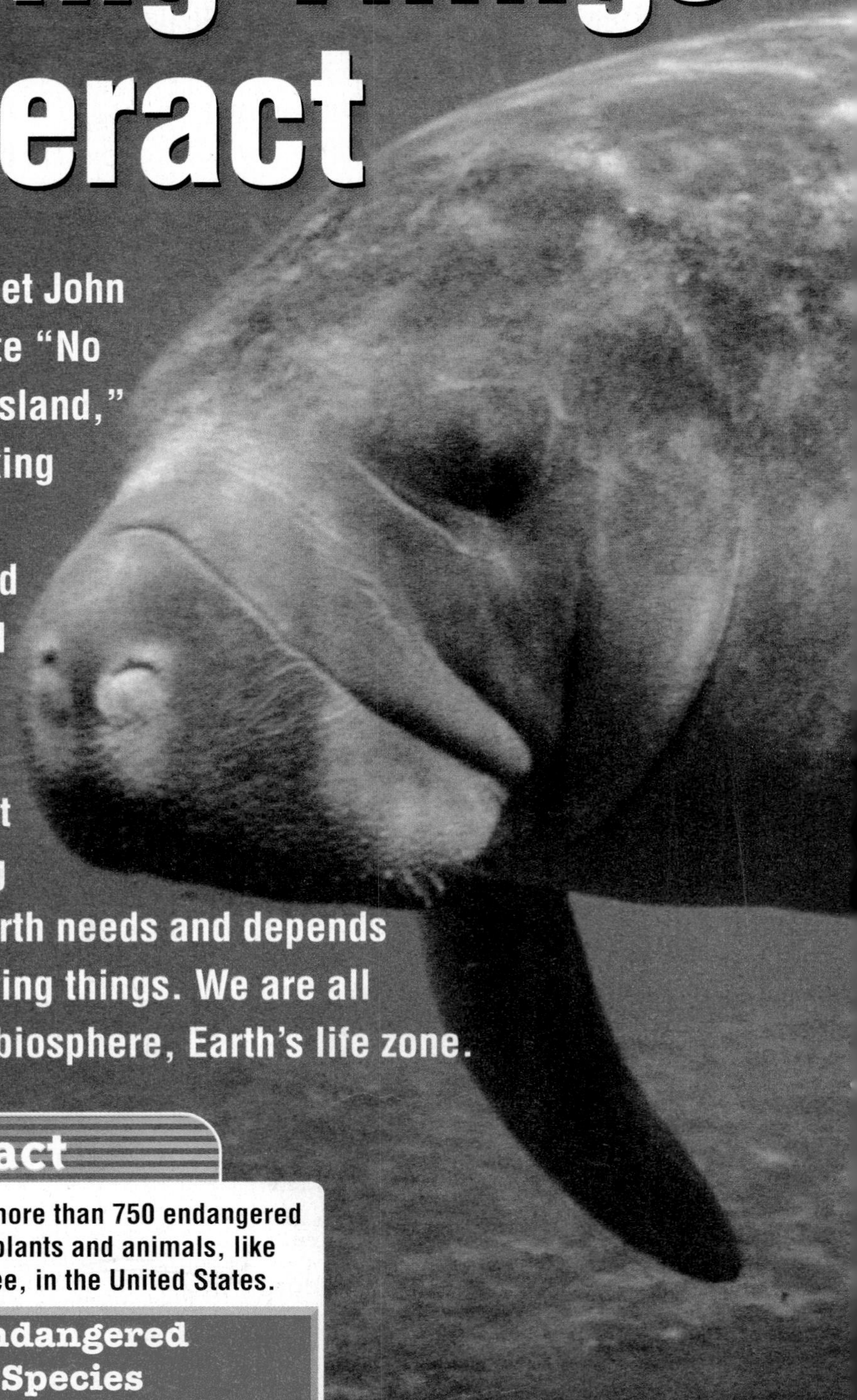

Fast Fact

There are more than 750 endangered species of plants and animals, like this manatee, in the United States.

Endangered Species

Type	Number
Mammals	55
Birds	74
Fish	65
Other animals	126
Plants	434

Most islands would have no plants or animals if they didn't arrive from other places. For example, the islands of Hawai'i are the most isolated islands on Earth. The native plants and animals that live there somehow reached the islands from the mainland of Central America.

In 1859 a settler released a few rabbits in Australia. Within a few years, millions of rabbits were competing for food with native birds and mammals. Although the rabbits have done well, some of these native Australian animals are now extinct.

What Are Ecosystems?

In this lesson, you can . . .

 INVESTIGATE a local environment.

 LEARN ABOUT how organisms live together in an ecosystem.

 LINK to math, writing, literature, and technology.

Prairie dogs live in large groups, called colonies. They feed on prairie plants.

INVESTIGATE

The Local Environment

Activity Purpose All living organisms interact with one another and with their environment. The environment includes all the nonliving things in an area, such as weather, soil, and water. In this investigation you will **observe** a local environment and note the interactions that occur in that environment.

Materials

- garden gloves
- meterstick
- 4 wooden stakes
- string
- hand lens
- aluminum pan
- wet paper towels
- garden trowel
- toothpick

CAUTION

Activity Procedure

1 **CAUTION** **Wear garden gloves to protect your hands.** Your teacher will send you to a grassy or lightly wooded area near your school. Once you are there, use the meterstick to **measure** an area of ground that is 1 m² (1 m × 1 m). Push a stake into each corner of the plot. Tie the string around the stakes. (Picture A)

2 Before observing the plot, **predict** what living organisms and nonliving things you might find in this environment. **Record** your prediction.

3 **Observe** the plot carefully. Use the hand lens to look for small things in the plot. **Record** your observations by making lists of the living organisms and the nonliving things in this environment.

4 Sit back and continue to **observe** the plot for a while. Look for living organisms, such as insects, interacting with other organisms or with the environment. Describe and **record** any interactions you observe.

5 Put wet paper towels in the aluminum pan, and use the garden trowel to scoop some soil onto them. Use a toothpick to sift through the soil. Be careful not to injure any living organisms with the toothpick. (Picture B)

6 **Record** what you **observe**, especially any interactions. Then return the soil to the plot of ground.

Picture A

Picture B

Draw Conclusions

1. How did what you **predicted** compare with what you **observed**?

2. What did you **observe** that showed living organisms interacting with one another or with the environment?

3. **Scientists at Work** Scientists often use prior knowledge to **predict** what they might find or what might happen. What prior knowledge did you use to predict what you would find in the plot of ground?

Investigate Further Sometimes you can **hypothesize** what interactions are occurring in an environment by **observing** what's in that environment. Choose an environment near your home or school. Observe what kinds of organisms live there, and hypothesize how they interact with one another and with the environment. Then **plan and conduct a simple investigation** to test your hypothesis.

Process Skill Tip

Scientists use what they already know to **predict** what they might find or what might happen. Careful observation also helps make a prediction more than a guess.

Ecosystems

Organisms and Their Environment

FIND OUT

• **about the parts of an ecosystem**

• **how the environment affects living organisms in an ecosystem**

VOCABULARY

individual
population
community
ecosystem
habitat
niche

The living organisms you observed in the investigation may stay in that small plot of land as long as the physical environment provides everything they need to survive. The physical environment includes all the nonliving things in an area, such as soil, weather, landforms, air, and water.

A single organism in an environment is called an **individual**. One grasshopper in a field is an individual. Individuals of the same kind living in the same environment make up a **population**. All the grasshoppers in a field are the grasshopper population. All the populations of organisms living together in an environment make up a **community**. A community may include many different populations. Each community interacts with its physical environment. Together, a community and its physical environment make up an **ecosystem**.

✔ **What are the two parts of an ecosystem?**

An individual caribou (KAR•uh•boo) (left) is part of a caribou population (right). Many plant and animal populations make up a community. The community interacts with the environment to make an ecosystem.

Habitats and Niches

Every population has a place where it lives in an ecosystem. This is its **habitat**. Think of a habitat as a neighborhood, and think of a community as the residents of that neighborhood. You might spot a golden eagle on a rocky mountain slope or near an open field that has tall trees around it. These areas are part of the golden eagle's habitat.

Many different populations can share a habitat. But each population has a certain role, or **niche** (NICH), in its habitat. For example, during the day eagles soar high above open ground, hunting for small animals such as mice. Great horned owls share the golden eagle's habitat, and they also hunt mice. But owls hunt at night. Because of their different hunting habits, golden eagles and great horned owls have different niches in the same habitat.

In a healthy ecosystem, populations are interdependent. That is, they depend on each other for survival. For example, great horned owls eat mice, which may eat the seeds of one type of plant. Since owls help keep the mouse population from getting too large, the plant population never dies out. In a similar way, the mice control the size of the owl population. If there are too many owls and not enough mice for them to eat, some of the owls will die.

In addition, the interactions of plants and animals help keep the balance of carbon dioxide and oxygen in the atmosphere. Plants and animals also give off water. This is an important part of the water cycle.

✔ **What is a niche?**

Red fox

Ground squirrel

B29

Limiting Factors

The environment largely determines what type of ecosystem will develop in an area. Soil conditions, temperature, and rainfall help determine what plants will grow. Cactus plants, for example, have adaptations for living in desert conditions. A desert environment has very little rain, and much of it drains away quickly in the sandy soil. But the shallow roots of cactus plants take in water quickly when it is available.

The kinds and numbers of plants in an ecosystem determine what animals will live there. Where there are only a few plants, the populations of animals that depend on plants for food are small.

Caribou, for example, graze on the few plants that grow in the cold Arctic ecosystems. Caribou must space themselves out, moving in small herds, or groups, from place to place to find enough food.

The amount of food—or any limited resource—in an ecosystem affects the size of

Southern Vermont/Brattleboro

■ Precipitation **Month** Temperature

Sandy desert soil has few nutrients and doesn't hold water. High temperatures and little rainfall mean that relatively few plants live in deserts. ▼

▲ The soil of eastern forests has a lot of organic matter. This type of soil holds water well and supports many organisms. Moderate temperatures and plenty of rain allow a variety of plants to grow.

Southern Arizona Tucson

■ Precipitation **Month** Temperature

a population. For example, one area may have enough food to support 100 caribou. Another area of the same size but with fewer plants may be able to support only 50 caribou. The *population density,* or number of animals in a certain area, is greater for the first area than it is for the second.

✓ **What is population density?**

Summary

Individuals of the same species make up a population. Populations of different organisms live together in a community. Communities of organisms together with the physical environment make up an ecosystem. Each organism in a habitat has its own niche. Limiting factors, such as the amount of food, affect population density.

Review

1. What is the relationship of a population to a community?

2. What is an ecosystem?

3. Use the data on page B30. How much warmer is it in June in the southern Arizona desert ecosystem than it is in the forest ecosystem of southern Vermont?

4. **Critical Thinking** The environment determines the ecosystem of an area. What things in the environment where you live determine your local ecosystem?

5. **Test Prep** Nonliving things that affect the organisms living in an ecosystem include weather, landforms, and —

   A habitat

   B niche

   C soil

   D population

LINKS

MATH LINK

Compare Numbers A scientist studied the habitat of a certain spider. She counted the number of spiders living in a field. On one hectare of a sunny, open section, she found 80 spiders. On one hectare of a shady, heavily wooded section, she found 10 spiders. How many times as great was the population density of spiders in the open area compared with the shady area?

WRITING LINK

Informative Writing—Narration Write a narration for a nature video about an ecosystem with which you are familiar. Before you begin your narration, make an outline of the living and nonliving things in the ecosystem.

LITERATURE LINK

What's a Penguin Doing in a Place Like This? by Miriam Schlein (Millbrook, 1998) tells how these interesting animals have adapted to a tropical ecosystem, which is very different from that of Antarctica. Read the book and share with your classmates how penguins came to live in this ecosystem.

GO ONLINE TECHNOLOGY LINK

Learn more about ecosystems by visiting the Harcourt Learning Site. **www.harcourtschool.com**

WELCOME TO THE LEARNING SITE

LESSON 2

How Does Energy Flow Through an Ecosystem?

In this lesson, you can . . .

 INVESTIGATE what eats what in ecosystems.

 LEARN ABOUT how energy is transferred in an ecosystem.

 LINK to math, writing, literature, and technology.

A hawk gets the energy it needs from eating this field mouse.

What Eats What In Ecosystems

Activity Purpose All animals must eat to survive. The energy from food is needed for all life processes. Some animals eat plants, and some eat other animals. Any food energy that isn't used by an animal is stored in its body tissue. When an animal is eaten, this stored energy is passed on to the animal that eats it. In this investigation you will **classify** and **order** organisms to see what eats what in a prairie ecosystem.

Materials

- index cards
- markers
- pushpins
- bulletin board
- yarn

Activity Procedure

1 Your teacher will assign you an organism from a prairie ecosystem. Use an encyclopedia to find out what your organism eats. Then **classify** your organism into one of the following groups:
- plants
- plant-eating animals
- meat-eating animals
- animals that eat both plants and meat
- animals that eat dead organisms

2 Use markers to draw your organism or write its name on an index card.

Picture A

Picture B

3 Your teacher will now assign you to a class team. Each team will have at least one organism from each group listed in Step 1. With your teammates, **order** your team's cards to show what eats what in a prairie ecosystem. (Picture A)

4 When your team's cards are in order, pin them in a line on the bulletin board. Connect the cards with yarn to show what eats what—both within your team's group of organisms and between those of other teams. (Picture B)

Draw Conclusions

1. When your team put its cards in **order**, what kind of organism was first?

2. How would you **classify** the organism that came right after the first organism?

3. **Scientists at Work** When scientists **classify** things that happen in a particular order, it helps them understand how something works. Look again at your team's cards on the bulletin board. Could you classify or order them in any other way to explain what eats what in an ecosystem?

Investigate Further Find out what eats what in another ecosystem. Then make a drawing to show the flow of energy in that ecosystem. Share your drawing with the class.

Process Skill Tip

When you **classify** things, you can better see relationships among them. For example, you may notice that plants are always first in an ecosystem. Seeing the order of the other organisms in an ecosystem helps you figure out each organism's niche.

How Energy Is Transferred in an Ecosystem

Living Things Need Energy

FIND OUT

- how living things get the energy they need
- why energy is lost in the transfer between organisms

VOCABULARY

producer
consumer
food chain
decomposer
food web
energy pyramid

Cells get the energy they need from food. In the investigation you saw that animals eat plants or other organisms to get energy. The sun provides the energy for almost every ecosystem on Earth. Plants, or **producers**, use sunlight to make the food they need from carbon dioxide and water.

As all other organisms do, plants use food energy to grow and reproduce. Any energy not needed is stored in roots, stems, and leaves. All life in an ecosystem depends on producers to capture the energy of the sun, change it into living tissue, and pass it on to other organisms. All other organisms in an ecosystem community must eat to get the energy they need. So the animals in a community are **consumers**.

✓ **Why do all animals in a community depend on producers?**

Food Chain
The organisms in this prairie ecosystem are lined up in the order of what eats what. This is called a *food chain*.

Prairie grasses and wildflowers are the ecosystem's producers.

Grasshoppers eat producers. Grasshoppers are first-level consumers.

Food Chains

Energy is passed through communities by way of food chains. A **food chain** shows how the consumers in an ecosystem are connected to one another according to what they eat. A food chain has several levels. At the base of every food chain are the producers—usually plants. Consumers make up all the other levels. First-level consumers, called *herbivores,* or plant eaters, eat the producers. Second-level consumers, called *carnivores,* or meat eaters, eat first-level consumers. Third-level consumers eat second-level consumers, and so on. Each level of consumer eats organisms from the level below it. There are also consumers, called *omnivores,* that eat both meat and plants. They may be first-, second-, and third-level consumers.

Identifying the organisms and their place in a food chain can help you understand how energy moves through an ecosystem. For example, energy stored in a grass plant may become part of a grasshopper's body. The grasshopper uses some of this energy and stores the rest.

If a snake eats the grasshopper, it consumes, or uses up, the energy stored in the grasshopper's body. In this way energy moves up through each level of the food chain, from producer to first-level consumer, to second-level consumer, and so on.

Decomposers, such as mushrooms and bacteria, are consumers that break down the tissues of dead organisms. They use some nutrients from the dead tissue as food. What decomposers don't use becomes part of the soil. Soil that has a lot of nutrients helps the ecosystem's producers grow. In this way decomposers connect both ends of a food chain.

✔ **What kind of food does a first-level consumer eat?**

Snakes eat grasshoppers. Snakes are second-level consumers.

Hawks eat snakes. This makes hawks third-level consumers.

Decomposers, such as these mushrooms, get energy from dead organisms.

A Prairie Food Web

A food web shows the relationships between many different food chains in a single ecosystem. Prairie grass, for example, is a producer in several food chains. In one, bison eat the grass. Since few bison are eaten by carnivores, the food chain is short. But prairie grass is also eaten by mice, which in turn are eaten by snakes. And the snakes may be eaten by hawks. A food web shows how organisms may be part of several food chains at the same time. What food chains could you make from these prairie organisms?

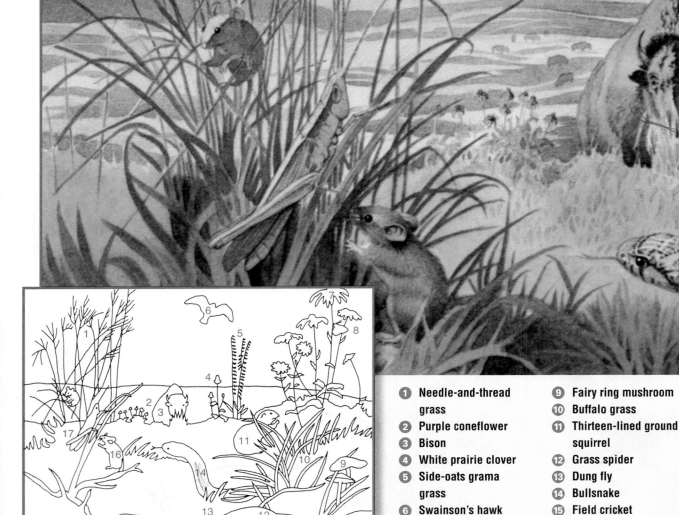

1. Needle-and-thread grass
2. Purple coneflower
3. Bison
4. White prairie clover
5. Side-oats grama grass
6. Swainson's hawk
7. Black-eyed Susan
8. Painted lady butterfly
9. Fairy ring mushroom
10. Buffalo grass
11. Thirteen-lined ground squirrel
12. Grass spider
13. Dung fly
14. Bullsnake
15. Field cricket
16. Western harvest mouse
17. Two-striped grasshopper

Energy Pyramids

In the food chains of most ecosystems, there are many more producers than there are consumers. Producers use about 90 percent of the food energy they make during photosynthesis for their life processes. Only 10 percent of the energy is stored in plant tissue. When a consumer eats the plant tissue, it uses about 90 percent of the plant's stored food energy to stay alive. It stores the other 10 percent in its body tissue. This huge loss of stored food energy occurs at each level in a food chain. An energy pyramid shows the amount of energy available to pass from one level of a food chain to the next.

Remember, only 10 percent of the energy at any level of a food chain is passed on to the next higher level. Since less energy is available to organisms higher up the food chain, there are usually fewer organisms at these levels. High-level consumers, such as wolves, have relatively small populations. There is not enough energy available to support a large population of wolves.

The size of each level of an energy pyramid is related to the sizes of the populations at that level. The producer population is usually the largest, since it provides energy for all consumer levels in the pyramid.

✓ **How much of the food energy that is taken in by an organism is used for its own life processes?**

Energy Pyramid

◀ **Third-level consumers** Hawks are at the top of this energy pyramid. They eat snakes. There are few hawks because most of the energy has been used at lower levels of the pyramid.

hawk

◀ **Second-level consumers** There are far fewer snakes than grasshoppers. This is because grasshoppers use 90 percent of the food energy they get for their own life processes.

snakes

◀ **First-level consumers** Since plants use 90 percent of the food energy they produce, there are fewer grasshoppers than there are grasses and other plants.

grasshoppers

◀ **Producers** Producers, such as grasses and other plants, form the base of an energy pyramid.

grass

▲ Vultures are called *scavengers*. They feed on the bodies of dead animals.

Summary

Producers use sunlight to make their own food energy. Consumers eat other organisms to get energy. A food chain may have several levels of consumers. Food webs show feeding relationships among several food chains. All organisms use most of the food energy they take in for themselves. Only 10 percent of the energy is passed on to organisms in the next higher level of an energy pyramid.

Review

1. In most ecosystems, what kinds of organisms are producers?
2. What benefit do decomposers provide for an ecosystem?
3. What is any organism that eats another organism called?
4. **Critical Thinking** Think of three things you like to eat. What level consumer are you for each of the foods you chose?
5. **Test Prep** Organisms at the bottom of an energy pyramid are always —
   A plant eaters
   B producers
   C hunters
   D scavengers

How Do Organisms Compete and Survive in an Ecosystem?

In this lesson, you can . . .

INVESTIGATE how body color helps animals survive.

LEARN ABOUT the ways in which organisms compete.

LINK to math, writing, literature, and technology.

Body Color

Activity Purpose An animal's physical characteristics, such as its body color, may give it a better chance of survival. For example, the body colors of many animals blend with their background. A green grasshopper in a grassy field may be nearly invisible to hungry snakes. In this investigation you will **gather data** and then **infer** how body color can help animals survive.

Materials

- colored acetate sheets: red, blue, green, yellow
- hole punch
- large green cloth
- clock with second hand

Activity Procedure

1 Copy the table on page B41. Use the hole punch to make 50 pieces from each of the acetate sheets. These colored acetate pieces will stand for insects that a bird is hunting. (Picture A)

2 **Predict** which color would be the easiest to find in grass. Predict which would be the hardest to find. **Record** your predictions.

3 Spread the cloth on the floor. Your teacher will randomly scatter the acetate "insects" over the cloth.

◀ Rattlesnakes eat kangaroo rats, limiting the size of the rat population in this desert ecosystem.

Number of Insects Found				
	Red	Blue	Green	Yellow
Hunt 1				
Hunt 2				
Hunt 3				
Total				

Picture A

4 Each member of the group should kneel at the edge of the cloth. You will each try to pick up as many colored acetate "insects" as you can in 15 seconds. You must pick them up one at a time. (Picture B)

5 Total the number of acetate pieces of each color your group collected. **Record** the data in the table.

6 Put aside the "insects" you collected. Repeat Step 4 two more times. After each 15-second "hunt," **record** the number of acetate pieces of each color your group collected. After the third hunt, total each column.

Picture B

Draw Conclusions

1. Look at the data you **recorded** for each hunt. What color of acetate was collected least? Were the results of each hunt the same, or were they different? Explain.

2. **Compare** the results with what you **predicted**. Do the results match your prediction? Explain.

3. **Scientists at Work** Scientists often **gather data** before they **infer** a relationship between things. Based on the data you gathered, what can you infer about the survival chances of brown-colored insects in areas where grasses and leaves turn brown in the fall?

Investigate Further Many insects have a body shape that allows them to blend in with their background. **Hypothesize** about what body shape might help an insect hide in a dead tree. Then **plan and conduct a simple investigation** to test your hypothesis.

Process Skill Tip

You can better **infer** relationships between things after you **gather data**. When scientists infer a relationship, they often conduct another experiment to gather more data.

Ways in Which Organisms Compete

FIND OUT

- how organisms compete for and share resources
- what symbiosis is
- how instincts and learned behaviors help animals survive

VOCABULARY

competition
symbiosis
instinct
learned behavior

Competition for Limited Resources

Food is a resource animals must have to survive. Because most ecosystems have limited supplies of food and other resources, there may be **competition**, or a contest, among organisms for these resources.

All organisms in a community compete in some way for resources. In the investigation you saw that body color may help some animals survive by making them nearly invisible to *predators*—animals that hunt them. Other animals use patterns of body color, or *camouflage* (KAM•uh•flahzh), to sneak up on *prey*—animals they hunt. Camouflage helps these animals compete for limited food resources. Animals also compete for water and shelter. Plants compete for water and sunlight.

Deer compete with each other for food, especially in winter.

Moray eels compete for shelter— a hole in a coral reef.

In dry months, fish compete for water in a swamp "gator hole."

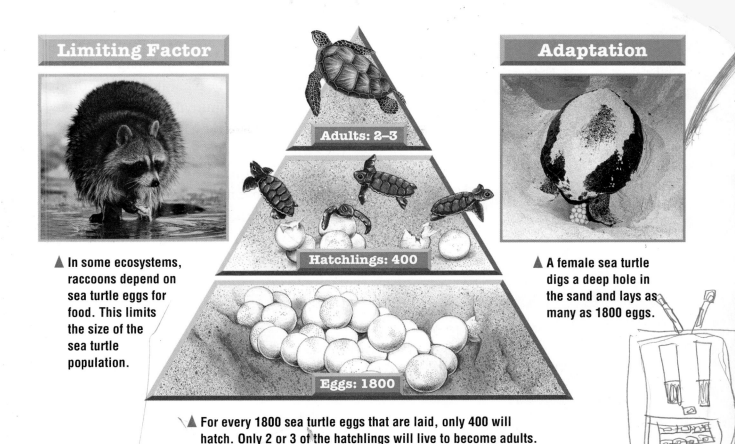

Adults: 2–3

Hatchlings: 400

Eggs: 1800

▲ In some ecosystems, raccoons depend on sea turtle eggs for food. This limits the size of the sea turtle population.

▲ A female sea turtle digs a deep hole in the sand and lays as many as 1800 eggs.

▲ For every 1800 sea turtle eggs that are laid, only 400 will hatch. Only 2 or 3 of the hatchlings will live to become adults.

Every organism has adaptations that help it compete for resources. For example, a cheetah's speed allows it to hunt and capture prey such as zebras and antelopes. Yet cheetahs, too, are limited by competition. Hyenas hunt prey in large packs. A pack of hyenas may chase away a single cheetah feeding on a zebra and then eat the zebra themselves. This adaptation—hunting in packs—helps hyenas compete with cheetahs.

If an organism competes successfully for resources, it is more likely to survive and reproduce. However, a balance usually exists between competing organisms, such as cheetahs and hyenas. Both compete for the same food resource, but each animal wins the contest often enough to survive.

✔ **What are two resources that organisms may compete for?**

Sharing Resources

Sea turtle eggs provide food for raccoons, while newly hatched sea turtles provide food for shorebirds. Although they share a resource, raccoons and shorebirds have different niches in the community.

In some communities animals live together and share resources. For example, many different herbivores eat the plants growing on the African plains. Giraffes eat from the higher branches of trees, antelopes eat from the middle branches, and rhinos eat from the lower branches.

At the same time, zebras and several other kinds of animals graze on the grasses. The reason the animals can all feed together is that they do not directly compete with each other. During a drought, when food is scarce, some animals will have to find other food supplies, or many will die.

Some trees provide food for several kinds of birds. All the birds eat insects, but in different parts of the tree.

The Blackburnian warbler spends more than half its feeding time eating insects at the top of the tree.

The bay-breasted warbler eats insects from the middle of the tree.

Myrtle warblers also eat insects. But they feed near the bottom of the tree.

Resources are shared in many ecosystems, including those in your own neighborhood. A single tree may be a habitat for hundreds of animals. Some animals, such as insects, may eat the leaves or bark of the tree, or they may lay their eggs in or on the tree. Birds may nest near the middle of the tree and eat the insects.

The tree at the left has three different kinds of warblers. Although the birds all feed on insects, they don't compete with each other for food. One kind of warbler feeds only in the top of the tree, while another feeds mainly in the middle branches. The third warbler feeds in the lower branches and along the tree's trunk.

In addition to the warblers, many other animals may find niches in the tree. Owls may sleep all day in the tree's upper branches and then sit on those same branches at night to watch for prey in a nearby field. Woodpeckers looking for insects may make holes in the tree's trunk. Then a squirrel may fill the holes with seeds or pine cones as part of its winter food supply. All of these animals share one resource, the tree, which provides them with food and shelter.

✔ **Why don't warblers compete for food, even though they all eat insects in the same tree?**

Ants herd aphids to fresh leaves where the aphids can feed and the ants can defend them against predators. When an ant rubs an aphid with its antennae, the aphid gives off a sweet juice that the ant eats. ▶

Symbiosis

Different kinds of organisms often live closely together for most or all of their lives. A long-term relationship between different kinds of organisms is called **symbiosis** (sim•be•OH•sis).

Symbiosis may benefit both organisms, or it may benefit one organism but not the other. A relationship where both organisms benefit is called *mutualism*. For example, a small fish called a cleaner fish picks bits of food from between sharks' teeth. The benefit is mutual. The cleaner fish get food, and the sharks get their teeth cleaned.

The relationship between flowers and bees is also an example of mutualism. Flowers produce nectar that bees eat. While the bees feed on the nectar, they pollinate the flowers.

One kind of African tree is protected by a mutual relationship with stinging ants. The ants live in the tree's large, hollow thorns and eat a sweet liquid the tree produces. Whenever another animal lands on or brushes up against the tree, the ants attack and sting the invader to death. The tree provides the ants with food and shelter, while the ants protect the tree.

✔ **What is symbiosis?**

◀ Sea anemones use long tentacles filled with poison to capture prey. Clown fish, however, are not harmed by the poison, so they can live among the anemone's tentacles. The fish attracts prey to the anemone, while the tentacles shelter the clown fish.

▲ Some spiders build webs. Building webs is an instinct. Webs trap insects that the spider eats. Without this instinct, some spiders could not survive.

Instincts and Learned Behaviors

If you have a pet, you're probably familiar with animal behavior. Maybe your dog can "shake hands" or your parrot can say a few words. Wild animals have certain behaviors, too. Most behaviors help animals survive in their communities.

Some behaviors are inherited and some are learned. An **instinct** is a behavior that an organism inherits. An instinct isn't unique to an individual. Instead, it is a behavior shared by an entire population, or by all the males or all the females of a population. Herding aphids, for example, is an instinct for certain populations of ants.

Behaviors for building shelters, finding mates, and hunting prey are usually instinc-tive. Canada geese, for example, fly south for the winter, mate for life, and eat grains and water plants. These behaviors are instinctive. Squirrels instinctively bury acorns and other seeds for their winter food. And birds instinctively build nests. But the nests are not all alike. Some birds weave their nests from twigs, while others hollow out holes in tree trunks. Knowing what kind of nest to build is not an instinct. It is learned.

Many animals show **learned behaviors,** which are behaviors they have learned from their parents, not inherited from them. Lions, for example, are born with the instinct to kill and eat other animals. To survive, however, young lions must learn hunting skills from adult lions. Both the instinct to hunt and the learned behavior, skillful hunting, help the lion survive.

✓ **What is the difference between an instinct and a learned behavior?**

This peregrine falcon is living on the ledge of a tall skyscraper in the middle of New York City. The falcon has learned to survive in the city, and it will teach its young how to survive in this habitat. ▼

Summary

Organisms may compete for limited resources in an ecosystem. The sizes of certain populations are limited by the amount of resources available. Sometimes organisms share resources, and sometimes they form relationships with other organisms. Instincts, which are inherited, and learned behaviors help organisms survive.

Review

1. Why does a female sea turtle lay more than a thousand eggs at a time?

2. How might the number of oak trees in a park affect the number of squirrels that can live there?

3. What resources are sometimes shared by squirrels and certain birds?

4. **Critical Thinking** Think of an animal that lives in your area. What behaviors does it have for survival?

5. **Test Prep** Which of the following is **NOT** a survival instinct for birds?

   A building nests

   B migrating

   C eating insects

   D learning to talk

LINKS

MATH LINK

Compare Numbers Look at the table. By how much did the population grow between 1650 and 1850? By how much will it grow between 1850 and 2050?

Year	Human Population
1650	0.5 billion
1850	1 billion
1930	2 billion
1980	4.5 billion
2050	14 billion (projected)

WRITING LINK

Expressive Writing—Poem Choose an animal you are familiar with, and write a poem about it for your class. Moving from head to tail, begin each line of the poem with the name of a body part of that animal. Then describe how the part helps the animal survive.

LITERATURE LINK

What Do You Do When Something Wants to Eat You? by Steven Jenkins (Houghton Mifflin, 1998) describes how behaviors help animals survive. Read and share what you learn with your class.

TECHNOLOGY LINK

Learn more about animal relationships by visiting the Harcourt Learning Site.
www.harcourtschool.com

WELCOME TO THE LEARNING SITE

What Is Extinction and What Are Its Causes?

In this lesson, you can . . .

INVESTIGATE
vanishing habitats.

LEARN ABOUT
extinction and its causes.

LINK to math,
writing, literature,
and technology.

◀ Hunting and habitat destruction have almost caused
the extinction of wolves in the United States.

INVESTIGATE

Vanishing Habitats

Activity Purpose Changing conditions in
an ecosystem may cause problems for plants and animals. Populations may decline, or become smaller.
They may even disappear. In this investigation you
will **use numbers** to **infer** how loss of habitat could
lead to the decline of animal populations in a South
American rain forest.

Materials

- globe or world map
- calculator
- graph paper
- graphing calculator or computer (optional)

Rain Forest Area and Human Population in Ecuador				
Year	1961	1971	1981	1991
Rain Forest (square km)	173,000	153,000	No data	112,000
Population (in millions)	5.162	7.035	No data	10.782

Activity Procedure

1 Locate Ecuador, a country in South America, on
the globe or world map. (Picture A)

2 Study the table above. It shows the size of
Ecuador's rain forests and the size of its human
population between 1961 and 1991.

3 **Calculate** and **record** the changes in rain-forest
area for each of the periods shown (1961–1971
and 1971–1991). Then calculate and record the
changes in the population size for the same
periods.

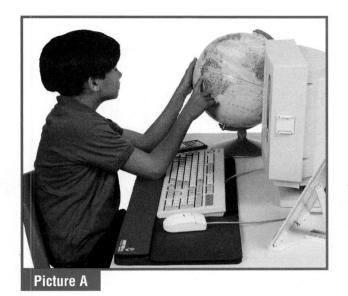

Picture A

Picture B

4 Using graph paper and a pencil, a graphing calculator, or a computer, make a double-bar graph that shows changes in forest area and population size for these periods. (Picture B)

Draw Conclusions

1. **Compare** the two sets of data in the double-bar graph. What relationship, if any, do you **observe** between the growth of the human population and the amount of rain forest in Ecuador?

2. Based on the **data collected**, what can you **infer** about the size of Ecuador's human population and the area of its rain forests in 1981?

3. According to the data, what do you **predict** the size of the rain forests in Ecuador will be in 2001 if the human population increases at the same rate as it has in the past?

4. **Scientists at Work** Scientists often **interpret data** to help them **infer** what may happen. If the size of the rain-forest habitat keeps getting smaller, what can you infer about the populations of animals that live there?

Investigate Further Research the changes in the size of the human population over several decades in your area. Then make a graph of the changes. **Hypothesize** how these changes in the human population might have affected animal populations in your area. **Plan and conduct a simple investigation** to test your hypothesis.

Process Skill Tip

Interpreting data about changes in habitat size can help you **infer** what effects these changes might have on populations living there.

Extinction and Its Causes

FIND OUT

- how changes in the environment may lead to the decline or extinction of populations
- how humans can help endangered populations

VOCABULARY

exotic
extinct
endangered
threatened

Population Decline

You observed in the investigation how an increase in human population may be related to a decrease in the size of an ecosystem. Loss of habitat causes a decline in population numbers of many organisms in a community.

Most declines in populations are caused by human activity. In the United States, hunting led to declines in the populations of bison, alligators, and wolves. Importing nonnative, or **exotic,** organisms into the country has brought in diseases that kill native populations. Building new roads, homes, and businesses also reduces the size of natural habitats, causing declines in many populations.

Natural events that change the environment—such as floods, fires, or droughts—also cause populations to decline. An erupting volcano or a strong hurricane may destroy habitats. A drought may kill producers in a food chain, which then causes consumer populations to decline. However, most natural changes are temporary, and healthy populations usually survive. But that is often not the case with changes caused by human activity.

✔ **Give two reasons why populations decline.**

Ivory is prized in many parts of the world. Even though selling ivory is illegal in every country, some people still kill elephants for their ivory tusks, shown at the right. ▼

Extinction Is Forever

A population of organisms can survive only if there are enough individuals to produce healthy offspring. If there are fewer than 50 individuals, the population is not likely to survive. As a result, some organisms become **extinct**. That is, the last individual in the population dies, and the organism is gone forever.

A number of natural processes cause extinction. Through all of Earth's history, disasters have resulted in the extinction of organisms. The extinction of dinosaurs is probably the best-known example. Natural processes usually cause the extinction of several species every thousand years or so. Today, however, habitat destruction causes the rate of extinction to be about 1000 times faster than normal. Scientists know of at least 50 kinds of birds and 75 kinds of mammals that have become extinct in the past 200 years.

Island organisms are especially in danger of extinction. If an organism lives only on one island, any change to its habitat may cause the organism to die out.

Organisms that have populations spread out over several areas have a better chance of avoiding extinction. Because of the islands' distance from other land areas, more species have become extinct in Hawai'i than in any other state.

For decades people in the United States have been working to reduce extinction. In 1973 Congress passed the Endangered Species Act. The act lists organisms according to how small their populations are.

Organisms listed as **endangered** have populations so small that they are likely to become extinct if steps to save them aren't taken right away. Places like state and national wildlife refuges protect endangered birds, mammals, reptiles, coral reefs, and plants.

Organisms listed as **threatened** are likely to become endangered if they are not protected. Threatened organisms, such as alligators, are protected by strict hunting laws. And some threatened organisms, such as bison, have been brought back into areas where there were once large populations.

✔ **What is the biggest cause of extinction today?**

Extinct, Endangered, and Threatened Animals of the United States

Extinct	Endangered	Threatened
Caribbean monk seal	Jaguarundi	American alligator
Mexican grizzly bear	Ridley's sea turtle	Bald eagle
Passenger pigeon	Florida manatee	California sea otter
Steller's sea cow	Mexican wolf	Peregrine falcon
Carolina parakeet	Whooping crane	Brown pelican
Tacoma pocket gopher	Florida panther	American bison
Arizona cotton rat	American crocodile	Spotted owl
Kansas bog lemming	California condor	Sandhill crane

In the 1800s there were billions of passenger pigeons in the United States. On September 1, 1914, the last one, named Martha, died at the Cincinnati Zoo in Ohio. ►

B51

Success Stories

During the 1940s people began using a poison called DDT to kill insects. It had many harmful effects on the environment that lasted a long time. One effect was the weakening of bald eagles' eggshells. Fewer and fewer offspring hatched, and the bald eagle population began to decline. Bald eagles were listed as endangered in the 1960s. In 1972 the Environmental Protection Agency made the use of DDT illegal. Scientists began raising bald eagles in captivity and releasing them back into the wild. Others worked to save and improve the habitats of bald eagles. Slowly, over many years, the bald eagle population has increased. Although still threatened, the bird that is our national symbol is no longer endangered.

In 1998 another endangered bird, the peregrine falcon, was removed from the endangered list. Like the bald eagle, the peregrine falcon population also declined as a result of DDT use. The falcon was listed as endangered in 1970. By 1975 there were only 324 pairs in the entire country. A program of saving and restoring habitats began. Today there are more than 1600 pairs of peregrine falcons in the wild.

A species that may or may not escape extinction is the California condor. The condor is a large scavenger whose natural habitat is open, hilly areas of southern California. In 1982, when scientists began breeding condors in captivity, only 30 birds were known to exist in the wild. Captive breeding is difficult, but some chicks hatched, grew to adulthood, and were released into the wild. Scientists still aren't sure if the California condor population will recover in its few remaining habitats near the crowded cities of Los Angeles and San Diego.

✔ **What two birds were successfully removed from the endangered list?**

◄ California condor chicks are cared for with a hand puppet that looks like a condor. This helps chicks learn to recognize and trust their own kind instead of humans.

◄ California condors weigh
as much as 45 kg (about
100 lb) and have wing-
spans of about 3 m (10 ft).

Summary

When the last individual dies, an organism is extinct. Extinction occurs naturally, but certain human activities result in a high rate of extinction among the world's plants and animals. An organism is endangered or threatened when its population is so small that it is in danger of becoming extinct. People have saved some organisms from extinction.

Review

1. Name a natural cause of decline in a population.
2. How is a threatened organism different from an endangered one?
3. How many living individuals are there in a population that is extinct?
4. **Critical Thinking** Think of an animal or plant in your state. What changes in the environment could cause it to become threatened or endangered? Give specific examples.
5. **Test Prep** It is impossible for an endangered organism to recover if —
   A its habitat is restored
   B its population is too small
   C hunting is stopped
   D it is bred in captivity

LINKS

MATH LINK

Estimate When peregrine falcons were first listed as endangered in 1975, there were about 325 pairs in the United States. When the birds were removed from the endangered list in 1998, there were about 1600 pairs. Estimate how many times more peregrine falcon breeding pairs there were in 1998 than in 1975.

WRITING LINK

Persuasive Writing—Opinion Should endangered organisms be protected? Are some organisms more important than others? Write an essay giving your opinion on this subject.

LITERATURE LINK

There's Still Time: The Success of the Endangered Species Act by Mark Galan (National Geographic, 1998) and *Back to the Wild* by Dorothy H. Patent (Gulliver, 1998) are two interesting and informative books about endangered organisms. Read one of these books. Then tell your classmates about it.

TECHNOLOGY LINK

Learn more about saving endangered animals by viewing *Yellowstone Wolves* on the **Harcourt Science Newsroom Video.**

The New Zoos

What if you were well fed and had a comfortable home but had nothing to do all day? At first you might really enjoy it, but pretty soon you would get bored. Zoo animals get bored, too, and often they show it. The big cats pace back and forth, and the chimps just loaf around, picking at their food and watching the people.

This chimp is using a twig as a tool to get insects out of this tree.

"Natural" Environments

Zoo animals need enriched environments that not only imitate their natural habitats but also give them the chance to behave as they would in the wild. Animal experts have come up with some clever ideas for keeping zoo animals happier and, as a result, healthier.

In the wild, chimpanzees use twigs to pry termites out of mounds. So the Lowry Park Zoo in Tampa, Florida, built their chimps some artificial termite mounds and filled them with honey and jelly. The chimps spend hours using twigs to scoop out their treats.

On African savannas, giraffes walk many miles each day to find baobab leaves to eat. At Disney's Animal Kingdom in Orlando, Florida, an imaginative system of mechanical baobab trees keeps the animals moving. Artificial branches with leaves spring out of a tree trunk, and the giraffes walk to them to eat. An hour later a branch pops out of another tree some distance away, and the giraffes are on the move again.

This polar bear needs a big pool to stay healthy.

Since lions are hunters, the Animal Kingdom freezes large chunks of meat inside blocks of ice. When a lion pounces on its "prey," the slippery ice block shoots away, and the lion has to chase it down.

Enriched Play

At the Central Park Wildlife Center in New York, Gus the polar bear now swims in a bigger pool. Zoo officials also added some big plastic floats that look like icebergs for Gus to climb on. The floats are always moving because Gus makes waves when he swims, so the bear's environment keeps changing, too.

Orangutans at the National Zoo in Washington, D.C., travel hand over hand just as they do through the trees in the rain forest. Surprisingly, they swing directly over visitors' heads on thick cables 13.5 m (about 45 ft) up in the air. The apes are free to come and go as they please from the Ape House. They cross the open space above a visitors' walkway on their way to a new play center called the Think Tank.

In the enriched environments of these zoos, animals behave more as they would in the wild. Experts hope that more zoos will develop ways to enrich their environments to keep their animals alert, healthy, and happy.

THINK ABOUT IT

1. How do the new zoo environments help meet animals' needs?
2. Suppose you ran a zoo. Make a list of some ways you would keep the animals happy and healthy. Be creative!

CAREERS
ZOO GUIDE

What They Do
Zoo guides take visitors on tours and may also work in school outreach programs. Some guides may also help with animal care and grounds work.

Education and Training
People wishing to be zoo guides need at least a high school diploma and should have taken courses in biology and other sciences. Zoos provide more training in working with the animals, leading tours, and keeping visitors safe.

 WEB LINK
For Science and Technology updates, visit the Harcourt Internet site.
www.harcourtschool.com

Dorothy McClendon
MICROBIOLOGIST

Dorothy McClendon works for the U.S. Army Tank Automotive Command (TACOM) in Warren, Michigan. She's not a soldier, however. She's a microbiologist. A microbiologist studies microorganisms—living things too small to be seen without a microscope—such as fungi and bacteria.

Microorganisms are important. For example, they are found in the digestive systems of most animals, including humans. People have learned how to make microorganisms work for them in many ways, such as in making cheese and in cleaning up oil spills. However, microorganisms can also be harmful to humans. Some cause disease. Others cause foods to spoil and materials to decay.

Ms. McClendon is a specialist known as an industrial microbiologist. She is in charge of research on microorganisms for the army. Her job is to develop ways to keep microorganisms from breaking down fuel oil and other materials the army stores. She is now working on the development of a new fungicide, a chemical that will kill fungi. It must do the job without being harmful to people.

Ms. McClendon was born in Louisiana and moved to Detroit, Michigan, where she became interested in science as a student in high school. She went on to major in biology in college and took advanced science courses at several universities. Before becoming a microbiologist, she was a teacher in Arizona and Arkansas.

THINK ABOUT IT

1. How are some microorganisms harmful to humans?
2. Why might it be difficult to develop a chemical that kills fungi but doesn't harm humans?

FEAST ON THIS!

How does an animal's diet affect the environment?

Materials
- sanitized owl pellet
- forceps
- toothpicks
- hand lens
- black paper
- glue

Procedure
1 Use the forceps and toothpicks to separate the materials in the owl pellet.

2 Sort the materials using the hand lens. Group together bones that look the same.

3 Reconstruct the skeletons on the black paper. When you are satisfied that all the bones are arranged correctly, glue the skeletons to the paper.

Draw Conclusions
How many skeletons did you find in the pellet? If an owl throws up one pellet a day, how many animals does the owl eat in a year? If all the owls were removed from an ecosystem, what would happen to the population of prey animals?

PYRAMIDS

Is lunch like an energy pyramid?

Materials
- food-guide pyramid
- energy pyramid

Procedure
1 Put the food-guide pyramid next to the energy pyramid. Compare them.

2 Look at today's menu from the school cafeteria. See if it also makes a pyramid according to the recommendations of the food-guide pyramid.

Draw Conclusions
How are the energy pyramid and the food-guide pyramid alike? Does the cafeteria menu meet the recommendations of the food-guide pyramid? What level consumers are people?

Vocabulary Review

Use the terms below to complete the sentences. The page numbers in ( ) tell you where to look in the chapter if you need help.

individual
population
community
ecosystem
habitat
niche
producers
consumers
food chain
decomposers

food web
energy pyramid
competition
symbiosis (B45)
instinct
learned behavior
exotic
extinct
endangered
threatened

1. "Shaking hands" and "playing dead" are examples of ____ in dogs.

2. Green plants are ____, or organisms that make their own food.

3. A ____ is the role a population has in its habitat.

4. Dead organisms are broken down by ____.

5. An ____ is a single member of a ____.

6. A population that begins to decline may be listed as ____.

7. An organism is ____ when all individuals are dead.

8. A ____ consists of all the populations of organisms in an ____.

9. A ____ shows the feeding relationships among food chains.

10. Organisms take part in ____ for the limited amount of resources in an ecosystem.

11. An ____ shows the amount of energy available at each level of a food chain.

12. Different kinds of organisms sharing a long-term, close relationship is called ____.

13. A non-native organism brought into a country is called an ____.

14. Organisms that eat other living things to survive are called ____.

15. Migrating south for the winter is an ____ for Canada geese.

16. Producers will always be the first organisms in any ____.

17. An ____ organism, such as a California condor, is at risk of becoming extinct.

18. The prairie is a ____ for animals such as snakes, hawks, bison, and mice.

Connect Concepts

Put the letter of each organism in the correct level of the Energy Pyramid.

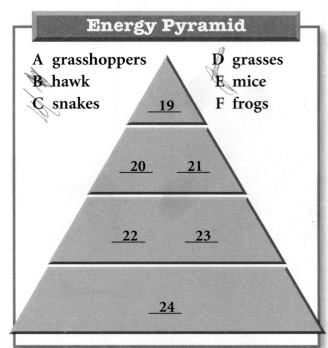

Energy Pyramid

A grasshoppers
B hawk
C snakes

D grasses
E mice
F frogs

19 ____

20 ____   21 ____

22 ____   23 ____

24 ____

Check Understanding

25. When a large volcano erupts, tons of dark ash often stay in the sky for months. If the ash blocks enough sunlight, producers will not be able to —

    A decompose dead organisms

    B perform photosynthesis

    C prey on consumers

    D none of the above

26. Habitat destruction is a major cause of —

    F extinction H instinct

    G competition J symbiosis

27. Organisms at the top of a food chain are predators and —

    A producers C first-level consumers

    B herbivores D carnivores

28. The oxpecker bird stands on the back of an ox and eats insects off the ox's back. Both the bird and the ox benefit. This relationship is called —

    F competition

    G learned behavior

    H parasitism

    J mutualism

29. If humans do not help endangered populations, the organisms are likely to become —

    A instinct C threatened

    B extinct D communities

Critical Thinking

30. Some people place bird feeders in their yards. What effect do you think this has on the bird populations of the local ecosystem?

31. What would be the effect of destroying most or all of the plants in an ecosystem?

32. Birds such as nightingales and mockingbirds imitate the songs of other birds in their environment. Is this behavior an instinct, or is it learned? Explain.

Process Skills Review

33. Wildlife experts know that wolves hunt and eat elk. What would wildlife experts **predict** about the elk population of Yellowstone National Park if all the wolves were killed? Explain.

34. Terns are shorebirds. When one tern's nest is attacked, all the terns in the area gather together and fight the predator. What can you **infer** about how this behavior helps terns survive?

35. A sundew is a green plant that traps and digests live insects. Do you think scientists would **classify** this plant as a consumer or as a producer? Explain.

Performance Assessment

Lunch Line

Choose one kind of food you like to eat, for example, cheeseburgers or pizza. On a sheet of paper, trace each ingredient in the food back to its source. Then make a poster that shows where the ingredients come from.

Biomes

You probably know that part of this country is desert, part is grassland, and part is forest. And you probably know that these areas normally aren't mixed together. Each area developed where favorable conditions for it existed.

Vocabulary Preview

biome
climate zone
intertidal zone
near-shore zone
open-ocean zone
estuary

Fast Fact

Wheat is the most important food crop of the grasslands. If all the wheat produced in the world were put into freight cars, the train would be more than 160,900 km (about 100,000 mi) long.

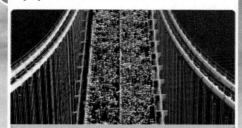
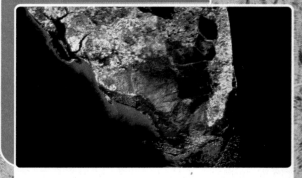

What Are Land Biomes?

In this lesson, you can . . .

INVESTIGATE
biomes and climates.

LEARN ABOUT
Earth's biomes.

LINK to math, writing, social studies, and technology.

Biosphere 2, near Tucson, Arizona, is a research center in which scientists have modeled several North American biomes. ▼

INVESTIGATE

Biomes and Climates

Activity Purpose The plants and animals where you live are adapted to live there. In North America there are six large-scale ecosystems called *biomes*. Each biome has characteristic plants and animals adapted to conditions there. In this investigation you will prepare one map of North American biomes and one of North American *climate zones*.

Climate zones are areas in which the long-term weather patterns are similar. Then you will **compare** the maps and **draw conclusions** about relationships between biomes and climate zones.

Materials

- map of North American climate zones
- map of North American biomes
- markers or colored pencils

Activity Procedure

1. On the map of North American climate zones, color the different climates as shown in the first chart on page B63. (Picture A)

2. On the map of North American biomes, color the biomes as shown in the second chart on page B63.

3. **Compare** the green areas on the two maps. How does the area with a warm, wet climate compare to the area of tropical rain forest? Compare other biomes and climate zones that are colored alike.

Picture A

North American Climate Zones		
Area	**Climate**	**Color**
1	More than 250 cm rain; warm all year	green
2	75–250 cm rain or snow; warm summer, cold winter	purple
3	20–60 cm rain or snow; cool summer, cold winter	blue
4	10–40 cm rain or snow; warm summer, cold winter	orange
5	Less than 10 cm rain; hot summer, cool winter	yellow
6	250 cm snow (25 cm rain); cold all year	brown

Draw Conclusions

1. How do areas on the climate map **compare** to areas shown in the same color on the biome map?

2. **Observe** the maps. If an area is too wet to be a desert but too dry to be a forest, what biome would you expect to find there?

North American Biomes		
Area	**Biome**	**Color**
A	Tropical rain forest	green
B	Deciduous forest	purple
C	Taiga	blue
D	Grassland	orange
E	Desert	yellow
F	Tundra	brown

3. **Order** the biomes from wettest to driest.

4. **Scientists at Work** When scientists **compare** sets of data, they can **draw conclusions** about relationships between the data sets. Conifers are the dominant plants of the taiga. Broad-leaved trees are the dominant plants of the deciduous forest. What conclusions can you draw about the water needs of conifers compared to those of broad-leaved trees?

Investigate Further Use a computer to make a chart showing the climates of the six biomes and a map combining climate zones and biomes.

Process Skill Tip

When scientists **compare** two different sets of data, they can sometimes find relationships between the data sets.

Land Biomes

Earth's Biomes

Suppose you suddenly found yourself in a region far from your home. The first thing you would probably be aware of is the weather. Is it hotter or colder than where you live? Is it wetter or drier? Later you might be aware of the plant and animal life. How is it different from the plant and animal life in your region?

You would be in a new biome. A **biome** is a large-scale ecosystem. Its climate and the plants and animals adapted to living in that climate are what make it different from other biomes. As you saw in the investigation, biomes roughly match up with climate zones. A **climate zone** is a region in which yearly patterns of temperature, rainfall, and the amount of sunlight are

FIND OUT

- about the Earth's biomes
- what determines the organisms of a biome
- how plants and animals are adapted to living in a biome

VOCABULARY

biome
climate zone

The photographs show a little bit of each biome.

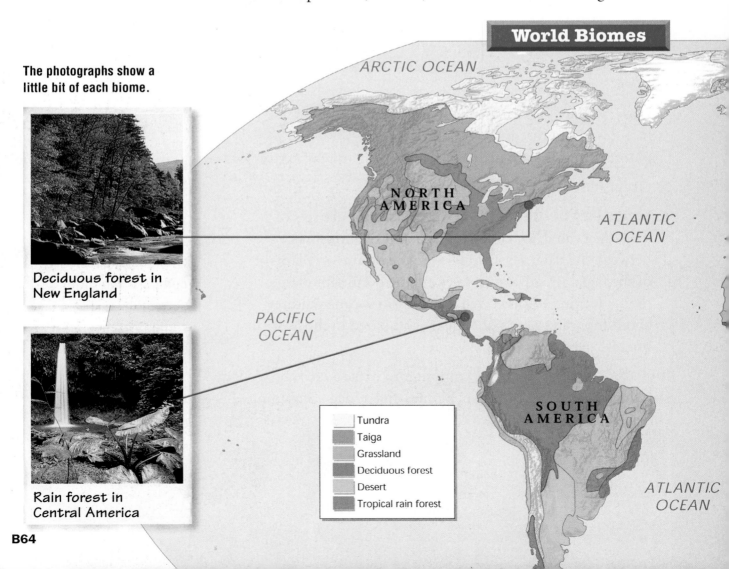

Deciduous forest in New England

Rain forest in Central America

World Biomes

ARCTIC OCEAN

NORTH AMERICA

ATLANTIC OCEAN

PACIFIC OCEAN

SOUTH AMERICA

ATLANTIC OCEAN

- Tundra
- Taiga
- Grassland
- Deciduous forest
- Desert
- Tropical rain forest

similar throughout. Wind patterns, land-forms, and closeness to large bodies of water help determine climate zones.

Earth has six major types of biomes: tropical rain forest, deciduous forest, grassland, desert, taiga (TY•guh), and tundra. Each type of biome occurs in several places on Earth. For example, North America, South America, Africa, Asia, and Australia all have desert biomes. All plants and animals that live in deserts have adaptations for living in dry climates. However, a certain organism may live only in a particular desert biome. For instance, lizards live in both Australian and North American deserts. But the collared lizard lives only in North America, while the frilled lizard lives only in Australia.

Differences also occur within biomes. All the plants and animals living in a biome may have similar adaptations for the climate of that biome. But different areas of the biome may have different plants and animals. One reason for these differences is that climate is not the only factor that affects what lives in a certain place. The type of soil, for example, helps determine which plants will grow well. The plant life, in turn, helps determine the kinds of animals that can live there.

✔ **What biome do you live in?**

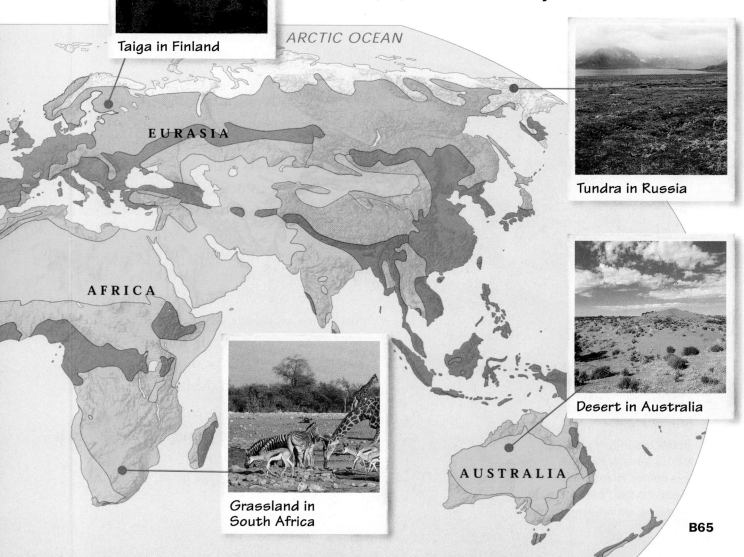

Taiga in Finland

ARCTIC OCEAN

EURASIA

AFRICA

Tundra in Russia

Desert in Australia

AUSTRALIA

Grassland in South Africa

Tropical Rain Forests

You can get an idea of what it feels like to be in a tropical rain forest by walking through a greenhouse. Tropical rain forests are found near the equator. There, Earth receives direct sunlight most of the year, so temperatures are always warm. The climate of tropical rain forests is also very wet. It rains almost every day.

The strong sunlight and warm, wet climate provide ideal growing conditions for a variety of plants. Tropical rain forests have about half of all the different kinds of plants on Earth. This amazing diversity, or variety, of life is one of the characteristics of tropical rain forests.

Producers in a rain forest are found in three layers. The tallest trees form the upper layer. Slightly lower, a second layer of trees forms a canopy, or roof, of leaves and tree branches. Under the canopy are a few shorter trees and many vines, orchids, and ferns. Very few plants live on the rain-forest floor because very little sunlight gets down through the thick canopy.

A tropical rain forest's animal life is just as diverse as its plant life. Many animals spend most of their lives in the branches of the canopy. Reptiles, amphibians, mammals, insects, fish, and birds all do well in a rain forest. The food webs they form are the most varied and complicated of all of the biomes.

✔ **What factors contribute to the diversity of plant and animal life in a tropical rain forest?**

Tucanette

In North America, tropical rain forests occur from southern Mexico through Panama, on many of the islands in the Caribbean Sea, and in Hawai'i.

Deciduous Forests

The forests of New England are famous for their autumn colors. The leaves of many trees turn red, orange, and yellow before they drop. These broad-leaved trees are deciduous—they shed their leaves each year. They are the dominant plants in deciduous forests. This biome occurs where there are moderate temperatures and moderate amounts of rainfall. Every continent except Africa and Antarctica has deciduous forests.

The varying amounts of sunlight Earth's surface receives at different times of the year cause changes of seasons in deciduous forests. The seasonal changes, in turn, cause a yearly cycle of plant growth. Warm temperatures in the spring and summer allow plants to grow and bloom. During the winter, temperatures often fall below freezing. The growing season in deciduous forests lasts about six months.

Several layers of plants can be found in deciduous forests. The tallest trees—oaks, maples, and hickories—form a thin canopy of leaves. Unlike the tropical rain forest, the deciduous forest lets enough sunlight get through the canopy to allow a layer of small trees and shrubs. Mosses, lichens, and ferns grow beneath the shrubs.

The different layers of plants provide a variety of habitats for animals. Many species of insects and birds live in the canopy. Rabbits, skunks, deer, and chipmunks are plant eaters of the forest floor. Toads, salamanders, and snakes also live on the forest floor. Foxes, coyotes, hawks, and a few other small carnivores prey on the herbivores.

✔ **What characteristic of deciduous forest trees is most obvious?**

Whitetail deer

Deciduous forests in North America occur mostly from southeastern Canada through the mountains of northern Georgia and west to the Mississippi River.

Grasslands

Imagine a sea of grass rippling in the wind like ocean waves. No matter which way you turn, you see tall grasses stretching away to the horizon. This is what you might see in the prairies, or grasslands, of North America. The temperatures are moderate, rainfall is light, and various grasses are the dominant plants. Grasslands are found on all continents except Antarctica.

Grasses have several adaptations that help them live without much rain. Their long, slender leaves allow little water loss. Their roots grow just below the surface of the soil, and they spread out to take in much of the rain that does fall. The few trees that grow in grasslands are usually found along streams and rivers, where they can get more water.

A number of small animals, such as rabbits, prairie dogs, gophers, badgers, rats, mice, snakes, and insects, live in grasslands. Herds of larger herbivores, such as deer, pronghorn, and bison, are also found in North American grasslands.

Grasslands play a major role in world agriculture. Thousands of farmers grow wheat, corn, rice, and other grains, all of which are types of grass. These grasses are used to make animal feed, bread, flour, and cereal. North American grasslands produce so much food that they are sometimes called the breadbasket of the world. Grasslands are also used to graze herds of livestock, such as cattle and sheep, which provide most of the animal products people eat.

✔ **How are grasses adapted to the grassland climate?**

Burrowing owl

North American grasslands stretch from central Canada through Texas and into Mexico.

Deserts

If you ever watch old westerns on TV, you know what a desert looks like. And if you visit the Sonoran Desert in Arizona, you will find that it's just as it looks in movies. The sun is always shining, it doesn't rain very often, and the soil and air are both very dry. Because deserts have little or no water, only a few kinds of plants can grow there.

Most deserts are very hot on summer days, but temperatures can drop below freezing on winter nights. Some deserts have no water at all. In others, streams or lakes form after a few heavy rainstorms, but they don't last long. All desert organisms have adaptations to extremes in temperature and very little water.

Desert plants have adaptations that help them conserve water. The cactus plants of North American deserts store water in their thick leaves or stems. Their roots lie close to the surface of the soil, so they can quickly absorb water from the occasional rains. Unlike the cactus, desert bushes such as the mesquite (mes•KEET) and the creosote (KREE•uh•soht) don't store water. Instead, their roots grow up to 15 m (about 50 ft) long to reach underground water.

Desert animals are also adapted to a dry climate. Reptiles, such as snakes and lizards, have tough, scaly skins that help prevent water loss. Some small mammals get all the water they need from the plants they eat. Most desert animals hide during the heat of the day. They come out to hunt for food at night, when it is cooler.

✔ **How are desert organisms adapted to a dry climate?**

Jackrabbit

Deserts in North America reach from the interior of southwestern Canada through northern Mexico.

Taiga

You can travel for miles in the taiga and see nothing but evergreen trees. The taiga is a forest of needle-leaved evergreens that extends in a broad belt across Eurasia and North America. Taiga winters are too long for most deciduous trees to survive. A few deciduous trees do grow in the taiga, but only around lakes and streams.

Evergreens, which include pines, firs, spruces, and hemlocks, are adapted to the taiga. The most important adaptation is their needlelike leaves. A waxy covering protects needles from the cold and limits the amount of water loss. And evergreens don't shed their needles all at once, so they can make food all year.

Unlike deciduous forests, the taiga has only two layers. The trees form an almost solid canopy. The forest floor is always covered with a thick mat of dead, dry needles. Even during a heavy rain, most water is caught and held in the canopy. Mosses and lichens are usually the only plants that grow below the canopy, either on the forest floor or on the trunks of the trees.

Insects, mammals, and birds all live in the taiga. The diversity of life, however, changes from season to season. Mosquito and fly populations increase during the summer months, and insect-eating birds return from the south. Owls, warblers, and woodpeckers live in the taiga year-round. Snowshoe hares, porcupines, and mice also live there year-round. Lynxes, weasels, and wolves prey on these other mammals. Bears may also live in the forest, eating nuts, leaves, and small animals.

✔ **Name two differences between deciduous forests and the taiga.**

Canada lynx

The taiga in North America stretches from Alaska across central Canada to the Atlantic Ocean.

Tundra

The tundra is a rolling plain that spreads across Greenland and the most northern areas of Eurasia and North America. It also covers the southern tip of South America and a small part of Antarctica.

Low temperatures and long winters in the tundra prevent trees from growing. Only smaller plants that send out roots in dense, shallow mats are able to survive on the tundra. Permafrost, a layer of permanently frozen soil just below the surface, is the reason larger plants cannot survive. In the spring, the surface of the ground above the permafrost begins to thaw. A few small plants grow in this layer of muddy, thawed ground. They grow low to the ground, away from the strong, drying winds.

The tundra is a region of dramatic seasonal changes. Because of its distance from the equator, the sun is rarely seen in the fall and winter. In most of the tundra, it disappears below the horizon in the fall and does not rise again for several months. Many animals, such as birds, caribou, and musk ox, migrate into the taiga for the winter. Animals that remain, like the arctic fox and arctic hare, have thick white coats that help them blend in with the snowy landscape.

In contrast, the sun shines all the time in summer. The constant light allows the tundra plants to sprout, grow, and bloom in only a few weeks. Herds of caribou and musk ox return to graze, and birds come back to their summer nesting grounds.

✓ **How are tundra plants adapted to the cold climate?**

Grizzly bear

In North America the tundra is limited to northern Alaska and Canada, and to the higher peaks of the Rocky Mountains.

Comparing Biomes

Starting at the poles, as you move toward the equator, biomes occur in this order: tundra, taiga, deciduous forest, grassland or desert, and tropical rain forest.

Biomes are in this order because the corresponding climate zones occur in this order. At the equator the sun is directly overhead most of the year, and the number of hours of daylight varies only a little. Because the climate zone near the equator receives more solar energy than other zones, it is warmer. It is also wetter, so it provides a climate in which tropical rain forests can grow.

As you move from the equator toward the poles, each climate zone receives a little less energy from the sun. Near the poles, sunlight reaches Earth at a sharp angle during the summer. No sunlight reaches those areas during the winter. Since little solar energy is available in these cold climate zones, tundra develops.

In temperate climate zones, there are different biomes, depending on the amount of water available. Temperate zones near oceans or other large bodies of water may have enough moisture for deciduous forests, while temperate zones farther from water may have only enough moisture for grasslands.

Variations in landforms also affect climate. High elevations, such as the Rocky Mountains, have local climates that result in taiga on their slopes and tundra on their peaks. When the wind forces moist air up over a mountain, the air cools, and any moisture condenses into clouds. The moisture then falls to Earth as rain or snow. By the time the air reaches the side of the

Wai'ale'ale in Hawai'i is the world's wettest place, receiving about 1150 cm (about 450 in.) of rain a year. ▼

The Atacama Desert in northern Chile is the world's driest place. Some areas receive no rain for as long as 20 years at a time. ▼

Amount of Rainfall	
Biome	**Yearly Precipitation**
Tropical rain forests	250 cm (about 100 in.)
Deserts	10 cm (about 4 in.)
Grasslands	10–40 cm (about 4–16 in.)
Deciduous forests	75–250 cm (about 30–100 in.)
Taiga	20–60 cm (about 8–24 in.)
Tundra	25 cm (about 10 in.)

mountain away from the wind, it is very dry. This dry area is called a *rain shadow.* Many deserts occur in the rain shadows of large mountain ranges.

✓ **Why does a certain type of biome occur only within a certain climate zone?**

Summary

The major land biomes are tropical rain forest, deciduous forest, grassland, desert, tundra, and taiga. The climate of each biome is unlike that of any other biome. Climate is affected by the amount of sunlight received, the amount of moisture, and the kinds of landforms. The coldest climate zones are near the poles, and the warmest zone is near the equator. Plants and animals show adaptations to the climate of their particular biome.

Review

1. In what order do biomes occur, from the poles to the equator?

2. How are areas within the same biome alike? How might they differ?

3. How is a tropical rain forest different from the taiga?

4. **Critical Thinking** The map of Earth's major biomes shows sharp borders between different biomes. Would you find this to be true if you traveled from one biome to another? Explain.

5. **Test Prep** The biome with the greatest diversity of plants and animals is the —
   A desert
   B tropical rain forest
   C deciduous forest
   D taiga

LINKS

MATH LINK

Solve Problems Large areas of the world's tropical rain forests are cut down each year. In Brazil alone, about 13,820 km² were cut down in 1990. At that rate, how much will have been cut from 1991 through 2000?

WRITING LINK

Informative Writing—Friendly Letter Write a letter to a relative who lives in a different biome. Describe the biome of your area, and ask the person to describe the biome of his or her area.

SOCIAL STUDIES LINK

Read Maps Work alone or with a partner. Write down one set of coordinates (latitude and longitude). Then locate those coordinates on a map or globe. Write down the name of the continent and the country or the ocean. Then find out what the climate is like and which biome occurs there.

TECHNOLOGY LINK

Learn more about the variety of life in a tropical rain forest by viewing *Rainforest Diversity* on the **Harcourt Science Newsroom Video.**

What Are Water Ecosystems?

In this lesson, you can . . .

 INVESTIGATE life in a pond community.

 LEARN ABOUT three different water ecosystems.

 LINK to math, writing, social studies, and technology.

The green heron is a consumer in several ecosystems. ▽

Life in a Pond Community

Activity Purpose Lakes, rivers, ponds, and oceans are all water ecosystems. In Lesson 1 you learned about the producers and consumers in each land biome. In this investigation you will **observe** some organisms in a pond community and **infer** whether they are producers or consumers.

Materials
- Microslide Viewer
- Microslide set of pond life
- Microslide set of ocean life

Alternate Materials
- pond water
- hand lens
- dropper
- slide
- coverslip
- microscope

Activity Procedure

1 Put the "Pond Life" Microslide in the Microslide Viewer. **Observe** the first photograph, which shows the fish and plants found in a pond. **Record** your observations by making a drawing and writing a short description of these organisms. You may use the information on the Microslide card to help you with your description. (Picture A)

2 The other photographs in the set show microscopic life in a pond. **Observe** each of the organisms. Then **record** your observations by making a drawing and writing a short description of each organism. (Picture B)

3 **Classify** each of the organisms as producer or consumer. **Record** this information on your drawings and in your descriptions.

4 Now put the "Marine Biology" Microslide in the Microslide Viewer. **Observe** each of the organisms, but don't read the information on the Microslide card yet. **Predict** which of the organisms are producers and which are consumers.

5 Now read the information on the Microslide card to see if your predictions were correct.

Picture A

Picture B

Draw Conclusions

1. **Compare** the two sets of organisms. Which pond organism was similar to the coral polyp? Which marine organisms were similar to the algae?

2. In what way were all the producers alike?

3. **Scientists at Work** Scientists often **infer** relationships between organisms after they **observe** them in their natural habitats. Think about your observations of pond life and ocean life. What organisms in a pond community have the same position in a pond food chain as zooplankton has in an ocean food chain?

Investigate Further Now that you have observed photographs of pond organisms, use the materials in the *Alternate Materials* list to **observe** a drop of water from a pond or other water ecosystem. Then **classify** as producers and consumers the organisms you observe. See page R3 for tips on using a microscope.

> ### Process Skill Tip
>
> Before you can **infer** a relationship between two organisms, you need to carefully **observe** the organisms in their natural habitats.

Water Ecosystems

Life in Water

FIND OUT

- about three types of water ecosystems
- about adaptations of plants and animals to the ecosystems in which they live

VOCABULARY

intertidal zone
near-shore zone
open-ocean zone
estuary

Living things are found in almost every body of water on Earth. Although there are many water ecosystems, they can be classified into three main types. Saltwater ecosystems include oceans and seas. Freshwater ecosystems include streams, rivers, lakes, and ponds. There are also *brackish*-water ecosystems—where salt water and fresh water mix.

Just as organisms of the various land biomes are adapted to conditions in their particular ecosystems, so are organisms living in water. Sunlight, for example, can reach to a depth of only about 200 m (about 650 ft). So plants can't grow below this depth. The amount of oxygen in the water is another limiting factor. Oxygen gets into water from the water's contact with air at its surface. In deep water, organisms must have adaptations that allow them to survive with less oxygen.

✓ **What are the three types of water ecosystems?**

Intertidal Zone | Near-shore Zone

Saltwater Ecosystems

Varieties of saltwater ecosystems exist because of differences in sunlight, nutrients in the water, the temperature of the water, and the movement of the water. Organisms in the ocean have adaptations to help them survive in their ecosystems.

At the ocean's edge, waves constantly lap at the shore and tides rise and fall each day. In this area, called the **intertidal zone**, the tide and the churning waves provide a constant supply of oxygen and nutrients that living organisms need. Animals of the intertidal zone, such as starfish, sea urchins, clams, and crabs, can live both in water and in moist sand.

Beyond the breaking waves, the **near-shore zone** extends out to waters that are about 180 m (about 600 ft) deep. Rivers that empty into the ocean provide most of the nutrients for this zone. The water is calm in this zone, and the temperature doesn't change much. Schools of fish, including anchovies, cod, and mackerel, feed on the large numbers of algae growing there. Organisms such as oysters and worms, which live on the ocean floor in this zone, rely on the steady "rain" of dead organisms from above for their food. This is because producers can live only as far down as sunlight reaches.

The **open-ocean zone** includes most of the ocean waters. In this zone the water is very deep, but most organisms live near the surface. Trillions of microscopic algae make up *phytoplankton* (FY•toh•plangk•tuhn), the beginning of the open-ocean food chain. Tiny herbivores, which make up *zooplankton* (ZOH•oh•plangk•tuhn), graze on the algae. Small fish eat the zooplankton and, in turn, are eaten by larger carnivores, such as sharks.

✔ **Name the three ocean zones.**

Open-ocean Zone

Few organisms live in the depths of the open-ocean zone, where it is dark and cold. Note: Diagram not to scale.

0 m–30 m

30 m–200 m

deeper than 200 m

B77

Freshwater Ecosystems

Lakes, ponds, streams, rivers, some marshes, and swamps are all freshwater ecosystems. The plants and animals in these ecosystems are adapted to life in fresh water only. They can't survive in salt water. Fresh- water plants include duckweed, waterlilies, cattails, and many different grasses. There are also many kinds of algae in fresh water. Trout, bass, catfish, frogs, crayfish, and tur- tles are a few of the more common fresh- water animals.

THE INSIDE STORY

Life in a Pond

On a hot summer day, a pond is a busy world of plants and animals that make up many complex food webs.

1 The roots of water plants are in the bottom of the pond.
2 When frogs are tadpoles, they feed on tiny pond plants, but as adults they catch insects.
3 Water striders, whirligig beetles, and mosquito larvae live at the surface of the water.
4 Turtles and small fish, such as bluegills, swim through the pond and feed on minnows and insects.
5 Bottom feeders and burrowing animals, such as snails, worms, and insect larvae, live in the bottom mud.
6 Birds may not live in the pond, but they go there to nest or to find food and water.
7 Microscopic organisms feed on the plants.

Water temperature and the speed at which the water moves, if it moves at all, determine the kinds of organisms that live in a freshwater ecosystem. In streams and rivers, the water moves fast. Fewer plants and animals live in fast-moving water than in still water such as lakes and ponds. The plants and animals that do live in rivers often have adaptations for anchoring themselves to the bottom. Algae attach themselves to rocks. Insects and crayfish often live under rocks.

✔ **What two factors determine the kinds of organisms living in freshwater ecosystems?**

Estuaries

Brackish water is a mixture of fresh water and salt water. Brackish water is usually found in an **estuary**, a place where a freshwater river empties into an ocean. At the mouth of the river, the water contains huge amounts of nutrients and organic matter. They make estuaries the most productive ecosystems on Earth. Salt marshes and mangrove swamps are two types of estuaries.

All estuaries have changing water conditions. At high tide, salty ocean water flows into the estuary. At low tide, estuaries are filled with fresh water or they become exposed, muddy flats. Organisms in estuaries have adaptations that allow them to survive in both fresh water and salt water.

Except for the slow rise and fall of tides, estuary waters are calm and still. The water is always fairly shallow, and sunlight easily reaches the bottom. These factors, along with the large amounts of nutrients, make estuaries ideal habitats for many plants and animals. Two-thirds of all the fish and shellfish harvested along the east coast of the United States depend on estuaries for their

▲ Mangroves grow along the coasts of Florida, Mexico, Central America, and other tropical areas. Their unique root structure provides a sheltered habitat for young fish and shellfish.

survival. Oysters, mussels, and shrimp feed on plants and decaying plant matter. They then become food for fish and birds.

The young of many fish and shellfish also start their lives in the calm, sunlit waters of estuaries. There is plenty of food, and the young animals are safe from large predators that can't live in brackish water.

The importance of estuaries wasn't noticed for many years. Besides their role as a water habitat, they also help prevent

Tall grasses are the main plants in salt marshes. These plants are able to live in brackish water because they get rid of salt through pores in their leaves. ▼

coastal flooding and the erosion of shorelines. Now that people recognize both their beauty and their importance, the remaining estuaries may be saved from fill-and-build practices that have destroyed many of these remarkable ecosystems.

✓ **What adaptations must all estuary organisms have?**

Summary

Water ecosystems occur in fresh water, salt water, and brackish water. Water organisms have adaptations to help them survive in their particular ecosystems. Saltwater ecosystems are the intertidal zone, the near-shore zone, and the open-ocean zone. Freshwater ecosystems occur in rivers, ponds, lakes, streams, some marshes, and swamps. Estuaries are brackish-water ecosystems where rivers empty into oceans.

Review

1. What factors determine the kinds of organisms that can live in a saltwater ecosystem?
2. What might be one adaptation of an organism that lives in a river?
3. Where do many shellfish and ocean fish spend the first part of their lives?
4. **Critical Thinking** Why are estuaries critical to both land and sea?
5. **Test Prep** The ocean zone that is the deepest is the —
   A near-shore zone
   B intertidal zone
   C open-ocean zone
   D estuary

LINKS

MATH LINK

Display Data Use a computer to make a circle graph based on the information below. It shows how much of Earth's water is salt water, ice water, and fresh water.

97 percent—salt water (oceans)
 2 percent—ice (glaciers and icecaps)
 1 percent—fresh water

WRITING LINK

Narrative Writing—Story Write a story about what life might be like in a coastal town. Describe the role that the ocean plays in your life and the lives of the townspeople. Then read your finished story to your classmates.

SOCIAL STUDIES LINK

Mangroves Perhaps the greatest value of mangrove swamps is their role as coastal protectors. But in some parts of the world, people cut mangroves and use the wood for fuel. Find out where mangroves are being destroyed and what is being done to protect them.

GO ONLINE TECHNOLOGY LINK

Learn more about ocean ecosystems by visiting the National Museum of Natural History Internet site.
www.si.edu/harcourt/science

⊛ Smithsonian Institution®

"SEE" FOOD

Scientists are now using a satellite to study ocean food chains. Images from this satellite provide valuable information about microscopic organisms that are the key to life in the oceans.

Links in a Chain

Life in the oceans—like life on land—depends on organisms that use energy from sunlight to produce food. These producers are the first link in the food chains that connect all living things.

In the ocean, the primary producers are floating algae called phytoplankton. In Greek, *phyto* means "plant" and *plankton* means "drifting." Phytoplankton are no bigger than a pinhead. Tiny consumers called zooplankton (drifting animals) eat the phytoplankton. Larger animals, such as shrimp and small fish, eat the zooplankton, adding another link to the ocean food chain. Larger fish eat the smaller ones, and the chain gets longer. The last link includes the ocean's largest predators, such as sharks and killer whales. It also includes humans looking for seafood din-

ners. But all these meat eaters would go hungry without the phytoplankton.

Phytoplankton grow in the warm, sunlit upper layers of the ocean. Changes in wind and weather can change the ocean's currents. The warm waters where phytoplankton grow best can shift location by hundreds of kilometers. When this happens, the animals—including humans who want to find the ocean's best fishing spots—must move.

An Eye in the Sky

Scientists have a new tool to help them find the places where phytoplankton are growing. It's a satellite called SeaWiFS, which stands for Sea-viewing Wide Field Sensor. SeaWiFS orbits more than 640 km (about 400 mi) above Earth. It senses the

A SeaWiFS image

color of ocean water. Ocean water with a healthy growth of phytoplankton is greener than surrounding water. Images from SeaWiFS can also show where pollution is damaging the ocean's food chains.

SeaWiFS surveys the entire planet every 48 hours. It can scan an entire ocean in less than one hour. "What SeaWiFS can see in one minute would take a decade to measure using ships," says a scientist who helped develop the satellite.

SeaWiFS helps scientists keep track of Earth's ocean "gardens." This allows them to help people plan to take advantage of the oceans' living resources without upsetting the balance that keeps them healthy and productive.

Phytoplankton

THINK ABOUT IT

1. Why are phytoplankton important?
2. How do satellites make it easier to observe ocean resources?

CAREERS
ECOLOGIST

What They Do
Ecologists study the relationships between living things, such as phytoplankton, and their environments.

Education and Training
People wishing to become ecologists should study subjects such as botany, zoology, and chemistry in college. They should also do a lot of research outdoors, where they can see how plants and animals react to changes in their environment.

GO ONLINE

WEB LINK
For Science and Technology updates, visit the Harcourt Internet site.
www.harcourtschool.com

B83

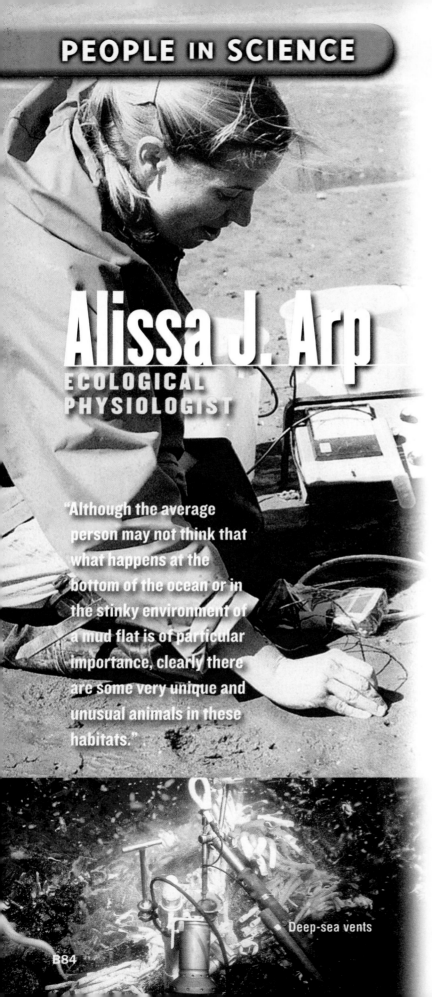

Alissa J. Arp
ECOLOGICAL PHYSIOLOGIST

"Although the average person may not think that what happens at the bottom of the ocean or in the stinky environment of a mud flat is of particular importance, clearly there are some very unique and unusual animals in these habitats."

Deep-sea vents

How can tube worms live in a zone of crushing pressure 7000 meters (about 23,000 ft) below sea level? How do clams live in the untreated sewage released into the ocean by some coastal cities? Why doesn't sulfur, a chemical normally poisonous to animals, kill black abalone? These are questions that Alissa J. Arp tries to answer.

Dr. Arp is an ecological physiologist. She studies marine animals that live under harsh conditions. She tries to learn how these animals can live in toxic chemicals, extremely cold temperatures, and total darkness. Her research takes her from polluted mud flats along the coast to cracks in the crust of the ocean floor. To reach these sea vents, where sulfurous water bubbles out into the near-freezing blackness, she dove in the U.S. Navy's deep-sea submarine, *Sea Cliff.*

Some of Dr. Arp's research may be important for humans. For example, animals who live in toxic chemicals have adaptations to get rid of the poisons. Humans may be able to use some of these animals to clean up polluted environments.

Currently Dr. Arp is a professor of biology and director of the Romberg Tiburon Center for Environmental Studies at San Francisco State University. Dr. Arp uses her position as a professor and research director to inspire young women to consider careers in science.

THINK ABOUT IT

1. How are the animals that Dr. Arp studies able to survive in toxic chemicals?

2. How might Dr. Arp's research be used to help humans living in industrial areas?

LAND BIOMES

What adaptations do animals from land biomes show?

Materials

- terrarium
- bedding
- water bottle
- food
- small animal: hamster, mouse, snake, or lizard

Procedure

❶ Set up the terrarium to meet the needs of the animal.

❷ Observe the animal in this environment for several days.

Draw Conclusions

What needs of the animal did you provide? What adaptations does the animal have for living in a land biome? What is the natural environment of the animal? How does the terrarium compare to the natural environment?

WATER ECOSYSTEMS

What interactions occur in water ecosystems?

Materials

- bucket
- collecting net
- large jar or aquarium
- air pump

Procedure

❶ With an adult, visit a stream or pond in your community.

❷ Use the bucket and the collecting net to scoop up sand, water, water plants, and water animals.

❸ Transfer the materials and organisms to the jar or aquarium.

❹ Set up the air pump, and observe the water ecosystem.

Draw Conclusions

List all the living and nonliving things in the ecosystem. How do the living things interact with each other? How do the living things and nonliving things interact?

Vocabulary Review

Use the terms below to complete the sentences. The page numbers in ( ) tell you where to look in the chapter if you need help.

biome (B64)
climate zone (B64)
intertidal zone (B77)
near-shore zone (B77)
open-ocean zone (B77)
estuaries (B80)

1. The ____ extends out into the ocean to a depth of about 180 m (600 ft).

2. A ____ is defined by its climate and the plants and animals that are adapted to that climate.

3. Most animals that live in the ____ can live both in water and in moist sand.

4. The deepest part of the ocean is the ____.

5. A ____ is a region with similar yearly patterns of temperature, rainfall, and sunlight.

6. ____ occur where fresh water and salt water mix.

Connect Concepts

Complete the chart using the choices below.

- Rivers and streams
- Near-shore zone
- Organisms are adapted to live in rapidly moving water.
- Intertidal zone
- Brackish water
- Estuaries such as saltwater marshes and mangrove swamps
- Many organisms can live both in water and in moist sand.
- In deep water, the lack of oxygen can be a factor.
- Open-ocean zone

Water Ecosystems	Characteristics
Fresh water	
7. ____	8. ____
Lakes and ponds	9. ____
Salt water	
10. ____	11. ____
12. ____	Light reaches much of this zone, allowing plants to grow.
13. ____	Most organisms live close to the surface, where light reaches.
14. ____	Areas where salt water mixes with fresh water
15. ____	Organisms can survive in salt water and fresh water.

Check Understanding

Write the letter of the best choice.

16. The biome that has a frozen layer of ground year-round is the —
    A taiga   C tundra
    B deciduous forest   D polar region

17. A biome is **NOT** characterized by —
    F its plants   H its climate
    G its animals   J its location

18. The biome where you would find the greatest number of tree species is the —
    A deciduous forest   C desert
    B tropical rain forest D grasslands

19. A water ecosystem that has brackish water is —
    F the near-shore zone
    G a river
    H the open-ocean zone
    J a mangrove swamp

20. An example of a freshwater biome is —
    A an estuary   C a pond
    B a taiga   D a tundra

21. Factors that affect water ecosystems include —
    F the amount of sunlight
    G the amount of oxygen
    H the temperature
    J all of the above

Critical Thinking

22. Since the Aswan Dam was built on the Nile River in Egypt, the waters of the Nile no longer reach the sea. How do you think that has affected the estuary at the river's mouth?

23. Deciduous beech and oak trees grow in the lowest regions of the Alps, a mountain range in Europe. Higher up, only conifers such as fir and pine grow. Even higher, tundra is found. What do you think causes this series of biomes?

Process Skills Review

24. Explain what you would need to **observe** in an area to determine which biome it is part of.

25. Write a brief paragraph in which you **compare** the climate and plant and animal life found in a desert and in a tropical rain forest.

Performance Assessment

Biome Mystery

Cut a sheet of paper into about 10 or more pieces. On each piece, write a biome clue or a water ecosystem clue. Write the name of the biome or water ecosystem on the back. Clues might be the name of a plant or animal that lives only in that biome or ecosystem, where on Earth the biome is found, the name of one water ecosystem, and so on. A list of clues might include the following: blue whale (ocean), pond (freshwater ecosystem), biome near the equator (tropical rain forest), and so on. Exchange your collection of clues with a classmate and challenge each other to guess the answers.

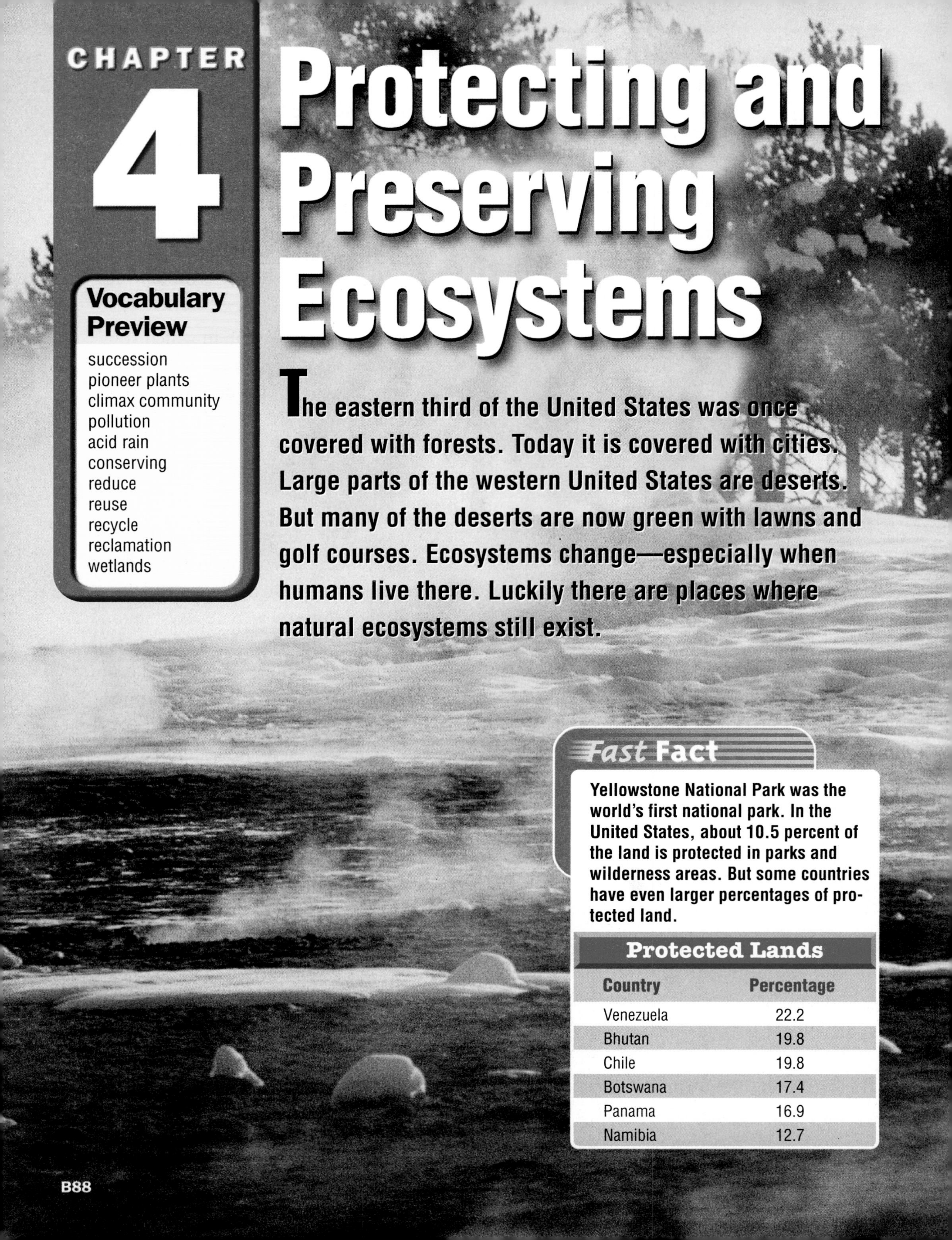

CHAPTER 4

Protecting and Preserving Ecosystems

Vocabulary Preview

succession
pioneer plants
climax community
pollution
acid rain
conserving
reduce
reuse
recycle
reclamation
wetlands

The eastern third of the United States was once covered with forests. Today it is covered with cities. Large parts of the western United States are deserts. But many of the deserts are now green with lawns and golf courses. Ecosystems change—especially when humans live there. Luckily there are places where natural ecosystems still exist.

Fast Fact

Yellowstone National Park was the world's first national park. In the United States, about 10.5 percent of the land is protected in parks and wilderness areas. But some countries have even larger percentages of protected land.

Protected Lands

Country	Percentage
Venezuela	22.2
Bhutan	19.8
Chile	19.8
Botswana	17.4
Panama	16.9
Namibia	12.7

Between 25,000 years ago and 10,000 years ago, huge glaciers covered the northern half of North America. As the ice melted, it left deposits of large rocks and thousands of lakes.

Every year about 60,000 km^2 (23,000 mi^2) of Earth becomes desert. That's an area about the size of West Virginia.

How Do Ecosystems Change Naturally?

In this lesson, you can . . .

INVESTIGATE how a pond changes over time.

LEARN ABOUT how ecosystems change.

LINK to math, writing, art, and technology.

This lone plant growing in a crack in the lava is a pioneer for a new ecosystem. ▽

How a Pond Changes

Activity Purpose In any ecosystem small changes occur every day. Those small changes sometimes lead to big changes over time. In this investigation you will **make a model** of a pond ecosystem. You will **observe** some of the changes that occur in a pond ecosystem over time.

Materials

- plastic dishpan
- potting soil
- water
- duckweed
- birdseed
- camera (optional)

Activity Procedure

1 Spread a layer of potting soil about 5 cm deep in the dishpan. Now bank the soil about 10 cm high around the edges of the dishpan. Leave a low spot, with about 1 cm of soil, in the center of the pan. (Picture A)

2 Slowly pour water into the low area of the pan until the water is about 4 cm deep. You may have to add more water as some of it soaks into the soil. Place some duckweed on the "pond."

3 Sprinkle birdseed over the surface of the soil. Don't worry if some of the seed falls into the water. Do not water the seed. Take a photograph or draw a picture to **record** how your pond looks. Put your pond model in a sunny window. (Picture B)

Picture A

Picture B

4 After three or four days, **measure** and **record** the depth of the water. Take another photograph or draw another picture. Then sprinkle more birdseed over the soil. Water the soil lightly.

5 After three or four more days, **observe** how your pond has changed. **Measure** and **record** the depth of the water. **Compare** your observations with the photographs you took or the pictures you drew.

Draw Conclusions

1. Describe any changes in the pond during the week. How did the depth of the water change?

2. **Compare** the changes in your model with those in a real pond. How are they the same? How are they different?

3. **Scientists at Work** By **observing** the changes that occur when they **use models**, scientists can **infer** changes that might occur in nature. From what you observed in your model, what do you infer might happen to a real pond over time?

Investigate Further An actual pond ecosystem has a greater diversity of plants and animals than your model. **Make a model** that includes a greater variety of living things.

> ### Process Skill Tip
>
> It is difficult to **observe** how an ecosystem changes, since these changes often occur over long periods of time. However, you can **use models** to **infer** changes that might take place.

Natural Succession

Primary Succession

In the investigation you observed the changes that occur in a pond ecosystem. All ecosystems—both water and land—change constantly. Small changes in climate, in soil conditions, or in plant and animal populations can change an ecosystem. Gradual change in an ecosystem—sometimes occurring over thousands of years—is called **succession**.

There are two types of succession. The first is *primary succession*. This type of succession occurs on bare, newly formed land. New land forms in a number of ways. Volcanic islands emerge from the sea. Glaciers melt, uncovering new land. **Pioneer plants** are the first plants to invade a bare area. Their sprouting and growth begins the process of succession. At the edge of a pond, for example, the roots of duckweed trap tiny bits of soil. As the duckweed dies and decays, more matter is added to the soil. Eventually, there is enough soil for a second community of plants, such as reeds and cattails, to take over. Over time the pond ecosystem grows smaller, and a land ecosystem takes its place.

FIND OUT

- **what happens in the stages of succession**
- **what happens to an ecosystem after a natural disaster**

VOCABULARY

succession
pioneer plants
climax community

As a glacier melts, rock that was covered with ice for thousands of years is exposed. ▼

Lichens, shown at the right, and small plants such as fireweed are common pioneer plants on glacier soil.

Glacier Bay, Alaska, is like a giant outdoor laboratory for studying primary succession. For the past 250 years, the glaciers have been melting and receding northward—leaving behind deposits of rock. The rock nearest the glaciers has been exposed for only a few weeks. Walking south—away from the glaciers and toward the bay—is like walking through time. As you walk, you pass through older stages of succession.

The first stage is the pioneer-plant stage. Pioneer organisms such as lichens—combinations of algae and fungi—grow nearest the glacier. As they die, their decaying matter adds nutrients to the ground. After a few years, a thin layer of soil forms and mosses take over. This is the second stage of succession, the *mossy stage.* Bits of organic matter and bird droppings become trapped in the dense moss. They add more nutrients to the slowly deepening soil.

Farther south, soil conditions have continued to improve. Grasses and flowering plants have taken root. A *grassy stage* is the third stage of succession. Farther still, the soil has become deep enough and rich enough to support the growth of alder and willow trees. Alders and willows gradually make the soil more acidic—producing favorable conditions for spruce trees to grow. The tall spruce trees begin to crowd out the alders as you continue south.

A spruce and hemlock forest makes up the **climax community**, the last stage of succession. If there are no disasters, such as volcanoes or fires, a climax community may stay the same for thousands of years. In the northeastern United States, the climax community is a deciduous forest. A prairie is the climax community in areas of the Midwest.

✓ **What are the first and last stages of primary succession?**

Grasses, shrubs, and small trees form transitional communities between a pioneer community and a climax community.

After 250 years, a climax community of spruce and hemlock has developed.

B93

Secondary Succession

On May 18, 1980, Mount St. Helens erupted in Washington state. The eruption was one of the most violent ever recorded in North America. It blanketed the surrounding land with a thick layer of ash and mud. However, *secondary succession*, the return of a damaged ecosystem to its natural climax community, soon began.

Under the ash and the mud were seeds and living roots. Rains washed away some of the ash, allowing the seeds and roots to sprout. Winds blew in more seeds, some of which sprouted and grew. By the summer of 1981, the slopes of the once-barren mountain blazed with pink fireweed flowers. In the fall, the dying fireweed helped to enrich the soil. As soil conditions improved, shrubs began to grow. Today a community of shrubs dominates the area. This community will probably last at least 20 more years. However, fir trees have already started to grow. They are a sign that a climax community of fir and hemlock trees is returning.

Forest fires burned much of Yellowstone National Park in 1988. Fires are another type of natural disaster that changes ecosystems. However, unlike volcanic eruptions, fires actually speed up the process of secondary succession.

▲ Shock waves from the 1980 eruption leveled the fir trees near Mount St. Helens. Secondary succession is already well underway.

Because of fires in Yellowstone National Park, a patchwork of new meadows and a mix of old and young forests exists. This mixture of plant life provides habitats for a variety of animals. ▼

The Yellowstone fires quickly burned the dead leaves and branches on the forest floor, releasing nutrients into the soil. After the fire, meadows of grasses sprouted in the rich soil. After a few years, a forest of lodgepole pines began growing, blocking out sunlight and gradually replacing the meadows. In the shade of the lodgepoles, a new climax community of spruce and fir has already started growing.

✔ **How are some forest fires helpful?**

Summary

The slow change of an ecosystem is called succession. Primary succession occurs on new, barren land. First, hardy pioneer plants grow. Eventually, most ecosystems reach a stable stage, called the climax community. Secondary succession occurs after a natural disaster has damaged an ecosystem.

Review

1. Describe the four stages of succession that occur after a glacier recedes.
2. What might you expect to find on Mount St. Helens 20 years from now?
3. Where would you find the pioneer stage of succession around a pond?
4. **Critical Thinking** How does a community of pioneer plants produce changes that cause its own destruction?
5. **Test Prep** The most stable stage of succession is the —
   A grassy community
   B pioneer stage
   C climax community
   D mossy stage

LINKS

MATH LINK

Organize and Display Data After a glacier recedes, it takes 50 years for thick stands of alders to appear. It takes 120 more years for a dense forest of spruce to replace the alders, and another 80 years for the climax community, a spruce-hemlock forest, to appear. Make a time line, beginning in 1750, of these stages of succession. Include historical events on your time line.

WRITING LINK

Persuasive Writing—Request Some people believe that forest fires in national parks should be put out to save the natural beauty of the parks. Others believe that fires should be allowed to burn because they benefit the natural ecosystems. Write a letter to the head ranger of a nearby national or state park. Ask the ranger to send you information about the fire policy in that park.

ART LINK

Succession Draw a series of pictures showing the stages of succession of abandoned fields in your area. Include in your drawings the plants and animals associated with each stage.

TECHNOLOGY LINK

Learn more about succession by visiting this Internet site.
www.scilinks.org/harcourt

How Do People Change Ecosystems?

In this lesson, you can . . .

INVESTIGATE how chemical fertilizers can affect an ecosystem.

LEARN ABOUT how some human activities affect ecosystems.

LINK to math, writing, art, and technology.

INVESTIGATE

How Chemical Fertilizer Affects a Pond

Activity Purpose Many people use chemical fertilizers on their fields, gardens, and lawns to help plants grow. However, not all of the fertilizer stays where it is put. Rain washes some of it into ponds, lakes, rivers, and streams. In this investigation you will **observe** what happens to pond water when fertilizer is added to it.

Materials

- marker
- 4 jars or cups with lids
- pond water
- liquid fertilizer
- dropper

Activity Procedure

1 Use the marker to label the jars 1, 2, 3, and 4. (Picture A)

2 Fill the jars with pond water.

3 Put 10 drops of liquid fertilizer in Jar 1, 20 drops in Jar 2, and 40 drops in Jar 3. Don't put any fertilizer in Jar 4. (Picture B)

◀ Trash that isn't disposed of properly can be harmful to wildlife.

Picture A

Picture B

4 Put the lids on the jars. Then place the jars in a sunny window.

5 **Observe** the jars every day for two weeks. **Record** your observations.

Draw Conclusions

1. What differences did you **observe** among the jars? Which jar had the most plant growth? Which had the least plant growth? How could you tell?

2. As organisms die and decay, they use up the oxygen in the water. Which cup do you **infer** will eventually have the least oxygen?

3. When water ecosystems are contaminated by fertilizer, fish and other animal populations begin to die off. Why do you think this happens?

4. **Scientists at Work** When scientists **identify and control variables**, they can **observe** the effects of one variable at a time. What variable were you observing the effect of in this investigation? What variables did you control?

Investigate Further Some fertilizers contain additional chemicals that are supposed to kill weeds. **Hypothesize** about the effects of using these chemicals on a lawn. Then **plan and conduct a simple experiment** to test your hypothesis.

How People Change Ecosystems

Damaging Ecosystems

In the investigation you observed the way one human activity—using chemical fertilizers—can change an ecosystem. There are other ways in which people change ecosystems. For example, some of the richest soil in the world is in the midwestern United States and Canada, where there were once grassland ecosystems. At one time there were several kinds of grasses and many different kinds of wildflowers. They supported a large variety of animal populations, including bison, deer, antelope, and prairie chickens. Now fields of corn, wheat, barley, and oats have replaced most of the natural producers. The diversity, or variety, of life has been greatly reduced.

Farming is vital to human survival. People have cultivated fields for thousands of years. But a growing human population increases the demand for food. This demand results in methods of agriculture that include the use of many different chemicals. In addition to fertilizers, pesticides and herbicides are used to

Chemical pesticides are sprayed on crops to kill insects. These pesticides may harm surrounding ecosystems. ▼

This thick green blanket of algae, called an *algal bloom*, was caused by chemical fertilizers running off nearby farmland. ▼

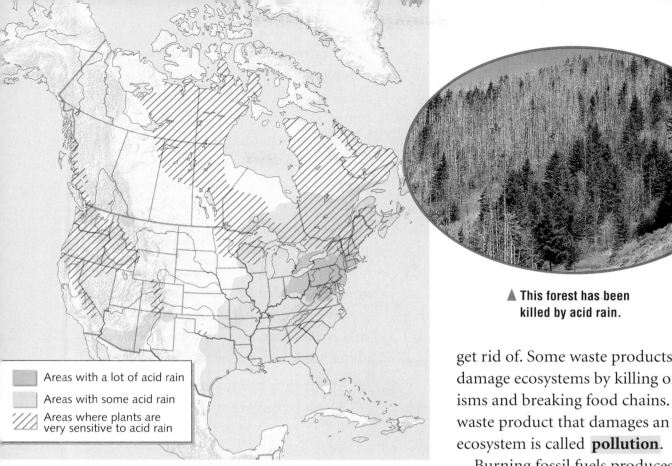

Legend:

■ Areas with a lot of acid rain

□ Areas with some acid rain

▨ Areas where plants are very sensitive to acid rain

▲ Winds can cause acid rain to fall far from the source of the pollution.

▲ This forest has been killed by acid rain.

kill a wide variety of unwanted plant and animal pests. The use of these chemicals can damage ecosystems.

In addition to farming, other human activities damage natural ecosystems. In growing human communities, for example, people build new roads, homes, schools, and shopping centers. New construction damages and often destroys natural habitats.

Obtaining the natural resources needed to make things also damages ecosystems. Many things people use today are made of wood or paper. To make wood and paper products, people cut down trees. Cutting entire forests damages ecosystems and destroys habitats.

Making things also produces wastes. And many wastes are harmful and difficult to get rid of. Some waste products damage ecosystems by killing organisms and breaking food chains. Any waste product that damages an ecosystem is called **pollution**.

Burning fossil fuels produces some of the most damaging pollution—air pollution and acid rain. Energy stations, some factories, and motor vehicles give off gases that include nitrogen oxides and sulfur dioxide. When water vapor in the air mixes with these gases, nitric acid and sulfuric acid form. The acids condense into clouds and fall to Earth as **acid rain**.

Many trees are damaged by acid rain, and some die from it. Acid rain also damages crops and destroys soil. Runoff from acid rain can kill plants and animals in lakes. Scientists estimate that about 4 percent of the lakes in North America are too acidic for fish to live in.

If ecosystems are not damaged too severely, some of them can slowly recover. A cut forest, for example, can become a forest ecosystem again through succession.

✔ **How does the making of things damage ecosystems?**

Catastrophic Changes

Some human activities can cause catastrophic (kat•uh•STRAHF•ik) changes to an ecosystem—changes so great that the ecosystem cannot recover. For example, one way to get rock and mineral resources from the ground is by strip mining. In this process, all the topsoil and overlying rock layers are removed until the resource is reached. Strip mining destroys all the communities and many of the nonliving parts of an ecosystem, such as streams and ponds.

Since 1977, however, the United States has required that all strip-mined areas be restored to their original condition. In most cases the soil is replaced, and forests or grasslands are replanted. In other cases the mine pits are turned into lakes. However, many older strip-mined areas have not been restored.

Catastrophic changes can also occur when highways, subdivisions, and shopping malls are built on small or fragile ecosystems. Large-scale construction projects often destroy habitats completely. Even when they don't, they often change conditions so much that natural communities can't survive. Some kinds of ecosystems, such as wetlands, are in danger of disappearing completely.

It is impossible for humans to be part of an ecosystem and not affect it. But people can live in ways that do less damage to natural ecosystems. You will find out more about some of those ways in Lesson 3.

✔ **What is a catastrophic change to an ecosystem?**

The Kennicott copper mine in Utah is the largest strip mine in the world. ▼

▲ In many areas people drain wetlands to build subdivisions and shopping centers.

Summary

Human activity has a huge effect on natural ecosystems. People need land for homes and natural resources to make things. These activities can damage ecosystems and cause pollution. Damaged ecosystems sometimes recover slowly, but catastrophic changes often destroy them.

Review

1. What human activities damage ecosystems?

2. What is acid rain?

3. Why is it difficult to recover land that has been strip-mined?

4. **Critical Thinking** Why do you think desert ecosystems are rarely affected by catastrophic changes?

5. **Test Prep** Acid rain is **NOT** caused by —

   A cars

   B energy stations

   C factories

   D farming

LINKS

MATH LINK

Compare Numbers Acidity is measured on a scale called a pH scale, with 0 being the most acidic and 14 being the least acidic. Each whole unit of the scale stands for an increase or decrease of ten times in acidity. Order the items in the list below from least acidic to most acidic.

lemon juice	2.3	vinegar	3.3
distilled water	7.0	acid rain	4.3
human blood	7.4	sea water	8.0

WRITING LINK

Informative Writing—Compare and Contrast Think of an ecosystem that has been changed by human activity. Write a paragraph in which you compare and contrast the appearance of the ecosystem before and after the change.

ART LINK

Collage Make a collage of items that you think symbolize our modern lifestyle. Cut photographs out of old magazines, or draw pictures of the items. Include pictures of ecosystems that might be changed to produce the items.

 GO ONLINE

TECHNOLOGY LINK

Learn more about damage to forest ecosystems by visiting the National Air and Space Museum Internet site.
www.si.edu/harcourt/science

 Smithsonian Institution®

How Can People Treat Ecosystems More Wisely?

In this lesson, you can . . .

INVESTIGATE what happens to trash in a landfill.

LEARN ABOUT using resources wisely.

LINK to math, writing, social studies, and technology.

Using beach crossovers is an easy way to treat a fragile ecosystem wisely.

KEEP OFF DUNES

INVESTIGATE

What Happens in a Landfill

Activity Purpose Do you know what happens to your trash once it's picked up? Most of it is taken to a landfill. There it is combined with the trash of everyone else in your community. In this investigation you will **make a model** of a landfill to find out what happens to trash.

Materials

- plastic gloves
- newspaper
- small pieces of trash, such as aluminum foil, tissues, plastic bags, Styrofoam cups, potato peels, bones, and apple cores
- shoe box
- plastic wrap
- potting soil
- tray
- measuring cup
- water
- watering can

CAUTION

Activity Procedure

1. Make a chart listing ten different items of trash. Allow space in your chart to **record** observations you will make later.

2. **CAUTION** **Put on the plastic gloves**. Spread newspaper on your work surface. Choose the ten items of trash listed on your chart to put in the model landfill. Lay the trash on the newspaper. (Picture A)

3. Now prepare the model landfill. First, line the shoe box with plastic wrap. Then put a layer of potting soil on the bottom of the box.

Picture A

Picture B

4 Take the pieces of trash from the newspaper, and place them on top of the soil. Then cover the trash completely with another layer of soil. (Picture B)

5 Set the model landfill on the tray. Use the watering can to sprinkle the soil each day with 50 mL of water.

6 After two weeks, put on plastic gloves and remove the top layer of soil. **Observe** the items of trash, and **record** your observations.

Draw Conclusions

1. Did you **observe** anything starting to decay? What items decayed the most? What items decayed the least?

2. Things that decay are said to be *biodegradable*. What items in your trash are biodegradable?

3. What do you **infer** might eventually happen to trash that is *not* biodegradable?

4. **Scientists at Work** Scientists often **draw conclusions** based on observations made while **using a model**. From your observations of a model landfill, what conclusions can you draw about using paper trash bags instead of plastic trash bags?

Investigate Further **Hypothesize** how quickly trash in landfills would decay if it were all biodegradable. **Plan and conduct a simple experiment** to test your hypothesis.

> **Process Skill Tip**
>
> Observations made while **using a model** can help you **draw conclusions** about real-world situations.

Using Resources Wisely

Reduce, Reuse, and Recycle

FIND OUT

- how to reduce your use of resources and how to recycle or reuse resources
- what landfills are

VOCABULARY

conserving
reduce
reuse
recycle

To help people treat ecosystems more wisely, scientists research and plan ways to protect ecosystems from catastrophic changes. To support these plans, governments pass laws to prevent strip mining, pollution, and overdevelopment. All new cars, for example, must have *catalytic converters,* devices that change some of the poisonous exhaust gases into carbon dioxide and water. New cars must also be more efficient—that is, they need to be able to go farther on less gasoline.

Changing human habits that damage ecosystems is just as important as passing new laws. Everyone can help protect ecosystems by saving, or **conserving**, resources. The three *Rs*— *reduce, reuse,* and *recycle*—are ways of conserving resources.

Reduce means to cut down on the use of resources. For example, appliances like clothes dryers, water heaters, and air

Reducing, reusing, and recycling are three ways to conserve resources and protect ecosystems. ▼

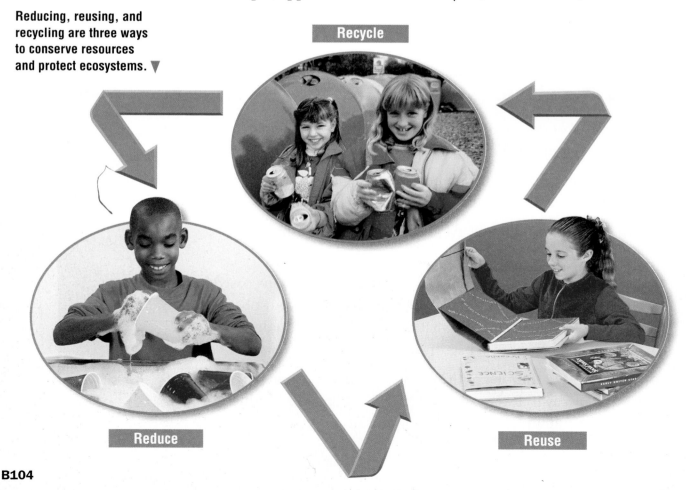

Recycle

Reduce

Reuse

conditioners use huge amounts of electricity. Using them wisely reduces the need for energy resources such as coal. Reducing the need for coal saves ecosystems from being destroyed by strip mining. Using appliances wisely also protects ecosystems by reducing air pollution. The burning of coal to make electricity is one of the main causes of acid rain.

Reuse means not to throw away items that can be used again. For example, cups and plates that can be washed and used again produce less waste than disposable ones. Reusing items also saves the resources needed to make new products.

Reusing also means using items for different purposes. For example, you can wash out milk cartons and juice bottles and use them as planters or bird feeders. You can also give to a resale shop toys or clothes you have outgrown. Buying

used items saves resources, reduces pollution, and protects ecosystems.

Recycle means to recover a resource from an item and to use the recovered resource to make a new item. Many resources can be conserved by recycling. Aluminum, glass, and paper can be ground up or melted down and then used over and over again. Recycling saves energy as well as resources. It takes less energy to make an item out of recycled material than it does to make the same item out of raw resources. Like reducing and reusing, recycling protects ecosystems from damage or destruction.

✓ **What are the three ways of conserving resources and protecting ecosystems?**

Today anyone can help protect ecosystems.

Landfills

What can't be recycled or reused usually goes to a landfill. Years ago, trash was either burned or dumped into a huge hole in the ground. These open dumps attracted birds, rats, and insects. When it rained, water filtered through the trash, carrying harmful chemicals into the groundwater. Today most open dumps have been replaced by landfills like the one shown here.

A landfill starts as a large hole in the ground. Unlike an open dump, the bottom and sides of a landfill are layered with heavy clay soil or plastic sheets. This helps keep harmful liquids from getting into groundwater.

Large trucks haul in the trash. Each layer of trash is flattened. Then it is covered with at least 15 cm (about 6 in.) of soil. This helps keep away insects and other animals.

Summary

Governments have passed many laws to reduce pollution and to protect ecosystems. However, people can also do things to protect ecosystems. For example, they can conserve resources using the three *R*s. That is, people can reduce the use of resources, reuse as many items as possible, and recycle. What cannot be reused or recycled should go to landfills.

Review

1. Explain the three *R*s of conserving resources.

2. What is a landfill?

3. How have cars become less harmful to ecosystems?

4. **Critical Thinking** What can people do to reduce the amount of coal burned to produce electricity?

5. **Test Prep** Catalytic converters —
   A reduce the air pollution from factory smokestacks
   B change some exhaust gases into carbon dioxide and water
   C reduce the amount of carbon dioxide in the air
   D change water into oxygen and carbon dioxide

LINKS

MATH LINK

Solve Problems The average American household throws away about 6.5 kg (14.3 lb) of trash each day. That's 4.5 billion kg (about 10 billion lb) of trash per week for all Americans. How many kilograms of trash does the average family produce each year? How many kilograms of trash are produced by all Americans?

WRITING LINK

Informative Writing—Report Research an environmental "tradeoff," a choice between two actions. For example, which is better for the environment, using disposable baby diapers or using cloth diapers? Cloth diapers don't fill up landfills, but cleaning them uses more water and energy. Report your findings to your class.

SOCIAL STUDIES LINK

Earth Day The first Earth Day was observed in 1970. Interview a parent, an older neighbor, or a teacher to find out how your community has changed since then. Use a tape recorder or video camera to record the interview. Then write a report.

GO ONLINE TECHNOLOGY LINK

Learn more about trash disposal by visiting the Harcourt Learning Site. **www.harcourtschool.com**

WELCOME TO **THE LEARNING SITE**

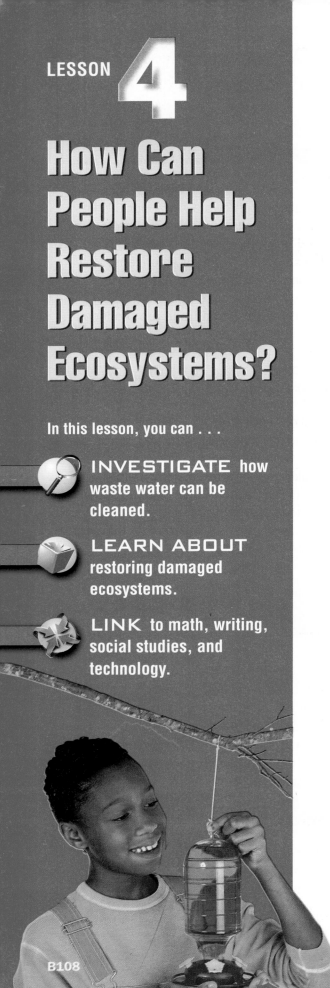

LESSON 4

How Can People Help Restore Damaged Ecosystems?

In this lesson, you can . . .

INVESTIGATE how waste water can be cleaned.

LEARN ABOUT restoring damaged ecosystems.

LINK to math, writing, social studies, and technology.

How Waste Water Can Be Cleaned

Activity Purpose Fifty years ago, most waste water was dumped directly into rivers, lakes, or other large bodies of water. But waste water can cause great damage to ecosystems. It contains pollutants such as harmful organisms and poisonous chemicals. Now waste water from homes and factories is treated before it is released into the environment. Treatment removes pollutants from the water. In this investigation you will **experiment** with a process that filters pollutants from waste water.

Materials

- plastic jar with lid
- spoon
- soil
- water
- paper clip
- 6 paper cups
- marker
- ruler
- gravel
- sand
- charcoal

Activity Procedure

1. Put several spoonfuls of soil in the jar. Then fill the jar with water and put the lid on. (Picture A)

2. Shake the jar for 15 sec. Then put the jar aside for about 5 min. A process called *sedimentation* is taking place in the jar. It is the first step in waste-water treatment. **Observe** the water in the jar. **Record** your observations.

3. Unbend the paper clip. Use it to punch 10 small holes each in the bottoms of 3 paper cups. Using the marker, label the cups *A*, *B*, and *C*.

◀ A simple way to help restore damaged ecosystems is to provide food for some of the animal populations.

B108

Picture A

Picture B

4. Using the spoon, put a 2.5-cm layer of gravel in Cup A. Put a 2.5-cm layer of sand and then a 2.5-cm layer of gravel in Cup B. Put a 2.5-cm layer of charcoal, then a 2.5-cm layer of sand, and finally a 2.5-cm layer of gravel in Cup C. (Picture B)

5. Put each cup with holes inside a cup without holes. Label the outer cups *A, B,* and *C* to match the inner cups. Then carefully pour equal amounts of water from the jar into the inner cups. Try not to shake the jar as you pour. A process called *filtering* is taking place in the cups. It is the second step in waste-water treatment.

6. Separate each set of cups, allowing all the water to drain into the outer cups. **Observe** the water in the outer cups. **Record** your observations.

Draw Conclusions

1. What did you **observe** happening during sedimentation?

2. What combination of materials did the best job of filtering the water?

3. What materials do you **infer** might not be filtered out of waste water?

4. **Scientists at Work** Scientists must **identify and control variables** when they **experiment**. In a real waste-water treatment plant, what variables might affect the filtering process?

Investigate Further **Hypothesize** what filter would best clean water that is "polluted" with food coloring. **Plan and conduct a simple experiment** to test your hypothesis.

Restoring Ecosystems

Rivers and Wetlands

FIND OUT

- how ecosystems are being reclaimed
- what you can do to help restore natural ecosystems

VOCABULARY

reclamation
wetlands

In the investigation you experimented with the best way to filter muddy water. By experimenting on a larger scale, scientists have developed more effective ways to treat waste water. This has helped to restore water ecosystems that had been polluted. In the 1960s, for example, the Hudson River, which flows from the Adirondack Mountains to New York Harbor, was dangerously polluted. Today, all waste water must be treated before being released into the river. The river is much cleaner now, and fish and wildlife populations have increased in size. The Hudson River ecosystem has been restored.

The process of restoring a damaged ecosystem is called **reclamation** (rek•luh•MAY•shuhn). Within the past 20 years, reclamation has occurred in many places. However, restoring most ecosystems takes a long time and a tremendous amount of work. For example, in many freshwater ecosystems, the bodies of fish contain high levels of poisons called PCBs. When carnivores eat these fish, PCBs enter their bodies. And when the fish die and decompose, the PCBs reenter the water. In this way poisons can remain in an ecosystem for many years, passing from one organism to another.

This wetland in California was built to filter waste water. ▼

Sometimes it isn't practical to restore natural ecosystems. The park at the right and the fountain above were once landfills. The lands have been adapted to new useful purposes.

Scientists have only recently learned the importance of saltwater marshes, mangrove swamps, and mud flats. These water ecosystems, called **wetlands**, provide habitats for marine organisms. They also act as natural filters that purify water. But 80 percent of the wetlands in the United States are already gone.

Scientists are now working on ways to protect the remaining wetlands and to restore damaged water ecosystems. The Florida Everglades, a mixture of marshes and mangrove swamps, once covered more than 1.6 million hectares (about 4 million acres). It covers only half that much area today. Since 1983 scientists have been working with the state of Florida and the Save Our Everglades program to help preserve the remaining ecosystem. They have also started buying farmland that was once part of the Everglades. They plan to restore that land to its original condition.

Scientists are also experimenting with ways to replace ecosystems that have already been destroyed. In 1986 the city of Arcata, California, completed construction of an artificial wetland. The wetland is used in the city's waste-water treatment.

Arcata's waste water is treated first by sedimentation and filtration. Then the water flows into two treatment marshes. The marshes contain plants that filter out most of the remaining pollutants. Only after this final filtering does the city's waste water flow into the ocean. Many wetland animals now live in the marshes, making this artificial environment a complete ecosystem.

✓ **Why are wetlands such important ecosystems?**

Your Own Back Yard

Local governments and civic organizations across the country are helping to restore natural ecosystems in schoolyards, public parks, and back yards. In midwestern states, for example, many people are replacing their lawns with grasses and flowers found in the area's original prairie ecosystem. Traditional lawns require the use of fertilizers and pesticides. As you have learned, fertilizers can get into groundwater, and pesticides can kill birds and other animals. Prairie lawns need little attention once they are established. And unlike traditional lawns, prairie lawns attract a wide variety of birds, butterflies, and other wildlife.

What was the natural ecosystem like in the area where you live? Have parts of it been saved or reclaimed? Reclaiming an ecosystem takes a lot of research, money, and time. The first steps in the process of reclamation are to learn about the causes of habitat loss and to investigate ways to restore native plants.

The dogwood, a flowering tree, is the state flower of Virginia. In the spring, the white blossoms cover large areas of Virginia forests. ▼

These students are working at the Atlanta Botanical Garden in Georgia.

But there are many little things that people can do to attract wildlife to an area. Planting a variety of wildflowers and native shrubs will provide food and shelter for birds, butterflies, and other small animals. Building a small pond will attract wildlife searching for water. The pond will also provide a habitat for frogs and insects.

✓ **How can people help to restore ecosystems in their own back yards?**

Summary

Reclamation is the restoring of a damaged ecosystem. Complete reclamation takes years of research and effort. The ecosystems that are still left must first be saved from destruction. Experimenting with new ways to restore ecosystems is also important. Reclaiming ecosystems takes the efforts of many people in an area.

Review

1. Name three types of wetlands.
2. How can research help to restore ecosystems?
3. What can people do to help restore ecosystems?
4. **Critical Thinking** Explain why government action may be needed to save or restore ecosystems.
5. **Test Prep** The recovery of natural ecosystems that have been damaged by human activity is called —
   - **A** restoration
   - **B** reclamation
   - **C** recovery
   - **D** reinstatement

LINKS

MATH LINK

Collect/Organize/Display Data Design and conduct a survey to determine people's interest in restoring a natural ecosystem in your area. Find out what people know about the original ecosystem and whether or not they are interested in restoring it. Also ask how much time they would be willing to commit each week. Compile the results of your survey, and summarize those results in a bar graph. You may want to use a computer program to make your graph.

WRITING LINK

Expressive Writing—Poem Write a poem about the reclamation of a damaged ecosystem. Describe how the area looks, smells, feels, and sounds. Then read your poem to your class.

SOCIAL STUDIES LINK

National Park System Since 1872 the National Park Service has established more than 330 parks. Find out how the park system tries to meet people's needs while preserving the environment. Report your findings to your class.

TECHNOLOGY LINK

Learn more about restoring natural ecosystems by viewing *Prairie Restoration* on the **Harcourt Science Newsroom Video.**

Major Events in Environmental Awareness

The bald eagle, America's national bird, was saved from extinction when Congress banned the use of DDT in 1972.

The History of Environmental Awareness

1872
The first national park is established.

1908
The Grand Canyon becomes a national monument.

100 B.C.	A.D. 1700	A.D. 1800	A.D. 1900

100 B.C.
The Chinese develop a natural insecticide made from dried flower parts.

1789
Gilbert White publishes the first ecology book, *The Natural History and Antiquities of Selborne.*

1962
Rachel Carson publishes *Silent Spring.*

The Industrial Revolution, which began in England in the 1700s and then spread to Europe and the United States, resulted in dramatic changes to the natural environment. Air, water, and land became more and more polluted, and Earth's natural resources were used much more rapidly. With these changes, some people began to develop a greater sense of responsibility for the environment.

Environmental Awareness Begins

In 1789 Englishman Gilbert White, often called the "father of ecology," wrote what is considered to be the first ecology book. In his book, White described the plants and animals of the English countryside.

By the mid-1800s the Industrial Revolution was in full swing on the east coast of the United States. At the same time, westward expansion of the country threatened to destroy the remaining wilderness areas. In 1872 President Ulysses S. Grant established the world's first national park—Yellowstone National Park.

A Book Sparks a Movement

Through the first half of the 1900s, the United States became more urban and more industrialized. Manufacturing plants dumped many kinds of pollutants into the environment.

Farmers used large amounts of chemicals to kill insect pests and weeds. In 1962 Rachel Carson published *Silent Spring,* in which she told that the use of DDT—a pesticide—was also killing birds, particularly the bald eagle. She also wrote that poisons in the environment can affect all living things, including people.

Laws that Protect

Largely because of Rachel Carson's work, the government and people of the United States began taking pollution seriously. Many laws were passed to control it. In 1972 Congress passed a law banning the use of DDT. In 1973 the Endangered Species Act was passed. This law helped save threatened and endangered wild plants and animals from extinction. Since then many more environmental laws have been passed, both in the United States and in countries around the world.

Many environmental problems affect the whole planet and require the cooperation of all nations to solve them. For example, in the late 1970s, scientists found that chemicals used in refrigerators and air conditioners destroy the atmosphere's protective ozone layer. Scientists from many nations met to find ways to help stop ozone destruction. The result was the development of new chemicals for refrigeration that do not destroy ozone.

Today the major environmental concern is global warming. Many scientists hypothesize that excess carbon dioxide, released into the air by the burning of fossil fuels, is raising the temperature of the atmosphere. If this hypothesis is correct, the world faces a great challenge, since modern societies depend on the burning of fossil fuels for industry and transportation.

THINK ABOUT IT

1. What started people thinking about ways to protect the environment?
2. Why is environmental protection a world-wide problem?

1970
The first Earth Day is held, and Congress passes the Clean Water Act.

1987
Twenty-four nations sign the Montreal Protocol, which states that nations must stop using chemicals that destroy ozone.

A.D. 2000

1976
Congress passes the Recycling Act.

1998
Representatives from many nations meet in Argentina to find ways to reduce excess carbon dioxide.

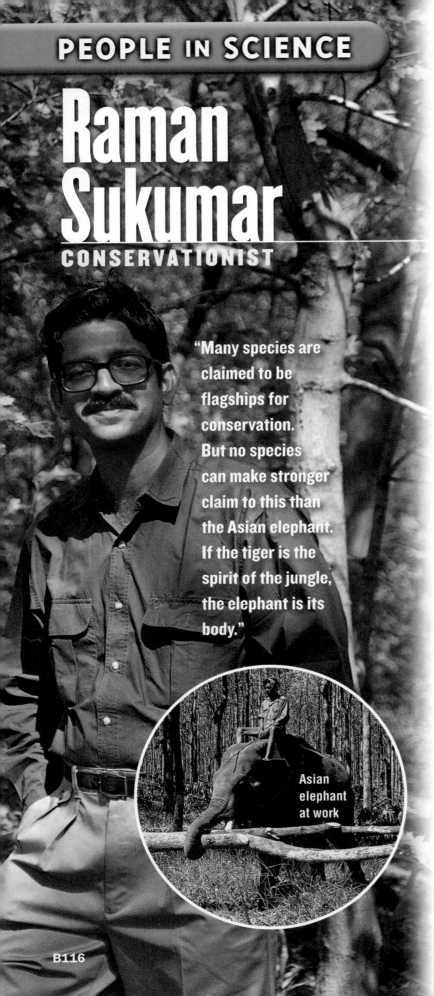

Raman Sukumar
CONSERVATIONIST

"Many species are claimed to be flagships for conservation. But no species can make stronger claim to this than the Asian elephant. If the tiger is the spirit of the jungle, the elephant is its body."

Asian elephant at work

Raman Sukumar is deputy chairperson of the Asian Elephant Specialist Group of the World Conservation Union. He is one of the world's leading authorities on Asian elephants. His work involves planning conservation strategies and finding ways to resolve conflicts between human and elephant use of the same land. He knows that unless these conflicts can be resolved, Asian elephants will not survive in the wild.

Mr. Sukumar believes deeply in the importance of protecting the Asian elephant. "Elephants are beloved locally and globally," he says. Mr. Sukumar stresses that the protection of the elephant will also help to preserve other species living in the elephant's habitat. "Elephants prosper in large forests that are home to a great number of plant and animal species," he says.

Mr. Sukumar first became interested in a career in conservation when he was in high school. It wasn't until college, however, that he began to study elephants. Since that time Mr. Sukumar has spent nearly two decades observing elephants in the wild to better understand their way of life.

Mr. Sukumar currently lives in India with his wife and daughters. Like many scientists, he uses the Internet to stay connected with colleagues around the world.

THINK ABOUT IT

1. What will happen to Asian elephants if conflicts over land use are not resolved?
2. Why will Mr. Sukumar's work help to preserve many other organisms in the Asian elephant's habitat?

ACID RAIN

How does acid rain affect art objects?

Materials

- chalk
- paper clip
- modeling clay
- vinegar
- dropper

Procedure

❶ Using the paper clip as a tool, carve the piece of chalk into a sculpture.

❷ Place your sculpture on a base of clay.

❸ Using the dropper, drop vinegar onto your sculpture and observe what happens.

Draw Conclusions

What effect does the vinegar, an acid, have on your sculpture? Chalk is similar to the limestone and marble of real art objects. What do you infer is happening to art objects around the world because of acid rain?

POWERFUL PLANTS

How can plants reclaim a damaged ecosystem?

Materials

- 2 small clay pots
- potting soil
- 6 bean seeds
- water
- flour

Procedure

❶ Fill both pots half-full of soil. Plant three bean seeds in each pot, and water them with equal amounts of water.

❷ Mix the flour and water until it forms a thick batter.

❸ Pour the batter into one pot, covering the soil and completely filling the space between the soil and the top of the pot.

❹ Place both pots in a warm, sunny place. Water the soil of the uncovered pot when it feels dry.

❺ Observe the pots every day for two weeks.

Draw Conclusions

Which pot is the control? What do you observe about the plants in the experimental pot? Where have you noticed plants growing in similar conditions in your neighborhood? How do plants help reclaim damaged ecosystems?

Vocabulary Review

Use the terms below to complete the sentences. The page numbers in ( ) tell you where to look in the chapter if you need help.

succession (B92)   **conserving** (B104)
pioneer plants (B92)   **reduce** (B104)
climax   **reuse** (B105)
community (B93)   **recycle** (B105)
pollution (B99)   **reclamation** (B110)
acid rain (B99)   **wetlands** (B111)

1. When you _____, you recover a resource from an item and use the resource to make a new item.

2. A spruce and hemlock forest is a final stage of succession, or a _____.

3. Reducing, reusing, and recycling are three ways of _____ resources.

4. If you cut down on the resources you use, you _____. If you _____ items, you use them for new purposes.

5. Primary _____ occurs on new, barren land, such as the land exposed by a receding glacier.

6. When pollutants such as nitrogen oxides and sulfur dioxide combine with water vapor and condense, _____ results.

7. Plants that grow during the first stage of succession are called _____.

8. The _____ of the Hudson River ecosystem has brought life back to the river, but it is not yet complete.

9. Untreated waste water, PCBs, and fertilizers form _____ that damages ecosystems.

10. Mangrove swamps, mud flats, and salt-water marshes are all types of _____.

Connect Concepts

Choose items from the list below to fill in the spaces in the concept map.

A an increase in population
B following the three *R*s
C catastrophic changes
D succession after a glacier, fire, or volcanic eruption
E researching ways to restore habitats
F pollution and acid rain
G passing laws that punish polluters

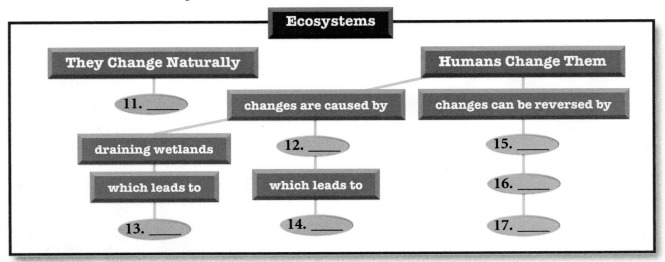

Ecosystems

They Change Naturally

11. _____

changes are caused by

Humans Change Them

changes can be reversed by

draining wetlands

12. _____

15. _____

which leads to

which leads to

13. _____

14. _____

16. _____

17. _____

Check Understanding

Write the letter of the best choice.

18. The last stage of succession is called —
    A the pioneer stage
    B the climax community
    C the third stage
    D the full-forest stage

19. An example of a pioneer plant is the —
    F hemlock tree   H fireweed
    G willow tree   J spruce tree

20. The causes of acid rain do **NOT** include —
    A pollution from cars
    B pollution from factories
    C pollution from energy stations
    D pollution from waste water

21. The three *R*s are —
    F refuse, reduce, and recycle
    G replace, recycle, and reuse
    H reduce, reuse, and recycle
    J reward, refuse, and reduce

22. The reclamation of ecosystems does **NOT** include —
    A passing laws like the Clean Water Act
    B civic projects like the Save Our Everglades program
    C research to find new ways to restore ecosystems
    D misusing resources

Critical Thinking

23. A pond is dug in an area where a deciduous forest is the climax community. If the pond is left alone, how will it change?

24. In what ways do you think your actions might affect an ecosystem?

25. Explain how reducing the amount of hot water you use could help to save an ecosystem.

Process Skills Review

26. Suppose you are sent to a river to find out whether it is polluted or not. How would you make your observations? Would you use any instruments to help you **observe**? What would you look for?

27. In Lesson 1 you made a pond model to study succession in a pond ecosystem. Suppose you wanted to find out whether the same thing happens in a river ecosystem. Describe how you could **make a model** of a river ecosystem.

28. Describe how you could **experiment** to test how well a certain fertilizer works in sandy soil, in red clay soil, and in black potting soil. What other **variables** would you need to **identify and control**? What problems might you encounter?

Performance Assessment

Algae Growth

In one jar, fertilizer was added to distilled water. The same amount of fertilizer was added to pond water in another jar. The jars were then put in a sunny spot and left undisturbed for two weeks. What variable was changed in this experiment? What variables were controlled? Predict which jar will have more growth. Explain. Then observe the two jars and draw conclusions.

UNIT B EXPEDITIONS

There are many places where you can study systems and interactions in nature. You can learn about systems and interactions by visiting the places below. You'll also have fun while you learn.

Oregon Dunes National Recreation Area

WHAT A large area of sand dunes, water, and forest ecosystems

WHERE Reedsport/Winchester Bay, Oregon

WHAT CAN YOU DO THERE? Explore the dunes, go camping, and observe the interactions of plants and animals.

Cumberland Island National Seashore

WHAT An island where the natural cycle of life has been left largely untouched

WHERE St. Marys, Georgia

WHAT CAN YOU DO THERE? Explore the island forests, estuaries, and seashore and observe interactions in the ocean and on the land.

GO ONLINE Plan Your Own Expeditions

If you can't visit Oregon Dunes National Recreation Area or Cumberland Island National Seashore, visit a recreation area or seashore near you. Or log on to The Learning Site at **www.harcourtschool.com** to visit these science sites and other places where you can study systems and interactions in nature.

Processes That Change the Earth

Processes That Change the Earth

UNIT EXPERIMENT

Wave Action

Earth's surface is constantly changed by natural processes. One of those processes, the action of waves crashing against a shore, can carry away large quantities of beach sand. While you study this unit, you can conduct a long-term experiment related to this process. Here are some questions to think about. How do artificial structures affect the action of waves? For example, can building jetties stop the loss of beach sand? Plan and conduct an experiment to find answers to these or other questions you have about wave action. See pages x–xvii for help in designing your experiment.

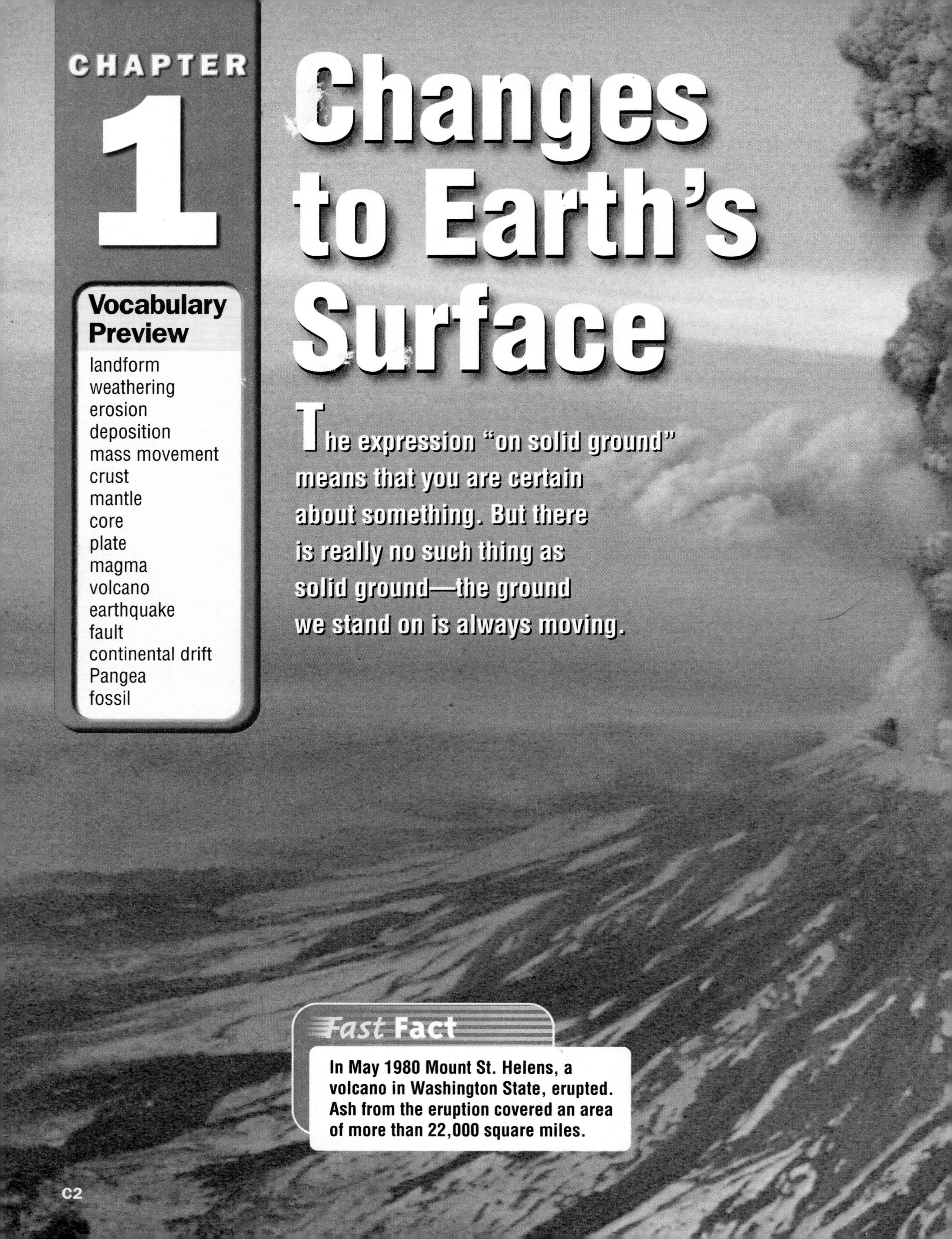

1

Changes to Earth's Surface

Vocabulary Preview

landform
weathering
erosion
deposition
mass movement
crust
mantle
core
plate
magma
volcano
earthquake
fault
continental drift
Pangea
fossil

The expression "on solid ground" means that you are certain about something. But there is really no such thing as solid ground—the ground we stand on is always moving.

Fast Fact

In May 1980 Mount St. Helens, a volcano in Washington State, erupted. Ash from the eruption covered an area of more than 22,000 square miles.

There are more than half a million earthquakes every year. Most occur at the bottom of the ocean and are too small to be felt. Only about 1000 earthquakes a year cause any damage.

Mauna Kea, a dormant volcano on the island of Hawai'i, is one of the tallest mountains in the world. From the floor of the Pacific Ocean it rises 9750 m (about 32,000 ft) to sea level and 4205 m (about 13,800 ft) above sea level, for a total height of nearly 14,000 m (about 46,000 ft). By comparison, Mount Everest is 8848 m (about 29,000 ft) high.

What Processes Change Landforms?

In this lesson, you can . . .

INVESTIGATE how water cuts through sand.

LEARN ABOUT how wind, water, and ice shape landforms.

LINK to math, writing, social studies, and technology.

▼ Window Rock, Arizona

INVESTIGATE

How Water Changes Earth's Surface

Activity Purpose Moving water is the most powerful force there is for changing Earth's surface. It can move soil, make cliffs fall down, and carve canyons in solid rock. In this investigation, you will **use a model**—a stream table—to **observe** how moving water can cut through sand.

Materials

- stream table
- sand
- 2 lengths of plastic tubing
- 2 plastic pails
- 3 wood blocks
- water

Activity Procedure

1. Place the stream table on a classroom table. Make sure the front end of the stream table is even with the edge of the table. Put the stream-table support under the back end of the stream table. (Picture A)

2. Fill the stream table with sand.

3. Using two fingers, make a path, or channel, down the middle of the sand.

4. Connect one end of one length of tubing to the front of the stream table. Let the other end of the tubing hang over the edge of the table. Place an empty pail on the floor under the hanging end of the tubing. (Picture B)

Picture A

Picture B

5 Place the other pail on two wood blocks near the raised end of the stream-table channel. Fill this pail $\frac{3}{4}$ full of water.

6 Put the second length of tubing into the pail, and fill it with water.

7 Start the water flowing through the tube from the pail to the stream table by lowering one end of the filled tube.

8 **Observe** any changes the water makes to the sand in the stream table. **Record** your observations.

9 Place the third wood block on top of the support under the stream table. Repeat Steps 7 and 8.

Draw Conclusions

1. In which setup was the speed of the water greater?

2. In which setup did you **observe** greater movement of sand from the channel?

3. **Scientists at Work** Scientists learn by **observing**. What did you learn about the way water can change the land by observing the channel in the stream table?

Investigate Further **Hypothesize** what would happen if you replaced the sand with soil. **Plan and conduct a simple experiment** to test your hypothesis.

Changes to Earth's Surface

Changing Landforms

Earth's surface is changing all around you. Rivers wear away rock and produce deep canyons. Waves eat away at sea cliffs, turning them into beach sand. Glaciers scrape away the tops of mountains, and winds carrying sand grind away desert rock. Earth's **landforms**, physical features on its surface, might seem as if they never change, but they do.

In the investigation, you saw how the force of flowing water can move sand. Forces such as flowing water, waves, wind, ice, and even movements inside the Earth are constantly changing landforms. Sometimes the changes happen fast enough for you to observe. For example, a volcano might erupt suddenly and blow away a mountaintop, or a powerful hurricane might sweep away a sandy beach. But most changes to Earth's landforms happen so slowly that you cannot observe them directly. Sometimes you can see only the results of past changes.

✔ **What are some of the forces that change landforms?**

FIND OUT

- how Earth's crust is broken down into soil
- how water, wind, and ice change landforms

VOCABULARY

landforms
weathering
erosion
deposition
mass movement

◀ Thousands of years of rain and wind shaped these landforms in Utah's Monument Valley.

Flowing water cuts into riverbanks and carries away soil. ▼

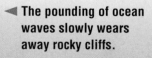
◀ The pounding of ocean waves slowly wears away rocky cliffs.

This satellite photo shows the delta the Mississippi River has built in the Gulf of Mexico. ►

Water

Much of Earth's surface is made of rock. The shaping of landforms starts when weathering wears away rock. **Weathering** is the process of breaking rock into silt, sand, clay, and other tiny pieces, called *sediment*. Water is an important agent, or cause, of weathering.

Water weathers rock in several ways. Fast-flowing rivers can carve deep canyons in rock. Arizona's Grand Canyon, carved by the action of the Colorado River, is 1.6 km (about 1 mi) deep. Also, ocean waves can weather cliffs and cause them to fall into the sea. Water can weather rock in other ways, too. When it rains, water seeps into tiny holes, or pores, and cracks in rock. If this water freezes, it expands, breaking the rock. Rain that becomes acidic because of pollution can dissolve rock. And flowing water tumbles rocks against each other, breaking them into smaller pieces and smoothing their edges.

After weathering has broken rock into sediment, erosion and deposition move the sediment around and leave it in new places. **Erosion** (ee•ROH•zhuhn) is the process of moving sediment from one place to another. **Deposition** (dep•uh•ZISH•uhn) is the process of dropping, or depositing, sediment in a new location.

Water is not only an important agent of weathering but also the chief agent of erosion. Water can erode great amounts of sediment. At the shore, sediment from weathered cliffs is eroded by waves and deposited as new sand on beaches. Rainfall erodes sediment and carries it into rivers and streams. Rivers pick up the sediment and move it downstream. Most rivers deposit sediment in flat areas along their banks. These *flood plains*, as they are called, are rich agricultural areas, but they are dangerous places for people to live because of periodic flooding. Some rivers deposit sediment in broad areas at their mouths. These areas of new land are called *deltas*. The Mississippi River delta is one of the largest in the world.

✔ **What is the difference between weathering and erosion?**

This dam, which forms Lake Lanier in north Georgia, reduces the chances of a damaging flood along the Chattahoochee River. The dam also provides a source of electric energy and recreation. ▼

C7

Wind

Wind is another agent of weathering and erosion. Have you ever seen a machine called a sandblaster? It uses a powerful jet of air containing sand to clean building surfaces. In a similar way, wind can carry bits of rock and sand that weather rock surfaces. Wind also moves sediment from place to place. If the wind blows hard, it can erode a lot of sediment.

In dry areas like the American Southwest, wind erosion has shaped some of the world's most unusual landforms—rocks that look like tables, arches, or columns. Wind erodes dry sediment more easily than it erodes particles of soil or damp rock. And there is little plant life in dry areas to hold sediment in place.

Wind erosion can also blow sand into large mounds called *dunes*. Huge dunes as much as 100 m (about 325 ft) high form in some deserts. Many sandy beaches have long lines of dunes on their land side. Beach dunes are built by the constantly blowing sea breezes. They help protect the land behind them during storms.

✔ **How does wind erosion change landforms?**

Ice

Ice in the form of glaciers can also change landforms. *Glaciers* are thick sheets of ice, formed in areas where more snow falls during the winter than melts during the summer. Glaciers seem to stand still, but they actually move. Because of a glacier's great size and weight, it erodes everything under it. Glaciers erode sediment from one place and deposit it in another.

There are two kinds of glaciers. *Valley glaciers* are found in high mountain valleys. They flow slowly down mountainsides, eroding the mountain under them and forming U-shaped valleys. Only a few valley glaciers remain in North America. And even those are melting rapidly.

Continental glaciers are ice sheets that cover large areas of Earth. They cover almost all of Greenland and Antarctica today. But thousands of years ago, when the climate was colder, continental glaciers covered Europe, Canada, and the northern United States.

✔ **What are glaciers?**

Dunes form where an obstacle, such as a plant or a rock, causes wind to slow and deposit the sand it is carrying. ▼

The Athabasca Glacier recedes about 13 m (43 ft) each year. Since 1890, it has receded about 1.6 km (1 mi). ▶

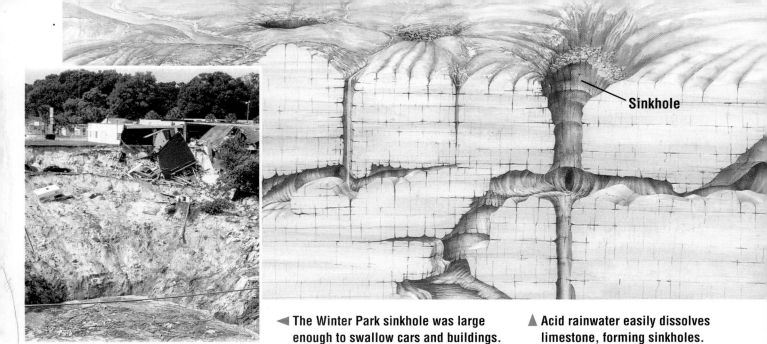

Sinkhole

◄ The Winter Park sinkhole was large enough to swallow cars and buildings.

▲ Acid rainwater easily dissolves limestone, forming sinkholes.

Mass Movement

During the winter of 1997–1998, heavy rains fell on much of the California coast. One night, families living in a small canyon heard a loud noise. When they went outside to see what had happened, they discovered that a mound of mud had slid down the steep sides of the canyon, covering part of a house. This mudslide occurred when a mass of soil that was full of water moved rapidly downhill.

A mudslide is one type of mass movement. **Mass movement** is the downhill movement of rock and soil because of gravity. Mass movements, such as mudslides and landslides, can change landforms quickly. Mudslides move wet soil. Landslides move dry soil and rock. Landslides occur when gravity becomes stronger than the friction that holds soil in place on a hill. The soil falls suddenly to the bottom of the hill.

Another type of mass movement—one that occurs slowly, as you might guess from its name—is called *creep*. Creep occurs when soil moves slowly downhill because of gravity. Creep is so slow that changes in landforms are hard to observe directly. The land may move only a few centimeters each year. But over time, creep can move fences, utility poles, roads, and railroad tracks.

One day in 1981, in the city of Winter Park, Florida, an area of land suddenly collapsed, or fell in on itself. The hole swallowed houses, swimming pools, and businesses, including a car dealership. Today there is a lake where there was once dry land. The process that led to the formation of the Winter Park sinkhole is different from that of other types of mass movement.

A sinkhole is a large hole in the ground that opens suddenly. Sinkholes form after rock under the surface has dissolved or become weak. Sinkholes often appear in areas of limestone rock, because limestone dissolves easily. Rain seeping into the ground combines with carbon dioxide from the air to form a weak acid called *carbonic acid*. Carbonic acid dissolves limestone, forming huge holes. When enough rock has dissolved, land over the weakened area collapses.

✔ **What is mass movement?**

New Landforms

Erosion and deposition can change landforms or produce new ones. Rivers can deposit sediment that builds deltas. They can also change their path, or course, producing new lakes on wide flood plains.

Glaciers are major forces for forming new landforms. As the glaciers of the last Ice Age moved forward, they pushed mounds of rock and soil in front of them. When the glaciers melted, they left behind at their lower ends long ridges of soil and rock, called *terminal moraines*. Long Island and Cape Cod are terminal moraines. They mark the leading edge of the glacier that covered much of North America.

New islands can be formed by volcanic eruptions. Underwater volcanoes increase their height by depositing melted rock and ash. In time, they build up enough to appear above the sea surface as islands. The Hawaiian Islands formed in this way. Almost constant eruptions of Kīlauea add daily to the size of the island of Hawai'i. Another volcano, now growing slowly on the ocean floor southeast of Hawai'i, will one day become the island of Loihi.

✔ **What new landforms are created by erosion and deposition?**

Old, slow-moving rivers form broad loops. ▼

The loops can become so broad that they meet. ▼

Because the river follows the shortest route, its flow cuts off the loop. The old loop forms a crescent-shaped body of water called an *oxbow lake*. ▼

Mississippi River, south of Memphis, Tennessee ▽

Summary

Weathering breaks down the rock of Earth's surface into soil, sand, and other small particles. Agents of erosion, such as water, wind, and ice, change Earth's landforms by moving rock and soil. Water can carve canyons and deposit sediment to form deltas. Wind can form sand dunes. Ice can carve U-shaped valleys and leave landforms such as terminal moraines. Even forces within the Earth, such as volcanoes, can produce new landforms.

Review

1. What is erosion?
2. What is deposition?
3. What forces cause erosion and deposition?
4. **Critical Thinking** Why is weathering so important to life on land?
5. **Test Prep** A type of mass movement is a —

   A glacier
   B delta
   C mudslide
   D terminal moraine

LINKS

MATH LINK

Organize/Display Data The Aletsch Glacier in Europe is 80 km^2. Malaspina Glacier in Alaska measures 1344 km^2. The Grinnell Glacier in Montana is about 2 km^2. Use a computer, if possible, to make a bar graph that compares these glaciers.

WRITING LINK

Informative Writing—Description During the 1930s huge dust storms eroded large areas of the Great Plains of the United States. Find out what caused the Dust Bowl, as the eroded region was called, and what problems it led to. Then describe how modern farming practices, such as contour plowing, can help prevent soil erosion.

SOCIAL STUDIES LINK

Topographic Maps Topographic maps use symbols and colors to represent landforms. These maps can tell you how the land looks—if you know how to read them. At the library, look for a topographic map of the area where you live. What kinds of symbols are used to show water, wetlands, and deserts?

GO ONLINE — TECHNOLOGY LINK

Learn more about landscapes and erosion by visiting this Internet site.

www.scilinks.org/harcourt

SCI LINKS
THE WORLD'S A CLICK AWAY

What Causes Mountains, Volcanoes, and Earthquakes?

In this lesson, you can . . .

INVESTIGATE the structure of Earth.

LEARN ABOUT what forms mountains and volcanoes.

LINK to math, writing, literature, and technology.

Volcanoes release melted rock from deep inside Earth. ▼

INVESTIGATE

Journey to the Center of Earth

Activity Purpose If you could slice Earth in half, you would see that it has several layers. Of course, you can't slice Earth in half, but you can make a model of it. In this investigation you will **make a model** that shows Earth's layers.

Materials

- 2 graham crackers
- 1 small plastic bag
- disposable plastic gloves
- 1 spoon
- 1 jar peanut butter
- 1 hazelnut or other round nut
- freezer
- plastic knife

Activity Procedure

1 Put the graham crackers in the plastic bag. Close the bag and use your hands to crush the crackers into crumbs. Then set the bag aside.

2 Put on the plastic gloves. Use the spoon to scoop a glob of peanut butter from the jar and put it in your gloved hand. Place the nut in the center of the peanut butter. Cover the nut with more peanut butter until there is about 2.5 cm of peanut butter all around the nut. Using both hands, roll the glob of peanut butter with the nut at its center into a ball. (Picture A)

Picture A

Picture B

3 Open the bag of crushed graham crackers, and roll the peanut butter ball in the graham cracker crumbs until the outside of the ball is completely coated.

4 Put the ball in the freezer for about 15 minutes. Remove the ball and cut into your model with the plastic knife. **Observe** the layers inside. You might want to take a photograph of your model for later review. (Picture B)

Draw Conclusions

1. The peanut butter ball is a model of Earth's layers. How many layers does Earth have in this model?

2. Which layer of Earth do the crushed graham crackers represent? Why do you think your model has a thick layer of peanut butter but a thin layer of graham cracker crumbs?

3. **Scientists at Work** Scientists can see and understand complex structures better by **making models** of them. What does the model show about Earth's layers? What doesn't the model show about Earth's layers?

Investigate Further Some geologists, scientists who study the Earth, say that Earth's center is divided into a soft outer part and a hard inner part. How could you **make a model** to show this?

Process Skill Tip

You cannot see Earth's layers. So **making a model** helps you understand how they look in relation to each other. In this activity, you need to cut open the model to see the layers.

Mountains, Volcanoes, and Earthquakes

Earth's Interior

FIND OUT

- how mountains form
- what causes volcanoes and earthquakes

VOCABULARY

crust
mantle
core
plate
magma
volcano
earthquake
fault

As the model you made in the investigation showed, Earth is not a solid ball of rock. It has three distinct layers. We live on Earth's crust. The **crust** is the outer layer, and it is made of rock. Earth's crust is very thin compared to the other layers. If Earth were the size of a chicken's egg, the crust would be thinner than the egg's shell.

The **mantle** is the layer of rock beneath Earth's crust. Just under the crust, the rock of the mantle is solid. But the mantle is very hot. This makes part of the mantle soft, like melted candy. No one has ever been to the mantle, but rock from the mantle sometimes reaches Earth's surface through volcanoes.

The **core** is the center layer of Earth. It is Earth's hottest layer. The core can be divided into two parts: an outer core of liquid, or *molten,* iron and an inner core of solid iron. Even though the core is very hot, great pressure at the center of Earth keeps the inner core solid.

✔ **What parts of Earth are solid?**

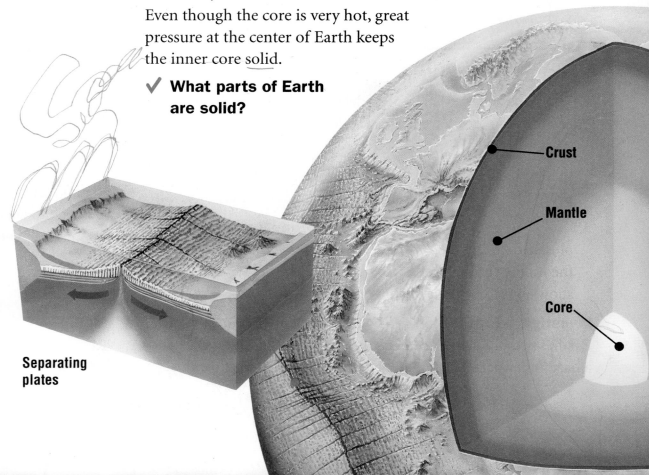

Separating plates

Crust

Mantle

Core

Earth's Crust Moves

Earth's surface is not a single piece of rock. Instead, it is made up of many plates. **Plates** are rigid blocks of crust and upper mantle rock. Most of North America, Greenland, and the western half of the North Atlantic Ocean are on the North American plate. Part of California and most of the Pacific Ocean make up the Pacific plate. There are 12 major plates in all. Earth's plates fit together like the pieces of a jigsaw puzzle.

Although these plates are enormous, they actually float on the soft rock of the mantle. Pressure and heat within the Earth produce currents in the soft rock of the mantle. As the mantle moves, the plates floating on it move, too.

Plate movement is very slow—only a few centimeters each year. But because plates are right next to each other, the movement of one plate affects other plates. Some plates push together. Some pull apart. Other plates slide past each other. As plates move around, they cause great changes in Earth's landforms.

Where plates collide, energy is released, and new landforms are produced. On land, mountains rise and volcanoes erupt. South America's Andes Mountains are a result of the Nazca and South American plates colliding. On the ocean floor, deep trenches form.

As plates pull apart on land, valleys dotted with volcanoes develop. Africa's Great Rift Valley was formed by the African and Arabian plates pulling apart. The rift, or crack, will one day result in a complete separation of part of eastern Africa from the rest of the continent. Where plates pull apart under the sea, ridges and volcanoes form. This spreading forms new sea floor at the ridges.

When plates scrape and slide past each other, they shake Earth's surface. Along the San Andreas (an•DRAY•uhs) fault in California, the Pacific plate is moving past the North American plate. As the plates grind past each other, they sometimes slip, causing earthquakes.

✔ **What are Earth's plates?**

Colliding ocean plates

Colliding continental plates

The Himalayas formed as the Indian plate pushed into the Eurasian plate. The plates are still pushing together, and the mountains are still getting taller.

Mountain Formation

Mountains are Earth's highest landforms. They form as the crust folds, cracks, and bends upward because of the movements of Earth's plates.

Many of the highest mountains form where continental plates collide. As the plates push together, their edges crumple and fold into mountains. The Himalayas (him•uh•LAY•uhz), Earth's highest mountain range, formed this way.

At some places, continental and oceanic plates collide. Because continental rock is less dense than seafloor rock, the continental plate moves up and over the oceanic plate. The Cascade Mountains, near the Pacific Ocean, formed this way.

Mountains do not form only at the edges, or boundaries, of plates. Some mountains form where pressure from movement at the boundaries pushes a block of rock upward. The Grand Tetons (TEE•tahnz) of Wyoming rise straight up from the flat land around them.

Plates that pull apart leave gaps between them. Magma bubbles up between the plates. **Magma** is molten rock from Earth's mantle. Magma builds up along the cracks, forming long chains of mountains under the ocean. These mountains are called *mid-ocean ridges*. The Mid-Atlantic Ridge is Earth's longest mountain range. It separates the North American and Eurasian plates in the North Atlantic and the South American and African plates in the South Atlantic.

✓ **How do many of the highest mountains form?**

Volcanoes

You have read that most volcanoes form at plate boundaries. A **volcano** is a mountain formed by lava and ash. *Lava* is magma that reaches Earth's surface. *Ash* is small pieces of hardened lava.

Chains of volcanoes form where a continental plate and an oceanic plate collide. The edge of the oceanic plate pushes under the edge of the continental plate. The leading edge of the oceanic plate melts as it sinks deep into the mantle. The melted rock becomes magma that forces its way up between the plates. The volcanoes of the Cascades, such as Mount St. Helens, formed this way.

Sometimes volcanoes form in the middle of plates, over unusually hot columns of magma. The magma melts a hole in the plate and rises through the hole, causing a volcanic eruption. The Hawaiian Islands are the tops of a chain of volcanoes that formed in the middle of the Pacific plate. As the Pacific plate continues moving over this hot spot, new volcanoes and new islands form. The big island of Hawai'i, with its active volcanoes, Kilauea and Mauna Loa, is the youngest island in the chain. Kure Atoll, an extinct volcano 2617 km (about 1625 mi) to the northwest, is the oldest island.

✓ **What is a volcano?**

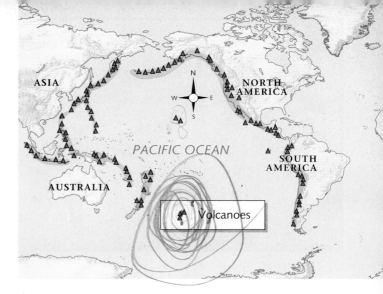

▲ Many volcanoes are located at plate boundaries around the Pacific plate. That's why this area is called the Ring of Fire.

THE INSIDE STORY

Volcanoes

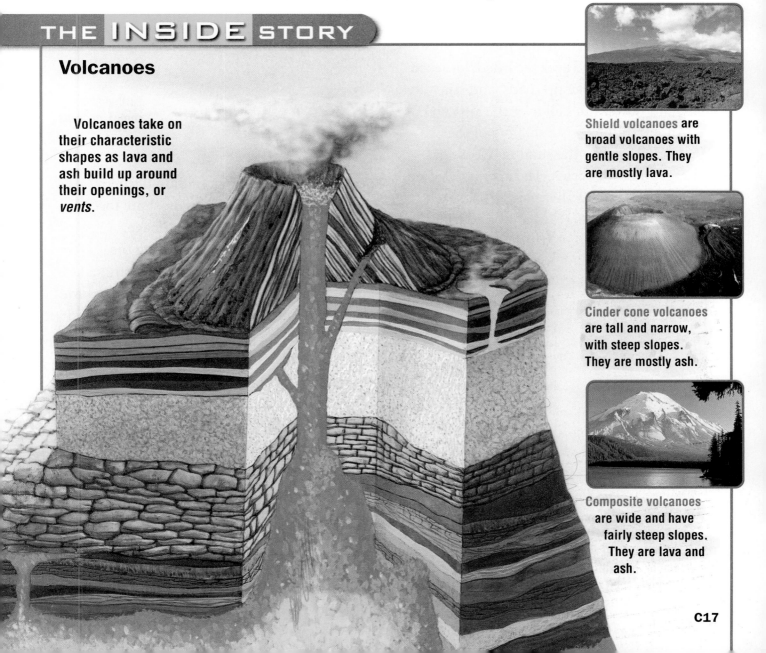

Volcanoes take on their characteristic shapes as lava and ash build up around their openings, or *vents*.

Shield volcanoes are broad volcanoes with gentle slopes. They are mostly lava.

Cinder cone volcanoes are tall and narrow, with steep slopes. They are mostly ash.

Composite volcanoes are wide and have fairly steep slopes. They are lava and ash.

C17

In 1964 a large earthquake hit Anchorage, Alaska. Streets split open, bridges collapsed, and houses slid downhill toward the sea.

Earthquake center, or *focus*

Fault

Earthquakes

On March 27, 1964, thousands of people in Anchorage, Alaska, were shaken as the ground rocked under them. A strong earthquake, possibly the most powerful one ever recorded, knocked down houses, broke up roads, and cut water, gas, and power lines all over the area.

An **earthquake** is a shaking of the ground caused by the sudden release of energy in Earth's crust. The energy released as plates crush together, scrape past each other, or bend along jagged boundaries can cause great damage. Earthquakes are very common. More than a million of them occur each year. However, most are too small to be felt or to cause damage.

Many earthquakes occur along the boundaries of the Pacific plate. Earthquakes also occur along faults in the crust. You have read that Earth's crust can bend or break in the middle of a plate as forces press in on it. These breaks can form **faults**, or places where pieces of the crust move.

An earthquake sends out energy in the form of *seismic* (SYZ•mik) *waves*. Seismic waves are like ripples that form on a pond when a stone is tossed in. Scientists measure and record seismic waves on an instrument called a *seismograph* (SYZ•muh•graf). These measurements can then be used to compare the relative strengths of earthquakes.

✔ **What is an earthquake?**

Major Earthquakes		
Magnitude	**Year**	**Location**
9.2	1964	Alaska
8.9	1933	Japan
8.4	1946	Japan
8.2	1976	China
8.1	1979	Indonesia
8.1	1985	Mexico
7.9	2001	India
6.9	1989	California

▲ The Richter scale is often used to measure relative strengths, or *magnitudes,* of earthquakes. On this scale an earthquake with a magnitude of 7.5, for example, is 32 times more powerful than an earthquake with a magnitude of 6.5.

◀ Sudden movement along a fault can cause an earthquake.

Summary

Earth has three layers: the crust, the mantle, and the core. Rock of the crust and upper mantle makes up plates that fit together like puzzle pieces. Earth's plates collide, pull apart, and slide past each other. Most mountains and volcanoes form at plate boundaries. Many earthquakes also occur at plate boundaries.

Review

1. Describe three ways in which Earth's plates interact.
2. What is magma and where does it come from?
3. How do volcanoes form where oceanic and continental plates collide?
4. **Critical Thinking** Assume that the overall size of Earth's crust stays the same. If one plate is pushing away from the plate next to it on one side, what must be happening at the boundary with another plate on the opposite side?
5. **Test Prep** Many strong earthquakes are caused by —
   - **A** plates sliding past each other
   - **B** lava flowing down the side of a volcano
   - **C** plates spreading apart
   - **D** hot magma

LINKS

MATH LINK

Estimate Each whole number on the Richter scale represents a force 32 times as strong as the next lower number. An earthquake of magnitude 7 is about 32 times as strong as one of magnitude 6. About how many times as strong is an earthquake of magnitude 8 compared with an earthquake of magnitude 5?

WRITING LINK

Informative Writing—Explanation The 1980 explosion of Mount St. Helens was a very powerful volcanic eruption. Find pictures in books and magazines of Mount St. Helens before, during, and after the eruption. Write captions for the pictures to explain what happened. Share your photo essay with your class.

LITERATURE LINK

Volcano: The Eruption and Healing of Mount St. Helens by Patricia Lauber (Bradbury Press, 1986) explains how and why Mount St. Helens erupted. It also describes the destruction the eruption caused, and how the land has since recovered.

TECHNOLOGY LINK

Learn more about volcanoes by viewing *Ring of Fire* and *Volcano Hunters* on the **Harcourt Science Newsroom Video.**

How Has Earth's Surface Changed?

In this lesson, you can . . .

INVESTIGATE the movement of continents.

LEARN ABOUT how Earth's surface has changed over time.

LINK to math, writing, art, and technology.

◁ Over millions of years, these trees have turned to stone.

INVESTIGATE

Movement of the Continents

Activity Purpose Earth's surface 100 million years ago probably looked much different than it does today. In the last lesson, you read that Earth's surface is made up of plates that move. In this investigation, you will **make a model** to find out how Earth's surface might have looked before these plates moved to their present locations.

Materials

- 3 copies of a world map
- scissors
- 3 sheets of construction paper
- glue
- globe or world map

Activity Procedure

1 Cut out the continents from one copy of the world map.

2 Arrange the continents into one large "supercontinent" on a sheet of construction paper. As you would with a jigsaw puzzle, arrange them so their edges fit together as closely as possible. (Picture A)

3 Label the pieces with the names of their present continents, and glue them onto the paper.

4 Use a globe or world map to locate the following mountains: Cascades, Andes, Atlas, Himalayas, Alps. Then draw these mountains on the supercontinent.

Picture A

Picture B

5. Use your textbook to locate volcanoes and places where earthquakes have occurred. Put a *V* in places where you know there are volcanoes, such as the Cascades. Put an *E* in places where you know that earthquakes have occurred, such as western North America.

6. Repeat Steps 1–5 with the second copy of the world map, but before gluing the continents to the construction paper, separate them by about 2.5 cm. That is, leave about 2.5 cm of space between North America and Eurasia, between South America and Africa, and so on. (Picture B)

7. Glue the third world map copy onto a sheet of construction paper. Then place the three versions of the world map in order from the oldest to the youngest.

Draw Conclusions

1. Where do the continents fit together the best?

2. Where are most of the mountains, volcanoes, and earthquake sites in relation to the present continents? Why do you think they are there?

3. **Scientists at Work** Scientists **use models**, such as maps, to better understand complex structures and processes. How did your models of Earth's continents help you **draw conclusions** about Earth's past? What limitations did your models have?

Investigate Further **Hypothesize** about the fact that the continents do not fit together exactly. Then **plan and conduct a simple investigation** to test your hypothesis.

> **Process Skill Tip**
>
> It is impossible to actually see Earth's surface as it looked millions of years ago. But by **using a model**, you can **draw conclusions** about how it may have looked.

How Earth's Surface Has Changed

Continental Drift

From evidence like the models you used in the investigation, scientists infer that Earth's surface has not always looked the way it does today. The surface is constantly changing because of continental drift. **Continental drift** is the theory of how Earth's continents move over its surface.

According to the theory, about 225 million years ago, all of the land on Earth was joined together in one "supercontinent" called **Pangea** (pan•JEE•uh). Evidence suggests that about 200 million years ago, Pangea broke into two big continents. The southern one, Gondwana, contained all the land that is now in the Southern Hemisphere. The northern continent, Laurasia, contained land that would become North America and Eurasia. Finally, Gondwana and Laurasia broke into smaller land masses, forming the continents we know today.

Since the continents are still moving, you might infer that the surface of Earth will be very different 200 million years from now. The Atlantic Ocean is getting wider, pushing Europe and North America apart. The Pacific Ocean is getting smaller. And Australia is moving north.

✔ **What is the theory of continental drift?**

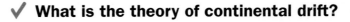

Continental Drift

200 million years ago
Pangea begins to break apart.

100 million years ago
Gondwana breaks into smaller continents earlier than Laurasia does.

Today
Earth's surface may look even different in the future.

The Rock Record

If you were floating down the Colorado River through the deepest part of the Grand Canyon, shown at the right, you would be looking up at layers of rock nearly 2 billion years old! The Grand Canyon is a mile-deep slice into Earth's history, cutting through 20 different layers of rock.

Some of the rocks of the canyon contain a fossil record of organisms from Earth's early history. **Fossils** are the remains or traces of past life found in some rocks. Scientists study fossils to find out how life on Earth has changed.

Scientists also depend on the fact that some things will always be the same. Processes that produced features like the Grand Canyon are still occurring today. Running water still erodes rock layers, and new layers of rock are still forming from deposited sediments.

From the position of certain rock layers, scientists can infer the relative ages of the rocks. Younger rock layers are found on top of older rock layers. The oldest rock layers are near the bottom of the Grand Canyon.

The walls of the Grand Canyon do not contain rock from the latest stages of Earth's history. Erosion has worn away more recent rock. If you stand on the canyon's north rim, you are standing on rock that is about 250 million years old.

✓ **Why is looking at the Grand Canyon like looking at Earth's history?**

The youngest rocks are at the top of the canyon walls.

The oldest rocks are at the bottom of the canyon.

How Fossils Show Changes

Fossils show us that life on Earth has not always been the same as it is now. Dinosaurs once roamed Earth, as did large, elephantlike animals called *woolly mammoths*. Scientists have drawn conclusions about these creatures from what they left behind—whole mammoths frozen in ice and fossilized bones and teeth of dinosaurs.

Most fossils, however, are not the actual remains of once-living organisms. Instead, they are traces left behind when dead plants and animals decayed or dissolved. When sediment buries an organism, it can produce a mold or cast as the sediment hardens into rock. A mold forms when underground water dissolves the organism, leaving only its shape behind in the rock. If sediments fill the empty space and harden, the fossil becomes a cast.

In addition to showing what kinds of organisms lived on Earth long ago, fossils also show that Earth's surface was different than it is today. Scientists have found fossils of sea organisms in rock at the tops of high mountains. They infer that those rocks were once under water.

Scientists use fossil evidence to support the theory of continental drift. Fossils of similar plants and animals have been found in Africa, South America, India, and Australia. This means that these widely separated continents must have been joined at one time.

✔ **How are fossils used to show changes?**

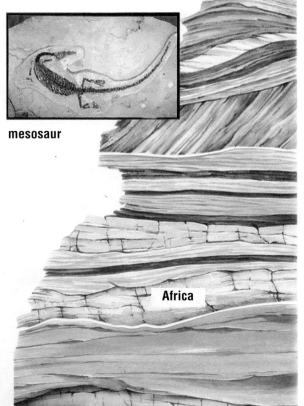

Similar rock layers and similar fossils, such as the mesosaur shown below, have been found in both South America and Africa. This provides evidence that the continents may once have been joined together.

South America

mesosaur

Africa

▲ Scientists called *paleontologists* study fossils to learn about life of the past.

Summary

Earth's continents once were joined to form a supercontinent called Pangea. Pangea broke apart and, over millions of years, the continents drifted to their present locations. Fossils, the remains and traces of dead organisms, show what Earth's life was like in the past. They also show that Earth's surface has changed.

Review

1. What was Pangea?
2. How old are the oldest rocks of the Grand Canyon?
3. How do we know that Earth's life was different in the past?
4. **Critical Thinking** Why is the Grand Canyon important to scientists studying Earth's past?
5. **Test Prep** The Southern continent that existed 200 million years ago was called —

   A Gondwana   C Laurasia
   B Precambria   D Eurasia

LINKS

MATH LINK

Collect/Organize/Display Data
Research Earth's history. Then make a chart showing the relative lengths of various eras. Your chart should show how long each era lasted and how long ago each occurred. Draw the chart to scale. For example, if an era lasted for half the time of Earth's history, it should cover half the chart.

WRITING LINK

Informative Writing—Compare and Contrast You learned that Earth's continents were once in different places. Where will they be in the future? Research what a map of the world might look like 100 million years from now. Then compare and contrast this map with a current map in a report for your teacher.

ART LINK

Past Life Look for illustrations of what Earth's surface might have looked like thousands, or even millions, of years ago. Compare what you find with the way Earth's surface looks today.

GO ONLINE TECHNOLOGY LINK

Learn more about changes to Earth's surface by visiting the National Air and Space Museum Internet site.
www.si.edu/harcourt/science

 Smithsonian Institution®

Exploring Earth's Surface from Space

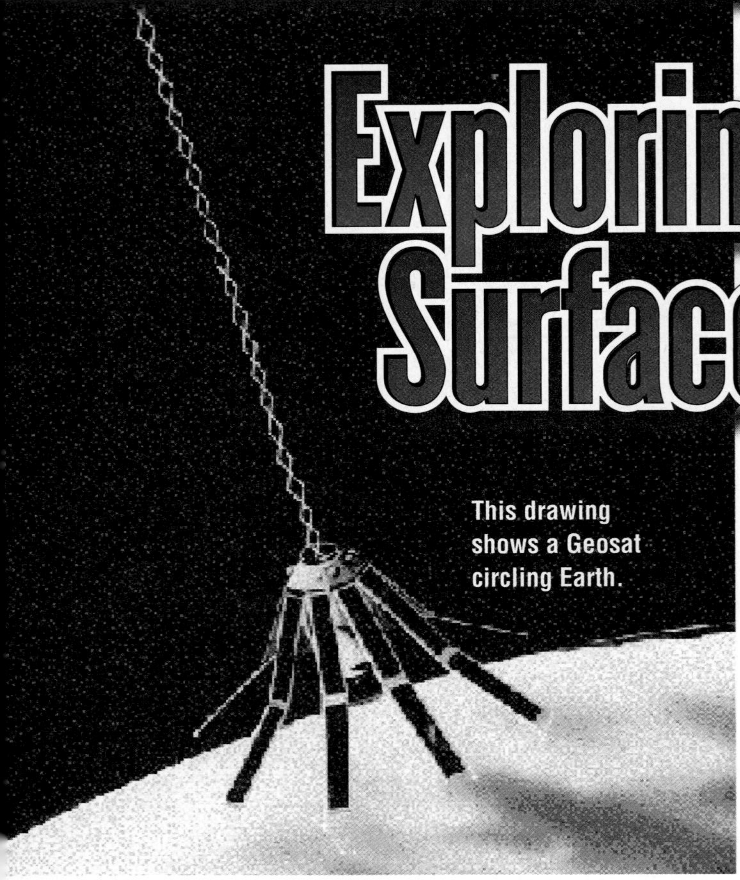

This drawing shows a Geosat circling Earth.

Newly released satellite images of the ocean floor are making scientists question old theories about the processes that change Earth's surface.

Satellite Secrets

Until recently, information collected by a U.S. government Geosat satellite was top secret. Now data gathered by this satellite has been released, and geologists are excited. However, they say it will take about ten years to analyze the satellite's images of Earth's geologic processes.

If you've ever sailed on the ocean, you probably couldn't tell that the water bulges up in certain places. It does this because of gravity. Rock on the ocean floor has a gravitational pull for the water around it. The more rock, the stronger the pull. The stronger the pull, the more the water bulges up. A 2000-m (about 6562-ft) underwater volcano causes a water bulge of about 2 m (6.6 ft).

Sensitive equipment on board a Geosat can measure these bulges from space. By measuring the surface of the ocean very precisely, the satellite produces clear gravity images of volcanoes, mountain ranges, plains, and other "landforms" on the ocean floor.

New Data Shakes Up Old Theories

Many areas of the ocean floor had never been surveyed before. About half of the underwater volcanoes shown by the Geosat's gravity imaging had not been known to exist. Gravity images of water bulges are also making scientists question old theories about how volcanic island chains form.

The old theory, called the "hot spot" model, said that there are hot areas in Earth's mantle. As Earth's plates pass slowly

Many of the volcanoes under the Pacific Ocean were discovered by gravity imaging.

over a hot spot, a long line of volcanoes forms. Each new volcano in the line is younger than the one just before it.

But the hot spot model can't explain some of the newly discovered volcano chains. For example, the Pukapuka Ridges, which extend for thousands of kilometers east of Tahiti, seem to have erupted all at the same time. Rock samples from different parts of the chain are all the same age.

Scientists are arguing about what these new discoveries mean in terms of the old theories about hot spots being correct. Many agree that the hot spot model may be wrong. All agree that there is much work ahead to develop more accurate theories based on this Geosat data.

THINK ABOUT IT

1. How does gravity imaging work?
2. Why do you think oil companies might be interested in gravity images?

Kia K. Baptist
GEOSCIENTIST

> "A key to being a scientist is to be unafraid to ask questions and unafraid that there may not be answers."

Kia Baptist can see what lies below Earth's surface. She is a geoscientist who works for an oil company. Her job is to help find oil and natural gas resources by finding clues in different kinds of data.

Ms. Baptist collects seismic data by creating small "earthquakes" in rock. Then she analyzes the sound signals that return and uses them to map the rock formations and structures underground.

Ms. Baptist also analyzes geochemical data to learn the chemical nature of the rock. This tells her what kind of rock it is, how old it is, and whether there is oil present. This information, along with computer technology, allows her to give advice to the oil companies on specific locations where oil and natural gas may be found.

Looking for clues is natural for Ms. Baptist. As a child growing up in Baltimore, Maryland, she was a mystery solver. She decided she wanted to help solve the mysteries of space by becoming an astronaut. Several times she worked as an intern at NASA, learning all she could about astronomy and physics. She took courses in many areas of science, believing that knowing about all branches of science would help her do her best work in one. When she began to study geology and chemistry, she realized her true interest lay in those areas. She hasn't stopped studying the Earth since then.

Ms. Baptist gives good advice to young scientists. She says, "Part of the process of science is attacking a problem and trying to find answers, but don't be intimidated if you don't find answers right away. Just keep learning."

THINK ABOUT IT

1. How could analyzing seismic data give clues about where oil is located?

2. Why is it important to know the specific location of oil?

MODEL EARTH

How can you model Earth's layers?

Materials

- rounded objects, such as
  - an apple
  - an avocado
  - a peach
  - a hard-boiled egg
  - a nectarine
  - a tennis ball
  - an orange
  - a plum
  - plain chocolates, or chocolate-covered peanuts

Procedure

1. Make two columns on a sheet of paper.

2. Label one column "Does Model Earth's Layers." Label the other column "Does Not Model Earth's Layers."

3. Decide what characteristics an object must have to model Earth's layers.

4. Examine each object. Then write the name of the object in the appropriate column.

Draw Conclusions

What characteristics must an object have to model Earth's layers? Which parts of the objects in the "Does Model Earth's Layers" column represent Earth's layers? What other objects can you think of that model Earth's layers?

FEATURING EARTH

How do landforms change?

Materials

- apple
- tape measure
- pan
- hotpad
- oven

Procedure

1. Measure the circumference of the apple.

2. Place the apple in a pan and, using the hot pad, put the pan in the oven and bake it for one hour at 300°F.

300° VEN

3. Your teacher or another adult will remove the apple from the oven. Allow it to cool, and measure it again.

4. Observe the features of the baked apple.

Draw Conclusions

In some ways, baked apples are a good model of how Earth's landforms change. Compare the circumference of the apple before and after you baked it. What happened to the peel as the apple cooled? What layer of Earth does the peel represent? What "landforms" can you identify on the apple peel? In what ways is the apple not a good model of Earth's changing landforms?

Vocabulary Review

Use the terms below to complete the sentences. The page numbers in ( ) tell you where to look in the chapter if you need help.

landform (C6)
weathering (C7)
erosion (C7)
deposition (C7)
mass movement (C9)
crust (C14)
mantle (C14)
core (C14)
plate (C15)

magma (C16)
volcano (C16)
earthquake (C18)
fault (C18)
continental drift (C22)
Pangea (C22)
fossils (C23)

1. An _____ is a sudden release of energy in Earth's _____, causing the ground to shake.

2. A rigid block of Earth's crust and upper mantle rock is a _____.

3. A _____ is a physical feature on Earth's surface, such as a mountain or valley.

4. The remains or traces of past life found in Earth's crust are called _____.

5. Molten rock from Earth's mantle is _____.

6. A _____ is a break in Earth's crust, along which pieces of the crust move.

7. _____ is the process of breaking rock into silt, sand, and other tiny pieces called sediment.

8. Lava is magma that reaches Earth's surface through an opening, called a _____, in Earth's crust.

9. The downhill movement of rock and soil because of gravity is _____.

10. The _____ is the layer of rock beneath Earth's crust.

11. The theory that the continents move over Earth's surface is _____.

12. _____ is the supercontinent that held all of Earth's land 225 million years ago.

13. _____ is the process of moving sediment from one place to another, and _____ is the process of dropping, or depositing, sediment in a new location.

14. The _____ is the center of Earth.

Connect Concepts

Use the Word Bank to complete the sentences.

deltas   beaches   tables   sinkholes   terminal moraines
arches   canyons   dunes   floodplains

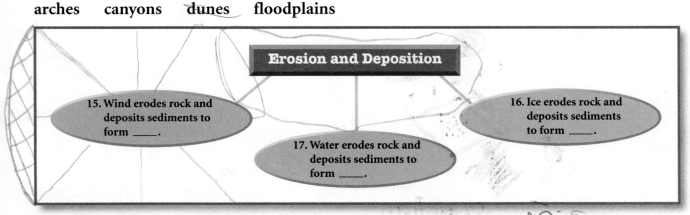

Erosion and Deposition

15. Wind erodes rock and deposits sediments to form _____.

16. Ice erodes rock and deposits sediments to form _____.

17. Water erodes rock and deposits sediments to form _____.

Check Understanding

Write the letter of the best choice.

18. Beginning with the outermost layer, Earth's layers are the —

  A crust, magma, and core

  B crust, mantle, and core

  C core, mantle, and crust

  D core, magma, and crust

19. Gondwana and Laurasia were formed by —

  F continental drift

  G erosion

  H deposition

  J earthquakes

20. Which of the following was **NOT** an ancient continent?

  A Pangea

  B Laurasia

  C Gondwana

  D Cenozoa

Critical Thinking

21. Explain why water erodes Earth's surface more than wind does.

22. If the mantle were solid rock, what feature would not form on Earth's surface? Explain.

23. Scientists have found many fossils of past life. Are fossils still being formed today? Explain.

Process Skills Review

24. What can you **observe** about these pieces of rock that shows you which one has been weathered and moved by water?

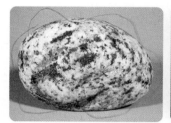 

25. How might you **make a model** of a volcano?

Performance Assessment

Plate Boundaries

Identify the three types of plate boundaries at A, B, and C in the illustration below. Explain what is happening at each boundary.

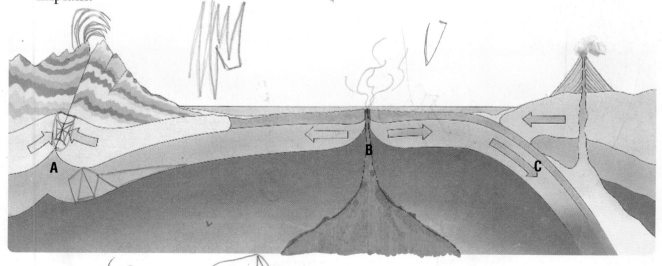

CHAPTER 2

Rocks and Minerals

Vocabulary Preview

mineral
streak
hardness
luster
rock
igneous rock
sedimentary rock
metamorphic rock
rock cycle

Rocks and minerals are all around you. The ground you walk on every day is made of rocks and minerals. They are in the soil. They are the gems that sparkle in jewelry. The Earth itself is made mostly of rocks and minerals.

Fast Fact

During your lifetime, you will use about 908,000 kilograms (2,000,000 lb) of rocks and minerals! This includes food, clothing, furniture, buildings, highways, and just about everything else a person uses.

Minerals Used by One Person During His or Her Life

Mineral	Amount Used (in kg)	(in lb)
Lead	400	880
Zinc	350	770
Copper	700	1500
Aluminum	1500	3300
Iron	41,000	90,400
Clay	12,250	27,000
Table salt	12,000	26,500
Coal	227,000	500,000
Stone, sand, gravel	454,000	1,000,000

All the gold known in the world would fit in a cube measuring about 18 meters (60 ft) on each side! But a little bit goes a long way. Twenty-eight grams (about 1 oz) of gold can be flattened into a thin sheet covering about 28 square meters (300 sq ft). That's enough to cover one-fourth of a tennis court!

Salt Salt
Salt Salt Salt

These pictures show equal weights of gold and salt. In ancient times, salt was so precious that it was traded ounce for ounce for gold! If you worked hard and you were "worth your salt," you were paid a "salary." This word meant "money for buying salt"!

This gravel quarry provides gravel for roads and buildings.

LESSON 1

What Are Minerals?

In this lesson, you can . . .

 INVESTIGATE mineral properties.

 LEARN ABOUT how minerals form and how we use them.

 LINK to math, writing, social studies, and technology.

Mineral Properties

Activity Purpose Chalk leaves a mark on a chalkboard because the board is harder than the chalk. Hardness is a property, or characteristic, of minerals, such as the calcite (KAL•syt) that makes up chalk. In this investigation you will **observe** that a mineral can be scratched by some things but not by other things. You will also test other mineral properties and then **classify** minerals by their properties.

Materials

- 6 labeled mineral samples
- hand lens
- streak plate
- copper penny
- steel nail

Activity Procedure

1 Copy the chart shown on page C33.

2 Use the hand lens to **observe** each mineral. Describe the color of each sample. **Record** your observations in the chart. (Picture A)

3 Use each mineral to draw a line across the streak plate. (Picture B) What color is the streak each made? **Record** your observations.

4 **CAUTION** Use caution with the nail, it is sharp. Test the hardness of each mineral by using your fingernail, the copper penny, and the steel nail. Try to scratch each mineral with each of these items. Then try to scratch each sample with each of the other minerals. **Record** your observations in the chart.

◀ A mineral can be different colors. Tourmaline (TOOR•muh•lin) can be pink, purple, green, black, or the mix of colors called watermelon, shown here. Tourmaline is often used in jewelry.

Picture A

Picture B

Mineral Sample	Color of the Mineral Sample	Color of the Mineral's Streak	Things That Scratch the Mineral
A			
B			
C			
D			
E			
F			

5 **Classify** the minerals based on each property you tested: color, streak, and hardness. Make labels that list all three properties for each mineral.

Draw Conclusions

1. How are the minerals you tested different from each other?

2. Which of the minerals you tested is the hardest? Explain your choice.

3. **Scientists at Work** Scientists **classify** things so it is easier to study them. How do you think scientists classify minerals?

Investigate Further Obtain five other unknown mineral samples. Determine the hardness, color, and streak of each. **Classify** all of the mineral samples after testing the new samples.

Process Skill Tip

When you **classify** things, you put them into groups based on ways they are alike. Organizing things in this way can make it easier to learn about them. Often, you can classify the same group of objects in many ways.

Minerals

How Some Minerals Form

To be a mineral, a material must have certain features. A **mineral** (MIN•er•uhl) is always a solid material with particles arranged in a repeating pattern. This pattern is called a crystal (KRIST•uhl). Almost all minerals are made from material that was never alive. Also, true minerals form only in nature. They are not made in a laboratory.

Minerals form in many ways. Some minerals form in Earth's mantle. There, high heat and pressure change carbon into hard, sparkling crystals called *diamond*. Diamonds have many uses. Some are cut and shaped to make jewelry. Most are used on cutting tools such as drills and saws.

Other minerals, such as *calcite*, can form at or near Earth's surface. Some calcite forms in the ocean when calcium, oxygen, and carbon combine in sea water. Some ocean animals form calcite shells or other body parts. Calcite also forms as water evaporates in limestone caves.

Water also plays a role in forming other minerals. *Galena* crystals form when hot, mineral-rich water moves slowly through cracks in Earth's crust, mixing with other minerals before it cools or evaporates.

✔ **What are some features a material must have to be called a mineral?**

FIND OUT

- what minerals are
- how to identify minerals
- how minerals are used

VOCABULARY

mineral
streak
luster
hardness

▲ Calcite is a mineral found in chalk.

◀ This shiny mineral is galena (guh•LEE•nuh), which is made of lead and sulfur. Galena crystals often form cubes.

The first compass needles were made from a mineral called *magnetite.* Magnetite is magnetic, as shown by the nail stuck to the sample. ▼

Mica is a mineral that splits easily into thin sheets. ▼

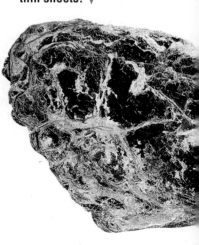

C36

Some Mineral Properties

You saw in the investigation that one property of a mineral is streak. **Streak** is the color of the powder left behind when you rub a mineral against a white tile called a streak plate. Usually the streak is the same color as the mineral. *Chalcopyrite* (chal•koh•PY•ryt), however, looks like shiny gold but has a black streak.

Luster (LUHS•tuhr) describes the way the surface of a mineral reflects light. Some minerals look shiny, like aluminum foil looks. These minerals have a *metallic* luster. Others look dull or dark. These minerals have a *nonmetallic* luster. The sparkling appearance of a diamond is known as a *brilliant* luster.

Hardness is a mineral's ability to resist being scratched. Mohs' hardness scale, shown at the right, lists minerals that have hardnesses from 1 to 10. A mineral with a higher number on the scale can scratch a mineral with a lower number.

✔ **Which minerals on Mohs' hardness scale can be scratched by quartz?**

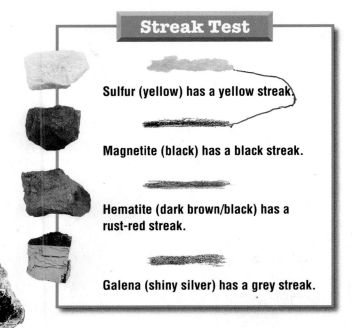

Streak Test

Sulfur (yellow) has a yellow streak.

Magnetite (black) has a black streak.

Hematite (dark brown/black) has a rust-red streak.

Galena (shiny silver) has a grey streak.

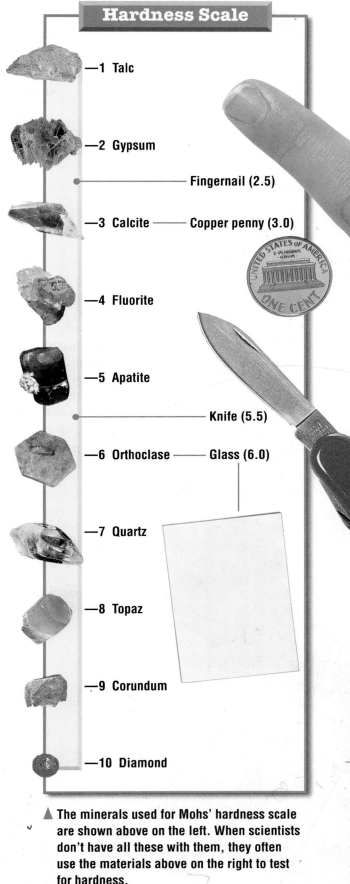

Hardness Scale

—1 Talc

—2 Gypsum

Fingernail (2.5)

—3 Calcite — Copper penny (3.0)

—4 Fluorite

—5 Apatite

Knife (5.5)

—6 Orthoclase — Glass (6.0)

—7 Quartz

—8 Topaz

—9 Corundum

—10 Diamond

▲ The minerals used for Mohs' hardness scale are shown above on the left. When scientists don't have all these with them, they often use the materials above on the right to test for hardness.

How We Use Minerals

Some minerals can be used in nearly the same form they have in nature. They don't need much refining, or processing to remove other materials. For example, silver and copper can be used to make musical instruments, electric wire, and jewelry. *Gypsum* can be used to make plaster and wallboard. *Graphite* is used in pencils. *Halite,* or table salt, can be used to flavor and preserve foods.

Pure silver is a very soft metal. It has a hardness of about 2 on the Mohs' hardness scale. Because it is so soft, it can be shaped easily. It also can be mixed with other metals to make beautiful jewelry or to cover musical instruments, such as this fluegelhorn.

Hematite is a mineral made of iron and oxygen. It has a hardness of 5 to 6.5 on the Mohs' hardness scale. Hematite is an important source of the iron used to make steel. Steel beams are used to make tall buildings strong.

Diamond is the hardest natural substance found on Earth. It has a hardness of 10 on Mohs' hardness scale. Some diamonds are used to make beautiful jewelry. Diamonds that are not good enough for jewelry are used on drills that dig deep into Earth's crust. The small cylinders all along the edges of this drill are industrial diamonds. They're hidden under the silver paint.

Some minerals are not useful in their natural form. They must be refined to be useful. The mineral *cuprite* (KOOP•ryt) is made of copper and oxygen. After cuprite is refined, the copper is used in making pennies, pots and pans, and water pipes.

✔ **What are five uses of minerals?**

Summary

Some minerals form in Earth's mantle, and others form at or near Earth's surface. Minerals can be identified by their properties. Some mineral properties are streak, hardness, and luster. People use minerals in many ways.

Review

1. List three features a material must have to be a mineral.
2. What is mineral hardness?
3. Name six ways people use minerals.
4. **Critical Thinking** You have a sample of an unknown mineral. It can scratch fluorite but not quartz. What is its approximate hardness?
5. **Test Prep** Which of the following minerals is the hardest?
   - A diamond
   - B apatite
   - C topaz
   - D talc

LINKS

MATH LINK

Choose Measuring Devices Collect six different mineral samples that are all about the same size. Use a balance to find the mass of each sample. Record each value in a table. Explain why minerals that are about the same size may have very different masses.

WRITING LINK

Expressive Writing—Poem A birthstone is the gem that stands for a particular month. Find a list of the birthstones for all the months, and make a poster about them. Draw a color picture of each gem next to its name. Write a poem for a family member about your birthday month and birthstone.

SOCIAL STUDIES LINK

Go West! Find out why so many Americans in the mid-1800s risked their lives riding west in covered wagons or sailing around Cape Horn to get to California. Make a map of the routes they took. Add pictures of what they did in California.

TECHNOLOGY LINK

Learn more about the mineral gold by viewing *Gold Mining* on the **Harcourt Science Newsroom Video.**

CNN
Turner
Le@rning®

LESSON 2

What Are Rocks?

In this lesson, you can . . .

 INVESTIGATE different kinds of rocks.

 LEARN ABOUT how rocks form.

 LINK to math, writing, physical education, and technology.

Identifying Rocks

Activity Purpose Have you ever helped make chocolate chip cookies? If so, you know that you put ingredients in a bowl, mix them, spoon the mixture onto a cookie sheet, and then bake it in an oven. The heat in the oven causes the ingredients to change and stick together to form something new—cookies. Some rocks form in a similar way. In this investigation you will **observe** some rocks and **classify** them by the ways they formed.

Materials

- 5 labeled rock samples
- hand lens
- dropper
- vinegar
- safety goggles
- paper plate
- paper towels

Activity Procedure

1 Make a chart like the one shown on page C41.

2 Use the hand lens to **observe** each rock. What color or colors is each rock? **Record** your observations in your chart.

◀ **Wind-blown sand and rain carved away bits of rock to form this arch in Arches National Park, Utah.**

Rock Sample	Color	Texture	Picture	Bubbles When Vinegar Added
1				
2				
3				
4				
5				

3 Can you see any grains, or small pieces, making up the rock? Are the grains very small, or are they large? Are they rounded, or do they have sharp edges? Do the grains fit together like puzzle pieces? Or are they just next to one another? **Record** your observations under *Texture* in your chart. Draw a picture of each rock in the *Picture* column.

4 **CAUTION** **Put on your safety goggles.** Vinegar bubbles when it is dropped on the mineral calcite. Put the rock samples on the paper plate. Use the dropper to put a few drops of vinegar on each rock. **Observe** what happens. **Record** your findings. (Picture A)

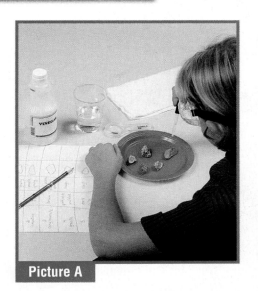

Picture A

5 **Classify** your rocks into two groups based on how the rocks are alike.

Draw Conclusions

1. What properties did you use to **classify** your rocks?

2. How does your classification system **compare** with those of two other students?

3. **Scientists at Work** One way scientists **classify** rocks is by how they formed. Choose one rock and describe how you think it might have formed.

Investigate Further **Plan and conduct a simple experiment** to test this **hypothesis:** Color is one of the best properties to use to identify rocks.

Process Skill Tip

Classifying is a way to study a large number of objects. You **classify** by grouping things, based on how they are alike. For rocks, their size, shape, color, and what has happened to them are all things that can be alike.

C41

Types of Rocks

Igneous Rocks

FIND OUT

- **how rocks form**
- **how people use rocks**

VOCABULARY

rock
igneous rock
sedimentary rock
metamorphic rock

Earth is made mostly of rocks. A **rock** is material made up of one or more minerals. Like minerals, some rocks form at or near Earth's surface. Others form deep in the crust or in Earth's middle layer, the mantle. There are many different kinds of rocks. But they all can be classified into three groups based on how they formed.

Rocks that form when melted rock hardens are called **igneous** (IG•nee•uhs) **rocks**. In Chapter 1 you learned that lava is magma that reaches Earth's surface through a volcano. Lava cools and hardens before large mineral crystals have time to form. Rocks formed from lava have small mineral pieces and are called *fine-grained*. Usually their mineral crystals can be seen only with a microscope.

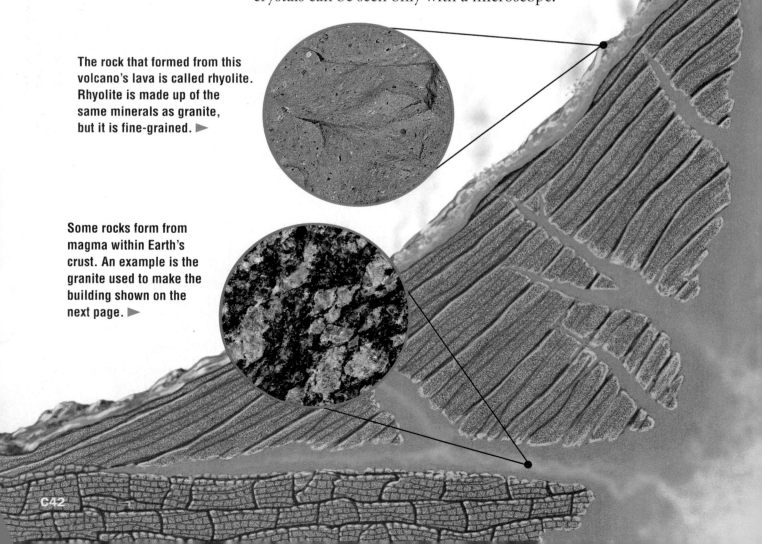

The rock that formed from this volcano's lava is called rhyolite. Rhyolite is made up of the same minerals as granite, but it is fine-grained. ▶

Some rocks form from magma within Earth's crust. An example is the granite used to make the building shown on the next page. ▶

▲ Basalt

▲ Gabbro

▲ Pumice

▲ Obsidian

Magma cools and hardens slowly. Its minerals can form large grains that are easy to see. Igneous rocks formed from slowly cooling magma are called *coarse-grained*.

Basalt (buh•SALT) is the most common igneous rock that forms from lava at Earth's surface. Basalt is a dark, greenish-black rock made up mostly of the minerals *feldspar* (FELD•spar) and *pyroxene* (py•RAHKS•een). *Gabbro* (GAB•roh) is an igneous rock that is also made up mostly of these two minerals. But gabbro has larger mineral grains than basalt. That's because gabbro forms inside Earth instead of at Earth's surface.

Pumice (PUHM•ihs) is another igneous rock. The tiny holes in pumice are caused by gases escaping from the lava as it cools. Pumice feels rough and scratchy. *Obsidian* (uhb•SID•ee•uhn) also forms from lava. The lava cools so quickly that the rock looks like black glass. When obsidian breaks, sharp edges form.

Granite is a common igneous rock that forms when magma cools slowly beneath Earth's surface. Most granite is made up of large grains of feldspar, *quartz,* and mica (MY•kuh). These mineral grains are joined together tightly, making granite a strong rock that lasts for a long time.

✔ **What are igneous rocks?**

◀ Granite is an igneous rock often used for building. Brookings Hall at Washington University in St. Louis, Missouri, is made of unpolished pink granite blocks.

C43

Sedimentary Rocks

Recall from Chapter 1 that rocks are broken down into smaller pieces by weathering. At Earth's surface the actions of wind, water, ice, and plant roots cause weathering.

After rocks are weathered into small pieces, blowing winds, flowing water, gravity, or slow-moving glaciers often move the pieces to other places, where they are deposited in layers.

When erosion is caused by water, over time the sediments drop to the bottoms of streams, rivers, or lakes. Over a long time, layers of sediments can form **sedimentary** (sed•uh•MEN•ter•ee) **rock** as they are squeezed and stuck together.

Most sediments are dropped by moving water when it slows down, such as when a river or stream enters a lake. The largest pieces of weathered rock are dropped first. *Conglomerate* (kuhn•GLAHM•er•it) is a type of sedimentary rock that can form from these larger pieces. The pieces in a conglomerate can be as big as boulders or as small as peas. In a conglomerate, the pieces are round and smooth. Most conglomerates form in shallow water.

Smaller sediments are carried farther by the water and dropped later. *Siltstone* is one type of rock made up of smaller sediments.

Limestone is a fine-grained sedimentary rock. It is made up mostly of the mineral calcite. Most limestone forms in oceans, sometimes from seashells. A few kinds of limestone form in lakes.

Many sedimentary rocks form in bodies of water like this stream. Sedimentary rocks may contain fossils. This happens when shells, bones, or other remains of once-living organisms are buried in sediment layers.

▲ Conglomerate

▲ Limestone

▲ Sandstone

▲ Shale

Sandstone is another kind of sedimentary rock. Sandstones, as you might guess from their name, are made up of minerals the size of sand grains. Nearly all sandstones are made up mostly of the mineral quartz.

Some sandstones are fine-grained. They feel smooth when you touch them. Other sandstones are coarse-grained. They feel rough against your skin. Sandstones can form in water or on land.

Shale is a fine-grained sedimentary rock made of very small sediments. The sediments in most shales are so small that you can see them only with a strong hand lens. Some shale sediments are so small that you can see them only with a microscope.

✔ **What processes help form sedimentary rocks?**

THE INSIDE STORY

Crossbedding

1. Many sandstones are *crossbedded*. Crossbeds can begin to form when wind blows sand grains in one direction for a long time. The grains pile up until the piles become so steep that sand begins to slide down the side away from the wind. These sand piles, or *dunes*, will become the first rock layer.

2. Over time, more sand covers the first layer. This new sand keeps the first layer from moving. Sand blown by the wind keeps filling the gaps between dunes.

3. When the wind changes direction, the next sand layer is put down at a different angle. As the wind keeps changing direction, new layers are put down at different angles. The rock layers that form from the sand layers will show these changes in wind direction.

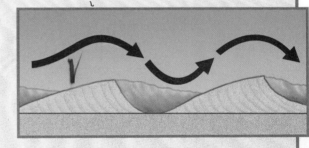
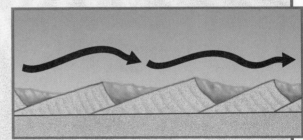
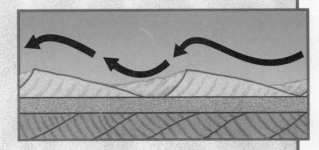

Metamorphic Rocks

High heat and great pressure can change the texture of rock—the way it looks and feels. They can also change the form of the minerals that make up the rock. These changed rocks are called **metamorphic** (met•uh•MAWR•fik) **rocks**. Metamorphic rocks can form from any kind of rock—sedimentary, igneous, or even other metamorphic rocks.

Some metamorphic rocks form when mountains are built up. *Schist* (SHIST) and *gneiss* (NYS) are two examples. Schist has wavy lines. It splits easily into layers. Gneiss forms when schist is heated and squeezed more. Gneiss often has bands of light and dark minerals.

Marble is another metamorphic rock. Marble forms when limestone is squeezed and heated. Artists often use marble to make statues. It also is used in buildings.

Slate is a metamorphic rock that forms when shale is under great pressure. Like shale, slate has layers. In the past, people used slate to make chalkboards for schools. Slate tiles are sometimes used to cover roofs.

Quartzite forms from sandstone when heat fuses the sand grains together. Quartzite usually has a milky color. Other minerals in the sandstone can give quartzite a gray or pink color.

✔ **How do metamorphic rocks form?**

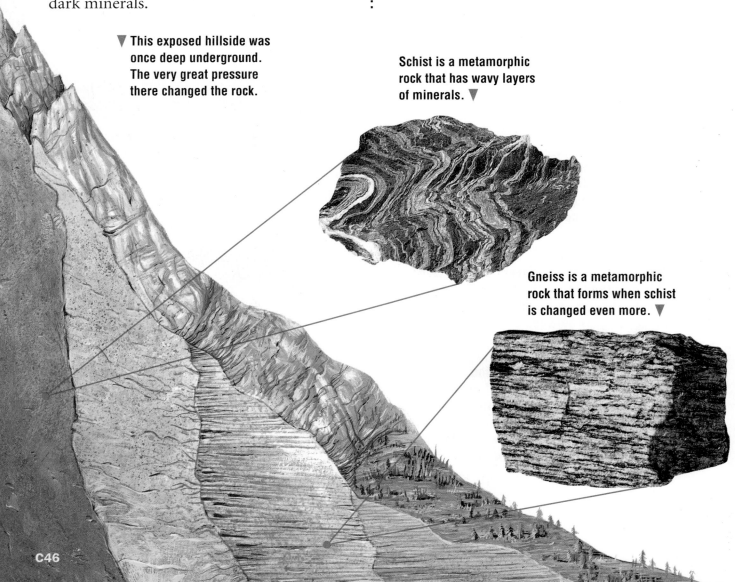

▼ This exposed hillside was once deep underground. The very great pressure there changed the rock.

Schist is a metamorphic rock that has wavy layers of minerals. ▼

Gneiss is a metamorphic rock that forms when schist is changed even more. ▼

Slate is a metamorphic rock that can be split into thin sheets. Slate pieces are used to cover roofs on houses.

Summary

Rocks are made up of one or more minerals. Rocks are classified by the way they form. Igneous rocks form when magma or lava cools and hardens. Sedimentary rocks are usually made of pieces of rock that have been squeezed and stuck together. Metamorphic rocks form when heat and pressure change rocks.

Review

1. What are rocks?
2. How are rocks classified?
3. In which type of rock are fossils found?
4. **Critical Thinking** You find a rock that is made of small grains. How can you tell whether it is igneous or sedimentary?
5. **Test Prep** Which kind of rock is granite?
   A igneous
   B metamorphic
   C layered
   D sedimentary

LINKS

MATH LINK

Use Mental Math A lake has three rivers flowing into it. Each river deposits 1 centimeter of sediment in one year. How deep will the sediments be after 10 years? If the lake is a meter deep, when will it be completely filled by sediment?

WRITING LINK

Informative Writing—Narration Use library reference materials to find out about the Navajo Sandstone crossbeds. Then write a story for your teacher describing the area while the crossbeds were forming.

PHYSICAL EDUCATION LINK

Rock Climbing Use library reference materials to find out the equipment needed for safe rock climbing. Make a list of safety rules for the sport of rock climbing. Tell how rock types affect climbing rules.

GO ONLINE TECHNOLOGY LINK

Learn more about rock types by visiting this Internet site.
www.scilinks.org/harcourt

SCI LINKS
THE WORLD'S A CLICK AWAY

What Is the Rock Cycle?

In this lesson, you can . . .

 INVESTIGATE how rocks can change.

 LEARN ABOUT ways in which rocks change.

 LINK to math, writing, technology, and other areas.

 **INVESTIGATE**

The Rock Cycle

Activity Purpose Do you recycle aluminum cans? After the recycling truck takes away the cans, they go through many changes before they become new products. In this investigation you will **make a model** to show how Earth's natural processes can change rocks.

Materials

- small objects—pieces of aquarium gravel, fake jewels, and a few pennies
- 3 pieces of modeling clay, each a different color
- 2 aluminum pie pans

Activity Procedure

1 The small objects stand for minerals. Press the "minerals" into the three pieces of clay. Each color of clay with its objects stands for a different igneous rock.

2 Now suppose that wind and water are weathering and eroding the "rocks." To **model** this process, break one rock into pieces (sediments) and drop the pieces into one of the pie pans (a lake). (Picture A)

◄ Giant's Causeway in Ireland began to form when lava quickly cooled and shrank to form basalt. Over many years, water and ice weathered the rock to form these spectacular, six-sided columns.

Picture A

Picture B

3 Drop pieces from the second rock on top of the first rock layer. Then drop pieces of the third rock on top of the second layer. Press the layers together by using the bottom of the empty pie pan. What kind of rock have you made?

4 Squeeze the "sedimentary rock" between your hands to warm it up. What causes the rock to change? Which kind of rock is it now? (Picture B)

Draw Conclusions

1. How did the igneous "rocks" change in this investigation?

2. What might weathering and erosion do to a metamorphic rock?

3. **Scientists at Work** Scientists often **make a model** to help them understand processes that occur in nature. What process did your hands represent in Step 4 of the activity?

Investigate Further **Plan and conduct a simple experiment** to test this **hypothesis:** Any type of rock can be changed into any other type of rock by natural processes within the Earth.

Process Skill Tip

If you **make a model**, you can often understand a natural process that is hard to observe. Because rocks change over a long time, it's hard to see the changes happening.

C49

How Rocks Change

Processes That Cause Change

Rocks are always changing. However, the changes usually happen so slowly that you would never notice them. It can take thousands of years for a rock to weather and erode. It can take many more years for the eroded pieces to be changed into sedimentary rock.

You learned in Lesson 2 that high heat and pressure can change rocks. Sometimes the rocks get hot enough to melt completely. When this melted rock cools and hardens, it has changed from metamorphic to igneous. It usually takes many years for rock to be buried deep enough inside Earth to melt.

A rock can begin as one type and be changed many times. You made a model of these changes in the investigation. Instead of a few minutes, however, changes can take many thousands of years. Some part of the first rock, however, will still be there after each change.

✔ **How does weathering affect rock?**

FIND OUT

- **about processes that change rocks**
- **how rocks change over time**

VOCABULARY

rock cycle

Follow the blue arrows to learn about the changes that might happen to one rock. ▼

◀ Basalt forms when lava quickly cools and hardens at Earth's surface. Basalt is the most common igneous rock on Earth.

Wind or rain carries the weathered pieces of basalt to the river. The river carries the pieces downstream. As they move, they bump into one another. Jagged edges are slowly rounded off. ▼

Tree roots weather the basalt by growing into the rock and breaking it into pieces. Freezing and thawing and rain also weather the rock. ▶

C50

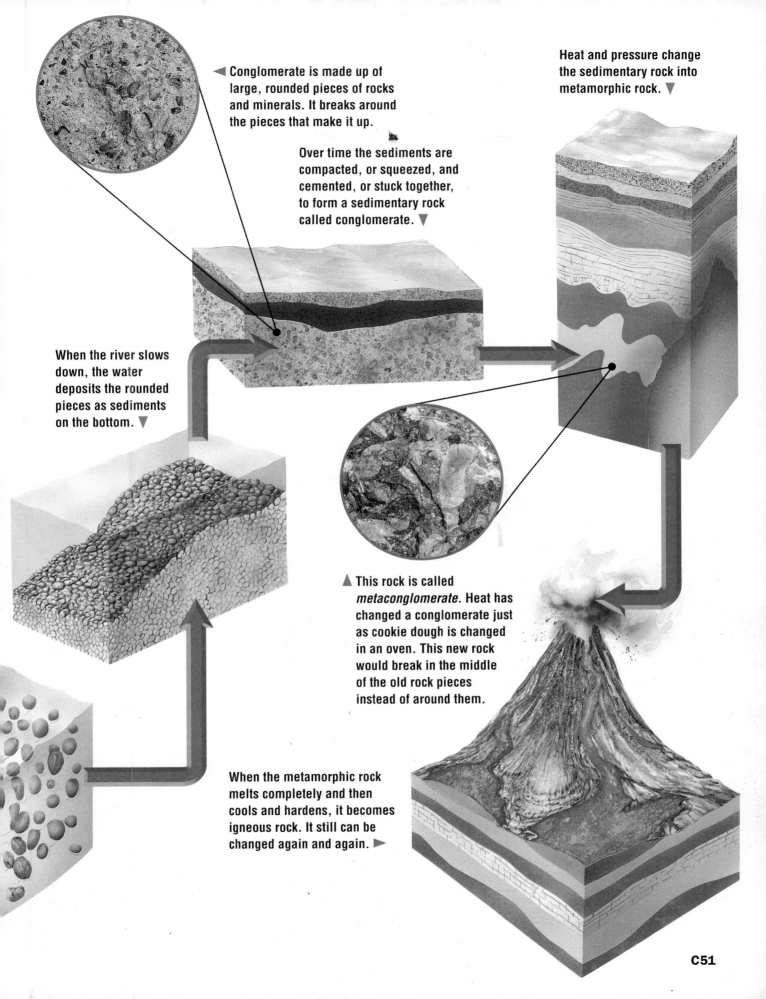

Conglomerate is made up of large, rounded pieces of rocks and minerals. It breaks around the pieces that make it up.

Over time the sediments are compacted, or squeezed, and cemented, or stuck together, to form a sedimentary rock called conglomerate. ▼

Heat and pressure change the sedimentary rock into metamorphic rock. ▼

When the river slows down, the water deposits the rounded pieces as sediments on the bottom. ▼

This rock is called *metaconglomerate*. Heat has changed a conglomerate just as cookie dough is changed in an oven. This new rock would break in the middle of the old rock pieces instead of around them.

When the metamorphic rock melts completely and then cools and hardens, it becomes igneous rock. It still can be changed again and again. ▶

C51

The Rock Cycle

The diagram below and on the next page shows the never-ending rock changes that are called the **rock cycle**. Notice that many arrows lead out from each rock type. This shows that there is more than one path through the rock cycle.

As rocks move through the rock cycle, the materials that make them up are used over and over. Look at the diagram. Try to find where rocks are squeezed. Also notice where sticking together might take place, where rocks melt, and where rocks are under heat and pressure. As you study the diagram, remember that all these processes take a very long time.

✔ **How can a metamorphic rock be changed into a different metamorphic rock?**

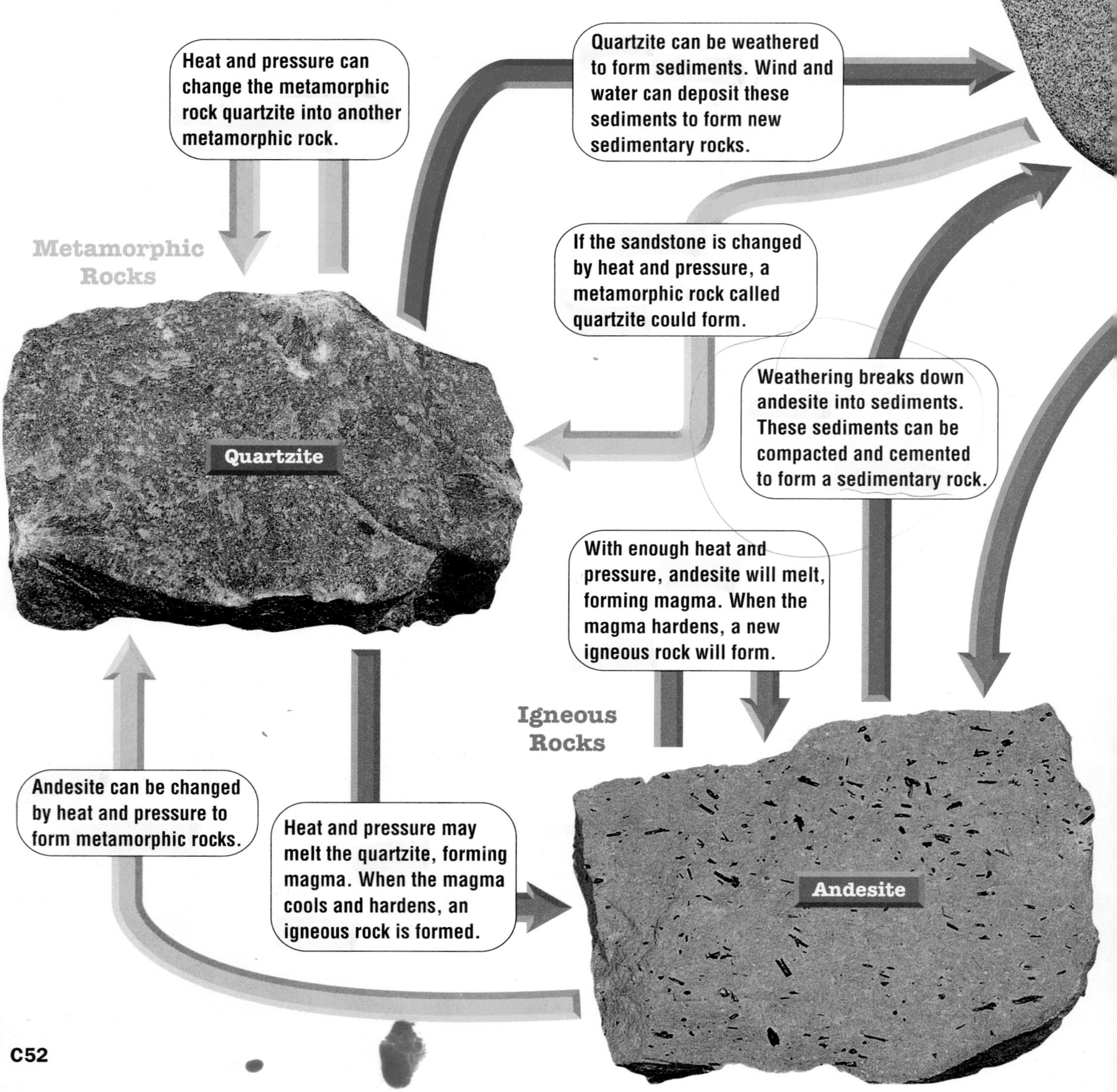

Metamorphic Rocks

Heat and pressure can change the metamorphic rock quartzite into another metamorphic rock.

Quartzite can be weathered to form sediments. Wind and water can deposit these sediments to form new sedimentary rocks.

If the sandstone is changed by heat and pressure, a metamorphic rock called quartzite could form.

Weathering breaks down andesite into sediments. These sediments can be compacted and cemented to form a sedimentary rock.

With enough heat and pressure, andesite will melt, forming magma. When the magma hardens, a new igneous rock will form.

Quartzite

Andesite can be changed by heat and pressure to form metamorphic rocks.

Heat and pressure may melt the quartzite, forming magma. When the magma cools and hardens, an igneous rock is formed.

Igneous Rocks

Andesite

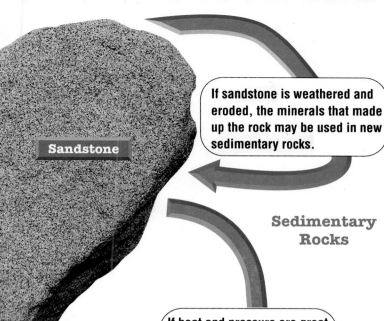

Sandstone

If sandstone is weathered and eroded, the minerals that made up the rock may be used in new sedimentary rocks.

Sedimentary Rocks

If heat and pressure are great enough, sandstone will melt, forming magma. When the magma hardens, a new igneous rock will form.

Summary

Rocks change from one kind to another in the rock cycle. Some of the processes in the rock cycle are weathering, erosion, melting, compaction, and cementation.

Review

1. What is the rock cycle?
2. What part do volcanoes play in the rock cycle?
3. What is one thing that can change a rock to metamorphic rock?
4. **Critical Thinking** How might a sandstone change into another sandstone?
5. **Test Prep** What starts the change from an igneous rock to a sedimentary rock?
   A heat
   B pressure
   C melting
   D weathering

LINKS

MATH LINK

Solve Problems A layer of sedimentary rock is 5 meters thick. The layer was laid down at the rate of 1 centimeter per year. How many years did it take to form?

WRITING LINK

Narrative Writing—Story For a younger child, tell about the "life" of a rock from the rock's point of view. Tell where the rock has been. Tell where it will go. Make sure the rock has been changed into each type of rock at least once.

SOCIAL STUDIES LINK

Building Materials Use library references to find out why some types of rocks are most often used as building materials in your city. Make a model or poster to show what you learned.

LITERATURE LINK

Everybody Needs a Rock Read the book *Everybody Needs a Rock* by Byrd Baylor. Make a list of rules to follow to find your own special rock.

GO **ONLINE** TECHNOLOGY LINK

Visit the Harcourt Learning Site for related links, activities, and resources.
www.harcourtschool.com

WELCOME TO THE LEARNING SITE

Diamond Coatings

Perhaps you've seen a ring that holds a diamond—a sparkling natural mineral. But did you know that diamonds can be made? These artificial diamonds aren't made for jewelry but for use by scientists and in factories.

Artificial Diamonds

In nature, diamonds form when carbon is kept at very high pressures and temperatures. It may take millions of years for the diamonds to reach Earth's surface. To make artificial diamonds, scientists imitate the natural process. They use enormous pressures and temperatures to make diamonds in a much shorter time than in nature. However, these diamonds are usually plain-looking and very small. These artificial diamonds have been made since the 1950s.

CVD

Now a new, easier way to make artificial diamonds has been found. It takes high temperature but not high pressure. The new method uses simple hydrocarbons (HY•droh•kar•buhnz). These are materials made of the elements hydrogen and carbon. Scientists heat these materials to very high temperatures. At these temperatures the materials become gases. When the gases cool, they form a thin layer of diamond crystals. This process is called chemical vapor deposition, or CVD. The thin layers of hard diamond crystals are used to protect softer materials.

A thin coating of artificial diamond can protect metal parts. Examples are airplane wings and parts of automobile engines. The coating makes the parts last longer. A thin diamond coating also lowers friction and improves speed. Perhaps someday golf clubs and racing boats will have diamond coatings.

Send Me a Wire

A group of scientists in England is working to develop diamond-coated wires and fibers. The coating adds very little weight but makes the coated materials much stronger. For example, the metal tungsten (TUHNG•stuhn) is too heavy to use as wire for some jobs. But a thin, lightweight wire coated with diamond would work as well as a thicker, heavier, uncoated wire.

Researchers also have removed the wire after it was coated. This leaves behind a very small, hollow diamond tube. These tubes might be used as fiber optic wires for computers, or they could be very fine needles for use by doctors and surgeons.

THINK ABOUT IT

1. Why would people want to make artificial diamonds?

2. Why is chemical vapor deposition useful?

▲ This microscope photograph shows a diamond crystal growing on a metal surface.

Mack Gipson, Jr.
STRUCTURAL GEOLOGIST

Mack Gipson grew up on a farm in South Carolina. He helped with farm work and was interested in nature. In junior high, he read a book about Earth and began to wonder how rocks were formed and what caused Earth's layers.

After finishing college with degrees in science and mathematics, Dr. Gipson became a high school teacher. He was drafted into the U.S. Army and trained as a radio technician. While he was with the army in Germany, he decided to go back to school and study geology. He decided he wanted to work outdoors as a geologist rather than spend all day indoors teaching.

One of Dr. Gipson's jobs in college was to test core samples. A core sample shows layers of soil and rock from underground. To get a core sample, a long metal tube is drilled into the ground.

Builders test core samples to make sure the ground can withstand the weight of a building or road. Dr. Gipson tested core samples for the building of runways at O'Hare International Airport in Chicago. He also studied rock layers near coal mines in Illinois.

After graduating from the University of Chicago, Dr. Gipson stayed to help study samples of rock and clay from the ocean floor. This study helped scientists learn about how the oceans have changed over time.

Dr. Gipson founded the Department of Geological Sciences at Virginia State University. In addition to teaching, he has done studies for the National Aeronautics and Space Administration (NASA). He studied pictures of pyramidlike mountains on Mars, concluding that the pictures show extinct volcanoes eroded by the wind.

THINK ABOUT IT

1. How might studying a core sample show how much weight the ground could safely support?

2. What skills do you think are needed to study worlds far from Earth?

Geologists studying core samples

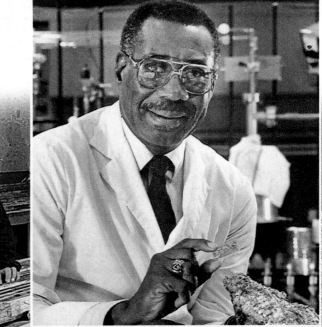

GROWING CRYSTALS

How are minerals left behind by evaporation?

Materials

- plastic gloves
- safety goggles
- apron
- 1 tablespoon of laundry bluing
- 1 tablespoon of water
- 1 tablespoon of ammonia
- 1 tablespoon of table salt
- plastic cup
- spoon
- sponge
- plastic bowl
- food coloring

Procedure

CAUTION Be sure to wear gloves, safety goggles, and an apron.

❶ Mix the bluing, water, ammonia, and salt in the plastic cup. Stir gently until the salt has dissolved.

❷ Place the sponge in the bowl. Pour the mixture over the sponge. Throw away the cup.

❸ Sprinkle 4 drops of food coloring over the sponge. Wait one day.

Draw Conclusions

Observe the sponge. Does it change? What is forming?

WEATHERING ROCK

How can you model weathering by using chalk?

Materials

- 2 pieces of chalk
- plastic jar with lid
- water
- strainer

Procedure

❶ Break each piece of chalk into about three pieces. Put all the chalk pieces except one into the jar.

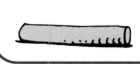

❷ Pour water into the jar until the chalk is covered. Put the lid on the jar. Make sure it is tightly sealed. Shake the jar for about 5 minutes to "weather" the chalk.

❸ Pour the water through the strainer to get the chalk pieces.

Draw Conclusions

Compare the strained pieces to the chalk that was left out. What happened? Why? Compare this model to real rocks, weathering, and erosion. How are they alike? How are they different?

Vocabulary Review

Use the terms below to complete the sentences. The page numbers in ( ) tell you where to look in the chapter if you need help.

mineral (C36) igneous rock (C42)
streak (C37) sedimentary rock (C44)
hardness (C37) metamorphic rock (C46)
luster (C37) rock cycle (C52)
rock (C42)

1. A natural, nonliving, solid material that has particles in a repeating pattern is a ____.

2. A ____ is made up of one or more minerals.

3. Limestone is a form of ____.

4. The ____ is the repeating of changes from one kind of rock to another over time.

5. A ____ is a rock changed by heat and pressure.

6. Melted rock cools and hardens to form ____.

7. The color of the powder left behind when you rub a mineral on a white porcelain plate is called the mineral's ____.

8. ____ is a mineral property that describes the way light reflects from the mineral's surface.

9. A mineral's ability to resist being scratched is its ____.

Connect Concepts

Fill in the blanks with the correct terms from the Word Bank.

color   luster   Mohs' hardness scale
hardness   streak

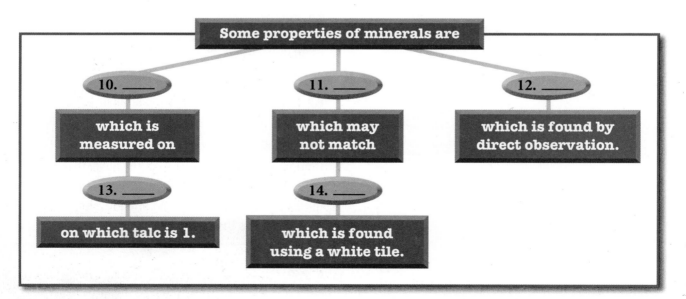

Some properties of minerals are

10. ____   11. ____   12. ____

which is measured on   which may not match   which is found by direct observation.

13. ____   14. ____

on which talc is 1.   which is found using a white tile.

Check Understanding

Write the letter of the best choice.

15. A rock forms in layers of small pieces. It is a _____ rock.
    A sedimentary C igneous
    B mineral   D metamorphic

16. Mohs' scale is used to identify a mineral's —
    F color   H streak
    G luster   J hardness

17. If you describe a mineral as being shiny, you are describing the property of —
    A streak   C hardness
    B luster   D color

18. A rock that has been changed by pressure and heat is called a(n) _____ rock.
    F sedimentary
    G metamorphic
    H igneous
    J metallic

19. Which of the following minerals is the hardest on Mohs' hardness scale?
    A talc   C diamond
    B gypsum   D quartz

20. Rocks change over time from one type to another. This process is called —
    F type changing
    G the rock cycle
    H erosion
    J melting

21. Particles in minerals form regular patterns called —
    A crystals   C conglomerates
    B layers   D shells

Process Skills Review

22. Based on the **model** you made of the rock cycle, what might happen to the "rock" if you made it hot enough to melt?

23. Why do scientists **classify** minerals?

24. How do scientists **classify** rocks?

Critical Thinking

25. How can a metamorphic rock be changed into an igneous rock?

26. Describe the path of a rock through the rock cycle.

Performance Assessment

Mineral Tests

Work with a partner. Use the hand lens to take a closer look at five mineral samples. Make a chart showing all the properties of each mineral. Tell how you tested for each property.

Weather and Climate

Vocabulary Preview

atmosphere
air pressure
humidity
precipitation
evaporation
condensation
local winds
prevailing winds
air mass
front
climate
microclimate
El Niño
greenhouse effect
global warming

Does weather begin or end? Or does it just keep moving from place to place? Many things contribute to making weather and to changing it.

Fast Fact

The United States is a country of many weather extremes. Below are some record-breaking weather measurements.

Heavy Weather

What	Where	How Much
Highest Temperature	Death Valley, CA	134°F
Lowest Temperature	Prospect Creek, AK	⁻79.8°F
Heaviest Snowfall	Mount Shasta, CA	189 in.
Most Snow in a Year	Mount Rainier, WA	1,224.5 in.
Strongest Wind	Mount Washington, NH	231 mi/hr
Most Rain in a Year	Kukui, HI	739 in.

Fast Fact

Each summer an average of 6–12 tropical storms form in the Atlantic Ocean, the Caribbean Sea, or the Gulf of Mexico and move toward the United States. If a storm's winds reach 74 miles an hour or more, the storm is called a hurricane.

Fast Fact

In 1816 a volcano in Asia blew huge amounts of dust into the atmosphere, blocking some of the sun's rays. That year average temperatures around the world dropped several degrees. In June there were even a few days of snow in the northeastern United States.

How Can You Observe and Measure Weather Conditions?

In this lesson, you can . . .

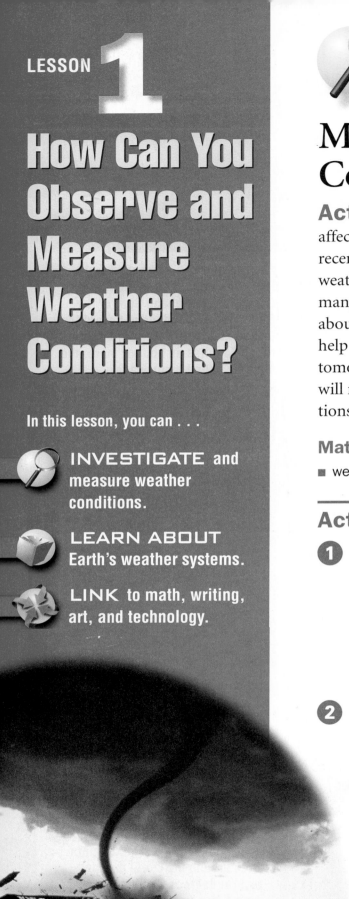

INVESTIGATE and measure weather conditions.

LEARN ABOUT Earth's weather systems.

LINK to math, writing, art, and technology.

◀ A Midwest tornado

INVESTIGATE

Measuring Weather Conditions

Activity Purpose People have always been affected by the weather. But it wasn't until fairly recently that scientists have been able to predict the weather accurately. Today's weather scientists use many instruments to **measure** and **collect data** about weather conditions. Then they use the data to help **predict** what the weather will be like today, tomorrow, or next weekend. In this investigation you will measure and collect data about weather conditions in your area.

Materials
- weather station

Activity Procedure

1 Make a copy of the Weather Station Daily Record table. You will use it to **record** the date, the time, the temperature, the amount of rain or snow, the wind direction and speed, and the cloud conditions each day for five days. Try to **record** the weather conditions at the same time each day.

2 Place the weather station in a shady spot, 1 m above the ground. **Record** the temperature. (Picture A)

3 Be sure the rain gauge will not collect runoff from any buildings or trees. **Record** the amount of rain or snow (if any).

Weather Station Daily Record

Date				
Time				
Temperature				
Rainfall or snowfall				
Wind direction and speed				
Cloud conditions				

Picture A

4 Be sure the wind vane is located where wind from any direction will reach it. **Record** the wind direction and speed. Winds are labeled with the direction from which they blow. (Picture B)

5 Describe and **record** the cloud conditions by noting how much of the sky is covered by clouds. Draw a circle and shade in the part of the circle that equals the amount of sky covered with clouds.

6 Use the temperature data to make a line graph showing how the temperature changes from day to day.

Draw Conclusions

1. Use your Weather Station Daily Record to **compare** the weather conditions on two different days. Which conditions were about the same? Which conditions changed the most?

2. From the **data** you **gathered** in this activity, how might scientists use weather data to **predict** the weather?

3. **Scientists at Work** Scientists learn about the weather by **measuring** weather conditions and **gathering data.** What did you learn by measuring the amount of rain your area received during the week of your observations?

Investigate Further Find a newspaper weather page, and note the temperatures in various cities throughout the United States. **Hypothesize** why there are different temperatures in different cities. **Plan and conduct a simple investigation** to find out.

Picture B

Process Skill Tip

Measurements are a kind of observation. You **measure** when you use a tool, such as a thermometer or rain gauge, to **gather data** about something.

Weather Systems

Where Weather Occurs

Almost all weather occurs in the lowest layer of air, or **atmosphere**, that surrounds Earth. The atmosphere stretches about 1000 km (620 mi) from the Earth's surface to outer space. The lowest layer of the atmosphere, called the *troposphere*, is where most water is found and where most clouds form. The troposphere is about 15 km (9 mi) thick at the equator.

Very little weather occurs above the troposphere. There is a little water in the *stratosphere,* the next higher layer, so a few clouds form there. But more important is the stratosphere's ozone layer, about 22.5 km (14 mi) above the Earth's surface. Ozone protects life on Earth by absorbing some of the sun's harmful rays. From the stratosphere to the edge of space, there is no water and too little air for any weather to occur.

✔ **In what layer of the atmosphere does most of Earth's weather occur?**

Blizzards, at the left, and hurricanes, at the right, are among the largest and most powerful weather systems of Earth's troposphere, shown below.

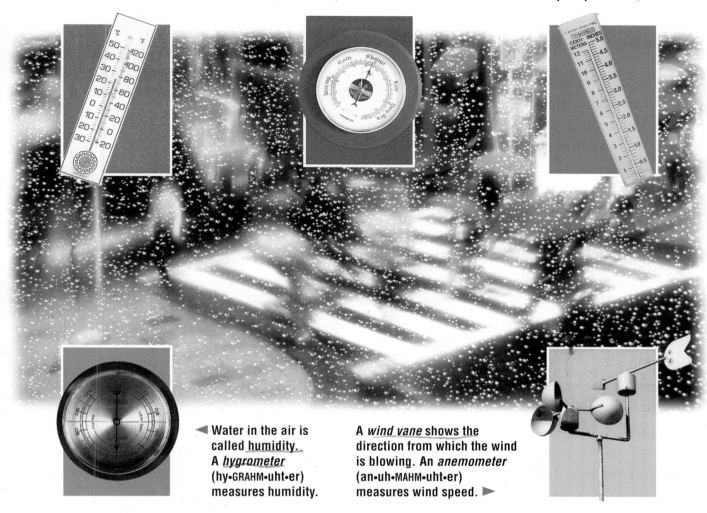

A *thermometer* measures air temperature. ▼

Air pressure is the weight of the atmosphere. A *barometer* measures air pressure. ▼

A *rain gauge* measures the amount of precipitation. ▼

◄ Water in the air is called humidity. A *hygrometer* (hy•GRAHM•uht•er) measures humidity.

A *wind vane* shows the direction from which the wind is blowing. An *anemometer* (an•uh•MAHM•uht•er) measures wind speed. ►

Measuring Atmospheric Conditions

The weather changes because the atmosphere is constantly changing. Sometimes the air is cold and sometimes it's warm. As air warms, its weight, or **air pressure**, lessens. And warm air holds more water, or can have more **humidity**, than cold air. These and other conditions of the atmosphere can be observed and measured.

The weather instruments shown on this page can be used to measure atmospheric conditions—air temperature, air pressure, **precipitation** (rain or snow), humidity, wind direction, and wind speed. Other atmospheric conditions, such as cloud type, are observed directly.

Why do people measure atmospheric conditions? One reason is to predict what the weather will be. For example, a change in air pressure or cloud type often means there will be a change in the weather.

✔ **What are some atmospheric conditions that can be measured?**

Air Pressure

You probably don't feel the atmosphere weighing you down. But air does have weight. The atmosphere pushes on you all the time, and this weight is air pressure.

There are several types of barometers for measuring air pressure. A mercury <u>barometer</u>, like the ones shown at the right, consists of a glass tube about 1 m (3 ft) long. Air is removed from the tube, and the glass is sealed at the top. Then the tube is turned upside down, and the open end is placed in a dish of mercury. The weight of the air pushing down on the mercury in the dish pushes mercury up into the glass tube. The mercury rises in the tube until its weight exactly balances the weight of the air pushing down on the mercury in the dish. The height of the mercury in the tube is a measure of air pressure. This measure is compared to a standard, or average, air pressure of about 76 cm (30 in.) of mercury.

Recall that warm air weighs less than cold air. A mass of cold air, called a *high-pressure area,* will measure more than 76 cm of mercury. A mass of warm air, called a *low-pressure area,* will measure less than 76 cm of mercury.

Weather changes because high- and low-pressure areas move. In the winter, areas of high pressure often move from northwestern Canada toward the southeastern United States, bringing cool, dry weather conditions. In the summer, areas of low pressure often move from the Gulf of Mexico to the northeastern United States, bringing warm, wet weather conditions.

As these high-pressure and low-pressure areas move, barometer readings in their paths change. Therefore, changing

HIGH AIR PRESSURE

The mercury in this barometer is high. Areas of high pressure usually have fair weather.

LOW AIR PRESSURE

The mercury in this barometer is low. Areas of low pressure often have stormy weather.

barometer readings can be used to predict changes in weather. If the barometer is rising, the weather will probably become fair. If the barometer is falling, stormy weather is probably coming.

✔ **How can changing air pressure be used to predict changing weather conditions?**

Water in the Air

In addition to temperature and air pressure, humidity, or the amount of water in the air, is an important factor in describing weather conditions. But how does water get into the air?

Earth's oceans are the biggest source of water. As the sun heats the oceans, liquid water changes into an invisible gas called *water vapor,* which rises into the air. The process of liquid water changing to water vapor is called **evaporation**. High up in the atmosphere, where the air is cooler, water vapor turns back into liquid drops of water, forming clouds. This process is called **condensation**.

When cloud drops come together, gravity returns the water to the Earth's surface as precipitation—usually rain. If the temperature in the clouds is below freezing, the precipitation is sleet, hail, or snow. This transferring of water from the Earth's surface to the atmosphere and back is called the *water cycle.*

THE INSIDE STORY

The Water Cycle

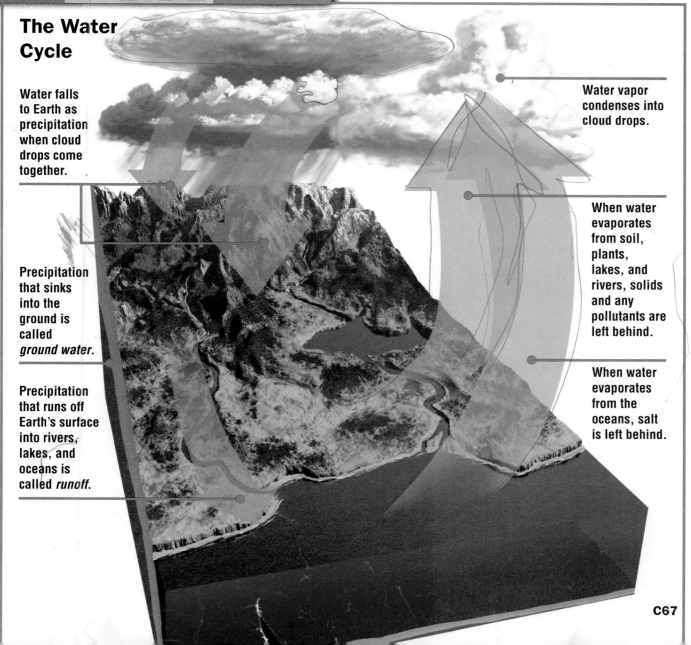

Water falls to Earth as precipitation when cloud drops come together.

Precipitation that sinks into the ground is called *ground water.*

Precipitation that runs off Earth's surface into rivers, lakes, and oceans is called *runoff.*

Water vapor condenses into cloud drops.

When water evaporates from soil, plants, lakes, and rivers, solids and any pollutants are left behind.

When water evaporates from the oceans, salt is left behind.

On clear nights, when the surface of the Earth cools quickly, water vapor may condense to form a cloud near the ground. This low cloud is called *fog*. If you have ever walked through fog, you know what the inside of a cloud is like.

Whether a cloud forms near the ground or high in the atmosphere, it forms in the same way. Water vapor condenses onto dust and other tiny particles in the air when it rises and cools. Another way in which air cools enough for water vapor to condense is by moving from a warm place to a colder place. For example, moist air that moves from over a warm body of water to over cooler land forms clouds or fog.

Even though all clouds form by condensation, different weather conditions produce different types of clouds. Weather scientists, or *meteorologists* (meet•ee•uhr•AHL•uh•juhsts),

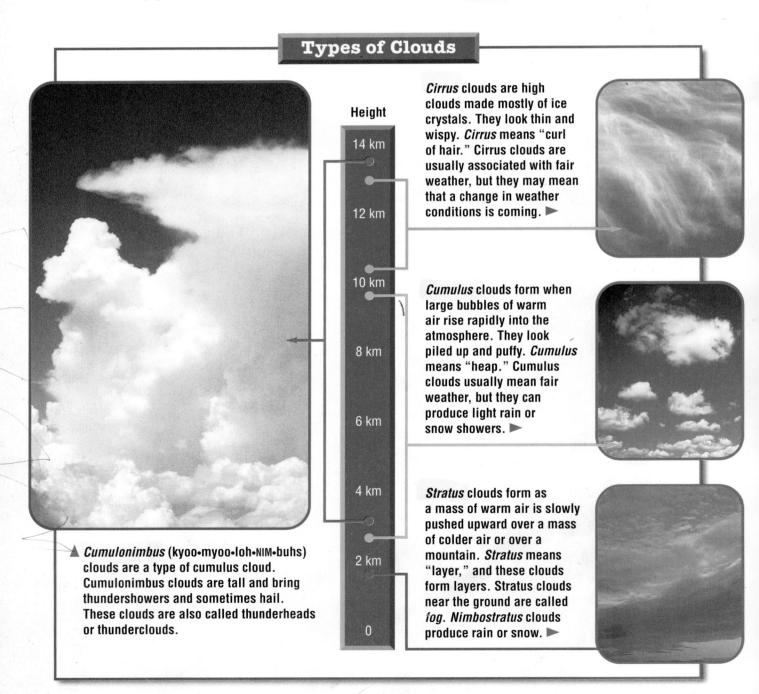

Types of Clouds

Height

14 km

12 km

10 km

8 km

6 km

4 km

2 km

0

Cirrus clouds are high clouds made mostly of ice crystals. They look thin and wispy. *Cirrus* means "curl of hair." Cirrus clouds are usually associated with fair weather, but they may mean that a change in weather conditions is coming. ▶

Cumulus clouds form when large bubbles of warm air rise rapidly into the atmosphere. They look piled up and puffy. *Cumulus* means "heap." Cumulus clouds usually mean fair weather, but they can produce light rain or snow showers. ▶

Stratus clouds form as a mass of warm air is slowly pushed upward over a mass of colder air or over a mountain. *Stratus* means "layer," and these clouds form layers. Stratus clouds near the ground are called *fog. Nimbostratus* clouds produce rain or snow. ▶

▲ *Cumulonimbus* (kyoo•myoo•loh•NIM•buhs) clouds are a type of cumulus cloud. Cumulonimbus clouds are tall and bring thundershowers and sometimes hail. These clouds are also called thunderheads or thunderclouds.

give clouds three basic names—cirrus (SEER•uhs), cumulus (KYOO•myoo•luhs), and stratus. Along with other information, the types of clouds in the atmosphere can be used to help predict weather changes. Some basic types of clouds and their descriptions are shown on page C68.

✓ **How do clouds form?**

Summary

Most of Earth's weather takes place in the troposphere, the lowest layer of the atmosphere. Weather conditions such as temperature, air pressure, humidity, wind speed and direction, and the amount of precipitation can be observed and measured. Certain weather conditions, such as changing air pressure and types of clouds, can be used to predict changes in the weather.

Review

1. How do weather scientists **observe** and **measure** weather conditions?

2. How is water recycled in the water cycle?

3. What causes clouds to form?

4. **Critical Thinking** It is a gray, cloudy day, and a light rain is falling. What type of clouds would you expect to see? Explain your answer.

5. **Test Prep** The process by which water vapor turns into liquid water drops is known as —

   A condensation
   B evaporation
   C precipitation
   D the water cycle

LINKS

MATH LINK

Multiply/Divide Decimals Many meteorologists in the United States measure air pressure in units called *millibars*. At sea level, standard air pressure is 1013.2 millibars. If 1013.2 millibars equals 76 cm of mercury, what would a barometer reading of 75 cm of mercury equal in millibars?

WRITING LINK

Informative Writing—Report Suppose that you are a meteorologist who has just spotted a large cumulonimbus cloud moving toward a city. Write a weather report for the city's residents.

ART LINK

Stormy Weather Make a drawing that includes one or more of the cloud types shown on page C68. Show the weather conditions that are associated with those cloud types.

TECHNOLOGY LINK

ONLINE

Learn more about Earth's atmosphere by visiting the Harcourt Learning Site.

www.harcourtschool.com

WELCOME TO THE LEARNING SITE

What Causes Weather?

In this lesson, you can . . .

INVESTIGATE the rates at which water and soil absorb and release heat.

LEARN ABOUT uneven heating of the Earth's surface and the movement of air masses as the causes of weather.

LINK to math, writing, music, and technology.

INVESTIGATE

The Sun's Energy Heats Unevenly

Activity Purpose If you've ever walked barefoot from pavement to grass on a sunny day, you know that different materials absorb heat differently. On a larger scale, uneven heating like this is what produces wind. In this investigation you will **predict** which material heats up and cools off faster—water or soil. Then you will test your predictions.

Materials

- 2 tin cans (lids removed)
- water
- dry soil
- spoon
- 2 thermometers

Activity Procedure

1 Fill one can about $\frac{3}{4}$ full of water and the other can about $\frac{3}{4}$ full of soil. (Picture A)

2 Place one thermometer in the can of water and the other in the can of soil. Put the cans in a shady place outside. Wait for 10 minutes, and then **record** the temperatures of the water and the soil.

3 Put both cans in sunlight. **Predict** which of the cans will show the faster rise in temperature. **Record** the temperature of each can every 10 minutes for 30 minutes. In which can does the temperature rise faster? Which material—soil or water—heats up faster? (Picture B)

◄ Energy to fly this kite starts with the sun.

Picture A

4. Now put the cans back in the shade. **Predict** in which of the cans the temperature will drop faster. Again **record** the temperature of each can every 10 minutes for 30 minutes. In which can does the temperature drop faster? Which material—soil or water—cools off faster?

5. Make line graphs to show how the temperatures of both materials changed as they heated up and cooled off.

Picture B

Draw Conclusions

1. How did your results match your predictions? Which material—water or soil—heated up faster? Which cooled off faster?

2. From the results you **observed** in this investigation, which would you **predict** heats up faster—oceans or land? Which would you predict cools off faster? Explain.

3. **Scientists at Work** Scientists learn by **predicting** and then testing their predictions. How did you test your predictions about water and soil?

Investigate Further **Hypothesize** how fast materials, such as moist soil, sand, or salt water, heat up and cool off. **Plan and conduct a simple experiment** to test your hypothesis.

Process Skill Tip

A prediction is based on previous observations. Before you **predict**, think about what you have already observed.

The Causes of Weather

Uneven Heating

FIND OUT

- what causes the wind
- about Earth's wind patterns
- about air masses and fronts

VOCABULARY

local winds
prevailing winds
air mass
front

The illustration below shows how the sun's rays strike the Earth's surface and the atmosphere. The atmosphere absorbs some of the sun's energy and reflects some of it back into space. Some of the energy that reaches the Earth's surface is reflected back into the atmosphere. However, much of the sun's energy is absorbed by the Earth's surface.

In the investigation you discovered that soil heats up faster and cools off faster than water. In the same way, when the sun's rays strike the Earth's surface, land absorbs the sun's energy more quickly and heats up faster than bodies of water, such as lakes, rivers, and oceans. And land releases heat and cools off faster when the sun goes down than bodies of water do.

✔ **What happens to the energy from the sun's rays that reach Earth?**

The atmosphere absorbs energy directly from the sun and from energy reflected from the Earth's surface. ▼

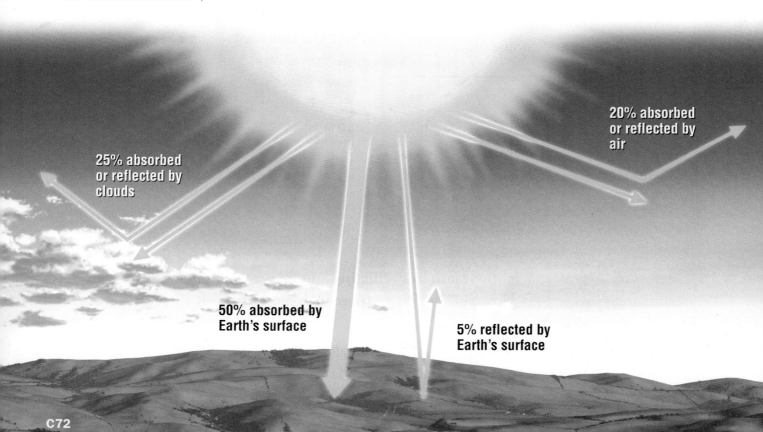

25% absorbed or reflected by clouds

20% absorbed or reflected by air

50% absorbed by Earth's surface

5% reflected by Earth's surface

Local Winds

Because the Earth's surface is heated unevenly, the air above it is in constant motion. Cold air is heavier than warm air, so it sinks, forcing lighter, warm air to rise. The upward movement of warm air in the atmosphere produces *updrafts*. You may have seen birds soaring on updrafts.

At the surface, two places can often have differences in temperature and, therefore, differences in air pressure. These differences cause air to move from the area of higher pressure to the area of lower pressure. This horizontal movement of air is called *wind*. Winds can be local, affecting small areas, or global, affecting large parts of the Earth.

Local winds depend on local changes in temperature. The illustrations below show an example of local winds at the seashore. During the day, the land heats up more quickly than the water does, so the breezes blow from the sea to the land. But at night, air over the water is warmer than air over the land, so the breezes blow from the land to the sea.

✔ **What causes local winds?**

▲ Uneven heating of the Earth's surface produces air masses of different temperatures. Cold air sinks, forcing warm air to rise.

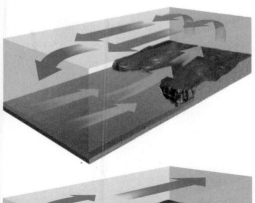

◄ During the day, the land heats up faster than the sea. Cooler sea air moves toward the land. This is called a sea breeze.

◄ At night, the land loses heat faster than the sea. Cooler air over the land moves toward the sea. This is called a land breeze.

Prevailing Winds

In the age of sailing ships, sailors relied on prevailing winds to carry them across the oceans. **Prevailing winds** are global winds that blow constantly from the same direction. Prevailing winds are caused by the uneven heating of large parts of Earth's atmosphere and by Earth's rotation.

To understand prevailing winds, first suppose an Earth that doesn't rotate. The sun warms the air over the equator, while air over the North and South Poles is very cold. The cold, heavy polar air flows toward the equator, forcing an upward movement of the warmed air at the equator. This air then flows north and south toward the poles. Far from the equator, the warm air cools and sinks at the poles, where it once again flows toward the equator. This flow from the equator to the poles and then back again is continuous.

The global winds that blow over most of the United States are the prevailing westerlies.

Polar easterlies

Prevailing westerlies

Northeast trades

Southeast trades

Prevailing westerlies

Polar easterlies

ARCTIC OCEAN

ARCTIC OCEAN

EURASIA

NORTH AMERICA

ATLANTIC OCEAN

PACIFIC OCEAN

AFRICA

Equator

SOUTH AMERICA

INDIAN OCEAN

PACIFIC OCEAN

ATLANTIC OCEAN

AUSTRALIA

ANTARCTICA

Now suppose Earth rotating from west to east. This rotation makes north and south winds curve. You can see this by placing a sheet of paper on a turntable. As the paper spins, try drawing a straight line from the center of the turntable to its edge.

Winds that blow toward the poles curve east. Winds that blow toward the equator curve west. In most of the United States, the prevailing winds curve to the east, producing west winds, or *westerlies.*

The prevailing westerlies cause most weather systems in the United States to move from west to east. This helps forecasters with their predictions because weather conditions in Oregon today often move to Kansas tomorrow and from there to Virginia the next day.

Since most weather systems in the United States move from west to east, this blizzard in Chicago may affect Buffalo tomorrow, and Boston the next day. ▶

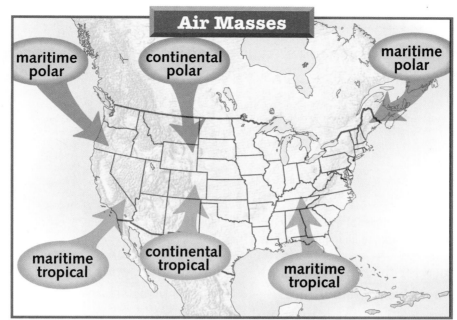

Air Masses

A continental polar air mass forms over land near the poles. It contains cold, dry air.

maritime polar

continental polar

maritime polar

A maritime polar air mass forms over bodies of water near the poles. It contains cold, moist air.

A maritime tropical air mass forms over bodies of water near the equator. It contains warm, moist air.

maritime tropical

continental tropical

maritime tropical

A continental tropical air mass forms over land near the equator. It contains warm, dry air.

Air Masses and Fronts

Most weather is associated with the boundaries between air masses. An **air mass** is a large body of air which has nearly the same temperature and humidity throughout.

The area over which an air mass forms determines its characteristics. Tropical air masses form near the equator, so they are warm. Polar air masses form near Earth's poles, so they are cold. Maritime air masses form over oceans. They contain moist air.

Air masses that form over land, called continental air masses, are dry.

Within an air mass weather conditions are fairly consistent. However, when two air masses that have different characteristics meet, the weather changes. The boundary between air masses is called a **front**. The area along a front is marked by a change in weather conditions.

The steep boundary of a cold front causes warm air to be quickly pushed up. Cumulonimbus clouds form and produce thunder, lightning, and, sometimes, severe storms. ▼

Cold front

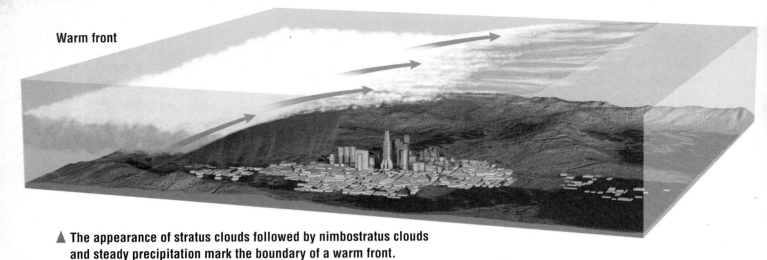

Warm front

▲ The appearance of stratus clouds followed by nimbostratus clouds and steady precipitation mark the boundary of a warm front.

A front is named for the type of air mass moving into an area. A *cold front* is the boundary line between a warm air mass and an approaching cold air mass. This type of front forms as cold air moves beneath warm air. The warm air is quickly pushed up and cools, forming cumulus clouds. Then cumulonimbus clouds form and produce brief, heavy precipitation and sometimes thunderstorms. After a cold front passes, the weather usually becomes clear and cooler.

Sometimes a warm air mass replaces a cold air mass, forming a *warm front*. Along a warm front, warm air slides up and over colder air. As the warm air is gently pushed up, stratus clouds form. Then nimbostratus clouds bring steady precipitation. Warmer weather follows the passage of a warm front.

Weather forecasters plot the movement of air masses on weather maps. Using symbols, they indicate where fronts are located and the direction that air masses are moving. Red half-circles indicate the position of warm fronts, while blue triangles show the location of cold fronts. The symbols point in the direction the air mass is moving. Weather maps also show temperature, precipitation, and areas of high and low pressure.

Weather in the United States usually moves from the west to the east. What kind of weather do you think Atlanta will have in the next day or so? Explain. ▶

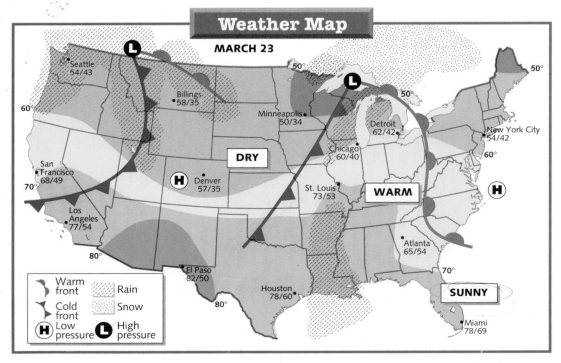

Weather Map

MARCH 23

Seattle 54/43
Billings 58/35
Minneapolis 50/34
Detroit 62/42
New York City 54/42
San Francisco 68/49
Denver 57/35
Chicago 60/40
St. Louis 73/53
Los Angeles 77/54
Atlanta 65/54
El Paso 82/50
Houston 78/60
Miami 78/69

DRY
WARM
SUNNY

Legend:
- Warm front
- Cold front
- **H** Low pressure
- **L** High pressure
- Rain
- Snow

Look at the weather map at the bottom of page C76. Weather forecasters use maps to show how weather systems move. Forecasters also use maps to help predict weather changes.

✓ **What causes weather conditions to change along fronts?**

Summary

Changes in air pressure, from uneven heating of Earth's surface and the air above it, cause the wind to blow. Local winds depend on local changes in temperature. Prevailing, or global, winds are caused by the sun's uneven heating of large parts of the atmosphere and by Earth's rotation on its axis. Prevailing winds in the United States are from the west, so air masses and fronts tend to move from west to east.

Review

1. How does uneven heating of Earth's surface produce wind?

2. Suppose you're at the seashore on a sunny summer day. In which direction is the wind blowing? Why?

3. How do the prevailing winds affect fronts in the United States?

4. **Critical Thinking** Shortly after daybreak at the seashore, the air temperature over sea and land is about the same. What sort of wind, if any, is blowing? Explain.

5. **Test Prep** A weather map can be used to show —
   A precipitation
   B fronts
   C temperature
   D all of these

LINKS

MATH LINK

Add and Subtract Percentages About 35 percent of the sun's rays that reach the Earth are reflected back into space. Another 15 percent are absorbed or reflected by the atmosphere. What percentage of the sun's rays reach the Earth's surface?

WRITING LINK

Expressive Writing—Friendly Letter Suppose you are on vacation. Write a postcard describing the weather to a friend. Include temperature, wind speed, and wind direction.

MUSIC LINK

Weather Songs Many songs are about the weather or compare something to the weather. Some examples are "You Are My Sunshine," "The Itsy Bitsy Spider," and "Sunny Day." Work with a partner to see how many weather songs you can list.

TECHNOLOGY LINK

Learn more about weather conditions and predictions by investigating *Umbrella or Not?* on the **Harcourt Science Explorations CD-ROM.**

3

What Is Climate and How Does It Change?

In this lesson, you can . . .

INVESTIGATE local weather conditions.

LEARN ABOUT climates and how they change.

LINK to math, writing, literature, and technology.

INVESTIGATE

Local Weather Conditions

Activity Purpose Why does the temperature change as you go from the city to the country? Why is a city park cooler than nearby streets and sidewalks? You know that different parts of the country often have different weather conditions. In this investigation you'll find out if places very close to each other can have different weather conditions, too.

Materials

■ 4 metersticks

■ 4 weather stations

Activity Procedure

1 Make a table like the one shown on page C79.

2 Choose four locations near your school to study. Select different kinds of locations, such as a shady parkway, a sunny playground, a parking lot on the south side of your school, and a ball field on the north side. For the same time on any given day, **predict** whether the temperature, wind direction, and wind speed will be the same or different at the different locations.

3 At the chosen time, four people should each take a meterstick and a weather station to a different one of the selected locations. Use the meterstick to locate a point 1 m above the ground. **Measure** and **record** the temperature at that point. Use the weather station to determine the wind direction and speed, too. Record the data in your table. (Pictures A and B)

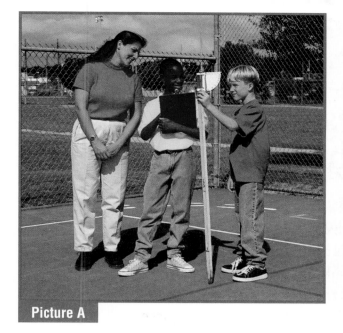

Picture A

Picture B

4 Make a double-bar graph to show the temperatures and wind speeds recorded at all the locations. Write the wind direction at each location on the appropriate wind-speed bar.

Draw Conclusions

1. Use your table to **compare** the temperature, wind direction, and wind speed at the different locations. What differences, if any, did you find? What conditions were the same?

2. Local weather conditions affect the organisms that live in a location. Do you think wind speed or temperature is more likely to affect living organisms? Explain.

3. Based on your investigation, how would you define the phrase *local weather conditions*?

4. **Scientists at Work** Scientists learn about local weather conditions by **comparing** weather data from different locations. **Draw conclusions** about local weather conditions, based on the locations you studied.

Investigate Further What other factors, in addition to temperature, wind direction, and wind speed, might affect local weather conditions? **Hypothesize** about a factor that might affect local weather conditions. Then **plan and conduct a simple experiment** to test your hypothesis.

Local Weather Conditions	1	2	3	4
Location				
Temperature				
Wind Direction				
Wind Speed				

Process Skill Tip

You **compare** before you **draw conclusions** about what is the same and what is different about weather conditions in different locations.

Climates and How They Change

Climate

The weather in your area probably changes from day to day and from season to season. Yet year after year many of the same weather conditions are repeated. These repeating conditions, or patterns, make up your area's climate. **Climate** is the average of all weather conditions through all seasons over a period of time. Temperature and precipitation are the major factors that determine climate. Wind speed and direction are also factors.

Temperature is also a major factor of microclimates. A **microclimate** is the climate of a very small area. You probably pass several microclimates on your way to school each day. If you live in a city, you may know that a wooded park has a cooler, wetter climate than a parking lot has. Observing microclimates, as you did in the investigation, is a good way to learn about climates.

These photos of Mount Wheeler, in New Mexico, show different climates on the slope of a high mountain. Notice that, in addition to certain weather conditions, each climate has its own typical plants and animals adapted to living in that climate.

✔ **What is climate?**

At the top of the mountain, you will find a cold, dry climate with few trees or animals. ▼

▲ On the sides of the mountain, the climate is cool and moist, and there are tall trees and forest animals.

▲ At the base of the mountain, the climate is warm and dry. Desert animals and plants such as sagebrush live there.

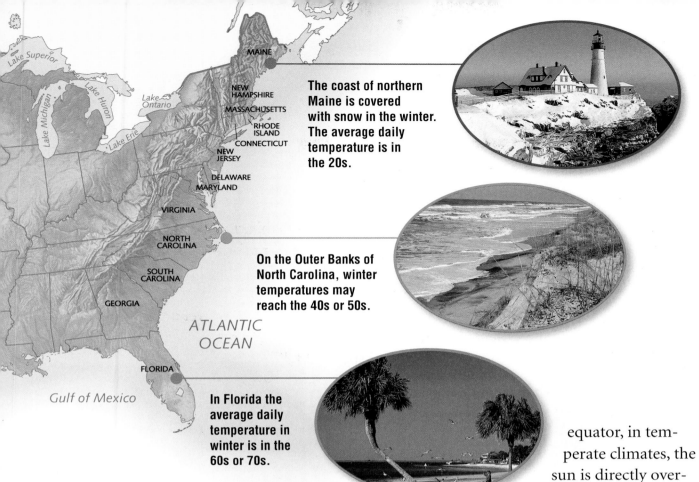

The coast of northern Maine is covered with snow in the winter. The average daily temperature is in the 20s.

On the Outer Banks of North Carolina, winter temperatures may reach the 40s or 50s.

In Florida the average daily temperature in winter is in the 60s or 70s.

Climate and Latitude

The United States has many different climates. There is the cold, *polar* climate of northern Alaska and the hot, *tropical* climate of Hawai'i and Puerto Rico. Most of the country has more moderate, or *temperate*, climates. But among temperate climates, there are big differences in average temperature and precipitation. Along the East Coast of the United States, for example, average temperatures vary quite a bit—from Florida, in the south, to Maine, in the north. These temperature differences are determined by *latitude*, or the distance a place is from the equator.

Most areas near the equator have tropical climates. There the sun is directly overhead nearly all year, which causes intense heating of the Earth's surface. Farther from the equator, in temperate climates, the sun is directly overhead only part of the year, causing less heating of the Earth's surface. These temperate climates have warm summers but cold winters. Near the poles the sun is never directly overhead. The decreased heating of the Earth's surface at latitudes far from the equator results in cold, polar climates.

In addition to latitude, precipitation causes differences among temperate climates. Most of the East Coast receives a lot of precipitation, allowing thick forests to grow. Farther west there is less precipitation. There are fewer trees and more grasslands, which require less water. Still farther west the grasslands give way to even drier, more desertlike climates that receive very little precipitation.

✔ **Why does Florida have a warmer average temperature than Maine?**

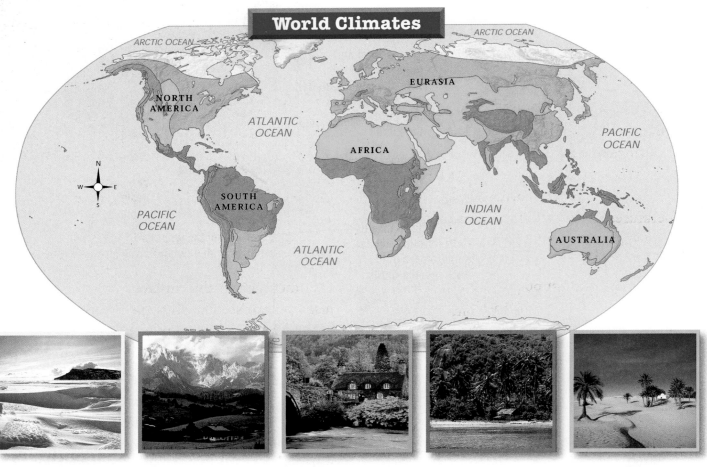

World Climates

Polar Zone
Cold all year; light precipitation

Mountain Zone
Cold winters, cool summers; moderate to heavy precipitation

Temperate Zone
Cold winters, warm summers; moderate precipitation

Tropical Zone
Hot all year; moderate to heavy precipitation

Desert Zone
Hot summers, cool winters; light precipitation

World Climates

So many factors affect an area's climate that no two places on Earth have exactly the same climate. Anything that affects temperature or precipitation affects climate.

Climate is also affected by prevailing winds. In the United States, the prevailing westerlies help to moderate the hot summer climate by pushing cooling air masses across the country.

Ocean currents can affect climate, too. On the West Coast, the cold California Current flows south from the North Pacific. It keeps the summers cool along the coastal areas of Washington, Oregon, and northern California.

Yet another factor that affects climate is the shape of the land itself. A mountain can have a wet climate on the side facing the prevailing winds and a dry climate on the other side.

Although no two places on Earth have exactly the same climate, Earth's climates can be grouped into five major zones—polar, mountain, temperate, tropical, and desert. Each zone has its own weather patterns and its own typical kinds of life. For example, a polar climate supports small plants and animals like the polar bear. A tropical climate supports lush forests and animals such as monkeys.

✔ **What are the five climate zones?**

Climate Changes

Have you ever heard an older relative say, "When I was young, the winters were much colder than they are now. Why, some days the snow was piled up to the windows."

Your relative may be right. Climate does change over time. Scientists have been measuring the Earth's winds, temperatures, and precipitation for many years. Based on this data and other evidence, they know that Earth's climate is slowly warming. As recently as 50 or 60 years ago, average temperatures in parts of the United States were a degree or two cooler than they are now.

Earth's climate hasn't always been warming up. About 20,000 years ago, Earth was in the middle of an Ice Age. When the climate cools enough, large areas of Earth are covered by sheets of ice, or *glaciers*. Earth has gone through many Ice Ages. During the most recent one, glaciers covered 30 percent of Earth's surface. Evidence of this period can still be seen in the glaciers of Greenland and the Canadian Rockies.

At other times, Earth has had a warmer climate than it does today. Look at the graph to see how Earth's temperature has increased and decreased over time.

Changes in Earth's temperature might be caused by a change in the size or shape of Earth's orbit or a change in the tilt of Earth's axis.

To determine which areas of North America were once covered by ice, scientists look for evidence of glacial erosion and deposition.

▲ One effect of El Niño's heavy rains is mudslides.

▲ During most winters, the weather in California is mild and cool, with only moderate precipitation.

Sometimes Earth's climate changes for just a year or so. The **El Niño** (EL NEEN•yoh) effect is a short-term climate change. Every two to ten years, weather conditions around the Pacific Ocean change dramatically because of changing ocean currents. The normally wet countries of Southeast Asia become dry, while heavy rains fall on the normally dry western coasts of Mexico and California. The photographs above show California during a normal winter and during a winter of heavy El Niño rains.

✔ **What evidence is there that Earth's climate is constantly changing?**

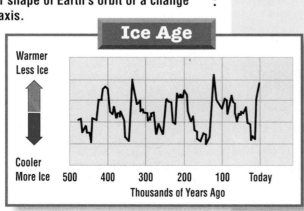

Ice Age

Warmer
Less Ice

Cooler
More Ice

500 400 300 200 100 Today
Thousands of Years Ago

Ice cover 18,000 years ago

Ice cover 10,000 years ago

Ice cover today

---- Ice Age coastline

Humans Affect Climate

You know that a city is warmer than the surrounding countryside. In fact, city temperatures may be as much as 8°C (15°F) warmer than surrounding areas. Cities are warmer for several reasons. Buildings, roads, and sidewalks hold heat longer than trees and grass. Cars, buses, and trucks increase city temperatures. Large buildings block winds that might otherwise blow warm air away. All of these factors combine to make a city an area of warm air surrounded by cooler air, or a *heat island.*

Warm air also results from an effect of the burning of fuels such as gasoline. Fuels give off carbon dioxide when burned. Carbon dioxide in the atmosphere absorbs some of the heat given off by Earth. This process, commonly called the **greenhouse effect**, is necessary for life. Without carbon dioxide and other gases in the atmosphere, all of Earth's heat would go off into space, leaving the planet too cold for life. However, too much carbon dioxide in the air may cause climate changes.

Many scientists hypothesize that excess carbon dioxide will lead to **global warming**, an abnormally rapid rise in Earth's average temperature. If Earth's average temperature rises just a few more degrees, the Greenland and Antarctic icecaps will begin to melt. The melting ice will raise the sea level around the world, flooding many coastal cities.

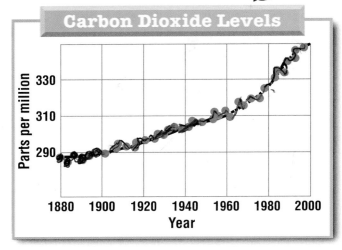

▲ The level of carbon dioxide (CO_2) in the atmosphere has increased over the past century.

▼ Earth's average temperature over the past century has increased at about the same rate.

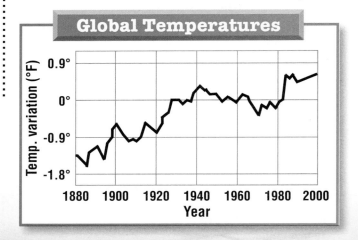

Cities have microclimates that are affected by humans. One reason is that a city has buildings, roads, and vehicles that hold or produce heat.

To reduce this possibility, many countries have agreed to try to reduce the amount of carbon dioxide released into the atmosphere. One way to do this is to burn less fuel.

✓ **What are some ways in which humans affect climate?**

Summary

Climate is the average of all weather conditions through all seasons over a period of time. Temperature and precipitation are the major factors that determine climate. Earth's climate has changed over time as average temperatures have risen and fallen. Human activities, such as burning fuels, can affect climate.

Review

1. What is the difference between climate and microclimate?
2. List four factors that affect climate.
3. What causes an Ice Age?
4. **Critical Thinking** During an Ice Age, what is likely to happen to the levels of oceans around the world?
5. **Test Prep** Burning fuels affects climate by —
   A reducing the number of trees
   B decreasing the amount of sunlight that reaches Earth's surface
   C raising Earth's average temperature
   D changing the prevailing winds

LINKS

MATH LINK

Estimate Look at the graph on page C84 showing global temperature variations. Find the highest and lowest values. Estimate how much Earth's average temperature has varied over the last 100 years.

WRITING LINK

Persuasive Writing—Request Do you think the recent measurements of Earth's temperatures are really evidence of global warming? Write a persuasive letter to the editor of a newspaper, requesting that your point of view be printed. Be sure to include facts to support your point of view.

LITERATURE LINK

Earthmaker's Tales Read *Earthmaker's Tales: North American Indian Stories About Earth Happenings* by Gretchen Will Mayo. Earth and its atmosphere are the subjects of this collection of Native American legends about the origins of thunder, tornadoes, and other weather features.

TECHNOLOGY LINK

Learn more about changes in climate by viewing *El Niño Erosion* and *Global Warming* on the **Harcourt Science Newsroom Video.**

Jacob Bjerknes discovered the warm current, called El Niño, that sometimes produces severe weather along the Pacific coast.

Major Events in Weather Forecasting

The History of Weather Forecasting

350 B.C.
Aristotle writes *Meteorologica*, a book about weather observations.

1835
Coriolis discovers what is later called the "Coriolis Effect."

1902
Scientists discover that the atmosphere has layers. The troposphere and stratosphere are identified.

400 B.C. | A.D. **1600** | A.D. **1700** | A.D. **1800**

1600
Early weather instruments are invented.

1849
The first weather report sent by telegraph is received by Joseph Henry, secretary of the Smithsonian Institution.

1890
Congress forms an agency called the Weather Bureau, later renamed the National Weather Service.

In ancient times, weather predictions were based on superstitions. It seemed to make sense that good weather depended on the happiness of the gods. Yet as early as the year 100, Egyptian scientists showed that air expanded when it was heated. This early discovery led to other advances in meteorology, the study of weather.

Observing Weather Systems

In 1735 scientists observed that the sun heated areas near the equator more strongly than areas north or south of the equator. They also discovered that as air above the equator expands, it moves toward the cooler latitudes. This movement results in a global wind pattern, which causes a global weather pattern.

This discovery was followed by the discovery of the "trade winds" north and south of the equator and other wind zones in the Northern Hemisphere. In 1835 French physicist Gustave Coriolis described the movement of air masses north and south of the equator. He showed how winds north or south of the equator curve in different directions. Coriolis realized that these curved air routes were caused by the rotation of Earth.

Modern Forecasting

Wind vanes had long been used to determine wind direction, but it wasn't until the 1600s that instruments were invented that could accurately measure other weather conditions. In 1644 the first barometer was made. In 1754 G. D. Fahrenheit made the first mercury thermometer.

At least 100 years ago, scientists knew that they could improve their forecasts if they had measurements from enough weather stations around the world. Today there are tens of thousands of weather stations. Each station takes many measurements—temperature, humidity, cloud cover, wind speed and direction, and barometric pressure. Modern communication systems allow scientists to share this information almost instantly. This allows warnings to be issued to people who might be affected by severe weather events.

Weather satellites, first launched in the 1960s, provide the most important data for modern weather forecasting. Satellite data helps scientists understand the global forces that cause local weather conditions. Today countries around the world share satellite weather data.

THINK ABOUT IT

1. What causes winds to curve?
2. What is the most important instrument for weather forecasters today? Explain.

1950s
Bjerknes makes the connection between the El Niño current and certain reversed weather patterns.

1980s
Doppler radar is first used.

A.D. 1900   A.D. 2000

1960s
The first weather satellites are launched.

1990s
International cooperation and the use of satellites increases understanding of worldwide weather patterns.

NIMBUS SPACECRAFT

Carolyn Kloth

METEOROLOGIST

"A lot of people tend to think that you need to be able to look out of a window to assess the weather. With the use of radar, weather satellites, and all of the other weather data available, you can do the job almost anywhere."

From the time she was in elementary school, Carolyn Kloth knew what she wanted to do—fly airplanes and chase storms. Today Ms. Kloth is doing both of these things as a pilot and a meteorologist at the National Severe Storms Forecast Center in Kansas City, Missouri. She specializes in tracking severe thunderstorms and giving information about them to airplane pilots.

At the severe storms center, Ms. Kloth receives weather data every hour from across North America. The data includes images of cloud patterns, locations of fronts, and the number of lightning strikes. She also studies measurements of air pressure, humidity, precipitation, and temperature, both at the ground and at various levels in the atmosphere. Once all the data has come in, Ms. Kloth uses computers to analyze it. Then she predicts where severe thunderstorms are likely to form across the continent and over nearby coastal waters.

Ms. Kloth issues severe storm warnings to pilots for any storm that has winds of more than 26 m/s, hail larger than 19 mm in diameter, or clouds that may form tornadoes. She finds that about 1 percent of all thunderstorms fit into one or more of those categories. The warnings that Ms. Kloth issues help pilots avoid thunderstorms and result in safer and more comfortable flights.

THINK ABOUT IT

1. How can Ms. Kloth gather weather data without looking out a window?
2. How do you think Ms. Kloth's experience as a pilot helps her in her job at the National Severe Storms Forecast Center?

AIR PRESSURE

How strong is air pressure?

Materials

- plastic sandwich bag
- drinking straw
- tape
- heavy book

Procedure

1 Put one end of the straw in the plastic bag. Then seal the bag shut with tape.

2 Put the plastic bag on a table and lay the book on part of the bag as shown.

3 Blow through the straw into the bag, and observe what happens.

Draw Conclusions

Describe what happened to the bag and the book. Explain what happened. Try to think of a situation where air pressure could be used like this.

SIDEWALK GRAPH

How does sunlight speed up evaporation?

Materials

- sunny sidewalk
- 500 mL water
- chalk
- clock

Procedure

1 Pour about 500 mL of water onto a sidewalk that is in full sunlight.

2 Draw a line around the outside of the puddle with the chalk.

3 Draw a new line around the puddle every 5 min for 20 min.

4 Repeat the experiment on a sidewalk in the shade.

Draw Conclusions

Compare the sizes of the puddles at each 5-min interval. Based on your observations, predict how long it would take for each puddle to evaporate.

Vocabulary Review

Use the terms below to complete the sentences. The page numbers in ( ) tell you where to look in the chapter if you need help.

atmosphere (C64)   air mass (C75)
air pressure (C65)   front (C75)
humidity (C65)   climate (C80)
precipitation (C65)   microclimate (C80)
evaporation (C67)   El Niño (C83)
condensation (C67)   greenhouse effect (C84)
local winds (C73)   global warming (C84)
prevailing winds (C73)

1. Liquid water changes to water vapor through the process of ____. Water vapor turns back into liquid drops of water through the process of ____.

2. Almost all weather occurs in the lowest layer of the ____.

3. Rain or snow is called ____.

4. Water in the air is called ____.

5. The weight of air is known as ____.

6. Global winds that blow constantly from the same direction are known as ____.

7. Winds that depend on local changes in temperature are called ____.

8. The climate of a small area is called a ____.

9. The boundary between air masses is called a ____.

10. The average of an area's weather conditions through all seasons over a period of time is called ____.

11. Excess carbon dioxide in the atmosphere may lead to ____.

12. The process by which carbon dioxide in the atmosphere absorbs some of the heat given off by Earth is called the ____.

13. One example of a short-term climate change is ____.

14. A body of air with nearly the same temperature and humidity throughout is an ____.

Connect Concepts

Copy and complete the idea clusters below, which describe weather and climate.

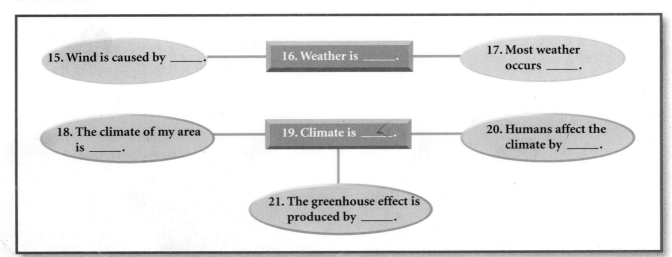

15. Wind is caused by ____.

16. Weather is ____.

17. Most weather occurs ____.

18. The climate of my area is ____.

19. Climate is ____.

20. Humans affect the climate by ____.

21. The greenhouse effect is produced by ____.

Check Understanding

Write the letter of the best choice.

22. As air warms, —
    A air pressure increases
    B air pressure decreases
    C temperature decreases
    D humidity changes

23. A wind vane indicates —
    F air pressure   H humidity
    G wind speed   J wind direction

24. Wind is caused when air —
    A moves from the land to the sea
    B moves from the sea to the land
    C moves from an area of higher
      pressure to an area of lower pressure
    D moves from an area of lower pressure
      to an area of higher pressure

25. Prevailing winds are caused by the
    uneven heating of Earth's atmosphere
    and by —
    F local winds   H Earth's rotation
    G air pressure   J temperature

26. Florida has a warmer climate than
    Maine because Florida —
    A is closer to the South Pole
    B is closer to the equator
    C is nearer to the Atlantic Ocean
    D receives more precipitation

27. Most of the eastern United States and
    the West Coast have a climate that is —
    F mountain   H desert
    G polar   J temperate

Critical Thinking

28. How does the location of Hawai'i, near
    the equator, affect its climate?

29. Suppose you live in the middle of the
    United States and are looking at a
    weather map. To the north and east of
    your location, it is warm and raining. To
    the west and south, the weather is cold
    and clear. What sort of weather can you
    expect before tomorrow? Explain.

Process Skills Review

30. A thermometer measures air tempera-
    ture. A barometer measures air pressure.
    A hygrometer measures humidity, and a
    rain gauge measures precipitation.
    Which two of these instruments are
    most useful for the **measurements** that
    determine a region's climate? Explain.

31. Which would you **predict** would heat
    up faster on a sunny day—a pond or a
    meadow? Explain.

32. **Compare** weather and climate.

Performance Assessment

Your Weather and Climate

Look at a map of the United States.
Explain where weather in your area comes
from. Describe any local conditions that
affect the weather. Then identify the climate
zone in which you are
located—polar, tropi-
cal, temperate,
desert, or mountain.
Explain what
determines
your climate
zone.

CHAPTER 4

Exploring the Oceans

Vocabulary Preview

- salinity
- water pressure
- wave
- current
- tide
- shore
- headland
- tide pool
- jetty
- scuba
- submersible
- sonar
- desalination

If you've ever been to the beach, it may have seemed to you that the water always moves toward the shore. But the movement of ocean water is more complex than that. In addition to causing waves, winds make ocean waters move in great loops around the world.

Fast Fact

In 1947 Thor Heyerdahl crossed the Pacific Ocean on a raft he named *Kon-Tiki*. He wanted to prove that natives of South America could have traveled thousands of miles to the islands of Polynesia by riding on ocean currents.

1

What Are the Oceans Like?

In this lesson, you can . . .

 INVESTIGATE how salt affects the freezing temperature of water.

 LEARN ABOUT oceans and seas, ocean water, and the ocean floor.

 LINK to math, writing, social studies, and technology.

Icebreakers help keep shipping lanes open in the frozen waters of the Arctic Ocean. ▼

Icy Water

Activity Purpose Have you ever skated on a frozen pond? In cold places, freshwater ponds and lakes often freeze in winter. Even in the coldest weather, however, ocean water rarely freezes, except in the very cold Arctic and Antarctic regions. In this activity you will **compare** the temperatures of icy fresh water and salt water. Then you will **predict** the temperature at which salt water will freeze.

Materials
- 2 plastic measuring cups
- wax pencil
- ice cubes
- water
- spoon
- salt
- thermometer

Activity Procedure

1 Make a copy of the chart shown below. You will use it to **record data** you collect.

Water Temperatures

Cup A		Cup B	
Spoonfuls of Salt	Temp.	Spoonfuls of Salt	Temp.
0		0	
0		2	
0		4	
0		6	

2 Use the wax pencil to label the cups A and B. Fill each cup with ice cubes. Then add equal amounts of water to each cup.

3 Wait 5 minutes, and then use the thermometer to **measure** the temperature of the water in each cup. Record the temperatures in the chart. (Picture A)

4 Stir two heaping spoonfuls of salt into cup B. (Picture B)

5 Wait 2 minutes, and then measure the temperature of the water in each cup again. Record these temperatures in the chart.

6 Repeat Steps 4 and 5 two more times. Each time, stir to dissolve the salt in cup B, and then measure and record the temperature of the water in each cup.

Picture A

Picture B

Draw Conclusions

1. **Compare** the final temperatures of the two cups of water. What happened to the temperature of the salt water as more salt was added to cup B?

2. Based on your results, **predict** the temperature at which the water in cup B would freeze.

3. **Scientists at Work** The Arctic Ocean tends to be less salty, on average, than the Atlantic Ocean. Scientists use this information to predict when winter temperatures will cause certain harbors and ports to freeze. Explain why cold winter temperatures would affect the formation of harbor ice differently in the two oceans.

Investigate Further **Hypothesize** how the amount of salt in water affects the temperature at which the water will freeze. Then **plan and conduct a simple experiment** using varying amounts of salt dissolved in water to test your hypothesis.

Earth's Oceans

Oceans and Seas

FIND OUT

- **the location of Earth's oceans and seas**
- **why oceans are salty**
- **about major features of the ocean floor**

VOCABULARY

salinity
water pressure

Nearly 71 percent of Earth's surface is covered with a continuous body of salty water. Geographers have divided this body into four oceans and many smaller seas. As you can see from the table below, the Pacific Ocean is the largest ocean. It is equal in size to the other three oceans combined. It is also the deepest ocean, with an average depth of 4188 m (about 13,740 ft). The Atlantic Ocean is shallower, with an average depth of only 3735 m (about 12,254 ft). Much of the surface of the Arctic Ocean, the smallest ocean, is covered with ice all year round. In ocean areas near Antarctica, the surface water freezes for at least part of the year.

Seas are smaller than oceans. Seas may be partly surrounded by land or separated from an ocean by a chain of islands. Some bodies of water, such as the Gulf of Mexico, are really seas, even though they have a different name.

✓ **Name Earth's four large oceans.**

Earth's Oceans	
Name	**Surface Area** (in millions of km²)
Pacific Ocean	166.0
Atlantic Ocean	82.4
Indian Ocean	74.0
Arctic Ocean	14.1

More than 70 percent of Earth's surface is covered by oceans and seas. ▼

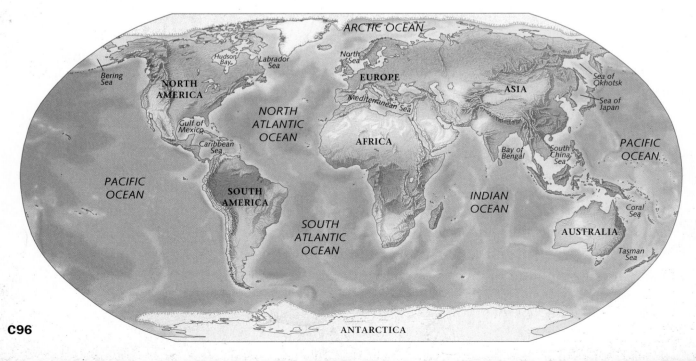

Characteristics of Ocean Water

The most obvious characteristic of ocean water is its **salinity**, or saltiness. The world's oceans and seas taste salty because of minerals dissolved in the water. The main mineral in ocean water is sodium chloride—ordinary table salt.

In addition to sodium chloride, ocean water has other minerals and gases dissolved in it. Many of the minerals in ocean water come from the weathering of rocks on land.

The salinity of ocean water varies from place to place. In warm, dry regions, evaporation of water from the ocean surface and little precipitation cause ocean water to have a high salinity. In cold regions, salinity is lower because less evaporation takes place and melting ice and snow add fresh water. Areas of lower salinity also occur where freshwater rivers enter the ocean.

Extreme pressure is another characteristic of ocean water. On land, air pressure is about

On Bonaire, an island in the Caribbean Sea near Venezuela, many evaporation ponds have been built for the collection of sea salts. After the water evaporates, salt is left behind.

14.7 lb per sq in. This amount of pressure is referred to as one atmosphere. Water weighs more than air. In the ocean, with each additional 10 m (about 33 ft) of depth, **water pressure**—the weight of the water pressing on an object—increases by one atmosphere. In the deepest parts of the oceans, water pressure can be as high as 1000 atmospheres. Exploration at these depths requires special equipment such as the bathyscaphe *Trieste* shown below.

✔ **What are some causes of high salinity in ocean water?**

◀ The cone-shaped window in *Trieste's* cabin was built to withstand the tremendous pressure of the water at depths to 15,240 m (about 50,000 ft). Its steel hull is about 17.5 cm (7 in.) thick.

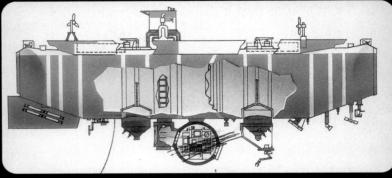

▲ The bathyscaphe *Trieste* holds the record for the world's deepest dive, 10,911 m (35,797 ft), in the Mariana Trench in the Pacific Ocean.

North America
continental shelf
continental slope
abyssal plain

The Ocean Floor

Features of the continents include mountains, hills, plains, and valleys. If you could remove the water from the oceans, you'd find that their floors have similar features. You would also see long mountain ranges, volcanoes, plateaus, and deep canyons called trenches.

Continental Shelf Around the edges of the continents, a shallow area called the *continental shelf* extends into the ocean for about 80 km (50 mi). It is no deeper than 140 m (about 460 ft), although it varies in width from 1.6 km (1 mi) to 1200 km (about 745 mi) in the arctic regions.

Continental Slope Beyond the continental shelf is a steep *continental slope* that drops sharply to a depth of 3000 m (about 10,000 ft). After that it slopes more gradually to a depth of 4000 m (about 13,000 ft). In some places the continental slope is deeply cut by canyons. Many of these canyons have been carved by large rivers entering the oceans.

Abyssal Plains The flattest parts of the ocean floor, which are also the flattest parts of Earth's surface, are the *abyssal plains*. They are at an average depth of 4500 m (about 16,000 ft). They are covered with a thick layer of ooze consisting of mud, sand, and decaying organic matter. The abyssal plains cover vast areas of the ocean floor.

Ridges, Volcanoes, and Trenches A ridge of underwater mountains rises up along the center of the three largest oceans. This ridge, from 1 to 3 km (about 0.6 to 2 mi) above the abyssal plains, forms a continuous undersea mountain chain 60,000 km (about 37,280 mi) long that winds through the Pacific, Atlantic, and Indian Oceans. The Mid-Atlantic Ridge has a deep valley, or *rift*, in its center. Here two of Earth's tectonic plates are pulling apart.

In some places huge volcanoes rise from the abyssal plain. The tops of some of these volcanoes extend above the ocean's surface, forming island chains. The deepest spots in the oceans are the trenches that often are found near these islands. The deepest known trench is the Mariana Trench, located near the Philippine Islands in the Pacific Ocean, 11,033 m (36,198 ft) below the surface.

✔ **Name the three main areas of the ocean floor.**

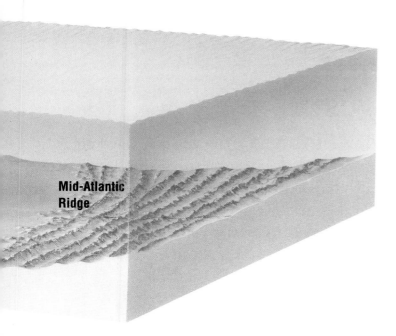

Mid-Atlantic Ridge

Summary

Four oceans and many seas make up one large body of salt water that covers more than 70 percent of Earth's surface. The salinity of ocean water comes mainly from minerals weathered from Earth's crust. Tremendous water pressure exists at the deepest parts of the ocean. Features of the ocean floor include a shallow shelf surrounding the continents, a steep slope, flat plains, volcanoes, trenches, and mountains.

Review

1. How are seas different from oceans?
2. Why is ocean water salty?
3. What are mid-ocean ridges?
4. **Critical Thinking** The plates that meet in the center of the Mid-Atlantic Ridge are gradually pulling apart. How will this affect the size of the Atlantic Ocean?
5. **Test Prep** Which of the following is **NOT** one of Earth's oceans?

   A Pacific   **C** Indian
   B Mediterranean   **D** Atlantic

LINKS

MATH LINK

Estimate Look at the table on page C96 showing the surface areas of major bodies of salt water. Estimate the total surface area of all the oceans listed in the table.

WRITING LINK

Narrative Writing—Story Write a first-person story from the point of view of an explorer making an underwater voyage across the Atlantic Ocean. Use a map of the ocean floor to help you plan your route. What challenges will you face on your expedition? What ocean features will you explore?

SOCIAL STUDIES LINK

Elevation Map Make a cross-sectional map of the floor of one of the world's oceans. Label the continents, and show the elevations of the ocean's major features, such as the continental shelves and slopes, abyssal plains, mid-ocean ridges, volcanoes, and trenches.

TECHNOLOGY LINK

Learn more about Earth's oceans by visiting the Harcourt Learning Site.
www.harcourtschool.com

How Do Ocean Waters Move?

In this lesson, you can . . .

INVESTIGATE waves.

LEARN ABOUT the movement of ocean waters.

LINK to math, writing, language arts, and technology.

INVESTIGATE

Waves

Activity Purpose Have you ever stood on a beach and watched the ocean? If so, you probably noticed that the water is always moving in waves. Waves can also move across a lake or a pond. You can even **observe** very small waves, called ripples, on a puddle. What causes waves? In the investigation, you will **use a model** of the ocean to find out.

Materials

- rectangular pan
- water
- straw

Activity Procedure

1. **Make a model** of the ocean by half-filling the pan with water. (Picture A)

2. Place your straw near one side of the pan, and gently blow across the surface of the water. What happens? (Picture B)

◀ Wind and waves work together to make windsurfing an exciting sport.

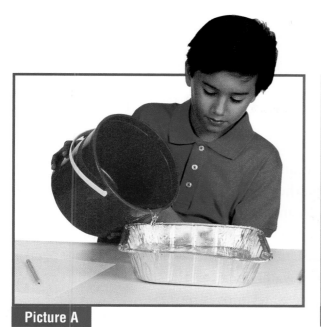

Picture A

Picture B

3 **Observe** the height and speed of the waves you make. **Record** your observations.

4 Repeat Step 2 several times, blowing a little harder each time. What do you **observe** about the waves you make? **Record** your observations.

Draw Conclusions

1. Use your observations to describe the relationship between how hard you blow and the height and speed of the waves.

2. From what you observed in this activity, what can you **infer** about the cause of waves on oceans and other bodies of water?

3. **Scientists at Work** Scientists often **use models** to learn about things they cannot **observe** directly. What did your model help you observe about waves?

Investigate Further **Hypothesize** how high the waves on a pond, a lake, or the ocean can be on a calm day or on a stormy day. Then **plan and conduct a simple experiment** to test your hypothesis.

Process Skill Tip

Observing is the most basic science skill. You **observe** when you use your senses to note the properties of an object or event, such as the effect of moving air on water.

How Ocean Waters Move

FIND OUT

- **how waves move**
- **what causes ocean currents**
- **what causes tides**

VOCABULARY

wave
current
tide

Wind and Waves

The waters of the ocean never stop moving. Most of the movement of water on the ocean's surface is due to waves. A **wave** is the up-and-down movement of surface water.

In the investigation you observed that wind produces waves. In fact, most waves are caused by wind. When wind blows over the surface of a body of water, it causes the surface of the water to move with it. Because water moves more slowly than air, the water piles up, forming a ripple. The wind then pushes on the side of the ripple, making it grow in height, and turning the ripple into a wave.

In the investigation you also observed that the height of a wave is related to how hard the wind blows. On a calm day, ocean waves may be less than 1.5 m (about 5 ft) high. But during a storm, waves can reach heights of 30 m (about 100 ft). That's as high as a ten-story building!

Even though the water in a wave may rise and fall by as much as 30 m, very little of the water moves forward. What moves across the ocean's surface is energy. Think about this: When you shake a rope, the rope moves up and down or side to side as waves travel to the

Water in a wave moves in circles, returning to about the place where it started. ▽

end of the rope. But the rope itself doesn't move forward. This motion is similar to what happens to water in the ocean. The waves move across the surface of the water, but the water stays in almost the same place.

✓ **What causes most waves in water?**

Other Kinds of Waves

Most ocean waves are caused by wind. But some waves can be caused by earthquakes and volcanoes, extremely low air pressure, or several things acting together.

Some of the biggest waves in the oceans are caused by earthquakes and volcanoes. These giant waves are called *tsunamis* (soo•NAH•meez). In the deep ocean, a tsunami may be more than 100 km (about 62 mi) long but less than 1 m (about 3 ft) high. These waves pass under ships without being noticed. But when a tsunami reaches a shore, friction with the ocean bottom slows the wave. This causes the wave to grow to as much as 25 m (about 82 ft), destroying everything in its path.

During hurricanes and tropical storms, large domes of water called *storm surges*

Hurricane winds produce huge waves that East Coast surfers enjoy before the storm arrives.

form. Low air pressure at the storm's center causes ocean water to rise. Strong winds form huge waves on top of the storm surge, and they push this high water ahead of the storm. If the storm is moving toward land, it may send a wall of water up to 10 m (about 33 ft) high crashing onto the beach.

Another kind of wave is called a rogue (ROHG) wave. This is a huge wave, much higher than the waves around it. Many rogue waves form when large storm waves join together.

✓ **Name three different kinds of waves, and tell what causes them.**

Tsunamis, such as the one that hit Hilo, Hawai'i, in 1946, cause great damage to buildings along the shore. ▼

Even large boats can be sunk by rogue waves. ▼

Currents

Although waves are the most easily seen kind of ocean movement, currents move much more water. An ocean **current** is a stream of water that flows like a river through the ocean. Unlike waves, currents actually move water forward, sometimes for long distances.

Large ocean currents, known as *surface currents,* flow across the surface of the oceans. Surface currents are usually caused by prevailing winds. As a prevailing wind blows across the surface of the ocean, the water begins to move as a stream. Some surface currents can be hundreds of kilometers wide and hundreds of meters deep. A single one of these "ocean rivers" can move more water than the Amazon, the largest river in the world.

A surface current can carry cold water to warm regions. It can also carry warm water to cold regions. One surface current is the Gulf Stream. This warm current flows northeast from the Caribbean Sea, past the East Coast of the United States, and across the North Atlantic. Even after its long trip across the cold Atlantic, there is enough warm water in this current to warm the climate of Great Britain and northern Europe. That's why palm trees can grow along the southern coast of England.

The warm waters that form the Gulf Stream are shown in orange and red in this satellite photograph. Colder waters are shown in green and blue. ▼

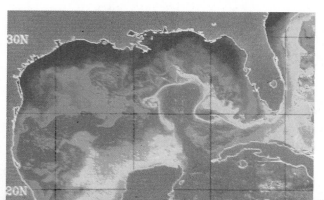

▲ Rip currents (red arrows) may flow away from a beach at 8 km/h (about 5 mi/h). If you get caught in a rip current, swim parallel to the shore until you move out of the current. The water on both sides of the rip current flows toward the beach.

Surface currents aren't the only currents flowing through the oceans. *Shoreline currents* are local currents that run along the coast. Local winds and shifting beach materials may cause shoreline currents to change from day to day.

A *rip current* is a shoreline current that flows away from the beach. A rip current is often caused by a sand spit, a long ridge of sand that forms offshore near a beach. Ocean waves flow over the sand spit and toward the beach. But water from the waves can't flow back over the sand spit. The water piles up, trapped by the sand spit, until a small break opens up in the sand spit. The water then flows rapidly out through the opening, producing a strong current.

When waves strike a shore at an angle, they move water forward along the shore. This movement of water parallel to the beach produces another type of shoreline current, called a longshore current. Longshore currents carry large amounts of beach materials from one place to another.

Surface Currents

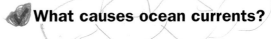

ARCTIC OCEAN — NORTH AMERICA — ATLANTIC OCEAN — EURASIA — ARCTIC OCEAN — PACIFIC OCEAN — AFRICA — SOUTH AMERICA — ATLANTIC OCEAN — INDIAN OCEAN — AUSTRALIA — PACIFIC OCEAN — ANTARCTICA

Greenland Current — Labrador Current — North Atlantic Drift — Oyashio Current — North Pacific Drift — California Current — Gulf Stream — Canary Current — North Equatorial Current — Kuroshio Current — North Equatorial Current — Equatorial Countercurrent — South Equatorial Current — Equatorial Countercurrent — Equatorial Countercurrent — South Equatorial Current — Peru Current — Brazil Current — Benguela Current — South Equatorial Current — South Equatorial Current — West Australian Current — East Australian Current — West Wind Drift — West Wind Drift

→ Warm current
→ Cold current

▲ This diagram shows how surface currents move. The red arrows show warm water, and the blue arrows show cold water.

Although wind blowing across the surface of an ocean can produce currents, these currents don't continue moving in the same direction as the wind. Earth's rotation causes ocean currents to bend to the right in the Northern Hemisphere and to the left in the Southern Hemisphere. The currents start moving in giant circles.

Not all ocean currents are caused by wind. Deep-ocean currents are caused by differences in water temperature. Cold water is heavier than warm water, so it sinks. The cold water then flows along the bottom of the ocean.

What causes ocean currents?

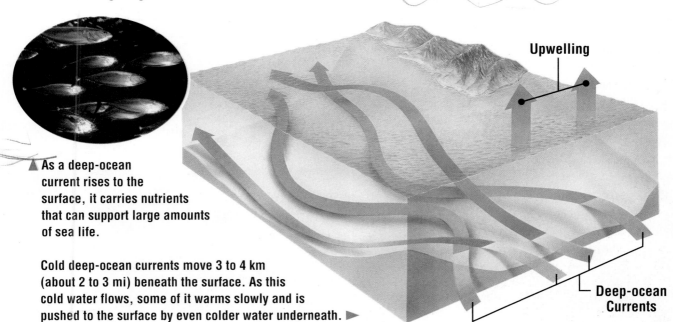

Upwelling

Deep-ocean Currents

▲ As a deep-ocean current rises to the surface, it carries nutrients that can support large amounts of sea life.

Cold deep-ocean currents move 3 to 4 km (about 2 to 3 mi) beneath the surface. As this cold water flows, some of it warms slowly and is pushed to the surface by even colder water underneath. ▶

Tides

Once or twice each day, ocean water rises and falls at every beach around the world. This repeated rise and fall in the level of the ocean is called the **tide**. Tides are caused by the pull of gravity of the sun and the moon on Earth's waters. Since the moon is closer to Earth than the sun, it has a greater effect on tides than the sun does.

The pull of the moon combines with Earth's rotation to produce traveling bulges of water. The moon's pull on the oceans is strongest on the side of Earth facing the moon. This causes Earth's shape to become slightly oval. Solid parts of Earth change very little. But the oceans bulge out on the side of Earth nearest the moon and on the side farthest from the moon. As Earth rotates, it pulls these bulges along.

The bulges of water on either side of Earth are called *high tides*. Low-water levels

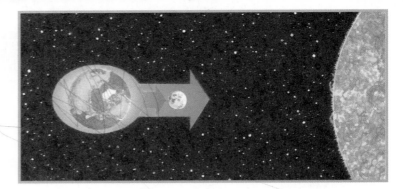
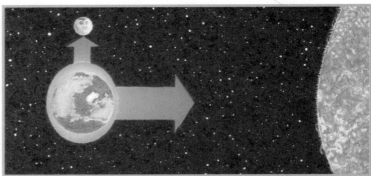

▲ Very high tides occur every 14 days when the moon and sun line up. Weaker tides occur when the moon, the sun, and the Earth form a right angle.

between high tides are called *low tides*. Most coastal areas have one or two low tides and one or two high tides every 24 hours. Low and high tides occur at regular times, which can be predicted. The table shows high and

In the Bay of Fundy, between Maine and Nova Scotia, the difference between high and low tides can be as much as 20 m (about 66 ft)!

Tides for the Bay of Fundy

Date	Time	Ht.	Time	Ht.	Time	Ht.	Time	Ht.
1/15/2002	0354	5.4	1003	24.7	1623	3.8	2232	23.6
1/16/2002	0437	4.8	1045	25.2	1705	3.3	2313	24.1
1/17/2002	0519	4.4	1126	25.6	1746	2.8	2354	24.5
1/18/2002	0600	4.0	1206	25.9	1826	2.4		
1/19/2002	0034	24.8	0642	3.7	1247	26.0	1908	2.2
1/20/2002	0115	25.0	0725	3.5	1329	26.0	1950	2.2
1/21/2002	0158	25.1	0810	3.5	1414	25.7	2035	2.4

low tides during one week in Canada's Bay of Fundy. The Bay of Fundy is famous for its extremely high and low tides, so knowing when tides will occur is very important for boaters.

✔ **What causes tides?**

Summary

The ocean is in constant motion. Ocean waters move as waves, currents, and tides. Most waves are caused by wind. Currents are streams of water caused by winds or differences in water temperature. Tides are caused by the gravitational pull of the moon and sun on Earth's oceans.

Review

1. How does the water in an ocean wave move?

2. Compare the causes of surface currents with those of deep-ocean currents.

3. How do the moon's gravity and Earth's rotation affect tides?

4. **Critical Thinking** For a science fair project, a student dissolves food coloring in a cup of cold water. Then the student pours the cold, colored water into a glass of warm water. **Predict** what will happen to the colored water. Explain your prediction.

5. **Test Prep** Tides are caused by —

   A ocean currents

   B waves and the prevailing winds

   C the gravitational pull of the moon and sun on the oceans

   D hurricanes and other tropical storms

LINKS

 MATH LINK

Describe Patterns Look at the tide table on page C106. Find the tides for January 20. At what times will high tide occur on that day? About how many hours apart are the two high tides?

 WRITING LINK

Narrative Writing—Story Do some research about an ocean current. Where does the current begin? Where does it go? What does the current carry? How does the current affect the lands it touches? Then write a short story for your teacher about the current.

 LANGUAGE ARTS LINK

Editing After you finish the first draft of your story about an ocean current, trade stories with a classmate for comments and corrections. Mark any errors in spelling or grammar. Then look for parts of the story that you like. Look also for parts that could be more exciting or that need to be explained better. Write any comments on the manuscript and give it back to your classmate.

GO ONLINE **TECHNOLOGY LINK**

Learn more about the effects of waves and currents by visiting this Smithsonian Institution Internet site. **www.si.edu/harcourt/science**

 Smithsonian Institution®

How Do Oceans Interact with the Land?

In this lesson, you can . . .

INVESTIGATE the effect of waves on a beach.

LEARN ABOUT how the oceans affect the shoreline.

LINK to math, writing, technology, and other areas.

INVESTIGATE

The Effect of Waves on a Beach

Activity Purpose Every day ocean waves keep pounding against the shore. How do waves change a shore? In this activity you will **make a model** so you can **observe** the effect of waves on a beach.

Materials
- stream table
- sand
- water

Activity Procedure

1 Use sand to **make a model** of a beach at one end of the stream table. The beach should have a gentle slope. (Picture A)

2 Slowly add water to the stream table until it is about half full. Try not to disturb the beach.

◄ Ocean waves will soon destroy this sand castle.

Picture A

Picture B

3 Make a wave by lifting the sand end of the stream table about 2 cm above the tabletop and then dropping it. What do you **observe** about the beach and the water? Repeat this several times. **Record** your observations.

4 Repeat Steps 1–3, but this time build a beach that is much steeper than the first one. **Record** your observations. (Picture B)

Draw Conclusions

1. Use your observations to explain how waves affect a beach.

2. Does the slope of the beach matter? Explain.

3. **Scientists at Work** Scientists often **make a model** to study how natural processes work. How did your model help you **observe** how waves affect a beach? What couldn't you observe about wave action with your model?

Investigate Further If possible, study the shore of a pond, a lake, or an ocean in your area. What do you **observe** about the shore? **Hypothesize** how waves affect the shore. **Plan and conduct a simple experiment** to test your hypothesis.

How Ocean Waters Shape the Shore

At the Shore

FIND OUT

- how ocean waves and currents shape the shore
- how human activities can change the shore

VOCABULARY

shore
headland
tide pool
jetty

The area from where waves begin to break to the highest place they reach on the beach is called the shore. The **shore** is the area where the ocean and land meet and interact. Anyone who has lived near the ocean knows that the shore is a place of constant change.

As you saw in the investigation, waves change the shore in several ways. One is by grinding pebbles and rocks against the shore. This action erodes the bottoms of cliffs, causing them to break apart and fall into the ocean. Another way waves change the shore is through water pressure. Each breaking wave hurls tons of water at the shore. This water pressure loosens pebbles and small rocks, which the outgoing waves carry into the ocean.

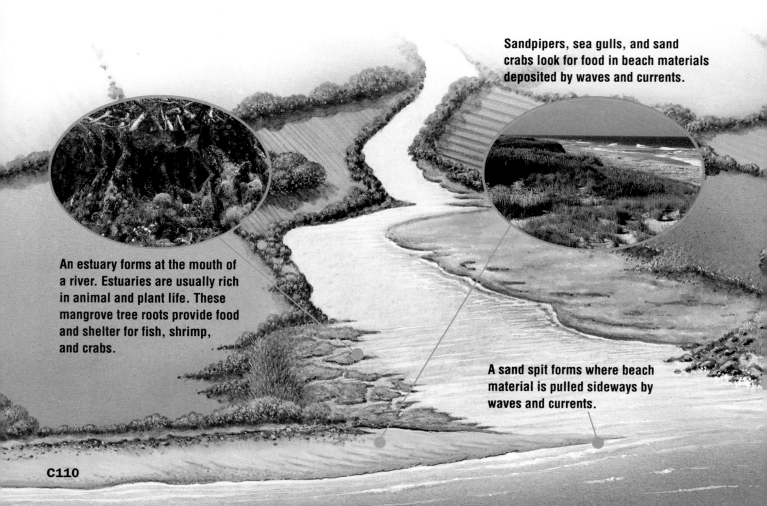

Sandpipers, sea gulls, and sand crabs look for food in beach materials deposited by waves and currents.

An estuary forms at the mouth of a river. Estuaries are usually rich in animal and plant life. These mangrove tree roots provide food and shelter for fish, shrimp, and crabs.

A sand spit forms where beach material is pulled sideways by waves and currents.

Where a shore is made of both soft rock and hard rock, erosion is uneven. Soft rock erodes faster than hard rock. Wave action may destroy the soft rock, forming small bays like those shown below. As the soft rock is washed away, the hard rock may be left as a rocky point, or **headland**. Sometimes the ocean cuts sea caves into a headland. If waves continue to erode the sea caves, a sea arch may form.

Currents also change a shore. If you've ever been swimming in the ocean, you may have noticed that when you came out of the water, you had to walk up and along the beach to the place where you left your towel. A longshore current carried you down the beach.

Longshore currents also move sand, pebbles, and shells along the shore. In places where the shore changes shape, a longshore current slows down and deposits beach materials. A new beach is formed, or the existing beach receives new sand and pebbles.

✓ **How do waves and currents change the shore?**

A tide pool is a pool of seawater found along a rocky shoreline. At high tide the pool is under water. This tide pool in California provides a habitat for a great variety of plants and animals.

Two sea caves have further eroded to form a sea arch like this one on Anacapa Island, in Channel Islands National Park, California.

Human Activities Affect the Shore

Human activities also change the shore. People in coastal communities often build structures to protect their beaches from erosion. These structures can block longshore currents and change the natural processes that erode and build up a shore.

At Cape Hatteras, along the coast of North Carolina, the Atlantic Ocean has eroded the beach so much that the lighthouse there was in danger of falling into the sea. The Cape Hatteras Lighthouse is one of the most famous lighthouses in the United States. To save the lighthouse, three small jetties, or groins were built along the water's edge to catch sand and build up the beach. A **jetty** is a wall-like structure made of rocks that sticks out into the ocean. Jetties are usually built on either side of an opening to a harbor. Groins are small jetties built along a beach.

A jetty protects a harbor by trapping sand and pebbles that normally flow down the coast with the longshore current. But jetties

These jetties were built to protect this beach from erosion. ▼

The Cape Hatteras Lighthouse was built in 1870 after many ships had sunk in the so-called Graveyard of the Atlantic. ▼

This was the Cape Hatteras Lighthouse in 1998. On parts of Hatteras Island, ocean waves wash away 4.3 m (about 15 ft) of beach each year. ▶

can also harm beaches. Although the beach above the jetty receives extra sand, beaches down the shore may lose their supply of sand and actually erode.

Cape Hatteras Lighthouse is safe for now. The lighthouse was moved farther from the ocean in 1999.

✔ **How do human activities affect the shore?**

Summary

The shore is changed by waves, currents, and human activities. Waves erode beaches and cliffs. Longshore currents deposit beach materials such as sand, pebbles, and shells along the shore. Jetties and other structures can affect the natural processes of shore change.

Review

1. How do waves erode beaches and cliffs?

2. How does a longshore current affect the shore?

3. What are two ways in which a jetty can affect a shore?

4. **Critical Thinking** A pier is built sticking out into the ocean. After a few years, sand builds up along one side of the pier. Explain why.

5. **Test Prep** An estuary is an area rich in plant and animal life that forms —

   A along a sandbar

   B along a jetty

   C at a headland

   D at the mouth of a river

Cumberland Island, Georgia, is a wide, beautiful barrier island. A barrier island is a long ridge of sand in the ocean running parallel to the shore. A barrier island gets its name from the fact that it blocks ocean waves and storm surges, protecting the low coastal mainland.

LINKS

MATH LINK

Estimate The Atlantic Ocean is eroding parts of Hatteras Island at the rate of 4.3 m per year. Estimate how many years it will take for 30 m of the island to be eroded.

WRITING LINK

Persuasive Writing—Opinion Take a stand for or against building jetties to save a beach. Prepare notes for a short speech explaining your point of view. Be sure to include facts and drawings or photographs to support your position. Present your speech to your classmates.

ART LINK

Shore Diagram Draw a picture showing how the ocean both erodes and builds up beaches.

SOCIAL STUDIES LINK

Shore Map Find a shore in your state to map. If you don't live near an ocean, map a large lake. Show natural features such as bays, estuaries, and beaches.

GO ONLINE TECHNOLOGY LINK

Learn more about the interactions of the ocean and the shore by visiting this Smithsonian Institution Internet site.
www.si.edu/harcourt/science

 Smithsonian Institution®

How Do People Explore the Oceans and Use Ocean Resources?

In this lesson, you can . . .

INVESTIGATE how scientists measure ocean depths.

LEARN ABOUT how people explore the oceans and use ocean resources.

LINK to math, writing, literature, and technology.

This copper diving helmet was first used in about 1819. ▷

INVESTIGATE

How Scientists Measure Ocean Depths

Activity Purpose In 1521 Portuguese explorer Ferdinand Magellan tried to measure the depth of the Pacific Ocean. He dropped 730 m (about 2400 ft) of weighted rope over the side of his ship. But this wasn't nearly enough rope to reach the bottom of the ocean. Today's scientists use *sonar*, or sound wave devices, to determine how deep the ocean is. In this activity you will learn about two ways to **measure** the depth of water—Magellan's way and a more modern way.

Materials

- shoe box
- sand, pebbles, small rocks
- construction paper
- scissors
- ruler
- string
- weight
- calculator

Activity Procedure

1 **Make a model** of the ocean floor by pouring sand and pebbles into the shoe box. Then scatter a few small rocks on top of the sand. (Picture A)

2 Cut a piece of construction paper large enough to cover the top of the box. This will stand for the sea surface.

3 With a pencil and ruler, draw a grid on the paper 4 squares wide by 8 squares long. Number the squares 1 through 32, and tape the lid onto the box. Tie the weight to a piece of string about twice as long as the box is deep.

4 Make a hole in the first square in any row and lower the weighted end of the string until the weight just touches the ocean floor. (Picture A)

5 Hold the string at sea level. **Measure** the length of string you pinched off to find the depth of the ocean. **Record** your measurement. Repeat Steps 4 and 5 for the remaining squares in that row.

6 Now copy the Sonar Data table. The "Time" is the number of seconds it takes for a sound to travel from a boat to the bottom of the ocean and back to the boat.

7 Use a calculator to multiply the Location 1 time by 1500 m/s (the speed of sound in water). Then divide the product by 2. This number is the depth of the water in meters at Location 1. This one has been done for you.

8 Repeat Step 7 for each location in the table. Then make a line graph of the depths. The graph will be a profile of the ocean floor.

Picture A

Sonar Data		
Location	Time (s)	Depth (m)
1	1.8	1350
2	2.0	
3	3.6	
4	4.5	
5	5.3	
6	2.3	
7	3.1	
8	4.6	
9	5.0	
10	5.2	

Draw Conclusions

1. Why do you think scientists today use sonar rather than weighted ropes to **measure** the depth of the ocean?

2. When using sonar, why must you divide each product by 2 to calculate the depth of the water?

3. **Scientists at Work** How could a scientist use sonar to **measure** the size of large objects on the ocean floor?

Investigate Further How could you find the depth of a pond, lake, or river? **Plan and conduct a simple investigation** to find out.

Process Skill Tip

You **measure** when you use a tool to find how deep the water is.

Exploring the Oceans and Using Ocean Resources

Exploring the Ocean

FIND OUT

- about ocean exploration
- about *Alvin,* the submersible that helped find RMS *Titanic*
- how people use ocean resources

VOCABULARY

scuba
submersible
sonar
desalination

Did you know that more than 70 percent of Earth is covered with water? Viewed from space, the continents we live on seem like big islands with oceans around them. People have been exploring the oceans for thousands of years. Early peoples took trips in small boats to search for food, to move to new homes, and to find better trade routes. Some went just for adventure. The time line below shows some of the ways in which people have explored the oceans in the past 600 years.

Scientists and explorers have been studying the oceans for hundreds of years. People designed diving suits as early as the

The voyage of HMS *Challenger* in 1872 started the modern science of oceanography (oh•shuhn•AWG•ruh•fee) —the scientific study of the oceans.

1400s	1500s	1600s	1700s	1800s

This diving suit was designed in the 1400s.

Sir Edmond Halley, an English astronomer, built this diving bell in 1690. Air was sent down to the bell using barrels and leather tubes. The bell shape trapped air for the divers to use.

1400s, and by 1690, divers could use Sir Edmond Halley's diving bell to explore to a depth of 18 m (about 60 ft) below sea level.

Detailed studies of the oceans began in 1872 with the voyage of the British ship HMS *Challenger*. Led by C. Wyville Thomson, six scientists spent about four years at sea. They took thousands of samples and measurements of the oceans. They studied the chemistry of sea water and collected ocean plants, animals, and minerals.

With simple methods like you used in the investigation, Thomson and his staff achieved many firsts. Using a weighted line and a steam engine, they measured a water depth of 8185 m (about 26,850 ft) in the western Pacific. They also captured and classified 4717 new species of marine life. The scientific reports of their expedition filled 50 books.

Today's scientists use many different technologies to explore the oceans. They dive beneath the water wearing **scuba** equipment. (The letters *s-c-u-b-a* stand for *self-contained **u**nderwater **b**reathing **a**pparatus*.) They travel in small, underwater vehicles called **submersibles**. Satellites are used to study ocean currents from space, and **sonar** (a device that uses sound waves) is used to map the ocean floor.

✔ **What technologies do scientists use to explore the oceans?**

In 1960 Jacques Piccard and Donald Walsh went down in the *Trieste II* to the deepest place in the Pacific Ocean. They reached a depth of about 10,910 m (35,800 ft). At this depth the top of Mount Everest would still be about 1525 m (5000 ft) below the ocean's surface.

Today, satellites can measure an ocean's salt content, temperature, wave heights, and current flows from thousands of kilometers in space. Sensors can even show where tiny organisms called plankton are found in ocean waters.

| 1900–1935 | 1935–1960 | 1960–2000 |

The Aqua-lung, an early form of scuba, was invented in 1942 by French explorer Jacques Cousteau. With scuba gear, a diver can move freely about underwater to a depth of about 60 m (200 ft).

The submersible *Alvin* has played an important role in exploring ocean depths. To reach the *Titanic* in 1986, it had to travel nearly 4000 m (about 13,000 ft) beneath the ocean's surface.

Submersibles

One of the best-known submersibles is *Alvin*, named in honor of ocean scientist Allyn Vine. In 1956 Vine convinced the United States government that scientists needed deep-diving vessels that could hold small crews. By the 1960s *Alvin* was exploring the oceans.

In 1977 scientists in *Alvin* discovered underwater vents along the Mid-Atlantic Ridge. In 1986 *Alvin* was used to explore the wreckage of the sunken ship RMS *Titanic*.

Alvin may have been the first submersible to explore *Titanic*, but it wasn't the last.

During the 1990s a team of French and American explorers used a newer submersible, *Nautile*, to continue the job *Alvin* started.

Nautile first visited the *Titanic* wreck in 1987, bringing up some objects from the site. In the 1990s even more objects were brought up, including a large part of the sunken ship itself.

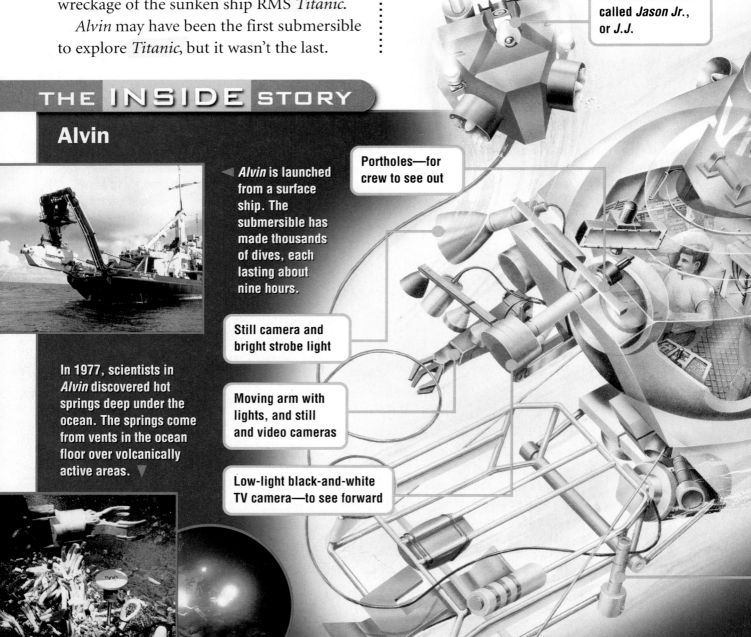

Remote-controlled underwater robot called *Jason Jr.*, or *J.J.*

THE INSIDE STORY

Alvin

Alvin is launched from a surface ship. The submersible has made thousands of dives, each lasting about nine hours.

In 1977, scientists in *Alvin* discovered hot springs deep under the ocean. The springs come from vents in the ocean floor over volcanically active areas. ▼

Portholes—for crew to see out

Still camera and bright strobe light

Moving arm with lights, and still and video cameras

Low-light black-and-white TV camera—to see forward

With space for crews of three—one pilot and two scientists each—*Alvin* and *Nautile* can work inside sea caves, shipwrecks, and other small spaces.

Crewed submersibles allow scientists to observe underwater objects up close. They have been able to make important scientific discoveries, as well as explore sunken ships.

But in the future, underwater exploration may be done with small, crewless submersibles. These underwater robots can fit into places too small for *Alvin* or *Nautile*. And they can dive deeper and stay longer on the ocean floor.

✔ **What kinds of places have scientists used submersibles to explore?**

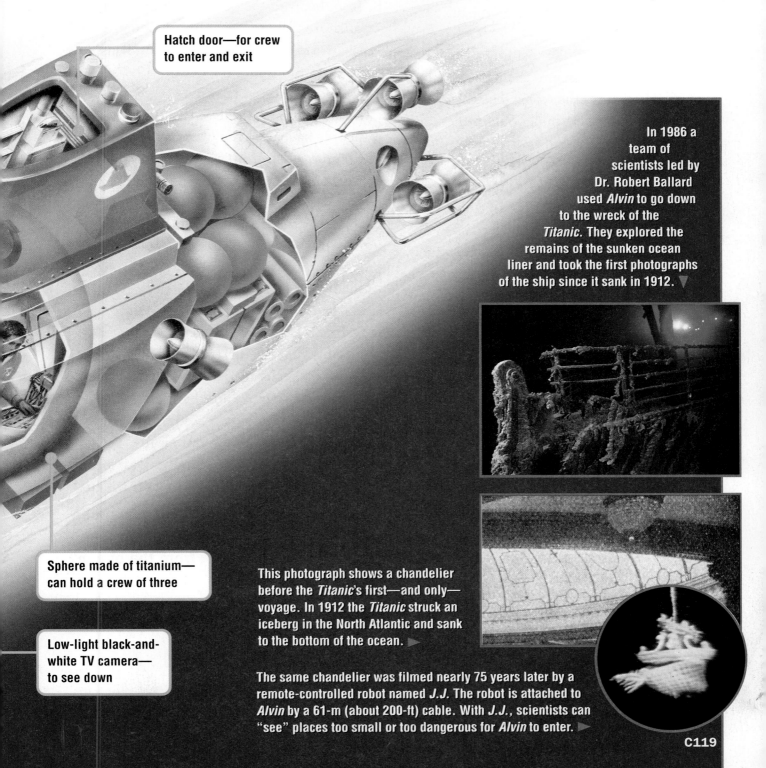

Hatch door—for crew to enter and exit

In 1986 a team of scientists led by Dr. Robert Ballard used *Alvin* to go down to the wreck of the *Titanic*. They explored the remains of the sunken ocean liner and took the first photographs of the ship since it sank in 1912. ▼

Sphere made of titanium—can hold a crew of three

This photograph shows a chandelier before the *Titanic*'s first—and only—voyage. In 1912 the *Titanic* struck an iceberg in the North Atlantic and sank to the bottom of the ocean. ▶

Low-light black-and-white TV camera—to see down

The same chandelier was filmed nearly 75 years later by a remote-controlled robot named *J.J.* The robot is attached to *Alvin* by a 61-m (about 200-ft) cable. With *J.J.*, scientists can "see" places too small or too dangerous for *Alvin* to enter. ▶

Using Ocean Resources

The importance of the oceans is not just in the discoveries they hold for scientists. The oceans contain huge amounts of natural resources. Ocean waters are filled with plants and animals. The ocean floor contains many minerals. Gas and oil are buried deep beneath the ocean floor. And in some places, sea water itself has become an important resource.

Among the ocean's most important resources are its fish and shellfish. Millions of people around the world feed their families by fishing from small boats. Others fish for large companies on factory ships—huge boats where fish can be cleaned, processed, and canned or frozen right on board.

Sea plants are another ocean resource. People eat some kinds of seaweed as food. Carrageenin (kar•uh•JEE•nuhn), a product made from seaweed, is used in foods, toothpaste, hand creams, and fertilizer.

As resources on land become scarce, people are beginning to mine underwater mineral deposits. Sand, gravel, and shells are easily obtained near the shore. Hundreds of millions of tons are dredged from the sea each year and used for road construction and building materials. Minerals containing iron, copper, manganese, nickel, and cobalt can be taken from lumps, or nodules, lying on the sea floor. These deep-sea nodules are difficult to mine, however, since they are located at depths of 4000 m (about 13,125 ft) or more.

Petroleum and natural gas are pumped from beneath the ocean floor using huge offshore drilling rigs. Almost a quarter of the world's petroleum and natural gas now comes from under the ocean.

Another useful resource, salt, is dissolved in the sea water itself. Since ancient times people have used the process of evaporation to remove salt from sea water. Much of the world's salt is still obtained using this natural process.

There is still another valuable ocean resource—water. In some parts of the world, freshwater supplies are so limited that water is taken from the ocean. The salt is removed from sea water by **desalination**. In one method, sea water is evaporated, leaving the minerals behind. The water vapor is then cooled and condensed back into fresh water. In another desalination method, sea water is passed through a plastic film that allows pure water, but not the dissolved salts, to go through.

✔ **What resources do people take from the ocean?**

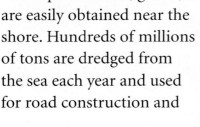

Offshore drilling rigs like this one may stand in water as deep as 300 m (about 1000 ft). ▶

▲ Desalination plants like this one provide water for drinking or industry. Right now the cost is usually too high to use desalinated water for farm irrigation.

Summary

Ocean exploration has a long history. Today's ocean scientists have a wide range of technology that they can use, including scuba equipment, submersibles, satellites, and sonar. The oceans also contain valuable natural resources such as fish, petroleum, minerals, and sea water itself.

Review

1. What did the crew of the *Challenger* study?

2. Why are submersibles such as *Alvin* valuable to ocean scientists?

3. What mineral resources are found in or beneath the ocean?

4. **Critical Thinking** The deeper you go in the ocean, the greater the water pressure. Use logical reasoning to **infer** why.

5. **Test Prep** Which word does NOT belong with the others?

   A seaweed

   B salt

   C manganese

   D iron

LINKS

MATH LINK

Solve Problems A typical dive with *Alvin* lasts about 9 hours. Of these 9 hours, 30 minutes are spent launching the craft. Another 30 minutes are spent recovering it from the water. The descent to the ocean floor takes $2\frac{1}{2}$ hours, and the ascent back to the surface takes another $2\frac{1}{2}$ hours. How long do the scientists have for research?

WRITING LINK

Narrative Writing—Story Choose an ocean resource to research. Find out more about this resource, including how it is obtained and how it is used. Then write a science fiction story for your class that describes a world where that resource has become scarce.

LITERATURE LINK

Exploring the **Titanic** The complete story of the *Titanic* expedition is told in this book by Robert D. Ballard. In 1985 Ballard and his team discovered the remains of the *Titanic* on the ocean floor. A year later the team returned to explore the ship in the submersible *Alvin*.

TECHNOLOGY LINK

Learn more about ocean exploration by viewing *Jacques Cousteau* on the **Harcourt Science Newsroom Video.**

Saltwater Agriculture

Who would grow crops in a desert? Scientists would, and they are using salt water to do it.

By the Sea

The first major use of salt water for growing crops was in Israel. At the end of World War II, Hugo and Elisabeth Boyko decided to live there. Elisabeth was a horticulturist, an expert in growing certain plants, and Hugo was an ecologist.

The Boykos used their skills to landscape a town near the Red Sea. They wanted to make it prettier so that more people would move there. Growing plants in the seaside town was a challenge. Most plants need rich soil and fresh water to grow, but here the land was sandy and the only water was from the sea. They pumped salt water from the sea to irrigate, or water, their plants. Many plants are killed by salt water, but the Boykos noticed that some plants survived in spite of the salt.

Since then other scientists have continued the Boykos' work. Some have teamed up with desert farmers in Mexico, India, and other countries to build experimental farms that practice saltwater agriculture.

A Growing Challenge

Why grow crops in a desert? And why use salty seawater instead of fresh water from

Glasswort is a halophyte. It can grow in salty soil.

This photograph shows a landscaped town along the Red Sea.

rivers or lakes? There are some very important reasons.

The world's population is increasing, so there are more and more people to feed. But Earth's supplies of good farmland and fresh water are shrinking. Every year it gets harder to raise enough food for everyone. Where could farmers find additional land and water? Areas of desert near an ocean seem like an excellent choice.

Saltwater Crops

Corn, wheat, rice, potatoes, and soybeans are the main crops that people eat. Salt water kills them all. What else is there? Halophytes. Halophytes are plants that grow in the wild and survive in salty soil. In fact, halophytes absorb salt and store it inside themselves. That's why some of them taste so salty.

One halophyte that could be used for food is called glasswort. This leafless plant can be fed to livestock. Its seeds contain protein and oil, and the oil has a nutlike taste. However, glasswort isn't the perfect crop—yet. Glasswort is so salty that it makes livestock thirsty. They have to drink more water than usual, which is not a good way to save fresh water, especially in a desert. Can scientists develop a less salty glasswort? Agronomists are trying.

THINK ABOUT IT

1. Why would it be useful to farm deserts near oceans?
2. What advantages and disadvantages are there to growing halophytes?

CAREERS
HYDROLOGIST

What They Do
Hydrologists test drinking water, issue flood warnings, check underground water supplies, and protect water in other ways. Many work in government agencies, city or state offices, consulting firms, and waste-treatment plants.

Education and Training
A person wishing to become a hydrologist needs to study physical or natural science or engineering and take courses in soils, marine biology, or other scientific fields. Math and computer skills are also helpful.

WEB LINK
For Science and Technology updates, visit the Harcourt Internet site.
www.harcourtschool.com

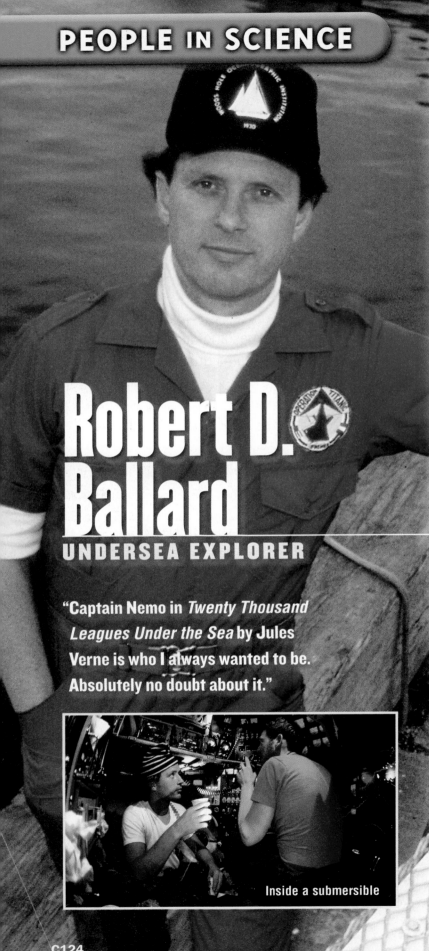

Robert D. Ballard
UNDERSEA EXPLORER

"Captain Nemo in *Twenty Thousand Leagues Under the Sea* by Jules Verne is who I always wanted to be. Absolutely no doubt about it."

Inside a submersible

Undersea explorer Robert D. Ballard made headlines around the world when he and his crew located the wreck of the R.M.S. *Titanic*. Although most people know of Dr. Ballard for making this discovery, his fellow scientists know him for discovering deep-ocean life forms and geologic processes never seen before.

Although geologists had hypothesized that thermal vents existed, no one had predicted that there would be so many kinds of organisms there. Dr. Ballard observed huge blood-red worms without eyes or mouths, clusters of giant clams, blind crabs, and other strange animals. These animals depend on bacteria, not on plants, for food.

Dr. Ballard's team is also recognized for discovering that all the water of the oceans is recycled over time through Earth's crust. This discovery has helped scientists explain why sea water is full of minerals.

Interested in becoming an undersea explorer from the time he was a boy, Dr. Ballard is thankful to the many people who taught and encouraged him throughout his career. "You need to pick out certain people you have great respect for and listen to them," he says. "At every critical point in my life, when I was ready to quit, I can point to someone who said, 'Keep it up.'"

THINK ABOUT IT

1. Why was discovering that all the water of the oceans is recycled through Earth's crust important?
2. Why is working as part of a team important to scientists?

WATER WORLD

What happens when waters meet?

Materials

- water
- 200-mL beaker
- food coloring
- hot plate
- tongs
- water-filled aquarium

Procedure

1 Fill the beaker half-full of water. Add food coloring to the water.

2 Using the hot plate, gently warm the water in the beaker.

3 Your teacher or another adult will use the tongs to lower the beaker straight down into the aquarium filled with cold water.

4 Observe the hot, colored water as it leaves the beaker.

Draw Conclusions

Describe what you observed. From your observations, what conclusions can you draw about areas in the ocean where warm currents flow through cooler waters?

OIL AND WATER

Why did ancient sailors use oil to calm the seas near their ships?

Materials

- glass bread pan
- water
- food coloring
- drinking straw
- cooking oil

Procedure

1 Fill the glass pan about half-full of water.

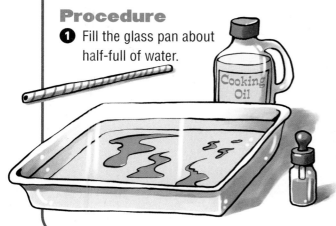

2 Add several drops of food coloring to the water.

3 Using the straw, gently blow across the surface of the water.

4 Now slowly pour oil into the water until it forms a layer of oil about 1 cm thick on top of the water.

5 Using the straw, blow gently across the surface again.

Draw Conclusions

Compare the waves produced in Step 3 with those produced in Step 5. What do you conclude to be the cause of any differences in the waves? Why would sailors pour oil on the water during rough weather?

Vocabulary Review

Use the terms below to complete the sentences. The page numbers in ( ) tell you where to look in the chapter if you need help.

salinity (C97)

water pressure (C97)

wave (C102)

current (C104)

tide (C106)

shore (C110)

tide pool (C111)

headland (C111)

jetty (C112)

scuba (C117)

submersible (C117)

sonar (C117)

desalination (C120)

1. The ____, which is the repeated rise and fall in the level of the ocean, is caused by the pull of gravity of the moon and the sun.

2. The area where the ocean and the land meet and interact is the ____.

3. Scientists can use self-contained underwater breathing apparatus, or ____, equipment to dive beneath the water.

4. In an ocean ____, a stream of water moves through the ocean like a river, but in a ____, water moves up and down in a circular motion.

5. A ____ is a small underwater vehicle used to explore the ocean.

6. The weight of overlying water is called ____.

7. Scientists can use ____ to map the ocean floor.

8. A pool of sea water found along a rocky shore is called a ____.

9. A ____ is a rocky point that juts out into the ocean.

10. A ____ is a wall-like structure made of rocks that sticks out into the ocean.

11. The process of ____ removes the salt from sea water.

12. The saltiness of ocean water is its ____.

Connect Concepts

Use terms from the Word Bank to complete the concept map below.

wave   tide   submersible
scuba   shore

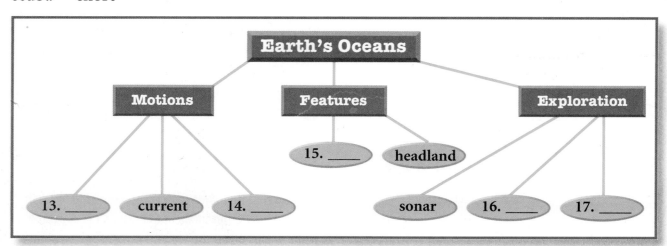

Check Understanding

Write the letter of the best choice.

18. A tsunami is a wave caused by —
    A an earthquake   C a storm surge
    B a high tide   D an ocean current

19. The main cause of tides is —
    F ocean waves
    G the moon's gravity
    H the sun's energy
    J longshore currents

20. Deep-ocean currents are caused by —
    A volcanoes deep under water
    B prevailing winds
    C the Earth's rotation
    D differences in water temperature

21. Shoreline currents are caused by —
    F local winds and conditions
    G prevailing winds
    H the saltiness of the water
    J sandspits

22. Most of the ocean floor is —
    A continental shelf
    B continental slope
    C abyssal plain
    D mid-ocean ridge

23. Detailed study of the oceans began with —
    F the discovery of the *Titanic*
    G the invention of scuba gear
    H the voyage of the *Challenger*
    J the scientists of the *Trieste*

24. Earth's oceans include the —
    A Atlantic   C Indian
    B Pacific   D all of the above

25. *Alvin* is a _____ that scientists used to discover hot springs deep under the ocean.
    F sailboat   H satellite
    G submersible   J robot

Critical Thinking

26. Suppose you drop a ball into the ocean in a place where there is no current. Will waves move the ball quickly away, or will it bob in place? Explain.

27. Suppose you have the choice of buying one of two houses. Both houses are built near the beach. One is 50 m from the ocean. The other is 100 m from the ocean. Which house would you choose? Explain.

28. Suppose you are an ocean miner. Tell how you might obtain a mineral that is on the ocean bottom, 1000 m below the surface.

Process Skills Review

29. How can you **make a model** of a tide pool?

30. Which method of **measuring** works better to determine the depth of the ocean—sonar or weighted ropes? Explain.

Performance Assessment

Waves

Using construction paper, glue, and two pieces of string, make a model to compare the way *energy* in waves travels with the way *water* in waves travels.

There are many places where you can find out more about processes that change the Earth. You can study weather and some of these Earth-changing forces at the places below. You'll also have fun while you learn.

National Weather Service Baltimore-Washington Forecast Office

WHAT A weather station where weather conditions are monitored and forecasts are made

WHERE Sterling, Virginia

WHAT CAN YOU DO THERE? Tour the weather station, see the equipment used to monitor the weather, and learn how weather forecasts are made.

Mammoth Cave National Park

WHAT The longest recorded cave system in the world, with more than 336 miles explored and mapped

WHERE Mammoth Cave, Kentucky

WHAT CAN YOU DO THERE? Take the tour of this cave system, see the many geologic formations, and learn how this cave was made.

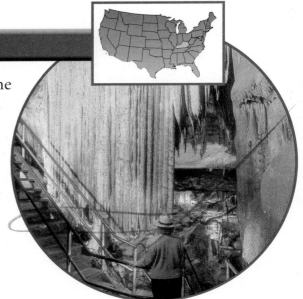

GO ONLINE Plan Your Own Expeditions

If you can't visit the National Weather Service Baltimore-Washington Forecast Office or Mammoth Cave National Park, visit a weather station or a cave near you. Or log on to The Learning Site at **www.harcourtschool.com** to visit these science sites and other places to find out more about processes that change the Earth.

The Solar System and Beyond

The Solar System and Beyond

UNIT EXPERIMENT

Designing Rockets

Scientists study the universe from Earth and from space. Studying the universe from space requires rockets that can send heavy payloads deep into space. While you study this unit, you can conduct a long-term experiment on rocket design. Here are some questions to think about. What rocket design will carry heavy payloads the farthest? For example, is one large rocket more powerful than several smaller rockets? Plan and conduct an experiment to find answers to these or other questions you have about designing rockets. See pages x–xvii for help in designing your experiment.

Earth, Moon, and Beyond

Although Earth moves through space very rapidly, it doesn't *seem* to move at all. That's why the sun and the moon both appear to move around Earth. It took astronomers a long time to realize that Earth actually moves around the sun.

Vocabulary Preview

revolve
orbit
rotate
axis
eclipse
solstice
equinox
planets
asteroids
comets
telescope
satellite
space probe

Fast Fact

Observatories located near growing cities are no longer very useful. The city lights and the pollution in the air make it impossible to see the stars clearly. But on the summit of Mauna Kea in Hawai'i, many miles from city lights and pollution, scientists can see the stars quite clearly.

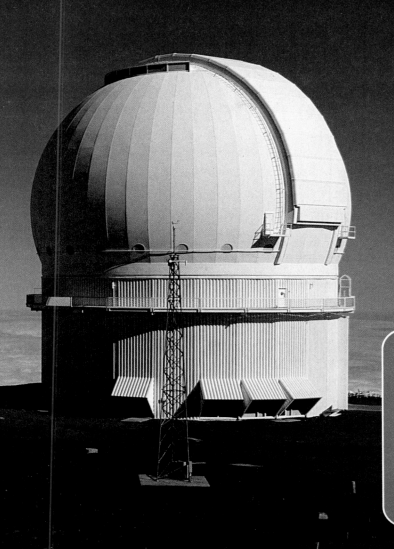

Fast Fact

It takes Earth 365.26 days to travel once around the sun. An adjustment to the calendar is made for the 0.26 day by adding a February 29 every four years. These longer years are called leap years.

Once Around the Sun

Planet	Earth Days
Mercury	88
Venus	224.7
Earth	365.26
Mars	687
Jupiter	4332.6
Saturn	10,759.2
Uranus	30,685.4
Neptune	60,189
Pluto	90,777.6

Fast Fact

The next total solar eclipse in the United States will take place on August 21, 2017. It will move across the country from Oregon to South Carolina. You can safely view a solar eclipse the way the photograph shows.

How Do the Earth and the Moon Compare?

In this lesson, you can . . .

 INVESTIGATE how the moon craters were formed.

 LEARN ABOUT Earth and its moon.

 LINK to math, writing, music, and technology.

Earth, from the surface of the moon ▼

INVESTIGATE

The Moon's Craters

Activity Purpose As Earth's nearest neighbor in space, the moon was the first object in the solar system that people studied. People **observed** that the moon's surface was very different from the Earth's surface. One difference was the large number of craters on the moon. In the investigation you will **make a model** of the moon's surface to **infer** how the craters formed.

Materials

- newspaper
- aluminum pan
- large spoon
- $\frac{1}{2}$ cup water
- 1 cup flour
- safety goggles
- apron
- marble
- meterstick

CAUTION

Activity Procedure

1 Copy the table below.

Trial	Height	Width of Craters
1	20 cm	
2	40 cm	
3	80 cm	
4	100 cm	

2 Put the newspaper on the floor. Place the pan in the center of the newspaper.

3 Use a large spoon to mix the water and flour in the aluminum pan. The look and feel of the mixture should be like thick cake batter. Now lightly cover the surface of the mixture with dry flour. (Picture A)

4 **CAUTION** **Put on the safety goggles and apron** to protect your eyes and clothes from flour dust. Drop the marble into the pan from a height of 20 cm. (Picture B)

5 Carefully remove the marble and **measure** the width of the crater. **Record** the measurement in the table. Repeat Steps 4 and 5 two more times.

6 Now drop the marble three times each from heights of 40 cm, 80 cm, and 100 cm. **Measure** the craters and **record** the measurements after each drop.

Picture A

Draw Conclusions

1. **Compare** the height from which each marble was dropped to the size of the crater it made. How does height affect crater size?

2. The Copernicus (koh•PER•nih•kuhs) crater on the moon is 91 km across. Based on your model, what can you **infer** about the object that formed this crater?

3. **Scientists at Work** Most of the moon's craters were formed millions of years ago. Scientists **use models** to **infer** events that occurred too long ago to **observe** directly. What did you infer from the model about how the moon's craters formed?

Investigate Further **Hypothesize** how using larger or smaller marbles would affect the size and shape of the craters. **Plan and conduct a simple experiment** to test your hypothesis.

Picture B

Process Skill Tip

You can **use a model** to **infer** how something happened a long time ago, such as how the moon's craters formed.

D5

How Earth and the Moon Compare

Earth and the Moon in Space

The moon is the brightest object in the night sky and Earth's nearest neighbor in space. Together, Earth and the moon are part of the sun's planetary system. Pulled by the sun's gravity, the Earth-moon system **revolves**, or travels in a closed path, around

FIND OUT

- about the Earth-moon system
- what causes lunar and solar eclipses
- how Earth and the moon are alike and different

VOCABULARY

revolve
orbit
rotate
axis
eclipse

3 FIRST QUARTER
About one week after a new moon, the moon looks like a half-circle. This phase is called the first quarter because the moon is a quarter of the way around Earth.

4 WAXING GIBBOUS
The word *gibbous* (GIB•uhs) comes from a word meaning "hump."

5 FULL MOON
About two weeks after a new moon, we see the entire sunlit half.

6 WANING GIBBOUS
A waning moon appears to get smaller.

7 LAST QUARTER
About three weeks after a new moon, the moon is three-fourths of the way around Earth.

the sun. The path Earth takes as it revolves is called its **orbit**. Earth's orbit is an ellipse, a shape that is not quite circular.

As Earth orbits the sun, it **rotates**, or spins on its axis. The **axis** is an imaginary line that passes through Earth's center and its North and South Poles. Earth's rotation results in day and night. When a location on Earth faces the sun, it is day in that place. When that location faces away from the sun, it is night.

Pulled by Earth's gravity, the moon revolves around Earth in an ellipse-shaped orbit. When the moon is closest to Earth, it is about 356,400 km (221,463 mi) away.

Like Earth, the moon rotates on its axis. However, the moon takes 27.3 Earth days to complete one rotation. This makes a cycle on the moon of one day and one night that is 27.3 Earth days long.

Even though the moon rotates, the same side of the moon always faces Earth. This is because the moon orbits Earth in 27.3 days—exactly the same amount of time it takes to rotate once on its axis.

Although the moon shines brightly at night, it does not give off its own light. We see the moon from Earth because sunlight is reflected off its surface. As the moon orbits Earth, its position in the sky changes. This produces the different shapes, or phases, of the moon we see each month. The phases of the moon, as seen from Earth, are shown in the photographs below and on page D6.

✔ **How do Earth and the moon move through space?**

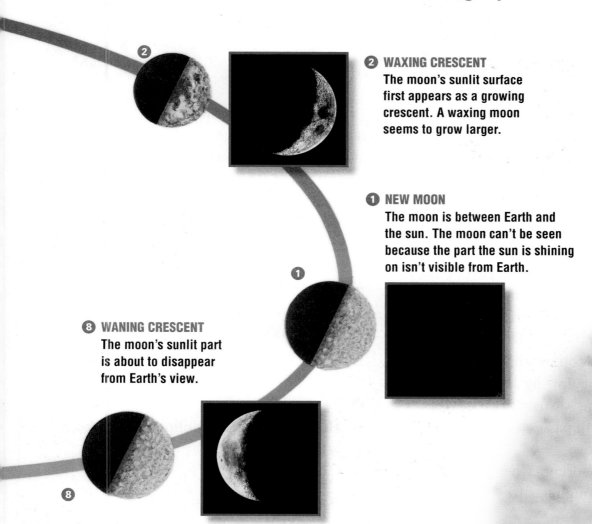

❷ **WAXING CRESCENT**
The moon's sunlit surface first appears as a growing crescent. A waxing moon seems to grow larger.

❶ **NEW MOON**
The moon is between Earth and the sun. The moon can't be seen because the part the sun is shining on isn't visible from Earth.

❽ **WANING CRESCENT**
The moon's sunlit part is about to disappear from Earth's view.

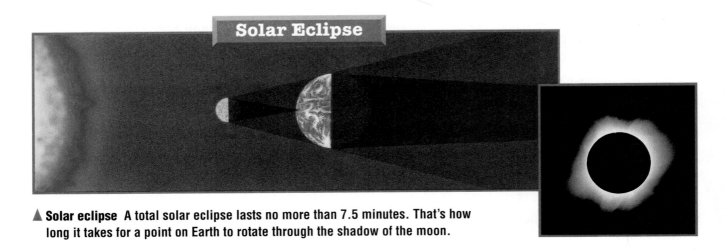

Solar Eclipse

▲ **Solar eclipse** A total solar eclipse lasts no more than 7.5 minutes. That's how long it takes for a point on Earth to rotate through the shadow of the moon.

Lunar Eclipse

▲ **Lunar eclipse** A total lunar eclipse lasts more than two hours. It may be seen from any place on Earth that is facing the moon.

Solar and Lunar Eclipses

All bodies in the solar system produce shadows in space. An **eclipse** (ee•KLIPS) occurs when one object passes through the shadow of another. A solar eclipse or a lunar eclipse occurs when Earth, the sun, and the moon line up.

A solar eclipse occurs when Earth passes through a new moon's shadow. During a total solar eclipse, the moon appears to completely cover the sun. The sky darkens, and only the sun's outer atmosphere is visible. It can be seen glowing as a bright circle around the moon. A partial solar eclipse occurs when Earth passes through part of the moon's shadow.

A lunar eclipse occurs when the full moon passes through Earth's shadow. When Earth passes between the sun and the moon, it blocks the sun's light. However, Earth's atmosphere bends certain colors of light, especially red. This makes the eclipsed moon look like a dim red circle.

You may wonder why eclipses do not occur twice each month—at every new moon and full moon. This is because the moon's shadow usually passes above or below Earth, or the moon passes above or below Earth's shadow. Only seven eclipses—two lunar eclipses and five solar eclipses—occur in a single year. And most of those are partial eclipses.

✔ **How does a solar eclipse differ from a lunar eclipse?**

The Moon's Surface

When the moon first formed, its surface was hot, molten rock. As the surface cooled, it formed a rocky crust. If you look at the moon through a telescope, you can see three types of landforms—craters, highlands, and dark, flat areas.

Some moon craters are very large. Tycho (TY•koh) crater, for example, is 87 km (about 54 mi) across. Other craters are so small that a hundred of them could fit on your fingernail.

The moon also has dark, flat areas known as *maria* (MAH•ree•uh). The word *maria* is Latin for "seas." For many years people thought these flat, dark areas on the moon were seas filled with water. But maria are really areas of hardened lava.

Maria formed when hot, molten rock flowed from the interior through cracks in the moon's surface. This molten rock over-flowed some craters and spread across the moon's surface. It then cooled to form a dark rock called *basalt*. The largest mare (MAH•ray) is 1248 km (about 775 mi) across. The illustration below shows craters and other landforms on the moon's surface.

✔ **What are some landforms found on the moon's surface?**

Lunar landforms include craters, maria, ray craters, rilles, highlands, and volcanic domes. Ray craters are thought to be new craters. The rays formed from rock that "splashed" out of the crater due to the impact of the object that made the crater. Rilles are lunar valleys. Some lunar highlands are as high as Earth's mountains. Volcanic domes may be like some volcanoes on Earth. ▶

volcanic dome

rilles

highlands

ray crater

crater

Comparing Earth's and the Moon's Features

Earth and its moon are alike in several ways. Both are rocky and fairly dense. The same materials that make up Earth—calcium, aluminum, oxygen, silicon, and iron—are found on the moon. Craters occur on both, although there are many more craters on the moon than on Earth.

There are also important differences between Earth and the moon. Unlike Earth, the moon has no atmosphere and no liquid water. Because of this, the moon's landscape has not been eroded by wind and water. The moon's surface weathers very slowly, staying the same for millions of years.

Comparing Earth and the Moon

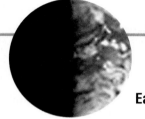

Earth

 Moon

Craters

Both Earth and the moon have craters. However, the surface of the moon has many more craters than the surface of Earth. Many meteorites burn up in Earth's atmosphere before they reach the surface, and weathering has eliminated many Earth craters.

Weathering

Since the moon has no wind or rain, footprints left by astronauts will remain on its surface for millions of years. Most footprints left on Earth's surface are worn away within a few days.

Water

Life on Earth depends on water. Since the moon has no liquid water, it has no life. However, frozen water has recently been discovered in craters at the moon's poles.

Look at the photographs on page D10 to compare features of the moon and Earth. The photographs on the right were taken on the moon. Those on the left were taken on Earth.

✓ **Compare and contrast features of Earth and the moon.**

Summary

The moon revolves around Earth, while the Earth-moon system orbits the sun. Both Earth and the moon rotate on axes and have day-night cycles. As Earth, the moon, and the sun travel through space, they sometimes line up to produce eclipses. Many of the features on Earth and the moon are different, although some landforms occur on both.

Review

1. Why does the same side of the moon always face Earth?
2. Describe a lunar eclipse.
3. How does a mare differ from a crater?
4. **Critical Thinking** Lunar rocks are very old and do not look as if they were eroded by water. Also, no rocks have been found that contain water combined with minerals, as are found on Earth. What can you **infer** about how long the moon has been without water?
5. **Test Prep** The path that Earth takes around the sun is called its —

   A axis
   B orbit
   C cycle
   D rotation

LINKS

MATH LINK

Use Fractions During a full moon, we see half of the moon's surface. During a first or third quarter, what fraction of the moon's surface do we see?

WRITING LINK

Narrative Writing—Story Some early people were afraid of solar eclipses. They believed that the sun might not return. They made up stories and myths to explain eclipses. For example, a myth might say that a dragon or wolf ate the sun and then spit it out again. Write a story or myth for your class explaining what happens during a solar eclipse.

MUSIC LINK

Moon Music The moon has given people many ideas for songs. Work with a group to list ideas for as many new titles of songs about the moon as you can think of. Then write a song about the moon. You may find it easier to write words to a tune you already know.

TECHNOLOGY LINK

Learn more about the discovery of ice near the moon's poles by viewing *Ice on the Moon* on the **Harcourt Science Newsroom Video.**

CNN
Turner
Le@rning.

What Else Is in the Solar System?

In this lesson, you can . . .

INVESTIGATE how Earth, the moon, and the sun move through space.

LEARN ABOUT objects in the solar system.

LINK to math, writing, literature, and technology.

The asteroid Ida is unique—it has its own moon! ▶

INVESTIGATE

How Earth, the Moon, and the Sun Move Through Space

Activity Purpose You may not feel as if you're moving right now, but you're actually speeding through space. Earth makes a complete spin once every 24 hours. So if you stand on the equator, you're moving at about 1730 km/hr (1075 mi/hr)! Earth also moves around the sun at about 107,000 km/hr (66,489 mi/hr). At the same time, the moon, which also spins, moves around Earth at about 3700 km/hr (2300 mi/hr). In the investigation you will **make a model** of Earth, the moon, and the sun to **compare** how they move through space.

Materials
- beach ball
- baseball
- Ping Pong ball

Activity Procedure

1. You will work in a group of four to **make a model** of the sun, Earth, and the moon in space. One person should stand in the center of a large open area and hold the beach ball over his or her head. The beach ball stands for the sun. A second person should stand far from the "sun" and hold the baseball overhead. The baseball stands for Earth. The third person should hold the Ping Pong ball near "Earth." The Ping Pong ball stands for the moon. The fourth person should **observe** and **record** what happens.

2 The real Earth moves around the sun in a path like a circle that has been pulled a little. This shape, called an *ellipse* (ee•LIPS), is shown here. For the model, Earth should move around the sun in an ellipse-shaped path. Earth should also spin slowly as it moves around the sun. The observer should **record** this motion. (Picture A)

ellipse

Picture A

3 While Earth spins and moves around the sun, the moon should move around Earth in another ellipse-shaped path. The moon should spin once as it moves around Earth. The same side of the moon should always face Earth. That is, the moon should spin once for each complete path it takes around Earth. The observer should **record** these motions. (Picture B)

Picture B

Draw Conclusions

1. Your model shows three periods of time—a year, a month, and a day. Think about the time it takes Earth to spin once, the moon to move around Earth once, and Earth to move around the sun once. Which period of time does each movement stand for?

2. **Compare** the movements of the moon to the movements of Earth.

3. **Scientists at Work** Scientists often **make models** to show **time and space relationships** in the natural world. However, models can't always show these relationships exactly. How was your model of Earth, the moon, and the sun limited in what it showed?

Investigate Further Plan and conduct a simple investigation to test this **hypothesis:** The amount of sunlight reaching Earth changes as Earth moves around the sun.

Process Skill Tip

Making a model of the sun-Earth-moon system enables you to **use time and space relationships** to learn how objects in space move and interact.

Cycles in the Solar System

Rotation and Time

You have observed that, each day, the sun appears to rise in the east, reach a high point around noon, and set in the west. This apparent motion of the sun is due to Earth's rotating on its axis. Recall the model you made of Earth and the sun. As Earth rotates, half of it always faces the sun. Locations on Earth's surface facing the sun experience daylight, while locations facing away from the sun experience darkness. Every location goes through a cycle of daylight and darkness in 24 hours. We call this cycle a day.

Our system of telling time is based on Earth's 24-hour rotation. For much of history, people did not need to know the exact time. They got up as the sun rose, ate their midday meal when the sun was overhead, and ended their day as the sun set. In the late 1800s the spread of railway systems produced a need for keeping exact time and schedules. People needed to know when trains would arrive and when they would leave. To solve this problem, 24 standard time zones were set up worldwide. Each time zone represents one of the hours in a day. All places within a particular time zone have the same time. If you travel from one time zone to the next going from east to west, the time will be one hour earlier. If you travel from one time zone to the next going from west to east, the time will be one hour later. The United States has seven time zones, from Puerto Rico in the east, to Hawai'i in the west. When families in Georgia are having dinner, students in Oregon, three time zones to the west, are just getting out of school.

✔ **How are time zones related to Earth's rotation?**

FIND OUT

- about time zones
- what causes seasons
- about planets, asteroids, and comets

VOCABULARY

solstice
equinox
planets
asteroids
comets

Earth's 360° circumference is divided into 24 time zones. When it is 7:00 A.M. in Atlanta, Georgia, it is only 4:00 A.M. in Portland, Oregon. ▼

Portland

Atlanta

Autumn equinox
September 21

Summer solstice
June 21

Spring equinox
March 21

Winter solstice
December 21

Earth's Seasons

Recall from Lesson 1 that Earth revolves around the sun, following a path called an orbit. It takes about 365 $\frac{1}{4}$ days, or one year, for Earth to complete its orbit. At the same time, Earth rotates once every 24 hours on its axis. However, Earth's axis isn't perpendicular, or straight up and down, in relation to its orbit. It is tilted about 23 $\frac{1}{2}$°. This tilt, along with Earth's changing position in its orbit, causes first the Northern Hemisphere and then the Southern Hemisphere to be pointed toward the sun.

For most places on Earth, this change in position causes changes in the number of hours of daylight and darkness. For example, when the Northern Hemisphere is pointed toward the sun, there are more hours of daylight than darkness, and the sun's rays strike the Earth very directly.

The day with the most daylight in the Northern Hemisphere, about June 21, is the summer solstice. It marks the first day of summer. In the Southern Hemisphere, this day is the winter solstice. Each point in Earth's orbit at which daylight hours are at their greatest or fewest is called a **solstice**. The winter solstice in the Northern Hemisphere is about December 21.

Halfway between the solstice points, neither hemisphere is pointed toward the sun. The hours of daylight and darkness are about equal everywhere. Each point in Earth's orbit at which the hours of daylight and darkness are equal is called an **equinox**. In the Northern Hemisphere, the autumn equinox, about September 21, marks the beginning of fall. The date of the spring equinox in the Northern Hemisphere is about March 21.

✔ **When is the spring equinox in the Northern Hemisphere?**

1. **Sun** The sun contains nearly all the matter in the solar system. Heat, light, and other forms of energy stream outward in all directions from its surface.

2. **Mercury** is so close to the sun that its temperature is about 425°C (800°F). Mercury does not have enough gravity to hold an atmosphere.

3. **Venus** is a hot planet with a thick atmosphere of carbon dioxide. Venus has a surface temperature of about 480°C (900°F), which is much too hot for life.

4. **Earth** With its oxygen-rich atmosphere and liquid surface water, Earth may be the only planet in the solar system able to support life.

5. **Mars** appears red because of the iron oxide, or rust, in its soil. Like Earth, Mars has frozen ice caps at its poles and deserts.

6. **Asteroid Belt** Asteroids are pieces of rock, perhaps left over from the formation of planets.

7. **Jupiter** is the largest planet in the solar system. Unlike the inner planets, Jupiter is a giant ball of liquid hydrogen and helium surrounded by several thin rings.

8. **Saturn** is another gas giant. Saturn has 18 moons and a huge system of rings, which are made up of ice chunks of varying sizes.

9. **Uranus** has more moons than any other planet and ten thin rings. It is tilted so far on its axis that it rotates on its side.

10. **Neptune** also has thin rings. Its color is similar to that of Uranus. One of Neptune's moons, Triton, is the largest in the solar system.

11. **Pluto** is small and icy. Part of Pluto's orbit passes inside that of Neptune, so at that time Neptune is the planet farthest from the sun.

12. **Comets** A comet has a solid, frozen core. As comets near the sun, their cores begin to melt, forming clouds of gas, which energy from the sun pushes into long tails.

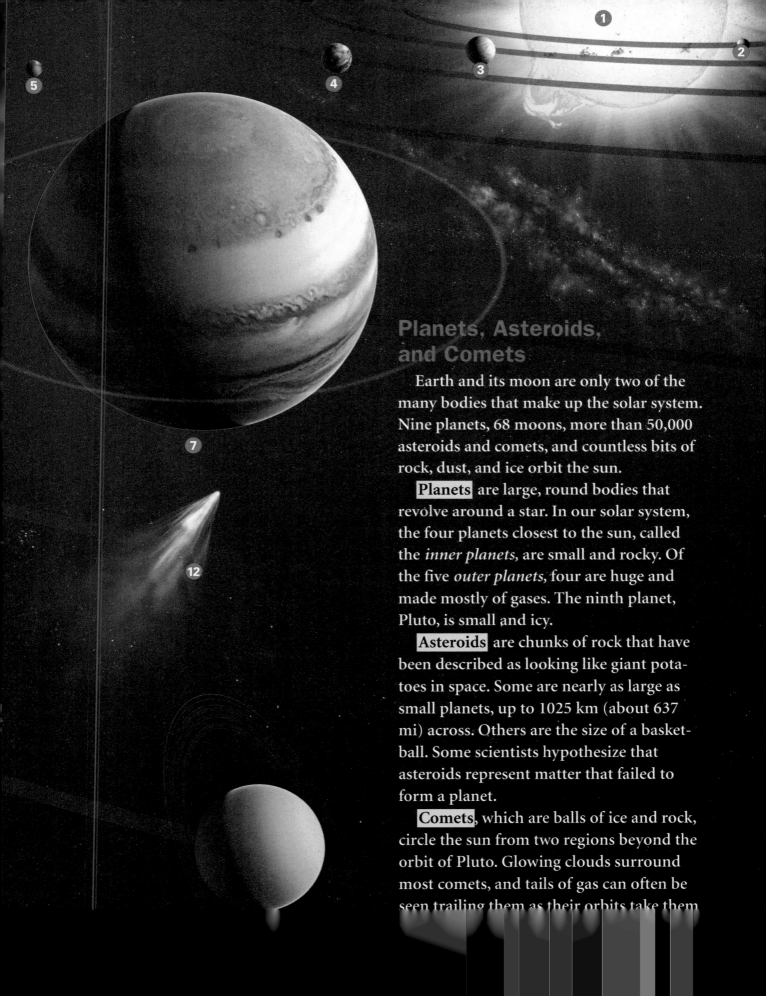

Planets, Asteroids, and Comets

Earth and its moon are only two of the many bodies that make up the solar system. Nine planets, 68 moons, more than 50,000 asteroids and comets, and countless bits of rock, dust, and ice orbit the sun.

Planets are large, round bodies that revolve around a star. In our solar system, the four planets closest to the sun, called the *inner planets*, are small and rocky. Of the five *outer planets,* four are huge and made mostly of gases. The ninth planet, Pluto, is small and icy.

Asteroids are chunks of rock that have been described as looking like giant potatoes in space. Some are nearly as large as small planets, up to 1025 km (about 637 mi) across. Others are the size of a basketball. Some scientists hypothesize that asteroids represent matter that failed to form a planet.

Comets, which are balls of ice and rock, circle the sun from two regions beyond the orbit of Pluto. Glowing clouds surround most comets, and tails of gas can often be seen trailing them as their orbits take them

Five planets of the solar system—Mercury through Saturn—are visible from Earth without using a telescope. To the unaided eye, these planets look very much like stars. Viewed through a telescope, as shown in the table below, the planets appear disk-shaped and have a steadier glow than stars.

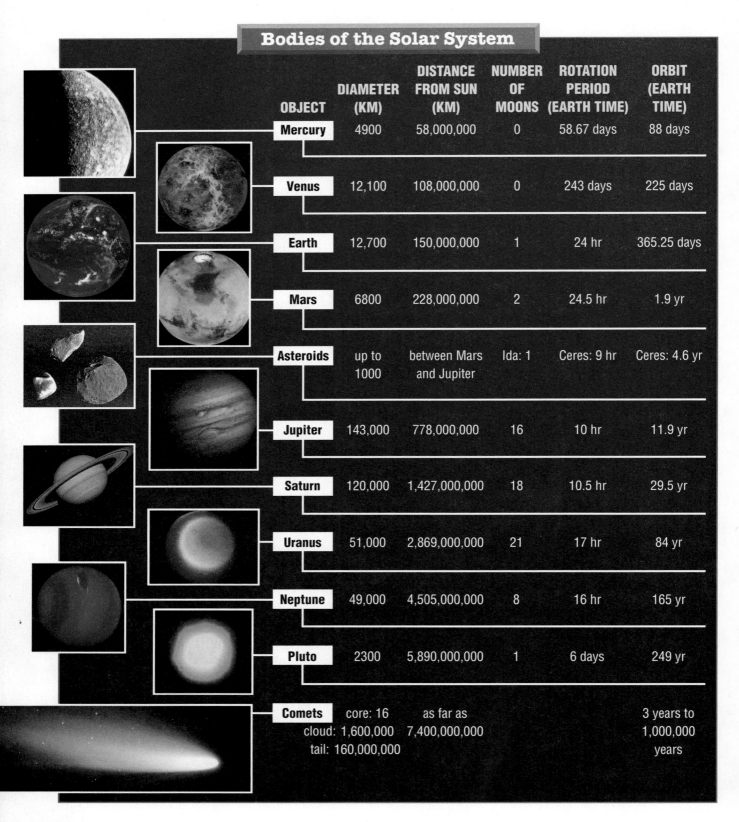

Bodies of the Solar System

OBJECT	DIAMETER (KM)	DISTANCE FROM SUN (KM)	NUMBER OF MOONS	ROTATION PERIOD (EARTH TIME)	ORBIT (EARTH TIME)
Mercury	4900	58,000,000	0	58.67 days	88 days
Venus	12,100	108,000,000	0	243 days	225 days
Earth	12,700	150,000,000	1	24 hr	365.25 days
Mars	6800	228,000,000	2	24.5 hr	1.9 yr
Asteroids	up to 1000	between Mars and Jupiter	Ida: 1	Ceres: 9 hr	Ceres: 4.6 yr
Jupiter	143,000	778,000,000	16	10 hr	11.9 yr
Saturn	120,000	1,427,000,000	18	10.5 hr	29.5 yr
Uranus	51,000	2,869,000,000	21	17 hr	84 yr
Neptune	49,000	4,505,000,000	8	16 hr	165 yr
Pluto	2300	5,890,000,000	1	6 days	249 yr
Comets	core: 16 cloud: 1,600,000 tail: 160,000,000	as far as 7,400,000,000			3 years to 1,000,000 years

▲ moon

Venus, as it appears from Earth without the use of a telescope. ▶ ✴

All the planets orbit the sun in the same direction as Earth. All the planets also rotate on their axes, though at very different speeds. The table on page D18 compares some of the important characteristics of the planets and other bodies in the solar system.

✓ **What bodies make up the solar system?**

Summary

Timekeeping on Earth is based on the division of Earth's surface into 24 standard time zones, each representing one of the 24 hours in a day. The position of Earth in its orbit and the tilt of its axis cause the change of seasons. The solar system contains the sun, planets and their moons, asteroids, and comets.

Review

1. What is the difference between a solstice and an equinox?

2. How are asteroids different from planets?

3. What causes a comet to have a tail?

4. **Critical Thinking** Why do astronomers consider Pluto an odd planet?

5. **Test Prep** The gas-giant planets are —

   A Venus, Jupiter, Uranus, Pluto

   B Venus, Jupiter, Saturn, Neptune

   C Jupiter, Saturn, Uranus, Neptune

   D Saturn, Uranus, Neptune, Pluto

LINKS

MATH LINK

Use Divisibility Rules Because distances in the solar system are so large, travel between the planets takes a very long time. If a spacecraft were traveling at 50,000 km/hr, how long would it take it to reach each of the inner planets from Earth? Use the table on page D18 for your information.

WRITING LINK

Informative Writing—Description About 65 million years ago, an asteroid striking Earth may have caused the extinction of the dinosaurs. At least 91 asteroids whose orbits cross Earth's have been identified. Find out how scientists are studying these asteroids and the probability of one of them actually hitting our planet. Then write a news story describing such an event.

LITERATURE LINK

Space Songs by Myra Cohn Livingston is a collection of poems on topics having to do with the sky, including the moon, the planets, and different times of day and weather. Read the poems in *Space Songs*. Then try making up your own space poem.

GO ONLINE **TECHNOLOGY LINK**

Learn more about planets and other objects in the solar system by visiting this Internet site.

www.scilinks.org/harcourt

SCI**L**INKS™
THE WORLD'S A CLICK AWAY

How Have People Explored the Solar System?

In this lesson, you can . . .

 INVESTIGATE how a telescope works.

 LEARN ABOUT how people explore the solar system.

 LINK to math, writing, art, and technology.

Astronaut working in space ▼

Make Your Own Telescope

Activity Purpose   Until Galileo invented the telescope in 1608, people were limited to the power of their eyes for viewing objects at a distance. Since then, people have used telescopes to observe objects in the night sky. To make his telescope, Galileo mounted a curved piece of glass, or lens, at each end of a long tube. In this investigation you will **make a model** telescope and use it to **observe** objects in greater detail.

Materials
- 2 sheets of construction paper
- two convex lenses
- tape
- modeling clay

Activity Procedure

1 Roll and tape a piece of construction paper to form a tube that is slightly larger in diameter than the lenses. Then make a second tube that is just enough larger in diameter for the smaller tube to fit snugly inside it.

2 Slide most of the small tube into the large tube. (Picture A)

3 Place one of the lenses in one end of the smaller tube, and use modeling clay to hold it in place. This lens will be the eyepiece of the telescope. (Picture B)

4 Place the other lens in the far end of the larger tube. Use clay to hold it in place. This lens will be the objective lens, or the lens closest to the object being viewed through the telescope.

5 Choose several distant objects to view with your telescope. You might look at a tree or a distant building. **CAUTION** **Do not look at the sun with your telescope. You could seriously damage your eyes.** Slide the smaller tube in and out until the object you are viewing comes into focus.

6 **Observe** each object twice, first using your eye alone and then using the telescope. **Record** your observations by making two drawings showing how the object appears when viewed with and without the telescope.

7 Repeat steps 5 and 6, observing the moon, a planet, or another object in space, using your telescope. Again make two drawings of the object, showing how it appears both with and without the telescope.

Picture A

Picture B

Draw Conclusions

1. **Compare** the drawings of each set. How does the appearance of each object change when viewed through the telescope? How does the use of the telescope affect your ability to observe details in those objects?

2. In which of the objects could more details be seen with the telescope than with the eye alone? In which of the objects, if any, were details NOT more visible?

3. **Scientists at Work** Scientists use many kinds of telescopes to **observe** objects in space. Some telescopes use curved mirrors instead of lenses to make objects appear larger. How is your model telescope limited in use for studying objects in space?

Investigate Further **Plan and conduct a simple experiment** to test this **hypothesis:** The curved surfaces of a lens bend the light rays that pass through it.

> **Process Skill Tip**
>
> **Making a model** of a telescope helps you **observe** the details of distant objects.

Space Exploration

Exploring the Solar System

Thousands of years ago, people observed the night sky and recorded their observations in cave paintings and rock art. These early observations were made without telescopes or other devices. About the only things early people could see were the phases of the moon and some of the moon's larger features. They could also see some of the planets and many stars. Then, about 400 years ago, the telescope was invented. It allowed people to observe objects in space in much greater detail.

FIND OUT

- **about the history of space exploration**
- **how spacesuits work**

VOCABULARY

telescope
satellite
space probe

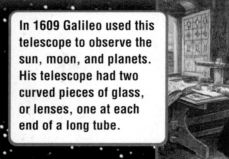

In 1609 Galileo used this telescope to observe the sun, moon, and planets. His telescope had two curved pieces of glass, or lenses, one at each end of a long tube.

900–1200	1200–1500	1500–1800

The Maya, in Central America, built many *observatories*, or places for viewing the stars and planets. This one at Chichén Itzá, in Mexico, was built about 900.

This telescope was designed by English scientist Sir Isaac Newton in 1668. It used two mirrors and one lens to produce sharper images than Galileo's telescope could.

In 1609 the Italian scientist Galileo (gal•uh•LEE•oh) was possibly the first person to use a new invention—the telescope—to observe the sky. A **telescope** is an instrument that magnifies, or makes larger, distant objects. With this telescope Galileo observed the moon and saw mountains, valleys, and craters that had never been seen before. He also observed the phases of Venus and four moons orbiting Jupiter. About fifty years later, English scientist Sir Isaac Newton used an even better telescope to observe other objects in space.

The modern age of space exploration began in 1957, when the Soviet Union launched *Sputnik I*, an artificial satellite. A **satellite** is any natural body, like the moon, or artificial object that orbits another object. *Sputnik,* which was about twice the size of a soccer ball, carried instruments to measure the density and temperature of Earth's upper atmosphere. The United States launched its own satellite the next year. Soon both countries were launching humans into space.

✔ **How did the telescope help people learn more about objects in space?**

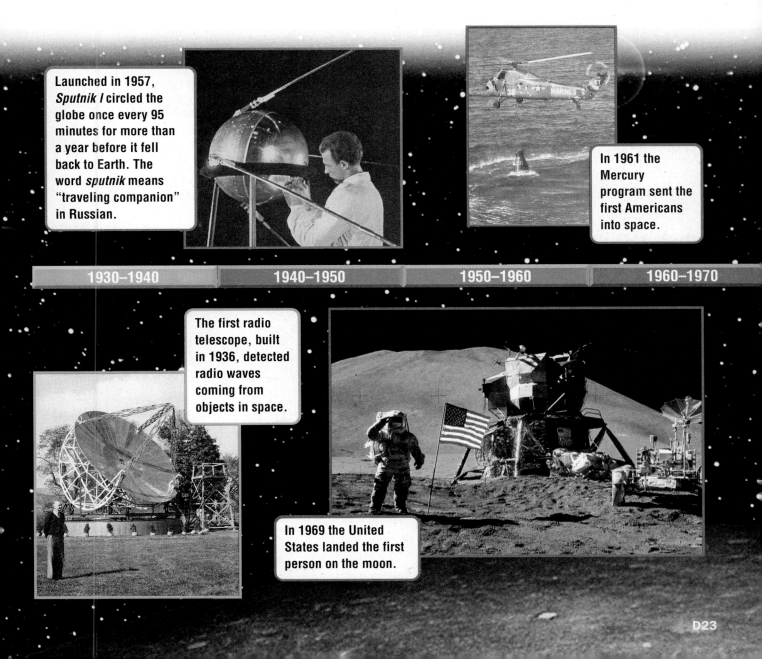

Launched in 1957, *Sputnik I* circled the globe once every 95 minutes for more than a year before it fell back to Earth. The word *sputnik* means "traveling companion" in Russian.

In 1961 the Mercury program sent the first Americans into space.

1930–1940   1940–1950   1950–1960   1960–1970

The first radio telescope, built in 1936, detected radio waves coming from objects in space.

In 1969 the United States landed the first person on the moon.

D23

To the Moon and Beyond

One of the best-known American space programs was Project Apollo. The Apollo missions landed 12 humans on the moon between 1969 and 1972. These astronauts set up experiments and brought back samples of rock. Their work helped scientists learn more about the moon.

In 1977 the *Voyager 1* and *Voyager 2* space probes were launched. A **space probe** is a robot vehicle used to explore deep space. The Voyager space probes have sent back pictures of Jupiter, Saturn, Uranus, and Neptune. Both Voyagers are still traveling through space beyond the solar system.

Other early space probes included *Viking I* and *Viking II,* which landed on Mars in 1976, and the Pioneer probes, which used instruments to "see" through thick clouds that cover Venus. Today's scientists use the Hubble Space Telescope, satellites, and space probes to better understand Earth, the solar system, and what lies beyond.

✔ **What was Project Apollo?**

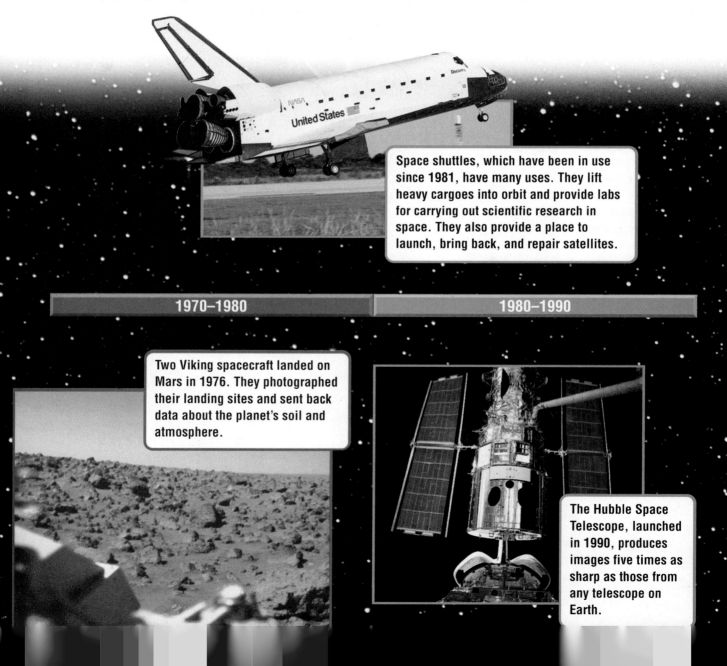

Space shuttles, which have been in use since 1981, have many uses. They lift heavy cargoes into orbit and provide labs for carrying out scientific research in space. They also provide a place to launch, bring back, and repair satellites.

1970–1980

1980–1990

Two Viking spacecraft landed on Mars in 1976. They photographed their landing sites and sent back data about the planet's soil and atmosphere.

The Hubble Space Telescope, launched in 1990, produces images five times as sharp as those from any telescope on Earth.

Spacesuits

The Apollo spacesuit below, once worn by Neil Armstrong, is a $10 million outfit made to protect an astronaut from the moon's hostile environment. The spacesuit must keep an astronaut from "cooking" in direct sunlight or freezing in cold shadows. It must provide the person who wears it with air, water, and waste removal for a moonwalk that may last up to eight hours. The spacesuit must also be flexible enough for an astronaut to walk, twist, turn, bend over, and pick up objects in the reduced gravity on the moon. Flightsuits, such as the one at the right, are much less bulky.

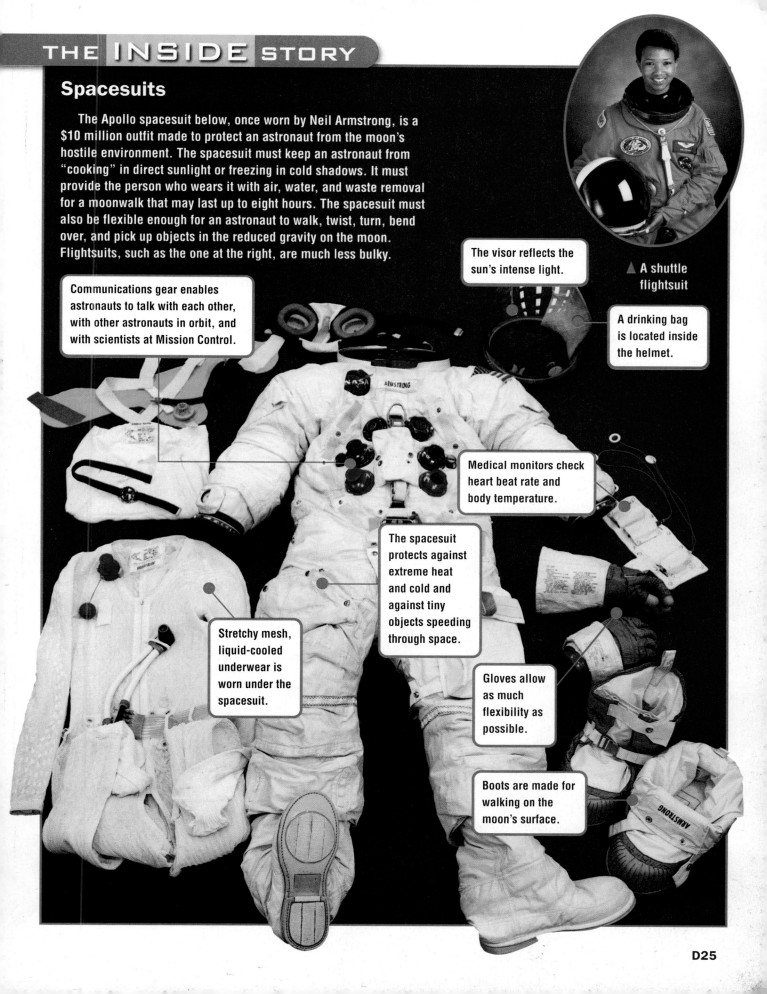

▲ A shuttle flightsuit

The visor reflects the sun's intense light.

A drinking bag is located inside the helmet.

Communications gear enables astronauts to talk with each other, with other astronauts in orbit, and with scientists at Mission Control.

Medical monitors check heart beat rate and body temperature.

The spacesuit protects against extreme heat and cold and against tiny objects speeding through space.

Stretchy mesh, liquid-cooled underwear is worn under the spacesuit.

Gloves allow as much flexibility as possible.

Boots are made for walking on the moon's surface.

Space Exploration in the Future

The arrival of the first scientists at the International Space Station, *Alpha,* in 2000 marked the beginning of a new era in space exploration. As many as seven scientists at a time will be able to live and work in space. When completed, *Alpha* will be nearly 80 m (about 260 ft) long and have a mass of more than 455,000 kg. In the future, larger stations could have room for a thousand people or more.

Settlements may one day be built on the moon, or even on Mars. Although there are as yet no plans to build bases on the moon, they could be possible by 2020.

A moon base could be used as a research station, like those in Antarctica. To save money, some materials needed to build and run the base could come from the moon itself. For example, some of the moon's rocks contain oxygen. This oxygen could be taken from the rocks and used by people living on the moon. Recently a probe discovered enough ice at the poles to supply a moon base with water. For electricity the base could use solar energy. And some minerals could be mined from the moon and sent back to Earth for processing.

✔ **How could people live on the moon?**

Living in space for long periods is now a reality with Space Station *Alpha,* shown here as a model.

1990–2000   2000–

Summary

People have observed and studied the moon and other objects in space since ancient times. The invention of the telescope allowed people to see features and objects that had never been seen before. Today scientists use telescopes, satellites, and space probes to study objects in the solar system and beyond. In the future, people may live and work on space stations and moon bases.

Review

1. What event marked the start of the space age?
2. What are space shuttles used for?
3. What problems have to be solved to build a permanent research station on the moon?
4. **Critical Thinking** A spacesuit weighs more than most astronauts. How can astronauts wear an outfit that is heavier than they are?
5. **Test Prep** The Apollo missions landed humans on —
   - **A** Mercury
   - **B** Venus
   - **C** Mars
   - **D** the moon

LINKS

MATH LINK

Solve Problems Earth spins once every 24 hours. A person standing still on the equator is moving with Earth's rotation at more than 1730 km/hr. How far does he or she move in a 24-hour day?

WRITING LINK

Persuasive Writing—Request Suppose that you have been invited to enter an essay contest. The winner will be the first student astronaut in space. Write a one-page essay to the judges requesting that they choose you. Explain why you are the best candidate.

ART LINK

Space Art Design a permanent space station or moon base. Draw a picture to show what it will look like. Label all the major parts, explaining how they will help people live and work in space or on the moon.

TECHNOLOGY LINK

Learn more about the solar system by investigating *Planet Hopping* on the **Harcourt Science Explorations CD-ROM.**

The History of Rockets and Spaceflight

As with many inventions, it is likely that the first rockets were produced partly by accident. Trying to scare off evil forces, the ancient Chinese lit bamboo tubes filled with a combination of charcoal, saltpeter, and sulfur. Perfectly sealed tubes produced loud explosions.

But once in a while an imperfectly sealed tube would shoot off into the air. At some point the Chinese began to produce these tubes, which they called "fire arrows," as weapons.

Rockets of War

Through the centuries, knowledge of how to make rockets spread through Asia, the Middle East, Europe, and the Americas. The "rockets' red glare" that Francis Scott Key wrote about in "The Star-Spangled Banner" were fired by British troops on Fort McHenry near Baltimore, Maryland, during the War of 1812.

The first liquid-fuel rockets were developed during the 1920s by American scientist Robert H. Goddard. These powerful rockets were a great advance in rocket technology. During World War II, a team of German scientists started the Space Age with the launch of the A4 rocket. It traveled 193 km (about 120 mi). Although it was designed to be a weapon of war, the A4 was the first modern rocket, a guided missile. After the war many German rockets were redesigned to collect data from Earth's upper atmosphere.

The Race to Space

In 1957 the Soviet Union used a German-designed rocket to launch *Sputnik*, the first Earth-orbiting satellite. The next year NASA (National Aeronautics and Space Administration) launched the first American satellite, *Explorer I*, and the space race was on. In 1961 a Soviet cosmonaut became the first person in space. Then President Kennedy promised that an American astronaut would be the first person to land on the moon. Competition between the

The History of Rockets and Spaceflight

300 B.C.
The Chinese use simple rockets as weapons.

1920s
Robert Goddard develops rockets powered by liquid fuel.

1950s
The two-stage rocket is developed.

300 B.C. — A.D. 1700 — A.D. 1800 — A.D. 1900

1700s
Sir William Congreve develops more powerful rockets for war.

1947
The first supersonic (faster than sound) flight is made aboard a rocket-powered airplane, the *X-1*.

Soviet Union and the United States was fierce. National pride was at stake. In 1964 the United States sent a space probe to Mars. In 1965 a Soviet cosmonaut became the first person to "walk" in space. In 1968 three American astronauts orbited the moon. Finally, in July 1969, the *Eagle* lander of *Apollo 11* touched down on the moon. Neil Armstrong became the first person to walk on another body in space.

Cooperation in Space

The space race ended with the flight of *Apollo 11*. Soon cooperation, not competition, became the key to space exploration. In 1988 Japan, Canada, the United States, Russia, and nine members of the European Space Agency agreed to construct the International Space Station. Many parts have already been built, and the process of launching them on American space shuttles and Russian rockets is underway. Once in orbit the parts are joined by astronauts from several countries.

Rockets began as weapons of war and were improved as sources of national pride. But they have become cargo carriers and transports for scientific research in space.

THINK ABOUT IT

1. Why do you think rockets were first used as weapons?

2. Why do you think the space race ended with *Apollo 11*?

The Mir space station

1962
John Glenn, in a Mercury capsule launched by an Atlas rocket, becomes the first American to orbit Earth.

1981
The first space shuttle, *Columbia*, is launched.

A.D. 2000

1969
Neil Armstrong becomes the first person to walk on the moon.

1986
The Soviet Union launches the Mir space station.

1998
Russia and the United States launch the first parts of the International Space Station.

Harrison Schmitt

GEOLOGIST, ASTRONAUT

Harrison (Jack) Schmitt is a geologist. He was also the first scientist to fly in space and the only scientist to do research on the moon. In 1971 he was the lunar module pilot for *Apollo 17*. The spacecraft landed in the Taurus-Littrow region of the moon. This area is noted for volcanic cinder cones and steep-walled valleys. At this location Dr. Schmitt collected samples of both young volcanic rock and older mountain rock.

Dr. Schmitt's involvement with the space program began at the United States Geological Survey's Astrogeology Center in Flagstaff, Arizona. There he developed geologic field techniques that were used by all Apollo crews. In 1965 Dr. Schmitt became an astronaut. As the only geologist-astronaut, he trained Apollo astronauts in geology observations. He also studied lunar rock samples and documented the geologic findings of each Apollo flight.

Following his resignation from NASA in 1975, Dr. Schmitt was elected to the United States Senate and served six years as senator from New Mexico. Today Dr. Schmitt is a consultant on issues concerning business, geology, space, and public safety.

THINK ABOUT IT

1. Why was it important for Apollo crew members to have a knowledge of geology?

2. What kinds of information do you think might be gained from samples of lunar rock?

Lunar Rover on the moon

PAPER MOON

How can the moon be used to make a calendar?

Materials

- clock
- 28 white paper plates
- scissors

Procedure

❶ Observe the moon at the same time each night for 4 weeks.

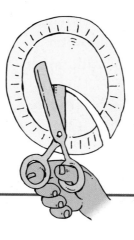

❷ Cut one paper plate each night to represent the shape of the moon as you observed it.

❸ Hang the paper-plate moons on a wall to make a record of your observations.

Draw Conclusions

How did the shape of the moon change over the length of your observations? What pattern do you notice about the changing shape of the moon? An Earth calendar has 12 months. How many months (moon cycles) would there be in a moon calendar?

SOLAR-SYSTEM DISTANCES

How far is it to Pluto?

Materials

- table of planets' distances from the sun
- roll of toilet paper
- wood dowel
- marker

Procedure

❶ Round off all distances on the table to the nearest million kilometers.

❷ Use one square of toilet paper to represent the distance from the sun to Mercury.

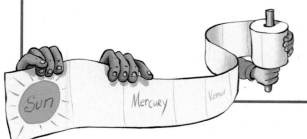

❸ Divide the distance from the sun to Mercury into all the other distances. The quotient for each problem will be how many toilet-paper squares each planet is from the sun.

❹ Put the dowel into the toilet-paper roll. Unroll the paper, count the squares of paper, and label the position for each planet.

Draw Conclusions

How many squares of toilet paper does it take to show the location of Pluto? How much farther from the sun is Pluto than Mercury? Distances in the solar system are huge. The toilet-paper model helps you visualize those distances. What kind of model could you make to show the sizes of the planets?

Vocabulary Review

Use the terms below to complete the sentences. The page numbers in ( ) tell you where to look in the chapter if you need help.

revolves (D6)　　**planets** (D17)
orbit (D7)　　　**asteroids** (D17)
rotate (D7)　　　**comets** (D17)
axis (D7)　　　　**telescope** (D23)
eclipse (D8)　　　**satellite** (D23)
solstice (D15)　　**space probe** (D24)
equinox (D15)

1. Any natural or artificial object that orbits another object is called a _____.

2. Both Earth and the moon have day-night cycles because they each _____, or spin on an _____.

3. The path the moon takes around Earth is its _____.

4. Galileo used a _____ to observe four of Jupiter's moons.

5. A _____ is a vehicle that is used to explore deep space.

6. As a planet travels around the sun, the planet _____.

7. During an _____, one object in space passes through the shadow of another object.

8. In one year, locations in the Northern Hemisphere experience a summer and a winter _____ and a spring and fall _____.

9. Objects in the solar system include nine _____ with their moons, thousands of _____ in orbits between Mars and Jupiter, and many _____, whose orbits take them far beyond Pluto.

Connect Concepts

Write terms and phrases from the Word Bank below where they belong in the Venn diagram.

revolve　　　　**weathering**
rotate　　　　　**almost no weathering**
life　　　　　　**craters**
no known life　　**rocky**
liquid water　　　**atmosphere**
no liquid water　　**no atmosphere**

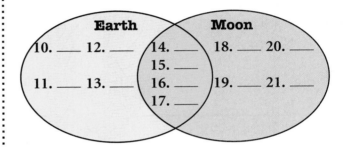

Check Understanding

Write the letter of the best choice.

22. The diagram below shows what season in the Northern Hemisphere?

Sun

A summer　　　　**C** winter
B spring　　　　　**D** autumn

23. During the new-moon phase, a person on Earth cannot see the moon because the sun is shining —

　F on the far side of the moon
　G on the Earth
　H on the moon's axis
　J from behind and below the moon

24. The diagram below shows a —

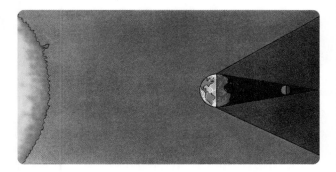

   A solar eclipse   **C** full moon

   B lunar eclipse   **D** new moon

25. The Apollo flights gave scientists first-hand knowledge of —

   F the moon

   G Earth's atmosphere

   H Mars

   J the sun

26. Which of the following must a spacesuit provide for an astronaut?

   A life support, including air

   B protection from intense heat and cold

   C a means to orbit the Earth

   D both A and B

Critical Thinking

27. Why does the moon appear to wax, or grow larger, and then wane, or get smaller?

28. Mercury has many craters that are millions of years old. Although Earth was hit by large objects from space, just as Mercury was, it has few such craters today. Explain why.

29. On Earth the moon appears to rise and set. If you could look at Earth from the moon, would Earth appear to rise and set? Explain why or why not.

Process Skills Review

30. How can you **use a model** to learn more about the moon?

31. You want to **compare** the moon's landforms with landforms on Earth. What processes will you consider? What tools can you use to **observe** the moon's landforms?

32. On the moon, the sun might rise on July 1 and not set until July 14. **Infer** the effects of such a long day on people living on a moon base.

Performance Assessment

On the Moon

Work with a partner to write a dialogue between an astronaut on the moon and Mission Control on Earth. From the astronaut's point of view, describe the moon's landforms and environment. Include a few details about your spacesuit, too.

CHAPTER

2

The Sun and Other Stars

Vocabulary Preview

photosphere
corona
sunspot
solar flare
solar wind
magnitude
main sequence
universe
galaxy
light-year

Have you ever looked up at night and seen the Milky Way Galaxy? It's hard to miss because it's the *only* thing you can see. All of the stars and planets visible to your eyes—including Earth—are part of it. Beyond the Milky Way Galaxy are hundreds of billions of other galaxies.

Fast Fact

On a clear night you can see more than 2000 stars without using a telescope. However, there are 50,000,000 times as many stars in the Milky Way Galaxy alone.

In 1989 the *Magellan* spacecraft was launched to Venus from a space shuttle. If you ever get to spend a day on Venus, take plenty of clean clothes. It takes just over 243 Earth days for Venus to rotate once on its axis.

Long Days, Short Days

Planet	Day
Jupiter	9 hr 50 min
Saturn	10 hr 39 min
Neptune	16 hr 3 min
Uranus	17 hr 14 min
Earth	23 hr 56 min
Mars	24 hr 37 min
Pluto	153 hr 18 min
Mercury	1392 hr 30 min
Venus	5832 hr 32 min

Fast Fact

Saturn's rings are made up of chunks of ice, some of which are bigger than most houses. The Voyager space probes showed that Jupiter, Uranus, and Neptune also have rings.

What Are the Features of the Sun?

In this lesson, you can . . .

INVESTIGATE
sunspots.

LEARN ABOUT
the sun's structure and
features.

LINK to math, writing,
and technology.

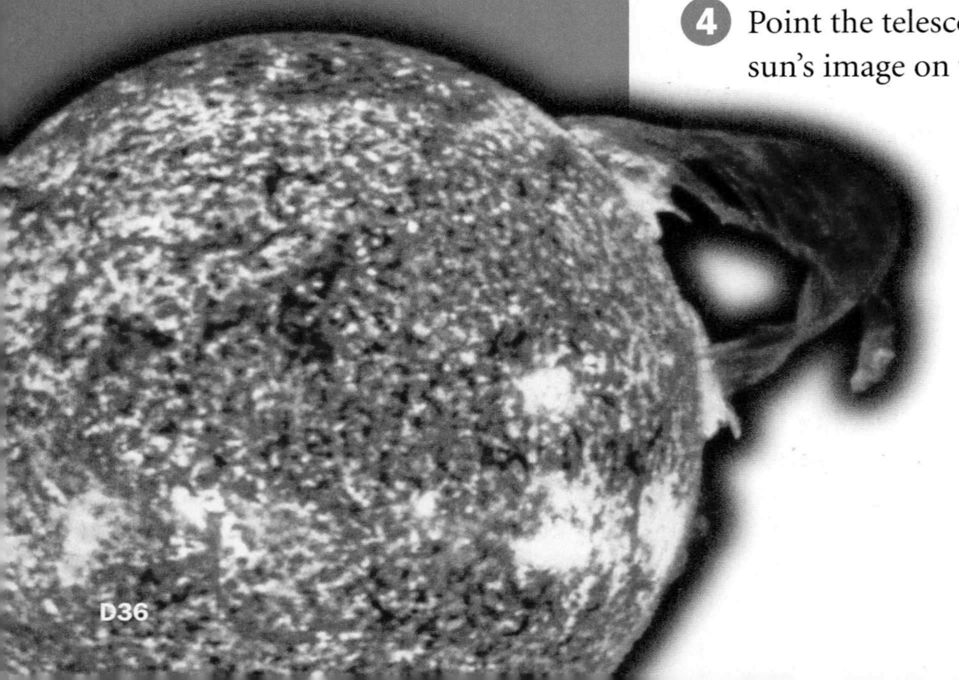

▼ The surface of the sun

INVESTIGATE

Sunspots

Activity Purpose The sun always seems the same from Earth. But is it always the same? What changes take place on the sun? You can find out about some of them as you **observe** sunspots in this investigation.

Materials

- white paper
- clipboard
- tape
- small telescope
- large piece of cardboard
- scissors

CAUTION

Activity Procedure

1 **CAUTION** **Never look directly at the sun. You can cause permanent damage to your eyes.** Fasten the white paper to the clipboard. Tape the edges down to keep the wind from blowing them.

2 Center the eyepiece of the telescope on the cardboard, and trace around the eyepiece.

3 Cut out the circle, and fit the eyepiece into the hole. The cardboard will help block some of the light and make a shadow on the paper.

4 Point the telescope at the sun, and focus the sun's image on the white paper. **Observe** the image of the sun on the paper. (Picture A)

5 On the paper, outline the image of the sun. Shade in any dark spots you see. The dark spots are called *sunspots.* **Record** the date and time on the paper. **Predict** what will happen to the sunspots in the next

Picture A

Picture B

day or two. *Note:* Since the image of the sun on the paper is reversed, any movement you **observe** will also be reversed. For example, movement from east to west, or from right to left on the image, represents movement from west to east on the sun.

6 Repeat Step 5 each sunny day for several days. **Record** the date, the time, and the positions of the sunspots each day. (Picture B)

Draw Conclusions

1. How did the positions of the sunspots change over several days?

2. What can you **infer** from the movement of sunspots?

3. **Scientists at Work** Scientists **draw conclusions** from what they **observe**. Galileo was the first scientist to observe that a sunspot takes about two weeks to cross from the left side of the sun's surface to the right side. Two weeks later, the sunspot appears on the left side of the sun's surface again. From this information, what conclusions can you draw about the time it takes the sun to make one complete rotation?

Investigate Further **Hypothesize** whether sunspots change in size. **Plan and conduct a simple investigation** to test this hypothesis.

The Sun

Energy from the Sun

VOCABULARY

photosphere
corona
sunspot
solar flare
solar wind

The sun is Earth's "local star"—the star at the center of the solar system. It has no permanent features, like Earth's mountains and oceans, because the sun is a huge ball of very hot gases.

The sun is the source of almost all energy on Earth. Plants are the link between the sun's energy and people. Plants use the sun's energy to make food energy. When an animal eats plants—or eats animals that have eaten plants—it gets food energy that comes from the sun.

When organisms die, they decay. Some organisms that died long ago became fuels. So the energy that lights many homes and runs most cars came originally from the sun.

The sun's energy is also the source of wind and other weather on Earth. Recall that when the sun's rays strike Earth's surface, land heats up faster than water. This uneven heating causes weather by producing differences in air pressure.

The sun is the source of most energy on Earth, but where does the sun's energy come from? On Earth, energy often comes from fuel. For example, burning gas or coal produces energy. But the sun's energy doesn't come from burning fuels. It comes from the fusing, or combining, of small particles to form larger ones.

Like all stars, the sun is a huge ball of gases, mostly hydrogen and helium. The temperature at the center of the sun is about

◄ **The sun is the source of most energy on Earth.**

Solar energy from the sun travels as waves. Some of these waves can be seen as light, while others can be felt as heat. ▼

15 million °C (27 million °F). At that temperature, and under enormous pressure, particles of hydrogen smash into each other and produce helium. Every time this happens, the sun releases energy as light and heat.

This process is called *fusion* because hydrogen particles fuse, or join together, to produce helium. The fusion of an amount of hydrogen the size of a pinhead releases more energy than the burning of 1000 metric tons of coal. And the sun fuses about 600 million metric tons of hydrogen every second.

Energy from the sun travels in waves, as shown in the illustration below. There are several kinds of waves. Each kind carries a different amount of energy. We see some of the waves as visible light. We feel infrared waves as heat, and ultraviolet waves tan or burn the skin. The sun even produces radio waves, which we hear as radio or TV static. Some of the sun's energy, such as X rays, is harmful to life on Earth. But the atmosphere keeps most of the harmful energy from reaching Earth's surface.

✔ **How does the sun affect life on Earth?**

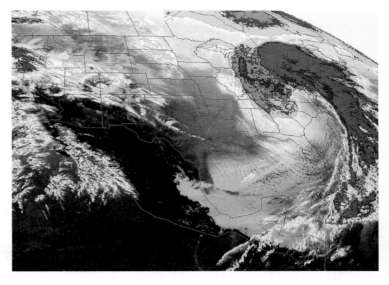

▲ Solar energy produces differences in air pressure, causing storms, such as hurricanes and blizzards. This photograph is a satellite image of a large winter storm.

Sometimes particles from the sun stream into space. When these particles reach Earth's atmosphere, they can produce colorful bands of light such as the *aurora borealis,* or northern lights. ▶

Through the process of photosynthesis, plants convert solar energy into food energy. ▼

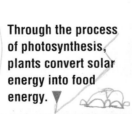

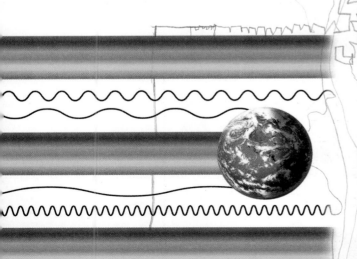

Exploring the Sun

The sun's diameter is 1.4 million km (about 870,000 mi)—more than 100 times that of Earth. The sun is large enough to hold 1 million Earths.

Since the sun is so much closer to Earth than other stars are, astronomers study it to understand stars. They have discovered that the sun has several layers of gases. The layers don't have definite boundaries. Instead, each layer blends into the next.

At the center of the sun is the *core*. As you can see in the illustration, the core is small in comparison to the entire sun. However, most of the sun's mass is in its core.

THE INSIDE STORY

The Sun's Structure

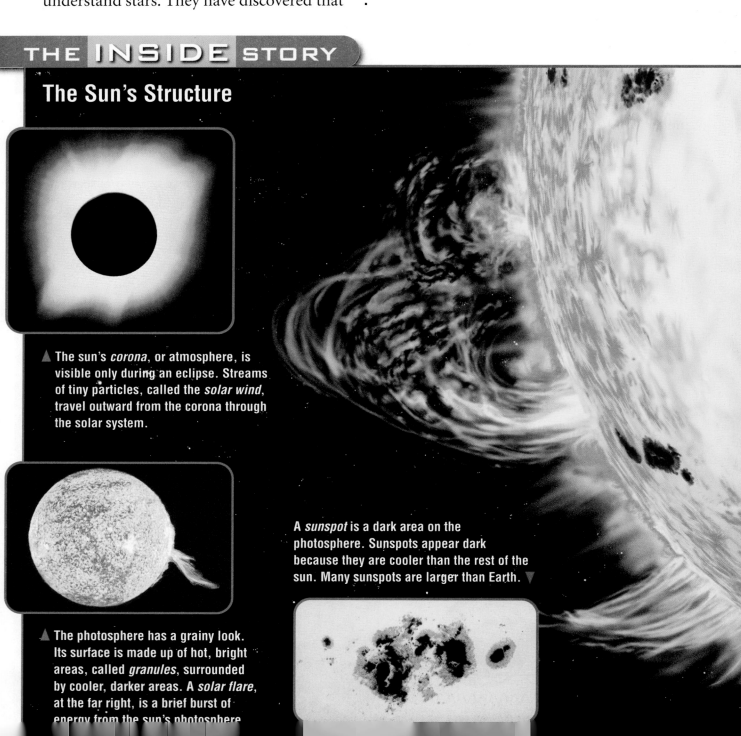

▲ The sun's *corona*, or atmosphere, is visible only during an eclipse. Streams of tiny particles, called the *solar wind*, travel outward from the corona through the solar system.

A *sunspot* is a dark area on the photosphere. Sunspots appear dark because they are cooler than the rest of the sun. Many sunspots are larger than Earth. ▼

▲ The photosphere has a grainy look. Its surface is made up of hot, bright areas, called *granules*, surrounded by cooler, darker areas. A *solar flare*, at the far right, is a brief burst of energy from the sun's photosphere

As energy from the sun's core moves outward, it passes through the *radiation zone.* Energy from the core heats this layer as a radiator heats the air in a room. From there it moves to the sun's outer layer, the *convection zone.* In the convection zone, energy moves to the surface by a process called convection. In convection, cooler particles are pulled down by gravity, pushing warmer particles up. This is the same way bubbles move energy to the surface of boiling water.

The surface of the sun is known as the **photosphere**, or "sphere of light." This is the surface of the sun we see. Above the photosphere is the sun's atmosphere, the **corona**. This area of hot gases extends 1 million km (about 600,000 mi) from the photosphere.

✔ **What are the layers of the sun?**

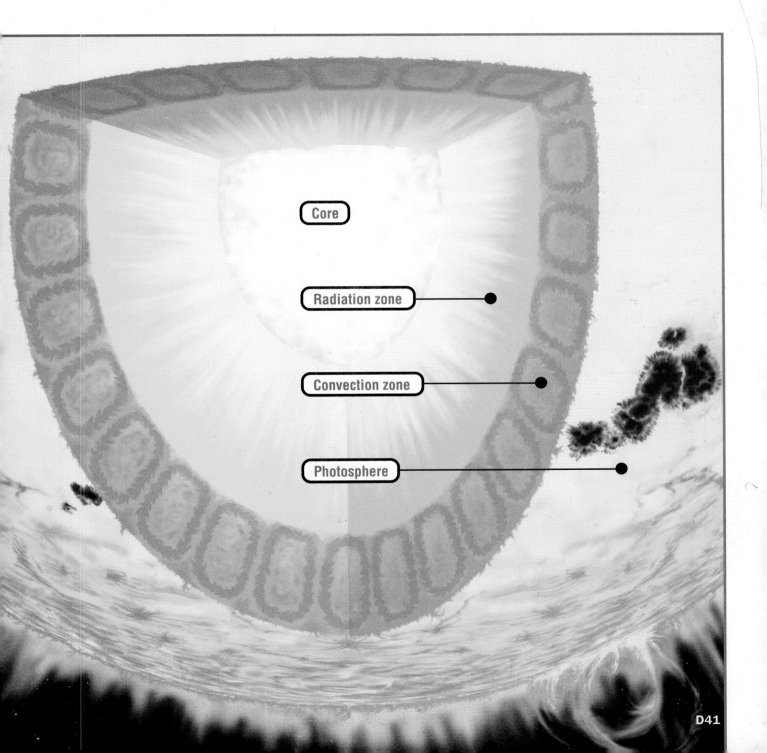

Core

Radiation zone

Convection zone

Photosphere

Solar Features

The sun has several features visible at different times at or near its surface. Bright spots on the photosphere are called *granules*. Granules are the tops of columns of rising gases in the convection layer. Darker areas between granules contain cooler gases.

Dark spots, called **sunspots**, are the most obvious features. Sunspots look dark because they are cooler than the rest of the photosphere. If you could see them by themselves, they would actually look very bright.

Scientists have observed sunspots for thousands of years. In the past few hundred years, they have recorded the number of sunspots observed each year. Scientists noticed that the number of sunspots increases and decreases over a period of about 11 years. This is called a sunspot cycle. The graph below shows sunspot cycles over a period of 300 years.

Sunspots can produce **solar flares**. These are brief bursts of energy from the photosphere. Much of a solar flare's energy is

ultraviolet waves, radio waves, and X rays. As the energy is released, a fast-moving stream of particles is thrown into space. These particles are called the **solar wind**. When the solar wind reaches Earth, the particles can cause magnetic storms. These storms disturb compasses and energy and communication systems. They also produce auroras in the northern skies.

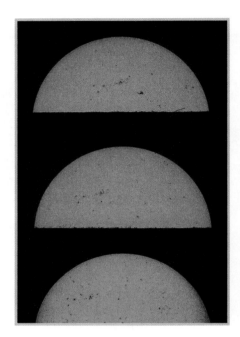

As the sun rotates, groups of sunspots seem to move across its surface. After a few days, the same spots are seen in a different location on the sun's surface, as you saw in the investigation. ▶

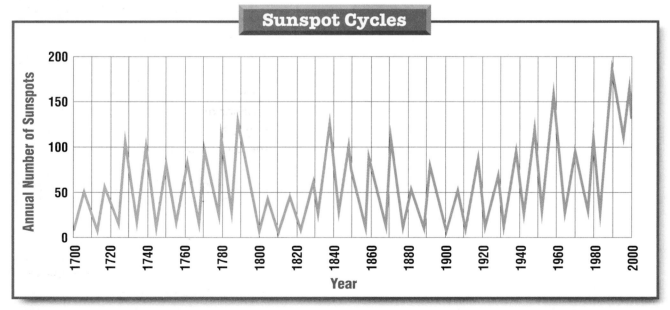

Sunspot Cycles

▲ The graph shows how the average number of sunspots varies in cycles. Years with a large number of sunspots are called *sunspot maximums*. Years with a low number of sunspots are called *sunspot minimums*.

A sun feature similar to a solar flare is called a *solar prominence*. A solar prominence is a bright loop or sheet of gas in the corona. It may hover there for days. Or it may explode and disappear in minutes. The photo on page D36 shows a spectacular solar prominence.

✓ **Compare sunspots, solar flares, and solar wind.**

Summary

The sun is a huge mass of hot gases that produces huge amounts of energy. It is the source of most of the energy on Earth. The sun has several layers: the core, the radiation zone, the convection zone, the photosphere, and the corona. Some of the visible features of the sun are solar prominences, solar flares, granules, and sunspots.

Review

1. How does life on Earth depend on the sun?

2. How is energy produced by the sun?

3. Draw a diagram of the sun, showing each layer.

4. **Critical Thinking** Suppose an astronomer observes a huge solar flare. Predict its effect on Earth in the next day or so.

5. **Test Prep** Solar prominences are loops of gas in the sun's —
   A corona
   B radiation zone
   C core
   D photosphere

LINKS

MATH LINK

Multiply Decimals Because distances in the solar system are so large, astronomers use a unit of measure called an astronomical unit, or AU. An AU is the distance between Earth and the sun, about 150 million km. At this distance, energy from the sun reaches Earth in about 8 minutes. Copy the table below, and complete it to show how long it takes the sun's energy to reach each planet.

Planet	Distance (AU)	Time (min)
Mercury	0.4	
Venus	0.7	
Earth	1.0	8
Mars	1.5	
Jupiter	5.2	
Saturn	9.5	
Uranus	19.2	
Neptune	30.0	
Pluto	39.5	

WRITING LINK

Informative Writing—Description Suppose scientists built a space probe that could withstand the sun's high temperatures. Write a description for your teacher of the information the probe might send back as it descends through the sun's layers to its core.

TECHNOLOGY LINK

Learn more about the sun by visiting this Internet site.

www.scilinks.org/harcourt

2

How Are Stars Classified?

In this lesson, you can . . .

INVESTIGATE the brightness of stars.

LEARN ABOUT how stars are classified.

LINK to math, writing, technology, and other areas.

Anyone can make discoveries in space using a simple telescope. ▼

INVESTIGATE

The Brightness of Stars

Activity Purpose Think about the last time you looked at a clear night sky. You probably saw millions of stars. Most stars are hot, bright balls of gas, like the sun. Yet some stars appear bright and some appear dim. Why? In this investigation you can **experiment** to find out.

Materials

- lamp with 40-watt bulb
- lamp with 60-watt bulb

Activity Procedure

1 Place the two lamps near the middle of a darkened hall. Turn the lamps on. (Picture A)

2 **Observe** the lamps from one end of the hall. **Compare** how bright they look. **Record** your observations.

3 Move the lamp with the 60-watt bulb to one end of the hall. **Observe** and **compare** how bright the two lamps look from the other end of the hall. **Record** your observations. (Picture B)

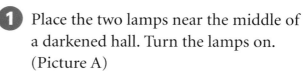

Picture A

Picture B

4. Now place the lamps side by side at one end of the hall. Again **observe** and **compare** how bright the two lamps look from the other end of the hall. **Record** your observations.

5. **Predict** the distances at which the two lamps seem to be equally bright. **Experiment** by placing the lamps at various places in the hall. **Observe** and **compare** how bright the two lamps look from a variety of distances. **Record** your observations.

Draw Conclusions

1. What two variables did you test in this experiment?

2. From what you **observed**, what two factors affect how bright a light appears to an observer?

3. **Scientists at Work** Scientists often **draw conclusions** when **experimenting**. Use the results of your experiment to draw conclusions about how distance and actual brightness affect how bright stars appear to observers on Earth.

Investigate Further Why can't you see stars during the day? **Plan and conduct a simple experiment** to test this **hypothesis:** Stars don't shine during the day.

Process Skill Tip

Drawing conclusions should be based on the results obtained while **experimenting** as well as any other information you have.

D45

How Stars Are Classified

Star Magnitude

FIND OUT

- about star magnitude
- about the types of stars
- how stars change

VOCABULARY

magnitude
main sequence

At night we can see thousands of stars, but during the day we see only one: the sun. The sun is so near that its brightness keeps us from seeing any other stars. As you learned in the investigation, how bright a star looks depends on two factors: its **magnitude**, or brightness, and its distance from Earth.

Suppose two stars that produce the same amount of light are different distances from Earth. They seem to have different magnitudes. The more distant star looks less bright when viewed from Earth, so its *apparent magnitude,* or how bright it seems to be, is less than its *absolute magnitude,* or how bright it really is.

✓ **Why do stars have different apparent magnitudes when viewed from Earth?**

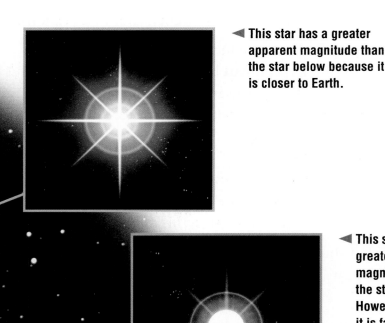

◀ This star has a greater apparent magnitude than the star below because it is closer to Earth.

◀ This star has a greater absolute magnitude than the star above. However, since it is farther from Earth, it looks less bright.

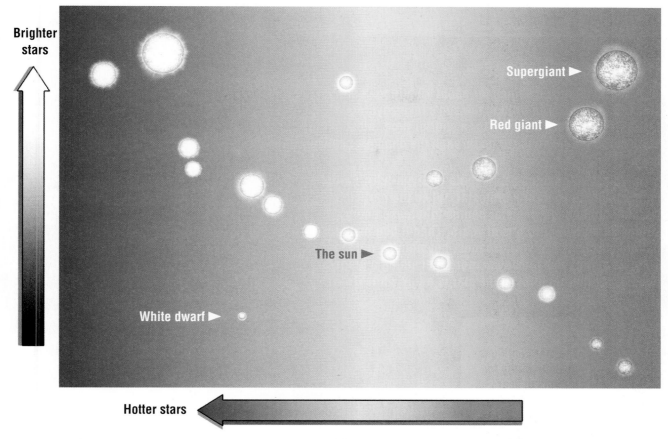

Brighter stars

Supergiant ▶

Red giant ▶

The sun ▶

White dwarf ▶

Hotter stars

▲ This diagram shows relationships between color, size, magnitude, and temperature of stars.

Types of Stars

On a clear, dark night, you can see that although most stars are white, some are blue and others look red. The color of a star is a clue to its surface temperature. Blue stars have the hottest surface temperatures. Red stars have the coolest. Astronomers use surface temperatures and absolute magnitudes to classify stars.

In the early 1900s, two astronomers—Ejnar Hertzsprung, a Dane, and Henry Russell, an American—classified stars. They used a diagram similar to the one above. The diagram shows the relationships between size, magnitude, temperature, and color.

The absolute magnitudes of stars are plotted from bottom to top. The brightest stars are at the top. The surface temperatures of stars are plotted from right to left.

The hottest stars are on the left. The color of a star is shown by its background color. The size of each star is shown by its relative size on the diagram.

Most stars are in a band that runs from the top left of the diagram to the bottom right. This band is called the **main sequence**. Look at the diagram. At the top left are bright, hot, blue stars. In the middle of the main sequence are less bright, cooler stars, such as the sun. These stars shine with a yellow-white light. At the lower right in the main sequence are dim, cool, red stars. About 95 percent of the stars scientists have observed can be classified as main-sequence stars.

✔ **What does a star's position in the main sequence tell you about that star?**

How Stars Change

A star like the sun shines for about 10 billion years. A star with a mass greater than the sun's fuses hydrogen faster. It shines brighter, but for a shorter time. Most of the stars in the main sequence go through the changes shown here.

A typical star begins as a nebula (NEB•yuh•luh). Particles clump together to form a protostar. When the particles become hot enough, the star begins to release energy. It shines steadily for billions of years. Then it begins to run out of hydrogen. The star expands, becoming a red giant. Then its corona expands even more, becoming a planetary nebula. All that remains of the star is a tiny white dwarf.

❶ NEBULA
A star begins within a huge cloud of hydrogen, helium, and tiny particles of dust.

❼ WHITE DWARF
The star continues to shine dimly for billions of years as it slowly cools.

A red giant is a very old star. When the sun becomes a red giant, it will expand until it consumes both Mercury and Venus. Earth will remain, but the planet will become too hot for life. ▼

❻ PLANETARY NEBULA
The red giant's atmosphere expands a million times. It forms a planetary nebula. At the center of the nebula, what is left of the star becomes a white dwarf.

Each wave of energy gives scientists information about the object it came from. For example, the kinds of waves absorbed or given off by a star can tell what it's made of. This is how scientists know that the sun and most other stars are mostly hydrogen and helium.

✔ **How do scientists learn about stars?**

Summary

Scientists classify stars by absolute magnitude, surface temperature, size, and color. Most stars are in the main sequence. Stars undergo a series of changes from nebula to protostar to main-sequence star to expanding star to red giant to planetary nebula and white dwarf. Scientists learn about stars by using telescopes and other instruments to study the energy that stars release into space.

Review

1. What is the difference between absolute magnitude and apparent magnitude?

2. How will the sun's cycle end?

3. Why does a star begin shining?

4. **Critical Thinking** Most of the stars in the main sequence are to the lower right of the sun. What can you conclude about the brightness of these stars and their temperatures?

5. **Test Prep** A star's apparent magnitude depends on —
   A brightness and size
   B absolute magnitude and distance from Earth
   C size and distance from Earth
   D absolute magnitude and size

LINKS

MATH LINK

Multiply Decimals Other than the sun, Proxima Centauri is the star closest to Earth. It is about 4.2 light-years away. A light-year is the distance light travels in one Earth year—about 9.5 trillion km. How far from Earth is Proxima Centauri?

WRITING LINK

Expressive Writing—Poem Write a poem about the stars for your classmates. Use what you have learned in this lesson about stars' magnitudes, temperatures, sizes, and colors.

LANGUAGE ARTS LINK

Star Questions Write a list of five questions you have about stars or other objects in space. If possible, find an astronomer at a local college or an amateur astronomy club. Ask the astronomer your questions.

ART LINK

Star Chart Make a diagram or a drawing to show the difference between absolute magnitude and apparent magnitude.

GO ONLINE TECHNOLOGY LINK

Learn more about stars by visiting the Harcourt Learning Site. **www.harcourtschool.com**

WELCOME TO THE LEARNING SITE

LESSON 3

What Are Galaxies?

In this lesson, you can . . .

INVESTIGATE the location of the sun in the Milky Way Galaxy.

LEARN ABOUT different types of galaxies.

LINK to math, writing, art, and technology.

These star tracks were made with time-lapse photography. ▼

The Sun's Location in the Milky Way Galaxy

Activity Purpose The sun is in a large grouping of stars called the Milky Way Galaxy. But where in this grouping is the sun? In this investigation you can **make a model** of the Milky Way Galaxy. You can **use the model** to help you find out where the sun is in the galaxy.

Materials

- scrap paper

Activity Procedure

1 Make about 70 small balls from scrap paper. These will be your "stars."

2 On a table, **make a model** of the Milky Way Galaxy. Arrange the paper stars in a spiral with six arms. Pile extra stars in the center of the spiral. Use fewer stars along the arms. (Picture A)

3 Look down at the model. Draw what you **observe**.

4 Position your eyes at table level. Look across the surface of the table at the model. Again, draw what you **observe**. (Picture B)

5 Look at the photographs at the bottom of page D55. One is of a spiral galaxy viewed from the edge. The other shows the galaxy viewed from the "top." **Compare** the pictures you drew in Steps 3 and 4 with the photographs of a spiral galaxy. Then look at page D54. **Observe** the photograph of a ribbon of stars. This is our view of the Milky Way Galaxy from Earth. Using your drawings and the photographs, **infer** where in the Milky Way Galaxy the sun is.

Picture A

Draw Conclusions

1. Suppose the sun is located "above" the Milky Way Galaxy. What view of the galaxy might we see from Earth?

2. If the sun is in one of the arms, what view might we see of the galaxy then?

Picture B

3. From your drawings and the photographs of a spiral galaxy, where in the Milky Way Galaxy do you **infer** the sun is?

4. **Scientists at Work** Scientists often **infer** when **using models** like the one you made. How did your model of the Milky Way Galaxy help you infer the sun's location in the galaxy?

Investigate Further Observe the Milky Way Galaxy in the night sky. You will need a clear, dark night, far away from city lights. Binoculars or a telescope will help you see some of the fainter stars.

Process Skill Tip

When you **infer** while **using models**, you base your inferences on everything you observe about the model. It's important to keep in mind that models are limited in how they show real-world situations.

Galaxies

The Milky Way Galaxy

FIND OUT ─────

- **about the Milky Way Galaxy**

- **about types of galaxies**

- **about galactic clusters and nebulae**

VOCABULARY

universe
galaxy
light-year

When you look at the sky on a clear, dark night, away from city lights, you can see millions of stars. But you are seeing only a small part of the universe. The **universe** is everything that exists—planets, stars, dust, gases, and energy. Although it seems crowded with stars, most of the universe is empty.

On some summer nights, you may see a bright ribbon of stars overhead. You are looking toward the center of Earth's galaxy. A **galaxy** is a group of stars, gas, and dust. Many galaxies rotate around a core. Most stars are part of galaxies, and the universe contains about a hundred billion galaxies.

Earth's galaxy is called the Milky Way Galaxy. It includes more than 100 billion stars, and it is one of the largest galaxies in the universe. It is so large that the light of a star on one side of the galaxy takes more than 100,000 light-years to reach the other side. As the Milky Way Galaxy rotates, the sun makes one complete turn around the center every 200–250 million Earth years.

✓ **What is a galaxy?**

This photograph of the Milky Way Galaxy was taken from Earth.

D54

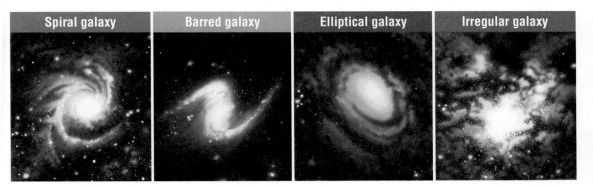

| Spiral galaxy | Barred galaxy | Elliptical galaxy | Irregular galaxy |

These drawings show the four types of galaxies. ▶

Types of Galaxies

Galaxies are classified by shape. There are four basic types: spiral, barred spiral, elliptical, and irregular.

The Milky Way Galaxy is a spiral galaxy. A spiral galaxy has a bright bulge of stars in the center and rotating arms. Earth's solar system is in one of the Milky Way Galaxy's spiral arms, about 30,000 light-years from the center of the galaxy. A **light-year** is the distance light travels in one Earth year, about 9.5 trillion km.

A spiral galaxy's arms contain young stars, protostars, dust, and gas. The thick bulge at the center contains older stars.

A barred spiral galaxy is similar to a spiral galaxy. The difference is that the spirals extend from a bar of stars that stretches from the center.

About half of all galaxies are elliptical. The shapes of elliptical galaxies range from almost a sphere, like a basketball, to a shape like a flattened football. Unlike spiral galaxies, elliptical galaxies don't seem to rotate. Irregular galaxies are groups of stars with no obvious shape.

✔ **What are the four basic shapes of galaxies?**

From the side a spiral galaxy looks like a thin rod with a center bulge. A spiral galaxy, seen from the "top," looks like a giant pinwheel spinning through space. The arms wind around the center as it turns, giving the galaxy its spiral appearance.

The Horsehead Nebula in Orion is a dark, dense swirl of dust. Behind the nebula, bright young stars flood the background with light.

Galactic Clusters and Nebulae

Have you ever seen a faint smudge or a misty patch of stars in the night sky? You may have been looking at a galactic cluster or a nebula.

A *galactic cluster* is a group of galaxies. The Milky Way Galaxy is one of about 30 galaxies in a cluster called the Local Group. The Milky Way Galaxy is one of the larger galaxies in this cluster. Most of the galaxies in the Local Group are small and elliptical or irregular.

Beyond the Local Group are other galactic clusters. Some of these are huge, with thousands of galaxies. One of the clusters closest to the Local Group is the Virgo Cluster, which is about 50 million light-years away.

You read about nebulae in Lesson 2. Astronomers hypothesize that stars form in nebulae. Unlike a galactic cluster, a nebula has no

◄ The Virgo Cluster contains more than 100,000 galaxies. At its center are three giant elliptical galaxies. One of these galaxies is about the same size as the entire Local Group.

light of its own. But if there is a hot star within a few light-years, the gases in the nebula shine. This is because hot stars emit a lot of ultraviolet waves. The energy of these waves is absorbed by the gases in the nebula. The gases then glow in different colors. The colors tell what gases are in the nebula. For example, hydrogen glows red, while oxygen and helium glow green. Different combinations of gases and dust create different effects, as in the Horsehead Nebula shown on page D56.

✔ **What is the difference between a galactic cluster and a nebula?**

Summary

A galaxy is a group of stars, gas, and dust. Many galaxies rotate around a central core. The sun is in the Milky Way Galaxy. The Milky Way Galaxy is part of a galactic cluster called the Local Group. Also visible in the night sky are nebulae, which are clouds of gas and dust in which stars form.

Review

1. What is the Local Group?
2. Describe the four basic shapes of galaxies.
3. What is a nebula?
4. **Critical Thinking** The Horsehead Nebula doesn't glow like some nebulae. Why not?
5. **Test Prep** The Virgo Cluster is a —
   A giant elliptical galaxy
   B nebula
   C Local Group
   D group of galaxies

LINKS

MATH LINK

Solve Problems It takes the sun about 250 million Earth years to travel around the center of the Milky Way Galaxy. If the sun is about 5 billion Earth years old, how many trips has it made?

WRITING LINK

Expressive Writing—Friendly Letter Suppose there are intelligent life forms in another galaxy. Write a letter to these life forms. Explain where you are in the Milky Way Galaxy, and tell the other life forms about life on Earth.

ART LINK

Galaxies on Stage Choose some of the information in this lesson. Rewrite it as a play. Present the play to other fifth-grade students in your school. Use dialogue, movement, and props in your play.

TECHNOLOGY LINK

Learn more about galaxies and how they move through space by viewing *Colliding Galaxies* on the **Harcourt Science Newsroom Video.**

Magnetars

Some people say "there's nothing new under the sun." Astronomers might laugh at this! They are always finding new things in the universe. One exciting discovery is a different kind of star. Stars of this kind spin rapidly and send out gigantic bursts of energy. They might also be the most powerful magnets in the universe. Astronomers call them magnetars.

This drawing of a magnetar shows its magnetic force field.

Surprise in the Sky

The first data about magnetars came from spy satellites. The U.S. government wanted to know when certain countries were testing nuclear weapons. So it launched a series of satellites to detect radiation from nuclear explosions. To government scientists' amazement, the satellites picked up radiation coming from outer space! Bursts of gamma rays seemed to be coming from everywhere in the universe. Government scientists communicated with civilian astronomers about this mysterious energy from space. Using satellites and radio telescopes, astronomers began measuring the energy bursts. Some of the larger bursts released as much energy in one second as the sun does in 1000 years!

A few astronomers hypothesized that these stars have solid crusts and magnetic fields so strong that they cause the crusts to crack, releasing radiation. So magnetars may have starquakes, just as Earth has earthquakes.

A Giant Magnet

What's so different about this new kind of star? For one thing, if you were close enough, a magnetar's huge magnetic field would rearrange the atoms in your body. You wouldn't be you anymore! Think of this star as a giant magnet. Even if it were as far away as the sun, it could pull metal objects, such as paper clips, out of your pockets. The pull of gravity on its surface would flatten you like a pancake. And a magnetar spins very, very fast! While Earth takes 24 hours to complete one rotation, some magnetars take less than 6 seconds.

Radio telescopes are also used to identify unknown energy sources from space.

Luckily for us, the closest magnetars are thousands of light-years away. Astronomers have identified several of them and hypothesize that there are millions of others. From studying magnetars, scientists can learn more about magnetism, gravity, and other forces. And, since magnetars seem to have formed after massive stars exploded, they might help scientists learn more about how stars develop and change.

THINK ABOUT IT

1. How are magnetars different from other stars?
2. Why would it be dangerous for a spacecraft to fly near a magnetar?

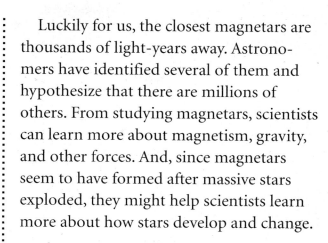

Julio Navarro
ASTRONOMER

"If you look at a galaxy far away, you're seeing the galaxy as it was many years ago. You're looking at the universe as it was when it was young."

Julio Navarro is a theoretical astronomer who studies galaxies. Instead of looking through telescopes, Dr. Navarro works with numerical data from the Hubble Space Telescope and from ground-based telescopes. He uses this data in computer models that help him study the formation of galaxies and other bodies in the universe.

Dr. Navarro explains that the light from distant galaxies can take billions of years to reach our telescopes. So we're not seeing those galaxies as they appear now, but as they appeared billions of years ago.

When he was growing up in Argentina, no one would have guessed that Dr. Navarro would become an astronomer. He was more interested in music. However, an essay assignment in high school changed everything. "I was looking through a lot of books, and I became interested in astronomy," says Dr. Navarro. He kept reading, and his interest grew.

Dr. Navarro earned a bachelor's degree and a Ph.D. in astronomy before leaving Argentina to work and study in North America and Europe. Today Dr. Navarro is at the University of Victoria, in British Columbia, Canada, where he teaches astronomy and does research on the formation of galaxies.

THINK ABOUT IT

1. Why does Dr. Navarro study distant galaxies?

2. How does Dr. Navarro gather data for his studies?

A MODEL SUN

What are some sun features?

Materials

- yellow construction paper
- ruler
- scissors
- markers
- black construction paper
- glue
- white legal-sized paper

Procedure

1. Cut a 20-cm circle from the yellow paper to represent the photosphere. Using markers, make sunspots on the photosphere.

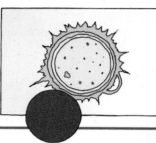

2. Cut a 20-cm circle from the black paper to represent the moon during a solar eclipse.

3. Glue the yellow circle to the white paper.

4. Using the markers, color jagged shapes around the sun to represent the sun's corona.

5. Use your black "moon" to eclipse the sun's photosphere to study its corona.

Draw Conclusions

Why did you cut out the moon for the total eclipse the same size as the sun? Scientists learn a great deal about the sun during total eclipses. Why is this an important time to study the sun? What benefits are there to blocking out the sun's photosphere?

ASTROLABE

How do people navigate by the stars?

Materials

- 15-cm cardboard square
- protractor
- pencil
- drinking straw
- tape
- 20-cm piece of string
- metal washer

Procedure

1. Using the protractor, and starting in one corner of the cardboard square, draw a line at an angle of 5°. Draw additional lines at 10°, 15°, and so on.

2. Tape the straw to the cardboard as shown.

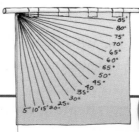

3. At the point where all the lines meet, make a hole in the cardboard. Push the string through the hole and tie a knot to keep it from pulling through the hole. Tie the washer to the other end of the string.

4. Look at the North Star through the straw. Measure the angle of the North Star by noting the angle of the string.

Draw Conclusions

The angle of the North Star tells you your latitude on the Earth. What is the angle of the North Star where you live? What is the latitude where you live?

Vocabulary Review

Use the terms below to complete the sentences. The page numbers in ( ) tell you where to look in the chapter if you need help.

- photosphere (D41)
- corona (D41)
- sunspot (D42)
- solar flare (D42)
- solar wind (D42)
- magnitude (D46)
- main sequence (D47)
- universe (D54)
- galaxy (D54)
- light-year (D55)

1. The sun's atmosphere is the ____.

2. A dark area on the sun that is caused by twists and loops in the sun's magnetic field is a ____.

3. A ____ is a brief burst of energy that occurs above a sunspot.

4. The ____ is a fast-moving stream of particles ejected into space.

5. Two stars the same distance from Earth that give off the same amount of light will appear to have the same ____.

6. The sun's ____ is the layer we see.

7. The classification group to which most stars belong is the ____.

8. The ____ is everything that exists.

9. A group of stars, gas, and dust is a ____.

10. A ____ is the distance light travels in one Earth year.

Connect Concepts

Use the terms in the Word Bank below to complete the chart of Your Place in Space.

solar system   universe   Earth
Local Group   Milky Way Galaxy

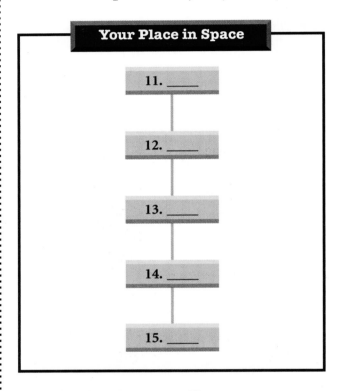

Your Place in Space

11. ____

12. ____

13. ____

14. ____

15. ____

Check Understanding

Write the letter of the best choice.

16. At the center of the solar system is a —
    - **A** galaxy
    - **B** moon
    - **C** planet
    - **D** star

17. The surface of the sun is the part we can see. It is called the —
    - **F** core
    - **G** photosphere
    - **H** chromosphere
    - **J** corona

18. Sunspots can cause brief bursts of energy known as solar —
    - **A** flares
    - **B** prominences
    - **C** auroras
    - **D** fusion

19. The sun is a huge mass of —
    F metals   H gases
    G light   J liquids

20. The hottest stars in the main sequence are also the —
    A brightest   C largest
    B least bright D smallest

21. The Milky Way Galaxy is located in the Local Group, a —
    F universe   H nebula
    G galactic cluster J main sequence

22. What type of galaxy is shown in the illustration?

    A elliptical   C spiral
    B irregular   D spiral barred

Critical Thinking

23. Infrared telescopes have detected new stars forming in the Orion Nebula. Why can't we see these stars forming?

24. Galaxies contain millions of stars. Yet they look faint to people on Earth. Explain why galaxies look so faint to observers on Earth.

25. A light-year is the distance light travels in one Earth year. Suppose you look at a star that is 100,000 light-years away. Explain why you are looking into the past.

Process Skills Review

26. Sunspots appear and disappear in cycles that average about 11 years. As the cycle starts, the number of sunspots increases for 5 to 6 years. Then it decreases for 5 to 6 years. Using what you know about the relationship between solar flares and sunspots, **hypothesize** when solar flares are most frequent.

27. Scientists believe that time spent in the main sequence is one of the stages of a star's "life." Most known stars are main-sequence stars. From this information, what can you **infer** about the amount of time a typical star spends in this stage?

28. How could you **model** changes in the apparent magnitude of stars?

Performance Assessment

Star Light, Star Bright

Make up a star. Draw a picture of your star, showing its color and its type—main sequence, red giant, white dwarf, or nebula. Label the drawing with the type of star. Draw another picture, showing the location of your star in a spiral galaxy as viewed from "above." From your drawing, infer the direction in which the galaxy rotates. Draw an arrow to show the direction.

There are many places where you can learn more about space. By visiting the places below, you can find out about the exploration of the solar system and beyond. You'll also have fun while you learn.

John C. Stennis Space Center

WHAT A collection of NASA spacecraft and exhibits about the exploration of space

WHERE I-10 Mississippi Welcome Station, Mississippi

WHAT CAN YOU DO THERE? See an Apollo-era Lunar Lander display, view other space exhibits, and try out the Space Shuttle and Mission to Mars simulators.

National Air and Space Museum

WHAT A museum with the world's largest collection of historic aircraft and spacecraft

WHERE Washington, D.C.

WHAT CAN YOU DO THERE? Tour the exhibits, see historic aircraft and spacecraft on display, and learn about the ongoing exploration of space.

GO ONLINE Plan Your Own Expeditions

If you can't visit the John C. Stennis Space Center or the National Air and Space Museum, visit a space exhibit or museum near you. Or log on to The Learning Site at **www.harcourtschool.com** to visit these science sites and other places where you can learn more about space.

Building Blocks of Matter

UNIT E PHYSICAL SCIENCE

Building Blocks of Matter

UNIT EXPERIMENT

Solubility

All matter has predictable physical and chemical properties. One of those properties is solubility, or the ability of one substance to dissolve in another substance. While you study this unit, you can conduct a long-term experiment in solubility. Here are some questions to think about. What substances dissolve in water? For example, do all white granules like salt dissolve? Plan and conduct an experiment to find answers to these or other questions you have about solubility. See pages x–xvii for help in designing your experiment.

Matter and Its Properties

Vocabulary Preview

matter
physical properties
mass
weight
volume
density
solubility
solid
liquid
gas
evaporation
condensation
reactivity
combustibility

Do you know why water, a liquid, can also be a solid (ice) and a gas (water vapor)? Actually, *every* substance can be a solid, a liquid, and a gas. The form a substance takes depends on its temperature and how fast particles of the substance move.

Fast Fact

Water expands as it freezes. Water freezing in tiny cracks in rocks makes the cracks bigger. Over millions of years, this process can turn a mountain into a pile of sand.

People used to think that glass was a liquid, not a solid, because old glass windows are thicker at the bottom than at the top. However, at normal temperatures, glass is still more like a solid than it is like a liquid.

How cold can it get? There is a lowest possible temperature, called absolute zero. At this temperature the particles that make up a substance stop moving.

Hot and Cold Temperatures

Temperature	Celsius	Farenheit
Absolute zero	-273.15°	-459.67°
Water freezes	0.0°	32.0°
Human body	37.0°	98.6°
Water boils	100.0°	212.0°

LESSON 1

How Can Physical Properties Be Used to Identify Matter?

In this lesson, you can . . .

 INVESTIGATE physical properties.

 LEARN ABOUT how to measure and use physical properties.

 LINK to math, writing, physical education, and technology.

Even apples have different physical properties. ▷

Using Physical Properties to Identify Objects

Activity Purpose Some objects, such as a tree and a rock, are so easy to identify that you almost don't have to think about it. But how do you identify two different trees? You have to **observe** their properties, or characteristics, more closely. In this investigation you will use properties to identify objects that are very similar.

Materials
- apples
- balance
- ruler
- string

Activity Procedure

1 Carefully **observe** the apple your teacher gave you. What properties of your apple can you discover just by observing it? **Record** all the properties you observe.

2 Use the balance, ruler, and string to **measure** some properties of your apple. **Record** the properties you measure. (Picture A)

3 Put your apple in the pile of apples on your teacher's desk. Don't watch while your teacher mixes up the apples.

Picture A

Picture B

4. Using the properties that you recorded, try to identify your apple in the pile. (Picture B)

5. Using the balance, ruler, and string, **measure** this apple. **Compare** the measurements to those you recorded earlier. Then decide whether the apple you chose from the pile is yours. If someone else chose the same apple, comparing measurements should help you decide whose apple it really is.

Draw Conclusions

1. **Compare** your apple with a classmate's apple. How are the two apples alike? How are they different?

2. Why was it helpful to **measure** some properties of your apple in addition to **observing** it?

3. How did you use the string to **measure** the apple?

4. **Scientists at Work** Scientists use both observations and measurements to identify substances. Which is faster, **observing** or **measuring**? Which provides more exact information?

Investigate Further **Compare** the list of your apple's properties with a classmate's list. Then, using your classmate's list, try to find his or her apple. Talk with your classmate about how he or she made the list. Did you and your classmate do things the same way?

Process Skill Tip

Some properties can only be observed. When you **observe**, you use only your senses. Some properties can be measured with instruments. Being able to **measure** something you are studying will help you identify it.

The Importance of Physical Properties

Matter and Physical Properties

FIND OUT

- what physical properties are
- how to measure some physical properties
- examples of physical properties that can be used to identify substances

VOCABULARY

matter
physical properties
mass
weight
volume
density
solubility

The objects you used in the investigation were all alike—they were all apples. But would you believe that apples, parrots, candy, computers, humans, and even the air around you are all alike in one way? They are all made of matter. **Matter** is anything that has mass and takes up space.

Objects made of matter can be very different from each other. Each object has its own set of characteristics, or *properties*. For example, one property of a piece of candy is its color. Another is its taste.

Physical properties are characteristics of a substance that can be observed or measured without changing the substance into something else. Color, hardness, and taste are examples of physical properties. An object's ability to conduct heat, sound, or electricity or to become a magnet are also physical properties.

Some physical properties, such as color, can be observed directly. Other physical properties, such as length, must be measured. Measurements are especially useful in science because they provide more exact descriptions of matter than direct observations do.

✔ **What are some examples of physical properties?**

◄ You can tell these balls apart by examining the physical properties of size, mass, and color.

Mass and Weight

One physical property that can be measured is mass. **Mass** is the amount of matter in an object. The mass of an 18-wheel truck is greater than the mass of a small car, because the truck has more matter. In this example you can easily see the difference in the amount of matter. Sometimes the difference in the amount of matter between two objects is very small. In fact, some matter may have so little mass that it is difficult to measure. But all matter has some mass.

It's easy to confuse mass with another physical property—weight. Weight depends on the amount of matter in an object. However, weight also depends on the force of gravity. So **weight** is a measure of the pull of gravity on an object. While the mass of an object is always the same, the weight of an object is not. For example, a car that weighs 12,000 newtons (about 2698 lb) on Earth would weigh only 2000 newtons (about 450 lb) on the moon! This is because the force of gravity is 6 times greater on Earth than it is on the moon. Because weight can vary,

▲ The mass of the foam, on the balance, will be the same no matter what shape it is given. The mass of the gel, in the container at the left, will also stay the same, even though it takes the shape of its container.

mass is a better measurement of the amount of matter in an object.

Different equipment is used to measure weight and mass. Weight is measured on a spring scale. How much the spring in the scale is squeezed or stretched depends on the pull of gravity and the mass of the object being weighed. Mass is measured on a balance to avoid also measuring the pull of gravity. On a balance the mass of an object is compared to a known mass.

✔ **How are mass and weight alike? How are they different?**

An astronaut weighs less on the moon than on Earth. However, the astronaut has the same mass on the moon as on Earth. ▶

Volume

Matter not only has mass but also takes up space. **Volume** is the amount of space that an object takes up. Volume can be measured in several ways.

The volume of a liquid can be measured using a graduated cylinder. A *graduated cylinder* is a clear tube that is marked in milliliters. When liquids are poured into a graduated cylinder, they stick slightly to the tube, forming a curved surface. To measure the volume of a liquid accurately, you need to read the volume at the bottom of this curve.

The volume of some solids can be calculated. First, measure the length, width, and height of the object. Then multiply as shown in this formula:

Volume = length × width × height

Volume is expressed in cubic units, such as cubic centimeters. For example, the volume of a box 38 cm long, 21 cm wide, and 13 cm high is 10,374 cm³.

Volume = 38 cm × 21 cm × 13 cm
= 10,374 cm³

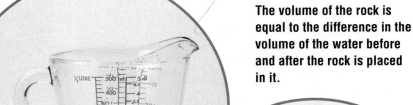

The volume of the rock is equal to the difference in the volume of the water before and after the rock is placed in it.

Although most solids do not have regular shapes, their volumes can still be measured. One way to do this is to measure the amount of liquid, such as water, that the solid *displaces*, or takes the place of. To do this, partially fill a measuring container with water and place the solid in the liquid. You will observe that the level of the liquid rises. The volume of the water and solid together is greater than the volume of the water alone. The volume of the solid is the difference between these two volumes.

✔ **What are two ways to measure the volume of a solid?**

◀ The 250 mL (about 8 oz) of juice in the box can be measured in a graduated cylinder. Notice that the volume of a liquid does not depend on the shape of the container.

Density

Mass and volume are physical properties that can be measured. By themselves, neither can be used to identify unknown objects or substances. However, if you have measured the mass and the volume of an object, you can calculate its density. You can then use this property to identify some objects.

Density is the concentration of matter in an object. It is the amount of matter in a certain volume. Density is calculated by using the following formula:

Density = mass ÷ volume

For example, the density of a substance with a mass of 10 g and a volume of 2 cm³ is 5 g/cm³ (5 grams per cubic centimeter).

Density = 10 g ÷ 2 cm³ = 5 g/cm³

Pure substances always have the same density when measured under the same conditions. The density of diamond, for example, is always 3.51 g/cm³.

copper

wood

aluminum

▲ The copper cube, made with the densest matter, has the greatest mass. The aluminum cube is less dense than the copper cube. The wooden cube is the same size but is made with the least-dense matter. It has the smallest mass.

Because density is always the same for a pure substance, this property can be used for identification. Suppose you were given a gemstone and didn't know whether it was a diamond or a zircon—a mineral that looks like a diamond but is much less valuable. If you had instruments that were exact enough, you could measure the gemstone's mass on a balance and find out its volume by the amount of water it displaced. Then you could calculate its density. If the density is 4.7 g/cm³, you have a zircon. If the density is 3.51 g/cm³, you have a diamond!

The Density of Copper			
Mass	8.96 g	89.6 g	134.4 g
Volume	1 cm³	10 cm³	15 cm³
Density	8.96 g/cm³	8.96 g/cm³	8.96 g/cm³

▲ No matter how large or how small a copper ball is, its density is always the same.

✔ **Will different volumes of the same substance have the same density or different densities?**

Mixtures and Solutions

Most of the objects around us are not pure substances. Instead, they are mixtures. A *mixture* is a combination of two or more different kinds of matter, each of which keeps its own physical properties.

In some mixtures it's easy to tell that each type of matter keeps its physical properties, because you can still see the parts of the mixture. If sugar and iron filings are mixed together, for example, you can still see the individual sugar grains and the iron filings.

Mixtures can be separated into the substances that make them up. The method used to separate a mixture depends on the physical properties of the substances in the mixture. In a mixture of iron filings and sugar, the iron filings keep their physical property of magnetism. Since sugar doesn't have this property, you can separate the mixture with a magnet.

If sugar is mixed with water, it's not easy to tell what is in the mixture. The sugar seems to disappear. But if you taste the mixture, you will find that the water is sweet. The sugar has kept its physical property of taste. In a mixture of sugar and water, the sugar dissolves in the water. When one substance dissolves in another, the two form a solution. A *solution* is a type of mixture in which particles of the two substances are mixed. Some solutions cannot be easily separated.

The **solubility** (sahl•yoo•BIL•uh•tee) of substances, or their ability to be dissolved, can be used to help identify them. Sugar, for example, is soluble in water, but ground black pepper is not.

The air in the diver's tank is a mixture of mostly nitrogen and oxygen ▶

Sea water is a mixture of salt and water. The salt in sea water can be separated from the water by evaporation.

Gases in Air

Other gases 1%

Oxygen 21%

Nitrogen 78%

Sand is a mixture of solids. You can still see the different types of solids after they are mixed together.

In the sugar and water solution, a solid is mixed with a liquid. Rubbing alcohol is a solution of two liquids: water and alcohol. But solutions don't have to include a liquid. Mixtures of metals are solutions of solids. Brass is a solution of zinc and copper. It is made by melting the two metals together. Gases can form solutions, too. Air is a solution of several gases, as the circle graph on page E10 shows.

✓ **What is an example of a mixture?**

Summary

Matter is anything that has mass and takes up space. Physical properties can be used to identify different types of objects and substances. Some physical properties (such as mass, volume, and density) can be measured. Physical properties such as density and solubility help scientists identify different substances.

Review

1. How can physical properties be used to identify objects and substances?
2. Does an object on Earth have the same mass as it does on the moon? Explain.
3. What physical properties are used to calculate the density of an object?
4. **Critical Thinking** Are all solutions mixtures? Are all mixtures solutions? Explain with examples.
5. **Test Prep** All of these are physical properties except —
   A mass
   B volume
   C density
   D time

LINKS

MATH LINK

Compare Numbers The International System of Units (SI) uses prefixes to tell you how many times to multiply or divide by 10. Put these measurements in order from shortest to longest: 2 dam, 4 m, 60 dm, 500 cm, 10,000 mm.

Prefix	Abbreviation	Multiply By
kilo	k	1000
hecto	h	100
deca	da	10
deci	d	$\frac{1}{10}$
centi	c	$\frac{1}{100}$
milli	m	$\frac{1}{1000}$

WRITING LINK

Informative Writing—Description Suppose you find an unknown substance growing out of the sidewalk in front of your home. Decide on its physical properties, and write a paragraph for your science teacher describing them.

PHYSICAL EDUCATION LINK

Swimming Research to find the dimensions of an Olympic-sized pool. Then figure out the volume of water it can hold.

GO ONLINE TECHNOLOGY LINK

Learn more about the physical properties of matter by visiting this Internet site.
www.scilinks.org/harcourt

SCI LINKS
THE WORLD'S A CLICK AWAY

LESSON 2

How Does Matter Change from One State to Another?

In this lesson, you can . . .

INVESTIGATE changes in states of matter.

LEARN ABOUT three states of matter.

LINK to math, writing, physical education, and technology.

Ice (water) changes state from a solid to a liquid when it is warmed by the heat of a human hand.

Changing States of Matter

Activity Purpose Liquid water, ice, and water vapor are all the same substance, but they have different physical properties. That's because they are all different states, or forms, of the same substance. In this investigation you will **observe** and **infer** changing states of matter.

Materials

- 5 ice cubes
- zip-top plastic bag
- balance
- thermometer
- glass beaker
- safety goggles
- hot plate

Activity Procedure

1 Place five ice cubes in a zip-top plastic bag. Be sure to seal the bag. Use the balance to **measure** the mass of the ice cubes and the bag. **Observe** the shape of the ice cubes. **Record** your observations and measurements. (Picture A)

2 Set the bag of ice cubes in a warm place. **Observe** what happens to the shape of the ice cubes. Use the balance to **measure** the mass of the melted ice cubes and the bag. Unzip the bag slightly and insert the thermometer. Measure the temperature of the water. **Record** your observations and measurements. Use your observations to **infer** that a change of state is occurring.

Picture A

Picture B

3 After the ice has completely melted, pour the water into a glass beaker. Put the thermometer in the beaker. **Observe** what happens to the water's shape, and **record** the water's temperature. (Picture B)

4 CAUTION **Put on the safety goggles.** Your teacher will use a hot plate to heat the water in the beaker until it boils. **Observe** what happens to the water when it boils. **Record** the temperature of the boiling water. Use your observations to **infer** that another change of state has occurred.

Draw Conclusions

1. Identify the different states of water at different points in this investigation.

2. **Compare** the mass of the ice to the mass of water after it melted. What does this show about changes in state?

3. What temperatures did you **record** as the water changed states?

4. **Scientists at Work** After scientists use their senses to **observe** the properties of substances, they can **infer** whether a change in state has taken place. What did you observe in this investigation? What did you infer about a change of state from each observation?

Investigate Further The physical change that happens to water when it is boiled produces water vapor—an invisible gas. **Plan and conduct a simple experiment** to test the following **hypothesis:** The mass of the water vapor is the same as the mass of the liquid water.

> **Process Skill Tip**
>
> When you **observe** the physical properties of a substance, you can use your observations to **infer** a change in its state.

Changes in State

Three States of Matter

In the investigation you learned that water exists in three states—solid, liquid, and gas. Most matter exists in one or more of these states. Which state it is in depends on the conditions at the time, such as temperature and pressure. A **solid** has a definite shape and a definite volume. A **liquid** has a definite volume but no definite shape. For example, when you pour orange juice, a liquid, from a jug into a glass, the shape of the juice changes to fit the container. The volume of juice, however, doesn't change. A **gas** does not have a definite shape or volume. If you put air into a tire, for example, it takes the same shape as the tire. But even when the tire seems full, you can put more air into it.

✔ **What are three states of matter?**

FIND OUT

- **what three states of matter are**
- **how substances change state**

VOCABULARY

solid
liquid
gas
evaporation
condensation

Two states of water are shown in this picture. A third can be inferred. The snow is solid water. Melted snow and ice are liquid water. Water vapor released into the air by the geysers (GY•zerz) is a gas. However, the steam that can be seen near the geysers is liquid water, not water vapor.

Particles of Matter

Why does a solid keep its shape? Why does a liquid flow? Why can the volume of a gas change? You can better understand the differences between states of matter if you think of matter as particles in motion.

In a solid the particles are very close together. Because there is very little space between particles, they can't be squeezed any closer together. This gives a solid a definite volume and shape. It also keeps particles in a solid from moving very much. In fact, they are packed together so tightly that each particle stays in the same place and just vibrates.

Particles are not packed together as tightly in a liquid, so they move more freely than they do in a solid. This enables a liquid to flow and take the shape of its container. You can see the motion of particles in a liquid by placing a drop of dye in a glass of water. As the particles bump into one another, the dye slowly spreads through the water.

The particles in a gas are packed together the least. Because the particles are freer to move around in gases than in solids or liquids, gas particles move the fastest. Like a liquid, a gas flows and takes the shape of its container. But the density of particles in a gas is so low that an increase in pressure can move the particles closer together. If the pressure is high enough, a gas becomes a liquid.

✔ **In which state of matter are the particles closest together? Farthest apart?**

A solid feels firm when you touch it because the particles that make it up are packed tightly together. A solid can be used to make gear that protects you, like this bicycle helmet.

The particles in a liquid move freely enough to slide past one another. This enables liquids to change shape, as the milk has done in this splash.

The particles in a gas are the farthest apart and move the fastest. Bubbles of carbon dioxide gas are lighter than the liquid in this glass, so they float to the top and escape into the air.

Changes Between States

You may be used to seeing many substances in only one state. Nitrogen is usually a gas, for example, and aluminum is usually a solid. But all substances can change states. Liquid nitrogen is used to cool other materials to very low temperatures. Liquid aluminum can be poured into molds to make objects.

You may have seen puddles freeze and turn to ice when it gets cold. *Freezing* changes a substance from a liquid to a solid.

When the sun comes out and warms the ice, it melts. *Melting* is a change in state from a solid to a liquid.

In the investigation you saw water boiling on a hot plate. *Boiling* changes a substance from a liquid to a gas. Even when the temperature of a liquid has not yet reached its boiling point, some of the particles near the surface may be moving fast enough to evaporate. **Evaporation** occurs when particles escape from a nonboiling liquid and become a gas.

THE INSIDE STORY

Changing States

When enough heat is removed from a liquid, it freezes. The particles slow down and move closer together. They become tightly packed and a solid is formed. ▼

As a solid melts, the addition of heat makes the particles move faster and farther apart. ▼

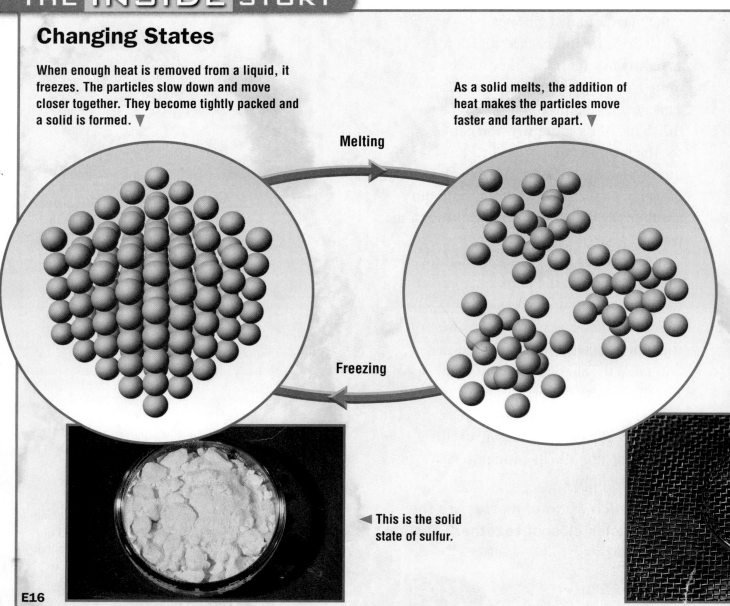

Melting

Freezing

◄ This is the solid state of sulfur.

Condensation (kahn•den•SAY•shuhn) changes a substance from a gas to a liquid. This is what happens when drops of water appear on the outside of a glass of cold water on a hot day. Water vapor in the air is cooled on the surface of the glass. It condenses, forming water drops.

Particles can also escape from the surface of a solid and become a gas. *Sublimation* (sub•luh•MAY•shuhn) is a change in state from a solid to a gas. Dry ice, which is solid carbon dioxide, sublimes. Without ever melting, in warm air it forms a cold gas that looks like smoke.

Changes in state do not change a substance. Water is still water whether it is a solid, a liquid, or a gas. Changes in state are also reversible.

Changes in state occur when heat is added or removed. When heat is added to a substance, the particles gain energy. They move faster, and farther apart. When heat is removed from a substance, the particles slow down. When enough heat has been removed, the particles move closer together.

✔ **What process is the opposite of evaporation?**

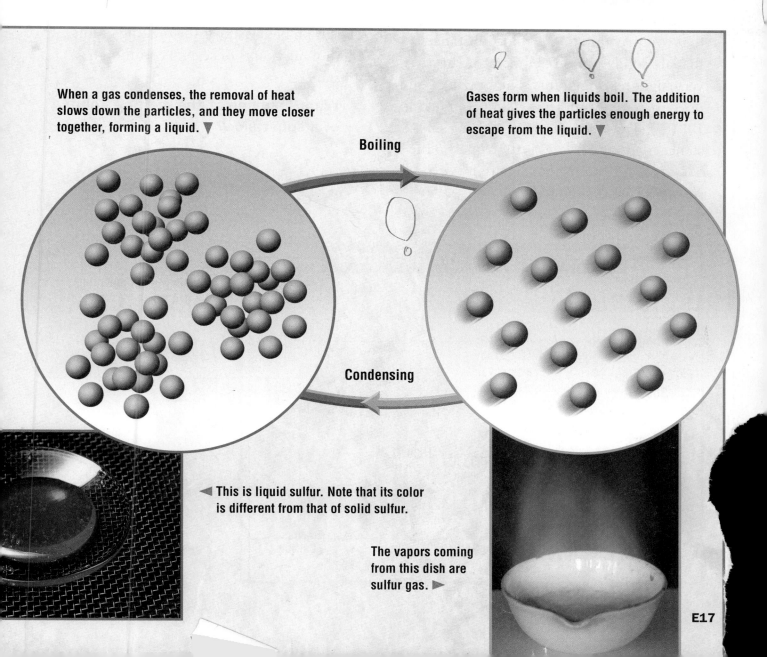

When a gas condenses, the removal of heat slows down the particles, and they move closer together, forming a liquid. ▼

Boiling

Gases form when liquids boil. The addition of heat gives the particles enough energy to escape from the liquid. ▼

Condensing

◀ This is liquid sulfur. Note that its color is different from that of solid sulfur.

The vapors coming from this dish are sulfur gas. ▶

E17

Melting and Boiling Points

Farmers who grow oranges and grapefruit worry when the outdoor temperature drops below 0°C (32°F). That's because all water, including the water inside the fruit, freezes at 0°C. Freezing and thawing can damage fruit, making it worthless.

When a weather forecaster says there will be freezing temperatures, the word *freezing* refers to the temperature at which water freezes. But every substance has its own temperature at which it changes from a liquid to a solid. This temperature is the substance's *freezing point*.

Not all freezing points are temperatures that you may think of as cold. Substances that are solids at room temperature have very high freezing points. The freezing point of copper, for example, is 1083°C (about 1981°F)! The temperature at which a substance melts and freezes is the same. So the *melting point* and the freezing point of a substance are the same.

The temperature at which a substance changes from a liquid to a gas is called its *boiling point*. The boiling point of water is 100°C (212°F). Boiling points are not always temperatures you would consider to be hot. Substances that are gases at room temperature have very low boiling points. The boiling point of oxygen, for example, is -183°C (about -297°F).

At normal air pressure, the temperatures at which a substance melts and boils are always the same. However, different substances melt and boil at different temperatures. So most substances can be identified by their melting points and boiling points. The graph below shows the melting points and boiling points of several common substances.

✓ **What happens at the melting point of a substance?**

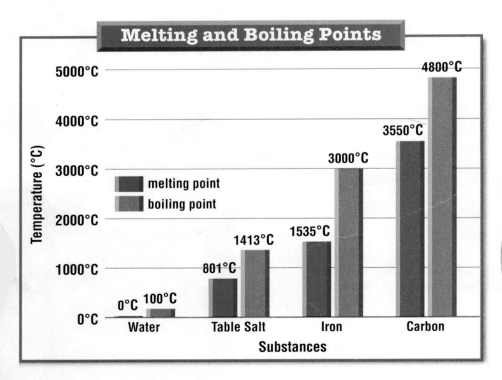

Melting and Boiling Points graph

Water freezes and melts at 0°C (32°F). ▼

Summary

Three states of matter are solid, liquid, and gas. Changes in state are physical changes. Particles of matter move faster as heat is added and slow down as heat is removed. Every substance has a melting point, the temperature at which it changes from a solid to a liquid. It also has a boiling point, the temperature at which it changes from a liquid to a gas.

Review

1. What are the three states in which most matter occurs?

2. List two substances that are solids, two that are liquids, and two that are gases at room temperature.

3. What happens to the particles of matter when a liquid changes to a gas?

4. **Critical Thinking** Why can boiling points and freezing points be used to identify substances?

5. **Test Prep** The process by which a liquid becomes a gas without boiling is called —

    A sublimation   **C** melting

    B precipitation   **D** evaporation

◀ **Water boils and condenses at 100°C (212°F).**

LINKS

MATH LINK

Solve Problems The volume of a gas varies with pressure. The higher the pressure, the smaller the volume. If a sample of gas has a volume of 150 mL, will its volume be larger or smaller if the pressure doubles?

WRITING LINK

Narrative Writing—Personal Story Suppose you are a particle in a substance. Write a story about what happens to you as the substance changes its state from a solid to a liquid and then to a gas. Read your story to your class.

PHYSICAL EDUCATION LINK

Sports and Water Many sports use water in different states. For example, hockey is played on solid water—ice. With a partner, make a list of as many sports as you can that use water in some state.

TECHNOLOGY LINK

Learn more about freezing points by viewing *Absolute Zero* on the **Harcourt Science Newsroom Video.**

How Does Matter React Chemically?

In this lesson, you can . . .

INVESTIGATE chemical properties of matter.

LEARN ABOUT changes in matter.

LINK to math, writing, social studies, and technology.

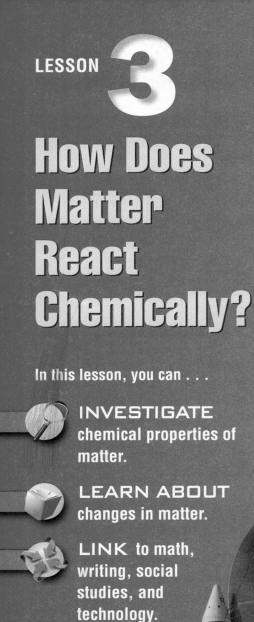

Heat and smoke are signs of chemical reactions that occur when the space shuttle lifts off. ▷

INVESTIGATE

Chemical Properties

Activity Purpose If you were in the kitchen at home and had to decide whether a cup of solid, white grains was sugar or salt, you could taste them. While tasting might be fairly safe in your own kitchen, you should never taste an unknown substance in a science laboratory. Tasting in the laboratory is very dangerous! Instead, you can use chemical properties to identify substances. *Chemical properties* are characteristics of a substance related to changing the substance into something else. In this investigation you will **experiment** to discover some chemical properties of matter.

Materials

- masking tape
- marking pen
- 3 test tubes
- apron
- safety goggles
- measuring spoon
- baking soda
- 3 droppers
- water
- vinegar
- iodine solution
- cornstarch
- talcum powder
- baking powder

CAUTION

Activity Procedure

1 Use the masking tape and marking pen to label your test tubes *water*, *vinegar*, and *iodine*.

2 **CAUTION** Put on the apron and safety goggles. Leave them on for the entire activity.

3 Put about $\frac{1}{3}$ spoonful of baking soda in each test tube. Add a dropper of water to the test tube labeled *water*. **Observe** and **record** what happens.

4 Add a dropper of vinegar to the test tube labeled *vinegar*. **Observe** and **record** what happens this time. (Picture A)

5 Add a dropper of iodine solution to the test tube labeled *iodine*. **CAUTION** **Iodine is poisonous if swallowed and can cause stains. Be careful not to spill or touch the iodine solution. Wash your hands if you get iodine on them.** **Observe** and **record** what happens.

6 Wash the test tubes with soap and water. Repeat Steps 3–5 three more times using cornstarch, talcum powder, and baking powder in the test tubes instead of baking soda. Be sure to wash the test tubes between tests. **Observe** and **record** what happens each time. (Picture B)

7 Get an "unknown" sample from your teacher. It will be one of the substances you have already tested. Test it with water, vinegar, and iodine solution, just as you did before. **Observe** and **record** what happens when you add each of the liquids. What is your unknown substance?

Picture A

Picture B

Draw Conclusions

1. How did you find out what your unknown sample was?

2. Vinegar is one of a group of substances called *acids*. Acids react with substances called *bases*. Of the substances you tested, which are bases? How can you tell?

3. Baking powder is not a pure substance. It is a mixture of two of the other substances you tested. Based on your results, what do you **infer** are the two substances in baking powder?

4. **Scientists at Work** Scientists **experiment** to find out if two substances react. What signs of reactions did your experiments produce? What **variables** did you **control**?

Investigate Further Suppose you wanted to discover some of the chemical properties of chalk. **Hypothesize** whether chalk is an acid or a base. Then **plan and conduct a simple experiment** to test your hypothesis.

Process Skill Tip

When you **experiment**, it is important to vary only one factor at a time. This helps make clear which factor is the cause of the results you observe. Varying one factor at a time is called **controlling variables**.

E21

Changes in Matter

Physical and Chemical Changes

VOCABULARY

reactivity
combustibility

When ice melts, it changes into liquid water. When liquid water boils, it changes into water vapor. But through all the changes, it is still water. Changes in which no new substances are formed are physical changes. All changes in state are physical changes.

When you shape clay on a potter's wheel, you change its form. This is a physical change. Cutting up a piece of paper is also a physical change. Gases such as hydrogen and oxygen can be cooled and squeezed until they become liquids. When this happens, the gases go through changes in state, volume, and density. These are all physical changes!

But if an electric current is sent through water, a different kind of change takes place. Gases are produced, but the gases are not water. They are oxygen and hydrogen, the substances that make up water. In the space shuttle's main engines, liquid oxygen and liquid hydrogen are mixed and burned as a fuel. Water—a new substance—is produced. Changes in which one or more new substances are formed are called chemical changes, or *chemical reactions*.

A marshmallow melting is an example of a physical change. A marshmallow burning is an example of a chemical change. ▼

Burning is one kind of chemical reaction. When charcoal burns, for example, carbon reacts with oxygen to produce carbon dioxide. Carbon and oxygen are *reactants*, the starting substances in a chemical reaction. Carbon dioxide is a *product* of the reaction. It is a new substance.

Some substances are more likely than others to react. Chlorine gas reacts chemically with many different substances. But neon gas does not. The ability of a substance to react chemically is called **reactivity**.

There are some clues that can help you identify chemical reactions. They include a change in color or the production of light, heat, or a gas. Paper turns black as it burns, for example. When baking soda is mixed with vinegar, it bubbles. This shows that carbon dioxide has been produced. A candle produces heat and light as it burns.

However, it's sometimes hard to tell the difference between a physical change and a chemical reaction. Cherry-flavored drink powder is pale pink. When you mix it with water, it turns bright red. But the powder has only dissolved. It has gone through a physical change, not a chemical reaction. When you open a cold soft drink, bubbles are produced. But a chemical reaction has not taken place. The carbon dioxide has simply come out of solution. And if you rub your hands quickly back and forth across a surface, they become hot. But the heat is due to friction, not a chemical reaction.

✔ **What is the difference between a physical change and a chemical reaction?**

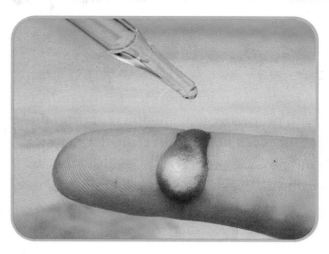

▲ Production of a different kind of gas shows that a chemical reaction has taken place. When hydrogen peroxide is used to clean a wound, it reacts with a substance in blood, forming oxygen and water.

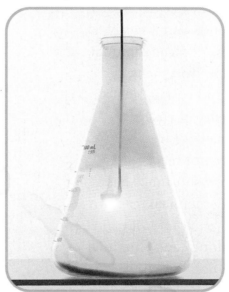

◄ When sodium combines with chlorine to make sodium chloride (salt), light is produced. This new product shows that a chemical reaction has occurred.

Steel wool burns, but only in pure oxygen, not in air. Steel wool is not as reactive as charcoal, which does burn in air. ▼

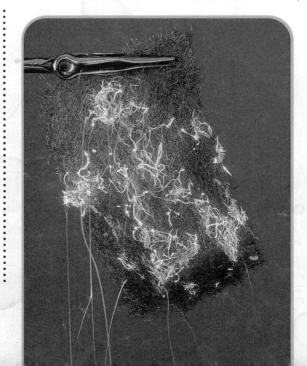

Using Physical and Chemical Properties

Chemical reactions often form products with properties that are different from those of the reactants. So observing the chemical and physical properties of a substance can help you decide whether a chemical change or a physical change has taken place.

For example, when iron rusts, it turns red or brown. But is this a chemical reaction or a physical change? Is rust a new substance, or is it still iron?

If you examine rust carefully, you will find that it is no longer shiny like iron. Rust is powdery, while iron bends and is easily formed into other shapes. Iron can conduct electricity, but rust cannot. Iron melts at 1535°C (about 2795°F), and rust at 1594°C (about 2901°F). The density of rust is 5.18 g/cm³, while the density of iron is 7.86 g/cm³. And rust does not react with oxygen as iron does. A new substance has definitely been formed. A chemical reaction has taken place.

Chemical properties alone can sometimes be used to identify substances. Since charcoal burns, it has the chemical property of **combustibility** (kuhm•buhs•tuh•BIL•uh•tee). Some substances can be identified by certain characteristics of their combustibility. Flame tests can be used to identify substances based on the color of the flame they produce when burned. Barium, for example, produces a green flame. Sodium produces a yellow flame, and potassium produces a violet flame.

Chemical properties are also important in deciding how certain substances can be used. For example, many solutions are either acids or bases. Acids are sour, and weak acids can be used to flavor foods. Weak bases can be used in cleaning products. However, strong acids and strong bases are dangerous. Therefore, it's important to be able to measure their strengths. The strengths of acids and bases are measured using dyes called *indicators*. Indicators react chemically with acids and bases and turn different colors depending on their strengths.

Physical and chemical properties can also be used to separate mixtures or to identify substances in mixtures. Remember that the

Gold can be separated from sand by panning, because gold is more dense than sand.

Acids can be used to identify limestone because they react easily with it, producing bubbles of carbon dioxide. Acid rain can damage limestone statues for the same reason; it reacts chemically with them.

substances that make up mixtures keep their physical properties. They also keep their chemical properties.

One industry that uses physical and chemical properties to separate mixtures is the mining industry. Metals must be separated from their ores before they can be made into useful products. An *ore* is a combination of a metal and other substances, such as oxygen, sulfur, carbon, or silicon. Several methods can be used to separate metals from their ores. Some impurities, or unwanted substances, are less dense than water, so they float in water and can be washed away. Others, like sulfur, can be burned away.

If a mixture contains a substance that is magnetic, a magnet can be used to separate the mixture. For example, a magnet can be used to separate steel from a mixture of car parts containing steel, aluminum, and plastics. The steel can then be recycled into new car parts.

Some liquid mixtures can be separated by spinning at very high speeds—up to 80,000 turns per minute. The force of the spinning pushes solids and other dense substances to the bottom of the container. This process can be used to separate heavy blood cells from the liquid, called plasma. It can also be used to separate the lighter cream from the heavier milk. This produces skim milk.

A solution of a solid and a liquid can be separated by boiling away the liquid, leaving the solid behind. When salt water is boiled, the water boils away and the salt is left as crystals in the container. The water can be recovered by collecting the water vapor and condensing it. This process is called *distillation*. Distillation is used to separate petroleum into products such as gasoline, motor oil, and asphalt.

Sometimes both a physical change and a chemical reaction are used to recover a substance from a mixture. For example, suppose you wanted to recover some copper from a mixture of copper, sugar, and charcoal. Since sugar is the only substance of the three that is soluble in water, water can be added to dissolve the sugar. The sugar water can be removed from the mixture by pouring it through filter paper. Sugar water will pass through the filter paper, but the large particles of copper and charcoal won't. After the charcoal-and-copper mixture dries, the charcoal can be burned away, leaving only copper.

✔ **What physical and chemical properties are used to separate metals from their ores?**

Conservation of Matter

Physical changes and chemical reactions cause matter to look different. But neither can change the amount of matter present. Matter is neither created nor destroyed during a physical change or a chemical change. Scientists call this the *law of conservation of matter*.

This law is easier to prove for some changes than it is for others. If you cut a piece of paper into tiny pieces, you have more pieces of paper, but you have not made more paper. However, when water changes from a liquid to a gas, there may appear to be more matter because the volume of water vapor is greater. But no new matter has been produced. The density of the water is less, so the same mass of water takes up more space. If you measured carefully, you would discover that the mass of the water before the change of state is equal to the mass of water vapor produced.

It may be harder to believe that matter is not produced or destroyed during a chemical change. The reactants seem to disappear and the products seem to appear. However, in the 1700s, Antoine Lavoisier (lah•vwah•ZYAY), a French chemist, was among the first scientists to carefully measure chemical reactions. He found that during a chemical change, the mass of the products equals the mass of the reactants. Because there is no change in mass after a chemical reaction, there is no more and no less matter than there was before the reaction.

Sometimes the masses involved in a chemical change may be harder to measure than those in a physical change. For example, one of the reactants of combustion reactions is oxygen from the air. If the oxygen is not included in the mass of the reactants, then the mass of the products appears to be greater than the mass of the reactants. It looks as if matter has been produced!

✔ **Give an example of a physical change, and explain how matter was neither created nor destroyed.**

When vinegar reacts with baking soda, the mass of the reactants before the reaction is equal to the mass of the products after the reaction.

Summary

Physical changes do not result in the formation of new substances. However, new substances are formed during chemical changes. Physical and chemical properties can be used to identify substances and to separate mixtures. Matter is neither produced nor destroyed during physical and chemical reactions.

Review

1. Give an example of a physical change and a chemical change for iron.

2. Give an example of a chemical change that produces light and heat.

3. Does distillation produce a chemical change or a physical change in petroleum? Explain your answer.

4. **Critical Thinking** Describe how to use physical properties to separate a mixture of ice cubes and nails.

5. **Test Prep** The law which says that matter is neither produced nor destroyed in a physical or chemical reaction is the law of —

   A conservation of matter
   B metallurgy
   C chemical properties
   D physical changes

LINKS

MATH LINK

Solve Problems Sometimes it is easier to calculate the mass of a gas involved in a chemical reaction than it is to measure it. If 56 g of iron react with oxygen gas to produce 80 g of rust, calculate the mass of the oxygen that reacted.

WRITING LINK

Persuasive Writing—Opinion Scientists sometimes don't agree whether a certain change is physical or chemical. They use data from experiments to support their positions. Choose an example that you think is a physical or chemical change, and then write a persuasive paragraph for your teacher using experimental data to support your opinion.

SOCIAL STUDIES LINK

History The progress of science is often affected by politics. Research the life of Antoine Lavoisier to find out how the politics in France during the late 1700s may have affected the progress of science.

TECHNOLOGY LINK

Learn more about physical and chemical changes by investigating *Matter Mania* on the **Harcourt Science Explorations CD-ROM.**

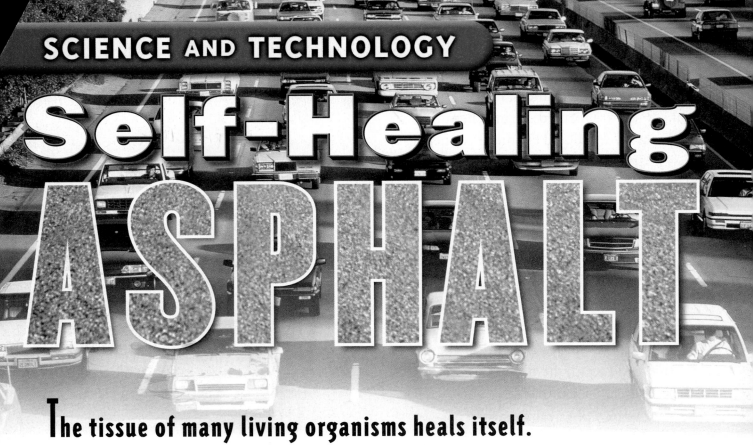

Self-Healing ASPHALT

The tissue of many living organisms heals itself. Trim away branches of a tree, for example, and it quickly produces new shoots. Can nonliving things also repair themselves? Some asphalt seems to.

Tired Pavement

Asphalt is the sticky, black stuff used to pave roads and parking lots. It is made from petroleum and crushed rock. After it dries, fresh asphalt feels smooth under the wheels of a car. As it gets old, however, asphalt cracks and crumbles from the weight of many vehicles rolling over it.

This cracking and crumbling is called fatigue. If the cracks widen and deepen, potholes appear. Eventually the road falls apart. In some places, however, asphalt cracks just seem to disappear. Researchers have conducted tests to find out why some asphalt repairs itself.

In one test a heavy machine imitates traffic on test pavement. Then engineers measure how much cracking has occurred. A day later they measure the pavement again. Remarkably, the cracks in some of the test pavement "heal" overnight. Somehow resting gives some kinds of asphalt a chance to recover.

Cracking the Mystery

Why does some asphalt heal itself? Molecules in any material—asphalt, glass, or anything else—bond with molecules around them. When a material cracks, the bonds between molecules break. Why do molecules

Highway repair takes a lot of time, money, and machinery.

in some kinds of asphalt reconnect after the asphalt rests, but the bonds in other asphalt do not? Scientists are studying the ingredients in different asphalts. They hope to find out which ones produce healing.

Some researchers hypothesize that they can speed up asphalt healing with microwaves. Heating the asphalt causes more molecules to reconnect. But it would be impractical to do this on a large scale. Engineers suggest building wider roads. During the day, driving lanes could alternate, giving each lane a rest period. Whichever process is used, self-healing roads could save taxpayers millions of dollars in repairs each year.

THINK ABOUT IT

1. What are some ways the healing process in roads could be speeded up?
2. Why do you think asphalt gets more "rest" in some locations than others?

CAREERS
HIGHWAY ENGINEER

What They Do Highway engineers plan, design, construct, and inspect highways, tunnels, and other structures. They analyze speed limits, study the soil, and work with asphalt mixtures.

Education and Training To become a highway engineer, a person needs to study civil and environmental engineering. Math, chemistry, physics, and computer studies are also important.

WEB LINK
For Science and Technology updates, visit the Harcourt Internet site.
www.harcourtschool.com

Theophilus Leapheart
CHEMIST

"No one can put the whole puzzle together alone. Chemists, engineers, mathematicians, and physicists all need to work together to solve problems and to develop new products. To be successful, you have to know how to work with others."

Theophilus Leapheart is the leader of a group of chemists who make new chemical compounds. An important part of this job is finding out the structures of the compounds being made. To do this, Mr. Leapheart's team uses the technology of NMR spectroscopy. The letters *NMR* stand for *nuclear magnetic resonance*.

When the team is ready to test a new compound, they take a sample and dissolve it in a solvent. Then they place the sample in the NMR machine, which produces a strong magnetic field. The magnetic field causes molecules of the sample compound to line up in a certain way, just as Earth's magnetic field causes a compass needle to point north.

The NMR spectrum of a compound is like its fingerprint—no two compounds produce exactly the same spectrum. By looking at an NMR spectrum, Mr. Leapheart can tell which atoms are present and how many are present. In this way he can determine the structure of even the most complicated molecules.

THINK ABOUT IT

1. How does an NMR spectrum help identify a compound?
2. Why is it important for chemists to communicate the processes they use and the results of their work?

DENSITY COLUMN

Why do some liquids separate?

Materials

- 250-mL graduate
- 50 mL cooking oil
- 50 mL water
- blue food coloring
- 50 mL corn syrup
- 50 mL alcohol
- small cork
- glass marble
- small rock
- wood cube
- metal nut

Procedure

❶ Add the food coloring to the water.

❷ Pour the liquids into the graduate in order: corn syrup, colored water, oil, and alcohol.

❸ Predict in which layers the cork, marble, rock, wood, and metal will end up.

❹ Gently drop in the cork, marble, rock, wood, and metal and observe.

Draw Conclusions

Why do the liquids separate into four layers? In which liquid does each of the objects end up? How does this match your predictions? Why do some of the objects sink, while others float?

MIX IT UP

How can some mixtures be separated?

Materials

- coffee filter
- scissors
- 3 different-colored water-soluble markers
- small paper cups
- water

Procedure

❶ Cut the coffee filter into three strips, each 3 cm X 10 cm.

❷ Touch a different-colored marker near one end of each of the pieces of filter paper.

❸ Put the bottom edge of each piece of filter paper in a paper cup containing a small amount of water. Do not let the marker spot touch the water.

❹ Observe what happens.

Draw Conclusions

Most inks are mixtures of different-colored pigments. As water traveled up the filter papers, the pigments separated. Which pigments made up the colors you tested? Why do you think some of the pigments traveled farther up the paper than others?

Vocabulary Review

Use the terms below to complete the sentences. The page numbers in ( ) tell you where to look in the chapter if you need help.

matter (E6)   solid (E14)
physical
  properties (E6)   liquid (E14)
mass (E7)   gas (E14)
weight (E7)   evaporation (E16)
volume (E8)   condensation (E17)
density (E9)   reactivity (E23)
solubility (E10)   combustibility (E24)

1. _____ is a measure of the amount of matter in an object.

2. _____ is the amount of space that an object takes up.

3. A substance's ability to be dissolved is its _____.

4. A measure of the pull of gravity on an object is _____.

5. _____ are properties that can be observed or measured without changing a substance into a new substance.

6. The concentration of matter in an object is its _____.

7. Particles escape from a nonboiling liquid and become a gas during _____. _____ is a change in state from a gas to a liquid.

8. _____ is anything that has mass and takes up space.

9. Three states of matter are _____, _____, and _____.

10. _____ is a kind of _____ that refers to a substance's ability to burn.

Connect Concepts

Diagrams that stand for three states of matter are shown below. Fill in the blanks (11–13) to identify each state shown. Describe how changes in state take place by labeling the arrows between the diagrams (14–19). The mass of a substance in one state is given. Give the mass of the substance in the other two states by filling in the blanks (20, 21). Add arrowheads to the lines labeled *volume* and *density* to show the direction in which they increase (22, 23).

_____ (11)   _____ (12)   _____ (13)

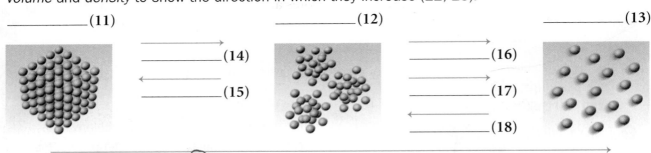

_____ (14)   _____ (16)

_____ (15)   _____ (17)

_____ (18)

_____ (19)

mass = _____ (20)   mass = 20g   mass = _____ (21)

volume (22)

density (23)

Check Understanding

Write the letter of the best choice.

24. Which of the following is **NOT** a physical property of an iron nail?
    A It rusts.   C It bends.
    B It's shiny.   D It's a solid.

25. Bill weighs 135 lb and Rodney weighs 175 lb. Bill's mass is _____ Rodney's mass.
    F more than   H the same as
    G less than   J unknown

26. If solid copper sulfate is mixed with water, _____ is formed.
    A a mixture   C a solvent
    B a solution   D both **A** and **B**

27. A substance seems to completely fill a container, but more can be forced in. The substance is a —
    F solid   H liquid
    G gas   J none of these

28. A liquid is usually _____ a gas.
    A denser than
    B less dense than
    C the same density as
    D lighter than

29. Nitrogen can be compressed and cooled into a liquid at a very low temperature. So, nitrogen normally exists as a —
    F solid   H gas
    G liquid   J none of these

30. The melting point of gold is 1064°C. The freezing point of gold —
    A is 1064°C
    B is greater than 1064°C
    C is less than 1064°C
    D cannot be determined from the information given

31. Because paper will burn, it has the property of —
    F combustibility   H evaporation
    G condensation   J sublimation

Critical Thinking

32. Choose an object in the room, and describe some of its physical and chemical properties.

33. Explain a possible way to separate a mixture of water, ethanol, and sand.

Process Skills Review

34. What properties of your apple were you able to **observe**? What properties of your apple were you able to **measure**?

35. What change of state can you **infer** when you **observe** that the water level in a pan is lower after the water has boiled for ten minutes?

36. In your **experiment** with baking powder, which substance did you vary?

Performance Assessment

Matter Models

Work with two other students. Use marbles and boxes of different sizes to make models that show the density and behavior of particles in solids, liquids, and gases.

Atoms and Elements

Vocabulary Preview

nucleus
proton
neutron
electron
element
atom
molecule
periodic table
compound

The Statue of Liberty has stood in New York Harbor for more than one hundred years—but it has never been completely still. Every particle of the statue is constantly in motion. These particles are so small that they can barely be seen with the most powerful microscopes.

Fast Fact

Oxygen makes up about half of the mass of Earth's water, soil, and rocky crust. However, it's not the most common substance in Earth's atmosphere.

The Composition of Air

Gas	Percent of Air
Nitrogen	78.00
Oxygen	20.90
Argon	0.93
Carbon dioxide	0.03
All other gases	0.14

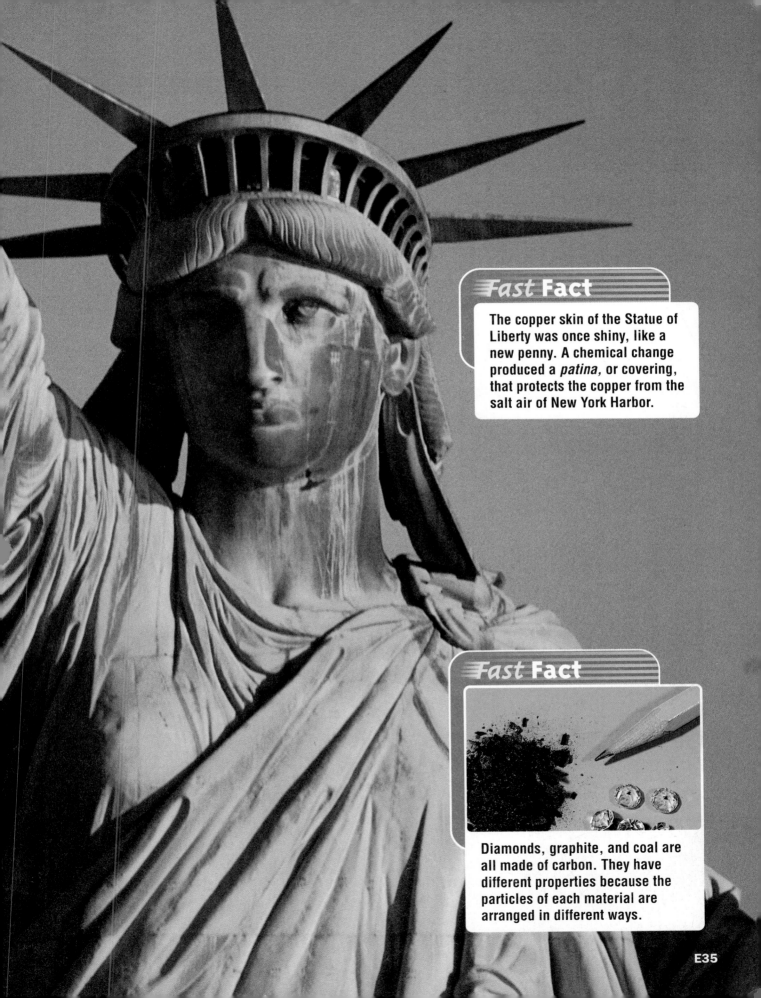

Fast **Fact**

The copper skin of the Statue of Liberty was once shiny, like a new penny. A chemical change produced a *patina,* or covering, that protects the copper from the salt air of New York Harbor.

Fast **Fact**

Diamonds, graphite, and coal are all made of carbon. They have different properties because the particles of each material are arranged in different ways.

1

What Are Atoms and Elements?

In this lesson, you can . . .

INVESTIGATE
objects you cannot see or touch.

LEARN ABOUT
atoms and elements.

LINK to math, writing, health, and technology.

Many of the treasures in this chest are metals and other natural materials. ▽

INVESTIGATE

Mystery Boxes

Activity Purpose It's easy to study the characteristics of an object you can see and touch. You can **observe** them directly. You can pick up the object to see patterns and feel textures. You can also **measure** its mass, volume, and dimensions. In this investigation you will study characteristics of an object you can't see or touch. You will have to **infer** information from indirect observations.

Materials

■ sealed box provided by your teacher
■ ruler
■ balance
■ magnet

Activity Procedure

1 With a partner, **observe** the sealed box your teacher gave you. **Record** any observations you think might help you learn about what's inside the box.

2 Use the ruler to **measure** the outside of the box. Use the balance to find the mass of the box. **Record** your results. (Picture A)

3 Carefully tilt and shake the box. How many objects do you **infer** are in the box? How big do you infer the objects are? **Record** your inferences and the reasons for them.

4 Hold the magnet to the surface of the box. Then tilt the box. Are any of the objects in the box attracted to the magnet? Repeat this at several places on the surface of the box. (Picture B)

Picture A

Picture B

5 What objects do you **infer** are inside the box? Base your inferences on your measurements and observations.

6 What do you **infer** about the inside of the box? Draw a picture of what you think the inside of the box looks like.

7 Now open the box. **Compare** your inferences about the objects in the box with the objects the box really contains. Also compare your inferences about what the box looks like inside with what it really looks like.

Draw Conclusions

1. How did what you **inferred** about the objects inside the box **compare** with what was really inside?

2. How did what you **inferred** about the inside of the box **compare** with the way it really looked inside?

3. **Scientists at Work** Different scientists may **infer** different things about objects they can't **observe** directly. Compare your inferences about the contents and the inside of the box with the inferences of other pairs. How were your inferences similar? How were they different?

Investigate Further Construct your own mystery box, and place various objects inside it. Give your box to a classmate. Your classmate will **observe** the box and **form a hypothesis** about its contents.

Process Skill Tip

When you can't **observe** something directly, you may be able to **infer** some of its characteristics. To do this, you might observe how the object reacts under certain conditions.

Atoms and Elements

The Atomic Theory

In the investigation you probably found it difficult to identify an object you couldn't see. Early scientists had the same difficulty in trying to understand what matter was made of.

The theory that matter is made of tiny particles that can't be divided was first proposed by a Greek philosopher, Democritus (di•MAHK•ruh•tuhs), in 400 B.C. The particles Democritus proposed were too small to be seen. Aristotle (AIR•is•taht•uhl), a Greek philosopher who lived after Democritus, believed that matter was not made of particles. This theory was widely accepted for 2000 years. However, neither of these theories was based on experimental evidence.

By the early 1800s, scientists had begun to measure chemical reactions. The measurements made it possible for John Dalton, an English chemist, to propose an atomic theory of matter that was based on experimental evidence. Dalton's atomic theory is that all matter is made up of tiny particles called *atoms*.

✓ **What is the atomic theory?**

The helium in these balloons is one of more than a hundred different kinds of atoms. ▼

The Structure of an Atom

How small is an atom? About 5 million atoms could be lined up across the period at the end of this sentence. When Dalton proposed his theory, it was thought that atoms were the smallest particles of matter. There was no evidence of smaller particles.

Scientists now know that atoms are made up of even smaller particles called *subatomic particles*. The **nucleus** (NOO•klee•uhs) is the very tiny center of an atom. The nucleus is made up of protons and neutrons. A **proton** (PROH•tahn) is a subatomic particle with a positive charge. A **neutron** (NOO•trahn) is a subatomic particle with no charge. The rest of an atom is made up of electrons, which surround the nucleus. An **electron** (ee•LEK•trahn) is a subatomic particle with a negative charge.

In 1913, Niels Bohr proposed a model of the structure of an atom. In his model, electrons circle the nucleus at fixed distances from it. The paths in which the electrons move are called *orbits*. They are also referred to as *energy levels*, because their distance from the nucleus depends on the energy of the electrons in them. Low-energy electrons orbit close to the nucleus. High-energy electrons orbit farther away.

Although the nucleus is very tiny, almost all of an atom's mass is in its nucleus. The mass of a proton is nearly 2000 times the mass of an electron. Protons and neutrons have about the same mass.

Although their masses are very different, electrons and protons have charges that are equally strong. Part of what holds atoms together is the attraction between the positive protons and the negative electrons. If an atom has more protons than electrons, it has a positive charge. If it has more electrons than protons, it has a negative charge. An atom with the same number of protons and electrons is called a *neutral atom*, because the positive and negative charges cancel each other.

✔ **What subatomic particles make up an atom?**

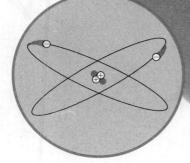

The Bohr model of a helium atom shows electrons orbiting the nucleus, much as planets orbit the sun.

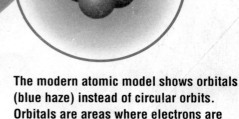

The modern atomic model shows orbitals (blue haze) instead of circular orbits. Orbitals are areas where electrons are likely to be found.

Elements

An **element** (EL•uh•muhnt) is a substance made up of only one kind of atom. For example, gold is an element. If a single atom is taken from a nugget of gold, that single atom is still gold. An **atom** is the smallest unit of an element that has all the properties of that element.

Each element has an *atomic number,* which is the number of protons in one atom of that element. There are more than 100 elements. An atom of each element has a specific number of protons in its nucleus. The nucleus of a hydrogen atom, for example, has only one proton. So the atomic number of hydrogen is 1. The atomic

number of plutonium is 94. All atoms that have 94 protons are plutonium atoms.

In their pure form, most elements are solids at room temperature. A few elements, such as oxygen, nitrogen, and helium, are gases. Only mercury and bromine are liquids.

The atoms of some elements do not occur alone. Instead, they are linked together. Two or more atoms linked together form a **molecule**. When atoms are linked only to atoms of the same kind, they are in a pure state. Oxygen gas, for example, is made up of oxygen molecules. Oxygen molecules are made up of two oxygen atoms linked together.

✓ **What is an element?**

◄ Diamond, graphite, and anthracite are all made up of carbon atoms, which have six protons. These materials have different properties because their carbon atoms are arranged differently.

This diagram of a carbon atom shows six protons and six neutrons in the nucleus. The six, fast-moving electrons are somewhere in the "cloud" surrounding the nucleus. ▼

Diamond

Graphite

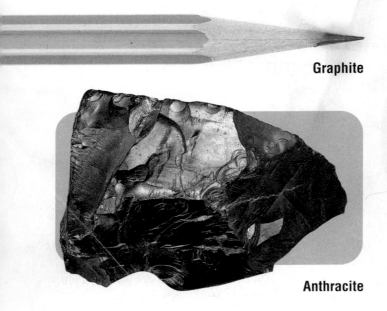

Anthracite

Common Elements

NAME	NUCLEUS MODEL	USES
Oxygen Oxygen is a colorless gas. It makes up about 20 percent of Earth's atmosphere. Oxygen is the most common element in Earth's crust. It is combined with other elements in many metal ores and minerals.	Atomic number 8	The mask supplies oxygen for the pilot.
Sodium Sodium is a silver-colored metal. It is a soft solid at room temperature, but it becomes brittle as the temperature falls. Sodium combines easily with nonmetals to form salts such as sodium chloride—table salt.	Atomic number 11	The sodium vapor in this light glows when electricity passes through it.
Aluminum Aluminum is a silver-colored metal solid. Because it combines easily with oxygen, it is never pure in nature. Aluminum is the third most common element in Earth's crust.	Atomic number 13	Most baseball bats are now made of aluminum, instead of wood.
Silicon Silicon is a dark nonmetal solid. It is the second most common element in Earth's crust. Silicon combines mainly with oxygen to form a mineral that is found in many beach sands.	Atomic number 14	Electric circuits are printed on thin pieces of silicon.
Chlorine Chlorine is a greenish yellow gas with a sharp odor. It is 2.5 times as dense as air, and it forms a pale yellow solution in water. Chlorine combines easily with metals to form salts, such as sodium chloride—table salt.	Atomic number 17	Chlorine bleach is a solution of sodium hypochlorite in water.
Iron Iron is a silver-white metal solid. There are large amounts of minerals containing iron in Earth's crust. Many useful materials, such as steel, are made from iron. Iron is also found in blood. It carries oxygen to cells.	Atomic number 26	Iron can be shaped more easily if it is red hot.

Metals

Elements are classified by their properties. About one-fourth of all elements are classified as nonmetals. The rest are metals. All metals except mercury are solid at room temperature.

Metals have many familiar properties. Gold is used in jewelry because of its high *luster,* or shininess. Most metals, like silver and nickel, have a gray or silver luster.

Most metals are said to be *malleable* (MAL•ee•uh•buhl). They can be hammered or rolled into thin sheets. The foil used to cover and store food is a thin sheet of aluminum. Metals are also *ductile* (DUHK•til). They can be formed into wires. Copper and aluminum are used in electric wiring.

Copper and aluminum are used in electric wiring because of another property. Metals *conduct,* or transfer, electricity. The electrons farthest from the nucleus of a metal atom are not held by just that atom. They are free to move to other metal atoms. This freedom of electrons allows metals to conduct electricity.

Electrons in materials such as glass, plastic, and rubber are bound tightly to their atoms. These materials conduct hardly any electricity. They are *insulators.*

Metals also conduct heat. Have you ever noticed that when a car has been sitting in the sun, its metal parts are much hotter than its plastic parts? Metal conducts heat better than plastic does. For this reason the

▼ Metal can be rolled into very thin sheets, called foil, that can be used to decorate buildings.

▼ Copper is often used on the bottom of pans because it conducts heat easily.

Metals such as aluminum and copper are good conductors of electricity. Most electric wiring is made of these metals.

handles of pots and pans are often made of plastic.

Some substances we think of as metals are not pure metal elements. They are actually *alloys,* or mixtures of metals. Bronze is an alloy of copper and tin. Steel is an alloy of iron and carbon. Brass is an alloy of copper and zinc.

✔ **What are five properties of metals?**

Summary

Matter is made up of tiny particles called atoms. Atoms are made of smaller, subatomic particles called protons, neutrons, and electrons. Elements are substances made up of only one kind of atom. Metals are elements that have luster, are malleable and ductile, and conduct electricity and heat.

Review

1. If you were to add all the missing elements to the table on page E41, how many would there be between silicon and chlorine? What would their atomic numbers be?

2. What subatomic particles make up the nucleus of an atom?

3. How do atoms with different atomic numbers differ from each other?

4. **Critical Thinking** Choose a metal you know, and list three uses that illustrate three properties of metals.

5. **Test Prep** Which are **NOT** a part of atoms?

   A protons

   B electrons

   C neutrons

   D elements

LINKS

MATH LINK

Estimate Twelve atomic mass units (abbreviated as *amu*) is equal to the mass of one carbon atom. Estimate how many amu there are in 20 atoms of carbon and in 200 atoms of carbon.

WRITING LINK

Informative Writing—Report The development of the atomic theory is central to the development of chemistry. Suppose you are a newspaper reporter, and John Dalton has just published his atomic theory. Research the history of the development of the atomic theory, and write an article for your school newspaper announcing John Dalton's new theory.

HEALTH LINK

Essential Elements Many elements, such as iron, are needed for human health. Find out which ones are in multivitamin tablets. How much of each element does a vitamin tablet contain? Report your findings to your class.

TECHNOLOGY LINK

Learn more about metals by viewing *Intermetallics* on the **Harcourt Science Newsroom Video.**

LESSON 2

What Are Compounds?

In this lesson, you can . . .

 INVESTIGATE how elements are grouped.

 LEARN ABOUT the periodic table and compounds.

 LINK to math, writing, language arts, and technology.

Mixing chemicals often produces unexpected results. ▼

Grouping Elements

Activity Purpose Suppose you have 100 baseball cards, and you want to know whether the players at certain positions have anything in common. If you group the cards by player position, you will be able to **infer** common characteristics about each group more quickly. Scientists have grouped elements by their properties. In this investigation you will learn how elements can be grouped.

Materials

- aluminum foil
- copper wire
- steel (iron) paper clip
- sulfur
- graphite pencil "lead"
- lead solder
- helium-filled balloon

Activity Procedure

CAUTION

1. Copy the chart on page E45. You will use it to **record** the properties of the elements you **observe**.

2. What elements do the objects represent? **Record** your answers in the second column of the chart.

3. **Observe** each element. Is it a solid, a liquid, or a gas at room temperature? **Record** your observations in the column labeled "Phase" of the chart.

4. What is the color of each element? (Carefully release some of the helium from the balloon.) **Record** what you **observe** in the chart. (Picture A)

5. Which elements have luster? (Which are shiny?) **Record** what you **observe** in the fifth column of the chart.

Picture A

Picture B

Object	Element	Phase	Color	Luster	Malleability
foil					
wire					
paper clip					
sulfur					
graphite					
solder					
balloon					

6 Which elements bend easily? **Record** what you **observe** in the column labeled "Malleability." **CAUTION** **Wash your hands after handling the objects in this investigation.** (Picture B)

Draw Conclusions

1. What similar properties did you **observe** in different elements?

2. Consider the properties you **observed** to form groups. Which elements could you group together? Explain.

3. **Scientists at Work** Scientists have made a periodic table, in which elements are grouped by their properties. Using your observations, **predict** which elements from the activity are near each other in the periodic table.

Investigate Further Think of other properties that could be used to group elements. Are there any you could test? **Plan and conduct a simple investigation** of one group of elements from this activity using these new tests.

Elements and Compounds

FIND OUT

- how elements are grouped in the periodic table
- how compounds form

VOCABULARY

periodic table
compound

The Periodic Table

As you learned in the investigation, some elements can be grouped together because they have similar properties. In 1869 a Russian chemist named Dmitri Mendeleev (duh•MEE•tree men•duh•LAY•uhf) organized elements by their atomic masses. Mendeleev noticed that if elements were put in order of atomic mass, some properties appeared in predictable patterns.

Scientists later found that using an order based on the number of protons in one atom of an element—atomic number—is better than one based on atomic mass.

THE INSIDE STORY

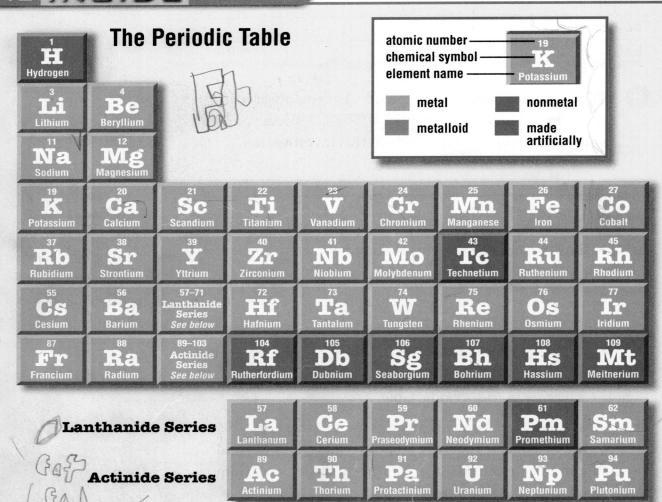

The Periodic Table

atomic number
chemical symbol
element name

19
K
Potassium

metal   nonmetal
metalloid   made artificially

1 **H** Hydrogen	

3 **Li** Lithium	4 **Be** Beryllium
11 **Na** Sodium	12 **Mg** Magnesium

19 **K** Potassium	20 **Ca** Calcium	21 **Sc** Scandium	22 **Ti** Titanium	23 **V** Vanadium	24 **Cr** Chromium	25 **Mn** Manganese	26 **Fe** Iron	27 **Co** Cobalt
37 **Rb** Rubidium	38 **Sr** Strontium	39 **Y** Yttrium	40 **Zr** Zirconium	41 **Nb** Niobium	42 **Mo** Molybdenum	43 **Tc** Technetium	44 **Ru** Ruthenium	45 **Rh** Rhodium
55 **Cs** Cesium	56 **Ba** Barium	57–71 Lanthanide Series *See below*	72 **Hf** Hafnium	73 **Ta** Tantalum	74 **W** Tungsten	75 **Re** Rhenium	76 **Os** Osmium	77 **Ir** Iridium
87 **Fr** Francium	88 **Ra** Radium	89–103 Actinide Series *See below*	104 **Rf** Rutherfordium	105 **Db** Dubnium	106 **Sg** Seaborgium	107 **Bh** Bohrium	108 **Hs** Hassium	109 **Mt** Meitnerium

Lanthanide Series

57 **La** Lanthanum	58 **Ce** Cerium	59 **Pr** Praseodymium	60 **Nd** Neodymium	61 **Pm** Promethium	62 **Sm** Samarium

Actinide Series

89 **Ac** Actinium	90 **Th** Thorium	91 **Pa** Protactinium	92 **U** Uranium	93 **Np** Neptunium	94 **Pu** Plutonium

In the modern **periodic table**, elements are arranged in order of atomic number. They are also arranged so that elements with similar properties are in the same column. The elements in a column are part of a *group*. Elements in the same group often have the same number of electrons in the outer energy levels of their atoms. The arrangement of electrons gives elements their chemical properties.

All the elements on the left side of the periodic table, except hydrogen, are metals. All the elements on the far right are non-metals. A change of color separates metals from nonmetals. Some elements have properties of both metals and nonmetals. These elements are called *metalloids*.

Notice that every element in the table has an abbreviation, called a *chemical symbol*.

When the periodic table was first set up, it had empty spaces. The spaces were for elements that had not yet been discovered. As new elements were found, scientists filled in the spaces. Using the periodic table, Mendeleev correctly predicted that three new elements with certain properties would be discovered. Even today, new elements are being added to the table. However, now most new elements are made artificially.

✔ **Which two things determine the arrangement of elements in the periodic table?**

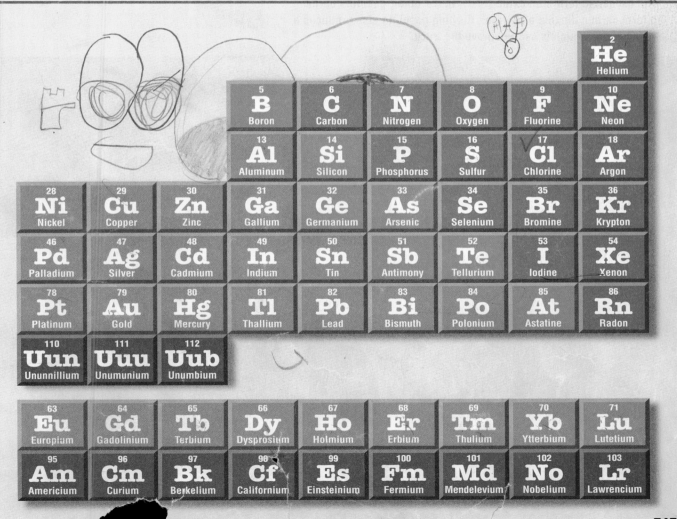

Compounds

In nature most elements are joined with other elements in compounds. A **compound** is a substance made of the atoms of two or more elements. Water is one of the most common compounds. It contains hydrogen and oxygen atoms. Table salt, sodium chloride, contains sodium and chlorine atoms.

A *chemical formula* shows which elements and how many atoms of each are in a compound. The chemical formula for water is H_2O. The small 2 next to the H means that there are 2 hydrogen atoms in every water molecule. Each water molecule also has 1 atom of oxygen. The chemical formula for table salt is NaCl. Salt has 1 sodium atom and 1 chlorine atom. The chemical formula for glucose, a simple sugar, is $C_6H_{12}O_6$. In each molecule of glucose, there are 6 carbon atoms, 12 hydrogen atoms, and 6 oxygen atoms.

When atoms join to form a compound, they undergo a chemical change. The properties of the compound are different from those of the elements in it. Hydrogen and oxygen, both gases, combine to form water, a liquid compound. Compounds can also react with each other. When compounds react, they change, and form new products. For example, hydrochloric acid contains hydrogen and chlorine atoms. It reacts with

Two chemical reactions are happening here. In one, iron combines with oxygen to form iron oxide (rust). In the other, gasoline burns to form carbon dioxide and water. Burning gasoline also produces a lot of energy, which is used to move the truck. ▼

Combustion

Gasoline + Oxygen →
Carbon Dioxide + Water + energy

Oxidation

Iron + Oxygen → Iron Oxide (rust)

sodium hydroxide, which contains sodium, oxygen, and hydrogen atoms. The products are sodium chloride, which contains sodium and chlorine atoms, and water, which contains hydrogen and oxygen atoms.

✓ **What does a chemical formula show?**

Summary

In the periodic table, elements are arranged by atomic number and properties. The table shows names, chemical symbols, and atomic numbers for all the known elements. A compound is a combination of two or more different elements. A chemical formula shows the number of atoms of each element in one molecule of a compound.

Review

1. Using the periodic table on pages E46 and E47, find the name of the element that has 36 protons.

2. In what form are most elements in nature? What does this mean?

3. What information is shown in a chemical formula?

4. **Critical Thinking** Using their placement in the periodic table, classify these elements as metals or nonmetals: iron, cobalt, sodium, oxygen, chlorine, and helium.

5. **Test Prep** Which of these is **NOT** found in the periodic table?
   A name
   B atomic number
   C luster
   D chemical symbol

LINKS

MATH LINK

Use Fractions Molecular formulas give the number of atoms in compounds. From this information you can calculate what fraction of the atoms in a compound are atoms of one element. For example, the molecular formula for ammonia is NH_3. What fraction of the atoms in ammonia are nitrogen atoms?

WRITING LINK

Informative Writing—Description From the periodic table, choose an element. Research the element, and write a description for your teacher. Include the element's properties and uses.

LANGUAGE ARTS LINK

Word Origins The chemical symbols for some elements don't seem to make sense. Many, such as Au for gold, are based on the Latin name of the element. Use a dictionary of word origins to look up other elements with strange symbols. Make a list of these elements and the origins of their symbols.

TECHNOLOGY LINK

Learn more about molecules and compounds by visiting the National Museum of American History Internet site.
www.si.edu/harcourt/science

 Smithsonian Institution®

Discovering Elements

Ancient cultures believed that matter was made up of just four or five elements. The Greeks believed these elements were water, fire, earth, and air. The Chinese added wood as a fifth element. These beliefs continued to be held for many centuries.

About 2000 years ago, the practice of alchemy (AL•kuh•mee) began in Egypt. Although the goal of alchemy—changing one substance into another—was not possible, it led to the discovery of new chemical substances. It also marked the beginning of a new science—chemistry.

Atoms and Elements

Alchemy continued for the next 1600 years. Then in 1661, Robert Boyle, a British scientist, stated that matter is made up of tiny particles. He later proposed that all matter could be broken down into elements but that elements could not be broken down into simpler substances. Within the next century, oxygen and hydrogen were both identified as elements. Scientists also discovered that elements could combine to form compounds, such as water.

The History of Elements

350 B.C.
Aristotle suggests that all substances are made of fire, water, wind, or earth.

400
The term *chemistry* is first used by Egyptian alchemists to describe the practice of changing matter.

1808
Dalton states his atomic theory.

| 400 B.C. | | A.D. 500 | A.D. 1000 | | A.D. 1600 | A.D. 1700 | A.D. 1800 |

100
Gold, silver, copper, lead, iron, tin, and mercury are known.

880
A Muslim chemist, al-Razi, classifies chemical substances into mineral, vegetable, animal, and derivative.

1661
Boyle's book, *The Sceptical Chymist,* proves the ancient "four elements" theory wrong.

1869
The periodic table of the elements is published.

In 1808 John Dalton published his atomic theory, in which he stated that every element is made up of atoms and that each type of atom has a unique set of properties. Dalton also showed that each element has a specific mass.

The Periodic Table

After the First International Chemical Congress met in 1860, chemists began grouping elements by atomic mass. Dmitri Mendeleev was the first to publish his groupings. The chart, known as the periodic table of the elements, showed each element's symbol and atomic mass in a clear, orderly arrangement.

More Elements

In 1911 the atomic nucleus was discovered. Protons and neutrons were discovered soon after. These discoveries led scientists to define elements not only by atomic mass but also by atomic number—the number of protons in each atom. Grouping atoms by atomic number became a feature of the periodic table.

During the rest of the 1900s, many elements were added to the periodic table. Scientists continue to find new elements. Knowledge of chemistry and atomic structure has even allowed scientists to make elements that don't occur in nature. And equipment such as the scanning tunneling microscope has made it possible to photograph the structure of some elements, revealing their ordered arrays of atoms.

THINK ABOUT IT

1. How were alchemists different from chemists?
2. Why is the number of elements in the periodic table not fixed?

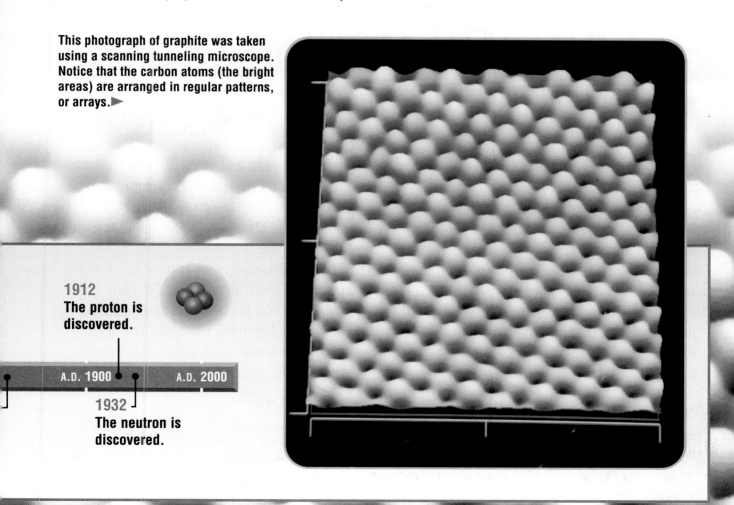

This photograph of graphite was taken using a scanning tunneling microscope. Notice that the carbon atoms (the bright areas) are arranged in regular patterns, or arrays. ▶

1912
The proton is discovered.

A.D. 1900   A.D. 2000

1932
The neutron is discovered.

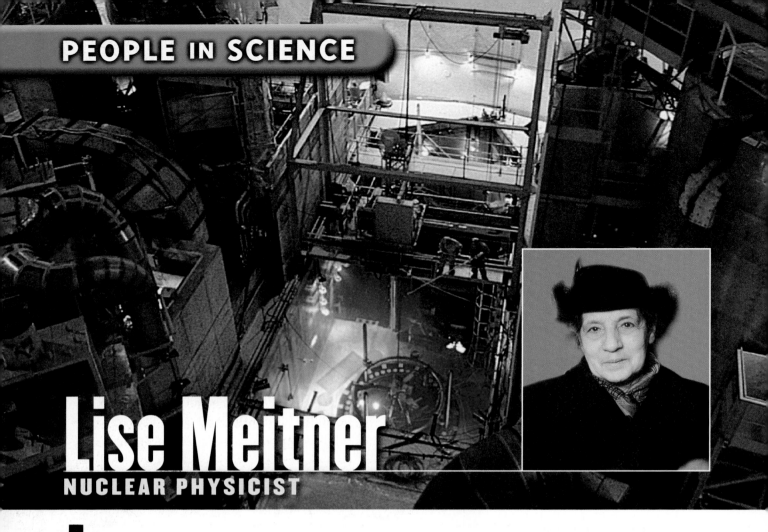

Lise Meitner
NUCLEAR PHYSICIST

Lise Meitner was a shy, quiet woman whose love of science made her go against the accepted ideas of her day. First, she insisted on going to college at a time when most women didn't even go to high school. Second, she chose to study physics, a subject that at the time was studied only by men. Third, she earned a doctoral degree, which had been given to only 13 other women in 541 years.

Born in Vienna, Austria, in 1878, Dr. Meitner grew up dreaming of becoming a scientist like Marie Curie. After finishing her doctoral studies at the University of Vienna, she went to Germany, where she worked as a researcher at the Kaiser-Wilhelm Institute in Berlin. While working there, she and chemist Otto Hahn discovered the element with atomic number 91, protactinium. After leaving Germany in 1938, Dr. Meitner continued her research in Sweden with her nephew,

Otto Frisch. It was while working with Frisch that Dr. Meitner made her most famous discovery— that the splitting of a uranium nucleus produces energy. This process is called nuclear fission and is the basis of nuclear energy.

Although Dr. Meitner's work on nuclear fission led in time to the development of the nuclear bomb, she refused to work on it. A peaceful person who had been forced to flee Germany just before World War II, she didn't want to see her discovery used to make a weapon. The development of nuclear-energy stations was more what she wanted her research to lead to.

THINK ABOUT IT

1. Why did Dr. Meitner go against the customs of her time?

2. Do you think a scientist can control the way his or her research is used? Explain.

ESCAPING GAS

How can you release dissolved gas?

Materials
- 250-mL beaker
- 200 mL carbonated soft drink
- 1 teaspoon sugar

Procedure
❶ Pour the carbonated drink into the beaker.

❷ Add the sugar.

❸ Observe what happens.

❹ Repeat the procedure with different brands of soft drinks.

Draw Conclusions
Carbonated soft drinks contain flavorings, colorings, water, and dissolved carbon dioxide gas. You probably heard some of the gas escape when you opened the can or bottle the soft drink came in. The remainder of the carbon dioxide comes out of the soft drink slowly over time. What happened when you added sugar to the drink? What do you think the foam is made of? Did different carbonated drinks behave differently when the sugar was added? Explain.

PERIODIC TABLE

Where are various elements found?

Materials
- a copy of the periodic table
- poster board
- tape
- string
- various objects, such as a helium-filled balloon, a piece of charcoal, an aluminum can, a glass bottle, garden fertilizer, an eggshell, a steel nail, an old penny, a fishing weight

Procedure
❶ Mount the periodic table on the poster board.

❷ Tape one end of a piece of string to the balloon, and the other end to *He* (helium) on the periodic table.

❸ Tape string to all the objects.

❹ Tape the other end of each string to the correct element on the periodic table.

Draw Conclusions
Which elements are found in these common objects? Why can't you find objects for all the elements on the periodic table?

Vocabulary Review

Use the terms below to complete the following passage. The page numbers in ( ) tell you where to look in the chapter if you need help.

nucleus (E39)
proton (E39)
neutron (E39)
electron (E39)
element (E40)

atom (E40)
molecule (E40)
periodic table (E47)
compound (E48)

The atomic theory states that matter is made up of tiny particles. One of these particles is called a(n) __1.__ . At the center of an atom is a tiny __2.__ . A(n) __3.__ , a positively charged subatomic particle, and a(n) __4.__ , a subatomic particle with no charge, are in the nucleus. A(n) __5.__ is a subatomic particle with a negative charge. It is found outside the nucleus. If an atom has a different number of protons from another atom, it is an atom of a different __6.__ . The elements are arranged in the __7.__ by atomic number. In nature, most elements are joined together in a(n) __8.__ . Two or more atoms joined together form a(n) __9.__ .

Connect Concepts

Using the Periodic Table, complete the table below.

Common Elements

Element	Chemical Symbol	Atomic Number	Number of Protons	Number of Electrons	Metal or Nonmetal	Example Compound
oxygen	(10)	8	(11)	(12)	(13)	(14), water
(15)	Ba	56	56	(16)	metal	$BaSO_4$, barium sulfate
(17)	S	16	(18)	(19)	nonmetal	(20), sulfur dioxide
sodium	(21)	(22)	(23)	11	(24)	(25), sodium chloride
(26)	C	(27)	(28)	(29)	nonmetal	CH_4, methane
iron	Fe	(30)	26	(31)	metal	FeO, iron oxide
(32)	(33)	(34)	1	(35)	nonmetal	(36), water
nitrogen	N	7	7	7	(37)	NH_3, ammonia
(38)	(39)	(40)	17	(41)	(42)	NaCl, sodium chloride
lead	(43)	82	(44)	82	metal	$PbSO_4$, lead sulfate

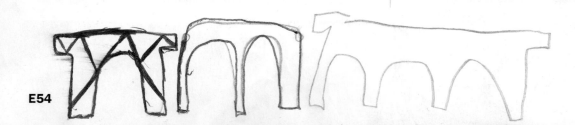

Check Understanding

Write the letter of the best choice.

45. Theories in science —
    A are based on philosophy
    B are based on experimental evidence
    C are never proved wrong
    D never change

46. The atomic theory states that matter is made up of —
    F atoms
    G earth and air
    H elements
    J earth, air, fire, and water

47. If an element has a gray luster and can be drawn into a wire, it is probably a —
    A nonmetal   C metal
    B gas   D alloy

48. What elements does the compound $MgCl_2$, magnesium chloride, contain?
    F chloride only
    G magnesium only
    H magnesium and calcium
    J magnesium and chlorine

Process Skills Review

49. What did you **observe** about the sealed box in the Lesson 1 investigation?

50. What did you **infer** about the contents and the inside shape of the sealed box?

51. What properties of elements can you **observe**?

Critical Thinking

Use the following information to answer the questions below.

- Fluorine is a pale yellow, poisonous gas. It does not conduct electricity. It has an atomic number of 9.

- Oxygen is a colorless gas. It does not conduct electricity. It has an atomic number of 8.

- Iron is a solid with a gray luster at room temperature. It is malleable and conducts electricity. It reacts with oxygen. It has an atomic number of 26.

- Sulfur is a bright yellow solid at room temperature. It is brittle and does not conduct electricity. It reacts with oxygen. It has an atomic number of 16.

- Gold is a yellow solid with a luster. It is malleable and conducts electricity. It has an atomic number of 79.

- Phosphorus can be a white solid at room temperature. It does not conduct electricity. It reacts with oxygen. It has an atomic number of 15.

52. Divide the elements into groups based on their properties. Explain how you grouped them.

53. Which of the elements are metals?

54. Which of the elements are nonmetals?

Performance Assessment

Element Detective

Divide into teams of five. Your teacher will give each student an element clue card. Using your clue, decide the name of your element. Discuss your reasoning with other members of your team. Then line up in order of atomic number.

There are many places where you can study the building blocks of matter. You can find out about the properties of matter and atoms and elements by visiting the places below. You'll also have fun while you learn.

The Discovery Center of Science & Technology

WHAT A museum featuring science exhibits and hands-on science learning

WHERE Bethlehem, Pennsylvania

WHAT CAN YOU DO THERE? See the exhibits, find out about the many activities, and ask about information that can make understanding matter simple for you.

Thomas Jefferson National Accelerator Facility

WHAT A research laboratory where the structure of matter is studied

WHERE Newport News, Virginia

WHAT CAN YOU DO THERE? Take a tour and visit the experimental labs, see the accelerator, and learn about atomic particles.

GO ONLINE Plan Your Own Expeditions

If you can't visit the Discovery Center of Science & Technology or the Thomas Jefferson National Accelerator Facility, visit a museum or research facility near you. Or log on to The Learning Site at **www.harcourtschool.com** to visit these science sites and other places where you can study the building blocks of matter.

Energy and Motion

Energy and Motion

UNIT EXPERIMENT

Changing Pitch

Energy exists in many forms, such as heat, light, and sound. One type of sound—music—can be produced by changing a sound's pitch. While you study this unit, you can conduct a long-term experiment on pitch. Here are some questions to think about. What is the relationship between pitch and the frequency of a vibrating string? For example, if the length of a string is shortened by a certain amount, will the pitch of the note be changed by an equal amount? Plan and conduct an experiment to find answers to these or other questions you have about changing pitch. See pages x–xvii for help in designing your experiment.

Forces

Have you ever wondered why things fall down instead of up? Or why you can't just keep going when you jump up? In fact, nothing just falls. Instead, everything is pulled toward the center of Earth.

Vocabulary Preview

force
friction
magnetism
gravitation
balanced forces
unbalanced forces
net force
work
power
machine

Fast Fact

The biggest problem in traveling to the moon is breaking free of Earth's gravity. A spacecraft such as this Apollo/Saturn rocket must reach a speed of about 40,000 km/hr (25,000 mi/hr) to leave Earth.

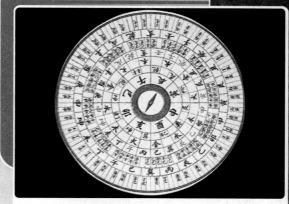

LESSON 1

What Forces Affect Objects on Earth Every Day?

In this lesson, you can . . .

INVESTIGATE magnetism.

LEARN ABOUT the forces of friction, magnetism, and gravity.

LINK to math, writing, social studies, and technology.

▲ When a magnet pulls objects to it, it exerts a force on the objects.

F4

INVESTIGATE

Magnetism

Activity Purpose Earth and everything on it are affected by forces. One of the forces that affects your life every day is magnetism. Cassette tapes, computer disks, electric motors, and televisions are just some of the things that work because of magnetism. A magnet produces a force field, called a *magnetic field,* around itself. This magnetic field affects certain objects. In this investigation you will **experiment** to find out what types of objects are affected by magnetic fields.

Materials
- test objects
- 2 bar magnets
- compass

Activity Procedure

1. Make a chart that has three columns. Label the columns *Object, Prediction,* and *Test Result.*

2. From the group of objects, choose one to test. Write the name of the object on your chart. **Predict** whether this object will be attracted, or pulled, by one of the magnets. **Record** your prediction on your chart. (Picture A)

3. Place the object on a desk. Slide a magnet slowly toward the object until the magnet touches it. In your chart, **record** whether the object is attracted to the magnet or not.

4. Repeat Steps 2 and 3 for each of the test objects.

5. Bar magnets have two different ends, called poles. One is labeled *N* for north seeking, and the other is labeled *S* for south seeking.

Observe what happens when you bring the north-seeking pole of one magnet near the south-seeking pole of another magnet. Then observe what happens when you bring two north-seeking poles or two south-seeking poles together. **Record** your observations.

6 Now place the compass on the desk. Slowly slide one of the magnets toward the compass. **Observe** what happens to the compass needle. Now move the magnet around the compass and observe what happens. **Record** your observations. (Picture B)

Picture A

Draw Conclusions

1. What characteristic of an object determines whether or not it is attracted by a magnet?

2. **Infer** what characteristic of a compass needle accounts for your observations of the compass and the magnet.

3. **Scientists at Work** Scientists often **hypothesize** about why things happen. Then they **plan and conduct investigations** to test their hypotheses. Form a hypothesis about why unlike magnetic poles attract each other while like magnetic poles repel, or push away, each other. Then plan and conduct an investigation to test your hypothesis.

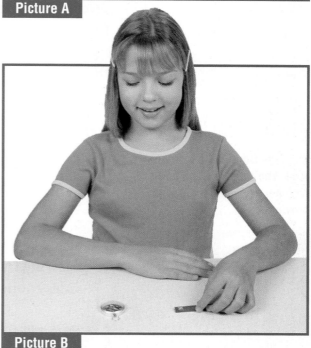
Picture B

Investigate Further **Experiment** to find out if this **hypothesis** is correct: A compass needle always points to the north.

Process Skill Tip

After you **hypothesize** about why something happens, you can **plan and conduct an investigation** to test your hypothesis.

F5

Everyday Forces

Forces

FIND OUT

- **what forces are and what they do**

- **how the forces of friction, magnetism, and gravity act in our everyday lives**

VOCABULARY

force
friction
magnetism
gravitation

In the investigation you experimented with magnetic force. A **force** is any push or pull that causes an object to move, stop, or change speed or direction. An object starts to move, stops moving, or changes speed or direction *only* when a force acts on it.

Some forces act on objects directly. When you push on a door, you directly apply the force that makes the door open. Other forces, such as gravity and magnetism, act on objects at a distance. In the investigation you saw objects move toward the magnet even if the magnet wasn't touching them. The force of the magnetic field attracted objects to the magnet.

✔ **What is a force?**

The luge (LOOZH) is a type of sled. The rider exerts a force with her arms to get the luge moving. ▼

Friction, Magnetism, and Gravity

Three of the forces that affect objects on Earth every day are friction, magnetism, and gravity. **Friction** is a force that opposes, or acts against, motion when two surfaces rub against each other. When a baseball player slides into second base, the friction of his or her legs rubbing on the dirt provides enough force to stop the slide.

There is little friction between the luge's runners and the ice. The force of gravity pulls the luge downhill. ▼

When the rider wants to stop, he pulls up on the runners and puts his feet down. The increased friction stops the luge. ▼

Earth is surrounded by a magnetic field.

Magnetic forces act along field lines. Iron filings align themselves along these lines, as shown in these photographs. When like poles are brought together (top), the lines bend away from each other. When unlike, or opposite, poles are brought together (bottom), the lines join. Lines of magnetic force never cross each other.

However, a sled on ice keeps on moving for quite a while. There is very little friction from ice.

Another force that affects us every day is magnetic force, or magnetism. **Magnetism** is the force of attraction between magnets and magnetic objects.

Every magnet has two poles. A bar magnet hanging from a string will turn so that one end points north and one points south. The end that points north is the magnet's north-seeking pole. The end that points south is the magnet's south-seeking pole.

Every magnet has a magnetic field around it. You can think of a magnetic field as lines of force that run from the north-seeking pole to the south-seeking pole of the magnet.

Why do a magnet's poles point north and south? It's because Earth is a huge magnet. On Earth the magnetic north and south poles are about 1500 km (930 mi) from the geographic North and South Poles. Earth's magnetic field causes the needle of a compass to point north and south.

The north- and south-seeking poles of two magnets attract each other—magnetic force pulls them together. But if you try to bring like poles (two north-seeking poles or two south-seeking poles) of two magnets together, they will repel each other. Magnetic force pushes them apart.

How does an object become a magnet? An iron magnet that has been broken in half becomes two magnets. This is because every piece of iron magnet has groups of atoms that produce magnetic fields. Each group has its own north and south poles. In iron that isn't a magnet, each group of atoms has a different magnetic field. These magnetic fields cancel each other out. In an iron magnet, the magnetic fields are lined up. The north-seeking poles all point in the same direction. The south-seeking poles all point in the opposite direction. So each piece of magnetized iron becomes a magnet.

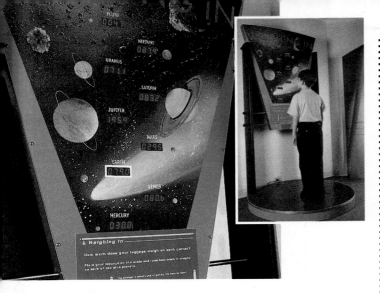

▲ A scale measures the force of gravity pulling you and Earth toward each other. Jupiter has more mass than Earth. On Jupiter the force of gravity would be much greater, and you would be much heavier.

A third force that affects objects on Earth all the time is gravity, or gravitation. **Gravitation** is the force that pulls all objects in the universe toward one another. This is the force that holds things to the surface of Earth.

Even two Ping Pong balls sitting side by side on a table pull on each other with gravitation. The force of gravity acting on them is smaller than the force of friction keeping them apart, so the balls don't move toward each other.

Earth and a Ping Pong ball pull on each other with a much stronger force, so they stay together. This is because the strength of the gravitation between two objects depends on the mass of the objects. The total mass of two Ping Pong balls is small, so the force between them is small. The total mass of a Ping Pong ball and Earth is very large, so the force between them is much larger.

The strength of gravitation between two objects also depends on the distance between the objects. When two objects are close to each other, they are pulled together by a greater force than if they were far apart. The greater the distance between two objects, the less the force of gravitation acts on them.

Earth and the moon have a lot of mass. The moon is kept in orbit around Earth by gravity. However, if Earth and the moon were much farther apart, gravity would not be enough to keep the moon in orbit around Earth.

Keep in mind that the force of gravitation between two objects pulls on *both* objects. When you toss a ball into the air, gravity pulls the ball toward

Gravitation pulls objects toward each other's centers. So the meteors both fall toward the center of Earth. ▼

Earth. Gravity also pulls Earth toward the ball. Earth, however, has so much mass that its movement toward the ball is not enough to be measured. So even though a gravitational force pulls on both objects, the smaller object does most of the moving.

✓ **What three forces affect Earth and objects on Earth every day?**

Summary

A force is a push or a pull that can make an object move, stop, or change speed or direction. Some forces are direct, while others act at a distance. Where two surfaces rub against each other, the force of friction opposes motion. Magnetism pulls magnets and magnetic objects together. Gravitation pulls objects toward each other. The strength of gravitation depends on the masses of the objects and how far apart the objects are.

Review

1. What starts an object moving or stops it if it is already moving?
2. Name three forces that affect you every day.
3. What force keeps the moon in orbit around Earth?
4. **Critical Thinking** Suppose you push a cart toward the west. In what direction does the force of friction push on the cart's wheels?
5. **Test Prep** The force of gravitation between two objects is less when —
   A the total of their masses is greater
   B friction between them is greater
   C the force of magnetism is greater
   D the distance between them is greater

Forces That Interact

Activity Purpose In Lesson 1 you learned about three forces that affect objects on Earth: gravitation, friction, and magnetism. Two or more of these forces often interact, or act at the same time. In this investigation you will **experiment** with two opposing forces—the force of gravity pulling down on an object and the force of a spring pulling up on the same object.

Materials

- clipboard
- graph paper
- tape
- ring stand
- spring
- weight
- marker

Activity Procedure

1 Tape the graph paper to the clipboard. Across the bottom of the graph paper, draw a line and label it *Seconds*. Starting at one end of the line, make a mark every 2.5 cm.

2 Tape the spring to the ring stand. Then tape the weight to the free end of the spring. Tape the marker to the bottom of the weight so that its tip points toward the back of the setup.

3 Have a partner hold the clipboard with the graph paper taped to it behind the weight. The marker point should just touch the graph paper. Pull the weight until the spring is fully stretched. (Picture A)

LESSON 2

What Are Balanced and Unbalanced Forces?

In this lesson, you can . . .

 INVESTIGATE how forces interact.

 LEARN ABOUT forces that act together.

 LINK to math, writing, physical education, and technology.

Balanced forces are at work in this pyramid.

Picture A

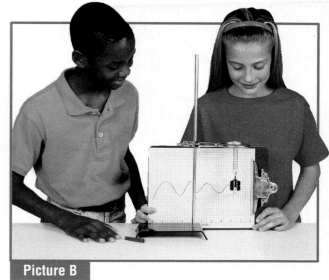
Picture B

4. Have your partner slide the clipboard across a table at a steady rate of about 2.5 cm/sec. As soon as the clipboard starts to move, drop the weight. As it bounces, it traces its movements on the graph paper. (Picture B)

5. **Interpret the data** on your graph. Identify and mark the points where the weight was not moving up or down for an instant. Identify and mark the direction (up or down) the weight was moving along each sloping line. Identify and mark the places where the weight was moving most rapidly.

Draw Conclusions

1. At what points was the weight not moving?

2. At what point was the weight moving most rapidly?

3. **Scientists at Work** Scientists often **draw conclusions** after they **interpret data** they have collected. After studying your graph, draw conclusions to answer the following question: What is the point at which the force of the spring was the greatest.

Investigate Further **Hypothesize** how your graph would look if you repeated the activity with a heavier weight. **Plan and conduct a simple experiment** to test your hypothesis.

F11

Forces That Act Together

Balanced and Unbalanced Forces

FIND OUT

- **what balanced and unbalanced forces are**
- **how to calculate the net force when more than one force acts on an object**

VOCABULARY

balanced forces
unbalanced forces
net force

In the investigation you made a graph of two forces acting on an object. Most of the time, forces act together. Imagine a car moving along a highway. Many forces are interacting in this situation. A force exerted by the ground is holding up the car. The force of gravity is pulling the car down. A force exerted by the engine is turning the wheels to make the car move forward. And the force of friction with the road and with the air around the car is holding the car back.

Sometimes the forces acting on an object balance each other. **Balanced forces** are equal in size and opposite in direction. As a result, they cancel each other out. When balanced forces act on an object, they do not change the object's motion or direction. If the object is stopped, it will remain stopped. If it is moving, it will keep moving at the same speed and in the same direction. Because balanced forces are equal in size and opposite in direction, it seems as if no force is acting on the object.

Suppose you exert a force by pushing on a very heavy object, such as a sturdy wall. The wall doesn't move because it is exerting an opposite force that exactly balances the force you exert while pushing against it. Even though the wall doesn't move, you are still exerting a force.

The force of friction and the wheelchair's mass are overcome by the force the boy exerts on the wheelchair. The forces are unbalanced, so the wheelchair moves. ▼

The force exerted by the woman pushing against the railroad car is balanced by the force of friction and the car's large mass. So the car doesn't move. ▼

40

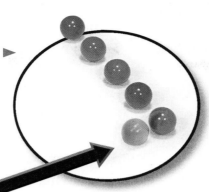

The blue marble will exert a force on the red marble, causing a change in its motion. ▶

▲ The red marble has also exerted a force on the blue marble, causing a change in its motion as well.

A bulldozer pushing against the same wall might exert a force large enough to over-come the force exerted by the wall. In this case, the forces are unbalanced. **Unbalanced forces** occur when one force is greater than its opposite force. When unbalanced forces act on an object, the object's motion changes. When the bulldozer pushes against the wall, unbalanced forces make the wall fall down.

Unbalanced forces can stop a moving object. When you catch a ball, you stop it by exerting a force greater than the force exerted by the moving ball.

Unbalanced forces can also speed up or slow down a moving object. A person riding a bicycle up a hill may be slowed by the force of gravity even though he or she exerts a strong force on the pedals of the bicycle. If the hill is steep enough, the force of gravity becomes the greater force. The forces are unbalanced, and the cyclist slows down. Once the cyclist gets to the top of the hill and starts down the other side, the unbalanced force of gravity may cause the bicycle to speed up. When unbalanced forces act on an object, the object starts to move, speeds up, slows down, stops, or changes direction.

✔ **What happens to an object's motion when unbalanced forces act on it?**

Forces Act in Pairs

The change in motion of an object is always caused by a force or forces. One place to see forces in action is in games such as marbles, billiards, or croquet.

Suppose you are playing a game with a blue marble and a red marble. The blue marble is moving, and the red marble is not. When the blue marble hits the red marble, the red marble moves. The force to move the red marble is exerted by the blue marble. But what happens to the blue marble after it hits the red one? It slows down, changes direction, or stops. A force must act on the blue marble as well. The force that acts on the blue marble is exerted by the red marble it hit.

One of the basic laws of science is this: *Forces always act in pairs.* When one object acts on a second object, the second object also acts on the first object. When you walk, your feet push against the floor. The floor also pushes against your feet, partly through the force of friction. On ice, which has less friction to push back against your feet, walking is harder.

✔ **If you see an object change its motion, what has happened to it?**

▲ Both players push with the same amount of force but in opposite directions. Their forces exactly cancel each other out, so neither player moves.

▲ The players push in opposite directions, but the player on the left pushes with greater force. The players move to the right.

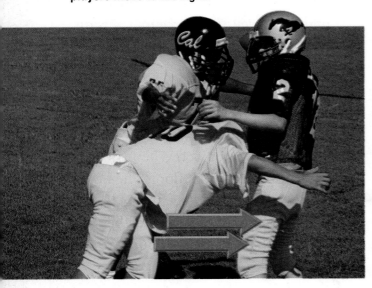

▲ The combined forces are acting in the same direction. In an instant, these forces will move the quarterback.

Net Force

When two forces act on an object at the same time, the forces may be balanced or unbalanced. Adding or subtracting the individual forces gives a value, called the **net force**, of the combined forces.

If two forces act on an object in the same direction, you add the forces to get the net force. For example, suppose two people who are moving a refrigerator push on the same side. Each pushes with a force of 120 newtons (N) toward the right.

$$\overrightarrow{120\,N} + \overrightarrow{120\,N} = \overrightarrow{240\,N}$$

The net force on the refrigerator equals 240 newtons to the right.

If two forces act on an object in opposite directions, you subtract the smaller force from the larger force to get the net force. The net force acts in the direction of the larger force.

In the case of the refrigerator, suppose the force of friction resisting the movement of the refrigerator is 100 newtons. This force acts in a direction opposite to the force acting to the right on the refrigerator.

$$\overrightarrow{240\,N} - \overleftarrow{100\,N} = \overrightarrow{140\,N}$$

The net force on the refrigerator equals 140 newtons to the right.

If two equal forces act on an object in opposite directions, the net force will be balanced and the object's motion will not change. To review the concept of net force, study the series of photographs at the left.

✔ **What is the net force when a force of 100 newtons pushes against a force of friction of 80 newtons?**

Summary

Balanced forces occur when two forces acting on an object are equal in size and opposite in direction. Unbalanced forces occur when forces acting on the same object are not opposite and equal. A net force occurs when forces are unbalanced. When you calculate the net force on an object, you must account for both the size and the direction of the forces.

Review

1. What happens to an object when balanced forces act on it?

2. A moving object speeds up. Are the forces acting on the object balanced? Explain.

3. Suppose you ride a bike along a flat, straight road at a constant speed. Are the forces acting on the bike balanced or unbalanced?

4. **Critical Thinking** Two bumper cars *collide. Both cars stop.* How do you know that a force has acted on both cars?

5. **Test Prep** Suppose a book weighs 35 newtons and you apply a force of 50 newtons to lift it. The net force acting on the book is —

   A 85 newtons, up
   B 50 newtons, up
   C 15 newtons, up
   D 35 newtons, down

LINKS

MATH LINK

Solve Problems Suppose two teams have a tug of war. The four players on Team A pull with these forces: 80 newtons (N), 120 N, 130 N, and 90 N. The four players on Team B pull with these forces: 100 N, 100 N, 90 N, and 90 N. Which team will win the tug of war?

WRITING LINK

Informative Writing—Explanation Have you ever heard the phrase "caught between a rock and a hard place"? Or "an unstoppable force meets an immovable object"? Both of these figures of speech refer to forces. What does each mean? Write a paragraph for a classmate that explains these phrases.

PHYSICAL EDUCATION LINK

Balanced Forces One type of exercise involves exerting a force against something that does not move. Press your palms together in front of your chest. Observe how balanced forces are exerted by the muscles in your arms. Design other exercises in which you exert balanced forces.

TECHNOLOGY LINK

Learn more about forces by visiting the National Air and Space Museum Internet site.
www.si.edu/harcourt/science

Smithsonian Institution®

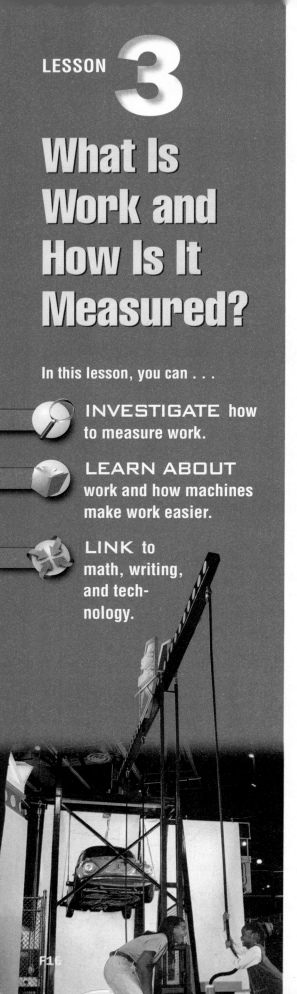

LESSON 3

What Is Work and How Is It Measured?

In this lesson, you can . . .

INVESTIGATE how to measure work.

LEARN ABOUT work and how machines make work easier.

LINK to math, writing, and technology.

◄ How much force does it take to lift a car?

INVESTIGATE

Measuring Work

Activity Purpose In Lesson 2 you learned that unbalanced forces affect the motion of an object. We say that an unbalanced force does *work* on the object it moves. In this investigation you will **measure** forces and **calculate** the amount of work done when you move objects, because work cannot be measured directly.

Materials

- heavy object
- spring scale
- meterstick
- flight of stairs
- calculator

Activity Procedure

1 Copy the table below.

Work			
Trial	Weight (newtons)	Height (meters)	Work (joules)
1			
2			
3			
4			

2 Weigh the object using the spring scale and **record** its weight in the table, next to *Trial 1*. (Picture A)

3 **Measure** the total height of the stairs in meters. **Record** the measurement in the table, also next to *Trial 1*. (Picture B)

F16

4 Work can be calculated as the product of force (in newtons) and distance (in meters). **Calculate** the number of newton-meters, or *joules*, of work you would do if you carried the object up the flight of stairs. **Record** the product in the table.

5 Suppose you carried the object up two flights of stairs. Beside *Trial 2* on the table, **record** the new height and **calculate** the work done.

6 For *Trial 3*, **calculate** how much work you would do if you carried the object up three flights every day for a week.

7 For *Trial 4,* suppose your weight is 300 newtons. **Record** this new data and **calculate** the work you do climbing the stairs without carrying the object.

Picture A

Picture B

Draw Conclusions

1. **Compare** the amount of work a person weighing 300 newtons does climbing one flight of stairs to the total amount of work the same person does climbing three flights of stairs every day for a week.

2. **Interpret** your **data**, and **draw conclusions** about how work is related to force and distance.

3. **Scientists at Work** When scientists **interpret data**, they often **draw conclusions** based on the data they collected. What can you conclude about the amount of work done by people who weigh more than 300 newtons?

Investigate Further *Power* is the measure of how quickly work is done. You can measure power in *joules per second.* **Hypothesize** about how much power you use walking up a flight of stairs compared to running up a flight of stairs. Then **plan and conduct an experiment** to test your hypothesis.

Process Skill Tip

When you **interpret data**, you should look for patterns in the results. You can then **draw conclusions** based on those patterns.

Work and Power

Work and Effort

FIND OUT

- how work is defined and measured
- how power is defined and measured
- what machines do

VOCABULARY

work
power
machine

How was work today? Have you finished your homework? You've probably heard questions like these before, but to a scientist, work may be somewhat different than what you're familiar with. To understand how scientists define *work*, think about the following situation.

Suppose a gardener is trying to pull an old tree stump out of the ground. He pulls and pulls until his face is red and he is soaked in sweat. But the stump doesn't move. Nearby a little girl on a tricycle rides from one corner of the block to the next, passing the gardener along the way. Who is exerting more effort? Who is doing work?

The gardener is clearly exerting more effort than the girl, because he is applying a much larger force. But according to the way scientists define *work*, he has done no work. **Work** is the use of a force to move an object through a distance. The girl, on the other hand, moves herself and her tricycle along the sidewalk. According to the definition, she has done work.

✔ **What is work?**

It takes the same amount of work to lift one piano two floors as it does to lift two pianos one floor. The table below shows how much work is done moving a piano in different situations.

Work Needed to Lift Pianos

Object to Be Moved	Force Needed (Weight of Object)	Distance to Be Moved	Work Done (Force × Distance)
1 piano	1000 N	1 floor (4 m)	1000 × 4 = 4000 J
1 piano	1000 N	2 floors (8 m)	1000 × 8 = 8000 J
2 pianos	2000 N	1 floor (4 m)	2000 × 4 = 8000 J
2 pianos	2000 N	2 floors (8 m)	2000 × 8 = 16,000 J

Calculating Work and Power

In the investigation you used a scale to measure force and you used a meterstick to measure distance. From these measurements you calculated the amount of work done. To calculate the amount of work done, multiply the force used to move an object by the distance the object moves.

The metric unit of work is the *joule* (JOOL). One joule is equal to a force of 1 newton exerted over a distance of 1 meter. For example, 1 joule is the amount of work it takes to lift a 1-newton weight 1 meter off the ground.

An average fifth grader does about 200 joules of work getting out of bed in the morning. When a 1000-newton (N) (about 225-lb) basketball star jumps 1 m (about 3 ft) to slam-dunk the ball, he or she does about 1000 joules (J) of work.

$$1000 \text{ N} \times 1 \text{ m} = 1000 \text{ J}$$

An average adult could probably push a small car along a flat road. The car's engine could also move the car along the same road. Even though the person and the engine do the same amount of work, the engine can do the work much more quickly. The engine has more power than a person. **Power** is the amount of work done for each unit of time. It is a measure of how quickly someone or something does work.

The metric unit of power is the *watt*. One watt is equal to doing 1 joule of work in 1 second. For example, lifting an apple

▲ The car's engine can produce about 100,000 watts of power. A well-trained bicycle racer can produce about 400 watts of power for a few seconds. A relaxed bicycle ride might use only 100 watts of power for the same period of time.

1 m requires about 1 joule of work. To lift that apple 1 m in 1 second takes about 1 watt (W) of power.

A person who weighs about 400 newtons (90 lb) does about 1200 joules of work climbing a 3-m (about 10-ft) flight of stairs.

$$400 \text{ N} \times 3 \text{ m} = 1200 \text{ J}$$

To run up the stairs in 3 seconds takes about 400 watts of power.

$$1200 \text{ J} \div 3 \text{ sec} = 400 \text{ J/sec} = 400 \text{ W}$$

✔ **Which requires more power, walking up a flight of stairs or running up the same flight of stairs? Explain.**

Machines and Work

The movers do a lot of work lifting a piano. But they can make this task easier for themselves by using a machine. A **machine** is something that makes a task easier by changing the size or direction of a force or the distance over which the force acts. There are six simple machines: pulley, lever, inclined plane, wedge, screw, and wheel and axle.

A machine makes a task seem easier by changing force into distance or distance into force. Using pulleys, for example, a person can lift a 1000-newton piano using only 100 newtons of force. But to lift the piano 1 m with the pulleys, that person would need to have a rope 10 m long.

$$1000 \text{ N} \times 1 \text{ m} = 1000 \text{ J}$$

$$100 \text{ N} \times 10 \text{ m} = 1000 \text{ J}$$

Pulleys, like all machines, do *not* reduce the amount of work to be done. The amount of work needed to lift the 1000-newton piano 1 m is still 1000 joules. Instead, a machine allows a person to do the same amount of work by exerting a smaller force over a longer distance. Other machines, such as a lever, allow a person to exert a larger force over a shorter distance. A lever increases the force, rather than the distance as the pulley did. Machines can also change the direction of a force. A screw with a wheel and axle, for example, can change a twisting force into a downward force.

✓ **A certain machine reduces the amount of force needed to move an object. What must it do to the distance through which the force is exerted?**

This strange machine makes use of many simple machines. Some of these are labeled and described.

A fixed pulley doesn't increase force or distance. Instead, it changes the direction of the force.

This wedge takes a downward force and changes it to an outward force to crack the egg.

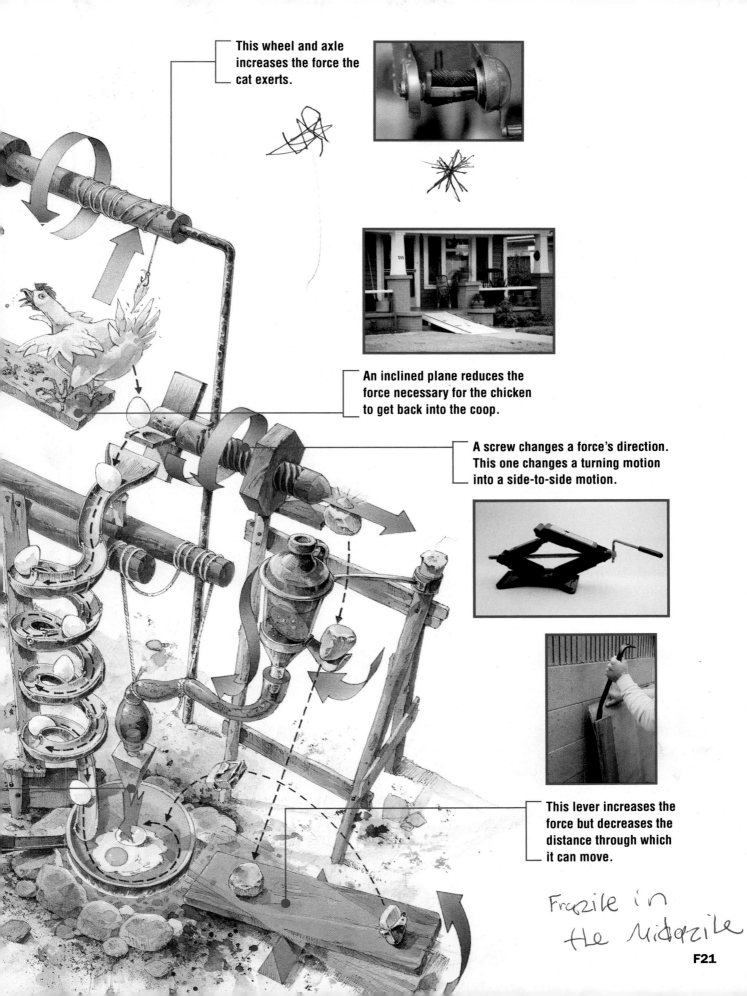

This wheel and axle increases the force the cat exerts.

An inclined plane reduces the force necessary for the chicken to get back into the coop.

A screw changes a force's direction. This one changes a turning motion into a side-to-side motion.

This lever increases the force but decreases the distance through which it can move.

Frazile in the Midezile

Everyday Machines

Most of the machines people use are compound machines. That is, they are made up of two or more simple machines. For example, a shovel is a wedge at the end of a lever. A hand-cranked pencil sharpener uses a wheel and axle to turn a set of wedges that cut.

Even a water faucet is made up of several simple machines. When you turn a faucet on or off, you are turning a wheel and axle that is attached to a metal screw. The metal screw is, in turn, attached to a rubber wedge.

Turning on a faucet lifts the rubber wedge, called a *washer*, and allows the water to flow. The more you turn the handle, the larger the opening becomes, allowing more water to flow.

When you turn the faucet off, the force of your hand turning the wheel and axle is moved along the screw threads. This presses the rubber wedge back down into its seat, stopping the flow of water.

✔ **What simple machines are part of a water faucet?**

THE INSIDE STORY

A Not-So-Simple Machine

The handle of the faucet is a wheel and axle—a type of lever. The larger the handle, the easier it is to turn.

The screw inside the faucet changes the turning force of the handle into a downward force. It also increases the force.

The rubber washer is a kind of wedge. It changes the downward force of the screw into an outward force that presses the rubber against the metal seat.

Summary

Work is the force applied to an object times the distance the object is moved. Work is measured in joules. Power is a measure of the speed at which work is done. Power is measured in watts. Machines are devices that make a task easier by changing the size or direction of a force. Pulleys, levers, wheels and axles, inclined planes, wedges, and screws are simple machines.

Review

1. How much work is done if you lift a 20-newton weight 10 meters?

2. Which involves speed—work or power?

3. Look at the table on page F18. How much power is needed to lift 1 piano 1 floor in 10 seconds?

4. **Critical Thinking** Explain how a set of pulleys could help the gardener mentioned on page F18 remove the tree stump.

5. **Test Prep** The amount of power needed to do 10 joules of work in 1 second is —

   A 1 watt

   B 10 joules

   C 10 watts

   D 1000 watts

LINKS

MATH LINK

Multiply Decimals The top of the Washington Monument is about 150 m above the ground. Gravity pulls on each pound of your body with a force of about 4.5 newtons. Calculate the amount of work you would do in climbing the stairs to the top of the Washington Monument. About how much power would you use if you climbed those stairs in 5 minutes?

WRITING LINK

Informative Writing—Compare and Contrast Write out definitions of *work* and *power* as you learned them in this lesson. Use each word in a sentence that clearly shows what the word means. Then look up the common meanings of these words in a dictionary. Write a paragraph for each word, comparing its everyday meaning with its scientific meaning. Then read the paragraph to your family.

GO ONLINE TECHNOLOGY LINK

Learn more about simple machines by visiting the Harcourt Learning Site. **www.harcourtschool.com**

WELCOME TO THE LEARNING SITE

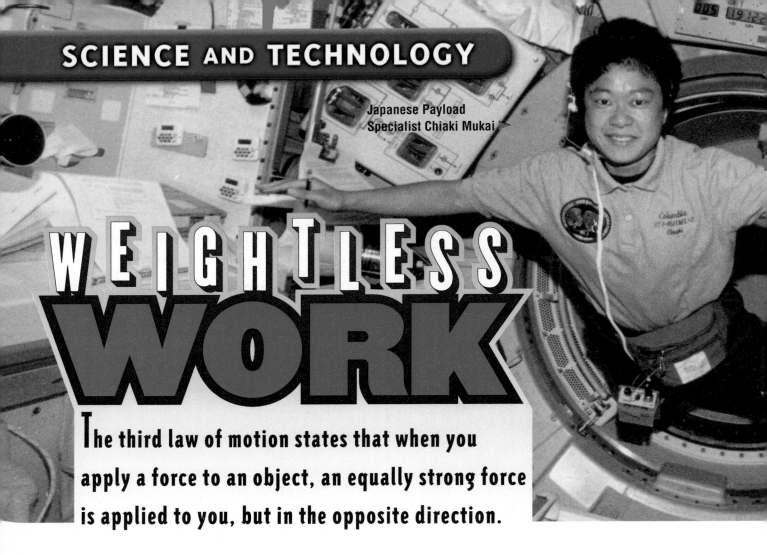

Japanese Payload Specialist Chiaki Mukai

WEIGHTLESS WORK

The third law of motion states that when you apply a force to an object, an equally strong force is applied to you, but in the opposite direction.

In Space, the Force Is Still With You

In space, a simple job—like loosening or tightening a screw—becomes a difficult task because your body tends to twist. On Earth, gravity keeps you firmly on the ground, so it's easy to resist the twisting. But in space, there is almost no gravity to hold you in place. Astronauts working in microgravity, as it is called, must use their arms or legs to brace themselves against something solid.

To build structures in space, engineers and scientists have developed new ways of working and new tools to work with. Working in space poses other problems, too. Joe Allen, who has spent more time working in space than any other American astronaut, says the pressurized space suits that astro-nauts wear squeeze you. "Every movement takes a lot of energy. The best way to get used to working in space," Allen says, "is to practice on Earth."

Practice in a Pool

Where do astronauts find a microgravity environment on Earth? In the Neutral Buoyancy Laboratory (NBL), the world's biggest swimming pool, located at the Johnson Space Center in Houston, Texas.

Six meters (about 20 ft) under water in the NBL, astronauts wearing space suits float as if they were in space. The NBL is big enough to hold a full-size model of the space shuttle cargo bay, so astronauts can spend several hours every day working in microgravity.

The RMS can be operated remotely. That means an astronaut inside a space shuttle can use simple hand controls (like joy sticks) to maneuver bulky cargo, such as satellites or parts of the International Space Station. Using cameras to guide the RMS, astronauts can make the fine movements needed to line up and connect huge pieces of the space station.

THINK ABOUT IT

1. Why are simple jobs, such as tightening or loosening screws, difficult in space?
2. Astronauts practicing in the Neutral Buoyancy Laboratory wear space suits filled with air. Why do you think they wear space suits in the water?

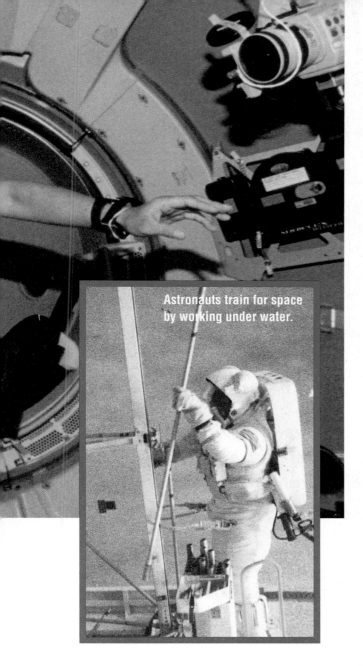

Astronauts train for space by working under water.

Working with the RMS

Astronauts need more than just practice to work in space. They need special tools, too. One of the most useful tools is the Remote Manipulator System, or RMS. Sometimes called the shuttle "arm," it was built for NASA by Canadian engineers. The RMS looks like the cranes used on construction sites on Earth, but it is much more than a crane. The RMS has a large grasping "hand" and joints that act like human wrist, elbow, and shoulder joints.

CAREERS
MISSION SPECIALIST

What They Do
Mission specialists perform the scientific experiments and construction projects on space shuttle flights.

Education and Training
Most astronauts have advanced degrees in sciences such as physics, chemistry, engineering, and medicine. Mission specialists also go through months or years of training for the specialized tasks they will perform in space.

▲ Mae Jemison

WEB LINK
For Science and Technology updates, visit the Harcourt Internet site.
www.harcourtschool.com

Ephraim Fischbach

PHYSICIST

"On the whole, the recent experiments do not point to the existence of a new force, although a number of the existing anomalies [unusual things] remain to be explained."

Among the most important ideas of modern science are the laws of motion. Although these laws were formulated in the 1600s, they are still used to calculate orbits for satellites and flight paths for space probes. The first three laws describe motion, and the fourth law describes gravity.

Is it possible that, in some cases, the fourth law might be wrong? Physics professor Ephraim Fischbach and a group of researchers at Purdue University have tried to answer that question for years. The scientists studied the idea that a force other than gravity might be at work in certain situations. Predictions based on the law of universal gravitation may not be accurate over all distances. So far, Dr. Fischbach's group has not found enough evidence to support the existence of what they hypothesize as a "fifth force." But

they have discovered exceptions to the fourth law that no one can explain yet.

In addition to being a professor and research scientist, Dr. Fischbach has also worked to develop the Physics Funfest, a physics show put on every year for people who live near the university. The shows have been so popular that they are now being taken to schools throughout Indiana. Dr. Fischbach has also worked on a project to establish a science and technology center at Purdue University, which will include a hands-on museum.

THINK ABOUT IT

1. What is the fourth law of motion?
2. Why is it important for scientists to continue testing ideas that are considered to be "laws" of science?

MAKING MAGNETS

How does an object become a magnet?

Materials

- compass
- sewing needle
- small piece of thin Styrofoam
- shallow bowl of water
- bar magnet

Procedure

1 Put the compass on the table. Observe the direction the north-seeking end points to.

2 Put the needle on the piece of Styrofoam, and float it in the bowl of water. Observe which way the needle points.

3 Now stroke the needle with the bar magnet.

4 Put the needle back on the floating Styrofoam. Which way does the needle point?

Draw Conclusions

Does the needle act like a compass in Step 2? Does it act like a compass in Step 4? How did you turn the needle into a magnet?

CENTER OF GRAVITY

How can you find an object's center of gravity?

Materials

- 10-cm square of paper
- flat toothpick
- 30 cm of 24-gauge wire
- cardboard cutout of your state

Procedure

1 Fold the paper in half, and then in half again. Balance the paper on your finger.

2 Balance the toothpick on your finger.

3 Straighten out the wire. Then fold the wire in

half. Wrap the midpoint of the wire tightly around the toothpick. Now balance the toothpick on your finger.

4 Using the cardboard cutout and what you have learned about balancing objects, find the geographic center of your state.

Draw Conclusions

An object's center of gravity is the point at which the force of gravity is evenly balanced. Where is the center of gravity of the toothpick? When you added weight (the wire) to the toothpick, what happened to its center of gravity? How did the cardboard cutout's center of gravity help you find the geographic center of your state?

Vocabulary Review

Use the terms below to complete the sentences. The page numbers in ( ) tell you where to look in the chapter if you need help.

force (F6)
friction (F6)
magnetism (F7)
gravitation (F8)
balanced forces (F12)
unbalanced forces (F13)

net force (F14)
work (F18)
power (F19)
machine (F20)

1. A _____ is a push or a pull and can make an object stop, speed up, slow down, or change direction.

2. The force of _____ attracts all objects toward each other.

3. When an object's motion changes, you know that the forces acting on it are _____.

4. A _____ makes a task easier by trading force for distance.

5. A force that acts on an object does _____ only when the object moves.

6. _____ act on an object without causing a change in the object's motion.

7. The watt is a unit of _____, which is a measure of how quickly work is done.

8. _____ is a force of attraction between magnets and magnetic objects.

9. When you slide one object over another, the force of _____ acts in the opposite direction.

10. Adding or subtracting individual forces gives a combined force called a _____.

Connect Concepts

Write the vocabulary terms or units that complete the concept map.

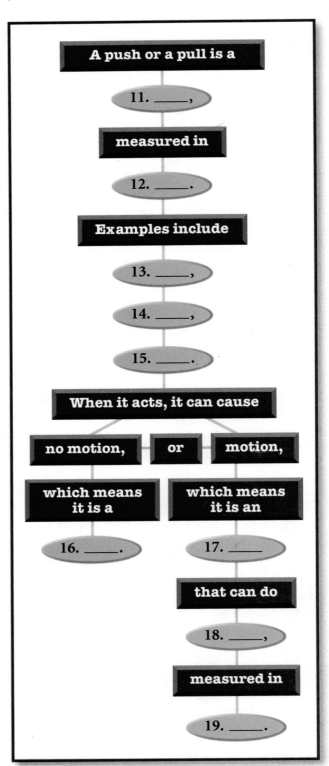

A push or a pull is a

11. _____,

measured in

12. _____.

Examples include

13. _____,

14. _____,

15. _____.

When it acts, it can cause

no motion,   or   motion,

which means it is a

which means it is an

16. _____.

17. _____

that can do

18. _____,

measured in

19. _____.

The greater a planet's mass, the greater its gravity. The table shows how much you would weigh on some planets if you weighed 100 pounds on Earth. An astronaut's weight on the moon is about $\frac{1}{6}$ his or her weight on Earth.

Weight on Planets

Planet	Weight (pounds)	Mass (kilograms)
Earth	100	45
Jupiter	264	45
Saturn	115	45
Venus	88	45
Mars	38	45
Pluto	0.6	45

Fast Fact

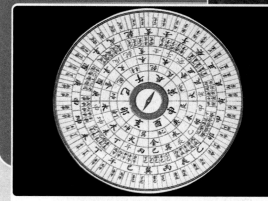

The earliest recorded use of magnetic compasses was on Chinese ships, around 1100. A small lodestone, a naturally magnetic rock, was probably placed on a piece of wood floating in a bowl of water. This compass was made about 1900.

Observe what happens when you bring the north-seeking pole of one magnet near the south-seeking pole of another magnet. Then observe what happens when you bring two north-seeking poles or two south-seeking poles together. **Record** your observations.

6 Now place the compass on the desk. Slowly slide one of the magnets toward the compass. **Observe** what happens to the compass needle. Now move the magnet around the compass and observe what happens. **Record** your observations. (Picture B)

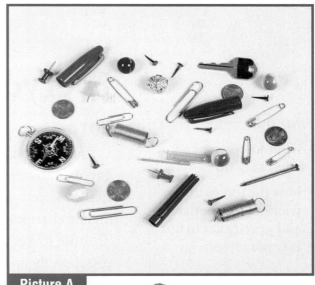
Picture A

Draw Conclusions

1. What characteristic of an object determines whether or not it is attracted by a magnet?

2. **Infer** what characteristic of a compass needle accounts for your observations of the compass and the magnet.

3. **Scientists at Work** Scientists often **hypothesize** about why things happen. Then they **plan and conduct investigations** to test their hypotheses. Form a hypothesis about why unlike magnetic poles attract each other while like magnetic poles repel, or push away, each other. Then plan and conduct an investigation to test your hypothesis.

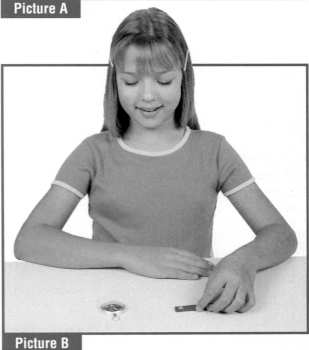
Picture B

Investigate Further **Experiment** to find out if this **hypothesis** is correct: A compass needle always points to the north.

Process Skill Tip

After you **hypothesize** about why something happens, you can **plan and conduct an investigation** to test your hypothesis.

Earth. Gravity also pulls Earth toward the ball. Earth, however, has so much mass that its movement toward the ball is not enough to be measured. So even though a gravitational force pulls on both objects, the smaller object does most of the moving.

✔ **What three forces affect Earth and objects on Earth every day?**

Summary

A force is a push or a pull that can make an object move, stop, or change speed or direction. Some forces are direct, while others act at a distance. Where two surfaces rub against each other, the force of friction opposes motion. Magnetism pulls magnets and magnetic objects together. Gravitation pulls objects toward each other. The strength of gravitation depends on the masses of the objects and how far apart the objects are.

Review

1. What starts an object moving or stops it if it is already moving?
2. Name three forces that affect you every day.
3. What force keeps the moon in orbit around Earth?
4. **Critical Thinking** Suppose you push a cart toward the west. In what direction does the force of friction push on the cart's wheels?
5. **Test Prep** The force of gravitation between two objects is less when —
   A the total of their masses is greater
   B friction between them is greater
   C the force of magnetism is greater
   D the distance between them is greater

LINKS

MATH LINK

Display Data In the United States, we measure weight in pounds. However, scientists everywhere measure weight in newtons. Gravity pulls on a 1-lb object with a force of about 4.5 newtons. Make a table that shows the weights of several objects in pounds and in newtons.

WRITING LINK

Informative Writing—Classification Every day you are affected by the forces of gravitation, friction, and magnetism. These forces start objects moving, stop objects that are already moving, and change the speed or direction of moving objects. For one day, keep a journal for your own use. Record and classify the forces you see in action.

SOCIAL STUDIES LINK

Magnetic North Earth's magnetic north pole is about 1500 km from its geographic North Pole (the point through which Earth's imaginary axis passes). Research the location of the magnetic north pole, and make a map that shows that location.

TECHNOLOGY LINK

Learn more about the effects of gravity by viewing *Microgravity* on the **Harcourt Science Newsroom Video.**

CNN
Turner
Le@rning

F9

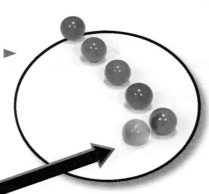
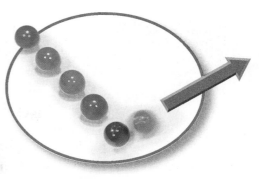

The blue marble will exert a force on the red marble, causing a change in its motion. ▶

▲ **The red marble has also exerted a force on the blue marble, causing a change in its motion as well.**

A bulldozer pushing against the same wall might exert a force large enough to overcome the force exerted by the wall. In this case, the forces are unbalanced. **Unbalanced forces** occur when one force is greater than its opposite force. When unbalanced forces act on an object, the object's motion changes. When the bulldozer pushes against the wall, unbalanced forces make the wall fall down.

Unbalanced forces can stop a moving object. When you catch a ball, you stop it by exerting a force greater than the force exerted by the moving ball.

Unbalanced forces can also speed up or slow down a moving object. A person riding a bicycle up a hill may be slowed by the force of gravity even though he or she exerts a strong force on the pedals of the bicycle. If the hill is steep enough, the force of gravity becomes the greater force. The forces are unbalanced, and the cyclist slows down. Once the cyclist gets to the top of the hill and starts down the other side, the unbalanced force of gravity may cause the bicycle to speed up. When unbalanced forces act on an object, the object starts to move, speeds up, slows down, stops, or changes direction.

✓ **What happens to an object's motion when unbalanced forces act on it?**

Forces Act in Pairs

The change in motion of an object is always caused by a force or forces. One place to see forces in action is in games such as marbles, billiards, or croquet.

Suppose you are playing a game with a blue marble and a red marble. The blue marble is moving, and the red marble is not. When the blue marble hits the red marble, the red marble moves. The force to move the red marble is exerted by the blue marble. But what happens to the blue marble after it hits the red one? It slows down, changes direction, or stops. A force must act on the blue marble as well. The force that acts on the blue marble is exerted by the red marble it hit.

One of the basic laws of science is this: *Forces always act in pairs.* When one object acts on a second object, the second object also acts on the first object. When you walk, your feet push against the floor. The floor also pushes against your feet, partly through the force of friction. On ice, which has less friction to push back against your feet, walking is harder.

✓ **If you see an object change its motion, what has happened to it?**

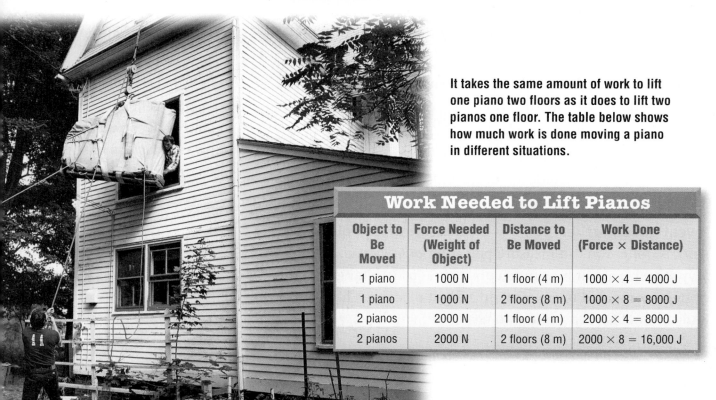

Everyday Machines

Most of the machines people use are compound machines. That is, they are made up of two or more simple machines. For example, a shovel is a wedge at the end of a lever. A hand-cranked pencil sharpener uses a wheel and axle to turn a set of wedges that cut.

Even a water faucet is made up of several simple machines. When you turn a faucet on or off, you are turning a wheel and axle that is attached to a metal screw. The metal screw is, in turn, attached to a rubber wedge.

Turning on a faucet lifts the rubber wedge, called a *washer*, and allows the water to flow. The more you turn the handle, the larger the opening becomes, allowing more water to flow.

When you turn the faucet off, the force of your hand turning the wheel and axle is moved along the screw threads. This presses the rubber wedge back down into its seat, stopping the flow of water.

✔ **What simple machines are part of a water faucet?**

THE INSIDE STORY

A Not-So-Simple Machine

The handle of the faucet is a wheel and axle—a type of lever. The larger the handle, the easier it is to turn.

The screw inside the faucet changes the turning force of the handle into a downward force. It also increases the force.

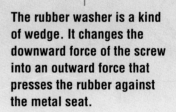

The rubber washer is a kind of wedge. It changes the downward force of the screw into an outward force that presses the rubber against the metal seat.

Check Understanding

Write the letter of the best choice.

20. When a leaf falls from a tree, the force acting on the leaf is —

   A friction   **C** magnetism

   B gravitation   **D** balanced

21. You can exert a force on an object, but only if the object moves do you —

   F make an effort   **H** do work

   G feel gravity   **J** exert power

22. When two forces act on an object in opposite directions and the object moves, it moves in the direction of the —

   A friction   **C** magnetic field

   B smaller force   **D** greater force

23. If you lift a 200-newton crate 1 meter off the floor, how much work do you do?

   F 100 joules   **H** 2000 joules

   G 200 joules   **J** 600 joules

24. The north and south poles of two magnets —

   A repel each other

   B magnetize each other

   C align with each other

   D attract each other

Critical Thinking

25. An object is not moving. Can you conclude that no forces are acting on it? Explain.

26. A dog chases a cat up a flight of stairs. The cat runs faster than the dog and gets away. Can you conclude that the cat is more powerful than the dog? Explain.

Process Skills Review

27. Compare the forces of gravitation and magnetism.

28. Hypothesize about whether your weight would be greater or less on top of Mount Everest than at sea level.

29. A line graph shows the speed of a race car during a short race. The horizontal axis shows time. The vertical axis shows speed. How would you **interpret the data** to identify the points at which the brakes were exerting the greatest force on the car's wheels?

30. Jamal and Janet climbed Mount Equinox together. Jamal weighs 120 newtons more than Janet. What can you **conclude** about who did more work?

Performance Assessment

Forces at Work

Slide a brick down an inclined plane. Analyze the forces that act on the brick as it slides and after it stops at the bottom of the ramp. Include as much detail as possible about the forces and the work they do. You may want to draw a diagram to help you communicate your findings.

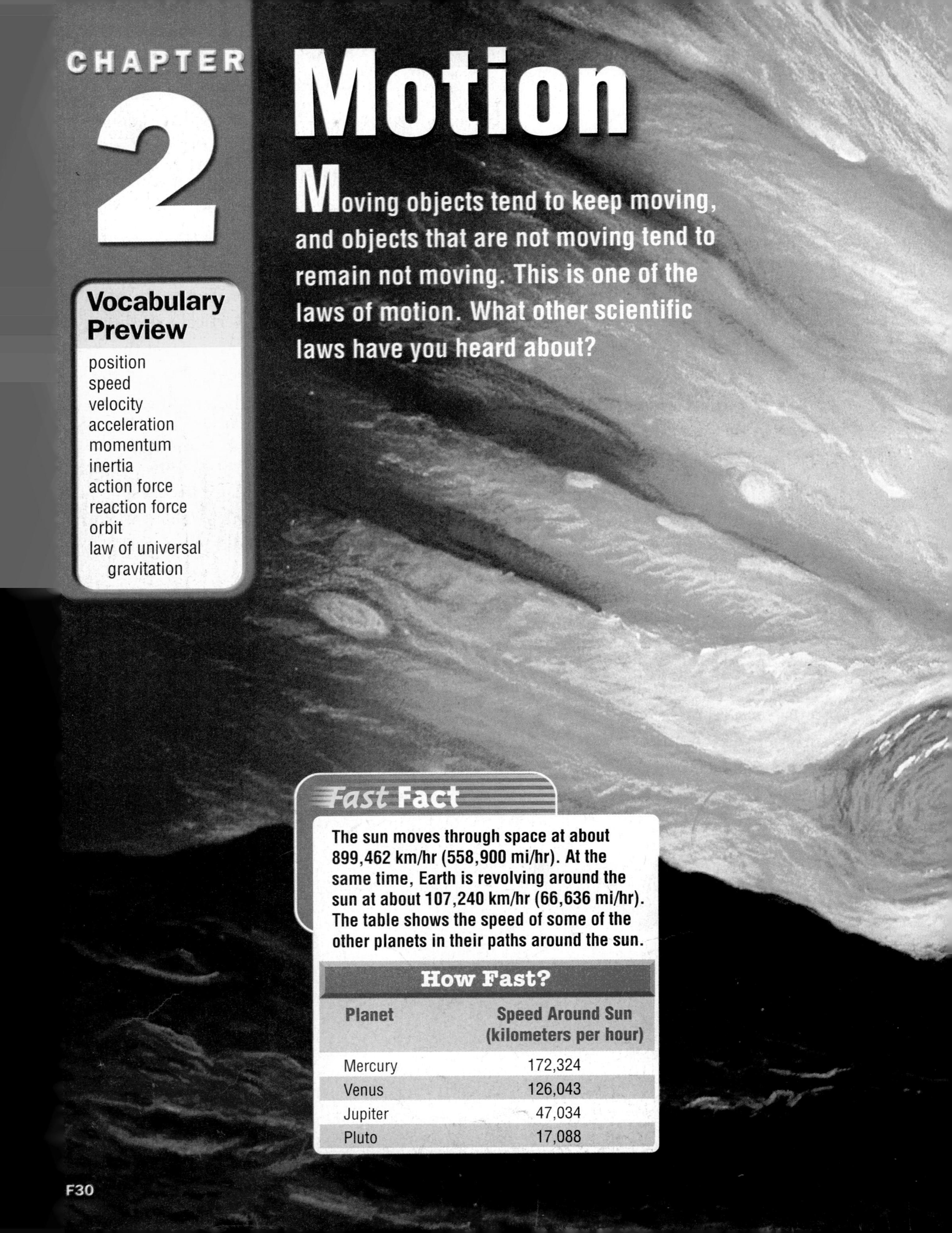

Motion

Moving objects tend to keep moving, and objects that are not moving tend to remain not moving. This is one of the laws of motion. What other scientific laws have you heard about?

Vocabulary Preview

position
speed
velocity
acceleration
momentum
inertia
action force
reaction force
orbit
law of universal
    gravitation

Fast Fact

The sun moves through space at about 899,462 km/hr (558,900 mi/hr). At the same time, Earth is revolving around the sun at about 107,240 km/hr (66,636 mi/hr). The table shows the speed of some of the other planets in their paths around the sun.

How Fast?

Planet	Speed Around Sun (kilometers per hour)
Mercury	172,324
Venus	126,043
Jupiter	47,034
Pluto	17,088

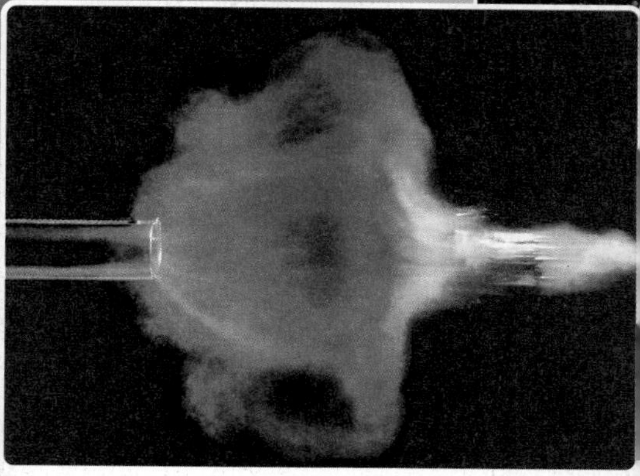

If a rifle is fired horizontally and a bullet is dropped from the same height at the same time, both bullets will hit the ground at the same time. The force of gravity is the same for both.

Jupiter from one
of its moons

A hovercraft floats on a cushion of air. The lack of friction means there are no brakes. The only way to stop it is to turn off the engine—or run into something.

How Are Motion and Speed Related?

In this lesson, you can . . .

INVESTIGATE the effects of changes in motion.

LEARN ABOUT speed, velocity, acceleration, and momentum.

LINK to math, writing, social studies, and technology.

The cheetah is the fastest land animal. Unlike most animals, it can change direction while running at top speed. ▼

INVESTIGATE

Changes in Motion

Activity Purpose Have you ever had to stand on a moving train or bus? It's hard to keep your balance when the vehicle starts, stops, speeds up, slows down, or turns. While standing on the moving train or bus, your body senses changes in direction and speed. In this investigation you will build and use a simple device to help you **observe** changes in motion.

Materials
- clear plastic bottle with cap
- water
- small piece of soap

Activity Procedure

1 Fill the bottle nearly to the top with water. Leave only enough space for a small air bubble. Add a small piece of soap to the water. This will keep the air bubble from sticking to the side of the bottle. Put the cap tightly on the bottle.

2 Lay the bottle on its side on a flat surface. You should see one small bubble in the bottle. Hold the bottle steady until the bubble moves to the center of the bottle and stays there. (Picture A)

3 **Predict** what will happen to the air bubble if you turn the bottle to the left or right. Turn the bottle and **observe** what happens. **Record** your observations.

Picture A

Picture B

4 Now **predict** what will happen to the air bubble if you move the bottle straight ahead at a steady speed. Move the bottle and **observe** what happens. **Record** your observations. (Picture B)

5 Repeat Step 4, but this time slowly increase the bottle's speed. **Observe** what happens to the air bubble. **Record** your observations.

Draw Conclusions

1. **Compare** your predictions and your observations. What happened when you turned the bottle to the left or right, or moved it forward?

2. From what you **observed**, how did a change in speed affect the bubble?

3. **Scientists at Work** Were you surprised by the way the air bubble moved? When scientists get surprising results, they often **hypothesize** about the cause of those results. Form a hypothesis about why the bubble moves the way it does.

Investigate Further **Hypothesize** about what will happen to the air bubble if the bottle is moving at a steady speed and its direction changes. **Plan and conduct an experiment** to test your hypothesis.

> ### Process Skill Tip
>
> As you investigate, you will often be surprised by what happens. **Hypothesize** about the causes of surprising results. Doing so can advance your thinking and increase your understanding.

Motion and Speed

Position and Motion

In the investigation you built a device that detected changes in motion. To observe motion, you must first determine an object's position. **Position** is an object's place, or location. If an object's position is changing, the object is in motion. However, whether you observe the motion depends on your *frame of reference*. That is, you must be able to observe the motion against a background that is *not* moving. For example, if you see a roller coaster moving, your frame of reference includes the track and the background, which are not moving.

For some objects in motion, several different frames of reference are possible. Suppose a person is sitting in a chair, reading a book. To the person reading, the book is not moving. But if the person reading the book is on a train, a person outside the train sees the book moving. The two people have different frames of reference. Suppose a third person is on a train going in the opposite direction. That person sees the book from yet another frame of reference. The motion of any object depends on your motion when you observe the object.

✓ **Why does motion need a frame of reference?**

FIND OUT

- the relationships among speed, velocity, acceleration, and momentum

- how speed, velocity, acceleration, and momentum are measured

VOCABULARY

position
speed
velocity
acceleration
momentum

Suppose you're observing this hiker. To decide whether she's moving or not, you need to compare her positions on the ground at two different times. ▶

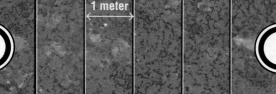

Speed				
Interval	0–6 m	6–16 m	16–22 m	22–30 m
Distance	6 m	10 m	6 m	8 m
Time	12 sec	5 sec	9 sec	32 sec
Speed (D/T)	0.5 m/sec	2 m/sec	0.67 m/sec	0.25 m/sec

As she moves down the hill, her speed increases. Her speed changes again when she reaches the bottom of the hill. It changes once more when she starts up the next hill.

1 meter

Speed and Velocity

One way to describe the motion of an object is to describe its speed. **Speed** is a measure of the distance an object moves in a given amount of time. Suppose you roll a ball along a sidewalk. If it travels 3 m in 1 sec, its speed is 3 m/sec.

In 5 sec, the ball's speed will probably vary. The ball starts fast and then slows down. *Average speed* is the total distance an object moves divided by the total amount of time. If the ball rolls 10 m in 5 sec, its average speed is calculated as follows:

$$10 \text{ m} \div 5 \text{ sec} = 2 \text{ m/sec.}$$

The motions of two cars going east at the same speed are the same. But if one car is going east and the other is going west, their motions are different. An object's speed in a particular direction is its **velocity**

▲ The bicyclists are on a curve. Their velocities are constantly changing because their directions are constantly changing.

(vuh•LAHS•uh•tee). For two objects to have the same velocity, they must be moving at the same speed *and* in the same direction.

✔ **If two bicyclists ride north at the same speed, do they have the same velocity? Explain.**

Acceleration

When an object starts, stops, speeds up, slows down, or turns left or right, it changes velocity. Any change in velocity is called **acceleration** (ak•sel•er•AY•shuhn).

Suppose that you are riding a bicycle. When you start pedaling, you accelerate. When you speed up going down a hill, you accelerate. And when you slow down going up a hill, you also accelerate. Slowing down is also known as *deceleration*. When you turn a corner, you accelerate, because you change direction. Finally, when you stop the bike, you accelerate, because your speed changes once again. The only time you are not accelerating is when you ride in a straight line at a constant speed.

✔ **If a car is driven along a curved stretch of road at a constant speed, is it accelerating? Explain.**

Momentum

When a car crashes, it stops almost instantly. Without seat belts or air bags, the passengers may be seriously hurt. A seat belt or an air bag stops a person who has a lot of momentum. **Momentum** (moh•MEN•tuhm) is a measure of how hard it is to slow down or stop an object. It is the product of an object's velocity and its mass.

If two objects have the same velocity, the one with the greater mass has more momentum. Which would be harder to stop—a toy truck moving in a straight line at 50 km/hr or a real truck with the same velocity? Obviously the real truck would be harder to stop, because its greater mass gives it more momentum than the toy truck.

If two objects have the same mass, the one with the greater velocity has more momentum. Which would be harder to stop—a baseball thrown gently or a hard line drive hit by a batter? The line drive would be harder to stop because of its greater velocity. The greater the velocity of an object, the greater its momentum.

High-speed crashes tend to cause more serious injuries than low-speed crashes. That's because high speed produces greater momentum. Velocity can give even small objects a lot of momentum. A bullet fired from a gun is dangerous because of its velocity.

✔ **Which has more momentum—a big car moving at 100 km/hr or a small car moving at the same speed?**

A large ship is hard to stop or turn because of its momentum. A personal watercraft may move at a higher speed, but it has much less mass. So it has less momentum than the ship and is easier to stop or turn.

Summary

Motion is a change in an object's position. Speed is a measure of the distance an object moves in a given amount of time. Velocity is speed in a particular direction. Acceleration is a change in velocity, either in direction or in speed. Momentum is a measure of how hard it is to slow down or stop an object. It is the product of an object's velocity and its mass.

Review

1. Two objects move for the same amount of time. Object A moves farther than Object B. Which object moved at a greater average speed?

2. Explain how velocity differs from speed.

3. An object speeds up. Then it slows down. Then it changes direction. Which of these are examples of acceleration?

4. **Critical Thinking** Use the idea of momentum to explain why a football coach might choose a large, fast runner to carry the ball.

5. **Test Prep** If you observe a change in an object's speed or direction, you are observing a change in its —
   A frame of reference
   B velocity
   C position
   D momentum

LINKS

MATH LINK

Use Formulas This is the formula for average speed:

$$\text{Average speed} = \text{total distance} \div \text{total time}$$

Light from the sun travels at 300,000 km/sec. The distance from the sun to Earth is 150,000,000 km. How long does it take sunlight to reach Earth?

WRITING LINK

Informative Writing—Classification
Keep track of your movements as you go from class to class, from home to school, or from school to home. In a journal, record and classify any changes in velocity you made. Then write a paragraph summarizing the changes.

SOCIAL STUDIES LINK

History The *Titanic* sank in the North Atlantic after hitting an iceberg. Research the events of the sinking. Then decide whether the collision was unavoidable because of the ship's momentum. Back up your conclusion with facts.

TECHNOLOGY LINK

GO ONLINE

Learn more about motion and speed by visiting this Internet site.
www.scilinks.org/harcourt

SCiLINKS
THE WORLD'S A CLICK AWAY

LESSON 2

What Are the Three Laws of Motion?

In this lesson, you can . . .

 INVESTIGATE how mass and velocity affect momentum.

 LEARN ABOUT the laws of motion.

 LINK to math, writing, technology, and other areas.

When the ball collides with the pins, the momentum it loses is equal to the momentum the pins gain. ▼

How Mass and Velocity Affect Momentum

Activity Purpose In Lesson 1 you read that mass is related to momentum. A moving object with a lot of mass has a lot of momentum. You also read that velocity is related to momentum. An object with a high velocity also has a lot of momentum. In this investigation you will **experiment** to see for yourself how mass and velocity affect momentum.

Materials
- gameboard
- several books
- meterstick
- small toy car
- dime
- quarter

Activity Procedure

1 Make a ramp by setting one end of the gameboard on a stack of books about 15 cm high. Place another book as a barrier about 10–15 cm from the bottom of the ramp. (Picture A)

2 Position the car at the top of the ramp. Put the dime on one end of the car. Let the car roll down the ramp and strike the barrier. **Observe** what happens to the dime. **Measure** and **record** its distance from the barrier. (Picture B)

3 Repeat Step 2, this time placing the quarter on the car instead of the dime. **Observe** what happens to the quarter. **Measure** and **record** its distance from the barrier.

Picture A

Picture B

4 Repeat Steps 2 and 3 several times. **Measure** and **record** the distance for each trial.

5 **Predict** how the results would differ if the ramp were higher. Add another book to the stack under the ramp, and repeat Steps 2 and 3 several times. **Measure** and **record** the distances for each trial.

Draw Conclusions

1. Make a table to organize your data. **Compare** the results for the dime with the results for the quarter. **Infer** how the mass of the coin is related to the distance it travels.

2. What happened to the distances the coins traveled when you made the ramp higher? Explain the results.

3. **Scientists at Work** While **gathering data**, scientists try to **identify and control variables**, or conditions, that may affect the results. In this investigation, what variables did you control in Steps 2 and 3? What variable did you test?

Investigate Further **Plan and conduct a simple investigation** to test various methods of keeping the coin on the car when it strikes the barrier. Carefully select the equipment you will need, and conduct several trials for each method you test.

Process Skill Tip

To **gather data** that is meaningful, it's important to **identify and control variables** in an experiment.

The Laws of Motion

Newton's Ideas

Isaac Newton was born in England in 1642. He introduced new ideas about forces and motion. By the time of his death in 1727, his ideas had changed the way scientists observe the natural world.

Before Newton, Aristotle, a Greek philosopher, described four basic "elements": earth, air, water, and fire. He believed that everything was made of one or more of these elements. It seemed reasonable to Aristotle that an object would try to move toward objects made of the same element. For example, Aristotle believed that smoke belonged to the air. He believed that smoke naturally rose to rejoin the air.

At the age of 23, Newton developed three laws of motion. These laws were the first to describe the movement of objects in terms of forces. For example, Newton didn't say that an apple falls from a tree because it is made of earth. He said that a force (gravitation) causes Earth and the apple to attract each other. The laws of motion describe the movement of objects on Earth. They also describe the movement of planets and moons.

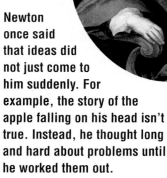

Newton once said that ideas did not just come to him suddenly. For example, the story of the apple falling on his head isn't true. Instead, he thought long and hard about problems until he worked them out.

✓ **According to Newton, why does a meteor fall to Earth?**

The two Voyager spacecraft, launched in the 1970s, have left our solar system. They will continue moving through space for thousands of years.

The First Law of Motion

Before Newton's time, scientists hypothesized that any moving object would stop moving unless something continued to push it. Newton saw things differently. He realized that a moving object would continue to move in a straight line until a force interfered with it. He also decided that an object that was not moving would remain motionless unless a force acted on it. These ideas became the first law of motion:

An object at rest will remain at rest, and an object in motion will continue moving in a straight line at a constant speed until an outside force acts on it.

Because of its great mass, this train has a lot of inertia. It takes a long time to speed up and a long time to stop.

According to this law, a ball rolling down a sidewalk stops because a force (friction) acts on it. In space there is very little friction. A spacecraft will continue moving at the same speed and in the same direction practically forever. Its motion will change only if forces from a nearby star or planet act on it.

The other part of this law states that an object at rest will remain at rest. This is easy to see if you place a ball on a flat, level surface. Unless you push the ball or tilt the surface, the ball will stay where it is.

The property of matter that keeps it moving in a straight line or keeps it at rest is called **inertia** (in•ER•shuh). An object's inertia resists any change in its motion.

Have you ever seen a performer pull a tablecloth from under a table setting? The items remain in place on the table, amazing the audience. How does the trick work? If the performer pulls the tablecloth quickly enough, the inertia of the objects on the table keeps them in place. If the objects are heavy, it is easier to pull the tablecloth off without disturbing them. This is because the amount of inertia in an object is related to its mass. The greater the mass, the greater the object's inertia.

✔ **What is the first law of motion?**

▲ As the ball approaches the bat, the ball and the bat exert forces in different directions.

▲ When the ball and the bat meet, the bat exerts a greater force.

▲ The force exerted by the bat accelerates the ball—its velocity changes. The more force the bat exerts, the faster the ball accelerates.

The Second Law of Motion

In Lesson 1 you read that acceleration is a change in an object's velocity—its speed or its direction. According to the laws of motion, the only thing that can cause acceleration is a force. The amount of acceleration depends on the size of the force *and* on the mass of the object. This is the second law of motion:

An object's acceleration depends on the size and direction of the force acting on it and on the mass of the object.

The size of the force A large force acting on an object will cause more acceleration than a small force. The harder a tennis player hits a ball, the more the ball's motion will change and the faster the ball will go.

The second law helps explain why race car drivers put the most powerful engines possible in their cars. A more powerful engine provides more force. It causes greater acceleration. So the car speeds up more quickly.

The direction of the force A force that acts on an object may cause it to speed up, slow down, stop, or change direction. A rolling soccer ball, for example, will speed up if it's kicked from behind. If the goalie blocks it from the front, it may slow down, stop, or change direction. If kicked from the side, the ball will change direction.

The mass of the object A force has more effect on an object with less mass than it has on an object with more mass. Cars that are used for drag racing are very light because a car with less mass accelerates faster.

To think about what this means, consider a model rocket and a space shuttle. The model rocket has much less mass than the shuttle. So a much smaller force is needed to lift it off the ground. Could the model rocket's engine lift the shuttle? What would the engine of the shuttle do to the model rocket?

✔ **What happens to an object's acceleration as the size of the force acting on the object increases?**

The Third Law of Motion

According to the laws of motion, if you push against a wall, there is an equal force that pushes back. For the wall to stop your push, there must be a force pushing against you. Forces always occur in pairs. Whenever an object (you) exerts a force on a second object (the wall), the second object also exerts a force on the first object. This is the third law of motion:

For every action, there is an equal and opposite reaction.

This law also applies to forces that produce motion. Think about an in-line skater holding a basketball. If the skater throws the ball really hard, the ball goes forward and the skater rolls backward.

The third law is also stated this way: For every action force, there is an equal and opposite reaction force. The first force is the **action force**. The force that pushes or pulls back is the **reaction force**.

The skater exerts an action force on the basketball by throwing it. The thrown ball exerts an equal reaction force on the skater, but in the opposite direction. The result is that the basketball moves in one direction and the skater moves in the other direction. These movements are a sure sign that forces have acted on both of them.

You can see the third law in action in many situations. When you run, your feet push against the ground. And the ground pushes back against your feet. If it didn't, you wouldn't go anywhere.

Space travel depends on the third law as well. A rocket engine pushes burning gases out the back of the rocket. The gases provide the force that moves the rocket forward. The

▲ The rowers' oars exert an action force on the water. The water exerts an equal reaction force on the oars, but in the opposite direction. This pushes the boat forward.

rocket provides the force that sends the gases backward. These two forces are equal in size and opposite in direction.

✔ **While sitting in a chair, you exert a force on the seat of the chair. What are the size and direction of the force the chair exerts on you?**

Conservation of Momentum

Curling is a game played on ice with large, rounded stones. A player from one team slides a stone toward a target on the ice. If the stone stops on or near the target, a player from the opposing team tries to knock it off the target by hitting it with a second stone.

If the second stone hits the first stone directly, it pushes the first stone away, and the second stone stops on the target. Why does the second stone stop, and the first stone start moving?

In Lesson 1 you read that the momentum of a moving object is equal to its mass times its velocity. When a moving object exerts a force on another object, the total momentum of the two objects remains the same. No momentum is produced, and none is lost. Scientists call this *conservation of momentum.* The second stone stops because its momentum is transferred to the first stone.

✓ **A moving car hits the back of a car stopped at a traffic light. The moving car stops, and the stopped car moves. What has happened to the momentum of the cars?**

Conservation of Momentum					
Mass	Speed			Mass	Speed
18 kg	2 m/sec			18 kg	2 m/sec
9 kg	2 m/sec			18 kg	1 m/sec
18 kg	2 m/sec			9 kg	4 m/sec

▲ The table shows that the red stone transfers all of its momentum to the yellow stone, setting it in motion. Since momentum equals mass times velocity, the momentum of the two stones together remains the same. Only the velocities of the stones change.

▲ Curling is a popular winter sport in many northern countries.

F44

Summary

Isaac Newton stated three laws that describe the motion of objects. The first law of motion is that an object at rest tends to remain at rest, and an object in motion tends to move in a straight line at a constant speed unless an outside force acts on it. The second law is that an object's acceleration depends on the mass of the object and on the size and direction of the force acting on it. The third law is that for every action, there is an equal and opposite reaction.

Review

1. If an astronaut throws an object into space, what happens to the object?
2. A truck and a falling leaf collide. The leaf accelerates rapidly. Why doesn't the truck?
3. Explain what happens when a person pushes on a stuck door.
4. **Critical Thinking** Suppose a golf ball and a bowling ball are rolled toward each other. When they collide, the bowling ball stops. How did the golf ball's speed compare with the bowling ball's speed?
5. **Test Prep** What is the property of matter that keeps it moving in a straight line at the same speed?

   A inertia

   B mass

   C momentum

   D velocity

LINKS

MATH LINK

Solve Problems Carl's mass is 35 kg. He is running north at 3 m/sec. What is his momentum?

WRITING LINK

Narrative Writing—Personal Story You have probably seen pictures of astronauts floating in space. Picture yourself "walking" in space outside an orbiting shuttle. Floating next to you is a satellite. You need to move the satellite into the shuttle's cargo bay. Write a story for your class describing what happens when you try to move the satellite.

HEALTH LINK

Buckle Up Use what you've learned about momentum and the laws of motion to explain why a car crash is dangerous to a person not wearing a seat belt.

LITERATURE LINK

Isaac Newton: The Greatest Scientist of All Time Read this book by Margaret J. Anderson to learn more about the life, work, and goals of Isaac Newton.

TECHNOLOGY LINK

Learn more about forces and motion by viewing *Baseball Physics* and *Egg Drop* on the **Harcourt Science Newsroom Video.**

CNN
Turner Le@rning.

Why Do the Planets Stay in Orbit?

In this lesson, you can . . .

INVESTIGATE
orbits and inertia.

LEARN ABOUT
the orbits of planets and moons.

LINK to math, writing, social studies, and technology.

This mechanical model, known as an *orrery* (OHR•er•ee), shows the solar system as it was known in the 1800s. ▽

Orbits and Inertia

Activity Purpose In Lesson 2 you learned about the laws of motion. The first law states that an object in motion will continue moving in a straight line at a constant speed until an outside force acts on it. In this investigation you will **make a model** to see how the first law helps explain why moons and planets stay in orbit.

Materials

- 2 m string
- metal washers
- safety goggles

Activity Procedure

1 Tie three or four metal washers securely to one end of the string.

2 **CAUTION** **Take the string with the washers outside to an open area. Be sure that you are far from any buildings or objects and that no one is standing close to you. Put on the safety goggles.** Hold the loose end of the string. Slowly swing the string and washers in a circle above your head. **Observe** the motion of the washers. (Picture A)

3 **Predict** what will happen if you let go of the string while swinging it in a circle.

4 **CAUTION** **Again, make sure that there are no people, buildings, or other objects near you.** Swing the string and washers in a circle again. Let the string slip through your fingers. **Observe** the motion of the washers. How does it **compare** with your prediction? (Picture B)

5 Using a drawing, **record** the motion of the washers in Steps 2 and 4. Be sure to show the forces acting in each situation. Now make a drawing of the moon orbiting Earth. **Compare** the two drawings.

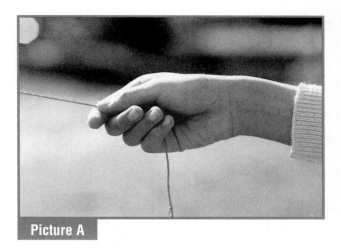
Picture A

Draw Conclusions

1. **Compare** the path of the washers while you were swinging them with their path once you let go of the string.

2. The string and washers can be used to **model** the moon orbiting Earth. **Compare** the motion of the washers circling your head with the motion of the moon orbiting Earth.

Picture B

3. **Scientists at Work** When scientists **experiment,** they must **communicate** their results to others. One way of doing this is with diagrams. Look at the drawing you made of the washers. What motions and forces does it show?

Investigate Further **Hypothesize** about the effect the length of the string has on the time the washers take to complete one revolution. Then **plan and conduct an experiment** to test your hypothesis.

Process Skill Tip

After you **experiment,** you need to **communicate** your results by using a graph, a chart, a table, a written summary, or a drawing.

The Orbits of Planets and Moons

FIND OUT

- how inertia and gravity interact to make an orbit
- what the law of universal gravitation is

VOCABULARY

orbit

law of universal gravitation

Orbits

In the investigation you made a model of an orbit. An **orbit** is the path one body in space takes as it revolves around another body. All of the planets in our solar system are in orbit around the sun. The moon orbits Earth. The orbit you modeled in the investigation was like the moon's orbit in two ways. First, the moon moves around Earth in much the same way as the washers moved around your head. Second, forces acted on the washers to keep them circling in the same way that forces act on the moon to keep it in orbit.

Think about what happened to the washers when you let go of the string. They flew away from you instead of continuing in a circle. This is an example of the first law of motion. A moving object will continue to move in a straight line until an outside force acts on it. The inertia of the washers made them fly away when you let go. In the

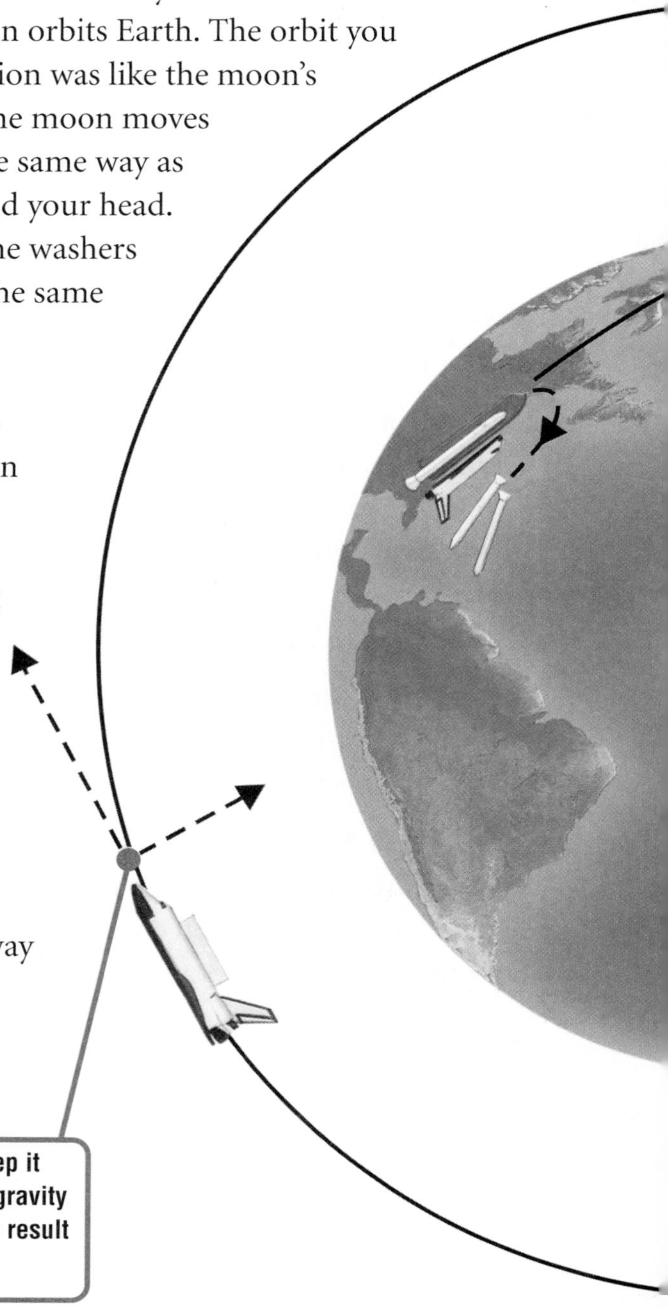

The shuttle's inertia tries to keep it moving in a straight line while gravity tries to pull it toward Earth. The result is that the shuttle orbits Earth.

same way, inertia would make the moon fly off in a straight line unless a force was acting on it.

What is that force? In your model it was the force exerted by the string, which pulled the washers toward your hand. In the moon's orbit, the force is gravitation

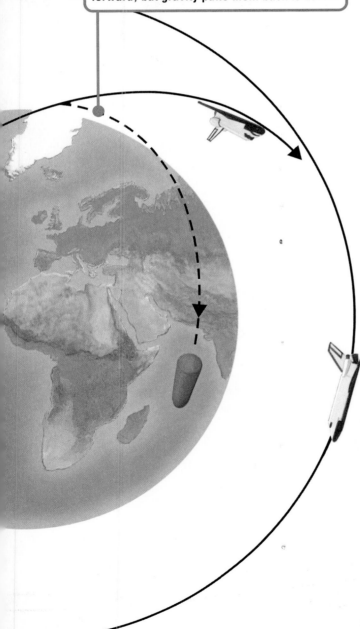

After launch, the shuttle separates from its booster rockets and then from its fuel tank. Inertia tries to keep the objects moving forward, but gravity pulls them back to Earth.

between Earth and the moon. The moon's orbit is the path that results when its inertia and the force of gravitation act together.

✓ **What keeps the moon in orbit around Earth?**

Universal Gravitation

In addition to three laws of motion, Isaac Newton stated a law of gravitation. The **law of universal gravitation** is that all objects in the universe are attracted to all other objects. This attraction is observable when the mass of at least one of the objects is huge. The masses of Earth and the moon produce a strong gravitational pull between them. The gravitational pull between two paperclips on a table isn't enough to pull them together because friction keeps them apart.

The law of universal gravitation, when combined with the property of inertia, also explains why planets orbit the sun. The size of a planet's orbit is related to the planet's speed and its mass. Earth moves around the sun at an average speed of about 30 km/sec. The outer planets move in much longer, slower orbits.

✓ **Why is gravitation between small objects not observed?**

In *Principia Mathematica,* Isaac Newton presented three laws of motion and the law of universal gravitation. ▼

Earth and the Moon

A moon is a body that orbits a planet. Earth has one moon. Some planets have no moons, while Jupiter has 17.

As a planet orbits the sun, the planet's moons orbit with it. In the same way, the planets move with the sun as it orbits the center of the Milky Way Galaxy.

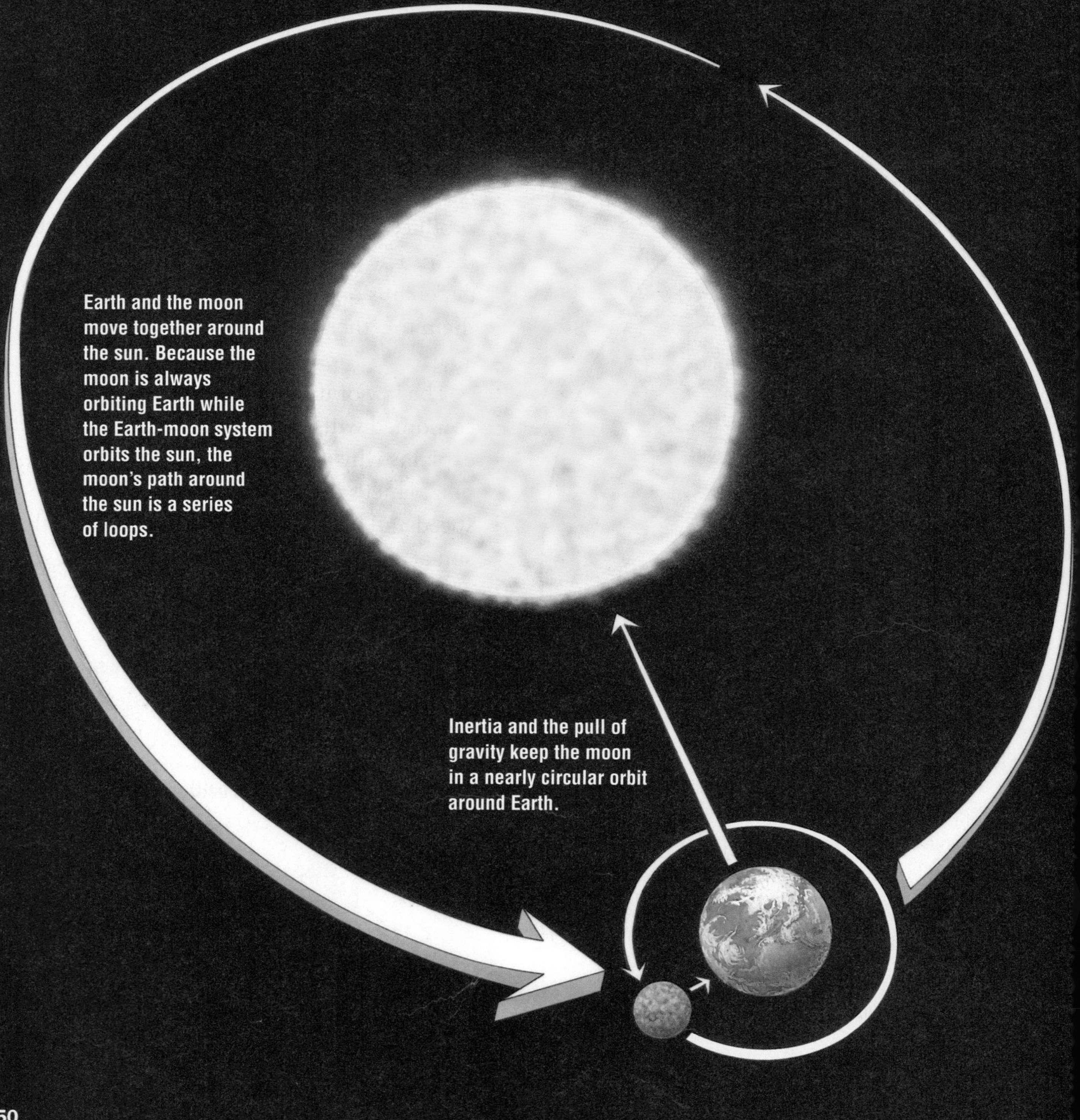

Earth and the moon move together around the sun. Because the moon is always orbiting Earth while the Earth-moon system orbits the sun, the moon's path around the sun is a series of loops.

Inertia and the pull of gravity keep the moon in a nearly circular orbit around Earth.

Newton saw the universe as a giant machine. This model of the solar system, built in 1712, reflects that view. Turning the crank, like winding a clock, sets the planets in motion. ▶

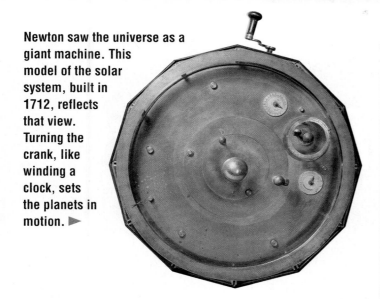

Summary

The moon circles Earth in a path called an orbit. Gravitation between Earth and the moon keeps the moon from flying off into space because of its inertia. The balance between inertia and gravitation keeps Earth in orbit around the sun. It also keeps other planets and moons in their orbits.

Review

1. What is an orbit?
2. What keeps Earth in orbit around the sun?
3. What is the law of universal gravitation?
4. **Critical Thinking** Suppose the gravitation between Earth and the sun suddenly stopped. What path would Earth follow?
5. **Test Prep** Gravitation between Earth and the moon pulls on the moon as the moon orbits. What property of the moon keeps it from crashing into the Earth?
   A gravitation
   B inertia
   C mass
   D momentum

Skipping Through SPACE

The HyperSoar could fly vacationers to Hawai'i from any city on the mainland in less than an hour.

Engineers have designed a new aircraft called the HyperSoar. It will be part rocket and part airplane. It will skip along the edge of space, like a flat stone on a smooth pond. When it becomes operational, the HyperSoar will take passengers anywhere on Earth in less than two hours.

No More Gas-Guzzlers

Rocket engines need oxygen to burn their fuel. When the space shuttle roars into orbit, it must carry its own oxygen because there isn't any in outer space. And every kilogram of oxygen means more fuel is needed. The space shuttle uses 50 kilograms of fuel to lift every kilogram of cargo (including oxygen) on board.

The HyperSoar will use what scientists call rocket-based combined cycle (RBCC) engines to get to the edge of space with a lot less fuel. The HyperSoar will fly in a skip-along style that will get people and packages from Chicago to Tokyo in 90 minutes instead of today's 10 hours.

The HyperSoar's RBCC engines won't need to carry oxygen because they will use air. The engines will be powerful enough to get the HyperSoar moving at speeds of more than 10,500 km/hr (about 6500 mi/hr). The HyperSoar will fly at nearly 40,000 m (about 130,000 ft) above Earth's surface. Then the engines will shut down because there is not enough air at that altitude for them to operate. The HyperSoar will then drift back into the upper atmosphere, restart its engines, and fly back up into space.

You may soon travel to the edge of space in the Hypersoar.

High-Speed Hopper

For a trip from Chicago to Tokyo, the HyperSoar would make two dozen of these skips into and out of space. Although friction will make the HyperSoar heat up when it's flying through the atmosphere, it will cool off again when it's in space.

As the HyperSoar leaves the atmosphere, passengers will feel nearly weightless. And with each skip into the atmosphere, they will feel as if they are accelerating from the bottom of a gentle roller coaster ride. After rocketing and gliding along at more than ten times the speed of sound, the Hyper-Soar will land just like a regular airplane.

Because its RBCC engines will breathe air, the HyperSoar will need only 3 kilograms of fuel for each kilogram of cargo. This will make it much less expensive to operate than a rocket-powered aircraft. And because it will go so fast, the HyperSoar will carry a lot more cargo and people around the world each day than a jet airplane. According to one of the HyperSoar's engineers, "Hyper-Soar has the potential of opening the space frontier to ordinary people."

THINK ABOUT IT

1. All engines need oxygen. Where will the HyperSoar get its oxygen?
2. Why will the HyperSoar be less expensive to operate than a rocket?

CAREERS
AERONAUTICAL ENGINEER

What They Do
Aeronautical engineers design the engines and wings that power and lift aircraft. They also design and build aircraft that are as light as possible so that they can carry a lot of passengers or cargo without using too much fuel.

Education and Training
People wishing to become aeronautical engineers should study subjects such as aerodynamics and engine design in college and graduate school.

WEB LINK
For Science and Technology updates, visit the Harcourt Internet site.
www.harcourtschool.com

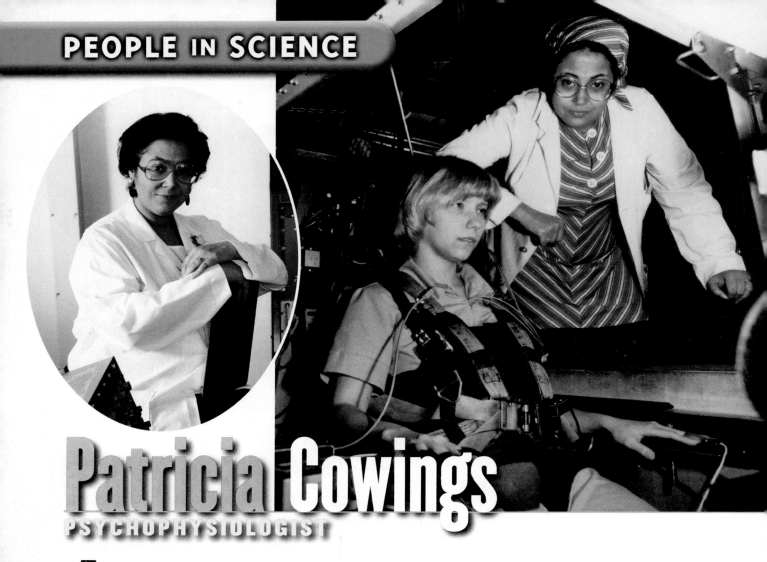

Patricia Cowings
PSYCHOPHYSIOLOGIST

Astronauts in space often experience physical problems, such as nausea and swelling of the legs and feet. The nausea, or "space sickness," is similar to the motion sickness some people feel while riding on an amusement park ride. One scientist trying to cut down on these problems or prevent them is Patricia Cowings. She is the director of psychophysiological research at NASA's Ames Research Center in California. As a psychophysiologist, she studies the science of mind and behavior.

In order to study the problems that astronauts experience, Dr. Cowings produces conditions on Earth that are similar to conditions in space. For example, to study nausea, she straps an astronaut into a seat that spins very rapidly. By observing the changes that occur in the astronaut's body just before he or she becomes nauseated, Dr. Cowings can teach the astronaut to use biofeedback to prevent the nausea. Biofeedback is a technique that allows a person to control certain body functions, such as heart rate, blood pressure, and breathing rate. If, for example, an astronaut's breathing rate increases just before the feeling of nausea, he or she can learn to slow the breathing rate and perhaps prevent the nausea.

THINK ABOUT IT

1. Why is it important to know how an astronaut's body changes just before he or she feels nauseated?

2. Why do you think astronauts experience nausea in space?

IT'S THE LAW

How does a rocket demonstrate the third law of motion?

Materials
- 5 m of string
- drinking straw
- rubber balloon
- double-backed tape

Procedure

❶ Thread the string through the straw. Then hold the ends of the string or tie them to stationary objects.

❷ Blow up the balloon and pinch the end.

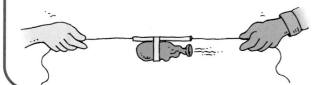

❸ While you hold the balloon, have a partner tape the balloon to the straw.

❹ When the balloon is taped to the straw, release the balloon. Observe the balloon.

Draw Conclusions

What is the third law of motion? What is the action force in your balloon rocket? What is the reaction force? Do you think the action force and the reaction force are equal? In what direction did the air push out? How could you make a more powerful balloon rocket?

SPIN FACTOR

What forces act on a spinning object?

Materials
- fishing weight
- string
- paper-towel tube
- rubber band

Procedure

CAUTION Do this activity in an open area, away from buildings and other people.

❶ Tie the weight to one end of the string. Tie the rubber band to the other end of the string. Then thread the weight through the paper-towel tube.

❷ Holding the paper-towel tube with one hand and the rubber band with your other hand, carefully spin the weight in a circle over your head. Observe the rubber band.

❸ As you spin the weight, slowly pull the string through the tube. Try to keep the weight spinning at the same rate.

❹ Observe what happens to the stretch of the rubber band.

Draw Conclusions

The variables you are experimenting with are the momentum, velocity, and mass of the weight and the radius of the weight's orbit. When you pulled the string through the tube, which variable changed? How did changing that variable change the forces acting on the weight?

Vocabulary Review

Use the terms below to complete the sentences. The page numbers in ( ) tell you where to look in the chapter if you need help.

position (F34)
speed (F35)
velocity (F35)
acceleration (F35)
momentum (F36)
inertia (F41)
action force (F43)
reaction force (F43)
orbit (F48)
law of universal gravitation (F49)

1. A statement of the ____ might be this: Everything is attracted to everything else.

2. An object's ____ is the product of its velocity and its mass.

3. How far an object moves in a given amount of time is a measure of its ____.

4. When an object undergoes ____, it speeds up, slows down, stops, or changes direction.

5. Newton's third law of motion can be stated this way: For every ____, there is an equal and opposite ____.

6. The property of matter that resists any change in an object's motion is ____.

7. Speed in a particular direction is ____.

8. An object's place or location is called its ____.

9. An ____ is the path a body in space takes as it revolves around another body.

Connect Concepts

This Venn diagram shows how some of the measurements from this chapter are related. Copy the Venn diagram. Write each term from the Word Bank in its proper place in the diagram.

velocity   speed
acceleration   inertia
average speed   momentum

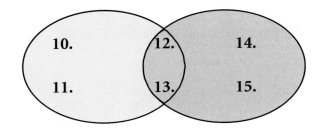

10.
11.
12.
13.
14.
15.

Check Understanding

Write the letter of the best choice.

16. The property of matter that makes it difficult to push a stopped car is —
    A acceleration
    B action forces
    C reaction forces
    D inertia

17. Unlike speed, velocity includes —
    F direction
    G acceleration
    H mass
    J time

18. A golf ball hits a tennis ball. The golf ball stops, but the tennis ball rolls away. This is an example of —
    A gravitation
    B conservation of momentum
    C equal and opposite forces
    D velocity

19. A person driving a car and a person walking have different views of the motion of an object. Each person has a different —

 F acceleration

 G position

 H frame of reference

 J orbit

20. If gravitation suddenly stopped, Earth would move —

 A in the same orbit

 B in the opposite direction

 C nowhere

 D in a straight line

21. If you throw a ball up, it moves up in a straight line until gravity slows it and pulls it back down to Earth. This is an example of —

 F the first law of motion

 G the second law of motion

 H the third law of motion

 J the law of universal gravitation

Critical Thinking

22. Two ice skaters stand facing each other. One pushes the other, and both move in opposite directions. Explain why both skaters move instead of just the skater who is pushed.

23. If gravitation attracts all objects in the universe toward each other, why don't all of the clothes hanging in a closet cling together?

24. If Earth pulls on a grapefruit with a force of 1 newton, the grapefruit also exerts a force of 1 newton on Earth. Explain why this is true.

Process Skills Review

25. You roll a basketball and a bowling ball directly toward each other at the same speed. **Predict** what will happen to each after the two collide. Use what you know about momentum and Newton's laws of motion.

26. Two cars are driven next to each other along 1 km of straight road. **Compare** the cars' velocities.

27. An engineer wants to compare the damage low-speed collisions do to three cars. Which **variable** should she **control** in her experiment?

28. Which would be more useful to **communicate** how an object's velocity changes—a drawing with arrows, or a table? Explain.

Performance Assessment

Demonstrating the Laws of Motion

Your teacher will give you two balls. Use them to demonstrate each of Newton's three laws of motion. You may refer to pages F41–F43 in Lesson 2 of this chapter.

Forms of Energy

What do a flashlight battery, snow on a mountainside, and a match have in common? Each has a form of stored energy. What do a beam of light, an avalanche, and a fire have in common? Each is energy in action.

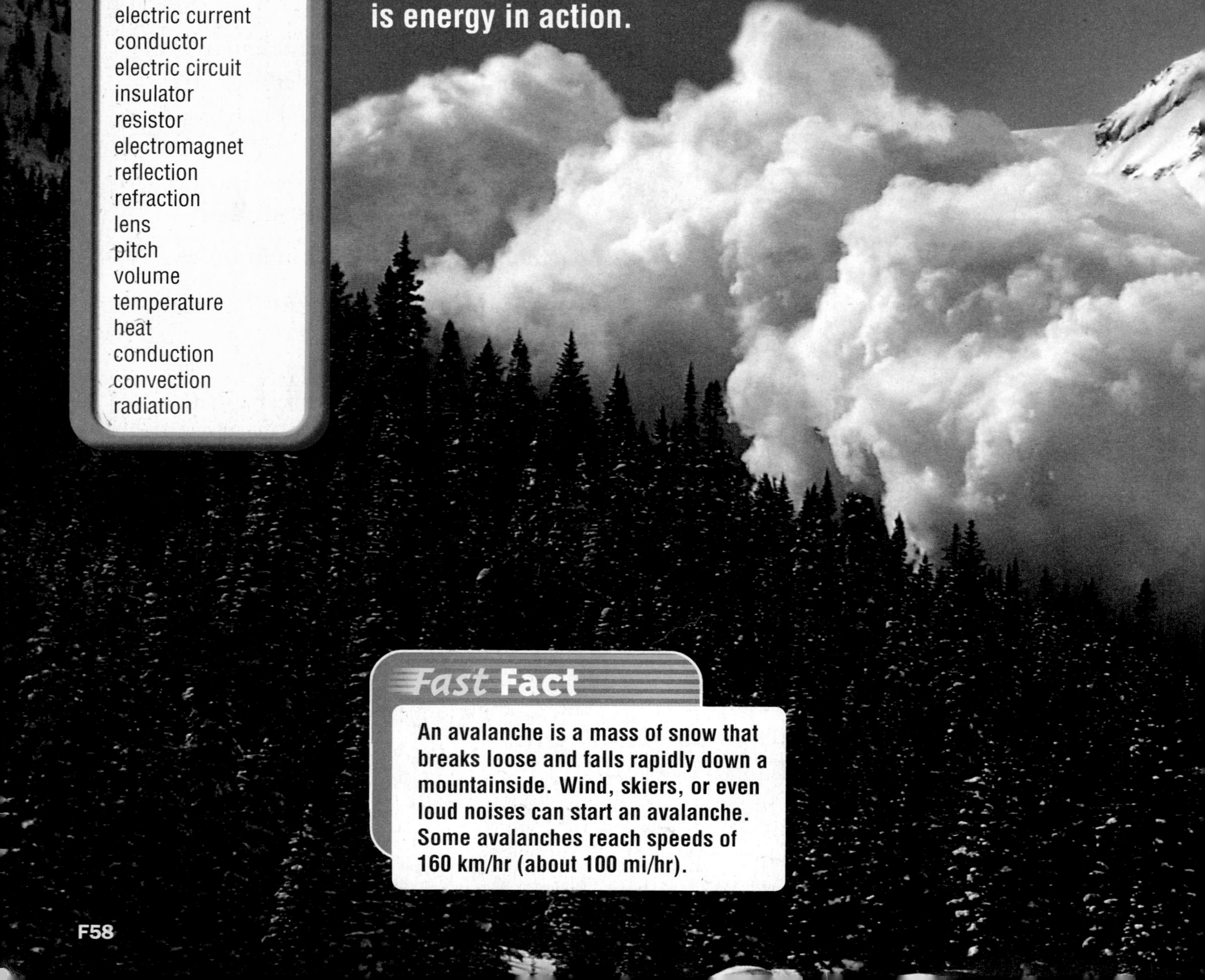

Vocabulary Preview

energy
kinetic energy
potential energy
electric charge
electric force
electric current
conductor
electric circuit
insulator
resistor
electromagnet
reflection
refraction
lens
pitch
volume
temperature
heat
conduction
convection
radiation

Fast Fact

An avalanche is a mass of snow that breaks loose and falls rapidly down a mountainside. Wind, skiers, or even loud noises can start an avalanche. Some avalanches reach speeds of 160 km/hr (about 100 mi/hr).

4. Repeat Steps 2 and 3 several times. Use a different-colored marker to **record** each trial.

5. Replace the paper and repeat Steps 1–4, but this time drop the ball from a height of 100 cm.

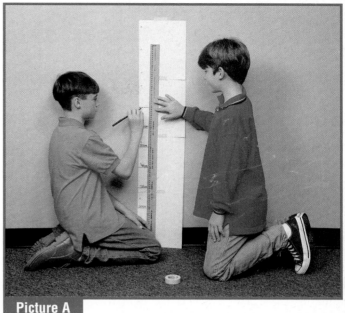
Picture A

Draw Conclusions

1. **Compare** the drop height to the bounce height for each trial in the experiment. How are the heights related?

2. When you hold the ball in the air before dropping it, it has *potential energy* because of its position and because of gravitation. When you let go of the ball, it has *kinetic energy* because of its movement. **Infer** the point at which the ball has the most kinetic energy.

3. **Draw a conclusion** about how potential energy and kinetic energy are related in the bouncing ball.

4. **Scientists at Work** Scientists often use computers to help them **interpret data** and **communicate** the results of an experiment. Use a computer graphing program to **compare** the height of each bounce and the number of bounces from one trial of 50-cm drops and one trial of 100-cm drops. Make a different-colored line graph for each trial.

Picture B

Investigate Further Analyze the data you graphed in Step 4, and **hypothesize** how high and how many times a ball dropped from a height of 200 cm will bounce. Then **experiment**, and compare your results to your hypothesis.

> **Process Skill Tip**
>
> Using a computer to help you **compare** and **interpret data** is one way to **communicate** the results of an experiment to others.

Energy

Kinetic and Potential Energy

Have you ever heard someone say that a person has a lot of energy? What is energy? **Energy** is the ability to cause changes in matter. In the investigation energy caused matter (the tennis ball) to move. Energy can also change matter in other ways. For example, energy can change solid ice into liquid water.

There are two basic kinds of energy—the energy of motion and the energy of position or condition. The energy of motion, or energy in use, is **kinetic energy**. Any matter in motion has kinetic energy. When you let go of the tennis ball, it gained kinetic energy as it moved faster and faster toward the floor. It also had kinetic energy after it bounced back up from the floor. When the ball reached the top of each bounce, it stopped for an instant between rising and falling again. At this point its kinetic energy was zero.

While bouncing up, the ball gained energy of position. When the ball stopped at the top of a bounce, it had potential energy. **Potential energy** is the energy an object has because of where it is or because of its condition. Once the ball reached the top of its bounce, it fell again, changing more and more of its potential energy back into kinetic energy. If you caught the ball at the top of a bounce, it would keep that potential energy until you dropped it again.

FIND OUT

- **what kinetic and potential energy are**
- **about different forms of energy**

VOCABULARY

energy
kinetic energy
potential energy

❶ The potential energy of food is changed into kinetic energy by the pole vaulter's muscles as he runs toward the bar.

❷ When the vaulter sticks his pole in the ground, much of this kinetic energy is changed to potential energy in the bent pole.

❸ As the pole straightens, it releases that potential energy as kinetic energy to lift him up toward the bar.

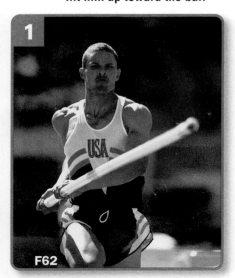

The snow that has fallen high in the mountains has a lot of potential energy. During an avalanche, that potential energy is suddenly changed to kinetic energy, and the fast-moving snow can cause a lot of damage.

The change of the ball's energy back and forth between kinetic energy and potential energy is called the *transformation of energy*. Although energy often is transformed, or changed, from one form to another, the total amount of energy doesn't change. Energy can't be created or destroyed. This is the *law of conservation of energy*.

Energy can change forms several times during one activity. Look at the series of photographs of the pole vaulter. According to the law of conservation of energy, the amount of energy is always the same, but its form keeps changing.

Both the tennis ball in the investigation and the pole vaulter eventually stopped. However, it wasn't because energy was destroyed. With each bounce some of the ball's energy was lost as sound and heat. The heat caused by the friction of the ball hitting the floor warmed the air and the floor slightly. Eventually, the results of bouncing turned all of the ball's energy into other forms.

✔ **At what point in the process does the pole vaulter have his greatest kinetic energy?**

❹ As the vaulter goes up and over the bar, kinetic energy is changed to potential energy.

❺ As he falls, potential energy becomes kinetic energy until he hits the ground. While on the ground, he has no potential energy.

Forms of Energy

The kinetic energy that moving objects have is also called *mechanical energy*. A spinning top, a rolling bicycle, a flying airplane, and flowing water all have mechanical energy. But mechanical energy isn't the only form of kinetic energy. Kinetic energy can have many different forms.

Thermal energy is another form of kinetic energy. The movement of molecules of matter is thermal energy. Another form of kinetic energy, *electric energy,* is caused by the movement of electrons. Electric energy can be felt in a shock. It also produces the picture and sound on a television. *Light energy* from the picture moves to your eyes in waves. Your ears receive vibrations produced by the television speakers as *sound energy.*

Potential energy also takes several forms. *Elastic potential energy* is the energy stored in compressed springs, stretched rubber bands, and bent vaulting poles. In fact, any object that can be forced into a shape that's different from its natural shape can store elastic potential energy—if it has the ability to return to its natural shape.

Gravitational potential energy is the energy an object has when it's in an elevated position. The tennis ball in the investigation had gravitational potential energy at the top of its bounce and elastic potential energy at the bottom of its bounce. Water behind a dam, a "balanced" rock, or any object that can fall has gravitational potential energy.

Most of Earth's energy comes from the sun. Plants absorb light energy and store it as *chemical energy* in the food they make. When a pole vaulter starts running, chemical energy stored in his muscles is changed into *thermal energy* and *mechanical energy.*

✔ **Name three forms of energy.**

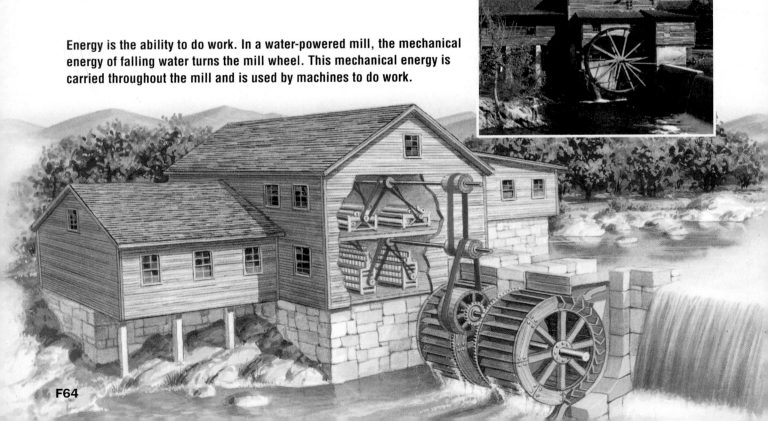

Energy is the ability to do work. In a water-powered mill, the mechanical energy of falling water turns the mill wheel. This mechanical energy is carried throughout the mill and is used by machines to do work.

The flashlight's dry cells (also called batteries) store chemical energy. When you flip the switch, chemical energy is changed to electric energy that moves through the light bulb. In the light bulb's filament, electric energy becomes thermal energy and light energy.

Summary

Energy is the ability to cause changes in matter. There are two basic types of energy—kinetic energy and potential energy. Electric energy, thermal energy, mechanical energy, light energy, and sound energy are all forms of kinetic energy. Chemical energy, gravitational potential energy, and elastic potential energy are forms of potential energy. The law of conservation of energy says energy can change form, but it can't be created or destroyed.

Review

1. What is energy?
2. What is kinetic energy?
3. You use mechanical energy to walk around. What form did this energy have before your body changed it to mechanical energy?
4. **Critical Thinking** If you toss a ball in the air, at what point does it have the most potential energy?
5. **Test Prep** Which law states that energy can't be created or destroyed?
   A the law of mechanical energy
   B the law of conservation of energy
   C the law of kinetic energy
   D the law of potential energy

LINKS

MATH LINK

Use Formulas To calculate kinetic energy, you can use the following formula:

Energy = (mass × speed × speed) ÷ 2

Suppose a 1-kg object is moving at 10 m/sec. If the object speeds up to 20 m/sec, does its energy double?

WRITING LINK

Expressive Writing—Poem Brainstorm a list of words related to forms of kinetic and potential energy, such as *rush, shining,* and *loud.* Then use your favorite words to write a poem about using energy, such as in pole vaulting. Read your poem to a classmate.

SOCIAL STUDIES LINK

Energy Crisis In the 1970s the United States had an "energy crisis." There were fears that there would not be enough energy to run our cars, light and heat our homes, and meet other needs. Learn more about what caused this energy crisis. Report on your findings to your classmates.

GO ONLINE TECHNOLOGY LINK

Learn more about kinetic and potential energy by visiting this Internet site.

www.scilinks.org/harcourt

SCILINKS
THE WORLD'S A CLICK AWAY

What Is Electric Energy?

In this lesson, you can . . .

 INVESTIGATE electric circuits.

 LEARN ABOUT electric charges, currents, and circuits and electromagnets.

 LINK to math, writing, art, and technology.

INVESTIGATE

Electric Circuits

Activity Purpose   Electricity is one form of energy. It results from the force of electrons being attracted or repelled. To use this energy, you need to make an *electric circuit*—a path of wires and devices that electrons can follow back to their source. In this investigation you will **make a model** of two different electric circuits and **compare** them.

Materials

- 4 lengths of insulated wire with bare ends
- 2 light-bulb holders
- battery holder
- 2 light bulbs
- batteries

Activity Procedure

1. To make electricity flow between the terminals, or charged ends, of a dry cell or battery, you need to connect the terminals in some way, such as with a wire. Electricity will then flow through any device you put along this path. Connect the wires, bulb holders, and battery holder as shown. (Picture A)

2. Insert the light bulbs and batteries. **Observe** what happens and **record** your observations.

3. Remove one of the bulbs from its holder. **Observe** and **record** what happens to the other bulb.

4. Now reconnect the wires, bulb holders, and battery holder as shown. **Observe** what happens and **record** your observations. (Picture B)

◀ Van de Graaff generators use friction to rub off electrons and build up electric charges on the spheres. These are the "lightning machines" used in old science-fiction movies.

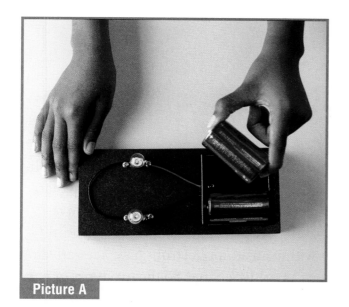

Picture A

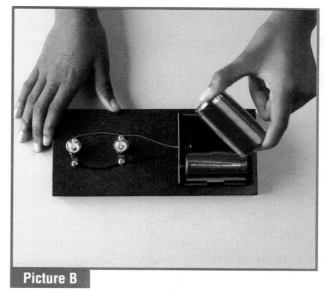

Picture B

5 Again remove one of the bulbs from its holder. **Observe** and **record** what happens to the other bulb.

6 Draw diagrams of both of the circuits you built. Use arrows to **compare** the path of the electric current in each circuit.

Draw Conclusions

1. What happened to the other bulb when one bulb was removed from the first circuit?

2. What happened to the other bulb when one bulb was removed from the second circuit?

3. **Scientists at Work** Scientists often **compare** results before they **draw a conclusion**. Cross out one bulb in each of your drawings. Then diagram the path the electric current must take if it can't pass through the bulb you crossed out. Compare your diagrams, and then draw a conclusion about which type of circuit would be better to use for a string of lights.

Investigate Further In the investigation you demonstrated that electricity flowing through a circuit produces light and heat (the glowing bulbs were warm). Now **plan and conduct a simple investigation** to demonstrate that electricity flowing through a circuit can also produce sound and magnetism. Decide what equipment you will need to use in your investigation.

> ### Process Skill Tip
>
> If you **compare** the results of different experiments before you **draw a conclusion**, you will have more information on which to base your conclusion.

Electric Energy

Electric Charges

VOCABULARY

electric charge
electric force
electric current
conductor
electric circuit
insulator
resistor
electromagnet

Electric energy runs computers, televisions, radios, and appliances, and it lights homes and streets. It is also the energy that produces lightning. Electric energy is produced by the movement of electrons.

You may recall that within an atom, electrons have a negative charge and protons have a positive charge. So the two types of particles attract each other. Most objects have equal numbers of protons and electrons. Sometimes, however, electrons are attracted to the protons of another object and rub off. When an object gains or loses electrons, it has an **electric charge**. An object that has gained electrons has a negative electric charge because it has more electrons than protons. An object that has lost electrons has a positive electric charge because it has more protons than electrons.

For example, when you drag your feet across a carpet on a dry day, electrons rub off your shoes and onto the carpet. The loss of these electrons results in a positive charge on your body, which makes it attract more electrons. When you reach for an object such as a doorknob, your body attracts electrons from that object. When this attraction is great enough, the electrons jump from the doorknob to your hand. You feel a shock and may even see a small spark.

✓ **What causes an electric charge?**

When the boy rubs the balloon on his hair, electrons rub off the balloon and it becomes positively charged. Opposite charges on the balloon and the boy's sweater make the two objects attract each other.

Electric Force

Most objects have no charge because most objects have about the same numbers of protons and electrons. If an object has a charge, it attracts objects with the opposite charge. Similar to magnetic force, unlike charges attract each other, and like charges repel each other. This attraction or repulsion is called **electric force**. If two objects have large electric charges, they produce a large electric force. Like gravitational force, electric force depends on distance. Two charged objects produce a larger electric force when they are close together.

Charged objects have potential electric energy. This is sometimes called *static electricity*, because the electrons aren't moving. When charged objects are close to each other, potential energy can become kinetic energy. If the charges on the objects are the same, the objects repel each other. If the charges are opposite, the objects are drawn together. If the objects touch or come very close to each other, electrons may flow from one object to the other.

Electrons flow from negatively charged objects to positively charged objects. The

The Van de Graaff generator produces a large static charge by building up electrons on the sphere. The girl touching the sphere is also charged. You can see the effect of this charge in her hair. Since electrons all have the same charge, they repel each other, causing the girl's hairs to separate.

flow of electrons is called **electric current**. Once electrons have moved from one object to the other, the attraction between the objects is gone. The charges are balanced, and there is no electric force.

✔ How do charges interact?

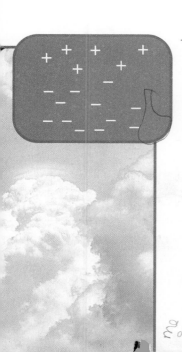

◀ As updrafts in a thunderstorm carry rain along, friction rubs electrons off the drops. The bottom of the thundercloud has extra electrons. The top has lost electrons. There is potential electric energy between the top and bottom of the cloud.

When the attraction between positive and negative charges becomes great enough, electrons move rapidly through the air between these areas. The potential electric energy becomes electric current. The cloud then gives off its energy in a flash of lightning. ▶

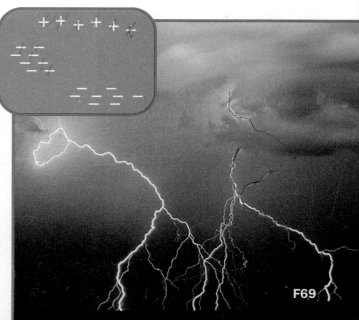

◄ A wall socket is an extension of the terminals of a generator.

Electric Current

Unlike static electricity, which does not move, an electric current is a flow of electrons. The shock you get by touching a doorknob is a small electric current. A lightning bolt is a brief but strong electric current.

To light a light bulb or run a computer, a continuous electric current must be produced. This requires a constant electric force, so a source of electrons is needed. A dry cell, a battery, or a generator can be the source of electrons.

In a dry cell or a battery, two different metals in a chemical bath build up opposite charges. In a generator, some outside force turns coils of wires between two magnets to produce opposite charges. Opposite charges build up on the terminals of a battery or generator.

Electrons are attracted from one terminal to the other. Connecting the two terminals allows an electric current to flow between them. Electric current flows through many kinds of matter if the electric force is strong enough. But some kinds of matter conduct, or carry, electrons more easily than others. Material that conducts electrons easily is called a **conductor**.

 What is a conductor?

THE INSIDE STORY

Comparing Circuits

For electrons to flow, a circuit has to complete a path between two terminals of opposite charges. Strings of lights can be wired between these terminals in series circuits or in parallel circuits.

In a *series circuit*, there is only one path for the electrons. If one of the bulbs burns out, all the other bulbs go out because the circuit is broken, and the electric current stops flowing.

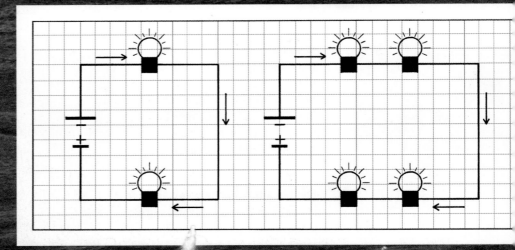

Electric Circuits

A conductor is used in the wire that makes an electric circuit. An **electric circuit** is any path along which electrons can flow. Copper and aluminum are often used as conductors. Metals are good conductors of electric current because their atoms don't hold electrons tightly. This allows electrons to move along from one atom to the next. An electric current flows through good conductors with little resistance.

The conductor in a circuit is wrapped with a material called an insulator (IN•suh•layt•er). An **insulator** is a material that doesn't carry electrons. Rubber, plastic, glass, and air are good insulators. They resist the flow of electrons through them. Insulation keeps wires from touching each other and completing an electrical circuit before the electrons can reach a device. When this happens, it is called a *short circuit*.

Some materials are neither conductors nor insulators. Inside many appliances are materials that don't completely stop the flow of electrons. However, they resist the flow in some way. These materials are called **resistors** (rih•ZIS•terz). Materials that resist electric current are important because they allow electric energy to be changed into other forms.

The filament in a light bulb, for example, resists the flow of electrons. This resistance produces heat. The filament gets hot enough to glow. Electrons flowing in an electric circuit can produce heat, light, sound, or movement. People use all these results in electric devices.

✓ **What materials make good conductors?**

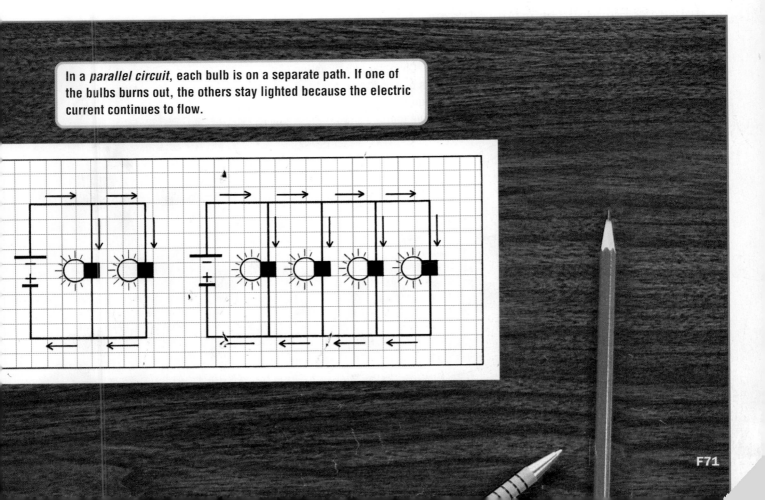

In a *parallel circuit*, each bulb is on a separate path. If one of the bulbs burns out, the others stay lighted because the electric current continues to flow.

Magnets and Electricity

Magnets are used to generate, or produce, electricity. Spinning a coil of wire inside a magnetic field produces an electric force between the ends of the coil. In a similar way, an electric current produces a magnetic field around it. A compass placed next to a wire carrying an electric current will point to the wire.

A current-carrying wire wrapped in a coil of more wire makes a strong magnet. A coil of current-conducting wire wrapped around an iron bar makes an even stronger magnet. Around the coil is a magnetic field much like the one around a bar magnet. But a bar magnet is always magnetized, while a coil wrapped around an iron bar is a magnet only when electric current flows through the coil. For this reason it is called an **electromagnet** (ee•LEK•troh•MAG•nit).

This link between electricity and magnetism allows motion to be produced from

▲ A junkyard is one place to see an electromagnet in action. This huge one picks up scrap metal when current flows through it. When the crane operator wants to drop the scrap, he or she will simply shut off current to the electromagnet.

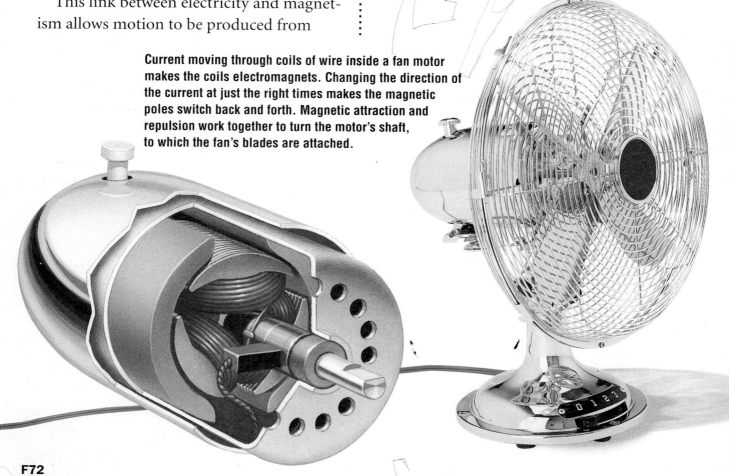

Current moving through coils of wire inside a fan motor makes the coils electromagnets. Changing the direction of the current at just the right times makes the magnetic poles switch back and forth. Magnetic attraction and repulsion work together to turn the motor's shaft, to which the fan's blades are attached.

electric energy. An electric motor uses electromagnets. By changing the direction of the electric current back and forth, these electromagnets alternately attract and repel each other. This causes the motor to turn.

✓ **What forms around a wire carrying an electric current?**

Summary

Electric energy is the movement of electrons between areas that have opposite charges. When objects with opposite charges are close enough together, or when the charges are very large, electrons move between the objects. Electric current moves through an electric circuit. When electric current flows through a conductor, it produces a magnetic field, turning the conductor into an electromagnet.

Review

1. How do like electric charges react to each other?

2. Why are insulators placed around electric conductors?

3. What are resistors, and why are they important?

4. **Critical Thinking** Are the lights in your school connected in series circuits or parallel circuits? Explain.

5. **Test Prep** A coil that is magnetized only when an electric current flows through it is —

   A a battery
   B a generator
   C a conductor
   D an electromagnet

LINKS

MATH LINK

Solve Problems Power is measured in *watts*. A 60-watt light bulb uses 60 watts of power every second. Use a calculator to determine how much power a 60-watt light bulb would use in a year if it were never turned off.

WRITING LINK

Informative Writing—Narration
Alessandro Volta, Michael Faraday, Georg Simon Ohm, Charles Coulomb, Joseph Henry, and Nikola Tesla all added to our understanding of electricity and magnetism. Learn more about one of these scientists, and write a short biography to share with your class.

ART LINK

Wiring Diagrams Electrical engineers use a set of symbols to stand for electric devices when they draw circuits. Learn more about these symbols, including the symbols for a battery, a light bulb, a resistor, and a switch. Use these symbols to redraw the circuit diagrams you did in the investigation.

GO ONLINE — TECHNOLOGY LINK

Learn more about electricity by visiting the Smithsonian Institution Internet site. **www.si.edu/harcourt/science**

Smithsonian Institution®

What Are Light and Sound Energy?

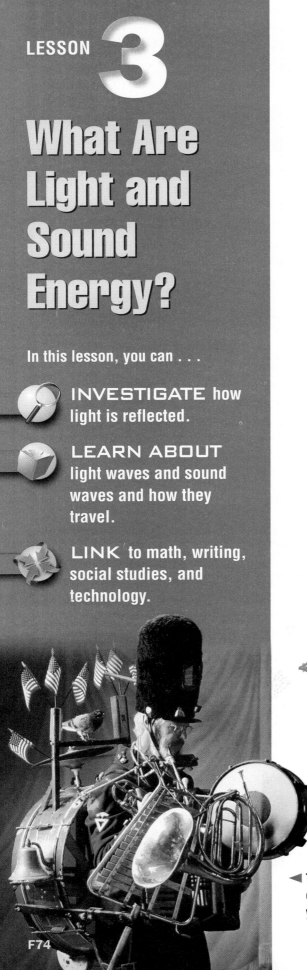

In this lesson, you can . . .

INVESTIGATE how light is reflected.

LEARN ABOUT light waves and sound waves and how they travel.

LINK to math, writing, social studies, and technology.

◄ This one-person band can send both sound energy and light energy your way. Your ears and eyes receive this energy, and your brain turns it into an image and sound.

INVESTIGATE

The Path of Reflected Light

Activity Purpose You probably use a mirror every day. But looking at a reflection as a scientist would can help you learn something about light. In this investigation you will **observe** and **measure** the angle at which light is reflected by a mirror.

Materials
- piece of corrugated cardboard, 10 cm × 10 cm
- small mirror
- masking tape
- ruler
- 3 pushpins of different colors
- protractor

Activity Procedure

1. Lay the cardboard flat. Use tape to attach the mirror vertically to one end of the cardboard. Push two of the pins into the cardboard, about 5 cm from the mirror. (Picture A)

2. Position yourself at eye level with the mirror. Align yourself so that your view of one pin lines up with the reflection of the other pin. Push a third pin into the cardboard at the edge of the mirror, right in front of where you see the reflection of the second pin. The first pin, the third pin, and the reflection of the second pin should appear to be in a straight line.

3. Draw lines on the cardboard to connect the three pins. These lines show how the reflected light from the first pin traveled to your eye. (Picture B)

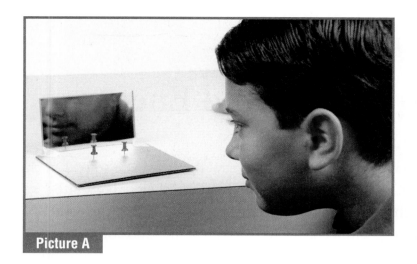

Picture A

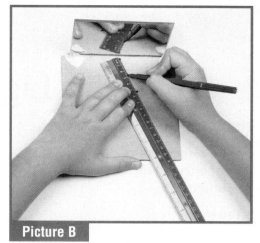

Picture B

4 Using the protractor, **measure** the angle between each line and the edge of the mirror. You will probably have to trace the edge of the mirror and then move it out of your way to make this measurement. **Record** your results.

5 Now remove the original pins and place two of them 10 cm from the mirror. Repeat Steps 2–4 with this new arrangement of pins. **Measure** the angles of the new lines, and **record** your results.

6 Now draw diagrams to **communicate** the results of the two experiments. Each diagram should show the locations of the pins and the mirror and the path of the reflected light.

Draw Conclusions

1. **Compare** the two angles you **measured** in each experiment.

2. The angle at which light strikes a mirror is the *angle of incidence*. The angle at which it reflects from the mirror is the *angle of reflection*. **Draw a conclusion** about the angle of incidence and the angle of reflection from a flat surface.

3. **Scientists at Work** When scientists **observe** a pattern that seems to always be true, they try to come up with a clear, simple rule. This helps them **predict** what will happen in the future. Predict what the angle of incidence and the angle of reflection would be if the pins were 20 cm from the mirror.

Investigate Further **Hypothesize** how light would be reflected from a mirror that was not flat. Then **plan and conduct a simple experiment** to test your hypothesis.

Process Skill Tip

If you **observe** that something always happens the same way under the same conditions, you will be able to **predict** what will happen in the future if the conditions are the same.

F75

Light and Sound Energy

Light Energy

We usually think about light as rays that start at a source, such as the sun, and travel in a straight line until they strike something, such as Earth. Light rays are a form of energy that can travel through empty space or through some kinds of matter. For example, light passes easily through gases in the atmosphere and through clear glass windows.

Sometimes light energy is absorbed when it strikes matter. Most objects absorb some colors of light. Other colors bounce off objects as a **reflection**. The colors of light that objects reflect are the colors we see.

A green leaf, for example, absorbs much of the sunlight that strikes it. The rest of the light—the green part—reflects off the leaf. That's why a leaf looks green to us. A mirror, however, reflects all colors.

In space, light energy from the sun travels at about 300,000 km/sec (186,000 mi/sec). When light passes through a glass window, it slows down. This change in speed causes light rays to bend. This bending of light rays is called **refraction**.

Light often refracts when it moves from one substance to another. For example, a pencil in a glass of water appears to bend at the water's surface. This is because light rays traveling from the pencil to your eyes bend as they move from the water, through the glass, and into the air.

✔ **What is reflection?**

FIND OUT

- **the characteristics of light energy and sound energy**
- **the wave characteristics of light and sound**

VOCABULARY

reflection
refraction
lens
pitch
volume

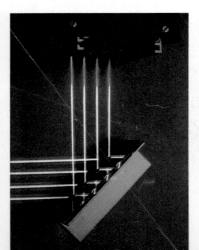
A mirror reflects all the light that strikes it. ▼

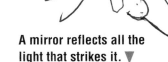

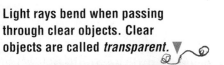

Light rays bend when passing through clear objects. Clear objects are called *transparent*. ▼

Some objects absorb all colors of light, producing a shadow. These objects are called *opaque*. ▼

Lenses

Many people wear corrective lenses—glasses or contacts—to improve their vision. A **lens** is a piece of clear material that bends, or refracts, light rays passing through it. There are two kinds of lenses. A *convex lens* is thicker in the middle than at the edges. When light passes through a convex lens, the rays bend toward each other. The hand lens you use for investigations is a convex lens. It makes nearby objects look larger.

People who are farsighted have trouble seeing things that are close to them, like print on a page. Glasses or contacts with convex lenses magnify the print, allowing these people to read more easily.

Movie projectors and slide projectors also use convex lenses. As light from the bulb shines through the film, light rays spread apart. As these rays pass through the projector lens, they bend toward each other again.

The other type of lens is a *concave lens*. This lens is thicker around the edges than in the middle. When light rays pass through a concave lens, they bend away from each other. This makes distant objects seem nearer and smaller. Some cameras have a concave lens in their viewfinders. When you look through the viewfinder, you see a small version of what the final photograph will look like.

Concave lenses help people who are nearsighted. These people have trouble seeing distant objects. Concave lenses bend light rays outward just enough to make distant objects seem closer.

✔ **Compare the shapes of convex lenses and concave lenses.**

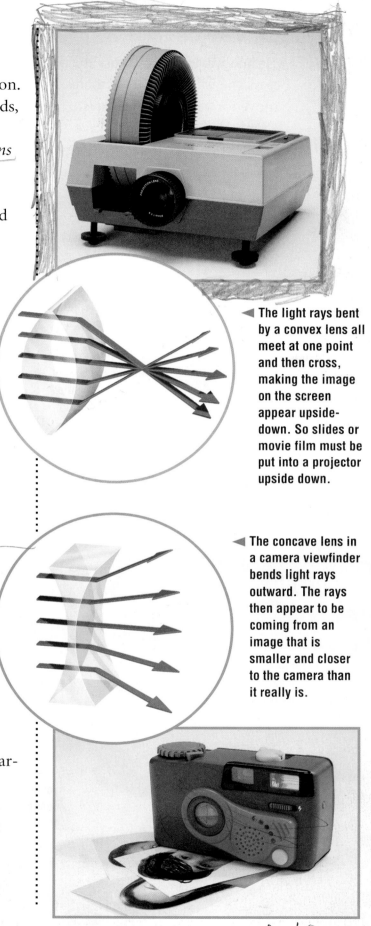

◄ The light rays bent by a convex lens all meet at one point and then cross, making the image on the screen appear upside-down. So slides or movie film must be put into a projector upside down.

◄ The concave lens in a camera viewfinder bends light rays outward. The rays then appear to be coming from an image that is smaller and closer to the camera than it really is.

Light Waves

When waves move across the ocean, the water doesn't actually move forward with the wave. Only the energy of the wave moves forward. Light energy moves as waves called *electromagnetic waves.* Electro-

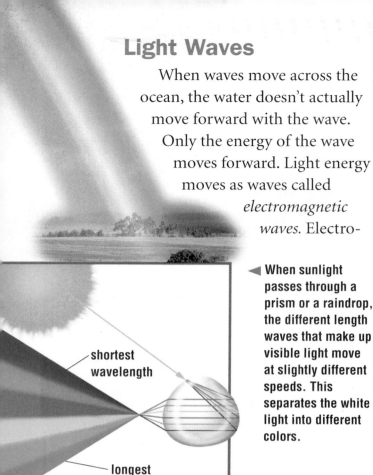

◄ When sunlight passes through a prism or a raindrop, the different length waves that make up visible light move at slightly different speeds. This separates the white light into different colors.

shortest wavelength

longest wavelength

magnetic waves are produced when electrons inside an atom vibrate and give off energy.

Visible light waves—those we can see—are just a small part of the electromagnetic waves produced in the universe. Radio waves, microwaves, infrared waves, ultraviolet waves, and X rays are also types of electromagnetic waves. Unlike water waves, electromagnetic waves don't need matter to move through. They move fastest, in fact, when there is no matter to slow them down, such as in space.

Within the range of visible light waves are different wavelengths that humans sense as different colors of light. We sense long wavelengths as red, and short wavelengths as violet. Between red and violet are all the colors of the rainbow.

✔ **How are electromagnetic waves produced?**

THE INSIDE STORY

Light and Sound

Your eyes gather light waves, and your ears gather sound waves. In these organs the energy waves are changed into nerve impulses. Your brain interprets these impulses, and you see images and hear sounds.

Lens Light passes through the clear *lens*, which can thicken to help focus light from nearby objects.

Iris The colored *iris* widens in darkness and narrows in bright light to control the amount of light that enters through the *pupil.*

Cornea Light enters through the clear *cornea*, which acts as a convex lens and bends light rays.

Retina An upside-down image falls on the *retina*, where cells change light energy to electrical and chemical energy in the form of nerve impulses.

Sound Waves

Sound also moves as waves. However, like water waves, sound waves are carried by vibrating matter.

Most of the sound waves we hear travel through air. But sound waves also travel through liquids, such as water, and even through solids. If you click two stones together while underwater, you can hear the sound quite clearly.

As a sound wave travels through matter, molecules in the matter vibrate in the direction the sound wave is moving. As the sound moves forward, the molecules are squeezed together. This is called *compression*. After the first compression passes, pressure on the molecules drops. This is called *rarefaction* (rer•uh•FAK•shuhn). The wavelength of a sound is the distance between two compressions. If a sound is continuous, both compression and rarefaction are repeated again and again, producing a series of sound waves.

As the harp string vibrates, it moves quickly from side to side. Short strings vibrate faster than long strings, and produce a higher pitch.

The frequency at which sound waves move determines the **pitch** of the sound. The higher the frequency, the higher the pitch. In music, pitch is labeled with letters called notes. As you move from left to right on a piano keyboard, pitch increases.

Another way of measuring sound waves is to measure their strength. The more the molecules are squeezed during compression, the louder the sound is. The loudness of a sound is called **volume**.

✔ **How are sound waves carried?**

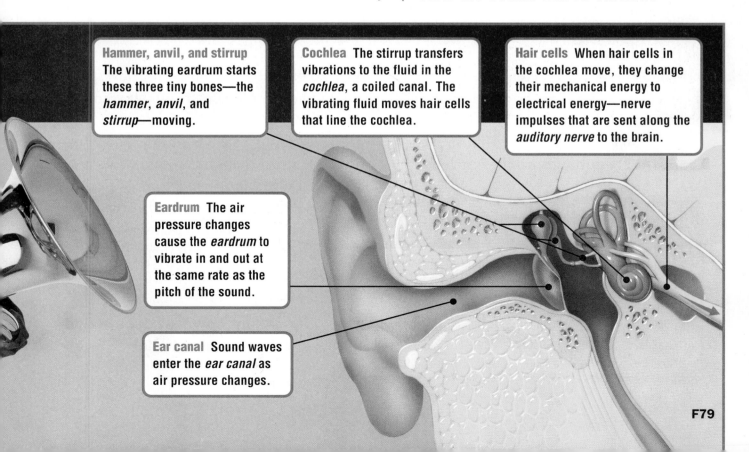

Hammer, anvil, and stirrup The vibrating eardrum starts these three tiny bones—the *hammer*, *anvil*, and *stirrup*—moving.

Cochlea The stirrup transfers vibrations to the fluid in the *cochlea*, a coiled canal. The vibrating fluid moves hair cells that line the cochlea.

Hair cells When hair cells in the cochlea move, they change their mechanical energy to electrical energy—nerve impulses that are sent along the *auditory nerve* to the brain.

Eardrum The air pressure changes cause the *eardrum* to vibrate in and out at the same rate as the pitch of the sound.

Ear canal Sound waves enter the *ear canal* as air pressure changes.

Sound Energy

Like water waves, sound waves are waves of energy moving through matter. And like water waves, sound waves move molecules back and forth without carrying them along with the wave.

Because sound waves are vibrations of molecules, molecules must be present for sound to travel. Where there is no matter, such as in outer space, sound cannot travel.

The sounds we hear travel mostly as vibrations of the gas molecules in the air around us. When sound waves move through air, they travel about 340 m/sec (1100 ft/sec). When sound waves move through denser materials, such as liquids and solids, they move faster. You can compare some of these speeds by using the table below.

Denser objects carry sound energy farther as well as faster than less dense objects. Whales, for example, produce sounds that travel underwater for hundreds of kilometers. Only very loud sounds can travel that far through air.

Sound energy travels even better through most solids. The rich sounds made by a cello or a guitar are due partly to the vibrations of the wood in the instruments. This is called *resonance.* Try putting a ticking watch on

Humans see objects when light waves reflect off them. Animals such as dolphins and bats can use the reflection of sound waves to form "pictures" of objects around them. This sense is similar to humans using sonar to "see" objects on the ocean floor.

one end of a table and observing how clearly you can hear the ticking if you put your ear against the other end of the table.

However, not all solids carry sound vibrations. Materials that carry sound waves are called sound *conductors.* Materials that don't carry sound are called sound *insulators.* Materials with a lot of air spaces in them, such as fabrics and plastic foam, are good sound insulators.

✔ **About how fast does sound travel through air?**

Speed of Sound Waves Through Different Materials

Material	Speed of Sound in Material
Air	340 m/sec (about 1100 ft/sec)
Water	1500 m/sec (about 4900 ft/sec)
Silver	2650 m/sec (about 8700 ft/sec)
Granite	3950 m/sec (about 13,000 ft/sec)
Steel	5000 m/sec (about 16,400 ft/sec)

Summary

Light energy is electromagnetic energy that travels through space and through certain materials. When light waves strike an obstacle, they are absorbed, reflected, or refracted. Lenses are curved pieces of transparent matter that refract light rays. Sound energy is vibrations that travel through matter. Solids and liquids conduct sound better than gases.

Review

1. What is refraction?
2. What type of lens would you use to magnify your view of a butterfly?
3. What is a sound wave?
4. **Critical Thinking** If a bright, loud explosion took place in space, would it be seen or heard on Earth?
5. **Test Prep** Which part of the eye has cells that change light energy to nerve impulses?
   A the iris
   B the blind spot
   C the lens
   D the retina

LINKS

MATH LINK

Estimate Suppose a thunderstorm is coming. First you see a flash of lightning. You hear the thunder 22 seconds later. Knowing the speed of sound in air, estimate how far away the storm is.

WRITING LINK

Informative Writing—Classification Make a list of all the uses of lenses you can think of. Classify the lens in each case as *concave* or *convex*. Exchange lists with a classmate, and talk about any differences between your lists.

SOCIAL STUDIES LINK

Law of Refraction The Egyptian astronomer Ptolemy stated the first law of refraction. But it was Willebrord Snell who finalized the law now known as Snell's law. Research these men, and write a short report about Snell's law of refraction.

TECHNOLOGY LINK

Learn more about light energy by viewing *Pscholograms* on the **Harcourt Science Newsroom Video.**

LESSON 4

What Are Thermal and Chemical Energy?

In this lesson, you can . . .

INVESTIGATE the way heat moves through different materials.

LEARN ABOUT how thermal energy is transferred and how chemical energy is stored.

LINK to math, writing, social studies, and technology.

INVESTIGATE

Heat

Activity Purpose In this lesson you will learn about heat. In this investigation you will **experiment** to help you understand the ways heat moves through different materials.

Materials
- margarine
- metal butter knife
- Styrofoam cup
- hot water
- clock
- plastic knife

CAUTION

Activity Procedure

1. Place a dab of cold margarine near the middle of the metal knife. Place another dab of margarine the same size near the tip of the knife's blade.

2. **CAUTION** **Be careful when pouring the hot water.** Half-fill the cup with hot water. Put the metal knife's handle into the water. The dabs of margarine should be above the level of the water. (Picture A)

3. **Predict** which dab of margarine will melt first—the one near the middle of the knife or the one near the end of the knife.

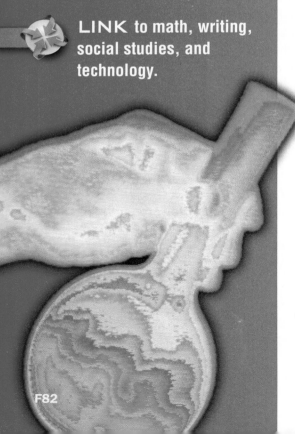

◄ This is a *thermogram*, a photo that records thermal energy. The purple, red, and orange areas are warmer than the blue and green areas.

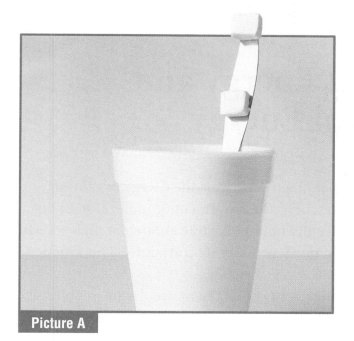

Picture A

Picture B

4️⃣ **Observe** the metal knife for ten minutes, and **record** your observations.

5️⃣ Repeat Steps 1–4, using the plastic knife. (Picture B)

6️⃣ **Experiment** to find out which material transfers heat faster—metal or plastic. Be sure to **identify and control variables** that might affect the results.

Draw Conclusions

1. **Draw conclusions** about how heat moves through the metal knife.

2. **Draw conclusions** about which material transfers heat faster.

3. **Scientists at Work** Scientists **identify and control variables** in an experiment to see how changing one variable affects the results. What variables did you control in your experiment? What variable did you test?

Investigate Further **Hypothesize** about which knife will lose heat more quickly. Then **experiment** to test your hypothesis.

Process Skill Tip

To be sure that the results of an experiment are valid, you must **identify and control** all **variables** that might affect the results.

Thermal Energy and Chemical Energy

Thermal Energy

FIND OUT

- **what thermal energy is and how it moves**

- **what chemical energy is**

VOCABULARY

temperature
heat
conduction
convection
radiation

You may recall that kinetic energy is the energy of motion. Kinetic energy is present in the movement of molecules. In liquids and gases, molecules bounce off one another at high speeds. Even in solid matter, molecules vibrate constantly. This kinetic energy of molecules is *thermal energy.*

The average kinetic energy of all the molecules in an object is the object's **temperature**. The higher the average kinetic energy, or the faster the molecules move, the higher the temperature. It's important to note that temperature and thermal energy aren't the same. For example, a large pot of boiling water and a small pot of boiling water have the same temperature, but the large pot has more thermal energy because it has more molecules.

When rapidly moving molecules (those in a hot substance) bump into slowly moving molecules (those in a cold substance), they transfer, or give off, some of their thermal energy to the slower molecules. The transfer of thermal energy from one substance to another is called **heat**. Thermal energy always flows in the same direction—from the warmer substance to the cooler substance. As you observed in the investigation, heat warms the cooler substance, raising its temperature. Heat can also change the state of a substance, making a solid melt or a liquid evaporate.

✔ **What is heat?**

The molecules in the milk are moving slowly. Their thermal energy is low, so the liquid feels cold. ▼

The molecules in the hot cocoa are moving quickly. Their thermal energy is high, so the liquid feels hot. ▼

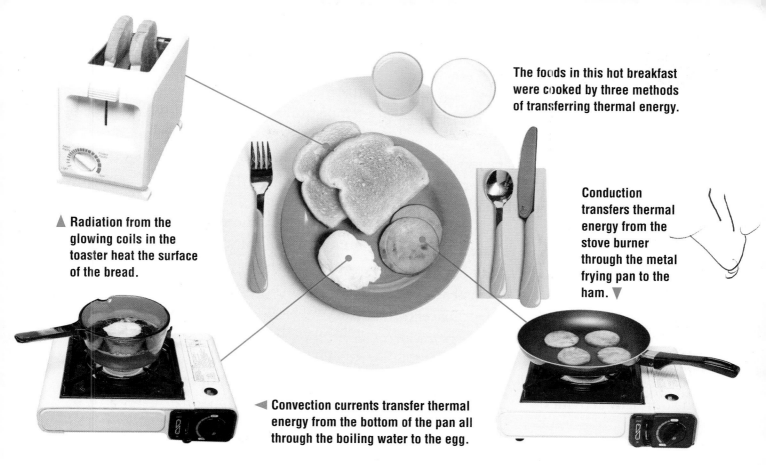

The foods in this hot breakfast were cooked by three methods of transferring thermal energy.

▲ Radiation from the glowing coils in the toaster heat the surface of the bread.

Conduction transfers thermal energy from the stove burner through the metal frying pan to the ham. ▼

◄ Convection currents transfer thermal energy from the bottom of the pan all through the boiling water to the egg.

Transferring Thermal Energy

Thermal energy can be transferred between objects in three ways: conduction, convection, and radiation.

Conduction (kuhn•DUHK•shuhn) is the direct transfer of thermal energy between objects that touch. A frying pan in direct contact with an electric-stove burner gets hot because the burner is hot.

When solids transfer thermal energy to other solids, it is usually by conduction. Materials that conduct heat easily are called *conductors*. Metals are good heat conductors. Materials that do a poor job of conducting heat are called *insulators*. Air is a good heat insulator. For example, double-paned windows have a layer of air between two layers of glass. This air slows down the rate at which heat can be conducted into or out of a building.

Convection (kuhn•VEK•shuhn) is thermal energy transfer as a result of the mixing of a liquid or a gas. When you heat a pan of water on a stove, the water at the bottom of the pan heats up first. The hot water becomes less dense, and cold water from the top of the pan sinks below it. As the hot water rises, it cools and sinks. This movement of hot water rising, cooling, sinking, being reheated, and rising again transfers thermal energy throughout the pan.

Radiation (ray•dee•AY•shuhn) is the transfer of thermal energy by electromagnetic waves. Energy from the sun is transferred to Earth by electromagnetic waves. Some of that energy is thermal energy. Conduction and convection can transfer thermal energy through matter, but only radiation can transfer thermal energy through space.

✓ **What are the three ways thermal energy can be transferred?**

Chemical Energy

Some chemical reactions give off energy. Others take in energy. Energy is stored in the bonds between atoms when they join together to form molecules. This energy is stored as a form of potential energy called *chemical energy*. Chemical energy can be released as kinetic energy when molecules break apart.

Chemical energy can be released as several forms of kinetic energy. Batteries, for example, contain chemical energy that can be used to produce electricity. During cellular respiration, your body changes chemical energy stored in the food you eat into mechanical energy that allows you to carry on your daily activities.

Other body processes change chemical energy into thermal energy. Some of that thermal energy is used to keep your body temperature at about 37°C (98.6°F). The table shows the amount of chemical energy stored in some of the foods you eat.

The potential energy of foods is measured in units called Calories (C). A Calorie is the amount of heat needed to raise the temperature of 1000 g of water by 1°C.

Chemical energy can also be released as light and heat when wood and other fuels are burned. You will learn more about the release of chemical energy from fuels in Chapter 4.

✔ **What is chemical energy?**

Potential Energy in Foods

Food (1 serving)	Energy (in Calories)	Food (1 serving)	Energy (in Calories)
Fruits		**Dairy Products**	
Apple	80	Ice cream	270
Banana	105	Cheese	110
Orange	80	Yogurt	230
Meats		**Vegetables**	
Chicken, roasted	140	Carrots	30
Hot dog	145	Corn	85
Pork chop	275	French fries	220
Roast beef, lean	175	Green beans	35
Salmon, baked	140	Lettuce	5
Shrimp, fried	240	Tomato	25
Bread and Cereal		**Snacks**	
Bread, white	65	Peanut butter	95
Macaroni and cheese	430	Pizza, cheese	290
Oatmeal	105	Popcorn, plain	30
Rice, white	180	Pretzel sticks	10

Grass stores energy from sunlight as chemical energy. By eating grass, the cow takes in this stored energy. Some of it becomes thermal energy, and some becomes mechanical energy. Some of it is stored as chemical energy in the cow's milk. ▼

Summary

Thermal energy is the kinetic energy of molecules. The average kinetic energy of the molecules in an object is the object's temperature. Heat is the transfer of thermal energy from one object to another. Conduction is the direct transfer of heat between objects that touch. Convection is the transfer of heat through currents in a gas or a liquid. Radiation is the transfer of energy by electromagnetic waves. When atoms join to form molecules, thermal energy can be stored as chemical energy. Chemical energy can be released as kinetic energy.

Review

1. What is convection?
2. What type of heat transfer takes place when you burn your hand on a stove?
3. Two atoms absorb thermal energy when joining together to form a molecule. What happens to that thermal energy?
4. **Critical Thinking** Suppose you drop an ice cube into a warm drink, and it melts. How is thermal energy transferred?
5. **Test Prep** Which form of energy transfer allows you to feel the warmth of the sun on your face?

   A radiation
   B conduction
   C convection
   D chemical energy

LINKS

MATH LINK

Draw Conclusions Which has a higher temperature, a 100-g ice cube or 10 g of water at 1°C? Which has more thermal energy?

WRITING LINK

Informative Writing—Explanation Write two or three paragraphs for your teacher explaining how the transfer of energy from the sun provides most of Earth's energy.

SOCIAL STUDIES LINK

History of Calories Scientists once thought of heat as a fluid, called *caloric*, that flowed from one object to another. Benjamin Thompson, also known as Count Rumford, came up with the idea that, because heat could be caused by motion, heat and motion must be different forms of the same thing (energy). Research Count Rumford's experiments and his ideas about heat, and report to your class.

GO ONLINE TECHNOLOGY LINK

Learn more about thermal and chemical energy by visiting the Harcourt Learning Site. **www.harcourtschool.com**

WELCOME TO THE LEARNING SITE

Sounds and Images

People have long been fascinated by the properties of sound and light. Over time, this interest has led inventors to develop many devices for producing sounds and images.

Early Musical Instruments

Early musical instruments, such as the 5000-year-old lyre, produced music through the vibration of strings. About 1000 years after the introduction of the lyre, necks and hollow bodies were added to stringed instruments to enable performers to produce louder musical sounds. These new designs led to the development of plucked instruments, such as the guitar, and bowed instruments, such as the violin.

Better Vision

In the late 1200s, the invention of eyeglasses helped bring the world into focus for people with blurry vision. Eyeglasses produced at that time had small glass lenses that bulged outward. These convex lenses helped correct the vision of far-sighted people, or people who could not see nearby objects clearly. They did this by bending light rays so that an image would focus on the eye's retina. Over time, eyeglass makers found that a combination of lenses could magnify images.

The Dutch built on this discovery, inventing the compound microscope in 1590 and the telescope in 1608. Less than a year later, Galileo used one of these early telescopes to study the moon. He observed mountains, valleys, and craters that had never been seen before.

The History of Sounds and Images

3200 B.C.
The lyre, one of the earliest known musical instruments, is developed.

1590
Hans and Zacharias Janssen invent the compound microscope.

1608
Hans Lippershey invents the telescope. A year later Galileo Galilei builds the first astronomical telescope.

3000 B.C. · **A.D. 1200** · **A.D. 1300** · **A.D. 1400** · **A.D. 1600** · **A.D. 1800**

1285
Lenses to help people with poor eyesight are invented.

1876
Alexander Graham Bell invents the telephone, which sends speech as electric signals through wires.

Transmitting Sounds and Images

In the late 1700s and early 1800s, people discovered that information could be sent from place to place over electric wires. In 1837, Samuel F. B. Morse invented the telegraph, a device that used electric current to transmit coded messages. Morse's telegraph looked like a simple electric switch. At the press of a button, current passed through the telegraph's wires. The current stopped when the button was released.

Morse invented a code known as Morse code, to enable messages to be sent over the telegraph. The code, still in use today, represents each letter of the alphabet as a series of long and short clicks. The clicks are translated by the telegraph into a series of dots and dashes. These marks then are transferred to paper by an electrically controlled pencil.

In 1876, Canadian inventor Alexander Graham Bell transmitted his own voice electrically over wire. This was the beginning of the modern telephone.

In the late 1800s and early 1900s, Thomas Edison, perhaps America's greatest inventor, developed many devices for storing and transmitting sounds and images. Edison's inventions included the phonograph, for recording and playing back sounds, and the kinetoscope, for producing motion pictures. Also among his more than 1000 inventions were the mimeograph—an early copying machine—the battery, and improved versions of Morse's telegraph and Bell's telephone.

Since then, the introduction of new technologies has led to new ways of transmitting information. In the early 1900s, Italian inventor Guglielmo Marconi perfected a wireless telegraph and a shortwave radio. By 1928, American Philo Farnsworth successfully transmitted video images—the first television.

Today voice and data, as well as radio and television signals, are sent through the air as electromagnetic waves. Other signals are transmitted as pulses of light through thin glass or plastic tubes called fiber optic cables. These cables can carry more signals with less energy loss than wire cables can.

THINK ABOUT IT

1. How did the addition of necks and hollow bodies improve early stringed instruments?

2. How did the Dutch build on the discovery that different lenses, used together, could magnify objects?

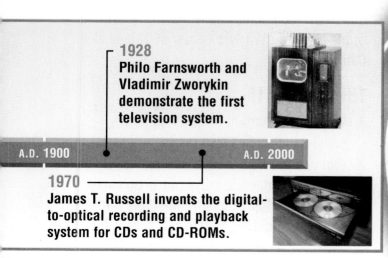

1928
Philo Farnsworth and Vladimir Zworykin demonstrate the first television system.

A.D. 1900   A.D. 2000

1970
James T. Russell invents the digital-to-optical recording and playback system for CDs and CD-ROMs.

Grinding lenses

Jean M. Bennett
PHYSICIST

Jean M. Bennett is a physicist who has done a great deal of work in the study of light scattering. Light scattering occurs when a beam of light strikes an uneven surface and is reflected in many different directions. This scattering is not at all like the parallel rays of light that are reflected by a smooth surface.

Dr. Bennett's work has many real-life uses, especially for optical equipment such as lenses. Most lenses used in optical equipment are polished to a very smooth finish. Then the lenses are treated with a thin coating to help prevent "ghost" reflections. If you have ever seen a faint double image on a television screen instead of one sharp image, you have an idea of what a ghost reflection is. However, the thin coating also gives a lens a surface that is not perfectly smooth, which causes the light to scatter. Dr. Bennett has worked with lens manufacturers to make lenses with smoother surfaces and coatings that scatter less light. This research helps people who wear glasses to be able to see better, especially at night.

In addition to working on light scattering, Dr. Bennett has also done research on the physics of Earth's atmosphere. She is currently an important member of the research department of the Naval Air Warfare Center at China Lake, California.

THINK ABOUT IT

1. Why is it important to develop better coatings as lenses also get better?

2. Can you think of another situation in which doing something to solve one problem caused another problem? Describe the situation and the problem.

SOUND WAVES

How do sound waves travel?

Materials

- glass pie pan with 200 mL water
- overhead projector
- tin can
- tuning fork
- uncooked rice
- balloon
- Slinky

Procedure

❶ Put the pie pan with water on the projector. Turn the projector on.

❷ Tap the tuning fork on a solid object. Place the end of the fork in the water. Observe the waves on the screen.

❸ Now stretch the balloon over the tin can.

❹ Sprinkle rice on top of the stretched balloon.

❺ Tap the tuning fork, and gently touch the end of the fork to the balloon. Observe the action of the rice.

❻ Stretch the Slinky out on a smooth surface. Gather some coils at one end. Then let them go. Observe how the compression waves travel.

Draw Conclusions

In Step 2, how did the sound waves travel from the tuning fork? How did Step 5 show that sound waves are energy waves? Sound waves travel as compression waves, like those you made with the Slinky. Describe the movement of compression waves.

THE EYES HAVE IT

How does the brain receive images?

Materials

- flashlight
- small toy car
- hand lens
- small, round fishbowl
- sheet of white paper

Procedure

❶ Line up the materials in the order shown.

❷ Darken the room. Turn on the flashlight.

❸ Shine the light on the toy car.

❹ Focus the shadow through the lens and the fishbowl, and onto the white paper. Observe the image formed on the paper.

Draw Conclusions

What organ does this model represent? What parts of that organ does each part of the model represent? What happens to the shadow of the toy car projected onto the paper? When an image is received on the retina and sent to the brain, what does the brain do with this image?

Vocabulary Review

Use the terms below to answer Questions 1 through 12. The page numbers in ( ) tell you where to look in the chapter if you need help.

energy (F62)
kinetic energy (F62)
potential energy (F62)
electric charge (F68)
electric force (F69)
electric current (F69)
conductor (F70)
electric circuit (F71)
insulator (F71)
resistor (F71)
electromagnet (F72)

reflection (F76)
refraction (F76)
lens (F77)
pitch (F79)
volume (F79)
temperature (F84)
heats (F84)
conduction (F85)
convection (F85)
radiation (F85)

1. The three ways in which thermal energy is transferred are _____, _____, and _____.

2. A _____ is a clear material that bends light rays.

3. _____ causes changes in matter.

4. A _____ carries electric current easily, while an _____ does not.

5. A sound's _____ is determined by the frequency of its energy waves, while _____ is determined by the strength of the waves.

6. When an _____ flows through a coil of wire wrapped around a bar of iron, it makes an _____.

7. When a piece of wood burns, energy from the burning wood _____ the air.

8. The energy of motion is _____, while the energy of position is _____.

9. The bouncing of light rays off an object is called _____. The bending of light rays by an object is called _____.

10. A path for electricity, called an _____, may include a _____ that changes electric energy into other forms of energy.

11. The attraction or repulsion of an _____ is called an _____.

12. The average kinetic energy of all the molecules in an object is the object's _____.

Connect Concepts

Write the terms from the Word Bank that belong in the concept map.

potential   kinetic   static   thermal
radiation   sound   light   convection
chemical   electric   current   conduction

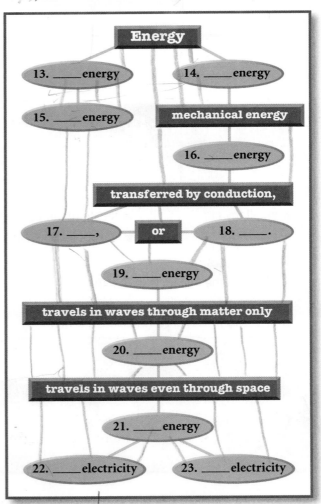

Energy

13. _____ energy
14. _____ energy
15. _____ energy
mechanical energy
16. _____ energy
transferred by conduction,
17. _____,   or   18. _____.
19. _____ energy
travels in waves through matter only
20. _____ energy
travels in waves even through space
21. _____ energy
22. _____ electricity
23. _____ electricity

Check Understanding

Write the letter of the best choice.

24. Metals and other materials that transfer heat and electricity easily are called —

A insulators   **C** radiators

B resistors   **D** conductors

25. The color you see in an object is the color of light the object —

F absorbs   **H** refracts

G reflects   **J** conducts

26. Because there is no matter in space, thermal energy moves from the sun to Earth by —

A radiation   **C** insulation

B convection   **D** conduction

27. Lightning and the spark you may see when you touch a doorknob on a dry day are both caused by —

F thermal energy

G static electricity

H electromagnetism

J resistors

28. An object with a positive charge will attract another object with —

A a negative charge

B a positive charge

C a positive or a negative charge

D no charge

Critical Thinking

29. Suppose you throw a ball high into the air and then it falls to the ground. Describe where the ball has the greatest potential energy and where it has the greatest kinetic energy.

30. If energy can be neither created nor destroyed, what happens to the sunlight that falls on Earth?

Process Skills Review

31. You touch a lamp cord and get a shock. **Draw a conclusion** about the insulation on the cord.

32. You record the temperature in a pan of water as it heats. You want to **make a graph** to display your results. What type of graph should you use?

33. You conduct an experiment with parallel and series electric circuits. What is one way you could **communicate** about the circuits you built?

34. You want to **compare** two materials to see which is the better conductor of thermal energy. Name two quantities you will measure.

35. You want to **plan and conduct an experiment** to show convection. Name two items you could use in your experiment.

36. You experiment to compare the colors of light reflected by different substances. Name one **variable** you must **control**.

Performance Assessment

Energy Audit

Take ten minutes to identify as many forms of energy around you right now as possible. Make a list of these forms and of how they are being transferred or changed from one form to another during those ten minutes.

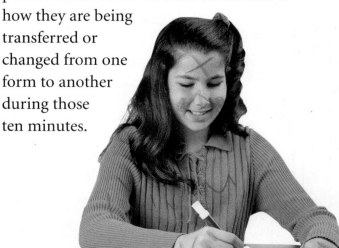

CHAPTER 4

How People Use Energy

Vocabulary Preview

chemical bonds
hydroelectric energy
tidal energy
biomass
nuclear energy
geothermal energy
solar energy
fusion energy

Early humans used energy mostly for heating and for cooking. When they learned how to work with metal, their energy use increased. Each new technology led them to use more energy. This is still true today. Every year people use about two percent more energy than they did the year before.

Fast Fact

Most of the world's energy is used by a small number of countries. The United States, for example, uses one-fourth of all the energy in the world.

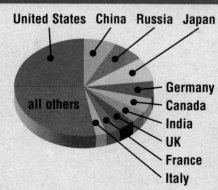

Energy Use

United States   China   Russia   Japan

all others

Germany
Canada
India
UK
France
Italy

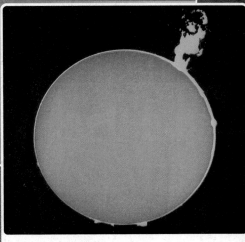

Less than one-billionth of the sun's energy reaches the surface of Earth. Yet one hour's worth of solar energy is more energy than everyone on Earth uses in an entire year.

Fast Fact

ENIAC, the first electronic digital computer, required huge amounts of electricity. Fifty years later, some hand-held computers use less energy than a portable radio.

How Do People Use Fossil Fuels?

In this lesson, you can . . .

INVESTIGATE how stored energy is released from chemical compounds.

LEARN ABOUT how fossil fuels are used.

LINK to math, writing, health, and technology.

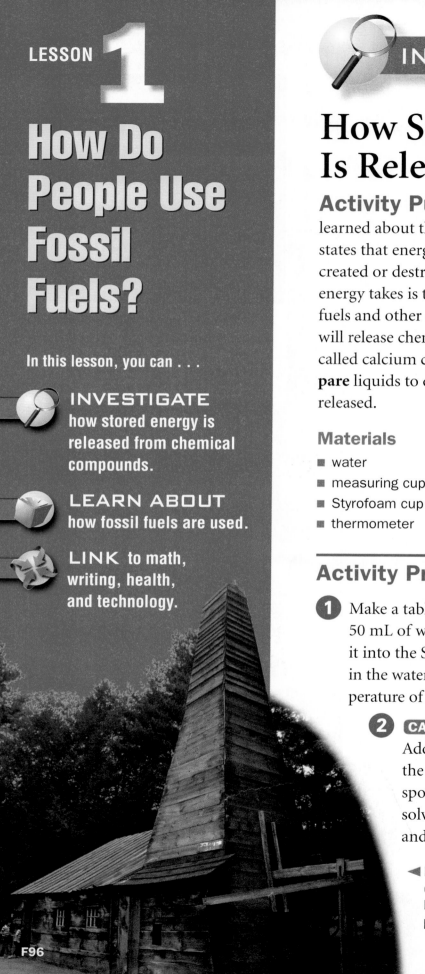

In 1859 E. L. Drake drilled the first producing oil well, at Oil Creek in Titusville, Pennsylvania. Most of the oil was used to produce kerosene for lamps.

INVESTIGATE

How Stored Energy Is Released

Activity Purpose In a previous chapter you learned about the law of conservation of energy. It states that energy can change forms but cannot be created or destroyed. One of the forms that potential energy takes is the chemical energy stored in fossil fuels and other compounds. In this investigation you will release chemical energy stored in a compound called calcium chloride. You will **observe** and **compare** liquids to determine what form of energy is released.

Materials

- water
- measuring cup
- Styrofoam cup
- thermometer
- clock with second hand
- safety goggles
- calcium chloride
- spoon

CAUTION

Activity Procedure

1 Make a table like the one on page F97. Measure 50 mL of water in the measuring cup, and pour it into the Styrofoam cup. Put the thermometer in the water. After 30 seconds, **measure** the temperature of the water and **record** it in the table.

2 **CAUTION** Put on the safety goggles. Add 2 spoonfuls of calcium chloride to the cup of water. Stir the water with the spoon until the calcium chloride dissolves. Wait 30 seconds. Then **measure** and **record** the temperature. (Picture A)

Substance	Temperature
Water without chemical	
Water with chemical after 30 seconds	
Water with chemical after 60 seconds	
Water with chemical after 120 seconds	

3 **Measure** and **record** the temperature of the water two more times, after 60 seconds and again after 120 seconds. Then **compare** the temperature of the water before and after you added calcium chloride. (Picture B)

Picture A

Draw Conclusions

1. How did the temperature of the water change when you added calcium chloride?

2. **Infer** whether the calcium chloride gives off heat or absorbs heat as it dissolves in water.

3. What do you **infer** might have caused the water temperature to change?

4. **Scientists at Work** Scientists **observe** and **measure** to gather as much data as they can from an experiment. What did you learn from this experiment about how the chemical energy in some compounds can be released?

Picture B

Investigate Further **Hypothesize** what will happen when a different chemical, such as magnesium sulfate (Epsom salts), is placed in water. Then **plan and conduct a simple experiment** to test your hypothesis.

Process Skill Tip

When you **observe** and **measure** carefully, the data you gather will be more useful.

F97

Fossil Fuel Use

Burning Fuels Produce Heat

As a tree grows, it uses energy from sunlight to build the chemical compounds it needs. Solar energy is stored in the tree's molecules. If molecules are broken apart, energy is released. In the investigation you observed that much of that energy is thermal energy, or heat. Burning wood or fossil fuels also breaks apart molecules and releases heat. *Fossil fuels* are fuels that formed from the remains of once-living organisms. They include coal, natural gas, and petroleum.

Stored solar energy, as chemical energy, exists in all living organisms. Most of it is stored in the **chemical bonds** that join atoms of carbon to each other and to atoms of other elements, such as hydrogen. When living matter from forests, swamps, and shallow seas is buried under sediments for long periods of time, the chemical energy is buried as well. When fossil fuels are taken from the ground, their chemical energy can be converted to thermal energy by burning.

✓ **How is the chemical energy stored in fossil fuels released?**

Solar energy is stored as chemical energy in living organisms. This energy can be released by burning. Wood was used as a fuel for heating and for cooking during much of America's history, but it doesn't really release much heat. The table shows the amount of heat released by burning different fuels.

Heat Released Burning 1 kg of Fuel

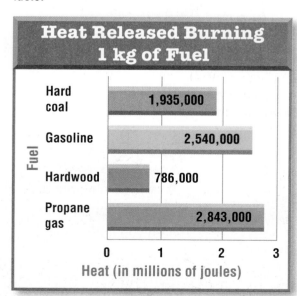

Fuel	Heat (in millions of joules)
Hard coal	1,935,000
Gasoline	2,540,000
Hardwood	786,000
Propane gas	2,843,000

Heat (in millions of joules)

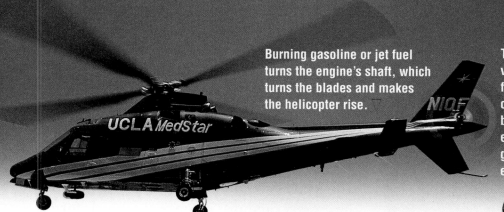

Burning gasoline or jet fuel turns the engine's shaft, which turns the blades and makes the helicopter rise. ▽

This generator is a smaller version of what you might find at an energy station. It changes the energy of burning fuel into mechanical energy (for turning the generator) and then into electric energy. ▽

Using Fossil Fuels

Fossil fuels are the main source of energy for industrial nations like the United States. Coal is taken from Earth's crust by strip mining or by deep mining. Wells are drilled into the crust to obtain natural gas or petroleum.

As the graph on page F98 shows, fossil fuels release large amounts of thermal energy when they're burned. People use this energy in many ways. In homes, offices, and schools, thermal energy is used to heat water or the air. On cold days the heat that comes from your classroom's radiators or air vents was probably produced by burning coal, oil, or natural gas.

In a gas stove, natural gas or bottled gas, such as propane, is burned to provide heat for cooking food. Natural gas is usually distributed through underground pipelines. Bottled gas is brought in by truck to fill local storage tanks.

Petroleum is the main source of energy for transportation. Cars, trucks, buses, trains, and planes have engines that burn fuel made from petroleum, such as gasoline or diesel fuel. As gasoline burns, it expands rapidly. The resulting force turns the engine's crankshaft. Through

a series of gears, this movement turns the wheels that push the vehicle.

Similar engines are used in electric energy stations. As you learned in an earlier chapter, when these engines run, they turn electric generators.

Much of the energy for generating electricity in the United States comes from burning fossil fuels, especially coal. Fossil fuels are also used for purposes other than thermal energy production. Plastics, fertilizers, chemicals, and some medicines are made partly from petroleum and coal. Even your shoes and clothes may be made partly from petroleum.

✔ **Name four uses of fossil fuels.**

Fossil fuels are used in making plastics, such as the ones in this kayak, paddle, and helmet. ▼

Alternatives to Fossil Fuels

Experts disagree about how much fossil fuel is still buried in the Earth, but the supply is limited. The remains of living organisms take millions of years to become petroleum or coal. However, in just a few years, a geologist can find a fossil-fuel deposit, a company can sell the fuel, and users can burn it. Since fossil fuels form so slowly but are used so quickly, they are considered *nonrenewable resources*.

Scientists don't know how small the supplies of fossil fuels are, but there are good reasons to use other sources of energy. One reason is that fossil fuels are needed more and more to make things, such as new types of plastics. Fossil fuels may also turn out to have uses not yet discovered.

Another reason for using other sources of energy is that burning fossil fuels releases large amounts of carbon dioxide into the air. Some scientists are concerned that the carbon dioxide may trap heat in Earth's

▲ This playground equipment is made of recycled soft drink bottles and other plastic items. Recycling plastics can reduce the use of fossil fuels.

An electric car produces no carbon dioxide itself. But the electricity to charge the car's battery may be produced by burning fossil fuels. ▼

atmosphere and cause environmental changes such as global warming.

To reduce the use of fossil fuels, many companies are developing alternative sources of energy. These include wind energy and geothermal energy (heat from within the Earth). In California and other places, some utility companies generate large amounts of electricity from these inexhaustible energy sources. Another method of using less fossil fuels is to recycle plastics and oils, such as the oil from car engines.

✔ **Why are fossil fuels considered nonrenewable resources?**

Summary

Coal, natural gas, and petroleum are fossil fuels formed from once-living matter that has been buried for millions of years. Fossil fuels are used to heat homes, move vehicles, and generate electricity. Because fossil fuels take millions of years to form, they are nonrenewable.

Review

1. Name three types of fossil fuels.
2. How is the chemical energy in fossil fuels changed to electric energy?
3. In what way does the energy in fossil fuels come from sunlight?
4. **Critical Thinking** Why isn't it correct to say that fossil fuels *make* thermal energy?
5. **Test Prep** Gasoline is produced from —

   A coal   **C** kerosene

   B natural gas **D** petroleum

LINKS

MATH LINK

Solve Problems A *calorie* is a unit of heat. One calorie is the amount of heat needed to raise the temperature of 1 g of water by 1°C. Suppose you fill a kettle with 1000 g of water at 20°C. Then you heat the water until it reaches 100°C. How many calories are needed to do this?

WRITING LINK

Expressive Writing—Friendly Letter Send e-mail to a friend. In the e-mail, describe all the energy changes that have occurred over millions of years to produce the electricity to send the e-mail.

HEALTH LINK

Comparing Calorie Content When you read on a food label that a snack has a certain number of Calories, you are learning about the chemical energy stored in that food. Each food Calorie (*Calorie* with a capital *C*) is the amount of energy needed to raise the temperature of 1 kg of water 1°C. Make a table that compares the energy stored in equal amounts of different foods.

TECHNOLOGY LINK

Learn more about generating electricity by visiting the National Museum of American History Internet site.
www.si.edu/harcourt/science

Smithsonian Institution®

How Can Moving Water Generate Electricity?

In this lesson, you can . . .

 INVESTIGATE the power of falling water.

 LEARN ABOUT how the energy of falling water is changed to electric energy.

 LINK to math, writing, social studies, and technology.

◀ The water behind Hoover Dam has a lot of potential energy. The dam's hydroelectric plant will change this potential energy to kinetic energy and then to electric energy.

 **INVESTIGATE**

Water Power

Activity Purpose To produce electricity, an energy station must change some other form of energy. In some cases, the mechanical energy of falling water is used. In this investigation you will **make a model** of a water wheel. Then you will **plan and conduct a simple investigation** to determine the amount of energy in falling water.

Materials

- two 10-cm plastic disks
- stapler
- scissors
- pencil sharpened at both ends
- 0.5-m length of string
- 30-g mass
- basin
- 1-L plastic bottle filled with water
- meterstick
- stopwatch

Activity Procedure

1. **CAUTION** **Be careful when using scissors.** Staple the plastic disks together near their centers. Using the scissors, cut four 3-cm slits into the disks as shown. At each slit, fold the disks in opposite directions to form a vane. (Picture A)

2. Again using the scissors, punch a 0.5-cm hole at the center of the disks. Insert the pencil. It will serve as the axle on which the water wheel rotates.

3. Use the scissors to make a smaller hole next to the pencil hole. Insert one end of the string into the hole, and tie a knot in the string to keep it in place. Tie the mass to the other end of the string.

4. Place the basin near the edge of the desk. Hold your water wheel over the basin. Your fingertips should hold the pencil points so the pencil can turn. The mass on the string should hang over the edge of the desk. (Picture B)

5. Have a partner slowly pour water over the wheel from a height of about 10 cm. Using the stopwatch, **measure** and **record** the time it takes for the mass to reach the level of the desk. Repeat this step several times.

6. Now repeat Steps 4 and 5, but have your partner pour the water from a height of about 20 cm. Again, **measure** and **record** the time it takes for the mass to reach the level of the desk.

Picture A

Draw Conclusions

1. What **variables** did you **control** in your investigation? What variable did you change?

2. Recall that the greater the power, the more quickly work is done. Which of your trials produced more power? Why?

3. **Scientists at Work** Scientists often look beyond the results of an investigation. For example, how does the height from which the water is poured affect the speed at which the water wheel turns? **Plan and conduct a simple investigation** to find out. Be sure to **identify and control variables,** changing only the height from which the water falls.

Picture B

Investigate Further **Hypothesize** about the rate of flow and the speed at which the water wheel turns. Then **plan and conduct a simple experiment** to test your hypothesis. Be sure to **identify and control variables,** changing only the rate of flow of the water.

Electricity and Moving Water

Hydroelectric Energy

Recall that energy cannot be created or destroyed, but that it can change forms. An electric generator works by changing mechanical energy into electric energy. Generators can be connected to any source of mechanical energy that makes their parts spin. One of these sources is falling water. Electricity generated from the force of falling water is called **hydroelectric energy**. *Hydro* means "water."

For thousands of years, people have used the energy of falling water to turn wheels along streams and rivers. The first water wheels probably powered mills that ground grain. During the

Hydroelectric dams often produce large lakes, which can be used for recreation. ▼

Fish swimming upstream can't get past a hydroelectric dam, so many dams have small rivers around them. Other dams have "fish ladders"—stepped waterfalls that fish can jump up, step by step, to get past the dam.

The water that moves through the dam (above) flows through turbines (at the right), setting them spinning. The turbines turn the electric generators.

▲ High-tension lines carry electricity produced at the energy station to places where it is needed.

Industrial Revolution of the 1700s and 1800s, water wheels provided the energy that turned the machines in many factories. Today about one-fifth of the world's energy is hydroelectric energy.

Hydroelectric energy stations use the energy of falling water to spin turbines. A *turbine* is an improved form of the water wheel you made in the investigation. Water strikes the blades of a turbine and makes it spin. The rotating turbine then spins the shaft of an electric generator. The electricity produced by the generator is then sent over power lines to homes, schools, and factories.

The energy that spins a hydroelectric turbine comes from the potential energy of water under pressure. Water near the surface of a lake exerts a force on the water below it. The greater the depth of the water, the greater the energy the water has due to this pressure. So people build dams across rivers to increase the depth of the water. The dam has openings, or gates, at the bottom that allow water to flow through. As water flows through a gate, it spins the vanes of the turbine.

Like almost all energy on Earth, hydroelectric energy can be traced back to the sun. The sun provides the energy that evaporates water from lakes and oceans and carries water vapor high into the air. When this water vapor condenses, it falls back to Earth as rain or snow. As runoff water flows into lakes, it compresses the water beneath it, passing on its potential energy. Rivers below the turbines carry the water back to the oceans. The water cycle is complete, and people have an inexhaustible source of energy.

✓ **What form of energy goes into a hydroelectric energy station? What form comes out?**

Tidal Energy

Along much of Earth's coastlines, tides rise and fall twice a day. In some places these changes in water level are especially large. There the mechanical energy of the moving water can be used to produce electricity. This is a form of hydroelectric energy called **tidal energy**.

Tidal energy plants depend on the difference in water height between high tide and low tide. They produce electricity by holding back water at high tide and letting it fall through turbines at low tide. For a tidal energy station to be efficient, the difference between water level at high tide and low tide must be large.

One place that is famous for its tides—sometimes called *supertides*—is the Bay of Fundy, in Canada. Supertides occur where

The world's first commercial tidal energy station was built at the mouth of the Rance River in Brittany, France. The station produces enough electricity for a city of 300,000 people. ▼

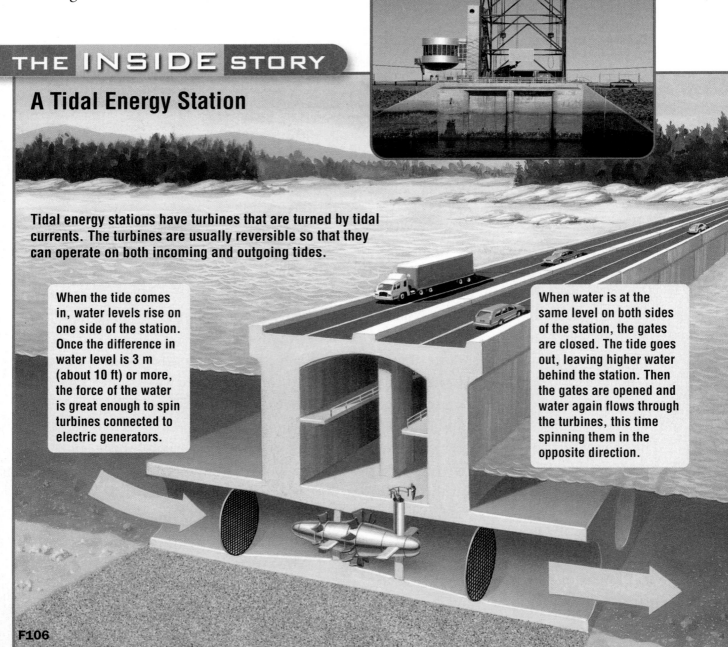

THE INSIDE STORY

A Tidal Energy Station

Tidal energy stations have turbines that are turned by tidal currents. The turbines are usually reversible so that they can operate on both incoming and outgoing tides.

When the tide comes in, water levels rise on one side of the station. Once the difference in water level is 3 m (about 10 ft) or more, the force of the water is great enough to spin turbines connected to electric generators.

When water is at the same level on both sides of the station, the gates are closed. The tide goes out, leaving higher water behind the station. Then the gates are opened and water again flows through the turbines, this time spinning them in the opposite direction.

spin freely on its axle. Now suspend the axle and turbine from the ring stand arm with two bent paper clips.

4 Fill the flask with water. Put the stopper with the bent glass tube in the flask. Set the flask on the hot plate. Point the open end of the glass tube toward the vanes on the bottom of the turbine. (Picture B)

5 **CAUTION** **Put on the safety goggles, and use caution around the steam.** Turn on the hot plate. **Observe** and **record** your observations of the turbine as the water begins to boil. Draw a diagram of your turbine to **communicate** your results. Be sure to include labels and arrows to show what happens.

Picture A

Draw Conclusions

1. **Infer** the source of energy for turning the turbine.

2. **Communicate** in a short paragraph how the energy from the source was changed to turn the turbine.

3. **Scientists at Work** When scientists **communicate,** they try to show clearly or describe what is happening. In what two ways did you communicate the results of this investigation? Which way was clearer?

Investigate Further **Plan and conduct a simple experiment** to determine how much work your turbine can do. Decide what **hypothesis** you will need to test and what equipment you will need to use.

Picture B

Process Skill Tip

Including arrows on a diagram can be a clear way to **communicate** information about motion and direction.

Other Energy Sources

Energy for Today

FIND OUT

- what other energy sources are used in the United States
- what energy sources we may rely on in the future

VOCABULARY

biomass
nuclear energy
geothermal energy
solar energy
fusion energy

Fossil fuels and hydroelectric energy are major energy sources in much of the world. Other energy sources may be less common, but they are still important. These include biomass, nuclear, wind, geothermal, and solar energy.

Biomass In some parts of the world, biomass is an important source of energy. **Biomass** is organic matter, such as wood, that is living or was recently alive. Biomass is often burned directly. However, as you saw in the graph on page F98, burning wood doesn't release much energy. In the United States, a major source of biomass is garbage. Burning garbage doesn't release much energy either, but it is basically a free energy source. Heat from burning biomass is used to boil water. The steam then turns turbines that run electric generators.

Biomass can also be made into liquid fuels. Alcohol made from wood or corn is mixed with gasoline to produce a fuel called gasohol. Other plants produce oils that can be burned in modified gasoline or diesel engines.

Nuclear Energy Energy is released when the nucleus of an atom is split apart. This energy is called **nuclear energy**. Splitting nuclei releases a large amount of energy. A nuclear energy station uses this energy to boil water. The resulting steam is directed through turbines and electric generators.

A nuclear energy station produces a large amount of electric energy from a small amount of fuel. However, the fuel and the waste products of the nuclear reactions can be dangerous to living organisms.

Wind Energy Wind energy is one of the oldest forms of energy used by people. Wind is still used all over the world. In the United States, for example, many farmers use windmills to pump

Wood, a type of biomass, is still used as a source of energy in some places. ▼

This pool of water is used to store fuel for a nuclear energy station. ▼

water from below the ground for irrigation. Some windmills on farms also generate small amounts of electricity.

A different kind of farm—a wind farm—uses modern windmills, or wind turbines, connected to electric generators. A wind farm can produce electricity wherever there is a steady wind. To get as much energy from the wind as possible, the blades of some wind turbines are 100 m (about 330 ft) across.

The advantage of using windmills or wind turbines to generate electricity is that the fuel—the wind—is free, nonpolluting, and inexhaustible. However, wind turbines are expensive, and the strength of the wind usually isn't constant.

Geothermal Energy In some parts of the world, people use heat from inside the Earth, called **geothermal energy**, to heat homes and produce electricity. Geothermal energy occurs where underground water lies close to hot magma. The water boils, and the steam forces its way to the surface. There it is used to turn turbines to generate electric energy. Sometimes steam or very hot water is piped directly to buildings to provide heat. In the United States, there are several geothermal energy stations near San Francisco, California.

▲ At The Geysers, north of San Francisco, underground water is heated by nearby magma. The escaping steam is directed to turbines to generate electricity.

▲ Solar panels change light energy directly into electricity.

Solar Energy The energy of sunlight is called **solar energy**. There are several ways to use solar energy. Solar collectors absorb and focus the sun's energy to heat water. Solar-heated water is often used to heat

This wind farm at Altmont Pass in California relies on a strong, steady wind to drive a set of 300 wind turbines.

homes and busi-
...is piped to faucets
...building.

...lar energy stations heat water
...it boils. The steam is then used to spin
turbines connected to electric generators.

Solar energy can also be changed directly
into electricity by *solar cells*. These cells,
arranged in flat panels, are made in layers.
Sunlight frees electrons from one layer. They
are attracted to the other layer. This produces an electric potential that can turn on
lights or run motors. Large panels of solar
cells are used to power satellites and space
stations. Strips containing just a few cells
provide the small amount of electricity
needed to run a calculator.

Although solar energy is free, solar collectors and cells can be expensive. And many
places do not have enough sunny days to
make it possible to use solar energy.

✔ **What are the advantages and disadvantages of each source of energy?**

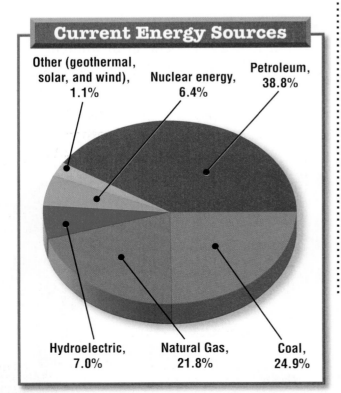

Current Energy Sources

Other (geothermal,
solar, and wind),
1.1%

Nuclear energy,
6.4%

Petroleum,
38.8%

Hydroelectric,
7.0%

Natural Gas,
21.8%

Coal,
24.9%

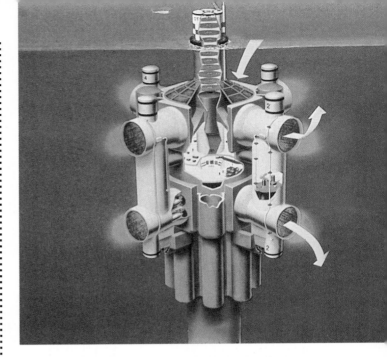

▲ Ocean thermal energy conversion (OTEC) uses
thermal energy from the ocean to produce electricity.
This experimental system uses differences in
temperature between warm upper layers and cold
lower layers of ocean water.

Energy for Tomorrow

New sources of energy are always being
developed. Scientists look for sources low in
cost and low in risk to humans and to the
environment.

One of these future sources is fusion.
Fusion energy is released when the nuclei
of two small atoms are forced together to
form a larger nucleus. This is the same
process that happens in the core of the sun.
The heat you feel on a sunny day has fusion
energy as its source.

Unfortunately, the temperature needed to
start fusion is so high that no known material can contain it. Success with fusion has so
far been limited to small experiments using
force fields to hold the atoms.

◀ Energy sources such as wind, geothermal, and solar
make up a larger percent of world energy production
today than in the past. In the future they will
probably be even more important.

Another promising source of energy for the future is hydrogen, which can be burned like fossil fuels. Ocean water could provide an almost limitless source of hydrogen. Today the best way to separate hydrogen from water is by using electricity. However, using electricity to produce another energy source is expensive.

Scientists are also working on ways to release thermal energy from water to produce electricity. This process is called ocean thermal energy conversion, or OTEC.

✓ **What is the biggest problem with developing fusion power?**

Summary

In addition to fossil fuels and hydroelectric energy, the United States uses small amounts of energy from other sources. These sources include biomass, nuclear energy, wind, geothermal energy, and solar energy. Researchers continue to work on new sources of energy, such as fusion.

Review

1. What is the disadvantage of nuclear energy?
2. Why is geothermal energy not an energy source that can be used in all areas?
3. In what ways are wind and solar energy similar?
4. **Critical Thinking** How is the nuclear energy now in use different from fusion energy?
5. **Test Prep** Many forms of energy are used to heat water, producing —

   A fuel   **C** hydrogen
   B wind   **D** steam

LINKS

MATH LINK

Draw Conclusions For a windmill to produce electric energy, the wind speed should be at least 13 km/hr. The wind should also be constant. Research the wind conditions in your area by using the weather station from an earlier chapter or by looking at the weather page of a local newspaper. Decide whether wind energy is a possible source for producing electricity where you live.

WRITING LINK

Persuasive Writing—Business Letter Write a letter to your electric company. Ask for information on your area's use of alternative sources of energy, such as biomass, nuclear energy, wind energy, geothermal energy, or solar energy. Be sure to ask clearly, to explain why you are asking, and to thank the person for his or her time.

LITERATURE LINK

Poem: "The Wind" Read "The Wind," a poem by Robert Louis Stevenson. What words does the poet use to describe the wind's energy?

TECHNOLOGY LINK

Learn more about alternatives to using fossil fuels by viewing *Wind Power and Electric Cars* on the **Harcourt Science Newsroom Video.**

CANOLA MOTOR OIL

What can you do with vegetable oil, besides making a salad or frying something for supper? Soon you will be able to put it in your family's car! At least that's the hope of the scientists developing vegetable motor oil.

Did You Say Vegetable Oil?

The engine of a car has many moving parts. To reduce the friction produced when those parts rub together, oil lubricates them, or keeps them slippery. Motor oil helps a car work by keeping the engine running smoothly. The oil now used for this purpose is a petroleum product. Petroleum oil works well in engines. Why replace it with something different? Why use vegetable oil?

Duane Johnson, an agronomist, or crop scientist, wanted to help Colorado farmers. He was looking for a crop they could grow to make money for themselves and their communities. He realized that canola might be that crop. For years people had grown canola plants, crushed their seeds to extract the oil, and used it for cooking. Colorado farmers could raise canola, and the oil could be processed in nearby towns.

But all the canola needed for cooking oil was already being grown. Growing more canola would simply drive down the price. So Johnson started thinking about other ways to use canola oil. For example, would it work in an engine?

A field of canola

The Advantages of Canola Motor Oil

After several years of research, he developed a canola-based motor oil and tested it in various cars. It worked! As word of his invention spread, mechanics from as far away as New Zealand wanted to buy canola motor oil.

▲ Canola oil can be used in place of petroleum-based oil in most vehicles.

People were eager to try it because they recognized its advantages. One advantage is that it helps protect the environment. Engines using petroleum-based motor oils make a lot of pollution. Switching to canola motor oil reduces the amount of pollution from car engines by up to 40 percent. Also, canola oil spills aren't harmful to organisms as petroleum spills are. Still another advantage is that after the oil has been used in car engines, drivers can dispose of it easily, since it isn't a hazardous waste. Like recycled petroleum oils, it can be made into chain oils and other lubricants, or it can be burned as a low-grade fuel oil. But unlike recycled petroleum oil, recycled canola oil doesn't cause pollution.

Perhaps the biggest advantage is that canola is a renewable resource. It can be grown year after year. Scientists hope that growing canola and other renewable energy sources will help meet future needs now filled by petroleum products. Some European buses have been using seed-oil fuels. Think about exhaust fumes that smell like popping corn!

THINK ABOUT IT

1. What are some advantages of using canola motor oil?
2. Why are crop fuels renewable resources, but fossil fuels are not?

CAREERS
AUTO MECHANIC

What They Do
Auto mechanics repair and maintain cars, buses, and trucks. They work at service stations, garages, auto centers, and public transportation agencies.

Education and Training
Many mechanics get their start by taking old cars apart and putting them back together. High schools, community colleges, and automobile manufacturers have auto mechanic classes and training seminars. On-the-job training at a service station is also possible.

GO ONLINE

WEB LINK
For Science and Technology updates, visit the Harcourt Internet site.
www.harcourtschool.com

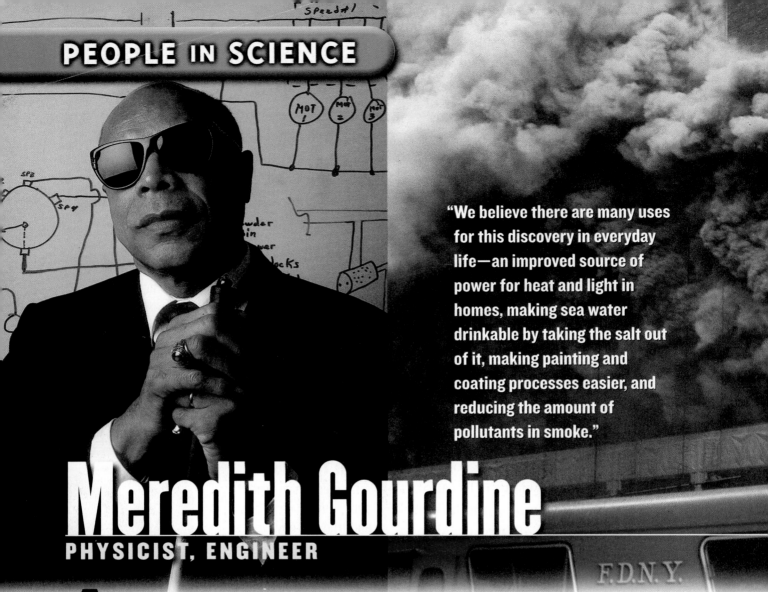

"We believe there are many uses for this discovery in everyday life—an improved source of power for heat and light in homes, making sea water drinkable by taking the salt out of it, making painting and coating processes easier, and reducing the amount of pollutants in smoke."

Meredith Gourdine

PHYSICIST, ENGINEER

As an undergraduate at Cornell University, Meredith Gourdine majored in engineering physics and served as captain of the track team. His performance as an athlete was so outstanding that he won a silver medal at the 1952 Olympic Games. Then he went on to earn a doctorate at the California Institute of Technology.

Over the next 30 years, Dr. Gourdine developed a career as a pioneer researcher and inventor in the field known as electrogasdynamics. Electrogasdynamics is the generation of energy from the motion of gas molecules that have been electrically charged under high pressure. Dr. Gourdine held about 30 patents for inventions, such as a system for removing smoke from burning buildings and a method for removing fog from airport runways. Both of these inventions work by giving particles in the air a negative charge. The charged particles are then attracted to the ground by electromagnets.

Before his death in 1998, Dr. Gourdine worked to perfect a generator that uses moving gas particles to convert low-voltage electricity into high-voltage electricity. Dr. Gourdine's generator may provide a much-needed new source of energy in the future.

THINK ABOUT IT

1. Why is it important to give airborne particles such as smoke and fog a negative charge?
2. Why do you think Dr. Gourdine's generator might be important in the future?

SAVING ENERGY

What materials make good heat insulators?

Materials

- 4 tin cans
- 4 thermometers
- cotton batting
- newspaper
- Styrofoam peanuts

Procedure

1. Put a thermometer in each can. Record the temperature of each can.

2. Pack cotton batting around one thermometer, shredded newspaper around another, and Styrofoam peanuts around a third. The control can will have a thermometer only.

3. Predict which item will be the best heat insulator.

4. Put all four cans in a sunny window.

5. Record the temperature of each can every minute for 10 min.

Draw Conclusions

In this experiment you tested three items that could help conserve energy. Which material was the best insulator? Home builders try to build energy-efficient homes. Design an energy-efficient house for an outdoor pet. Remember that the house may need to protect the pet from cold weather as well as hot weather.

CLEAN IT UP

What materials can be used to contain and clean up an oil spill?

Materials

- small bowl of water
- 20 mL vegetable oil
- rubber bands
- string
- cotton batting
- paper towels

Procedure

1. Carefully pour a small amount of oil on top of the water in the bowl.

2. Brainstorm different ways to use the materials to contain the spill or clean up the oil.

3. Try out your ideas.

Draw Conclusions

To protect the environment from damage, an oil spill must be contained quickly. Then the oil must be removed from the water. Which of the items you tested were most helpful in containing the oil spill? Which of the items were most helpful in cleaning up the oil spill? Research to find out what materials are actually used.

Vocabulary Review

Use the terms below to complete the sentences. The page numbers in ( ) tell you where to look in the chapter if you need help.

chemical bonds (F98)
hydroelectric energy (F104)
tidal energy (F106)
biomass (F110)
nuclear energy (F110)
geothermal energy (F111)
solar energy (F111)
fusion energy (F112)

1. One alternative energy source is ____, organic matter that is burned or may be turned into liquid fuel.

2. One future energy source is ____, which is the same process the sun uses.

3. One of the biggest disadvantages of ____ is that the fuel used and the waste produced are dangerous to organisms.

4. The energy in fossil fuels is stored in ____ that join atoms of carbon together.

5. A ____ station produces energy by holding water at high tide and releasing it through turbines at low tide.

6. In some areas people use ____ from water heated by hot magma.

7. A solar cell turns ____ directly into electricity.

8. A ____ station produces electricity from the energy of falling water.

Connect Concepts

Write the terms from the Word Bank below in the correct column of the concept map.

nuclear energy
geothermal energy
tidal energy
fusion energy

wind
hydroelectric energy
solar energy
biomass

fossil fuels
ocean thermal energy conversion (OTEC)

Energy Sources			
Energy from Sunlight	**Energy from Atoms**	**Energy from Earth**	**Energy from Forces in Space**
9. _____	15. _____	17. _____	18. _____
10. _____	16. _____		
11. _____			
12. _____			
13. _____			
14. _____			

Check Understanding

Write the letter of the best choice.

19. The energy in fossil fuels that is turned into thermal energy when it burns is —
    A chemical   C heat
    B electric   D mechanical

20. The energy at the bottom of a waterfall is the same energy that is turned into electric energy in a —
    F hydroelectric energy station
    G nuclear energy station
    H solar energy station
    J coal energy station

21. Solar cells are dependent on the weather from day to day, as are —
    A hydroelectric energy stations
    B nuclear energy stations
    C geothermal energy stations
    D wind farms

22. The thermal energy from many sources is turned into —
    F chemical energy
    G electric energy
    H solar energy
    J mechanical energy

Critical Thinking

23. Fossil fuels form from once-living matter. Why are they considered *nonrenewable* sources of energy?

24. Suppose you are an engineer designing a hydroelectric energy station. You can build the dam 10 m high or 25 m high. Which would you choose? Explain.

25. Suppose you are going to build a wind farm. What decisions will you need to make about its location? Explain.

Process Skills Review

26. Your family is going to build a new house. What three features might you **compare** in choosing an energy source for heating the house?

27. You plan to **measure** the thermal energy released during a chemical reaction. What tool would you use?

28. You decide to **plan and carry out a simple investigation** to decide the best place for a solar collector at your home. What are two factors you should test for in each area you investigate?

29. You want to **compare** the amounts of heat released by gasoline and kerosene. What **variables** should you **identify and control** when you experiment?

30. For a report on fossil fuels, you plan to **communicate** the steps necessary to produce electricity from coal. Choose a type of display—a table, a chart, a diagram, or a graph. Explain why this is the best way to communicate the steps.

Performance Assessment

Producing Light Energy

Draw a diagram that traces the energy in this light back through the steps it took in getting to you. Show the different forms the energy took on its journey.

There are many places where you can find out more about energy and motion. By visiting the places below, you can explore the forces of motion and find out some of the ways that electricity is produced. You'll also have fun while you learn.

The National Science Center

WHAT A science center that has fun-filled exhibits and attractions

WHERE Augusta, Georgia

WHAT CAN YOU DO THERE? See the displays and investigate some of the interactive exhibits.

New Madrid Power Plant

WHAT A coal-based electric energy station

WHERE New Madrid, Missouri

WHAT CAN YOU DO THERE? Find out what it takes to produce electricity, explore some of the scientific principles concerning electricity, and find out what goes on each day at an energy station.

GO ONLINE **Plan Your Own Expeditions**

If you can't visit The National Science Center or the New Madrid Power Plant, visit a science center or an energy station near you. Or log on to The Learning Site at **www.harcourtschool.com** to visit these science sites where you can find out more about energy and motion.

References

Science Handbook

Using Science Tools

Using a Hand Lens

A hand lens magnifies objects, or makes them look larger than they are.

1. Hold the hand lens about 12 centimeters (5 in.) from your eye.

2. Bring the object toward you until it comes into focus.

Using a Thermometer

A thermometer measures the temperature of air and most liquids.

1. Place the thermometer in the liquid. Don't touch the thermometer any more than you need to. Never stir the liquid with the thermometer. If you are measuring the temperature of the air, make sure that the thermometer is not in line with a direct light source.

2. Move so that your eyes are even with the liquid in the thermometer.

3. If you are measuring a material that is not being heated or cooled, wait about two minutes for the reading to become stable. Find the scale line that meets the top of the liquid in the thermometer, and read the temperature.

4. If the material you are measuring is being heated or cooled, you will not be able to wait before taking your measurements. Measure as quickly as you can.

Caring for and Using a Microscope

A microscope is another tool that magnifies objects. A microscope can increase the detail you see by increasing the number of times an object is magnified.

Caring for a Microscope

- Always use two hands when you carry a microscope.
- Never touch any of the lenses of a microscope with your fingers.

Using a Microscope

1. Raise the eyepiece as far as you can using the coarse-adjustment knob. Place your slide on the stage.

2. Always start by using the lowest power. The lowest-power lens is usually the shortest. Start with the lens in the lowest position it can go without touching the slide.

3. Look through the eyepiece, and begin adjusting it upward with the coarse-adjustment knob. When the slide is close to being in focus, use the fine-adjustment knob.

4. When you want to use a higher-power lens, first focus the slide under low power. Then, watching carefully to make sure that the lens will not hit the slide, turn the higher-power lens into place. Use only the fine-adjustment knob when looking through the higher-power lens.

You may use a Brock microscope. This is a sturdy microscope that has only one lens.

1. Place the object to be viewed on the stage.

2. Look through the eyepiece, and begin raising the tube until the object comes into focus.

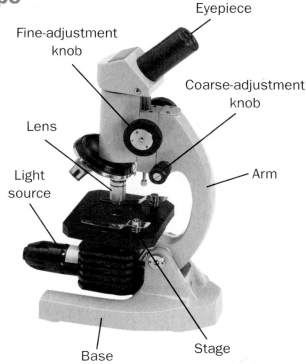

Eyepiece

Fine-adjustment knob

Coarse-adjustment knob

Lens

Light source

Arm

Base

Stage

A Light Microscope

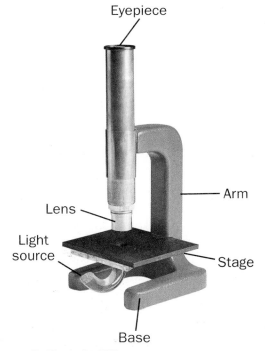

Eyepiece

Arm

Lens

Light source

Stage

Base

A Brock Microscope

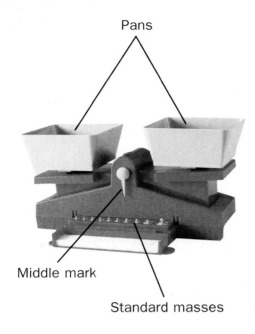

Pans

Middle mark

Standard masses

Using a Balance

Use a balance to measure an object's mass. Mass is the amount of matter an object has.

1. Look at the pointer on the base to make sure the empty pans are balanced.

2. Place the object you wish to measure in the left pan.

3. Add the standard masses to the other pan. As you add masses, you should see the pointer move. When the pointer is at the middle mark, the pans are balanced.

4. Add the numbers on the masses you used. The total is the mass in grams of the object you measured.

Using a Spring Scale

Use a spring scale to measure forces such as the pull of gravity on objects. You measure weight and other forces in units called newtons (N).

Measuring the Weight of an Object

1. Hook the spring scale to the object.

2. Lift the scale and object with a smooth motion. Do not jerk them upward.

3. Wait until any motion of the spring comes to a stop. Then read the number of newtons from the scale.

Measuring the Force to Move an Object

1. With the object resting on a table, hook the spring scale to it.

2. Pull the object smoothly across the table. Do not jerk the object.

3. As you pull, read the number of newtons you are using to pull the object.

Measuring Liquids

Use a beaker, a measuring cup, or a graduate to measure liquids accurately.

1. Pour the liquid you want to measure into a measuring container. Put your measuring container on a flat surface, with the measuring scale facing you.

2. Look at the liquid through the container. Move so that your eyes are even with the surface of the liquid in the container.

3. To read the volume of the liquid, find the scale line that is even with the surface of the liquid.

4. If the surface of the liquid is not exactly even with a line, estimate the volume of the liquid. Decide which line the liquid is closer to, and use that number.

Beaker   **Graduate**

Using a Ruler or Meterstick

Use a ruler or meterstick to measure distances and to find lengths of objects.

1. Place the zero mark or end of the ruler or meterstick next to one end of the distance or object you want to measure.

2. On the ruler or meterstick, find the place next to the other end of the distance or object.

3. Look at the scale on the ruler or meterstick. This will show the distance you want or the length of the object.

Using a Timing Device

Use a timing device such as a stopwatch to measure time.

1. Reset the stopwatch to zero.

2. When you are ready to begin timing, press start.

3. As soon as you are ready to stop timing, press stop.

4. The numbers on the dial or display show how many minutes, seconds, and parts of seconds have passed.

Measurement Systems

SI Measures (Metric)

Temperature
Ice melts at 0 degrees Celsius (°C)
Water freezes at 0°C
Water boils at 100°C

Length and Distance
1000 meters (m) = 1 kilometer (km)
100 centimeters (cm) = 1 m
10 millimeters (mm) = 1 cm

Force
1 newton (N) = 1 kilogram ×
   1 meter/second/second (kg-m/s^2)

Volume
1 cubic meter (m^3) = 1m × 1m × 1m
1 cubic centimeter (cm^3) =
   1 cm × 1 cm × 1 cm
1 liter (L) = 1000 milliliters (mL)
1 cm^3 = 1 mL

Area
1 square kilometer (km^2) =
   1 km × 1 km
1 hectare = 10,000 m^2

Mass
1000 grams (g) = 1 kilogram (kg)
1000 milligrams (mg) = 1 g

Rates (Metric and Customary)
km/h = kilometers per hour
m/s = meters per second
mi/h = miles per hour

Customary Measures

Volume of Fluids
8 fluid ounces (fl oz) = 1 cup (c)
2 c = 1 pint (pt)
2 pt = 1 quart (qt)
4 qt = 1 gallon (gal)

Temperature
Ice melts at 32 degrees
   Fahrenheit (°F)
Water freezes at 32°F
Water boils at 212°F

Length and Distance
12 inches (in.) = 1 foot (ft)
3 ft = 1 yard (yd)
5280 ft = 1 mile (mi)

Weight
16 ounces (oz) = 1 pound (lb)
2000 pounds = 1 ton (T)

Health Handbook

Good Nutrition

The Food Guide Pyramid

No one food or food group supplies all the nutrients you need. That's why it's important to eat a variety of foods from all the food groups. The Food Guide Pyramid can help you choose healthful foods in the right amounts. By choosing more foods from the groups at the bottom of the pyramid, and few foods from the group at the top, you will eat nutrient-rich foods that provide your body with energy to grow and develop.

**Fats, oils, and sweets
Eat sparingly.**

**Meat, poultry, fish, dried beans, eggs, and nuts
2–3 servings**

Milk, yogurt, and cheese 2–3 servings

**Fruits
2–4 servings**

**Vegetables
3–5 servings**

Breads, cereals, rice, and pasta 6–11 servings

Understanding Serving Size

The Food Guide Pyramid suggests a number of servings to eat each day from each group. But a serving isn't necessarily the amount you eat at a meal. A plate full of macaroni and cheese may contain three or four servings of pasta (macaroni) and three servings of cheese. That's about half your bread group servings and all your milk servings at one sitting! The table below can help you estimate the number of servings you are eating.

Food Group	Amount of Food in One Serving	Easy Ways to Estimate Serving Size
Bread, Cereal, Rice, and Pasta Group	$\frac{1}{2}$ cup cooked pasta, rice, or cereal 1 ounce ready-to-eat (dry) cereal 1 slice bread, $\frac{1}{2}$ bagel	ice-cream scoop large handful of plain cereal or a small handful of cereal with raisins and nuts
Vegetable Group	1 cup of raw, leafy vegetables $\frac{1}{2}$ cup other vegetables, cooked or chopped raw $\frac{3}{4}$ cup vegetable juice $\frac{1}{2}$ cup tomato sauce	about the size of a fist ice-cream scoop
Fruit Group	medium apple, pear, or orange $\frac{1}{2}$ large banana, or one medium banana $\frac{1}{2}$ cup chopped or cooked fruit $\frac{3}{4}$ cup of fruit juice	about the size of a baseball
Milk, Yogurt, and Cheese Group	$1\frac{1}{2}$ ounces of natural cheese 2 ounces of processed cheese 1 cup of milk or yogurt	about the size of two dominoes $1\frac{1}{2}$ slices of packaged cheese
Meat, Poultry, Fish, Dried Beans, Eggs, and Nuts Group	3 ounces of lean meat, chicken, or fish 2 tablespoons peanut butter $\frac{1}{2}$ cup of cooked dried beans	about the size of your palm
Fats, Oils, and Sweets Group	1 teaspoon of margarine or butter	about the size of the tip of your thumb

Preparing Foods Safely

Fight Bacteria

You probably already know to throw away food that smells bad or looks moldy. But food doesn't have to look or smell bad to make you ill. To keep your food safe and yourself from becoming ill, follow the procedures shown in the picture below. And remember—when in doubt, throw it out!

Food Safety Tips

Tips for Preparing Food

- Wash hands in hot, soapy water before preparing food. It's also a good idea to wash hands after preparing each dish.
- Defrost meat in the microwave or the refrigerator. Do NOT defrost meat on the kitchen counter.
- Keep raw meat, poultry, fish, and their juices away from other food.
- Wash cutting boards, knives, and countertops immediately after cutting up meat, poultry, or fish. Never use the same cutting board for meats and vegetables without thoroughly washing the board first.

Tips for Cooking Food

- Cook all food thoroughly, especially meat. Cooking food completely kills bacteria that can make you ill.
- Red meats should be cooked to a temperature of 160°F. Poultry should be cooked to 180°F. When done, fish flakes easily with a fork.
- Eggs should be cooked until the yolks are firm. Never eat food that contains raw eggs. Never eat cookie dough made with raw eggs.

Tips for Cleaning Up the Kitchen

- Wash all dishes, utensils, and countertops with hot, soapy water. Use a disinfectant soap, if possible.
- Store leftovers in small containers that will cool quickly in the refrigerator. Don't leave leftovers on the counter to cool.

Being Physically Active

Planning Your Weekly Activities

Being active every day is important for your overall health. Physical activity strengthens your body systems and helps you manage stress and maintain a healthful weight. The Activity Pyramid, like the Food Guide Pyramid, can help you choose a variety of activities in the right amounts to keep your body strong and healthy.

 **The Activity Pyramid**

Sitting for more than thirty minutes at a time: Only Once in a While

Flexibility and Strength: Two to Three Times a Week

Light Exercise: Two to Three Times a Week

Twenty-plus minutes of continuous aerobic activity: Three to Five Times a Week

Stay active: Every Day

Guidelines for a Good Workout

There are three things you should do every time you are going to exercise—warm up, workout, and cool down.

Warm-Up When you warm up, your heart rate, respiration rate, and body temperature gradually increase and more blood begins to flow to your muscles. As your body warms up, your flexibility increases, helping you avoid muscle stiffness after exercising. People who warm up are also less prone to exercise-related injuries. Your warm-up should include five minutes of stretching, and five minutes of a low-level form of your workout exercise. For example, if you are going to run for your primary exercise, you should spend five minutes stretching, concentrating on your legs and lower back, and five minutes walking before you start running.

Workout The main part of your exercise routine should be an aerobic exercise that lasts twenty to thirty minutes. Some common aerobic exercises include walking, bicycling, jogging, swimming, cross-country skiing, jumping rope, dancing, and playing racket sports. You should choose an activity that is fun for you and that you will enjoy doing over a long period of time. You may want to mix up the types of activities you do. This helps you work different muscle groups, and provides a better overall workout.

Cool-Down When you finish your aerobic exercise, you need to give your body time to return to normal. You also need to stretch again. This portion of your workout is called a cool-down. Start your cool-down with three to five minutes of low-level activity. For example, if you have been running, you may want to jog and then walk during this time. Then do stretching exercises to prevent soreness and stiffness.

Being Physically Active

Warm-Up and Cool-Down Stretches

Before you exercise, you should always warm up your muscles. The warm-up stretches shown here should be held for at least fifteen to twenty seconds and repeated at least three times. At the end of your workout, spend about two minutes repeating some of these stretches.

► **Hurdler's Stretch**
HINT—Keep the toes of your extended leg pointed up.

▲ **Shoulder and Chest Stretch** HINT—Pulling your hands slowly toward the floor makes this stretch more effective. Keep your elbows straight, but not locked!

▼ **Sit-and-Reach Stretch**
HINT—Remember to bend at the waist. Keep your eyes on your toes!

▲ **Upper Back and Shoulder Stretch**
HINT—Try to stretch your hand down so that it lies flat against your back.

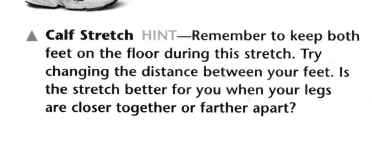

▼ **Thigh Stretch** HINT—Keep both hands flat on the floor. Try to lean as far forward as you can.

▲ **Calf Stretch** HINT—Remember to keep both feet on the floor during this stretch. Try changing the distance between your feet. Is the stretch better for you when your legs are closer together or farther apart?

Tips for Stretching

- Never bounce when stretching.
- Remember to hold each stretch for fifteen to twenty seconds.
- Breathe normally. This helps your body get the oxygen it needs.
- Stretch only until you feel a slight pull, NOT until it hurts.

Being Physically Active

Building a Strong Heart and Lungs

Aerobic activities, those that cause deep breathing and a fast heart rate for at least twenty minutes, help both your heart and your lungs. Because your heart is a muscle, it gets stronger with exercise. A strong heart doesn't have to work as hard to pump blood to the rest of your body. Exercise also allows your lungs to hold more air. With a strong heart and lungs, your cells get oxygen faster and your body works more efficiently.

◀ **Swimming** Swimming may provide the best overall body workout of any sport. It uses all the major muscle groups, and improves flexibility. The risk of injury is low, because the water supports your weight, greatly reducing stress on the joints. Just be sure to swim only when a lifeguard is present.

▶ **In-Line Skating** In-line skating gives your heart and lungs a great workout. Remember to always wear a helmet when skating. Always wear protective pads on your elbows and knees, and guards on your wrists, too. Learning how to skate, stop, and fall correctly will make you less prone to injuries.

▶ **Tennis** To get the best aerobic workout from tennis, you should run as fast, far, and hard as you can during the game. Move away from the ball so that you can step into it as you hit it. Finally, try to involve your entire body in every move.

▲ **Bicycling** Bicycling provides good aerobic activity that places little stress on the joints. It's also a great way to see the countryside. Be sure to use a bike that fits and to learn and follow the rules of the road. And *always* wear your helmet!

▶ **Walking** A fast-paced walk is a terrific way to build your endurance. The only equipment you need is a good pair of shoes and clothes appropriate for the weather. Walking with a friend can make this exercise a lot of fun.

Safety in Emergencies

Fire Safety

Fires cause more deaths than any other type of disaster. But a fire doesn't have to be deadly if you prepare your home and follow some basic safety rules.

- Install smoke detectors outside sleeping areas and on any additional floors of your home. Be sure to test the smoke detectors once a month and change the batteries in each detector twice a year.

- Keep a fire extinguisher on each floor of your home. Check monthly to make sure each is properly charged.

- Work with your family to make a fire escape plan for each room of your home. Ideally, there should be two routes out of each room. Sleeping areas are most important, because most fires happen at night. Plan to use stairs only; elevators can be dangerous in a fire.

- Pick a place outside for everyone to meet. Designate one person to call the fire department or 911 from a neighbor's home.

- Practice crawling low to avoid smoke. If your clothes catch fire, follow the three steps listed below.

1. STOP

2. DROP

3. ROLL

Earthquake Safety

An earthquake is a strong shaking of the ground. The tips below can help you and your family stay safe in an earthquake.

Before an Earthquake	During an Earthquake	After an Earthquake
• Secure tall, heavy furniture, such as bookcases, to the wall. Store the heaviest items on the lowest shelves. • Check for potential fire risks. Bolt down gas appliances, and use flexible hosing and connections for both gas and water utilities. • Reinforce and anchor overhead light fixtures to help keep them from falling.	• If you are outdoors, stay outdoors and move away from buildings and utility wires. • If you are indoors, take cover under a heavy desk or table or in a doorway. Stay away from glass doors and windows and heavy objects that might fall. • If you are in a car, drive to an open area away from buildings and overpasses.	• Continue to watch for falling objects as aftershocks shake the area. • Adults should have the building checked for hidden structural problems. • Check for broken gas, electric, and water lines. If you smell gas, an adult should shut off the gas main and leave the area. Report the leak.

Thunderstorm Safety

Thunderstorms are severe storms. Lightning associated with thunderstorms can injure or kill people, cause fires, and damage property. Here are some thunderstorm safety tips.

- **If you are inside, stay there.** The best place to take cover is inside a building.
- **If you are outside, try to take shelter.** If possible, get into a closed car or truck. If you can't take shelter, crouch in a ditch or low area, if possible.
- **If you are outside, stay away from tall objects.** Don't stand under a lone tree, in an open field, on a beach, or on a hilltop. Find a low place to stay.
- **Stay away from water.** Lightning is attracted to water, and water conducts electricity.
- **Listen for weather bulletins and updates.** The storms that produce lightning may also produce tornadoes. Be ready to take shelter in a basement or interior hallway away from windows and doors.

First Aid

The tips on the next few pages can help you provide simple first aid to others or yourself. Always tell an adult about any injuries that occur.

For Choking . . .

If someone else is choking . . .

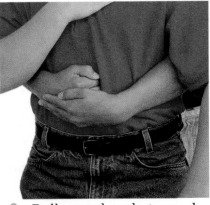

1. Recognize the Universal Choking Sign—grasping the throat with both hands. This sign means a person is choking and needs help.

2. Stand behind the choking person, and put your arms around his or her waist. Place your fist above the person's belly button.
Grab your fist with your other hand.

3. Pull your hands toward yourself, and give five quick, hard, upward thrusts on the person's stomach.

If you are choking when alone . . .

1. Make a fist, and place it above your belly button. Grab your fist with your other hand. Pull your hands up with a quick, hard thrust.

2. Or, keep your hands on your belly, lean your body over the back of a chair or over a counter, and shove your fist in and up.

For Bleeding . . .

If someone else is bleeding . . .

Wash your hands with soap, if possible.

Put on protective gloves, if available.

Wash small wounds with soap and water. Do *not* wash serious wounds.

Place a clean gauze pad or cloth over the wound. Press firmly for ten minutes. Don't lift the gauze during this time.

If you don't have gloves, have the injured person hold the gauze or cloth in place with his or her hand for ten minutes.

If after ten minutes the bleeding has stopped, bandage the wound. If the bleeding has not stopped, continue pressing on the wound and get help.

If you are bleeding . . .

- Wash your wound if it is a small cut. If it is a serious wound, do *not* wash it.
- Place a gauze pad or clean cloth over the wound, and hold it firmly in place for ten minutes. Don't lift the gauze or cloth until ten minutes have passed.
- If you have no gauze or cloth, apply pressure with your hand.
- If after ten minutes the bleeding has stopped, bandage the wound. If the bleeding has not stopped, continue pressing on the wound and get help.

Sense Organs

Eyes

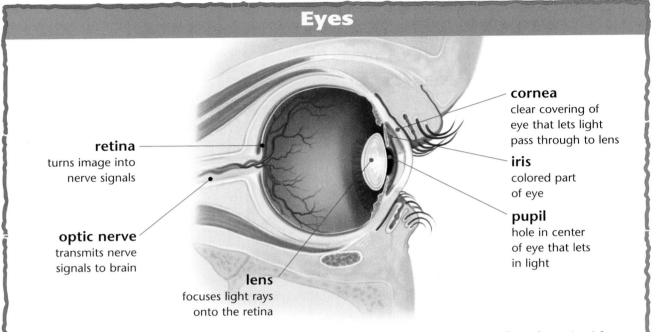

retina
turns image into
nerve signals

optic nerve
transmits nerve
signals to brain

lens
focuses light rays
onto the retina

cornea
clear covering of
eye that lets light
pass through to lens

iris
colored part
of eye

pupil
hole in center
of eye that lets
in light

Light rays bounce off objects and enter your eye through your pupil. A lens inside your eye focuses the light rays, and the image of the object is projected onto the retina at the back of your eye. In the retina the image is turned into nerve signals. Your brain analyzes the signals to tell you what you're seeing.

Ears

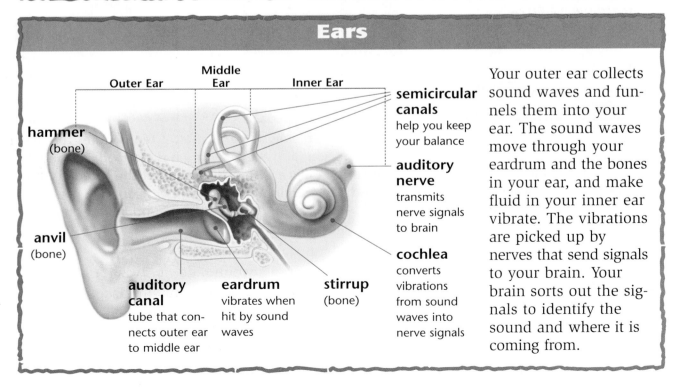

Outer Ear

Middle
Ear

Inner Ear

hammer
(bone)

anvil
(bone)

**auditory
canal**
tube that con-
nects outer ear
to middle ear

eardrum
vibrates when
hit by sound
waves

stirrup
(bone)

**semicircular
canals**
help you keep
your balance

**auditory
nerve**
transmits
nerve signals
to brain

cochlea
converts
vibrations
from sound
waves into
nerve signals

Your outer ear collects sound waves and funnels them into your ear. The sound waves move through your eardrum and the bones in your ear, and make fluid in your inner ear vibrate. The vibrations are picked up by nerves that send signals to your brain. Your brain sorts out the signals to identify the sound and where it is coming from.

Nose

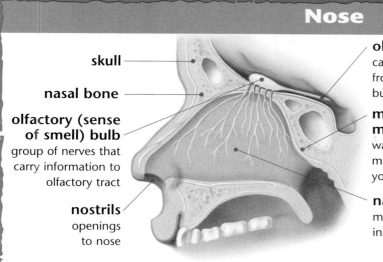

skull

nasal bone

olfactory (sense of smell) bulb
group of nerves that carry information to olfactory tract

nostrils
openings to nose

olfactory tract
carries information from olfactory bulb to brain

mucous membrane
warms and moistens air you breathe in

nasal cavity
main opening inside nose

When you breathe in, air is swept upward to nerve cells in your nasal cavity. Your nasal cavity is the upper part of your nose inside your skull. Different nerve cells respond to different odors in the air and send signals to your brain.

Skin

The skin is made of three layers, the outer epidermis, the middle dermis, and the lower subcutaneous layer. Nerve cells in your skin signal your brain about stimuli (conditions around you) that affect your skin.

Merkel's endings
respond to medium pressure

epidermis

dermis

subcutaneous layer

Krause's endings
cold and mechanoreceptors

Pacini's endings
react to heavy pressure

free nerve endings
react to painful stimuli

Meissner's endings
respond to light pressure and small, fast vibration

Ruffini's endings
sense changes in temperature and pressure

Caring for Your Senses

Injuries to your brain can affect your senses. Protect your brain by wearing safety belts in the car and helmets when playing sports or riding your bike.

Tongue

Your tongue is covered with about 10,000 tiny nerve cells, or taste buds, that pick out tastes in the things you eat and drink. Different taste buds respond to different tastes and send signals to your brain.

taste buds

Activity

With a partner, toss a table tennis ball back and forth 15 times. Then put a patch over one eye and toss the ball again. Was it easier to catch the ball when you had both eyes open or only one eye open?

Skeletal System

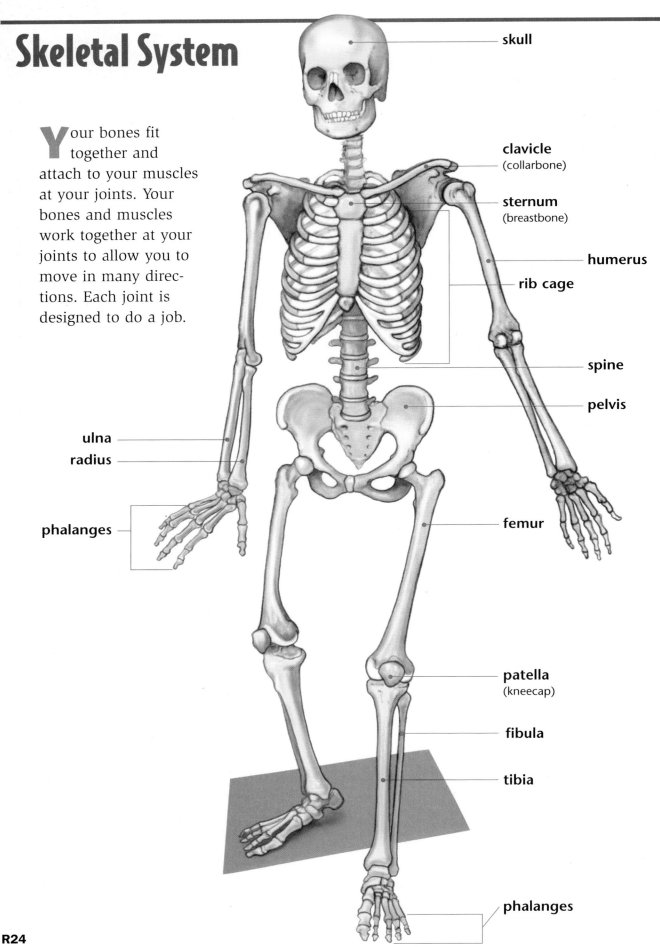

Your bones fit together and attach to your muscles at your joints. Your bones and muscles work together at your joints to allow you to move in many directions. Each joint is designed to do a job.

skull

clavicle
(collarbone)

sternum
(breastbone)

humerus

rib cage

spine

pelvis

ulna

radius

phalanges

femur

patella
(kneecap)

fibula

tibia

phalanges

Bones and Joints

Kinds of Bones Bones come in four basic shapes: long, short, flat, and irregular. Long bones, such as those in your legs, arms, and fingers, are narrow with large ends and are slightly curved. These bones can support the most weight. Short bones, found in your wrists and ankles, are chunky and wide. These bones allow maximum movement around a joint. Flat bones, such as your skull and ribs, are platelike. They provide protection for especially delicate parts of your body. Irregular bones, such as those in your spine and your ears, have unique shapes that don't fit into any other category.

flat bone (rib)

irregular bone (vertebra)

short bone (wrist)

long bone (femur)

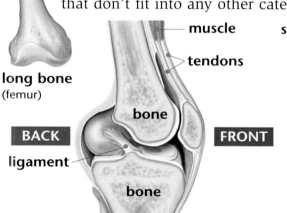

muscle

tendons

bone

BACK

FRONT

ligament

bone

Parts of a Joint A joint has several parts. Ligaments are tough, elastic bands that attach one bone to another. Ligaments give flexibility for bending and stretching. Cartilage is a cushioning material at the ends of bones that meet in a joint. Cartilage helps the bones move smoothly and absorbs some of the impact when you move. Tendons are dense cords that connect bones to muscles.

Caring for Your Skeletal System

- Move and flex your joints regularly through exercise. If you don't, they might get injured or become stiff and sore. Be sure to warm up and cool down whenever you exercise.

- You can injure a joint by using it too much or moving it in a way it is not designed to move.

- Calcium is necessary for healthy bones. You can get calcium from milk, dairy products like yogurt and cheese, or some dark green, leafy vegetables.

Activities

1. **Build a model of a long bone and a short bone. Use a sheet of construction paper. Cut off a strip about 1 inch (2.5 cm) wide. Roll the strip and the remainder of the sheet into tight cylinders. Test their strength by putting objects on top of them.**

2. **Make a model of a joint. Cut out two strips of cardboard and join them together using a round metal fastener. What does the fastener represent?**

Muscular System

The muscles that make your body move are attached to bones. When one of these muscles contracts, or gets shorter, it pulls on the bone it's connected to and the bone moves.

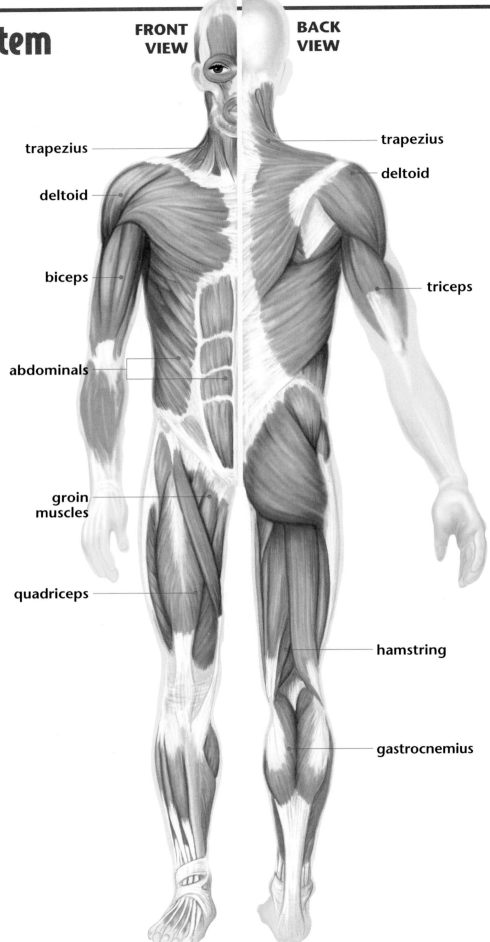

trapezius

deltoid

biceps

abdominals

groin muscles

quadriceps

trapezius

deltoid

triceps

hamstring

gastrocnemius

Muscles and Bones

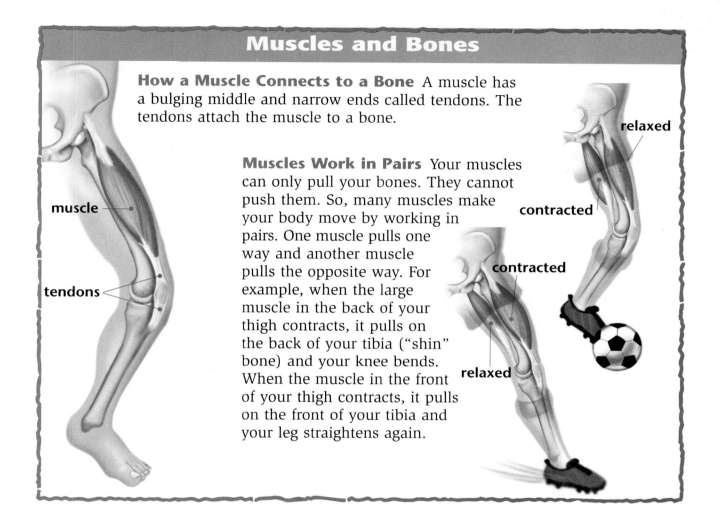

How a Muscle Connects to a Bone A muscle has a bulging middle and narrow ends called tendons. The tendons attach the muscle to a bone.

Muscles Work in Pairs Your muscles can only pull your bones. They cannot push them. So, many muscles make your body move by working in pairs. One muscle pulls one way and another muscle pulls the opposite way. For example, when the large muscle in the back of your thigh contracts, it pulls on the back of your tibia ("shin" bone) and your knee bends. When the muscle in the front of your thigh contracts, it pulls on the front of your tibia and your leg straightens again.

muscle

tendons

relaxed

contracted

contracted

relaxed

Caring for Your Muscular System

- Take a brisk five-minute walk and do gentle stretches before you start to play a sport to loosen your tendons, ligaments, and muscles and help prevent injuries.

- You should ease out of exercise too. Because your muscles contract during exercise, they need to be stretched when you finish.

Activities

1. Wrap your fingers around your upper arm, so you can feel both the top and bottom of your arm. Slowly bend and straighten your arm several times. Which muscles are working as a pair?

2. Write a paragraph about which muscles work in pairs when you play your favorite sport.

Digestive System

Digestion is the process of breaking food into tiny pieces that are absorbed by your blood and carried to all parts of your body. Each part of your digestive system does a different job.

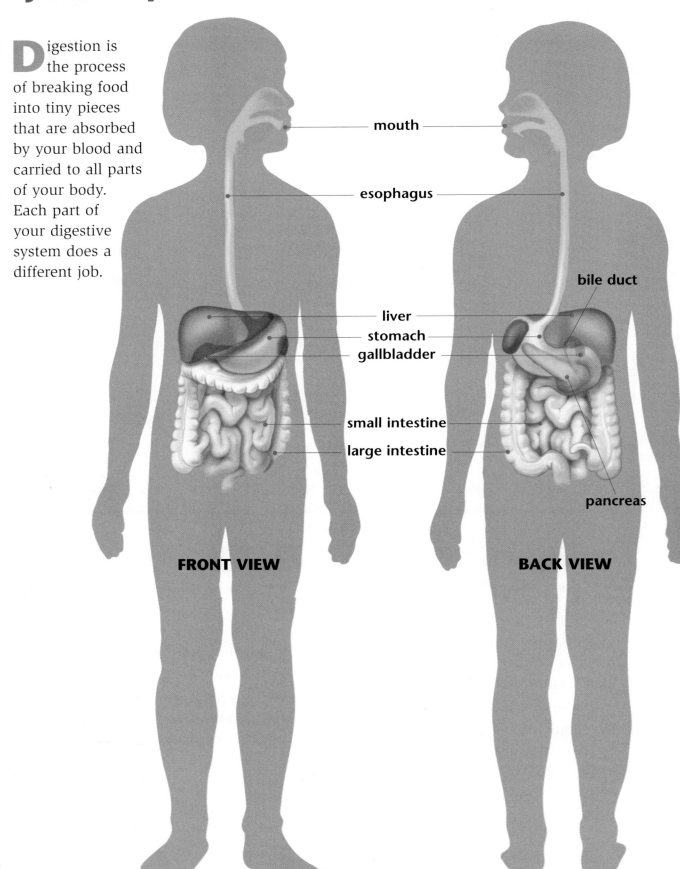

mouth

esophagus

bile duct

liver

stomach

gallbladder

small intestine

large intestine

pancreas

FRONT VIEW

BACK VIEW

Some Digestive Organs

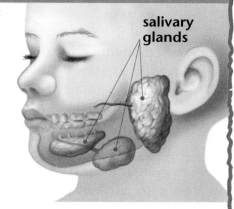

salivary glands

Esophagus When you swallow, the chewed and moistened food goes down a tube to your stomach. This tube, called the esophagus, is about 10 inches (25.4 cm) long. The food is pushed down the esophagus by a squeezing muscle action, similar to squeezing a tube of toothpaste. When you swallow, your airway is protected by the epiglottis and your vocal cords. If you try to talk and swallow, you cough or choke.

esophagus

Stomach The walls of your stomach are made of very strong muscles. Once food reaches the stomach, more chemicals are added that digest the food more thoroughly. At the same time, the stomach muscles squeeze the liquid food mixture.

stomach

Food leaves your stomach in two stages. First, the top of your stomach squeezes the liquid food mixture into the small intestine. Second, the solid particles are pushed into the small intestine by the muscles in the lower part of your stomach.

Salivary Glands When you chew your food, it is moistened with saliva. The saliva comes from three sets of glands: one set under your tongue, one on each side of your head in front of your ear, and one on each side of your head under your jaw.

Saliva is mostly water, but it does contain a chemical called *amylase* that helps digest starches. Saliva also helps keep your mouth clean and helps control infection.

Caring for Your Digestive System

- Try to drink at least six to eight glasses of water a day. Water helps food move through your digestive system.

- Chew your food thoroughly. Large pieces of food are more difficult to digest, and the large pieces might cause you to choke.

Activities

1. **Chew a cracker and then hold it in your mouth for about a minute. Move it around. How has the taste changed?**

2. **Record the amount of water you drink every day for three days. Are you drinking at least six glasses of water every day?**

Circulatory System

Blood is carried throughout your body by arteries, veins, and capillaries. Arteries deliver blood with needed materials, such as oxygen and nutrients, to parts of your body. Veins carry blood with waste or unused materials, such as carbon dioxide. Capillaries are microscopic blood vessels that allow needed substances to seep into your body's tissues.

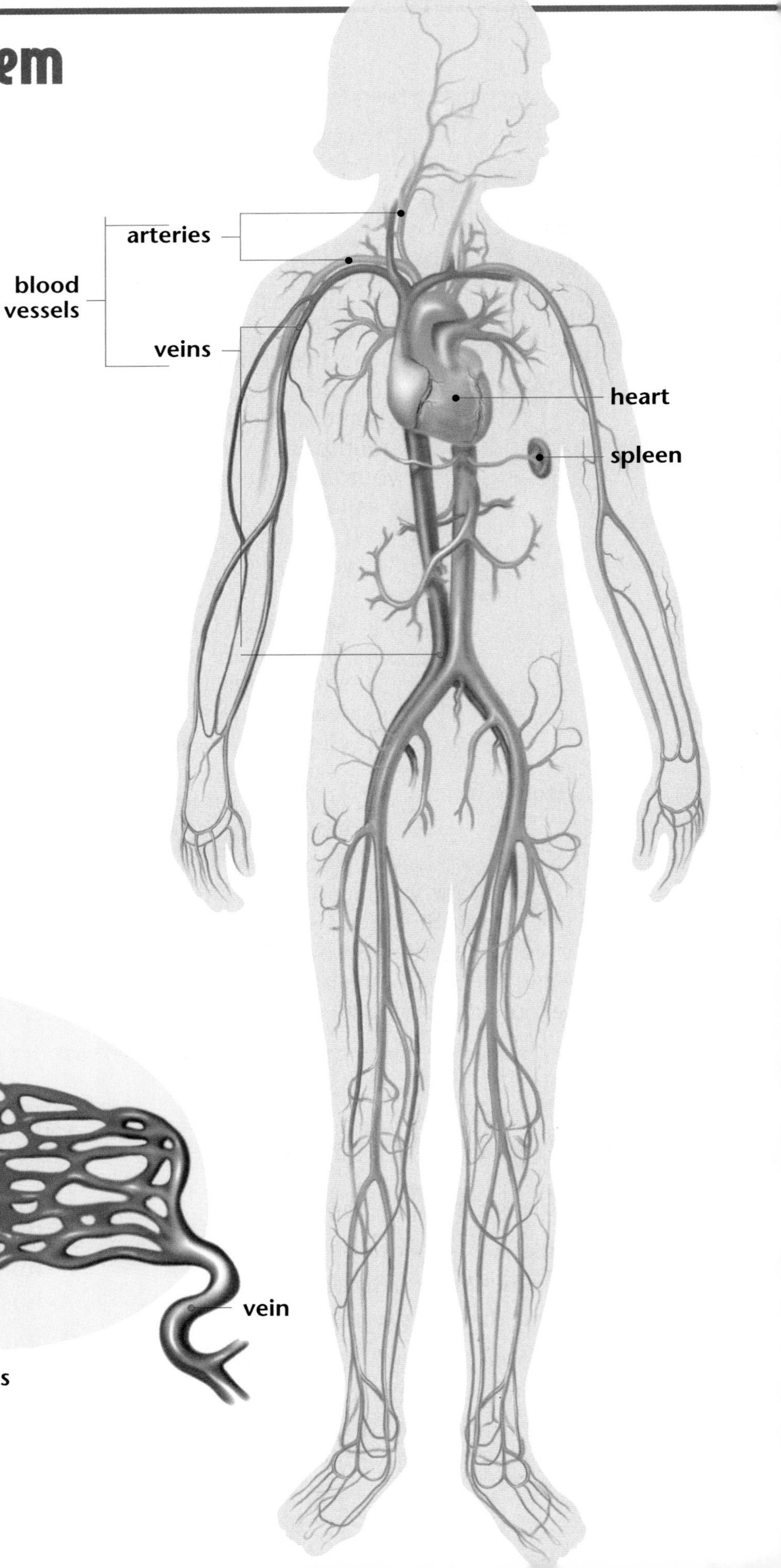

arteries

blood vessels

veins

heart

spleen

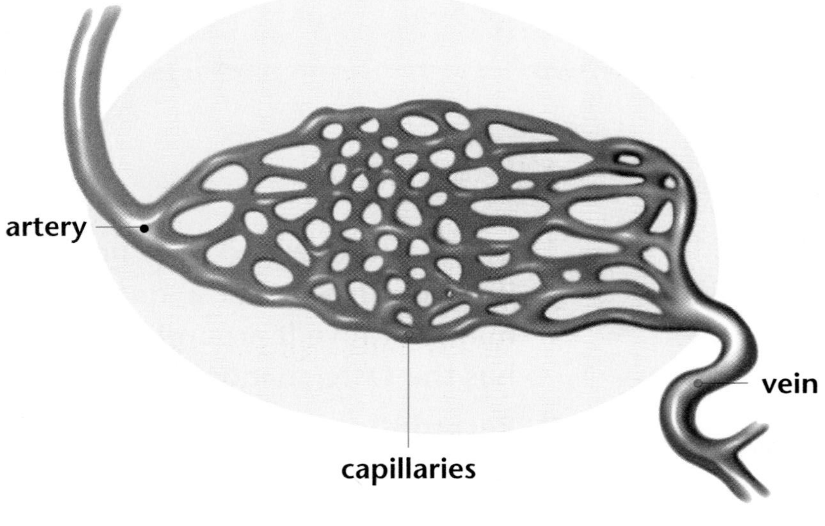

artery

vein

capillaries

How Blood Moves in Your Heart

Your heart has four chambers. The upper chambers are called atria. The lower chambers are called ventricles. Here is how blood moves through the heart.

1. Blood comes from your body into the right atrium. Blood comes from your lungs into the left atrium. The atria squeeze.

2. Two valves open, and the blood moves into the ventricles. When both ventricles have filled with blood, the valves shut. The ventricles squeeze.

3. Two different valves then open. The right ventricle sends blood through one valve to the lungs. The left ventricle sends blood through the other valve to the body. The "lub-dub" of your heartbeat is the sound of valves slamming shut.

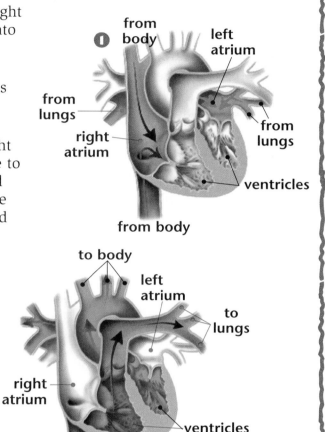

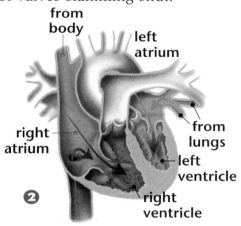

Caring for Your Circulatory System

- Don't ever smoke. Smoking narrows blood vessels and can cause high blood pressure.

- Remember, your heart is a constantly working muscle. Exercise strengthens your heart by making it beat harder, which makes the heart muscles larger and able to push more blood with each "squeeze" or "beat."

Activities

1. Take your pulse for ten seconds. Multiply that number by six to find how many times your heart beats in a minute. How many times does your heart beat in a day?

2. Feel your pulse in various places—your wrist, your neck, behind your knee. Where is it easiest to feel?

Respiratory System

Your lungs are filled with air tubes, air sacs, and blood vessels. The air tubes and blood vessels in your lungs divide until they are very small. At the ends of the tiny air tubes are air sacs called alveoli. The smallest blood vessels, capillaries, surround the alveoli.

Blood coming from your body (blue) delivers waste gases to your lungs. It then picks up oxygen (red) and takes it to your body.

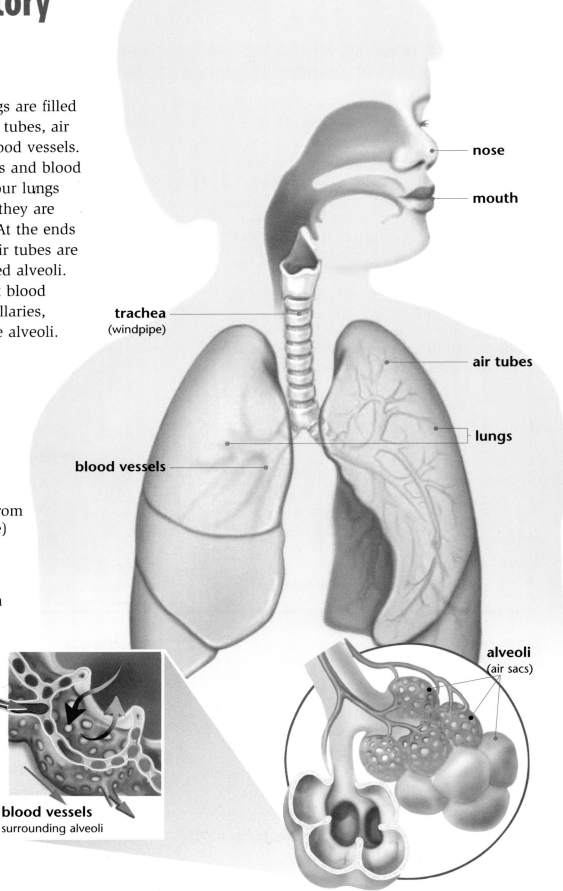

nose

mouth

trachea (windpipe)

air tubes

lungs

blood vessels

alveoli (air sacs)

blood vessels
surrounding alveoli

How Oxygen Travels to Your Body Parts

Your heart and lungs are connected by veins and arteries. The blood your heart pumps out to the rest of your body comes directly from your lungs, where it is filled with oxygen. The blood delivers the oxygen and picks up carbon dioxide. When the blood returns to your heart, it needs oxygen. Your heart sends the blood to your lungs, where oxygen is added and carbon dioxide is removed.

Tiny blood vessels in your lungs release carbon dioxide into the alveoli and absorb oxygen from the air inside the alveoli. The replenished blood returns to the heart, and the process starts over.

It takes just one minute for blood to circulate around your entire body.

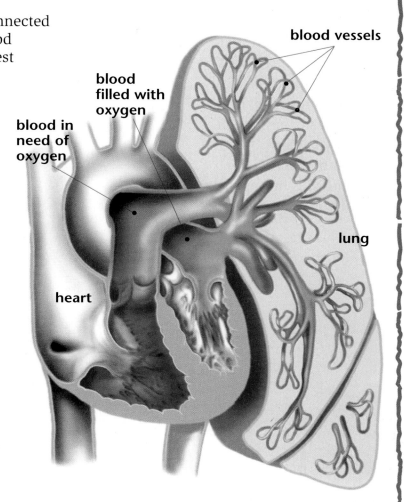

blood vessels

blood filled with oxygen

blood in need of oxygen

lung

heart

Caring for Your Respiratory System

- Don't ever smoke. The tar in cigarettes damages the lungs. Avoid environmental tobacco smoke too. Inhaling someone else's smoke can be as dangerous as smoking a cigarette yourself, especially for people with asthma.

- If you exercise so hard that you can't talk or you feel dizzy, your body is not getting enough oxygen. Slow down.

Activities

1. List three sports you think would exercise your respiratory system the most and three sports you think would exercise it the least.

2. Survey people you know about their thoughts on cigarettes and health. Record their answers.

3. Write the words to a jingle for an anti-smoking commercial.

R33

Nervous System

brain

Your nervous system is responsible for all of your thoughts and your body's activity. It makes your heart beat and your lungs work. It allows you to see, hear, smell, taste, and touch. It lets you learn, remember, and feel emotions. It moves all of your muscles.

spinal cord

nerves

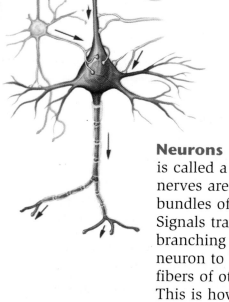

Neurons A nerve cell is called a neuron. Your nerves are made up of bundles of neurons. Signals travel along branching fibers of one neuron to branching fibers of other neurons. This is how messages are transmitted to and from your brain.

Your Nervous System

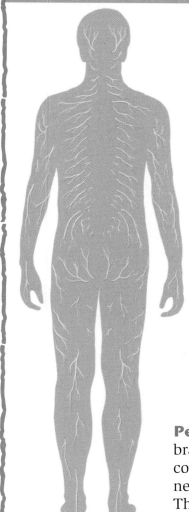

Autonomic Nervous System Your autonomic nervous system keeps your body's systems functioning and in balance. Masses of nerves called ganglia receive messages from your brain and relay those messages to organs like your heart, lungs, and kidneys.

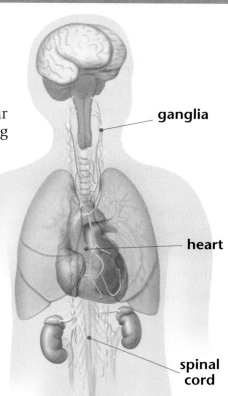

ganglia

heart

spinal cord

Peripheral Nervous System Major nerves branch off your brain and spinal cord. They continue to branch and form a complicated network that spreads throughout your body. This is your peripheral nervous system.

Caring for Your Nervous System

- Do not take any drugs unless given by your parents or guardian or a doctor. Some drugs can affect your brain cells.

- Eat a well-balanced diet. Your nervous system cannot work properly without certain nutrients.

- Learning new skills builds new nerve connections in your brain.

Activities

1. Put one hand in a bowl of very warm water and one hand in a bowl of cold water. Then put both hands in a bowl of warm water. How does each hand feel?

2. Blindfold a friend. Touch your friend's back with two fingers and your friend's palm with two fingers. Can your friend tell how many fingers you used in each place?

Immune System and Endocrine System

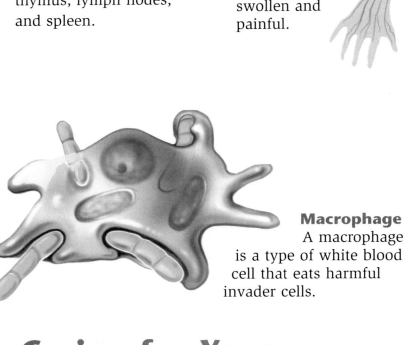

tonsils

thymus

lymph nodes

spleen

long bone marrow

Your immune system defends your body from harmful invaders, such as organisms that cause infection. White blood cells, which are your immune system's primary infection fighters, are produced in your bone marrow, thymus, lymph nodes, and spleen.

Tonsils Your tonsils are also lymph tissue. They produce white blood cells. When your body has an infection, lymph nodes can become infected. Infected lymph nodes become swollen and painful.

Macrophage A macrophage is a type of white blood cell that eats harmful invader cells.

Caring for Your Immune System

One way to help your body fight disease is through immunization (shots that protect you from certain diseases). You were required to have some immunizations as an infant and "boosters" before you started school.

Activity

Find out what immunizations are recommended at various ages. What will you need next?

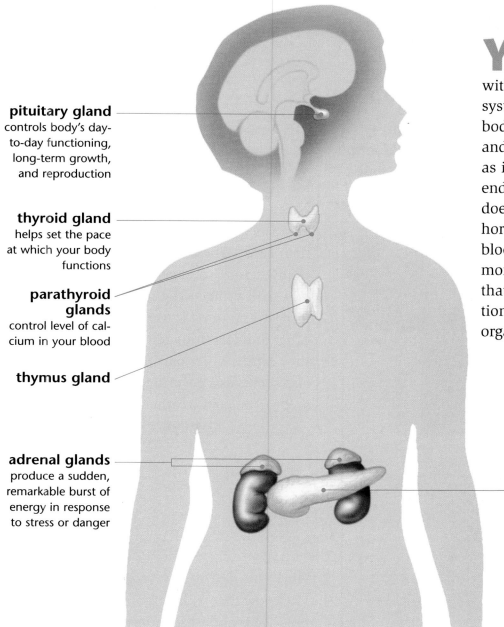

pituitary gland
controls body's day-
to-day functioning,
long-term growth,
and reproduction

thyroid gland
helps set the pace
at which your body
functions

**parathyroid
glands**
control level of cal-
cium in your blood

thymus gland

adrenal glands
produce a sudden,
remarkable burst of
energy in response
to stress or danger

pancreas
helps regulate the
amount of sugar in
your bloodstream

Your endocrine system works with your nervous system to help your body grow normally and work and react as it should. The endocrine system does this by releasing hormones into your bloodstream. Hormones are chemicals that deliver instructions to various organs and tissues.

Caring for Your Endocrine System

Some drugs, such as steroids, can harm your endocrine system. Avoid these drugs.

Activity

The next time you are startled, feel your heartbeat. How is it different from normal?

Using Science Reading Strategies

Some strategies work better than others when it comes to reading science topics. Below are some good strategies to use, and how you might use them.

Flowering Vascular Plants

Most of the plants you are familiar with are flowering plants, or **angiosperms** (AN•jee•oh•spermz). There are more than 235,000 kinds of angiosperms on Earth. These include grasses, herbs, shrubs, and many trees. Flowering plants are important sources of wood, fiber, and medicine. Nearly all the food that people eat comes directly or indirectly from flowering plants.

Flowers are an adaptation that is important to the success of angiosperms. They help make sure that pollen gets from the male part of a flower to the female part. Unlike gymnosperms, which are pollinated only by the wind, angiosperms are also pollinated by insects and other small animals. The colors, shapes, and odors of flowers attract these animals, which carry pollen from one flower to another as they move about.

Angiosperm seeds are also an adaptation for success. Unlike the gymnosperms, which produce unprotected seeds, angiosperms produce fruits that protect their seeds. These fruits include apples, oranges, tomatoes, peanuts, and acorns.

A fruit protects the seed or seeds inside it in several ways. It usually keeps birds and other animals from getting at them, even if they eat the outer part of the fruit. A fruit also serves as a covering that protects the seeds from cold weather. In addition, a rotting fruit provides extra food for a new plant when it begins to grow.

✔ What is an angiosperm?

▲ An apple begins as a flower.

◀ There are more than 235,000 kinds of flowering plants. Flowers are important to the success of angiosperms.

▲ The seeds of the apple tree are protected by the fruit. As the fruit rots, it provides extra food for the growth of a new apple tree.

A103

A good strategy to use is...
USE PRIOR KNOWLEDGE

Think about questions like these:

• What new information are you learning?

• How does the information fit in with what you already know about this scientific topic?

When reading a text like this...

Angiosperm seeds are also an adaptation for success. Unlike the gymnosperms, which produce unprotected seeds, angiosperms produce fruits that protect their seeds. These fruits include apples, oranges, tomatoes, peanuts, and acorns.

A fruit protects the seed or seeds inside it in several ways. It usually keeps birds and other animals from getting at them, even if they eat the outer part of the fruit. A fruit also serves as a covering that protects the seeds from cold weather. In addition, . . .

page A103

What you might say to yourself...

"I know that fruit contains seeds. I've seen apple seeds and tomato seeds. I also know that these seeds can grow into apple trees and tomato plants. But I've always thought that fruit was just a kind of food for people and animals. I never thought about what purpose fruit had for the plant itself. Now that I think of it, though, growing fruit around its seeds is the perfect way for a plant to make sure that new seeds are safe and have a chance to grow."

When reading a text like this...

Activity Purpose
In Lesson 1 you learned about three forces that affect objects on Earth: gravitation, friction, and magnetism. Two or more of these forces often interact, or act at the same time. In this investigation you will experiment with two opposing forces—the force of gravity pulling down on an object and the force of a spring pulling up on the same object.

Materials
- clipboard
- spring
- graph paper
- weight
- tape
- marker
- ring stand

Activity Procedure

1 Tape the graph paper to the clipboard. Across the bottom of the graph paper, draw a line and label it *Seconds*. Starting at one end of the line, make a mark every 2.5 cm.

2 Attach the spring to the ring stand. Then attach the weight to the free end of the spring. Tape the marker to the bottom of the weight so that its tip points toward the back of the setup.

page F10

A good strategy to use is...

ADJUST READING RATE

Think about the kind of science text you are reading.

- Something that is new to you or complicated should be read slowly.

- Something that is familiar can be read more quickly.

What you might say to yourself...

"I see three kinds of text on this page: The first paragraph describes the reason for doing the activity. The next kind of text is a list of what I'll need for the investigation. The last kind of text tells me what I need to do, step by step.

"I can probably read the description once and read it pretty quickly—just to get an idea of the reason for doing the activity.

"I'll glance through the list quickly, even though I may look back at it more than once. I want to make sure I have everything I need.

"I'll have to slow down and carefully read all the directions. Then I'll have to reread and check them a few times. I want to be sure I do the investigation the right way."

When reading a text like this...

The Causes of Weather

Uneven Heating

The illustration below shows how the sun's rays strike the Earth's surface and the atmosphere. The atmosphere absorbs some of the sun's energy and reflects some of it back into space. Some of the energy that reaches the Earth's surface is reflected back into the atmosphere. However, much of the sun's energy is absorbed by the Earth's surface.

page C72

A good strategy to use is...

SELF-QUESTION

Think about questions you could ask yourself to be sure you understand what you're reading. As you read your science textbook, one way to check yourself is to turn headings into questions that you answer as you read.

What you might say to yourself...

"I can turn both of these headings into questions that I'll try to answer as I read. My first question would be, 'What are the causes of weather?' I'll wait to fully answer that question when I finish the whole section.

"The question I'll answer first, after I read a few paragraphs, comes from the second heading. That question is, 'How does uneven heating cause weather?'"

When reading a text like this...

Think about an in-line skater holding a basketball. If the skater throws the ball really hard, the ball goes forward and the skater rolls backward. . . . The skater exerts an action force on the basketball by throwing it. The thrown ball exerts an equal reaction force on the skater, but in the opposite direction. The result is that the basketball moves in one direction and the skater moves in the other direction.

page F43

A good strategy to use is...

CREATE MENTAL IMAGES

Think about how an artist might draw a picture of what a passage describes. If you can picture what each part of a process looks like, you can tell if you are understanding what you are reading.

What you might say to yourself...

"First, I'm picturing an in-line skater. Now I see that she passes a basketball, hard, to someone standing in front of her. The ball goes forward, pushed by her arms and wrists. That's the action force. At the same time, she is pushed backward by the force of the pass. That's the reaction force."

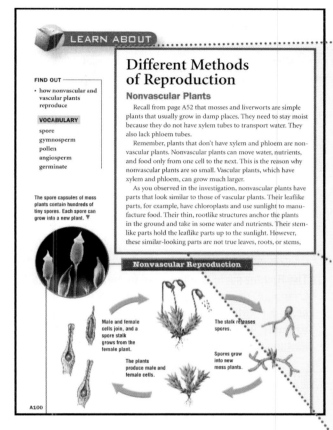

A100

When reading a text like this...

Different Methods of Reproduction

Nonvascular Plants

Recall from page A52 that mosses and liverworts are simple plants that usually grow in damp places. They need to stay moist because they do not have xylem tubes to transport water. They also lack phloem tubes.

Remember, plants that don't have xylem and phloem are nonvascular plants. Non-vascular plants can move water, nutrients, and food only from one cell to the next. This is the reason why nonvascular plants are so small. Vascular plants, which have *xylem* and *phloem*, can grow much larger.

page A100

What you might say to yourself...

"The first heading makes me think that this material is organized to show how plants reproduce. The second heading indicates that the first grouping of plants I'll read about are nonvascular plants.

"As I read this section, I see I'm right. The paragraph tells me how nonvascular plants are different from vascular plants."

A good strategy to use is...

USE TEXT STRUCTURE AND FORMAT

Think about how the information is arranged in the section you are reading. What headings and captions are used? How did the author organize the paragraphs?

- Do the paragraphs tell about causes and effects?

- Do they show the sequence in a process?

- Do they compare two or more things?

- Do they classify concepts?

Recognizing how the information is arranged helps you understand it more easily.

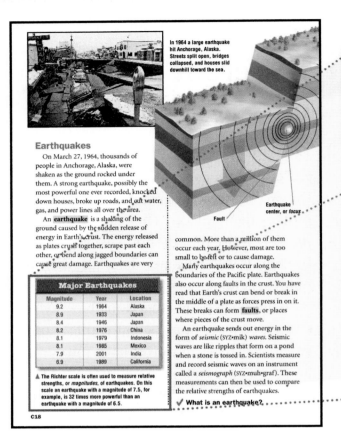

Major Earthquakes

Magnitude	Year	Location
9.2	1964	Alaska
8.9	1933	Japan
8.4	1946	Japan
8.2	1976	China
8.1	1979	Indonesia
8.1	1985	Mexico
7.9	2001	India
6.9	1989	California

▲ The Richter scale is often used to measure relative strengths, or *magnitudes,* of earthquakes. On this scale an earthquake with a magnitude of 7.5, for example, is 32 times more powerful than an earthquake with a magnitude of 6.5.

page C18

A good strategy to use is...

USE GRAPHIC AIDS

Look at any pictures, graphs, tables, diagrams, or time lines that are included with the text. Think about why the author included graphic aids.

• Are they there to help you organize the information you are learning? If so, use them as you read.

• Are they there to add new information? If so, take time to read them carefully, to learn the new information.

What you might say to yourself...

"The table and caption accompany text that talks about earthquakes in general. The information here is additional, so I'd better study the table and examine the caption.

"The title of the table tells me what it's about. The headings indicate that the table is comparing the magnitude of major earthquakes. It also tells where and when they occurred. I'm not sure what *magnitude* means, but I notice that it's defined in the caption.

"Now that I know what the table is about, I can start comparing entries. Were any earthquakes the same magnitude? Yes, I see that two were. I also notice that certain areas of the world seem to have powerful earthquakes over and over."

When reading a text like this...

Electric Charges

You may recall that within an atom, electrons have a negative charge and protons have a positive charge. So the two types of particles attract each other. Most objects have equal numbers of protons and electrons. Sometimes, however, electrons are attracted to the protons of another object and rub off. When an object gains or loses electrons, it has an **electric charge**. An object that has gained electrons has a negative electric charge. An object that has lost electrons has a positive electric charge.

page F68

A good strategy to use is...

REREAD

Think about whether you are understanding what you're reading. If something you read doesn't make sense to you, you may need to go back and read it again. Maybe the passage involves something you learned in an earlier chapter. You may have to look back at that chapter to remember what you learned before.

What you might say to yourself...

"Wait. I'm getting confused. I'd better not read more until I reread this paragraph.

"Now that I've reread it, I see that I need to be clear about the structure of an atom. I'm having trouble remembering exactly what protons and electrons are. I'd better look back at Chapter 2 to remind myself. Then I'll reread this paragraph to see if I understand it."

When reading a text like this...

Why Use Plants to Make Plastic?

Products made from plastics make life simpler, but plastics can cause problems, too. Most plastics are made from petroleum, and when you throw them away, they aren't really gone. Petroleum-based plastics don't decompose (break down) in the environment. Each year people throw away almost 20 million tons of plastic. That's a lot of trash. Now scientists . . .

page A114

A good strategy to use is...

SUMMARIZE AND PARAPHRASE

Think about how you could shorten a passage without leaving out any key ideas.

- Can you sum up the main points of a section in your own words?
- Is there a chapter summary to help you recall the main points?

What you might say to yourself...

"When I summarize this section, I want to include all the important points. I also want to keep it as short as possible. Here is my summary.

"Most plastics are petroleum-based. They don't decompose, so they harm the environment."

Building a Science Vocabulary

Reading and understanding a new science word can be a challenge. One way to make things easier is to use what you already know. First, look at the words that appear near the new word in a sentence or paragraph. Can any of them give you a clue? Next, look at the new science word itself. Have you seen that word—or part of it—before? If so, how was the word used? Using what you already know can help you to learn and remember the meaning of new science words.

Use the Context

Look for Clues in a Sentence or Paragraph

When you see a science word for the first time, look at words that appear near it in a sentence or paragraph. Often, they will provide clues about the meaning of the new word.

For example, look at the vocabulary word *precipitation* in the following sentence:

> Seventy inches of rain and sixty-five inches of snow helped Johnson County set a record for annual **precipitation**.

The sentence refers to rain and snow. You know what both of those things are. So you might be able to figure out that *precipitation* means "water that falls from the clouds."

Look Both Ways

Context clues don't always come before a vocabulary word. Sometimes, clues come after the word. When you see a science word for the first time, don't stop there. Keep reading, and keep your eyes open for context clues.

How could you figure out the meaning of the vocabulary word *submersible* in the following passage?

> To learn more about life in the North Atlantic, scientists will use a **submersible**. Safe inside this underwater vehicle, researchers can look closely at fish and other undersea animals.

If you read beyond the vocabulary word, you will find out that a *submersible* is an underwater vehicle.

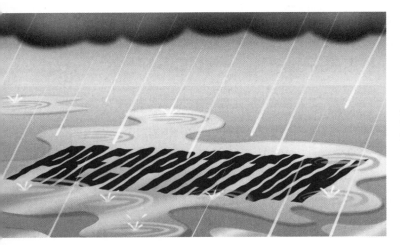

Same Words, New Uses

Scientists often use familiar words to describe new things or ideas.

- The word *current*, for example, has long been used to describe flowing water. When scientists needed a word to describe the amount of electricity flowing through a circuit, they chose *current*.

- As science vocabulary words, *crust* and *core* might be unfamiliar to you. But you have used both words before. You know that the crust is the outer surface of a loaf of bread. You also know that the core is the center of an apple.

So, which part of the earth is the crust? You guessed it—the outer surface. And which part is the core? Right—the center!

Other science terms that use familiar words:
greenhouse effect
continental drift
telescope lens
space shuttle

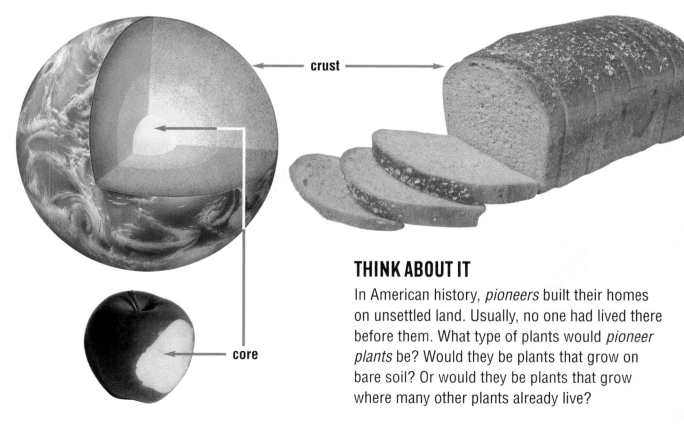

crust

core

THINK ABOUT IT

In American history, *pioneers* built their homes on unsettled land. Usually, no one had lived there before them. What type of plants would *pioneer plants* be? Would they be plants that grow on bare soil? Or would they be plants that grow where many other plants already live?

Greek and Latin Roots in Scientific Terms

Many scientific words in English come from ancient Greek and Latin—two languages used long ago. Scientists often use Greek and Latin roots, or word parts, to make new words.

Consider the word *photosynthesis*. It is used to describe the process by which plants use light to make food for themselves. It comes from the Greek root *photo*, which means "light."

Knowing a word's root can help you figure out its meaning. It can also help you to read long words. Once you recognize a word part like *photo*, there's a better chance that you'll be able to pronounce and understand the remaining part of the word. Other scientific words that use the root *photo* include *photography*, *phototropism*, *photosphere*, and *photometer*.

Photosynthesis

Sunlight is taken in by chlorophyll. Light energy is turned into chemical energy, which is used to split water into hydrogen and oxygen. In a series of reactions, hydrogen combines with the carbon dioxide to form glucose and oxygen.

carbon dioxide and water

sunlight and chlorophyll

glucose and oxygen

Latin and Greek Roots in Science Vocabulary

Root	Meaning	Vocabulary Term(s)	Other Scientific Terms
bios	life	biomass, biome, symbiosis	antibiotic, biochemistry, biology, biosphere
cycle	circle	carbon-oxygen cycle, life cycle, nitrogen cycle, recycling, water cycle	cyclotron, cyclone, cyclometer
derma	skin	epidermis	dermal, dermatology
geo	earth	geothermal, Pangea	geology, geography, geomagnetism
hydro	water	hydroelectric energy	dehydrate, hydraulic, hydrofoil, hydrodynamics
vas	duct	vascular, nonvascular	blood vessel, cardiovascular, vascular bundle

Other Common Roots in Scientific Words

Root	Meaning	Example Words
aero	air	aerobic, aerodynamics, aerometer, aeronautics, aerospace
dec	ten	decahedron, decimal
genes	born	genetic, genome
log	study of	biology, geology, physiology, zoology
meso	middle	mesoderm, mesosphere, Mesozoic
pod	foot	arthropod, podiatry, pseudopod
spirare	to breathe	respire, respiratory, transpiration
trope	turn	tropism, phototropism

THINK ABOUT IT

Imagine that you have been hired to name a new invention. The invention is a system of pipes that will carry water to farmers' fields. Which of the following names would be best for the invention?

- Dermal Hydrator
- Hydrocyclon
- Hydrovasculator

Can you use Greek and Latin roots to come up with an even better name? Try using roots to come up with names for imaginary inventions of your own!

Phonics: Sounds and Spellings in Scientific Terms

When you encounter an unfamiliar science word, you need to be able to read and pronounce it correctly. Here are some pointers to help you out.

Some letters and letter combinations always sound the same. In English, some letters and letter combinations almost always stand for the same sound each time they appear.

- The letter combination *th* almost always stands for the sound you hear at the beginning of *thick*. You can find the *th* letter combination in the following vocabulary terms: *an**th**racite, ear**th**quake, geo**th**ermal energy, pho**t**osyn**th**esis, **th**reatened,* and *wea**th**ering.*

- The letter combination *ph* almost always stands for the same sound as the letter *f*. You can find this letter combination in the following vocabulary terms: *atmos**ph**ere, chloro**ph**yll, metamor**ph**osis, ne**ph**rons, **ph**loem, **ph**otosphere, **ph**otosynthesis, **ph**ototropism,* and ***ph**ysical properties.*

Silent *e* makes a vowel long. In English, a silent *e* at the end of a syllable usually means that the vowel that comes before it is a long sound. That means that the vowel "says its own name." You can actually hear the letter name when you say a word with a long vowel. The word *plate*, for example, ends in silent *e*. This means that the *a* that comes before it is a long *a*. Do you hear the *a* when you say *plate*? You can use the silent *e* rule to help you pronounce science words such as *gen**o**me* (long *o*), *sp**o**re* (long *o*), *photosph**e**re* (long *e*), *precipit**a**te* (long *a*), and *bi**o**me* (long *o*).

A letter can stand for different sounds, depending on the letter that follows it.

- When the letter *g* is followed by the vowels *a, o,* or *u*, it usually sounds like the *g* in *got*. It also sounds this way when it is followed by a consonant. When the letter *g* is followed by *e, i,* or *y*, it usually sounds like the *g* in *general*.

  Use this rule to pronounce the *g* sound in the following vocabulary terms: *energy, galaxy, gas, gene, germinate, global warming, grafting, gymnosperm, ligament,* and *magma.*

- When the letter *c* is followed by the vowels *a, o,* or *u*, it sounds like the *k* sound in *can*. The letter *c* sounds the same way when it is followed by most consonants. When the letter *c* is followed by the letters *e, i,* or *y*, it sounds like the *s* sound in *nice*.

  Use this rule to pronounce the *c* sound in the following vocabulary terms: *acid rain, action force, cell, climate, competition, core, eclipse, ecosystem, extinct, friction,* and *precipitation.*

THINK ABOUT IT

Consider the vocabulary word *recycle.* Are the two *c*'s in the word pronounced in the same way? Why or why not?

Rule-breakers can be a challenge. Some letters and letter combinations don't seem to obey any rules at all.

Take the letter combination *ch*, for example. Most of the time, you pronounce it like the *ch* in *chin*. But in many cases, *ch* stands for the *k* sound you hear in the word *echo*. And in words such as *chute*, *ch* can even sound like the *sh* in *ship*.

Use the glossary in your book to help you pronounce these vocabulary terms: *chemical bonds, chlorophyll, chromosome, electric charge, machine, niche,* and *pitch*.

When in doubt, use a glossary or a dictionary. A glossary or a dictionary is the best resource for learning how to pronounce a new science word. Each word in a dictionary appears next to its pronunciation. A guide to the symbols used in the pronunciation usually appears at the front of a dictionary. When you find a new science word and can't figure out how to pronounce it, go straight to a dictionary.

AH-CHOO?
AH-KOO?
AH-SHOO?

Glossary

As you read your science book, you will notice that new or unfamiliar words have been respelled to help you pronounce them quickly while you are reading. Those respellings are *phonetic respellings*. In this Glossary you will see a different kind of respelling. Here, diacritical marks are used, as they are used in dictionaries. *Diacritical respellings* provide a more precise pronunciation of the word.

When you see the ′ mark after a syllable, pronounce that syllable with more force than the other syllables. The page number at the end of the definition tells where to find the word in your book. The boldfaced letters in the examples in the Pronunciation Key that follows show how these letters are pronounced in the respellings after each glossary word.

PRONUNCIATION KEY

a	**a**dd, m**a**p	m	**m**ove, see**m**	u	**u**p, d**o**ne
ā	**a**ce, r**a**te	n	**n**ice, ti**n**	û(r)	b**ur**n, t**er**m
â(r)	c**a**re, **air**	ng	ri**ng**, so**ng**	yo͞o	f**u**se, f**ew**
ä	p**a**lm, f**a**ther	o	**o**dd, h**o**t	v	**v**ain, e**v**e
b	**b**at, ru**b**	ō	**o**pen, s**o**	w	**w**in, a**w**ay
ch	**ch**eck, cat**ch**	ô	**o**rder, j**a**w	y	**y**et, **y**earn
d	**d**og, ro**d**	oi	**oi**l, b**oy**	z	**z**est, mu**s**e
e	**e**nd, p**e**t	ou	p**ou**t, n**ow**	zh	vi**s**ion, plea**s**ure
ē	**e**qual, tr**ee**	o͝o	t**oo**k, f**u**ll	ə	the schwa, an
f	**f**it, hal**f**	o͞o	p**oo**l, f**oo**d		unstressed vowel
g	**g**o, lo**g**	p	**p**it, sto**p**		representing the sound
h	**h**ope, **h**ate	r	**r**un, poo**r**		spelled
i	**i**t, g**i**ve	s	**s**ee, pa**ss**		*a* in **a**bove
ī	**i**ce, wr**i**te	sh	**s**ure, ru**sh**		*e* in sick**e**n
j	**j**oy, le**dg**e	t	**t**alk, si**t**		*i* in poss**i**ble
k	**c**ool, ta**k**e	th	**th**in, bo**th**		*o* in mel**o**n
l	**l**ook, ru**l**e	t̶h̶	**th**is, ba**th**e		*u* in circ**u**s

Other symbols:
• separates words into syllables
′ indicates heavier stress on a syllable
′ indicates light stress on a syllable

R50

acceleration [ak•sel′ər•ā′shən] A change in motion caused by unbalanced forces or a change in velocity **(F35)**

acid rain [as′id rān′] Precipitation resulting from pollution condensing into clouds and falling to Earth **(B99)**

action force [ak′shən fôrs′] The first force in the third law of motion **(F43)**

air mass [âr′ mas′] A large body of air that has nearly the same temperature and humidity throughout **(C75)**

air pressure [âr′ presh′ər] The weight of air **(C65)**

alveoli [al•vē′ə•lē] Tiny air sacs located at the ends of bronchi in the lungs **(A18)**

amphibians [am•fib′ē•ənz] Animals that have moist skin and no scales **(A44)**

angiosperm [an′jē•ō•spûrm′] A flowering plant **(A103)**

asexual reproduction [ā•sek′shoo•əl rē′prə•duk′shən] Reproduction by simple cell division **(A67)**

asteroids [as′tə•roidz] Chunks of rock that look like giant potatoes in space **(D17)**

atmosphere [at′məs•fir] The layer of air that surrounds Earth **(C64)**

atom [at′əm] The smallest unit of an element that has all the properties of that element **(E40)**

axis [ak′sis] An imaginary line that passes through Earth's center and its North and South Poles **(D7)**

balanced forces [bal′ənst fôrs′əz] The forces acting on an object that are equal in size and opposite in direction, canceling each other out **(F12)**

biomass [bī′ō•mas′] Organic matter, such as wood, that is living or was recently alive **(F110)**

biome [bī′ōm′] A large-scale ecosystem **(B64)**

birds [bûrdz] Vertebrates with feathers **(A45)**

bone marrow [bōn′ mar′ō] A connective tissue that produces red and white blood cells **(A24)**

capillaries [kap′ə•ler′ēz] The smallest blood vessels **(A17)**

carbon–oxygen cycle [kär′bən ok′sə•jən sī′kəl] The process by which carbon and oxygen cycle among plants, animals, and the environment **(B8)**

cell [sel] The basic unit of structure and function of all living things **(A6)**

cell membrane [sel′ mem′brān′] The thin covering that encloses a cell and holds its parts together **(A8)**

chemical bonds [kem′i•kəl bondz′] The forces that join atoms to each other **(F98)**

chlorophyll [klôr′ə•fil′] A pigment, or coloring matter, that helps plants use light energy to produce sugars **(A96)**

chromosome [krō′mə•sōm′] A threadlike strand of DNA inside the nucleus **(A65)**

classification [klas′ə•fə•kā′shən] The grouping of things by using a set of rules **(A38)**

climate [klī′mit] The average of all weather conditions through all seasons over a period of time **(C80)**

climate zone [klī′mit zōn′] A region throughout which yearly patterns of temperature, rainfall, and amount of sunlight are similar **(B64)**

climax community [klī′maks′ kə•myoō′nə•tē] The last stage of succession **(B93)**

combustibility [kəm•bus′tə•bil′ə•tē] The chemical property of being able to burn **(E24)**

comets [kom′its] Balls of ice and rock that circle the sun from two regions beyond the orbit of Pluto **(D16)**

community [kə•myoō′nə•tē] All the populations of organisms living together in an environment **(B28)**

competition [kom′pə•tish′ən] The contest among organisms for the limited resources of an ecosystem **(B42)**

compound [kom′pound] A substance made of the atoms of two or more different elements **(E48)**

condensation [kon′dən•sā′shən] The process by which a gas changes back into a liquid **(B14, C67, E17)**

conduction [kən•duk′shən] The direct transfer of heat between objects that touch **(F85)**

conductor [kən•duk′tər] A material that conducts electrons easily **(F70)**

conserving [kən•sûrv′ing] The saving or protecting of resources **(B104)**

consumer [kən•soō′mər] An organism in a community that must eat to get the energy it needs **(B34)**

continental drift [kon′tə•nen′təl drift′] A theory of how Earth's continents move over its surface **(C22)**

convection [kən•vek′shən] The transfer of heat as a result of the mixing of a liquid or a gas **(F85)**

core [kôr] The center of the Earth **(C14)**

corona [kə•rō′nə] The sun's atmosphere **(D41)**

crust [krust] The thin, outer layer of Earth **(C14)**

current [kûr′ənt] A stream of water that flows like a river through the ocean **(C104)**

cytoplasm [sīt′ō•plaz′əm] A jellylike substance containing many chemicals that keep a cell functioning **(A9)**

decomposer [dē′kəm•pōz′ər] Consumer that breaks down the tissues of dead organisms **(B35)**

density [den′sə•tē] The concentration of matter in an object **(E9)**

deposition [dep′ə•zish′ən] The process of dropping, or depositing, sediment in a new location **(C7)**

desalination [dē•sal′ə•nā′shən] The process of removing salt from sea water **(C120)**

diffusion [di•fyoō′zhən] The process by which many materials move in and out of cells **(A10)**

direct development [də•rekt′ di•vel′əp•mənt] A kind of growth where organisms keep the same body features as they grow larger **(A72)**

dominant trait [dom′ə•nənt trāt′] A strong trait **(A79)**

E

earthquake [ûrth′kwāk′] A shaking of the ground caused by the sudden release of energy in Earth's crust **(C18)**

eclipse [i•klips′] The passing of one object through the shadow of another **(D8)**

ecosystem [ek′ō•sis′təm] A community and its physical environment together **(B28)**

electric charge [i•lek′trik chärj′] The charge obtained by an object when it gains or loses electrons **(F68)**

electric circuit [i•lek′trik sûr′kit] The path along which electrons can flow **(F71)**

electric current [i•lek′trik kûr′ənt] The flow of electrons from negatively charged objects to positively charged objects **(F69)**

electric force [i•lek′trik fôrs′] The attraction or repulsion of objects due to their charges **(F69)**

electromagnet [i•lek′trō•mag′nit] A temporary magnet made by passing electric current through a wire coiled around an iron bar **(F72)**

electron [ē•lek′tron′] A subatomic particle with a negative charge **(E39)**

element [el′ə•mənt] A substance made up of only one kind of atom **(E40)**

El Niño [el nēn′yō] A short-term climate change that occurs every two to ten years **(C83)**

endangered [en•dān′jərd] A term describing a population of organisms that is likely to become extinct if steps are not taken to save it **(B51)**

energy [en′ər•jē] The ability to cause changes in matter **(F62)**

energy pyramid [en′ər•jē pir′ə•mid] Shows the amount of energy available to pass from one level of a food chain to the next **(B38)**

equinox [ē′kwi•noks] Point in Earth's orbit at which the hours of daylight and darkness are equal **(D15)**

erosion [i•rō′zhən] The process of moving sediment from one place to another **(C7)**

estuary [es′chōō•er′ē] The place where a freshwater river empties into an ocean **(B80)**

evaporation [ē•vap′ə•rā′shən] The process by which a liquid changes into a gas **(B14, C67, E16)**

exotic [ig•zot′•ik] An imported or nonnative organism **(B50)**

extinct [ik•stingkt′] No longer in existence; describes a species when the last individual of a population dies and that organism is gone forever **(B51)**

F

fault [fôlt] A break or place where pieces of Earth's crust move **(C18)**

fiber [fī′bər] Any material that can be separated into threads **(A112)**

fish [fish] Vertebrates that live their entire lives in water **(A44)**

food chain [fōōd′ chān′] The ways in which the organisms in an ecosystem interact with one another according to what they eat **(B35)**

food web [fōōd′ web′] Shows the interactions among many different food chains in a single ecosystem **(B36)**

force [fôrs] A push or pull that causes an object to move, stop, or change direction **(F6)**

fossil [fos′əl] The remains or traces of past life found in sedimentary rock **(C23)**

friction [frik′shən] A force that opposes, or acts against, motion when two surfaces rub against each other **(F6)**

front [frunt] The boundary between air masses **(C75)**

fungi [fun′jī′] Living things that look like plants but cannot make their own food; example, mushrooms **(A39)**

fusion energy [fyōō′zhən en′ər•jē] The energy released when the nuclei of two atoms are forced together to form a larger nucleus **(F112)**

galaxy [gal′ək•sē] A group of stars, gas, and dust **(D54)**

gas [gas] The state of matter that does not have a definite shape or volume **(E14)**

gene [jēn] Structures on a chromosome that contain the DNA code for a trait an organism inherits **(A80)**

genus [jē′nas] The second-smallest name grouping used in classification **(A40)**

germinate [jûr′mi•nāt] the sprouting of a seed **(A105)**

geothermal energy [jē′ō•thûr′məl en′ər•jē] Heat from inside the Earth **(F111)**

global warming [glō′bəl wôrm′ing] The hypothesized rise in Earth's average temperature from excess carbon dioxide **(C84)**

grain [grān] The seed of certain grasses **(A110)**

gravitation [grav′i•tā′shən] The force that pulls all objects in the universe toward one another **(F8)**

greenhouse effect [grēn′hous′ i•fekt′] Process by which the Earth's atmosphere absorbs heat **(C84)**

gymnosperm [jim′nə•spûrm′] Plant with unprotected seeds; conifer or cone-bearing plant **(A102)**

habitat [hab′ə•tat′] A place in an ecosystem where a population lives **(B29)**

hardness [härd′nis] A mineral's ability to resist being scratched **(C37)**

headland [hed′land′] A hard, rocky point of land left when softer rock is washed away by the sea **(C111)**

heat [hēt] The transfer of thermal energy from one substance to another **(F84)**

humidity [hyōō•mid′ə•tē] A measure of the amount of water in the air **(C65)**

hydroelectric energy [hī′drō•ē•lek′trik en′ər•jē] Electricity generated from the force of moving water **(F104)**

igneous rock [ig′nē•əs rok′] A type of rock that forms when melted rock hardens **(C42)**

individual [in′də•vij′ōō•əl] A single organism in an environment **(B28)**

inertia [in•ûr′shə] The property of matter that keeps it moving in a straight line or keeps it at rest **(F41)**

inherited trait [in•her′it•əd trāt′] A characteristic that is passed from parent to offspring **(A78)**

instinct [in′stingkt] A behavior that an organism inherits **(B46)**

insulator [in′sə•lāt′ər] A material that does not carry electrons **(F71)**

intertidal zone [in′tər•tīd′əl zōn′] An area where the tide and churning waves provide a constant supply of oxygen and nutrients to living organisms **(B77)**

invertebrates [in•vûr′tə•brits] Animals without a backbone **(A45)**

jetty [jet′ē] A wall-like structure made of rocks that sticks out into the ocean **(C112)**

joint [joint] A place where bones meet and are attached to each other and to muscles **(A24)**

kinetic energy [ki•net′ik en′ər•jē] The energy of motion, or energy in use **(F62)**

kingdom [king′dəm] The largest group into which living things can be classified **(A39)**

landform [land′fôrm′] A physical feature on Earth's surface **(C6)**

law of universal gravitation [lô′ uv yōōn′ə•vûr′səl grav′i•tā′shən] Law that states that all objects in the universe are attracted to all other objects **(F49)**

learned behavior [lûrnd′ bē•hāv′yər] A behavior an animal learns from its parents **(B46)**

lens [lenz] A piece of clear material that bends, or refracts, light rays passing through it **(F77)**

ligament [lig′ə•mənt] One of the bands of connective tissue that hold a skeleton together **(A25)**

life cycle [līf′ sīkəl] all the stages of an organism's life **(A72)**

light-year [līt′yir′] The distance light travels in one Earth year; about 9.5 trillion km **(D55)**

liquid [lik′wid] The state of matter that has a definite volume but no definite shape **(E14)**

local winds [lō′kəl windz′] The winds dependent upon local changes in temperature **(C73)**

luster [lus′tər] The way the surface of a mineral reflects light **(C37)**

machine [mə•shēn′] Something that makes work easier by changing the size or the direction of a force **(F20)**

magma [mag′mə] Molten rock from Earth's mantle **(C16)**

magnetism [mag′nə•tiz′əm] The force of attraction between magnets and magnetic objects **(F7)**

magnitude [mag′nə•tōōd] Brightness of stars **(D46)**

main sequence [mān′ sē′kwəns] A band of stars that includes most stars of average color, size, magnitude, and temperature **(D47)**

mammals [mam′əlz] Animals that have hair and produce milk for their young **(A44)**

mantle [man′təl] The layer of rock beneath Earth's crust **(C14)**

mass [mas] The amount of matter in an object **(E7)**

mass movement [mas′ mōōv′mənt] The downhill movement of rock and soil because of gravity **(C9)**

matter [mat′ər] Anything that has mass and takes up space **(E6)**

meiosis [mi•ō′sis] The process that reduces the number of chromosomes in reproductive cells **(A68)**

metamorphic rock [met′ə•môr′fik rok′] A type of rock changed by heat or pressure but not completely melted **(C46)**

metamorphosis [met′ə•môr′fə•sis] A change in the shape or characteristics of an organism's body as it grows and matures **(A73)**

microclimate [mi′krō•kli′mit] The climate of a very small area **(C80)**

mineral [min′ər•əl] A natural, solid material with particles arranged in a repeating pattern **(C36)**

mitosis [mi•tō′sis] The process of cell division **(A65)**

molecule [mol′ə•kyōol′] A grouping of two or more atoms joined together **(E40)**

moneran [mō•ner′ən] The kingdom of classification for organisms that have only one cell and no nucleus **(A39)**

momentum [mō•men′təm] A measure of how hard it is to slow down or stop an object **(F36)**

near-shore zone [nir′shôr′ zōn′] The area beyond the breaking waves that extends to waters that are about 180 m deep **(B77)**

nephrons [nef′ronz′] Tubes inside the kidneys where urea and water diffuse from the blood **(A20)**

net force [net′ fôrs′] The result of two or more forces acting together on an object **(F14)**

neuron [nŏŏr′on′] A specialized cell that can receive information and transmit it to other cells **(A26)**

neutron [nŏŏ′tron′] A subatomic particle with no charge **(E39)**

niche [nich] The role each population has in its habitat **(B29)**

nitrogen cycle [ni′trə•jən si′kəl] The cycle in which nitrogen gas is changed into forms of nitrogen that plants can use **(B7)**

nonvascular plants [non•vas′kyə•lər plants] Plants that do not have tubes **(A52)**

nuclear energy [nŏŏ′klē•ər en′ər•jē] The energy released when the nucleus of an atom is split apart **(F110)**

nucleus [nŏŏ′klē•əs] 1 *(cell)* The organelle that controls all of a cell's activities 2 *(atom)* The center of an atom **(A8, E39)**

open-ocean zone [ō′pən•ō′shən zōn′] The area that includes most deep ocean waters; most organisms live near the surface **(B77)**

orbit [ôr′bit] The path one body in space takes as it revolves around another body; such as that of Earth as it revolves around the sun **(D7, F48)**

organ [ôr′gən] Tissues that work together to perform a specific function **(A12)**

osmosis [os•mō′sis] The diffusion of water and dissolved materials through cell membranes **(A10)**

Pangea [pan•jē′ə] A supercontinent containing all of Earth's land that existed about 225 million years ago **(C22)**

periodic table [pir′ē•od′ik tā′bəl] The table of elements in order of increasing atomic number, grouped by similar properties **(E47)**

phloem [flō'em] The tubes that transport food in the vascular plants **(A95)**

photosphere [fōt'ə•sfir'] The visible surface of the sun **(D41)**

photosynthesis [fōt'ō•sin'thə•sis] The process by which plants make food **(A96)**

physical properties [fiz'i•kəl prop'ər•tēz] The characteristics of a substance that can be observed or measured without changing the substance **(E6)**

pioneer plants [pī'ə•nir' plantz'] The first plants to invade a bare area **(B92)**

pitch [pich] An element of sound determined by the speed at which sound waves move **(F79)**

planets [plan'its] Large, round bodies that revolve around a star **(D16)**

plate [plāt] A rigid block of crust and upper mantle rock **(C15)**

pollen [pol'ən] Flower structures that contain the male reproductive cells **(A102)**

pollution [pə•lōō'shən] Waste products that damage an ecosystem **(B99)**

population [pop•yə•lā'shən] All the individuals of the same kind living in the same environment **(B28)**

position [pə•zish'ən] An object's place, or location **(F34)**

potential energy [pō•ten'shəl en'ər•jē] The energy an object has because of its place or its condition **(F62)**

power [pou'ər] The amount of work done for each unit of time **(F19)**

precipitation [pri•sip'ə•tā'shən] Any form of water that falls from clouds, such as rain or snow **(B15, C65)**

prevailing winds [prē•vāl'ing windz'] The global winds that blow constantly from the same direction **(C73)**

producer [prə•dōōs'ər] An organism that makes its own food **(B34)**

protist [prō'tist] The kingdom of classification for organisms that have only one cell and also have a nucleus, or cell control center **(A39)**

proton [prō'ton'] A subatomic particle with a positive charge **(E39)**

radiation [rā'dē•ā'shən] The transfer of thermal energy by electromagnetic waves **(F85)**

reaction force [rē•ak'shən fôrs'] The force that pushes or pulls back in the third law of motion **(F43)**

reactivity [rē'ak•tiv'ə•tē] The ability of a substance to go through a chemical change **(E23)**

receptors [ri•sep'tərz] Nerve cells that detect conditions in the body's environment **(A26)**

recessive trait [ri•ses'iv trāt'] A weak trait **(A79)**

reclamation [rek'lə•mā'shən] The process of restoring a damaged ecosystem **(B110)**

recycle [rē•sī'kəl] To recover a resource from an item and use the recovered resource to make a new item **(B105)**

reduce [ri•dōōs'] To cut down on the use of resources **(B104)**

reflection [ri•flek'shən] The light energy that bounces off objects **(F76)**

refraction [ri•frak'shən] The bending of light rays when they pass through a substance **(F76)**

reptiles [rep'tīlz] Animals that have dry, scaly skin **(A44)**

resistor [ri•zis′tər] A material that resists the flow of electrons in some way **(F71)**

respiration [res′pə•rā′shən] The process that releases energy from food **(B8)**

reuse [rē′yo͞oz′] To use items again, sometimes for a different purpose **(B105)**

revolve [ri•volv′] To travel in a closed path around an object such as Earth does as it moves around the sun **(D6)**

rock [rok] A material made up of one or more minerals **(C42)**

rock cycle [rok′ sī′kəl] The slow, never-ending process of rock changes **(C52)**

rotate [rō′tāt] The spinning of Earth on its axis **(D7)**

S

salinity [sə•lin′ə•tē] Saltiness of the ocean **(C97)**

satellite [sat′ə•līt′] A natural body, like the moon, or an artificial object that orbits another object **(D23)**

scuba [sko͞o′bə] Underwater breathing equipment; the letters stand for **s**elf-**c**ontained **u**nderwater **b**reathing **a**pparatus **(C117)**

sedimentary rock [sed′ə•men′tər•ē rok′] A type of rock formed by layers of sediments that were squeezed and stuck together over a long time **(C44)**

sexual reproduction [sek′sho͞o•əl rē′prə•duk′shən] The form of reproduction in which cells from two parents unite to form a zygote **(A68)**

shore [shôr] The area where the ocean and land meet and interact **(C110)**

solar energy [sō′lər en′ər•jē] The energy of sunlight **(F111)**

solar flare [sō′lər flâr′] A brief burst of energy from the sun's photosphere **(D42)**

solar wind [sō′lər wind′] A fast-moving stream of particles thrown into space by solar flares **(D42)**

solid [sol′id] The state of matter that has a definite shape and a definite volume **(E14)**

solstice [sol′stis] Point in Earth's orbit at which the hours of daylight are at their greatest or fewest **(D15)**

solubility [sol′yə•bil′ə•tē] The ability of one substance to be dissolved in another substance **(E10)**

sonar [sō′när′] A device that uses sound waves to determine water depth **(C117)**

space probe [spās′ prōb′] A robot vehicle used to explore deep space **(D24)**

species [spē′shēz] The smallest name grouping used in classification **(A40)**

speed [spēd] A measure of the distance an object moves in a given amount of time **(F35)**

spore [spôr] A single reproductive cell that grows into a new plant **(A101)**

streak [strēk] The color of the powder left behind when you rub a material against a white tile called a streak plate **(C37)**

submersible [sub•mûr′sə•bəl] An underwater vehicle **(C117)**

succession [sək•sesh′ən] A gradual change in an ecosystem, sometimes occurring over hundreds of years **(B92)**

sunspot [sun′spot′] A dark spot on the photosphere of the sun **(D42)**

symbiosis [sim′bē•ō′sis] A long-term relationship between different kinds of organisms **(B45)**

system [sis′təm] Organs that work together to perform a function **(A12)**

telescope [tel′ə•skōp′] An instrument that magnifies distant objects, or makes them appear larger **(D23)**

temperature [tem′pər•ə•chər] The average kinetic energy of all the molecules in an object **(F84)**

tendons [ten′dənz] Tough bands of connective tissue that attach muscles to bones **(A25)**

threatened [thret′ənd] Describes a population of organisms that are likely to become endangered if they are not protected **(B51)**

tidal energy [tīd′əl en′ər•jē] A form of hydroelectric energy that produces electricity from the rising and falling of tides **(F106)**

tide [tīd] The repeated rise and fall in the level of the ocean **(C106)**

tide pool [tīd′ pool′] A pool of sea water found along a rocky shoreline **(C111)**

tissue [tish′oo] Cells that work together to perform a specific function **(A12)**

transpiration [tran′spə•rā′shən] The process in which plants give off water through their stomata **(B15)**

unbalanced forces [un•bal′ənst fôrs′əz] Forces that are not equal **(F13)**

universe [yoon′ə•vûrs′] Everything that exists—planets, stars, dust, gases, and energy **(D54)**

vascular plants [vas′kyə•lər plants] Plants that have tubes **(A50)**

velocity [və•los′ə•tē] An object's speed in a particular direction **(F35)**

vertebrates [vûr′tə•brits] Animals with a backbone **(A44)**

villi [vil′ī] Projections sticking into the small intestine **(A19)**

volcano [vol•kā′nō] A mountain formed by lava and ash **(C16)**

volume [vol′yoom] **1** *(measurement)* The amount of space that an object takes up **2** *(sound)* The loudness of a sound **(E8, F79)**

water cycle [wôt′ər sī′kəl] The cycle in which Earth's water moves through the environment **(B14)**

water pressure [wôt′ər presh′ər] The weight of water pressing on an object **(C97)**

wave [wāv] An up-and-down movement of surface water **(C102)**

weathering [weth′ər•ing] The process of breaking rock into soil, sand, and other tiny pieces **(C7)**

weight [wāt] A measure of the pull of gravity on an object **(E7)**

wetlands [wet′landz′] The water ecosystems that include saltwater marshes, mangrove swamps, and mud flats **(B111)**

work [wûrk] The use of a force to move an object through a distance **(F18)**

xylem [zī′ləm] The tubes that transport water and minerals in vascular plants **(A95)**

Page Placement Key:
(l)-left, (r)-right, (t)-top, (c)-center, (b)-bottom, (bg)-background, (fg)-foreground, (i)-inset

Cover and Title Pages
Wolfgang Kaehler/Corbis; (bg) Eduardo Garcia/FPG International

Table of Contents
iv (t) Anup & Manoj Shah/Animals Animals; iv (bg) Grant V. Faint/The Image Bank; v (t) Zig Leszczynski/Animals Animals; v (bg) Karl Hentz/The Image Bank; vi (t) Eric & David Hosking/Photo Researchers; vi (bg) Bios (Klein-Hubert)/Peter Arnold, Inc; vii Telegraph Colour Library/FPG International; viii (t) Alvis Upitis/The Image Bank; viii (bg) Tim Crosby/Liaison International; ix (t) David Zaitz/Photonica; ix (bg) Stone;

Unit A
Unit A Opener (fg) Anup & Manoj Shah/Animals Animals; (bg)Grant V. Faint/The Image Bank; A2-A3 Image Shop/Phototake; A3 (l) Lawrence Migdale/Photo Researchers; A3 (c) Quest/Science Photo Library/Photo Researchers; A4 Charles D. Winters/Timeframe Photography, Inc./Photo Researchers; A6 (l) The Granger Collection, New York; A6 (c), (r) Courtesy of Hunt Institute for Botanical Documentation, Carnegie Mellon University, Pittsburgh, PA; A7 (tl) Ed Reschke/Peter Arnold, Inc.; A7 (tr) Michel Viard/Peter Arnold, Inc.; A7 (bl) Courtesy of Dr. Sam Harbo D.V.M., and Dr. Jurgen Schumacher D.V.M. , Veterinary Hospital, University of Tennessee; A7 (br) A.B. Sheldon/Dembinsky Photo Associates; A8 Dwight R. Kuhn; A9 Courtesy of Dr. Sam Harbo D.V.M., and Dr. Jurgen Schumacher D.V.M., Veterinary Hospital, University of Tennessee; A11 Skip Moody/Dembinsky Photo Associates; A14 Michael Newman/PhotoEdit; A16 (l) Dr. Tony Brain/Science Photo Library/Photo Researchers; A16 (r) Prof. P. Motta/Dept. of Anatomy/University "La Sapienza", Rome/Science Photo Library/Photo Researchers; A22 Gary Holscher/Stone; A28 D. Cavagnaro/DRK; A28 (i) Dr. Dennis Kunkel/Phototake; A29 Mark Richards/PhotoEdit; A30 NASA; A33 Charles D. Winters/Timeframe Photography, Inc./Photo Researchers; A34-A35 Gregory Ochocki/Photo Researchers; A35 (t) Dave Watts/Tom Stack & Associates; A35 (b) Frances Fawcett/Cornell University/American Indian Program; A36 Christian Grzimek/Okapia/Photo Reseachers; A38-A39 Bill Lea/Dembinsky Photo Associates; A38 (l) MESZA/Bruce Coleman, Inc.; A38 (c) Andrew Syred/SPL/Photo Researchers; A38 (r) Robert Brons/BPS/Stone; A39 (t) Bill Lea/Dembinsky Photo Associates; A39 (tc) Dr. E. R. Degginger/Color-Pic; A39 (c) S. Nielsen/Bruce Coleman, Inc.; A39 (bc) Robert Brons/BPS/Stone; A39 (b) Andrew Syred/SPL/Photo Researchers; A41 Daniel Cox/Stone; A42 Arthur C. Smith, III/Grant Heilman Photography; A44 (t) Ana Laura Gonzalez/Animals Animals; A44 (b) Tom Brakefield/The Stock Market; A44-A45 Runk/Schoenberger/Grant Heilman Photography; A45 (tl) Amos Nachoum/The Stock Market; A45 (tc) Hans Pfletschinger/Peter Arnold, Inc.; A45 (tr) Mark Moffett/Minden Pictures; A45 (br) Larry Lipsky/DRK; A46 (t) James Balog/Stone; A46 (b) Stephen Dalton/Photo Researchers; A48 Darrell Gulin/Stone; A50 Dr. E. R. Degginger, FPSA/Color-Pic; A51 Phil A. Dotson/Photo Researchers; A52 (t) Heather Angel/Biofotos; A52 (c) Runk Schoenberger/Grant Heilman Photography; A52-A53 Runk Schoenberger/Grant Heilman Photography; A54 Leonard Lee Rue III/Photo Researchers; A54-A55 S. J. Krasemann/Peter Arnold, Inc.; A55 (tl) Art Resource, NY; A55 (tr) Dr. E. R. Degginger/Photo Researchers; A55 (bl) Superstock; A55 (br) The Granger Collection, New York; A56 (t) Courtesy of Hunt Institute for Botanical Documentation, Carnegie Mellon University, Pittsburg, PA; A56 (b) Grant Heilman Photography; A60-A61 Rob & Ann Simpson/Visuals Unlimited; A61 (l) Dwight R. Kuhn; A61 (r) Dr. D. Spector/Peter Arnold, Inc.; A62 Ron Kimball; A64 (l) Jerome Wexler/Photo Researchers; A64 (cl), (c) Carolina Biological Supply Company/Phototake; A64 (cr) Jerome Wexler/Photo Researchers; A64 (r) Kenneth H. Thomas/Photo Researchers; A65 Conly L. Rieder/BPS/Stone; A66 (tl), (tc), (tr) Carolina Biological Supply Company/Phototake; A66 (c) Noble Proctor/Photo Researchers; A66 (b) Zig Leszczynski/Animals Animals; A67 (tl), (tc), (tr) Carolina Biological Supply Company/Phototake; A67 (b) Bob Gossington/Bruce Coleman, Inc.; A69 Carolina Biological Supply Company/Phototake; A70 J.H. Robinson/Photo Researchers; A72 (t) Peter A. Simon/Phototake; A72 (b) Dr. E.R. Degginger/Photo Researchers; A73 (l) Thomas Gulz/Visuals Unlimited; A73 (c) Dwight R. Kuhn; A73 (r) William J. Weber/Visuals Unlimited; A74 Harry Rogers/Photo Researchers; A75 Michael Fogden/Bruce Coleman, Inc.; A76 Paul Barton/The Stock Market; A78 Phil Savoie/The Picture Cube; A79 The Granger Collection, New York; A82 Tim Davis/Tony Stone Images; A83 (li) College of Veterinary Medicine/University of Florida; A83 (r) Zigy Kaluzny/Tony Stone Images; A84 Henry Friedman/HRW; A84 (i) Oliver Meckes/Photo Researchers; A88-A89 Tom Bean/Stone; A89 (t) Inga Spence/Visuals Unlimited; A89 (b) Ned Therrien/Visuals Unlimited; A90 James Randklev/Stone; A92 (l) Richard Choy/Peter Arnold, Inc.; A92 (r) Reinhard Siegel/Stone; A93 Norman Myers/Bruce Coleman, Inc.; A93 (li) Dr. E. R. Degginger/Color-Pic; A93 (ri) John Kaprielian/Photo Researchers; A95 Jane Grushow/Grant Heilman Photography; A96-A97 (t), A96 (ti) Runk/Schoenberger/Grant Heilman Photography; A96-A97 (b) Alan Levenson/Stone; A98 Darrell Gulin/Dembinsky Photo Associates; A100 Kim Taylor/Bruce Coleman, Inc.; A101, A102 (t) Runk/Schoenberger/Grant Heilman Photography; A102 (b) S.J. Krasemann/Peter Arnold, Inc.; A103 (t) Dr. E. R. Degginger/Color-Pic; A103 (b) Robert Maier/Earth Scenes; A104 (t) David Cavagnaro/Peter Arnold, Inc.; A104 (tc) E. R. Degginger/Bruce Coleman, Inc.; A104 (bc) Gregory K. Scott/Photo Researchers; A104 (b) Kevin Schafer Photography; A104 (bg) Jeff Lepore/Photo Researchers; A105 Runk/Schoenberger/Grant Heilman Photography; A106 (animal life cycle) (t) Gregory K. Scott/Photo Researchers; A106 (r) Harry Rogers/National Audubon Society; A106 (b) David M. Dennis/Tom Stack & Associates; A106 (l) Jen & Des Bartlett/Bruce Coleman, Inc.; A106 (plant life cycle) (t) Dr. E. R. Degginger/Color-Pic; A106 (r) Barry L. Runk/Grant Heilman Photography; A106 (b) Jane Grushow/Grant Heilman Photography; A106 (l) Dwight R. Kuhn; A112 (l) Alan & Linda Detrick/Photo Researchers; A112 (cr) Angelina Lax/Photo Researchers; A113 Grant Heilman Photography; A113 (i) Will & Deni McIntyre/Photo Researchers; A114-115 Dana Downie/AGStock USA; A115 (b) Mark Richards/PhotoEdit; A116 Dennis Carlyle Darling/ HRW; A118 Dr. E. R. Degginger/Color-Pic; A119 James Randklev/Stone; A120 (t) Jeff Greenberg/Unicorn Stock Photos; A120 (b) Jack Olson Photography;

Unit B
Unit B Opener (fg) Zig Leszczynski/Animals Animals; (bg) Karl Hentz/The Image Bank; B2 Clyde H. Smith/Peter Arnold, Inc.; B2-B3 Superstock; B3 Earl Roberge/Photo Researchers; B4 Wolfgang Kaehler Photography; B6 Randy Ury/The Stock Market; B7 Thomas Hovland/Grant Heilman Photography; B10 Wolfgang Kaehler Photography; B12 Michael Giannechini/Photo Researchers; B14-B15 Greg Vaughn/Stone; B16 (t) C. Vincent/Natural Selection Stock Photography; B16 (b) Bob Daemmrich Photography, Inc.; B16 (bi) Superstock; B18 John Shaw/Bruce Coleman, Inc.; B18-B19 Lee Rentz/Bruce Coleman, Inc.; B19 Ken Graham/Bruce Coleman, Inc.; B20 Sipa Press; B22 Greg Vaughn/Stone; B23 C. Vincent/Natural Selection Stock Photography; B24-B25 P & R Hagan/Bruce Coleman, Inc.; B25 (t) Tomas del Amo/Pacific Stock; B25 (b) Mitsuaki Iwago/Minden Pictures; B26 Tim Davis/Photo Researchers; B28 (li) Michael Giannechini/Photo Researchers; B28-B29 (bg) J.A. Kravlis/Masterfile; B28-B29 (ci) Ted Kerasote/Photo Researchers; B29 (ti) Superstock; B29 (bi) Mitsuaki Iwago/Minden Pictures; B30 (tl) David Muench Photography, Inc.; B30 (tr), (bl) Barry L. Runk/Grant Heilman Photography; B30 (br) David Muench Photography, Inc.; B32 Superstock; B34 (tli) V.P. Weinland/Photo Researchers; B34 (tri) Parviz M. Pour/Photo Researchers; B34-B35 (bi) Dembinsky Photo Associates; B34-B35 (bg) Larry Ditto/Bruce Coleman, Inc.; B35 (li) Tom McHugh/Photo Researchers; B35 (ri) Tom & Pat Leeson/Photo Researchers; B36-B37 Woods, Michael J./NGS Image Collection; B39 Bruce Coleman, Inc.; B40 (both) Joe McDonald/McDonald Wildlife Photography; B42 (bg) Stuart Westmorland/Stone; B42 (li) Roger Bickel/New England Stock Photo; B42 (ri) Bruce Coleman, Inc.; B43 (l) Kevin Schafer/Peter Arnold, Inc.; B43 (r) Mitsuaki Iwago/Minden Pictures; B44 (t) John Shaw/Bruce Coleman, Inc.; B44 (c) Hal H. Harrison/Photo Researchers; B44 (b) Wayne Lankinen/Bruce Coleman, Inc.; B45 (t) M. & C. Photography/Peter Arnold, Inc.; B45 (b) William Townsend/Photo Researchers; B46 (t) Vince Streano/The Stock Market; B46-B47 Ralph Ginzburg/Peter Arnold, Inc.; B48 Bryan & Cherry Alexander/Masterfile; B50 (t) Tim Davis/Photo Researchers; B50 (bl) Johnny Johnson/Tony Stone Images; B50 (br) Malcolm Boulton/Photo Researchers; B51 Tom McHugh/Photo Researchers; B52-B53 Ted Schiffman/Peter Arnold, Inc; B52 Roy Toft/Tom Stack & Associates; B54 Gunter Ziesler/Peter Arnold, Inc.; B55 (t) Doug Cheeseman/Peter Arnold, Inc.; B55 (b) Bonnie Kamin/PhotoEdit; B56 (i) Louisiana State University Chemistry Library Website; B56 Meckes/Ottawa/Photo Researchers; B60-B61 Craig Tuttle/The Stock Market; B61 (t) Jake Rajs/Stone; B61 (b) Earth Satellite Corporation/Science Photo Library/Photo Researchers; B62 Chromosohm/Sohm/Stone; B64 (t) David Muench Photography, Inc.; B64 (b) Gary Braasch/Stone; B65 (tl) Superstock; B65 (tr) Steve Kaufman/Peter Arnold, Inc.; B65 (bl) Joseph Van Os/The Image Bank; B65 (br) Colin Prior/Stone; B66 Wolfgang Kaehler Photography; B66 (i) Mark Moffett/Minden Pictures; B67 Superstock; B67 (i) Roger Bickel/New England Stock Photo; B68 David Muench Photography, Inc.; B68 (i) William Manning/The Stock Market; B69 Darrell Gulin/Stone; B69 (i) T. Eggers/The Stock Market; B70 David Muench Photography, Inc.; B70 (i) Joseph Van Os/The Image Bank; B71 Carr Clifton/Minden Pictures; B71 (i) Kennan Ward Photography; B72 (l) Nicholas DeVore, III/Bruce Coleman, Inc.; B72 (r) Tui De Roy/Minden Pictures; B74 Stan Osolinski/The Stock Market; B80 (t) Jim Brandenburg/Minden Pictures; B80 (b) David Muench Photography, Inc.; B82 (t) © Corel; B82-B83 Manfred Kage/Peter Arnold; B83 (t) NASA GSFC/Science Photo Library/Photo Researchers; B83 (bi) Pete Saloutos/The Stock Market; B84 (t) Romberg Tiburon Center; B84 (b) Emory Kristof/NGS Image Collection; B86 Jim Bradenburg/Minden Pictures; B88-B89 Gary Brettnacher/Stone; B89 (t) Jonathan Wallen; B89 (b) Argus Fotoarchiv/Peter Arnold, Inc.; B90 Frans Lanting/Minden Pictures; B92 Runk/Schoenberger/Grant Heilman Photography; B93 (t) Kennan Ward Photography; B93 (b) Ed Reschke/Peter Arnold, Inc.; B94 (t) Larry Nielsen/Peter Arnold, Inc.; B94 (c) John Marshall/Stone; B94 (b) Jeff & Alexa Henry/Peter Arnold, Inc.; B96 Art Wolfe/Stone; B98 Mark E. Gibson; B98 (i) Dr. E.R. Degginger/Color-Pic; B99 J.H. Robinson/Photo Researchers; B100 Francois Gohier/Photo Researchers; B101 Tony Arruza/Bruce Coleman, Inc.; B104 (c) Jim Corwin/Stone; B106 Tim Davis/Photo Researchers; B110 Mark E. Gibson; B111 (l) Bernard Boutrit/Woodfin Camp & Associates; B111 (r) Bill Tiernan/The Virginian-Pilot; B112 Courtesy of Atlanta Botanical Gardens; B112 (i) Kenneth Murray/Photo Researchers; B114 John Hyde/Bruce Coleman, Inc.; B114 (tli) Superstock; B114 (tri) Tom Bean/The Stock Market; B116 Centre For Ecological Studies; B116 (i) E. Hanumantha/Photo Researchers; B120 (t) Bill M. Campbell, MD; B120 (b) Graeme Teague Photography;

Unit C
Unit C Opener (fg) Eric & David Hosking/Photo Researchers; (bg) Bios (Klein-Hubert)/Peter Arnold, Inc.; C2-C3 Roger Werth/Woodfin Camp & Associates; C3 (t) John Livzey/Stone; C3 (b) Royal Oservatory, Edinburgh/Science Photo Library/Photo Researchers; C4 Tom Bean/Tom & Susan Bean, Inc.; C6 (tl) Helen Paraskevas; C6 (tr) Tom Bean/Tom & Susan Bean, Inc.; C6 (bi) Mark E. Gibson; C6-C7 Eric Neurath/Stock, Boston; C7 (t) NASA Photo/Grant Heilman Photography; C7 (b) Digital Visual Library/US Army Corps of Engineers; C8 (both) Mark E. Gibson; C9 M.T. O'Keefe/Bruce Coleman, Inc.; C10-C11 Michael Collier/Stock, Boston; C12 Soames Summerhays/Photo Researchers; C16 G. Gualco/Bruce Coleman, Inc.; C17 (t) Gregory G. Dimijian/Photo Researchers; C17 (c) Krafft/Explorer/Science Source/Photo Researchers; C17 (b) Tom & Pat Leeson/Photo Researchers; C18 UPI/Corbis-Bettmann; C20 M.P.L. Fogden/Bruce Coleman, Inc.; C23 Tom Bean/Tom & Susan Bean, Inc.; C24 A. J. Copley/Visuals Unlimited; C25 (t) R.T. Nowitz/Photo Researchers; C26 NASA; C27 (t) Walter H. F. Smith & David T. Sandwell/NOAA National Data Centers; C27 (b) David Young-Wolff/PhotoEdit; C28 (i) Santa Fabio/Black Star/Harcourt; C28 Tom Bean/Tom & Susan Bean, Inc.; C31 (l) Dr. E. R. Degginger/Color-Pic; C31 (r) Joyce Photographics/Photo Researchers; C32-C33 Dan Suzio/Photo Researchers; C33 (tl) Sam Ogden/Science Photo Library/Photo Researchers; C33 (br) Breck P. Kent/Earth Scenes; C34 The Natural History Museum, London; C36 (tl) Dr. E.R. Degginger/Color-Pic; C36 (bl) E.R. Degginger/Bruce Coleman, Inc.; C36 (bc) Joy Spurr/Bruce Coleman, Inc.; C36 (br), (cl) Dr. E.R. Degginger/Color-Pic; C37 (c2), (c3) E.R. Degginger/Bruce Coleman, Inc.; C37 (c5), (c6), (c8) Dr. E.R. Degginger/Color-Pic; C37 (c9) Mark A. Schneider/Dembinsky Photo Associates; C37 (c10) Dr. E.R. Degginger/Bruce Coleman, Inc.; C38 (tl) Dr. E.R. Degginger/Color-Pic; C38 (cl) Biophoto Associates/Photo Researchers; C38 (cr) Andy Sacks/Stone; C38 (bl) Dr. E.R. Degginger/Color-Pic; C38 (br) B. Daemmrich/The Image Works; C40 Joe McDonald/Bruce Coleman, Inc.; C42 (t) Dr. E.R. Degginger/Color-Pic; C42 (b) Phillip Hayson/Photo Researchers; C43 (tl), (tcl) Dr. E.R. Degginger/Color-Pic; C43

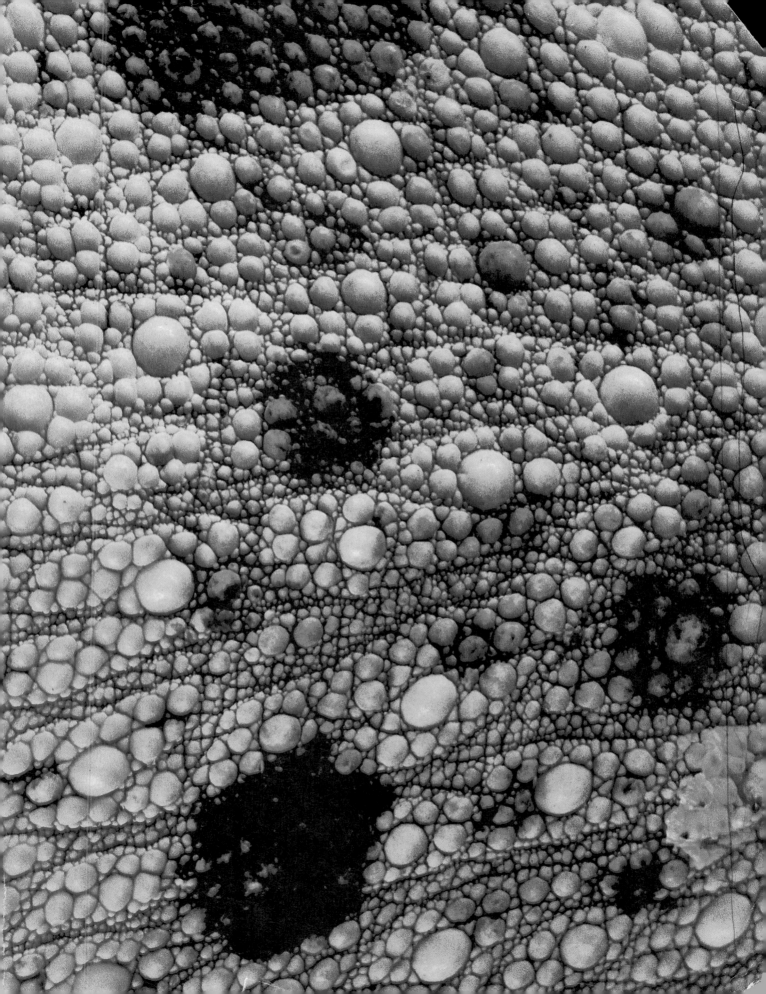